WALDEN
AND
CIVIL DISOBEDIENCE

AUTHORITATIVE TEXTS

BACKGROUND

REVIEWS AND ESSAYS IN CRITICISM

A NORTON CRITICAL EDITION

HENRY DAVID THOREAU

WALDEN
AND
CIVIL DISOBEDIENCE

AUTHORITATIVE TEXTS

BACKGROUND

REVIEWS AND ESSAYS IN CRITICISM

Edited by

OWEN THOMAS
UNIVERSITY OF CALIFORNIA, IRVINE

W · W · NORTON & COMPANY · INC · *New York*

Library of Congress Catalog Card No. 66-11310

ISBN 0 393 04276 6 Cloth Edition
ISBN 0 393 09665 3 Paper Edition
PRINTED IN THE UNITED STATES OF AMERICA
4 5 6 7 8 9 0

Contents

Preface

The fame of Henry David Thoreau rests primarily on the two works included in this volume. *Walden* is the artistic record of a man who confronted the natural world on its own terms; "Civil Disobedience" is an equally artistic record of the same man's confrontation with an imperfect society. Each of these works has become part of the fiber of the American character. Each of them has had an influence far beyond the boundaries of the mid-nineteenth century village of Concord, Massachusetts, where they were written.

This edition has two purposes: first, to present authoritative versions of the texts, and second, to provide annotations and secondary materials that will enable a reader to comprehend the texts more fully. The sources for the texts are discussed in brief notes following the texts themselves. The annotations seek to be complete without being unwieldy; I have tried to identify words, persons, and quotations that might not be familiar to the general reader, but I have not always identified brief quotations and paraphrases—such as, for example, the frequent reference to the Bible—when, in my opinion, such identification would not add to the reader's understanding of the passage or would not increase his awareness of the scope of Thoreau's reading. The background materials, reviews, and essays cover a period of more than a hundred years; they are representative of the diversity of opinion that has been expressed since the publication of *Walden* in 1854.

Like all new books on Thoreau, this one draws upon the work of several generations of scholars. Reginald L. Cook was the first to record Thoreau's annotations and corrections in the first edition of *Walden*; these are incorporated in the present text. Walter Harding and D. Gordon Rohman have both supplied annotations to *Walden*, the former in *The Variorum Walden* and the latter in an unpublished dissertation, "An Annotated Edition of *Walden*" (Syracuse University, 1960); their meticulous scholarship considerably simplifies the work of any editor. Thoreau's *Journal*, edited by Bradford Torrey and Francis H. Allen, has proved to be an essential source book. Thoreau's many biographers, particularly Ellery Channing, H. S. Salt, F. B. Sanborn, and H. S. Canby, provide much useful information as do the *Bulletins* and the *Booklets* of the Thoreau Society. I gratefully acknowledge my debt to these scholars.

In addition, I would like to thank M. H. Abrams and Edwin H. Cady for their helpful suggestions; Joseph McElrath for his careful proofreading of an earlier printing of this edition; the Oberlin College Library, which provided the copy of the first edition of *Walden* on which the present edition is based; the staff of the Indiana University Library, particularly Anthony Shipps, who was extremely helpful in identifying sources previously unidentified; and the Graduate School of Indiana University, which provided a grant that aided in the preparation of the manuscript.

OWEN THOMAS

Bloomington, Indiana

The Texts of

WALDEN

and

CIVIL DISOBEDIENCE

The Contents of Walden

Walden

I do not propose to write an ode to dejection, but to brag as lustily as chanticleer in the morning, standing on his roost, if only to wake my neighbors up.

Economy

When I wrote the following pages, or rather the bulk of them, I lived alone, in the woods, a mile from any neighbor, in a house which I had built myself, on the shore of Walden Pond, in Concord, Massachusetts, and earned my living by the labor of my hands only. I lived there two years and two months. At present I am a sojourner in civilized life again.

I should not obtrude my affairs so much on the notice of my readers if very particular inquiries had not been made by my townsmen concerning my mode of life, which some would call impertinent, though they do not appear to me at all impertinent, but, considering the circumstances, very natural and pertinent. Some have asked what I got to eat; if I did not feel lonesome; if I was not afraid; and the like. Others have been curious to learn what portion of my income I devoted to charitable purposes; and some, who have large families, how many poor children I maintained. I will therefore ask those of my readers who feel no particular interest in me to pardon me if I undertake to answer some of these questions in this book. In most books, the I, or first person, is omitted; in this it will be retained; that, in respect to egotism, is the main difference. We commonly do not remember that it is, after all, always the first person that is speaking. I should not talk so much about myself if there were any body else whom I knew as well. Unfortunately, I am confined to this theme by the narrowness of my experience. Moreover, I, on my side, require of every writer, first or last, a simple and sincere account of his own life, and not merely what he has heard of other men's lives; some such account as he would send to his kindred from a distant land; for if he has lived sincerely, it must have been in a distant land to me. Perhaps these pages are more particularly addressed to poor students. As for the rest of my readers, they will accept such portions as apply to them. I trust that none will stretch the seams in putting on the coat, for it may do good service to him whom it fits.

I would fain say something, not so much concerning the Chinese and Sandwich Islanders [1] as you who read these pages, who are said to live in New England; something about your condition, especially your outward condition or circumstances in this world, in this town, what it is, whether it is necessary that it be as bad as it is, whether it cannot be improved as well as not. I have travelled a good deal in Concord; and every where, in shops, and offices, and fields, the inhabitants have appeared to me to be doing penance in a thousand remarkable ways. What I have heard of Bramins [2] sitting exposed to four fires and looking in the face of the sun; or hanging suspended, with their heads downward, over flames; or looking at the heavens over their shoulders "until it becomes impossible for them to resume their natural position, while from the twist of the neck nothing but liquids can pass into the stomach;" or dwelling, chained for life, at the foot of a tree; or measuring with their bodies, like caterpillars, the breadth of vast empires; or standing on one leg on the tops of pillars,—even these forms of conscious penance are hardly more incredible and astonishing than the scenes which I daily witness. The twelve labors of Hercules [3] were trifling in comparison with those which my neighbors have undertaken; for they were only twelve, and had an end; but I could never see that these men slew or captured any monster or finished any labor. They have no friend Iolas [4] to burn with a hot iron the root of the hydra's head, but as soon as one head is crushed, two spring up.

I see young men, my townsmen, whose misfortune it is to have inherited farms, houses, barns, cattle, and farming tools; for these are more easily acquired than got rid of. Better if they had been born in the open pasture and suckled by a wolf, that they might have seen with clearer eyes what field they were called to labor in. Who made them serfs of the soil? Why should they eat their sixty acres, when man is condemned to eat only his peck of dirt? Why should they begin digging their graves as soon as they are born? They have got to live a man's life, pushing all these things before them, and get on as well as they can. How many a poor immortal soul have I met well nigh crushed and smothered under its load, creeping down the road of life, pushing before it a barn

1. A mid-nineteenth century name for the Hawaiian islanders.
2. Generally spelled Brahmin or Brahman; a member of the highest caste of Hindus.
3. The son of Zeus, in classical Greek mythology, known for his great strength and for the performance of twelve seemingly impossible tasks.
4. A servant to Hercules who helped him to overcome the many-headed monster, Hydra, by singeing with fire the stumps that remained after Hercules chopped off its heads.

seventy-five feet by forty, its Augean stables [5] never cleansed, and one hundred acres of land, tillage, mowing, pasture, and wood-lot! The portionless, who struggle with no such unnecessary inherited encumbrances, find it labor enough to subdue and cultivate a few cubic feet of flesh.

But men labor under a mistake. The better part of the man is soon ploughed into the soil for compost. By a seeming fate, commonly called necessity, they are employed, as it says in an old book, laying up treasures which moth and rust will corrupt and thieves break through and steal. It is a fool's life, as they will find when they get to the end of it, if not before. It is said that Deucalion and Pyrrha [6] created men by throwing stones over their heads behind them:—

> Inde genus durum sumus, experiensque laborum,
> Et documenta damus quâ simus origine nati.

Or, as Raleigh rhymes it in his sonorous way,—

> "From thence our kind hard-hearted is, enduring pain and care,
> Approving that our bodies of a stony nature are."

So much for a blind obedience to a blundering oracle, throwing the stones over their heads behind them, and not seeing where they fell.

Most men, even in this comparatively free country, through mere ignorance and mistake, are so occupied with the factitious cares and superfluously coarse labors of life that its finer fruits cannot be plucked by them. Their fingers, from excessive toil, are too clumsy and tremble too much for that. Actually, the laboring man has not leisure for a true integrity day by day; he cannot afford to sustain the manliest relations to men; his labor would be depreciated in the market. He has no time to be any thing but a machine. How can he remember well his ignorance—which his growth requires—who has so often to use his knowledge? We should feed and clothe him gratuitously sometimes, and recruit him with our cordials, before we judge of him. The finest qualities of our nature, like the bloom on fruits, can be preserved only by the most delicate handling. Yet we do not treat ourselves nor one another thus tenderly.

5. The home of thousands of cattle whose stalls had not been cleaned in years. As one of his tasks, Hercules was required to clean the stables in a single day.
6. The only human survivors when Zeus destroyed mankind with a flood. The Latin quotation is from Ovid's *Metamorphoses;* the translation from Sir Walter Raleigh's *History of the World.*

Some of you, we all know, are poor, find it hard to live, are sometimes, as it were, gasping for breath. I have no doubt that some of you who read this book are unable to pay for all the dinners which you have actually eaten, or for the coats and shoes which are fast wearing or are already worn out, and have come to this page to spend borrowed or stolen time, robbing your creditors of an hour. It is very evident what mean and sneaking lives many of you live, for my sight has been whetted by experience; always on the limits, trying to get into business and trying to get out of debt, a very ancient slough, called by the Latins *æs alienum*,[7] another's brass, for some of their coins were made of brass; still living, and dying, and buried by this other's brass; always promising to pay, promising to pay, to-morrow, and dying to-day, insolvent; seeking to curry favor, to get custom, by how many modes, only not state-prison offences; lying, flattering, voting, contracting yourselves into a nutshell of civility, or dilating into an atmosphere of thin and vaporous generosity, that you may persuade your neighbor to let you make his shoes, or his hat, or his coat, or his carriage, or import his groceries for him; making yourselves sick, that you may lay up something against a sick day, something to be tucked away in an old chest, or in a stocking behind the plastering, or, more safely, in the brick bank; no matter where, no matter how much or how little.

I sometimes wonder that we can be so frivolous, I may almost say, as to attend to the gross but somewhat foreign form of servitude called Negro Slavery, there are so many keen and subtle masters that enslave both north and south. It is hard to have a southern overseer; it is worse to have a northern one; but worst of all when you are the slave-driver of yourself. Talk of a divinity in man! Look at the teamster on the highway, wending to market by day or night; does any divinity stir within him? His highest duty to fodder and water his horses! What is his destiny to him compared with the shipping interests? Does not he drive for Squire Make-a-stir? How godlike, how immortal, is he? See how he cowers and sneaks, how vaguely all the day he fears, not being immortal nor divine, but the slave and prisoner of his own opinion of himself, a fame won by his own deeds. Public opinion is a weak tyrant compared with our own private opinion. What a man thinks of himself, that it is which determines, or rather indicates, his fate. Self-emancipation even in the West Indian provinces of the fancy and imagination,—what Wilberforce[8] is there to bring that about? Think, also, of the ladies of the land weaving toilet cushions

---

7. Literally, "another's brass"; metaphorically, "another person's money" or "debt."

8. William Wilberforce (1759–1833), leader of the anti-slavery forces in England.

against the last day, not to betray too green an interest in their fates! As if you could kill time without injuring eternity.

The mass of men lead lives of quiet desperation. What is called resignation is confirmed desperation. From the desperate city you go into the desperate country, and have to console yourself with the bravery of minks and muskrats. A stereotyped but unconscious despair is concealed even under what are called the games and amusements of mankind. There is no play in them, for this comes after work. But it is a characteristic of wisdom not to do desperate things.

When we consider what, to use the words of the catechism, is the chief end of man, and what are the true necessaries and means of life, it appears as if men had deliberately chosen the common mode of living because they preferred it to any other. Yet they honestly think there is no choice left. But alert and healthy natures remember that the sun rose clear. It is never too late to give up our prejudices. No way of thinking or doing, however ancient, can be trusted without proof. What every body echoes or in silence passes by as true to-day may turn out to be falsehood to-morrow, mere smoke of opinion, which some had trusted for a cloud that would sprinkle fertilizing rain on their fields. What old people say you cannot do you try and find that you can. Old deeds for old people, and new deeds for new. Old people did not know enough once, perchance, to fetch fresh fuel to keep the fire a-going; new people put a little dry wood under a pot, and are whirled round the globe with the speed of birds, in a way to kill old people, as the phrase is. Age is no better, hardly so well, qualified for an instructor as youth, for it has not profited so much as it has lost. One may almost doubt if the wisest man has learned any thing of absolute value by living. Practically, the old have no very important advice to give the young, their own experience has been so partial, and their lives have been such miserable failures, for private reasons, as they must believe; and it may be that they have some faith left which belies that experience, and they are only less young than they were. I have lived some thirty years on this planet, and I have yet to hear the first syllable of valuable or even earnest advice from my seniors. They have told me nothing, and probably cannot tell me any thing, to the purpose. Here is life, an experiment to a great extent untried by me; but it does not avail me that they have tried it. If I have any experience which I think valuable, I am sure to reflect that this my Mentors [9] said nothing about.

One farmer says to me, "You cannot live on vegetable food

9. The wise protector of Telemachus, the son of Odysseus in Homer's *Odyssey;* metaphorically, any wise teacher.

solely, for it furnishes nothing to make bones with;" and so he religiously devotes a part of his day to supplying his system with the raw material of bones; walking all the while he talks behind his oxen, which, with vegetable-made bones, jerk him and his lumbering plough along in spite of every obstacle. Some things are really necessaries of life in some circles, the most helpless and diseased, which in others are luxuries merely, and in others still are entirely unknown.

The whole ground of human life seems to some to have been gone over by their predecessors, both the heights and the valleys, and all things to have been cared for. According to Evelyn,[1] "the wise Solomon prescribed ordinances for the very distances of trees; and the Roman prætors have decided how often you may go into your neighbor's land to gather the acorns which fall on it without trespass, and what share belongs to that neighbor." Hippocrates[2] has even left directions how we should cut our nails; that is, even with the ends of the fingers, neither shorter nor longer. Undoubtedly the very tedium and ennui which presume to have exhausted the variety and the joys of life are as old as Adam. But man's capacities have never been measured; nor are we to judge of what he can do by any precedents, so little has been tried. Whatever have been thy failures hitherto, "be not afflicted, my child, for who shall assign to thee what thou hast left undone?"

We might try our lives by a thousand simple tests; as, for instance, that the same sun which ripens my beans illumines at once a system of earths like ours. If I had remembered this it would have prevented some mistakes. This was not the light in which I hoed them. The stars are the apexes of what wonderful triangles! What distant and different beings in the various mansions of the universe are contemplating the same one at the same moment! Nature and human life are as various as our several constitutions. Who shall say what prospect life offers to another? Could a greater miracle take place than for us to look through each other's eyes for an instant? We should live in all the ages of the world in an hour; ay, in all the worlds of the ages. History, Poetry, Mythology!—I know of no reading of another's experience so startling and informing as this would be.

The greater part of what my neighbors call good I believe in my soul to be bad, and if I repent of any thing, it is very likely to be my good behavior. What demon possessed me that I behaved so well? You may say the wisest thing you can old man,—you who have lived seventy years, not without honor of a kind,—I hear an

---

1. John Evelyn (1620–1706), British agricultural writer; the quotation is from *Sylva: or, a Discourse of Forest-Trees.*

2. An ancient Greek physician (fl. 300 B.C.), frequently called "the father of medicine."

irresistible voice which invites me away from all that. One generation abandons the enterprises of another like stranded vessels.

I think that we may safely trust a good deal more than we do.
We may waive just so much care of ourselves as we honestly bestow elsewhere. Nature is as well adapted to our weakness as to
our strength. The incessant anxiety and strain of some is a well
nigh incurable form of disease. We are made to exaggerate the
importance of what work we do; and yet how much is not done
by us! or, what if we had been taken sick? How vigilant we are!
determined not to live by faith if we can avoid it; all the day long
on the alert, at night we unwillingly say our prayers and commit
ourselves to uncertainties. So thoroughly and sincerely are we
compelled to live, reverencing our life, and denying the possibility
of change. This is the only way, we say; but there are as many
ways as there can be drawn radii from one centre. All change is a
miracle to contemplate; but it is a miracle which is taking place
every instant. Confucius [3] said, "To know that we know what we
know, and that we do not know what we do not know, that is
true knowledge." When one man has reduced a fact of the imagination to be a fact to his understanding, I foresee that all men
will at length establish their lives on that basis.

Let us consider for a moment what most of the trouble and
anxiety which I have referred to is about, and how much it is
necessary that we be troubled, or, at least, careful. It would be
some advantage to live a primitive and frontier life, though in the
midst of an outward civilization, if only to learn what are the
gross necessaries of life and what methods have been taken to
obtain them; or even to look over the old day-books of the merchants, to see what it was that men most commonly bought at the
stores, what they stored, that is, what are the grossest groceries. For
the improvements of ages have had but little influence on the
essential laws of man's existence; as our skeletons, probably, are
not to be distinguished from those of our ancestors.

By the words, *necessary of life*, I mean whatever, of all that
man obtains by his own exertions, has been from the first, or from
long use has become, so important to human life that few, if any,
whether from savageness, or poverty, or philosophy, ever attempt
to do without it. To many creatures there is in this sense but one
necessary of life, Food. To the bison of the prairie it is a few
inches of palatable grass, with water to drink; unless he seeks the
Shelter of the forest or the mountain's shadow. None of the brute
creation requires more than Food and Shelter. The necessaries
of life for man in this climate may, accurately enough, be dis-

3. Chinese philosopher and teacher (551?–478? B.C.) and one of Thoreau's favorite
authors.

tributed under the several heads of Food, Shelter, Clothing, and Fuel; for not till we have secured these are we prepared to entertain the true problems of life with freedom and a prospect of success. Man has invented, not only houses, but clothes and cooked food; and possibly from the accidental discovery of the warmth of fire, and the consequent use of it, at first a luxury, arose the present necessity to sit by it. We observe cats and dogs acquiring the same second nature. By proper Shelter and Clothing we legitimately retain our own internal heat; but with an excess of these, or of Fuel, that is, with an external heat greater than our own internal, may not cookery properly be said to begin? Darwin,[4] the naturalist, says of the inhabitants of Tierra del Fuego,[5] that while his own party, who were well clothed and sitting close to a fire, were far from too warm, these naked savages, who were farther off, were observed, to his great surprise, "to be streaming with perspiration at undergoing such a roasting." So, we are told, the New Hollander [6] goes naked with impunity, while the European shivers in his clothes. Is it impossible to combine the hardiness of these savages with the intellectualness of the civilized man? According to Liebig,[7] man's body is a stove, and food the fuel which keeps up the internal combustion in the lungs. In cold weather we eat more, in warm less. The animal heat is the result of a slow combustion, and disease and death take place when this is too rapid; or for want of fuel, or from some defect in the draught, the fire goes out. Of course the vital heat is not to be confounded with fire; but so much for analogy. It appears, therefore, from the above list, that the expression, *animal life*, is nearly synonymous with the expression, *animal heat*; for while Food may be regarded as the Fuel which keeps up the fire within us,—and Fuel serves only to prepare that Food or to increase the warmth of our bodies by addition from without,—Shelter and Clothing also serve only to retain the *heat* thus generated and absorbed.

The grand necessity, then, for our bodies, is to keep warm, to keep the vital heat in us. What pains we accordingly take, not only with our Food, and Clothing, and Shelter, but with our beds, which are our night-clothes, robbing the nests and breasts of birds to prepare this shelter within a shelter, as the mole has its bed of grass and leaves at the end of its burrow! The poor man is wont to complain that this is a cold world; and to cold, no less physical than social, we refer directly a great part of our ails. The summer,

4. Charles Darwin (1809–1882), an English naturalist who developed the theory of evolution.
5. An island at the southern tip of South America.

6. Mid-nineteenth century name for Australian aborigines.
7. Justus von Liebig (1803–1873), German organic chemist.

in some climates, makes possible to man a sort of Elysian life.[8] Fuel, except to cook his Food, is then unnecessary; the sun is his fire, and many of the fruits are sufficiently cooked by its rays; while Food generally is more various, and more easily obtained, and Clothing and Shelter are wholly or half unnecessary. At the present day, and in this country, as I find by my own experience, a few implements, a knife, an axe, a spade, a wheelbarrow, &c., and for the studious, lamplight, stationery, and access to a few books, rank next to necessaries, and can all be obtained at a trifling cost. Yet some, not wise, go to the other side of the globe, to barbarous and unhealthy regions, and devote themselves to trade for ten or twenty years, in order that they may live,—that is, keep comfortably warm,—and die in New England at last. The luxuriously rich are not simply kept comfortably warm, but unnaturally hot; as I implied before, they are cooked, of course à *la mode*.[9]

Most of the luxuries, and many of the so called comforts of life, are not only not indispensable, but positive hinderances to the elevation of mankind. With respect to luxuries and comforts, the wisest have ever lived a more simple and meagre life than the poor. The ancient philosophers, Chinese, Hindoo, Persian, and Greek, were a class than which none has been poorer in outward riches, none so rich in inward. We know not much about them. It is remarkable that *we* know so much of them as we do. The same is true of the more modern reformers and benefactors of their race. None can be an impartial or wise observer of human life but from the vantage ground of what *we* should call voluntary poverty. Of a life of luxury the fruit is luxury, whether in agriculture, or commerce, or literature, or art. There are nowadays professors of philosophy, but not philosophers. Yet it is admirable to profess because it was once admirable to live. To be a philosopher is not merely to have subtle thoughts, nor even to found a school, but so to love wisdom as to live according to its dictates, a life of simplicity, independence, magnanimity, and trust. It is to solve some of the problems of life, not only theoretically, but practically. The success of great scholars and thinkers is commonly a courtier-like success, not kingly, not manly. They make shift to live merely by conformity, practically as their fathers did, and are in no sense the progenitors of a nobler race of men. But why do men degenerate ever? What makes families run out? What is the nature of the luxury which enervates and destroys nations? Are we sure that there is none of it in our own lives? The philosopher is in

8. In Greek mythology, Elysium was the home of the blessed dead; also called the "Elysian fields."   9. In a fashionable style.

advance of his age even in the outward form of his life. He is not fed, sheltered, clothed, warmed, like his contemporaries. How can a man be a philosopher and not maintain his vital heat by better methods than other men?

When a man is warmed by the several modes which I have described, what does he want next? Surely not more warmth of the same kind, as more and richer food, larger and more splendid houses, finer and more abundant clothing, more numerous incessant and hotter fires, and the like. When he has obtained those things which are necessary to life, there is another alternative than to obtain the superfluities; and that is, to adventure on life now, his vacation from humbler toil having commenced. The soil, it appears, is suited to the seed, for it has sent its radicle downward, and it may now send its shoot upward also with confidence. Why has man rooted himself thus firmly in the earth, but that he may rise in the same proportion into the heavens above?—for the nobler plants are valued for the fruit they bear at last in the air and light, far from the ground, and are not treated like the humbler esculents, which, though they may be biennials, are cultivated only till they have perfected their root, and often cut down at top for this purpose, so that most would not know them in their flowering season.

I do not mean to prescribe rules to strong and valiant natures, who will mind their own affairs whether in heaven or hell, and perchance build more magnificently and spend more lavishly than the richest, without ever impoverishing themselves, not knowing how they live,—if, indeed, there are any such, as has been dreamed; nor to those who find their encouragement and inspiration in precisely the present condition of things, and cherish it with the fondness and enthusiasm of lovers,—and, to some extent, I reckon myself in this number; I do not speak to those who are well employed, in whatever circumstances, and they know whether they are well employed or not;—but mainly to the mass of men who are discontented, and idly complaining of the hardness of their lot or of the times, when they might improve them. There are some who complain most energetically and inconsolably of any, because they are, as they say, doing their duty. I also have in my mind that seemingly wealthy, but most terribly impoverished class of all, who have accumulated dross, but know not how to use it, or get rid of it, and thus have forged their own golden or silver fetters.

If I should attempt to tell how I have desired to spend my life in years past, it would probably surprise those of my readers who are somewhat acquainted with its actual history; it would cer-

tainly astonish those who know nothing about it. I will only hint
at some of the enterprises which I have cherished.

In any weather, at any hour of the day or night, I have been
anxious to improve the nick of time, and notch it on my stick too;
to stand on the meeting of two eternities, the past and future,
which is precisely the present moment; to toe that line. You will
pardon some obscurities, for there are more secrets in my trade
than in most men's, and yet not voluntarily kept, but inseparable
from its very nature. I would gladly tell all that I know about it,
and never paint "No Admittance" on my gate.

I long ago lost a hound, a bay horse, and a turtle-dove,[1] and
am still on their trail. Many are the travellers I have spoken concerning them, describing their tracks and what calls they answered
to. I have met one or two who had heard the hound, and the
tramp of the horse, and even seen the dove disappear behind a
cloud, and they seemed as anxious to recover them as if they had
lost them themselves.

To anticipate, not the sunrise and the dawn merely, but, if
possible, Nature herself! How many mornings, summer and winter, before yet any neighbor was stirring about his business, have I
been about mine! No doubt, many of my townsmen have met me
returning from this enterprise, farmers starting for Boston in the
twilight, or woodchoppers going to their work. It is true, I never
assisted the sun materially in his rising, but, doubt not, it was of
the last importance only to be present at it.

So many autumn, ay, and winter days, spent outside the town,
trying to hear what was in the wind, to hear and carry it express!
I well-nigh sunk all my capital in it, and lost my own breath into
the bargain, running in the face of it. If it had concerned either of
the political parties, depend upon it, it would have appeared in the
Gazette [2] with the earliest intelligence. At other times watching
from the observatory of some cliff or tree, to telegraph any new
arrival; or waiting at evening on the hill-tops for the sky to fall,
that I might catch something, though I never caught much, and
that, manna-wise, would dissolve again in the sun.

For a long time I was reporter to a journal,[3] of no very wide
circulation, whose editor has never yet seen fit to print the bulk
of my contributions, and, as is too common with writers, I got
only my labor for my pains. However, in this case my pains were
their own reward.

For many years I was self-appointed inspector of snow storms

---

1. Probably symbols for the unattainable things of life; critics differ over
whether the symbols have specific references.
2. A common name for a newspaper,
including the *Yeoman's Gazette* of Concord; by extension, any newspaper.
3. Either Thoreau's own *Journal* or the
transcendentalist magazine, *Dial.*

and rain storms, and did my duty faithfully; surveyor, if not of highways, then of forest paths and all across-lot routes, keeping them open, and ravines bridged and passable at all seasons, where the public heel had testified to their utility.

I have looked after the wild stock of the town, which give a faithful herdsman a good deal of trouble by leaping fences; and I have had an eye to the unfrequented nooks and corners of the farm; though I did not always know whether Jonas or Solomon worked in a particular field to-day; that was none of my business. I have watered the red huckleberry, the sand cherry and the nettle tree, the red pine and the black ash, the white grape and the yellow violet, which might have withered else in dry seasons.

In short, I went on thus for a long time, I may say it without boasting, faithfully minding my business, till it became more and more evident that my townsmen would not after all admit me into the list of town officers, nor make my place a sinecure with a moderate allowance. My accounts, which I can swear to have kept faithfully, I have, indeed, never got audited, still less accepted, still less paid and settled. However, I have not set my heart on that.

Not long since, a strolling Indian went to sell baskets at the house of a well-known lawyer in my neighborhood. "Do you wish to buy any baskets?" he asked. "No, we do not want any," was the reply. "What!" exclaimed the Indian as he went out the gate, "do you mean to starve us?" Having seen his industrious white neighbors so well off,—that the lawyer had only to weave arguments, and by some magic wealth and standing followed, he had said to himself; I will go into business; I will weave baskets; it is a thing which I can do. Thinking that when he had made the baskets he would have done his part, and then it would be the white man's to buy them. He had not discovered that it was necessary for him to make it worth the other's while to buy them, or at least make him think that it was so, or to make something else which it would be worth his while to buy. I too had woven a kind of basket of a delicate texture, but I had not made it worth any one's while to buy them. Yet not the less, in my case, did I think it worth my while to weave them, and instead of studying how to make it worth men's while to buy my baskets, I studied rather how to avoid the necessity of selling them. The life which men praise and regard as successful is but one kind. Why should we exaggerate any one kind at the expense of the others?

Finding that my fellow-citizens were not likely to offer me any room in the court house, or any curacy or living any where else, but I must shift for myself, I turned my face more exclusively than ever to the woods, where I was better known. I determined to go into business at once, and not wait to acquire the usual capital, using such slender means as I had already got. My purpose in going to Walden Pond was not to live cheaply nor to live dearly there, but to transact some private business with the fewest obstacles; to be hindered from accomplishing which for want of a little common sense, a little enterprise and business talent, appeared not so sad as foolish.

I have always endeavored to acquire strict business habits; they are indispensable to every man. If your trade is with the Celestial Empire,[4] then some small counting house on the coast, in some Salem [5] harbor, will be fixture enough. You will export such articles as the country affords, purely native products, much ice and pine timber and a little granite, always in native bottoms. These will be good ventures. To oversee all the details yourself in person; to be at once pilot and captain, and owner and underwriter; to buy and sell and keep the accounts; to read every letter received, and write or read every letter sent; to superintend the discharge of imports night and day; to be upon many parts of the coast almost at the same time;—often the richest freight will be discharged upon a Jersey shore;[6]—to be your own telegraph, unweariedly sweeping the horizon, speaking all passing vessels bound coastwise; to keep up a steady despatch of commodities, for the supply of such a distant and exorbitant market; to keep yourself informed of the state of the markets, prospects of war and peace every where, and anticipate the tendencies of trade and civilization,—taking advantage of the results of all exploring expeditions, using new passages and all improvements in navigation;—charts to be studied, the position of reefs and new lights and buoys to be ascertained, and ever, and ever, the logarithmic tables to be corrected, for by the error of some calculator the vessel often splits upon a rock that should have reached a friendly pier,—there is the untold fate of La Perouse;[7]—universal science to be kept pace with, studying the lives of all great discoverers and navigators, great adventurers and merchants, from Hanno [8] and the Phœnicians [9] down to our day; in fine, account of stock to be taken from time to time, to know how you stand. It is a labor to task the faculties of a man,—such problems of profit and loss, of interest, of tare and tret,[1] and gauging of all kinds in it, as demand a universal knowledge.

I have thought that Walden Pond would be a good place for

---

4. Common mid-nineteenth century name for China.
5. An important port on the Massachusetts coast.
6. The coast of New Jersey on which many ships were wrecked.
7. French explorer (1741–1788) whose ship was lost in the south Pacific.

8. Probably the Carthaginian explorer and navigator (ca. 500 B.C.).
9. Citizens of ancient Phœnicia (fl. 1200 B.C.), said to be excellent sailors.
1. In shipping, "tare" is a deduction for the weight of the container; "tret" is an allowance made to buyers for waste or damage.

business, not solely on account of the railroad and the ice trade; it offers advantages which it may not be good policy to divulge; it is a good port and a good foundation. No Neva [2] marshes to be filled; though you must every where build on piles of your own driving. It is said that a flood-tide, with a westerly wind, and ice in the Neva, would sweep St. Petersburg from the face of the earth.

As this business was to be entered into without the usual capital, it may not be easy to conjecture where those means, that will still be indispensable to every such undertaking, were to be obtained. As for Clothing, to come at once to the practical part of the question, perhaps we are led oftener by the love of novelty, and a regard for the opinions of men, in procuring it, than by a true utility. Let him who has work to do recollect that the object of clothing is, first, to retain the vital heat, and secondly, in this state of society, to cover nakedness, and he may judge how much of any necessary or important work may be accomplished without adding to his wardrobe. Kings and queens who wear a suit but once, though made by some tailor or dressmaker to their majesties, cannot know the comfort of wearing a suit that fits. They are no better than wooden horses to hang the clean clothes on. Every day our garments become more assimilated to ourselves, receiving the impress of the wearer's character, until we hesitate to lay them aside, without such delay and medical appliances and some such solemnity even as our bodies. No man ever stood the lower in my estimation for having a patch in his clothes; yet I am sure that there is greater anxiety, commonly, to have fashionable, or at least clean and unpatched clothes, than to have a sound conscience. But even if the rent is not mended, perhaps the worst vice betrayed is improvidence. I sometimes try my acquaintances by such tests as this;—who could wear a patch, or two extra seams only, over the knee? Most behave as if they believed that their prospects for life would be ruined if they should do it. It would be easier for them to hobble to town with a broken leg than with a broken pantaloon. Often if an accident happens to a gentleman's legs, they can be mended; but if a similar accident happens to the legs of his pantaloons, there is no help for it; for he considers, not what is truly respectable, but what is respected. We know but few men, a great many coats and breeches. Dress a scarecrow in your last shift, you standing shiftless by, who would not soonest salute the scarecrow? Passing a cornfield the other day, close by a hat and coat on a stake, I recognized the owner of the farm. He was only

2. St. Petersburg (now Leningrad) in Russia was built on the delta of the Neva River.

a little more weather-beaten than when I saw him last. I have heard of a dog that barked at every stranger who approached his master's premises with clothes on, but was easily quieted by a naked thief. It is an interesting question how far men would retain their relative rank if they were divested of their clothes. Could you, in such a case, tell surely of any company of civilized men, which belonged to the most respected class? When Madam Pfeiffer,[3] in her adventurous travels round the world, from east to west, had got so near home as Asiatic Russia, she says that she felt the necessity of wearing other than a travelling dress, when she went to meet the authorities, for she "was now in a civilized country, where——people are judged of by their clothes." Even in our democratic New England towns the accidental possession of wealth, and its manifestation in dress and equipage alone, obtain for the possessor almost universal respect. But they who yield such respect, numerous as they are, are so far heathen, and need to have a missionary sent to them. Beside, clothes introduced sewing, a kind of work which you may call endless; a woman's dress, at least, is never done.

A man who has at length found something to do will not need to get a new suit to do it in; for him the old will do, that has lain dusty in the garret for an indeterminate period. Old shoes will serve a hero longer than they have served his valet,—if a hero ever has a valet,—bare feet are older than shoes, and he can make them do. Only they who go to soirées and legislative halls must have new coats, coats to change as often as the man changes in them. But if my jacket and trousers, my hat and shoes, are fit to worship God in, they will do; will they not? Who ever saw his old clothes,—his old coat, actually worn out, resolved into its primitive elements, so that it was not a deed of charity to bestow it on some poor boy, by him perchance to be bestowed on some poorer still, or shall we say richer, who could do with less? I say, beware of all enterprises that require new clothes, and not rather a new wearer of clothes. If there is not a new man, how can the new clothes be made to fit? If you have any enterprise before you, try it in your old clothes. All men want, not something to· *do with*, but something to *do*, or rather something to *be*. Perhaps we should never procure a new suit, however ragged or dirty the old, until we have so conducted, so enterprised or sailed in some way, that we feel like new men in the old, and that to retain it would be like keeping new wine in old bottles. Our moulting season, like that of the fowls, must be a crisis in our lives. The loon retires to solitary ponds to spend it. Thus also the snake casts its slough, and the caterpillar its wormy coat, by an internal industry and expan-

3. A German woman who traveled around the world in the 1840's.

sion; for clothes are but our outmost cuticle and mortal coil. Otherwise we shall be found sailing under false colors, and be inevitably cashiered at last by our own opinion, as well as that of mankind.

We don garment after garment, as if we grew like exogenous plants by addition without. Our outside and often thin and fanciful clothes are our epidermis or false skin, which partakes not of our life, and may be stripped off here and there without fatal injury; our thicker garments, constantly worn, are our cellular integument, or cortex; but our shirts are our liber or true bark, which cannot be removed without girdling and so destroying the man. I believe that all races at some seasons wear something equivalent to the shirt. It is desirable that a man be clad so simply that he can lay his hands on himself in the dark, and that he live in all respects so compactly and preparedly, that, if an enemy take the town, he can, like the old philosopher, walk out the gate empty-handed without anxiety. While one thick garment is, for most purposes, as good as three thin ones, and cheap clothing can be obtained at prices really to suit customers; while a thick coat can be bought for five dollars, which will last as many years, thick pantaloons for two dollars, cowhide boots for a dollar and a half a pair, a summer hat for a quarter of a dollar, and a winter cap for sixty-two and a half cents, or a better be made at home at a nominal cost, where is he so poor that, clad in such a suit, *of his own earning*, there will not be found wise men to do him reverence?

When I ask for a garment of a particular form, my tailoress tells me gravely, "They do not make them so now," not emphasizing the "They" at all, as if she quoted an authority as impersonal as the Fates,[4] and I find it difficult to get made what I want, simply because she cannot believe that I mean what I say, that I am so rash. When I hear this oracular sentence, I am for a moment absorbed in thought, emphasizing to myself each word separately that I may come at the meaning of it, that I may find out by what degree of consanguinity *They* are related to *me*, and what authority they may have in an affair which affects me so nearly; and, finally, I am inclined to answer her with equal mystery, and without any more emphasis of the "they,"—"It is true, they did not make them so recently, but they do now." Of what use this measuring of me if she does not measure my character, but only the breadth of my shoulders, as it were a peg to hang the coat on? We worship not the Graces,[5] nor the Parcæ,[6] but Fashion. She spins and weaves and cuts with full authority.

4. In classical mythology, the three goddesses who control human destiny.
5. In classical mythology, the three goddesses of grace and beauty.
6. The name of the Fates in Roman mythology.

The head monkey at Paris puts on a traveller's cap, and all the monkeys in America do the same. I sometimes despair of getting any thing quite simple and honest done in this world by the help of men. They would have to be passed through a powerful press first, to squeeze their old notions out of them, so that they would not soon get upon their legs again, and then there would be some one in the company with a maggot in his head, hatched from an egg deposited there nobody knows when, for not even fire kills these things, and you would have lost your labor. Nevertheless, we will not forget that some Egyptian wheat is said to have been handed down to us by a mummy.

On the whole, I think that it cannot be maintained that dressing has in this or any country risen to the dignity of an art. At present men make shift to wear what they can get. Like shipwrecked sailors, they put on what they can find on the beach, and at a little distance, whether of space or time, laugh at each other's masquerade. Every generation laughs at the old fashions, but follows religiously the new. We are amused at beholding the costume of Henry VIII.,[7] or Queen Elizabeth,[8] as much as if it was that of the King and Queen of the Cannibal Islands. All costume off a man is pitiful or grotesque. It is only the serious eye peering from and the sincere life passed within it, which restrain laughter and consecrate the costume of any people. Let Harlequin [9] be taken with a fit of the colic and his trappings will have to serve that mood too. When the soldier is hit by a cannon ball rags are as becoming as purple.

The childish and savage taste of men and women for new patterns keeps how many shaking and squinting through kaleidoscopes that they may discover the particular figure which this generation requires to-day. The manufacturers have learned that this taste is merely whimsical. Of two patterns which differ only by a few threads more or less of a particular color, the one will be sold readily, the other lie on the shelf, though it frequently happens that after the lapse of a season the latter becomes the most fashionable. Comparatively, tattooing is not the hideous custom which it is called. It is not barbarous merely because the printing is skin-deep and unalterable.

I cannot believe that our factory system is the best mode by which men may get clothing. The condition of the operatives is becoming every day more like that of the English; and it cannot be wondered at, since, as far as I have heard or observed, the principal object is, not that mankind may be well and honestly

7. King of England from 1509 to 1547.
8. Elizabeth I, queen of England from 1558 to 1603.

9. A standard character in old Italian comedy, traditionally dressed in multi-colored tights.

clad, but, unquestionably, that the corporations may be enriched. In the long run men hit only what they aim at. Therefore, though they should fail immediately, they had better aim at something high.

As for a Shelter, I will not deny that this is now a necessary of life, though there are instances of men having done without it for long periods in colder countries than this. Samuel Laing [1] says that "The Laplander in his skin dress, and in a skin bag which he puts over his head and shoulders, will sleep night after night on the snow——in a degree of cold which would extinguish the life of one exposed to it in any woollen clothing." He had seen them asleep thus. Yet he adds, "They are not hardier than other people." But, probably, man did not live long on the earth without discovering the convenience which there is in a house, the domestic comforts, which phrase may have originally signified the satisfactions of the house more than of the family; though these must be extremely partial and occasional in those climates where the house is associated in our thoughts with winter or the rainy season chiefly, and two thirds of the year, except for a parasol, is unnecessary. In our climate, in the summer, it was formerly almost solely a covering at night. In the Indian gazettes a wigwam was the symbol of a day's march, and a row of them cut or painted on the bark of a tree signified that so many times they had camped. Man was not made so large limbed and robust but that he must seek to narrow his world, and wall in a space such as fitted him. He was at first bare and out of doors; but though this was pleasant enough in serene and warm weather, by daylight, the rainy season and the winter, to say nothing of the torrid sun, would perhaps have nipped his race in the bud if he had not made haste to clothe himself with the shelter of a house. Adam and Eve, according to the fable, wore the bower before other clothes. Man wanted a home, a place of warmth, or comfort, first of physical warmth, then the warmth of the affections.

We may imagine a time when, in the infancy of the human race, some enterprising mortal crept into a hollow in a rock for shelter. Every child begins the world again, to some extent, and loves to stay out doors, even in wet and cold. It plays house, as well as horse, having an instinct for it. Who does not remember the interest with which when young he looked at shelving rocks, or any approach to a cave? It was the natural yearning of that portion of our most primitive ancestor which still survived in us. From the

---

1. A British author (1780–1868) of several books on the Scandinavian countries; the Lapps were a nomadic Mongolian tribe who settled in northern Scandinavia.

cave we have advanced to roofs of palm leaves, of bark and boughs, of linen woven and stretched, of grass and straw, of boards and shingles, of stones and tiles. At last, we know not what it is to live in the open air, and our lives are domestic in more senses than we think. From the hearth to the field is a great distance. It would be well perhaps if we were to spend more of our days and nights without any obstruction between us and the celestial bodies, if the poet did not speak so much from under a roof, or the saint dwell there so long. Birds do not sing in caves, nor do doves cherish their innocence in dovecots.

However, if one designs to construct a dwelling house, it behooves him to exercise a little Yankee shrewdness, lest after all he find himself in a workhouse, a labyrinth without a clew, a museum, an almshouse, a prison, or a splendid mausoleum instead. Consider first how slight a shelter is absolutely necessary. I have seen Penobscot Indians,[2] in this town, living in tents of thin cotton cloth, while the snow was nearly a foot deep around them, and I thought that they would be glad to have it deeper to keep out the wind. Formerly, when how to get my living honestly, with freedom left for my proper pursuits, was a question which vexed me even more than it does now, for unfortunately I am become somewhat callous, I used to see a large box by the railroad, six feet long by three wide, in which the laborers locked up their tools at night, and it suggested to me that every man who was hard pushed might get such a one for a dollar, and, having bored a few auger holes in it, to admit the air at least, get into it when it rained and at night, and hook down the lid, and so have freedom in his love, and in his soul be free. This did not appear the worst, nor by any means a despicable alternative. You could sit up as late as you pleased, and, whenever you got up, go abroad without any landlord or house-lord dogging you for rent. Many a man is harassed to death to pay the rent of a larger and more luxurious box who would not have frozen to death in such a box as this. I am far from jesting. Economy is a subject which admits of being treated with levity, but it cannot so be disposed of. A comfortable house for a rude and hardy race, that lived mostly out of doors, was once made here almost entirely of such materials as Nature furnished ready to their hands. Gookin,[3] who was superintendent of the Indians subject to the Massachusetts Colony, writing in 1674, says, "The best of their houses are covered very neatly, tight and warm, with barks of trees, slipped from their bodies at those seasons when the sap is up, and made into great flakes, with pressure of weighty timber, when they are green. . . . The meaner

2. A tribe originally from northern Maine.   3. Daniel Gookin (1612–1687).

sort are covered with mats which they make of a kind of bulrush, and are also indifferently tight and warm, but not so good as the former. . . . Some I have seen, sixty or a hundred feet long and thirty feet broad. . . . I have often lodged in their wigwams, and found them as warm as the best English houses." He adds, that they were commonly carpeted and lined within with well-wrought embroidered mats, and were furnished with various utensils. The Indians had advanced so far as to regulate the effect of the wind by a mat suspended over the hole in the roof and moved by a string. Such a lodge was in the first instance constructed in a day or two at most, and taken down and put up in a few hours; and every family owned one, or its apartment in one.

In the savage state every family owns a shelter as good as the best, and sufficient for its coarser and simpler wants; but I think that I speak within bounds when I say that, though the birds of the air have their nests, and the foxes their holes, and the savages their wigwams, in modern civilized society not more than one half the families own a shelter. In the large towns and cities, where civilization especially prevails, the number of those who own a shelter is a very small fraction of the whole. The rest pay an annual tax for this outside garment of all, become indispensable summer and winter, which would buy a village of Indian wigwams, but now helps to keep them poor as long as they live. I do not mean to insist here on the disadvantage of hiring compared with owning, but it is evident that the savage owns his shelter because it costs so little, while the civilized man hires his commonly because he cannot afford to own it; nor can he, in the long run, any better afford to hire. But, answers one, by merely paying this tax the poor civilized man secures an abode which is a palace compared with the savage's. An annual rent of from twenty-five to a hundred dollars, these are the country rates, entitles him to the benefit of the improvements of centuries, spacious apartments, clean paint and paper, Rumford[4] fireplace, back plastering, Venetian blinds, copper pump, spring lock, a commodious cellar, and many other things. But how happens it that he who is said to enjoy these things is so commonly a *poor* civilized man, while the savage, who has them not, is rich as a savage? If it is asserted that civilization is a real advance in the condition of man,—and I think that it is, though only the wise improve their advantages,— it must be shown that it has produced better dwellings without making them more costly; and the cost of a thing is the amount of what I will call life which is required to be exchanged for it, immediately or in the long run. An average house in this neighbor-

4. Benjamin Thompson, Count Rumford (1753–1814), scientist, inventor and soldier-of-fortune.

hood costs perhaps eight hundred dollars, and to lay up this sum will take from ten to fifteen years of the laborer's life, even if he is not encumbered with a family;—estimating the pecuniary value of every man's labor at one dollar a day, for if some receive more, others receive less;—so that he must have spent more than half his life commonly before *his* wigwam will be earned. If we suppose him to pay a rent instead, this is but a doubtful choice of evils. Would the savage have been wise to exchange his wigwam for a palace on these terms?

It may be guessed that I reduce almost the whole advantage of holding this superfluous property as a fund in store against the future, so far as the individual is concerned, mainly to the defraying of funeral expenses. But perhaps a man is not required to bury himself. Nevertheless this points to an important distinction between the civilized man and the savage; and, no doubt, they have designs on us for our benefit, in making the life of a civilized people an *institution*, in which the life of the individual is to a great extent absorbed, in order to preserve and perfect that of the race. But I wish to show at what a sacrifice this advantage is at present obtained, and to suggest that we may possibly so live as to secure all the advantage without suffering any of the disadvantage. What mean ye by saying that the poor ye have always with you, or that the fathers have eaten sour grapes, and the children's teeth are set on edge?

"As I live, saith the Lord God, ye shall not have occasion any more to use this proverb in Israel."

"Behold all souls are mine; as the soul of the father, so also the soul of the son is mine: the soul that sinneth it shall die."

When I consider my neighbors, the farmers of Concord, who are at least as well off as the other classes, I find that for the most part they have been toiling twenty, thirty, or forty years, that they may become the real owners of their farms, which commonly they have inherited with encumbrances, or else bought with hired money,—and we may regard one third of that toil as the cost of their houses,—but commonly they have not paid for them yet. It is true, the encumbrances sometimes outweigh the value of the farm, so that the farm itself becomes one great encumbrance, and still a man is found to inherit it, being well acquainted with it, as he says. On applying to the assessors, I am surprised to learn that they cannot at once name a dozen in the town who own their farms free and clear. If you would know the history of these homesteads, inquire at the bank where they are mortgaged. The man who has actually paid for his farm with labor on it is so rare that every neighbor can point to him. I doubt if there are three such men in Concord. What has been said of the merchants, that a very large majority, even ninety-seven in a hundred, are sure to fail, is equally true of the farmers. With regard to the merchants, however, one of them says pertinently that a great part of their failures are not genuine pecuniary failures, but merely failures to fulfil their engagements, because it is inconvenient; that is, it is the moral character that breaks down. But this puts an infinitely worse face on the matter, and suggests, beside, that probably not even the other three succeed in saving their souls, but are perchance bankrupt in a worse sense than they who fail honestly. Bankruptcy and repudiation are the spring-boards from which much of our civilization vaults and turns its somersets, but the savage stands on the unelastic plank of famine. Yet the Middlesex Cattle Show [5] goes off here with *éclat* [6] annually, as if all the joints of the agricultural machine were suent.[7]

The farmer is endeavoring to solve the problem of a livelihood by a formula more complicated than the problem itself. To get his shoestrings he speculates in herds of cattle. With consummate skill he has set his trap with a hair springe to catch comfort and independence, and then, as he turned away, got his own leg into it. This is the reason he is poor; and for a similar reason we are all poor in respect to a thousand savage comforts, though surrounded by luxuries. As Chapman [8] sings,—

> "The false society of men —
> — for earthly greatness
> All heavenly comforts rarefies to air."

And when the farmer has got his house, he may not be the richer but the poorer for it, and it be the house that has got him. As I understand it, that was a valid objection urged by Momus [9] against the house which Minerva made, that she "had not made it movable, by which means a bad neighborhood might be avoided;" and it may still be urged, for our houses are such unwieldy property that we are often imprisoned rather than housed in them; and the bad neighborhood to be avoided is our own scurvy selves. I know one or two families, at least, in this town, who, for nearly a generation, have been wishing to sell their houses in the outskirts and move into the village, but have not been able to accomplish it, and only death will set them free.

Granted that the *majority* are able at last either to own or hire the modern house with all its improvements. While civilization

---

5. Middlesex is the county of which Concord is a part; the Agricultural Fair was an annual event.
6. Conspicuous success.
7. Also spelled "suant"; a dialect term meaning "running smoothly."

8. George Chapman (1559?–1634), English dramatist, translator, and poet; the quotation is from *The Tragedy of Caesar and Pompey*, V, ii.
9. The Greek god of pleasure.

has been improving our houses, it has not equally improved the men who are to inhabit them. It has created palaces, but it was not so easy to create noblemen and kings. And *if the civilized man's pursuits are no worthier than the savage's, if he is employed the greater part of his life in obtaining gross necessaries and comforts merely, why should he have a better dwelling than the former?*

But how do the poor *minority* fare? Perhaps it will be found, that just in proportion as some have been placed in outward circumstances above the savage, others have been degraded below him. The luxury of one class is counterbalanced by the indigence of another. On the one side is the palace, on the other are the almshouse and "silent poor." [1] The myriads who built the pyramids to be the tombs of the Pharaohs [2] were fed on garlic, and it may be were not decently buried themselves. The mason who finishes the cornice of the palace returns at night perchance to a hut not so good as a wigwam. It is a mistake to suppose that, in a country where the usual evidences of civilization exist, the condition of a very large body of the inhabitants may not be as degraded as that of savages. I refer to the degraded poor, not now to the degraded rich. To know this I should not need to look farther than to the shanties which every where border our railroads, that last improvement in civilization; where I see in my daily walks human beings living in sties, and all winter with an open door, for the sake of light, without any visible, often imaginable, wood pile, and the forms of both old and young are permanently contracted by the long habit of shrinking from cold and misery, and the development of all their limbs and faculties is checked. It certainly is fair to look at that class by whose labor the works which distinguish this generation are accomplished. Such too, to a greater or less extent, is the condition of the operatives of every denomination in England, which is the great workhouse of the world. Or I could refer you to Ireland, which is marked as one of the white or enlightened spots on the map. Contrast the physical condition of the Irish with that of the North American Indian, or the South Sea Islander, or any other savage race before it was degraded by contact with the civilized man. Yet I have no doubt that that people's rulers are as wise as the average of civilized rulers. Their condition only proves what squalidness may consist with civilization. I hardly need refer now to the laborers in our Southern States who produce the staple exports of this country, and are themselves a staple production of the South. But to confine myself to those who are said to be in *moderate* circumstances.

1. Any debtor; perhaps also one who tries to hide his debts and who refuses charity.
2. The rulers of ancient Egypt.

Most men appear never to have considered what a house is, and are actually though needlessly poor all their lives because they think that they must have such a one as their neighbors have. As if one were to wear any sort of coat which the tailor might cut out for him, or, gradually leaving off palmleaf hat or cap of woodchuck skin, complain of hard times because he could not afford to buy him a crown! It is possible to invent a house still more convenient and luxurious than we have, which yet all would admit that man could not afford to pay for. Shall we always study to obtain more of these things, and not sometimes to be content with less? Shall the respectable citizen thus gravely teach, by precept and example, the necessity of the young man's providing a certain number of superfluous glowshoes,[3] and umbrellas, and empty guest chambers for empty guests, before he dies? Why should not our furniture be as simple as the Arab's or the Indian's? When I think of the benefactors of the race, whom we have apotheosized as messengers from heaven, bearers of divine gifts to man, I do not see in my mind any retinue at their heels, any car-load of fashionable furniture. Or what if I were to allow— would it not be a singular allowance?—that our furniture should be more complex than the Arab's, in proportion as we are morally and intellectually his superiors! At present our houses are cluttered and defiled with it, and a good housewife would sweep out the greater part into the dust hole, and not leave her morning's work undone. Morning work! By the blushes of Aurora [4] and the music of Memnon,[5] what should be man's *morning work* in this world? I had three pieces of limestone on my desk, but I was terrified to find that they required to be dusted daily, when the furniture of my mind was all undusted still, and I threw them out the window in disgust. How, then, could I have a furnished house? I would rather sit in the open air, for no dust gathers on the grass, unless where man has broken ground.

It is the luxurious and dissipated who set the fashions which the herd so diligently follow. The traveller who stops at the best houses, so called, soon discovers this, for the publicans presume him to be a Sardanapalus,[6] and if he resigned himself to their tender mercies he would soon be completely emasculated. I think that in the railroad car we are inclined to spend more on luxury than on safety and convenience, and it threatens without attaining these to become no better than a modern drawing room, with its divans, and ottomans, and sunshades, and a hundred other oriental things, which we are taking west with us, invented for the ladies

3. Galoshes, waterproof overshoes.
4. In Roman mythology, the goddess of dawn.
5. A statue of an ancient Theban king which supposedly emitted musical sounds at dawn.
6. The last and corrupt king of ancient Assyria (d. 880 B.C.).

of the harem and the effeminate natives of the Celestial Empire, which Jonathan [7] should be ashamed to know the names of. I would rather sit on a pumpkin and have it all to myself, than be crowded on a velvet cushion. I would rather ride on earth in an ox cart with a free circulation, than go to heaven in the fancy car of an excursion train and breathe a *malaria* all the way.

The very simplicity and nakedness of man's life in the primitive ages imply this advantage at least, that they left him still but a sojourner in nature. When he was refreshed with food and sleep he contemplated his journey again. He dwelt, as it were, in a tent in this world, and was either threading the valleys, or crossing the plains, or climbing the mountain tops. But lo! men have become the tools of their tools. The man who independently plucked the fruits when he was hungry is become a farmer; and he who stood under a tree for shelter, a housekeeper. We now no longer camp as for a night, but have settled down on earth and forgotten heaven. We have adopted Christianity merely as an improved method of *agri*-culture. We have built for this world a family mansion, and for the next a family tomb. The best works of art are the expression of man's struggle to free himself from this condition, but the effect of our art is merely to make this low state comfortable and that higher state to be forgotten. There is actually no place in this village for a work of *fine* art, if any had come down to us, to stand, for our lives, our houses and streets, furnish no proper pedestal for it. There is not a nail to hang a picture on, nor a shelf to receive the bust of a hero or a saint. When I consider how our houses are built and paid for, or not paid for, and their internal economy managed and sustained, I wonder that the floor does not give way under the visitor while he is admiring the gewgaws upon the mantel-piece, and let him through into the cellar, to some solid and honest though earthy foundation. I cannot but perceive that this so called rich and refined life is a thing jumped at, and I do not get on in the enjoyment of the *fine* arts which adorn it, my attention being wholly occupied with the jump; for I remember that the greatest genuine leap, due to human muscles alone, on record, is that of certain wandering Arabs, who are said to have cleared twenty-five feet on level ground. Without factitious support, man is sure to come to earth again beyond that distance. The first question which I am tempted to put to the proprietor of such great impropriety is, Who bolsters you? Are you one of the ninety-seven who fail, or the three who succeed? Answer me these questions, and then perhaps I may look at your bawbles and find them ornamental.

---

7. A common mid-nineteenth century name for any American; also, "Brother Jonathan."

The cart before the horse is neither beautiful nor useful. Before we can adorn our houses with beautiful objects the walls must be stripped, and our lives must be stripped, and beautiful house-keeping and beautiful living be laid for a foundation: now, a taste for the beautiful is most cultivated out of doors, where there is no house and no housekeeper.

Old Johnson,[8] in his "Wonder-Working Providence," speaking of the first settlers of this town, with whom he was contemporary, tells us that "they burrow themselves in the earth for their first shelter under some hillside, and, casting the soil aloft upon timber, they make a smoky fire against the earth, at the highest side." They did not "provide them houses," says he, "till the earth, by the Lord's blessing, brought forth bread to feed them," and the first year's crop was so light that "they were forced to cut their bread very thin for a long season." The secretary of the Province of New Netherland,[9] writing in Dutch, in 1650, for the information of those who wished to take up land there, states more particu-larly, that "those in New Netherland, and especially in New England, who have no means to build farm houses at first accord-ing to their wishes, dig a square pit in the ground, cellar fashion, six or seven feet deep, as long and as broad as they think proper, case the earth inside with wood all round the wall, and line the wood with the bark of trees or something else to prevent the cav-ing in of the earth; floor this cellar with plank, and wainscot it overhead for a ceiling, raise a roof of spars clear up, and cover the spars with bark or green sods, so that they can live dry and warm in these houses with their entire families for two, three, and four years, it being understood that partitions are run through those cellars which are adapted to the size of the family. The wealthy and principal men in New England, in the beginning of the colonies, commenced their first dwelling houses in this fashion for two reasons; firstly, in order not to waste time in building, and not to want food the next season; secondly, in order not to dis-courage poor laboring people whom they brought over in numbers from Fatherland. In the course of three or four years, when the country became adapted to agriculture, they built themselves handsome houses, spending on them several thousands."

In this course which our ancestors took there was a show of prudence at least, as if their principle were to satisfy the more pressing wants first. But are the more pressing wants satisfied now? When I think of acquiring for myself one of our luxurious dwell-ings, I am deterred, for, so to speak, the country is not yet adapted to *human* culture, and we are still forced to cut our *spiritual* bread

8. Edward Johnson (1598–1672), early American historian.

9. Seventeenth-century name for what is now New York.

far thinner than our forefathers did their wheaten. Not that all architectual ornament is to be neglected even in the rudest periods; but let our houses first be lined with beauty, where they come in contact with our lives, like the tenement of the shellfish, and not overlaid with it. But, alas! I have been inside one or two of them, and know what they are lined with.

Though we are not so degenerate but that we might possibly live in a cave or a wigwam or wear skins to-day, it certainly is better to accept the advantages, though so dearly bought, which the invention and industry of mankind offer. In such a neighborhood as this, boards and shingles, lime and bricks, are cheaper and more easily obtained than suitable caves, or whole logs, or bark in sufficient quantities, or even well-tempered clay or flat stones. I speak understandingly on this subject, for I have made myself acquainted with it both theoretically and practically. With a little more wit we might use these materials so as to become richer than the richest now are, and make our civilization a blessing. The civilized man is a more experienced and wiser savage. But to make haste to my own experiment.

Near the end of March, 1845, I borrowed an axe and went down to the woods by Walden Pond, nearest to where I intended to build my house, and began to cut down some tall arrowy white pines, still in their youth, for timber. It is difficult to begin without borrowing, but perhaps it is the most generous course thus to permit your fellow-men to have an interest in your enterprise. The owner of the axe, as he released his hold on it, said that it was the apple of his eye; but I returned it sharper than I received it. It was a pleasant hillside where I worked, covered with pine woods, through which I looked out on the pond, and a small open field in the woods where pines and hickories were springing up. The ice in the pond was not yet dissolved, though there were some open spaces, and it was all dark colored and saturated with water. There were some slight flurries of snow during the days that I worked there; but for the most part when I came out on to the railroad, on my way home, its yellow sand heap stretched away gleaming in the hazy atmosphere, and the rails shone in the spring sun, and I heard the lark and pewee [1] and other birds already come to commence another year with us. They were pleasant spring days, in which the winter of man's discontent was thawing as well as the earth, and the life that had lain torpid began to stretch itself. One day, when my axe had come off and I had cut a green hickory for a wedge, driving it with a stone, and had placed the whole to soak in a pond hole in order to swell the

1. The meadowlark and the phoebe.

wood, I saw a striped snake run into the water, and he lay on the bottom, apparently without inconvenience, as long as I staid there, or more than a quarter of an hour; perhaps because he had not yet fairly come out of the torpid state. It appeared to me that for a like reason men remain in their present low and primitive condition; but if they should feel the influence of the spring of springs arousing them, they would of necessity rise to a higher and more ethereal life. I had previously seen the snakes in frosty mornings in my path with portions of their bodies still numb and inflexible, waiting for the sun to thaw them. On the 1st of April it rained and melted the ice, and in the early part of the day, which was very foggy, I heard a stray goose groping about over the pond and cackling as if lost, or like the spirit of the fog.

So I went on for some days cutting and hewing timber, and also studs and rafters, all with my narrow axe, not having many communicable or scholar-like thoughts, singing to myself,— [2]

> Men say they know many things;
> But lo! they have taken wings, —
> The arts and sciences,
> And a thousand appliances;
> The wind that blows
> Is all that any body knows.

I hewed the main timbers six inches square, most of the studs on two sides only, and the rafters and floor timbers on one side, leaving the rest of the bark on, so that they were just as straight and much stronger than sawed ones. Each stick was carefully mortised or tenoned by its stump, for I had borrowed other tools by this time. My days in the woods were not very long ones; yet I usually carried my dinner of bread and butter, and read the newspaper in which it was wrapped, at noon, sitting amid the green pine boughs which I had cut off, and to my bread was imparted some of their fragrance, for my hands were covered with a thick coat of pitch. Before I had done I was more the friend than the foe of the pine tree, though I had cut down some of them, having become better acquainted with it. Sometimes a rambler in the wood was attracted by the sound of my axe, and we chatted pleasantly over the chips which I had made.

By the middle of April, for I made no haste in my work, but rather made the most of it, my house was framed and ready for the raising. I had already bought the shanty of James Collins, an Irishman who worked on the Fitchburg Railroad,[3] for boards.

2. This poem, like all poems not enclosed within quotation marks, was written by Thoreau himself.

3. The Boston & Fitchburg Railroad which ran near Walden Pond.

James Collins' shanty was considered an uncommonly fine one. When I called to see it he was not at home. I walked about the outside, at first unobserved from within, the window was so deep and high. It was of small dimensions, with a peaked cottage roof, and not much else to be seen, the dirt being raised five feet all around as if it were a compost heap. The roof was the soundest part, though a good deal warped and made brittle by the sun. Doorsill there was none, but a perennial passage for the hens under the door board. Mrs. C. came to the door and asked me to view it from the inside. The hens were driven in by my approach. It was dark, and had a dirt floor for the most part, dank, clammy, and aguish, only here a board and there a board which would not bear removal. She lighted a lamp to show me the inside of the roof and the walls, and also that the board floor extended under the bed, warning me not to step into the cellar, a sort of dust hole two feet deep. In her own words, they were "good boards overhead, good boards all around, and a good window,"—of two whole squares originally, only the cat had passed out that way lately. There was a stove, a bed, and a place to sit, an infant in the house where it was born, a silk parasol, gilt-framed looking-glass, and a patent new coffee mill nailed to an oak sapling, all told. The bargain was soon concluded, for James had in the mean while returned. I to pay four dollars and twenty-five cents to-night, he to vacate at five to-morrow morning, selling to nobody else meanwhile: I to take possession at six. It were well, he said, to be there early, and anticipate certain indistinct but wholly unjust claims on the score of ground rent and fuel. This he assured me was the only encumbrance. At six I passed him and his family on the road. One large bundle held their all,—bed, coffee-mill, looking-glass, hens,—all but the cat, she took to the woods and became a wild cat, and, as I learned afterward, trod in a trap set for woodchucks, and so became a dead cat at last.

I took down this dwelling the same morning, drawing the nails, and removed it to the pond side by small cartloads, spreading the boards on the grass there to bleach and warp back again in the sun. One early thrush gave me a note or two as I drove along the woodland path. I was informed treacherously by a young Patrick [4] that neighbor Seeley, an Irishman, in the intervals of the carting, transferred the still tolerable, straight, and drivable nails, staples, and spikes to his pocket, and then stood when I came back to pass the time of day, and look freshly up, unconcerned, with spring thoughts, at the devastation; there being a dearth of work, as he said. He was there to represent spectatordom, and help make this

4. A common name for any Irishman.

seemingly insignificant event one with the removal of the gods of Troy.[5]

I dug my cellar in the side of a hill sloping to the south, where a woodchuck had formerly dug his burrow, down through sumach and blackberry roots, and the lowest stain of vegetation, six feet square by seven deep, to a fine sand where potatoes would not freeze in any winter. The sides were left shelving, and not stoned; but the sun having never shone on them, the sand still keeps its place. It was but two hours' work. I took particular pleasure in this breaking of ground, for in almost all latitudes men dig into the earth for an equable temperature. Under the most splendid house in the city is still to be found the cellar where they store their roots as of old, and long after the superstructure has disappeared posterity remark its dent in the earth. The house is still but a sort of porch at the entrance of a burrow.

At length, in the beginning of May, with the help of some of my acquaintances, rather to improve so good an occasion for neighborliness than from any necessity, I set up the frame of my house. No man was ever more honored in the character of his raisers than I. They are destined, I trust, to assist at the raising of loftier structures one day. I began to occupy my house on the 4th of July, as soon as it was boarded and roofed, for the boards were carefully feather-edged and lapped, so that it was perfectly impervious to rain; but before boarding I laid the foundation of a chimney at one end, bringing two cartloads of stones up the hill from the pond in my arms. I built the chimney after my hoeing in the fall, before a fire became necessary for warmth, doing my cooking in the mean while out of doors on the ground, early in the morning: which mode I still think is in some respects more convenient and agreeable than the usual one. When it stormed before my bread was baked, I fixed a few boards over the fire, and sat under them to watch my loaf, and passed some pleasant hours in that way. In those days, when my hands were much employed, I read but little, but the least scraps of paper which lay on the ground, my holder, or tablecloth, afforded me as much entertainment, in fact answered the same purpose as the Iliad.[6]

It would be worth the while to build still more deliberately than I did, considering, for instance, what foundation a door, a window, a cellar, a garret, have in the nature of man, and perchance never raising any superstructure until we found a better reason for it than our temporal necessities even. There is some of

5. The removal of the gods from Troy was a necessary prelude to the defeat of that ancient city.
6. The great epic poem by the ancient Greek poet, Homer, which tells of the fall of Troy and the defeat of the Trojans by the Greeks.

the same fitness in a man's building his own house that there is in
a bird's building its own nest. Who knows but if men constructed
their dwellings with their own hands, and provided food for
themselves and families simply and honestly enough, the poetic
faculty would be universally developed, as birds universally sing
when they are so engaged? But alas! we do like cowbirds and
cuckoos, which lay their eggs in nests which other birds have built,
and cheer no traveller with their chattering and unmusical notes.
Shall we forever resign the pleasure of construction to the carpenter? What does architecture amount to in the experience of the
mass of men? I never in all my walks came across a man engaged in so simple and natural an occupation as building his house.
We belong to the community. It is not the tailor alone who is the
ninth part of a man; it is as much the preacher, and the merchant,
and the farmer. Where is this division of labor to end? and
what object does it finally serve? No doubt another *may* also think
for me; but it is not therefore desirable that he should do so to
the exclusion of my thinking for myself.

   True, there are architects so called in this country, and I have
heard of one at least possessed with the idea of making architectural ornaments have a core of truth, a necessity, and hence a
beauty, as if it were a revelation to him. All very well perhaps
from his point of view, but only a little better than the common
dilettantism. A sentimental reformer in architecture, he began at
the cornice, not at the foundation. It was only how to put a core
of truth within the ornaments, that every sugar plum in fact
might have an almond or caraway seed in it,—though I hold that
almonds are most wholesome without the sugar,—and not how the
inhabitant, the indweller, might build truly within and without, and
let the ornaments take care of themselves. What reasonable man
ever supposed that ornaments were something outward and in the
skin merely,—that the tortoise got his spotted shell, or the shellfish its mother-o'-pearl tints, by such a contract as the inhabitants
of Broadway their Trinity Church? [7] But a man has no more to do
with the style of architecture of his house than a tortoise with
that of its shell: nor need the soldier be so idle as to try to paint
the precise *color* of his virtue on his standard. The enemy will
find it out. He may turn pale when the trial comes. This man
seemed to me to lean over the cornice, and timidly whisper his
half truth to the rude occupants who really knew it better than he.
What of architectural beauty I now see, I know has gradually
grown from within outward, out of the necessities and character
of the indweller, who is the only builder,—out of some unconscious truthfulness, and nobleness, without ever a thought for the

7. A famous church in New York City.

appearance; and whatever additional beauty of this kind is destined to be produced will be preceded by a like unconscious beauty of life. The most interesting dwellings in this country, as the painter knows, are the most unpretending, humble log huts and cottages of the poor commonly; it is the life of the inhabitants whose shells they are, and not any peculiarity in their surfaces merely, which makes them *picturesque*; and equally interesting will be the citizen's suburban box, when his life shall be as simple and as agreeable to the imagination, and there is as little straining after effect in the style of his dwelling. A great proportion of architectural ornaments are literally hollow, and a September gale would strip them off, like borrowed plumes, without injury to the substantials. They can do without *architecture* who have no olives nor wines in the cellar. What if an equal ado were made about the ornaments of style in literature, and the architects of our bibles spent as much time about their cornices as the architects of our churches do? So are made the *belles-lettres* [8] and the *beaux-arts* [9] and their professors. Much it concerns a man, forsooth, how a few sticks are slanted over him or under him, and what colors are daubed upon his box. It would signify somewhat, if, in any earnest sense, *he* slanted them and daubed it; but the spirit having departed out of the tenant, it is of a piece with constructing his own coffin, —the architecture of the grave, and "carpenter," is but another name for "coffin-maker." One man says, in his despair or indifference to life, take up a handful of the earth at your feet, and paint your house that color. Is he thinking of his last and narrow house? Toss up a copper [1] for it as well. What an abundance of leisure he must have! Why do you take up a handful of dirt? Better paint your house your own complexion; let it turn pale or blush for you. An enterprise to improve the style of cottage architecture! When you have got my ornaments ready I will wear them.

Before winter I built a chimney, and shingled the sides of my house, which were already impervious to rain, with imperfect and sappy shingles made of the first slice of the log, whose edges I was obliged to straighten with a plane.

I have thus a tight shingled and plastered house, ten feet wide by fifteen long, and eight-feet posts, with a garret and a closet, a large window on each side, two trap doors, one door at the end, and a brick fireplace opposite. The exact cost of my house, paying the usual price for such materials as I used, but not counting the work, all of which was done by myself, was as follows; and I give

8. Esthetic literature, i.e., poetry, drama, fiction, etc.
9. The fine arts.
1. A coin; perhaps a reference to the ancient Greek myth of giving a coin to the spirit who guides a corpse to the land of the dead.

the details because very few are able to tell exactly what their houses cost, and fewer still, if any, the separate cost of the various materials which compose them:—

Boards,	$8 03½,	mostly shanty boards.
Refuse shingles for roof and sides,	. 4 00	
Laths,	1 25	
Two second-hand windows with glass,	2 43	
One thousand old brick,	4 00	
Two casks of lime,	2 40	That was high.
Hair,	0 31	More than I needed.
Mantle-tree iron,	0 15	
Nails,	3 90	
Hinges and screws,	0 14	
Latch,	0 10	
Chalk,	0 01	
Transportation,	1 40	I carried a good part on my back.
In all,	$28 12½	

These are all the materials excepting the timber, stones and sand, which I claimed by squatter's right. I have also a small wood-shed adjoining, made chiefly of the stuff which was left after building the house.

I intend to build me a house which will surpass any on the main street in Concord in grandeur and luxury, as soon as it pleases me as much and will cost me no more than my present one.

I thus found that the student who wishes for a shelter can obtain one for a lifetime at an expense not greater than the rent which he now pays annually. If I seem to boast more than is becoming, my excuse is that I brag for humanity rather than for myself; and my shortcomings and inconsistencies do not affect the truth of my statement. Notwithstanding much cant and hypocrisy,—chaff which I find it difficult to separate from my wheat, but for which I am as sorry as any man,—I will breathe freely and stretch myself in this respect, it is such a relief to both the moral and physical system; and I am resolved that I will not through humility become the devil's attorney. I will endeavor to speak a good word for the truth. At Cambridge College [2] the mere rent of a student's room, which is only a little larger than my own, is thirty dollars each year, though the corporation had the advantage of building thirty-two side by side and under one roof, and the occupant suffers the inconvenience of many and noisy neighbors, and perhaps a residence in the fourth story. I cannot but think that if we had more true wisdom in these respects, not only less education would be needed, because, forsooth, more would already have been acquired, but the pecuniary expense of getting

2. Harvard College, Cambridge, Massachusetts; Thoreau's own college.

an education would in a great measure vanish. Those conveniences which the student requires at Cambridge or elsewhere cost him or somebody else ten times as great a sacrifice of life as they would with proper management on both sides. Those things for which the most money is demanded are never the things which the student most wants. Tuition, for instance, is an important item in the term bill, while for the far more valuable education which he gets by associating with the most cultivated of his contemporaries no charge is made. The mode of founding a college is, commonly, to get up a subscription of dollars and cents, and then following blindly the principles of a division of labor to its extreme, a principle which should never be followed but with circumspection, —to call in a contractor who makes this a subject of speculation, and he employs Irishmen or other operatives actually to lay the foundations, while the students that are to be are said to be fitting themselves for it; and for these oversights successive generations have to pay. I think that it would be *better than this*, for the students, or those who desire to be benefited by it, even to lay the foundation themselves. The student who secures his coveted leisure and retirement by systematically shirking any labor necessary to man obtains but an ignoble and unprofitable leisure, defrauding himself of the experience which alone can make leisure fruitful. "But," says one, "you do not mean that the students should go to work with their hands instead of their heads?" I do not mean that exactly, but I mean something which he might think a good deal like that; I mean that they should not *play* life, or *study* it merely, while the community supports them at this expensive game, but earnestly *live* it from beginning to end. How could youths better learn to live than by at once trying the experiment of living? Methinks this would exercise their minds as much as mathematics. If I wished a boy to know something about the arts and sciences, for instance, I would not pursue the common course, which is merely to send him into the neighborhood of some professor, where any thing is professed and practised but the art of life;—to survey the world through a telescope or a microscope, and never with his natural eye; to study chemistry, and not learn how his bread is made, or mechanics, and not learn how it is earned; to discover new satellites to Neptune,[3] and not detect the motes in his eyes, or to what vagabond he is a satellite himself; or to be devoured by the monsters that swarm all around him, while contemplating the monsters in a drop of vinegar. Which would have advanced the most at the end of a month,—the boy who had made his own jackknife from the ore which he had dug

---

3. The eighth planet from the sun; it has two satellites or moons.

and smelted, reading as much as would be necessary for this,—or the boy who had attended the lectures on metallurgy at the Institute in the mean while, and had received a Rogers'[4] pen-knife from his father? Which would be most likely to cut his fingers? . . . To my astonishment I was informed on leaving college that I had studied navigation!—why, if I had taken one turn down the harbor I should have known more about it. Even the *poor* student studies and is taught only *political* economy, while that economy of living which is synonymous with philosophy is not even sincerely professed in our colleges. The consequence is, that while he is reading Adam Smith,[5] Ricardo,[6] and Say,[7] he runs his father in debt irretrievably.

As with our colleges, so with a hundred "modern improvements;" there is an illusion about them; there is not always a positive advance. The devil goes on exacting compound interest to the last for his early share and numerous succeeding investments in them. Our inventions are wont to be pretty toys, which distract our attention from serious things. They are but improved means to an unimproved end, an end which it was already but too easy to arrive at; as railroads lead to Boston or New York. We are in great haste to construct a magnetic telegraph from Maine to Texas; but Maine and Texas, it may be, have nothing important to communicate. Either is in such a predicament as the man who was earnest to be introduced to a distinguished deaf woman, but when he was presented, and one end of her ear trumpet was put into his hand, had nothing to say. As if the main object were to talk fast and not to talk sensibly. We are eager to tunnel under the Atlantic and bring the old world some weeks nearer to the new; but perchance the first news that will leak through into the broad, flapping American ear will be that the Princess Adelaide[8] has the whooping cough. After all, the man whose horse trots a mile in a minute does not carry the most important messages; he is not an evangelist, nor does he come round eating locusts and wild honey. I doubt if Flying Childers[9] ever carried a peck of corn to mill.

One says to me, "I wonder that you do not lay up money; you love to travel; you might take the cars and go to Fitchburg[1] to-day and see the country." But I am wiser than that. I have learned that the swiftest traveller is he that goes afoot. I say to my friend, Suppose we try who will get there first. The distance is thirty miles; the fare ninety cents. That is almost a day's wages. I re-

4. A relatively costly knife manufactured by a famous firm in Sheffield, England.
5. Scottish economist (1723–1790).
6. David Ricardo, English economist (1772–1823).
7. Jean Baptiste Say, French economist (1767–1823).
8. Perhaps the Princess of Orleans, the sister of King Louis Philippe of France; figuratively, any famous but inconsequential person.
9. A famous English racehorse.
1. A town west of Concord.

member when wages were sixty cents a day for laborers on this very road. Well, I start now on foot, and get there before night; I have travelled at that rate by the week together. You will in the mean while have earned your fare, and arrive there some time to-morrow, or possibly this evening, if you are lucky enough to get a job in season. Instead of going to Fitchburg, you will be working here the greater part of the day. And so, if the railroad reached round the world, I think that I should keep ahead of you; and as for seeing the country and getting experience of that kind, I should have to cut your acquaintance altogether.

Such is the universal law, which no man can ever outwit, and with regard to the railroad even we may say it is as broad as it is long. To make a railroad round the world available to all man-kind is equivalent to grading the whole surface of the planet. Men have an indistinct notion that if they keep up this activity of joint stocks and spades long enough all will at length ride somewhere, in next to no time, and for nothing; but though a crowd rushes to the depot, and the conductor shouts "All aboard!" when the smoke is blown away and the vapor condensed, it will be perceived that a few are riding, but the rest are run over,—and it will be called, and will be, "A melancholy accident." No doubt they can ride at last who shall have earned their fare, that is, if they survive so long, but they will probably have lost their elasticity and desire to travel by that time. This spending of the best part of one's life earning money in order to enjoy a questionable liberty during the least valuable part of it, reminds me of the Englishman who went to India to make a fortune first, in order that he might return to England and live the life of a poet. He should have gone up garret at once. "What!" exclaim a million Irishmen starting up from all the shanties in the land, "is not this railroad which we have built a good thing?" Yes, I answer, *comparatively* good, that is, you might have done worse; but I wish, as you are brothers of mine, that you could have spent your time better than digging in this dirt.

Before I finished my house, wishing to earn ten or twelve dollars by some honest and agreeable method, in order to meet my unusual expenses, I planted about two acres and a half of light and sandy soil near it chiefly with beans, but also a small part with potatoes, corn, peas, and turnips. The whole lot contains eleven acres, mostly growing up to pines and hickories, and was sold the preceding season for eight dollars and eight cents an acre. One farmer said that it was "good for nothing but to raise cheeping squirrels on." I put no manure whatever on this land, not being the owner, but merely a squatter, and not expecting to cultivate so much again, and I did not quite hoe it all once. I got out several cords of stumps in ploughing, which supplied me with fuel for a long time, and left small circles of virgin mould, easily distinguishable through the summer by the greater luxuriance of the beans there. The dead and for the most part unmerchantable wood behind my house, and the driftwood from the pond, have supplied the remainder of my fuel. I was obliged to hire a team and a man for the ploughing, though I held the plough myself. My farm outgoes for the first season were, for implements, seed, work, &c., $14 72½. The seed corn was given me. This never costs any thing to speak of, unless you plant more than enough. I got twelve bushels of beans, and eighteen bushels of potatoes, beside some peas and sweet corn. The yellow corn and turnips were too late to come to any thing. My whole income from the farm was

$$\begin{array}{lr} & \$23\ 44. \\ \text{Deducting the outgoes, ...} & 14\ 72\frac{1}{2} \\ \hline \text{There are left, ...} & \$8\ 71\frac{1}{2}, \end{array}$$

beside produce consumed and on hand at the time this estimate was made of the value of $4 50,—the amount on hand much more than balancing a little grass which I did not raise. All things considered, that is, considering the importance of a man's soul and of to-day, notwithstanding the short time occupied by my experiment, nay, partly even because of its transient character, I believe that that was doing better than any farmer in Concord did that year.

The next year I did better still, for I spaded up all the land which I required, about a third of an acre, and I learned from the experience of both years, not being in the least awed by many celebrated works on husbandry, Arthur Young [2] among the rest, that if one would live simply and eat only the crop which he raised, and raise no more than he ate, and not exchange it for an insufficient quantity of more luxurious and expensive things, he would need to cultivate only a few rods of ground, and that it would be cheaper to spade up that than to use oxen to plough it, and to select a fresh spot from time to time than to manure the old, and he could do all his necessary farm work as it were with his left hand at odd hours in the summer; and thus he would not be tied to an ox, or horse, or cow, or pig, as at present. I desire to speak impartially on this point, and as one not interested in the success or failure of the present economical and social arrangements. I was more independent than any farmer in Concord, for I was not anchored to a house or farm, but could follow the bent of my genius, which is a very crooked one, every moment. Be-

2. British agricultural author.

side being better off than they already, if my house had been
burned or my crops had failed, I should have been nearly as well
off as before.

I am wont to think that men are not so much the keepers of
herds as herds are the keepers of men, the former are so much
the freer. Men and oxen exchange work; but if we consider
necessary work only, the oxen will be seen to have greatly the
advantage, their farm is so much the larger. Man does some of his
part of the exchange work in his six weeks of haying, and it is no
boy's play. Certainly no nation that lived simply in all respects,
that is, no nation of philosophers, would commit so great a blunder
as to use the labor of animals. True, there never was and is not
likely soon to be a nation of philosophers, nor am I certain it is
desirable that there should be. However, I should never have
broken a horse or bull and taken him to board for any work he
might do for me, for fear I should become a horse-man or a herdsman merely; and if society seems to be the gainer by so doing,
are we certain that what is one man's gain is not another's loss,
and that the stable-boy has equal cause with his master to be
satisfied? Granted that some public works would not have been
constructed without this aid, and let man share the glory of such
with the ox and horse; does it follow that he could not have
accomplished works yet more worthy of himself in that case?
When men begin to do, not merely unnecessary or artistic, but
luxurious and idle work, with their assistance, it is inevitable that
a few do all the exchange work with the oxen, or, in other words,
become the slaves of the strongest. Man thus not only works for
the animal within him, but, for a symbol of this, he works for the
animal without him. Though we have many substantial houses of
brick or stone, the prosperity of the farmer is still measured by the
degree to which the barn overshadows the house. This town is said
to have the largest houses for oxen, cows, and horses hereabouts,
and it is not behindhand in its public buildings; but there are very
few halls for free worship or free speech in this country. It should
not be by their architecture, but why not even by their power of
abstract thought, that nations should seek to commemorate themselves? How much more admirable the Bhagvat-Geeta [3] than all
the ruins of the East! Towers and temples are the luxury of
princes. A simple and independent mind does not toil at the bidding of any prince. Genius is not a retainer to any emperor, nor is
its material silver, or gold, or marble, except to a trifling extent. To
what end, pray, is so much stone hammered? In Arcadia,[4] when I

3. A sacred Hindu text, frequently
cited by Thoreau; also spelled "Bha-
gavad Gita."

4. Ancient Greek pastoral area; figuratively, any ideal land.

was there, I did not see any hammering stone. Nations are possessed with an insane ambition to perpetuate the memory of themselves by the amount of hammered stone they leave. What if equal pains were taken to smooth and polish their manners? One piece of good sense would be more memorable than a monument as high as the moon. I love better to see stones in place. The grandeur of Thebes [5] was a vulgar grandeur. More sensible is a rod of stone wall that bounds an honest man's field than a hundred-gated Thebes that has wandered farther from the true end of life. The religion and civilization which are barbaric and heathenish build splendid temples; but what you might call Christianity does not. Most of the stone a nation hammers goes toward its tomb only. It buries itself alive. As for the Pyramids,[6] there is nothing to wonder at in them so much as the fact that so many men could be found degraded enough to spend their lives constructing a tomb for some ambitious booby, whom it would have been wiser and manlier to have drowned in the Nile, and then given his body to the dogs. I might possibly invent some excuse for them and him, but I have no time for it. As for the religion and love of art of the builders, it is much the same all the world over, whether the building be an Egyptian temple or the United States Bank. It costs more than it comes to. The mainspring is vanity, assisted by the love of garlic and bread and butter. Mr. Balcom, a promising young architect, designs it on the back of his Vitruvius,[7] with hard pencil and ruler, and the job is let out to Dobson & Sons, stonecutters. When the thirty centuries begin to look down on it, mankind begin to look up at it. As for your high towers and monuments, there was a crazy fellow once in this town who undertook to dig through to China, and he got so far that, as he said, he heard the Chinese pots and kettles rattle; but I think that I shall not go out of my way to admire the hole which he made. Many are concerned about the monuments of the West and the East,—to know who built them. For my part, I should like to know who in those days did not build them,—who were above such trifling. But to proceed with my statistics.

By surveying, carpentry, and day-labor of various other kinds in the village in the mean while, for I have as many trades as fingers, I had earned $13 34. The expense of food for eight months, namely, from July 4th to March 1st, the time when these estimates were made, though I lived there more than two years,—not counting potatoes, a little green corn, and some peas, which I had raised, nor considering the value of what was on hand

---

5. Ancient capital of Upper Egypt, a standard symbol of grandeur.
6. Massive Egyptian tombs, one of the "wonders" of the ancient world.
7. Roman architect and author of a textbook on design.

at the last date, was

Rice, ...	$1 73½	
Molasses, . . .	1 73	Cheapest form of the saccharine.
Rye meal, . .	1 04¾	
Indian meal, .	0 99¾	Cheaper than rye.
Pork, ...	0 22	
Flour, ...	0 88 }	Costs more than Indian meal, both money and trouble.
Sugar, ...	0 80	
Lard, ...	0 65	
Apples, . . .	0 25	
Dried apple, . .	0 22	
Sweet potatoes,	0 10	
One pumpkin,	0 6	
One watermelon,	0 2	
Salt, ...	0 3	

All experiments which failed.

Yes, I did eat $8 74 all told; but I should not thus unblushingly publish my guilt, if I did not know that most of my readers were equally guilty with myself, and that their deeds would look no better in print. The next year I sometimes caught a mess of fish for my dinner, and once I went so far as to slaughter a woodchuck which ravaged my bean-field,—effect his transmigration, as a Tartar [8] would say,—and devour him, partly for experiment's sake; but though it afforded me a momentary enjoyment, notwithstanding a musky flavor, I saw that the longest use would not make that a good practice, however it might seem to have your woodchucks ready dressed by the village butcher.

Clothing and some incidental expenses within the same dates, though little can be inferred from this item, amounted to

$8 40¾

Oil and some household utensils, . . . 2 00

So that all the pecuniary outgoes, excepting for washing and mending, which for the most part were done out of the house, and their bills have not yet been received,—and these are all and more than all the ways by which money necessarily goes out in this part of the world,—were

House, ...	$28 12½
Farm one year, ...	14 72½
Food eight months, ...	8 74
Clothing, &c., eight months, ...	8 40¾
Oil, &c., eight months, ...	2 00
In all, ...	$61 99¾

8. A resident of Tartary, a region of Asia and eastern Europe; figuratively, any Oriental who believed in the transmigration of souls.

I address myself now to those of my readers who have a living to get. And to meet this I have for farm produce sold

$23 44
Earned by day-labor, ... 13 34
In all, ... $36 78,

which subtracted from the sum of the outgoes leaves a balance of $25 21¾ on the one side,—this being very nearly the means with which I started, and the measure of expenses to be incurred,—and on the other, beside the leisure and independence and health thus secured, a comfortable house for me as long as I choose to occupy it.

These statistics, however accidental and therefore uninstructive they may appear, as they have a certain completeness, have a certain value also. Nothing was given me of which I have not rendered some account. It appears from the above estimate, that my food alone cost me in money about twenty-seven cents a week. It was, for nearly two years after this, rye and Indian meal without yeast, potatoes, rice, a very little salt pork, molasses, and salt, and my drink water. It was fit that I should live on rice, mainly, who loved so well the philosophy of India. To meet the objections of some inveterate cavillers, I may as well state, that if I dined out occasionally, as I always had done, and I trust shall have opportunities to do again, it was frequently to the detriment of my domestic arrangements. But the dining out, being, as I have stated, a constant element, does not in the least affect a comparative statement like this.

I learned from my two years' experience that it would cost incredibly little trouble to obtain one's necessary food, even in this latitude; that a man may use as simple a diet as the animals, and yet retain health and strength. I have made a satisfactory dinner, satisfactory on several accounts, simply off a dish of purslane (*Portulaca oleracea*) which I gathered in my cornfield, boiled and salted. I give the Latin on account of the savoriness of the trivial name. And pray what more can a reasonable man desire, in peaceful times, in ordinary noons, than a sufficient number of ears of green sweet-corn boiled, with the addition of salt? Even the little variety which I used was a yielding to the demands of appetite, and not of health. Yet men have come to such a pass that they frequently starve, not for want of necessaries, but for want of luxuries; and I know a good woman who thinks that her son lost his life because he took to drinking water only.

The reader will perceive that I am treating the subject rather from an economic than a dietetic point of view, and he will not venture to put my abstemiousness to the test unless he has a well-stocked larder.

Bread I at first made of pure Indian meal and salt, genuine hoe-cakes, which I baked before my fire out of doors on a shingle or the end of a stick of timber sawed off in building my house; but it was wont to get smoked and to have a piny flavor. I tried flour also; but have at last found a mixture of rye and Indian meal most convenient and agreeable. In cold weather it was no little amusement to bake several small loaves of this in succession, tending and turning them as carefully as an Egyptian his hatching eggs. They were a real cereal fruit which I ripened, and they had to my senses a fragrance like that of other noble fruits, which I kept in as long as possible by wrapping them in cloths. I made a study of the ancient and indispensable art of bread-making, consulting such authorities as offered, going back to the primitive days and first invention of the unleavened kind, when from the wildness of nuts and meats men first reached the mildness and refinement of this diet, and travelling gradually down in my studies through that accidental souring of the dough which, it is supposed, taught the leavening process, and through the various fermentations there-after, till I came to "good, sweet, wholesome bread," the staff of life. Leaven, which some deem the soul of bread, the *spiritus* [9] which fills its cellular tissue, which is religiously preserved like the vestal fire,—some precious bottle-full, I suppose, first brought over in the Mayflower,[1] did the business for America, and its influence is still rising, swelling, spreading, in cerealian billows over the land,—this seed I regularly and faithfully procured from the village, till at length one morning I forgot the rules, and scalded my yeast; by which accident I discovered that even this was not indispensable,—for my discoveries were not by the synthetic but analytic process,—and I have gladly omitted it since, though most housewives earnestly assured me that safe and wholesome bread without yeast might not be, and elderly people prophesied a speedy decay of the vital forces. Yet I find it not to be an essential ingredient, and after going without it for a year am still in the land of the living; and I am glad to escape the trivialness of carrying a bottle-full in my pocket, which would sometimes pop and discharge its contents to my discomfiture. It is simpler and more respectable to omit it. Man is an animal who more than any other can adapt himself to all climates and circumstances. Neither did I put any sal soda, or other acid or alkali, into my bread. It would seem that I made it according to the recipe which Marcus Porcius Cato [2] gave about two centuries before Christ. "Panem depsticium sic

9. The life-giving force or spirit.
1. The ship on which the Pilgrims sailed to Massachusetts in 1620.

2. An ancient Roman writer on agriculture.

facito. Manus mortariumque bene lavato. Farinam in mortarium indito, aquæ paulatim addito, subigitoque pulchre. Ubi bene subegeris, defingito, coquitoque sub testu." Which I take to mean— "Make kneaded bread thus. Wash your hands and trough well. Put the meal into the trough, add water gradually, and knead it thoroughly. When you have kneaded it well, mould it, and bake it under a cover," that is, in a baking-kettle. Not a word about leaven. But I did not always use this staff of life. At one time, owing to the emptiness of my purse, I saw none of it for more than a month.

Every New Englander might easily raise all his own breadstuffs in this land of rye and Indian corn, and not depend on distant and fluctuating markets for them. Yet so far are we from simplicity and independence that, in Concord, fresh and sweet meal is rarely sold in the shops, and hominy and corn in a still coarser form are hardly used by any. For the most part the farmer gives to his cattle and hogs the grain of his own producing, and buys flour, which is at least no more wholesome, at a greater cost, at the store. I saw that I could easily raise my bushel or two of rye and Indian corn, for the former will grow on the poorest land, and the latter does not require the best, and grind them in a handmill, and so do without rice and pork; and if I must have some concentrated sweet, I found by experiment that I could make a very good molasses either of pumpkins or beets, and I knew that I needed only to set out a few maples to obtain it more easily still, and while these were growing I could use various substitutes beside those which I have named. "For," as the Forefathers sang,—

"we can make liquor to sweeten our lips
Of pumpkins and parsnips and walnut-tree chips." [3]

Finally, as for salt, that grossest of groceries, to obtain this might be a fit occasion for a visit to the seashore, or, if I did without it altogether, I should probably drink the less water. I do not learn that the Indians ever troubled themselves to go after it.

Thus I could avoid all trade and barter, so far as my food was concerned, and having a shelter already, it would only remain to get clothing and fuel. The pantaloons which I now wear were woven in a farmer's family,—thank Heaven there is so much virtue still in man; for I think the fall from the farmer to the operative as great and memorable as that from the man to the farmer;—and in a new country fuel is an encumbrance. As for a habitat, if I were not permitted still to squat, I might purchase one acre at the same price for which the land I cultivated was sold— namely, eight dollars and eight cents. But as it was, I considered that I enhanced the value of the land by squatting on it.

3. An anonymous poem, probably written by an early American colonist.

There is a certain class of unbelievers who sometimes ask me such questions as, if I think that I can live on vegetable food alone; and to strike at the root of the matter at once,—for the root is faith,—I am accustomed to answer such, that I can live on board nails. If they cannot understand that, they cannot understand much that I have to say. For my part, I am glad to hear of experiments of this kind being tried; as that a young man tried for a fortnight to live on hard, raw corn on the ear, using his teeth for all mortar. The squirrel tribe tried the same and succeeded. The human race is interested in these experiments, though a few old women who are incapacitated for them, or who own their thirds in mills,[4] may be alarmed.

My furniture, part of which I made myself, and the rest cost me nothing of which I have not rendered an account, consisted of a bed, a table, a desk, three chairs, a looking-glass three inches in diameter, a pair of tongs and andirons, a kettle, a skillet, and a frying-pan, a dipper, a wash-bowl, two knives and forks, three plates, one cup, one spoon, a jug for oil, a jug for molasses, and a japanned lamp. None is so poor that he need sit on a pumpkin. That is shiftlessness. There is a plenty of such chairs as I like best in the village garrets to be had for taking them away. Furniture! Thank God, I can sit and I can stand without the aid of a furniture warehouse. What man but a philosopher would not be ashamed to see his furniture packed in a cart and going up country exposed to the light of heaven and the eyes of men, a beggarly account of empty boxes? That is Spaulding's furniture. I could never tell from inspecting such a load whether it belonged to a so called rich man or a poor one; the owner always seemed poverty-stricken. Indeed, the more you have of such things the poorer you are. Each load looks as if it contained the contents of a dozen shanties; and if one shanty is poor, this is a dozen times as poor. Pray, for what do we *move* ever but to get rid of our furniture, our *exuviæ*;[5] at last to go from this world to another newly furnished, and leave this to be burned? It is the same as if all these traps were buckled to a man's belt, and he could not move over the rough country where our lines are cast without dragging them,—dragging his trap. He was a lucky fox that left his tail in the trap. The muskrat will gnaw his third leg off to be free. No wonder man has lost his elasticity. How often he is at a dead set! "Sir, if I may be so bold, what do you mean by a dead set?" If you are a seer, whenever you meet a man you will see all that he owns, ay, and much that he pretends to disown, behind

---

4. A widow's legal share of an inheritance is one-third; a mill is one-tenth of a cent.
5. Things cast off.

him, even to his kitchen furniture and all the trumpery which he saves and will not burn, and he will appear to be harnessed to it and making what headway he can. I think that the man is at a dead set who has got through a knot hole or gateway where his sledge load of furniture cannot follow him. I cannot but feel compassion when I hear some trig, compact-looking man, seemingly free, all girded and ready, speak of his "furniture," as whether it is insured or not. "But what shall I do with my furniture?" My gay butterfly is entangled in a spider's web then. Even those who seem for a long while not to have any, if you inquire more narrowly you will find have some stored in somebody's barn. I look upon England to-day as an old gentleman who is travelling with a great deal of baggage, trumpery which has accumulated from long housekeeping, which he has not the courage to burn; great trunk, little trunk, bandbox and bundle. Throw away the first three at least. It would surpass the powers of a well man nowadays to take up his bed and walk, and I should certainly advise a sick one to lay down his bed and run. When I have met an immigrant tottering under a bundle which contained his all—looking like an enormous wen which had grown out of the nape of his neck—I have pitied him, not because that was his all, but because he had all *that* to carry. If I have got to drag my trap, I will take care that it be a light one and do not nip me in a vital part. But perchance it would be wisest never to put one's paw into it.

I would observe, by the way, that it costs me nothing for curtains, for I have no gazers to shut out but the sun and moon, and I am willing that they should look in. The moon will not sour milk nor taint meat of mine, nor will the sun injure my furniture or fade my carpet, and if he is sometimes too warm a friend, I find it still better economy to retreat behind some curtain which nature has provided, than to add a single item to the details of housekeeping. A lady once offered me a mat, but as I had no room to spare within the house, nor time to spare within or without to shake it, I declined it, preferring to wipe my feet on the sod before my door. It is best to avoid the beginnings of evil.

Not long since I was present at the auction of a deacon's effects, for his life had not been ineffectual:—

"The evil that men do lives after them." [6]

As usual, a great proportion was trumpery which had begun to accumulate in his father's day. Among the rest was a dried tapeworm. And now, after lying half a century in his garret and other

---

6. From Antony's speech after the death of Caesar in Shakespeare's *Julius Caesar*.

dust holes, these things were not burned; instead of a *bonfire*, or purifying destruction of them, there was an *auction*, or increasing of them. The neighbors eagerly collected to view them, bought them all, and carefully transported them to their garrets and dust holes, to lie there till their estates are settled, when they will start again. When a man dies he kicks the dust.

The customs of some savage nations might, perchance, be profitably imitated by us, for they at least go through the semblance of casting their slough annually; they have the idea of the thing, whether they have the reality or not. Would it not be well if we were to celebrate such a "busk," or "feast of first fruits," as Bartram [7] describes to have been the custom of the Mucclasse Indians? "When a town celebrates the busk," says he, "having previously provided themselves with new clothes, new pots, pans, and other household utensils and furniture, they collect all their worn out clothes and other despicable things, sweep and cleanse their houses, squares, and the whole town, of their filth, which with all the remaining grain and other old provisions they cast together into one common heap, and consume it with fire. After having taken medicine, and fasted for three days, all the fire in the town is extinguished. During this fast they abstain from the gratification of every appetite and passion whatever. A general amnesty is proclaimed; all malefactors may return to their town.—"

"On the fourth morning, the high priest, by rubbing dry wood together, produces new fire in the public square, from whence every habitation in the town is supplied with the new and pure flame."

They then feast on the new corn and fruits and dance and sing for three days, "and the four following days they receive visits and rejoice with their friends from neighboring towns who have in like manner purified and prepared themselves."

The Mexicans also practised a similar purification at the end of every fifty-two years, in the belief that it was time for the world to come to an end.

I have scarcely heard of a truer sacrament, that is, as the dictionary defines it, "outward and visible sign of an inward and spiritual grace," than this, and I have no doubt that they were originally inspired directly from Heaven to do thus, though they have no biblical record of the revelation.

For more than five years I maintained myself thus solely by the labor of my hands, and I found, that by working about six weeks in a year, I could meet all the expenses of living. The whole of my winters, as well as most of my summers, I had free

7. William Bartram (1739–1823), an early American botanist.

and clear for study. I have thoroughly tried school-keeping, and found that my expenses were in proportion, or rather out of proportion, to my income, for I was obliged to dress and train, not to say think and believe, accordingly, and I lost my time into the bargain. As I did not teach for the good of my fellow-men, but simply for a livelihood, this was a failure. I have tried trade; but I found that it would take ten years to get under way in that, and that then I should probably be on my way to the devil. I was actually afraid that I might by that time be doing what is called a good business. When formerly I was looking about to see what I could do for a living, some sad experience in conforming to the wishes of friends being fresh in my mind to tax my ingenuity, I thought often and seriously of picking huckleberries; that surely I could do, and its small profits might suffice,—for my greatest skill has been to want but little,—so little capital it required, so little distraction from my wonted moods, I foolishly thought. While my acquaintances went unhesitatingly into trade or the professions, I contemplated this occupation as most like theirs; ranging the hills all summer to pick the berries which came in my way, and thereafter carelessly dispose of them; so, to keep the flocks of Admetus.[8] I also dreamed that I might gather the wild herbs, or carry evergreens to such villagers as loved to be reminded of the woods, even to the city, by hay-cart loads. But I have since learned that trade curses every thing it handles; and though you trade in messages from heaven, the whole curse of trade attaches to the business.

As I preferred some things to others, and especially valued my freedom, as I could fare hard and yet succeed well, I did not wish to spend my time in earning rich carpets or other fine furniture, or delicate cookery, or a house in the Grecian or the Gothic [9] style just yet. If there are any to whom it is no interruption to acquire these things, and who know how to use them when acquired, I relinquish to them the pursuit. Some are "industrious," and appear to love labor for its own sake, or perhaps because it keeps them out of worse mischief; to such I have at present nothing to say. Those who would not know what to do with more leisure than they now enjoy, I might advise to work twice as hard as they do,—work till they pay for themselves, and get their free papers. For myself I found that the occupation of a day-laborer was the most independent of any, especially as it required only thirty or forty days in a year to support one. The laborer's day ends with the going down of the sun, and he is then free to devote himself

8. In Greek mythology, the king of Pherae; the god Apollo was forced to serve as his serf. Figuratively, the myth serves as an allegory of the artist who is subjugated by society.

9. A style of architecture popular in Europe in the thirteenth and fourteenth centuries.

to his chosen pursuit, independent of his labor; but his employer, who speculates from month to month, has no respite from one end of the year to the other.

In short, I am convinced, both by faith and experience, that to maintain one's self on this earth is not a hardship but a pastime, if we will live simply and wisely; as the pursuits of the simpler nations are still the sports of the more artificial. It is not necessary that a man should earn his living by the sweat of his brow, unless he sweats easier than I do.

One young man of my acquaintance, who has inherited some acres, told me that he thought he should live as I did, *if he had the means.* I would not have any one adopt *my* mode of living on any account; for, beside that before he has fairly learned it I may have found out another for myself, I desire that there may be as many different persons in the world as possible; but I would have each one be very careful to find out and pursue *his own* way, and not his father's or his mother's or his neighbor's instead. The youth may build or plant or sail, only let him not be hindered from doing that which he tells me he would like to do. It is by a mathematical point only that we are wise, as the sailor or the fugitive slave keeps the polestar in his eye; but that is sufficient guidance for all our life. We may not arrive at our port within a calculable period, but we would preserve the true course.

Undoubtedly, in this case, what is true for one is truer still for a thousand, as a large house is not proportionally more expensive than a small one, since one roof may cover, one cellar underlie, and one wall separate several apartments. But for my part, I preferred the solitary dwelling. Moreover, it will commonly be cheaper to build the whole yourself than to convince another of the advantage of the common wall; and when you have done this, the common partition, to be much cheaper, must be a thin one, and that other may prove a bad neighbor, and also not keep his side in repair. The only coöperation which is commonly possible is exceedingly partial and superficial; and what little true coöperation there is, is as if it were not, being a harmony inaudible to men. If a man has faith he will coöperate with equal faith every where; if he has not faith, he will continue to live like the rest of the world, whatever company he is joined to. To coöperate, in the highest as well as the lowest sense, means *to get our living together.* I heard it proposed lately that two young men should travel together over the world, the one without money, earning his means as he went, before the mast and behind the plough, the other carrying a bill of exchange in his pocket. It was easy to see that they could not long be companions or coöperate, since one would not *operate* at all. They would part at the first interesting crisis in their adventures. Above all, as I have implied, the man who goes alone can start to-day; but he who travels with another must wait till that other is ready, and it may be a long time before they get off.

But all this is very selfish, I have heard some of my townsmen say. I confess that I have hitherto indulged very little in philanthropic enterprises. I have made some sacrifices to a sense of duty, and among others have sacrificed this pleasure also. There are those who have used all their arts to persuade me to undertake the support of some poor family in the town; and if I had nothing to do,—for the devil finds employment for the idle,—I might try my hand at some such pastime as that. However, when I have thought to indulge myself in this respect, and lay their Heaven under an obligation by maintaining certain poor persons in all respects as comfortably as I maintain myself, and have even ventured so far as to make them the offer, they have one and all unhesitatingly preferred to remain poor. While my townsmen and women are devoted in so many ways to the good of their fellows, I trust that one at least may be spared to other and less humane pursuits. You must have a genius for charity as well as for any thing else. As for Doing-good, that is one of the professions which are full. Moreover, I have tried it fairly, and, strange as it may seem, am satisfied that it does not agree with my constitution. Probably I should not consciously and deliberately forsake my particular calling to do the good which society demands of me, to save the universe from annihilation; and I believe that a like but infinitely greater steadfastness elsewhere is all that now preserves it. But I would not stand between any man and his genius; and to him who does this work, which I decline, with his whole heart and soul and life, I would say, Persevere, even if the world call it doing evil, as it is most likely they will.

I am far from supposing that my case is a peculiar one; no doubt many of my readers would make a similar defence. At doing something,—I will not engage that my neighbors shall pronounce it good,—I do not hesitate to say that I should be a capital fellow to hire; but what that is, it is for my employer to find out. What *good* I do, in the common sense of that word, must be aside from my main path, and for the most part wholly unintended. Men say, practically, Begin where you are and such as you are, without aiming mainly to become of more worth, and with kindness aforethought go about doing good. If I were to preach at all in this strain, I should say rather, Set about being good. As if the sun should stop when he had kindled his fires up to the splendor of a moon or a star of the sixth magnitude, and go about like a Robin Goodfellow,[1] peeping in at every cottage window, inspiring lunatics, and tainting meats, and making darkness visible, instead of steadily increasing his genial heat and beneficence till he is of such brightness that no mortal can look him in the face, and then, and in the mean while too, going about the world in his own orbit, doing it good, or rather, as a truer philosophy has discovered, the world going about him getting good. When Phaeton,[2] wishing to prove his heavenly birth by his beneficence, had the sun's chariot but one day, and drove out of the beaten track, he burned several blocks of houses in the lower streets of heaven, and scorched the surface of the earth, and dried up every spring, and made the great desert of Sahara, till at length Jupiter [3] hurled him headlong to the earth with a thunderbolt, and the sun, through grief at his death, did not shine for a year.

There is no odor so bad as that which arises from goodness tainted. It is human, it is divine, carrion. If I knew for a certainty that a man was coming to my house with the conscious design of doing me good, I should run for my life, as from that dry and parching wind of the African deserts called the simoom, which fills the mouth and nose and ears and eyes with dust till you are suffocated, for fear that I should get some of his good done to me,—some of its virus mingled with my blood. No,—in this case I would rather suffer evil the natural way. A man is not a good *man* to me because he will feed me if I should be starving, or warm me if I should be freezing, or pull me out of a ditch if I should ever fall into one. I can find you a Newfoundland dog that will do as much. Philanthropy is not love for one's fellow-man in the broadest sense. Howard [4] was no doubt an exceedingly kind and worthy man in his way, and has his reward; but, comparatively speaking, what are a hundred Howards to *us*, if their philanthropy do not help *us* in our best estate, when we are most worthy to be helped? I never heard of a philanthropic meeting in which it was sincerely proposed to do any good to me, or the like of me.

The Jesuits [5] were quite balked by those Indians who, being burned at the stake, suggested new modes of torture to their tormentors. Being superior to physical suffering, it sometimes chanced that they were superior to any consolation which the missionaries could offer; and the law to do as you would be done

1. In English folklore, a mischievous elf; also known as Puck.
2. In Greek mythology, the son of Helios (the sun).
3. Chief god in Roman mythology.

4. John Howard (1726?–1790), English prison reformer.
5. A religious order of the Roman Catholic faith which attempted to convert the Indians to Christianity.

by fell with less persuasiveness on the ears of those, who, for their part, did not care how they were done by, who loved their enemies after a new fashion, and came very near freely forgiving them all they did.

Be sure that you give the poor the aid they most need, though it be your example which leaves them far behind. If you give money, spend yourself with it, and do not merely abandon it to them. We make curious mistakes sometimes. Often the poor man is not so cold and hungry as he is dirty and ragged and gross. It is partly his taste, and not merely his misfortune. If you give him money, he will perhaps buy more rags with it. I was wont to pity the clumsy Irish laborers who cut ice on the pond, in such mean and ragged clothes, while I shivered in my more tidy and somewhat more fashionable garments, till, one bitter cold day, one who had slipped into the water came to my house to warm him, and I saw him strip off three pairs of pants and two pairs of stockings ere he got down to the skin, though they were dirty and ragged enough, it is true, and that he could afford to refuse the *extra* garments which I offered him, he had so many *intra* ones. This ducking was the very thing he needed. Then I began to pity myself, and I saw that it would be a greater charity to bestow on me a flannel shirt than a whole slop-shop on him. There are a thousand hacking at the branches of evil to one who is striking at the root, and it may be that he who bestows the largest amount of time and money on the needy is doing the most by his mode of life to produce that misery which he strives in vain to relieve. It is the pious slave-breeder devoting the proceeds of every tenth slave to buy a Sunday's liberty for the rest. Some show their kindness to the poor by employing them in their kitchens. Would they not be kinder if they employed themselves there? You boast of spending a tenth part of your income in charity; may be you should spend the nine tenths so, and done with it. Society recovers only a tenth part of the property then. Is this owing to the generosity of him in whose possession it is found, or to the remissness of the officers of justice?

Philanthropy is almost the only virtue which is sufficiently appreciated by mankind. Nay, it is greatly overrated; and it is our selfishness which overrates it. A robust poor man, one sunny day here in Concord, praised a fellow-townsman to me, because, as he said, he was kind to the poor; meaning himself. The kind uncles and aunts of the race are more esteemed than its true spiritual fathers and mothers. I once heard a reverend lecturer on England, a man of learning and intelligence, after enumerating her scientific, literary, and political worthies, Shakspeare, Bacon, Cromwell, Milton, Newton,[6] and others, speak next of her Christian heroes, whom, as if his profession required it of him, he elevated to a place far above all the rest, as the greatest of the great. They were Penn, Howard, and Mrs. Fry.[7] Every one must feel the falsehood and cant of this. The last were not England's best men and women; only, perhaps, her best philanthropists.

I would not subtract any thing from the praise that is due to philanthropy, but merely demand justice for all who by their lives and works are a blessing to mankind. I do not value chiefly a man's uprightness and benevolence, which are, as it were, his stem and leaves. Those plants of whose greenness withered we make herb tea for the sick, serve but a humble use, and are most employed by quacks. I want the flower and fruit of a man; that some fragrance be wafted over from him to me, and some ripeness flavor our intercourse. His goodness must not be a partial and transitory act, but a constant superfluity, which costs him nothing and of which he is unconscious. This is a charity that hides a multitude of sins. The philanthropist too often surrounds mankind with the remembrance of his own cast-off griefs as an atmosphere, and calls it sympathy. We should impart our courage, and not our despair, our health and ease, and not our disease, and take care that this does not spread by contagion. From what southern plains comes up the voice of wailing? Under what latitudes reside the heathen to whom we would send light? Who is that intemperate and brutal man whom we would redeem? If any thing ail a man, so that he does not perform his functions, if he have a pain in his bowels even,—for that is the seat of sympathy,—he forthwith sets about reforming—the world. Being a microcosm himself, he discovers, and it is a true discovery, and he is the man to make it,— that the world has been eating green apples; to his eyes, in fact, the globe itself is a great green apple, which there is danger awful to think of that the children of men will nibble before it is ripe; and straightway his drastic philanthropy seeks out the Esquimaux and the Patagonian,[8] and embraces the populous Indian and Chinese villages; and thus, by a few years of philanthropic activity, the powers in the mean while using him for their own ends, no doubt, he cures himself of his dyspepsia, the globe acquires a faint blush on one or both of its cheeks, as if it were beginning to be ripe, and life loses its crudity and is once more sweet and wholesome to live. I never dreamed of any enormity greater than I have com-

6. Francis Bacon (1561–1626), English philosopher and statesman; Oliver Cromwell (1599–1658), English general and statesman, Lord Protector of England; John Milton (1608–1674), English poet; Isaac Newton (1642–1727), English philosopher and mathematician.

7. William Penn (1644–1718), humanitarian and founder of Pennsylvania; John Howard (1726?–1790), English prison reformer; Elizabeth Fry (1780–1845), English prison reformer.
8. A native of the southernmost part of South America.

mitted. I never knew, and never shall know, a worse man than myself.

I believe that what so saddens the reformer is not his sympathy with his fellows in distress, but, though he be the holiest son of God, is his private ail. Let this be righted, let the spring come to him, the morning rise over his couch, and he will forsake his generous companions without apology. My excuse for not lecturing against the use of tobacco is, that I never chewed it; that is a penalty which reformed tobacco-chewers have to pay; though there are things enough I have chewed, which I could lecture against. If you should ever be betrayed into any of these philanthropies, do not let your left hand know what your right hand does, for it is not worth knowing. Rescue the drowning and tie your shoe-strings. Take your time, and set about some free labor.

Our manners have been corrupted by communication with the saints. Our hymn-books resound with a melodious cursing of God and enduring him forever. One would say that even the prophets and redeemers had rather consoled the fears than confirmed the hopes of man. There is nowhere recorded a simple and irrepressible satisfaction with the gift of life, any memorable praise of God. All health and success does me good, however far off and withdrawn it may appear; all disease and failure helps to make me sad and does me evil, however much sympathy it may have with me or I with it. If, then, we would indeed restore mankind by truly Indian, botanic, magnetic, or natural means, let us first be as simple and well as Nature ourselves, dispel the clouds which hang over our own brows, and take up a little life into our pores. Do not stay to be an overseer of the poor, but endeavor to become one of the worthies of the world.

I read in the Gulistan, or Flower Garden, of Sheik Sadi of Shiraz,[9] that "They asked a wise man, saying; Of the many celebrated trees which the Most High God has created lofty and umbrageous, they call none azad, or free, excepting the cypress, which bears no fruit; what mystery is there in this? He replied; Each has its appropriate produce, and appointed season, during the continuance of which it is fresh and blooming, and during their absence dry and withered; to neither of which states is the cypress exposed, being always flourishing; and of this nature are the azads, or religious independents.—Fix not thy heart on that which is transitory; for the Dijlah,[1] or Tigris, will continue to flow through Bagdad after the race of caliphs[2] is extinct: if thy hand has plenty, be liberal as the date tree; but if it affords nothing to give

9. A Persian poet of the twelfth century, admired by many transcendentalists.
1. A river in southwest Asia.

2. A caliph is a Moslem ruler: Bagdad is the capital of Iraq, located on the Dijlah (or Tigris) river.

away, be an azad, or free man, like the cypress."

COMPLEMENTAL VERSES.[3]

THE PRETENSIONS OF POVERTY.

"Thou dost presume too much, poor needy wretch,
To claim a station in the firmament,
Because thy humble cottage, or thy tub,
Nurses some lazy or pedantic virtue
In the cheap sunshine or by shady springs,
With roots and pot-herbs; where thy right hand,
Tearing those humane passions from the mind,
Upon whose stocks fair blooming virtues flourish,
Degradeth nature, and benumbeth sense,
And, Gorgon-like, turns active men to stone.
We not require the dull society
Of your necessitated temperance,
Or that unnatural stupidity
That knows nor joy nor sorrow; nor your forc'd
Falsely exalted passive fortitude
Above the active. This low abject brood,
That fix their seats in mediocrity,
Become your servile minds; but we advance
Such virtues only as admit excess,
Brave, bounteous acts, regal magnificence,
All-seeing prudence, magnanimity
That knows no bound, and that heroic virtue
For which antiquity hath left no name,
But patterns only, such as Hercules,
Achilles, Theseus. Back to thy loath'd cell;
And when thou seest the new enlightened sphere,
Study to know but what those worthies were."

T. Carew.

Where I Lived, and What I Lived for

At a certain season of our life we are accustomed to consider
every spot as the possible site of a house. I have thus surveyed
the country on every side within a dozen miles of where I live. In
imagination I have bought all the farms in succession, for all
were to be bought, and I knew their price. I walked over each
farmer's premises, tasted his wild apples, discoursed on husbandry
with him, took his farm at his price, at any price, mortgaging it to
him in my mind; even put a higher price on it,—took every thing
but a deed of it,—took his word for his deed, for I dearly love to

3. The poem is by Thomas Carew (1595?–1645); Thoreau added the title and
modernized the spelling.

talk,—cultivated it, and him too to some extent, I trust, and withdrew when I had enjoyed it long enough, leaving him to carry it on. This experience entitled me to be regarded as a sort of real-estate broker by my friends. Wherever I sat, there I might live, and the landscape radiated from me accordingly. What is a house but a *sedes*, a seat?—better if a country seat. I discovered many a site for a house not likely to be soon improved, which some might have thought too far from the village, but to my eyes the village was too far from it. Well, there I might live, I said; and there I did live, for an hour, a summer and a winter life; saw how I could let the years run off, buffet the winter through, and see the spring come in. The future inhabitants of this region, wherever they may place their houses, may be sure that they have been anticipated. An afternoon sufficed to lay out the land into orchard, woodlot, and pasture, and to decide what fine oaks or pines should be left to stand before the door, and whence each blasted tree could be seen to the best advantage; and then I let it lie, fallow perchance, for a man is rich in proportion to the number of things which he can afford to let alone.

My imagination carried me so far that I even had the refusal of several farms,—the refusal was all I wanted,—but I never got my fingers burned by actual possession. The nearest that I came to actual possession was when I bought the Hollowell place,[1] and had begun to sort my seeds, and collected materials with which to make a wheelbarrow to carry it on or off with; but before the owner gave me a deed of it, his wife—every man has such a wife—changed her mind and wished to keep it, and he offered me ten dollars to release him. Now, to speak the truth, I had but ten cents in the world, and it surpassed my arithmetic to tell, if I was that man who had ten cents, or who had a farm, or ten dollars, or all together. However, I let him keep the ten dollars and the farm too, for I had carried it far enough; or rather, to be generous, I sold him the farm for just what I gave for it, and, as he was not a rich man, made him a present of ten dollars, and still had my ten cents, and seeds, and materials for a wheelbarrow left. I found thus that I had been a rich man without any damage to my poverty. But I retained the landscape, and I have since annually carried off what it yielded without a wheelbarrow. With respect to landscapes,—[2]

> "I am monarch of all I *survey*,
> My right there is none to dispute."

I have frequently seen a poet withdraw, having enjoyed the

1. Before deciding on Walden Pond, Thoreau nearly bought this farm, which is on the Sudbury River in Concord.

2. William Cowper (1731–1800). Thoreau italicized the final word of the first line to emphasize the pun.

most valuable part of a farm, while the crusty farmer supposed that he had got a few wild apples only. Why, the owner does not know it for many years when a poet has put his farm in rhyme, the most admirable kind of invisible fence, has fairly impounded it, milked it, skimmed it, and got all the cream, and left the farmer only the skimmed milk.

The real attractions of the Hollowell farm, to me, were; its complete retirement, being about two miles from the village, half a mile from the nearest neighbor, and separated from the highway by a broad field; its bounding on the river, which the owner said protected it by its fogs from frosts in the spring, though that was nothing to me; the gray color and ruinous state of the house and barn, and the dilapidated fences, which put such an interval between me and the last occupant; the hollow and lichen-covered apple trees, gnawed by rabbits, showing what kind of neighbors I should have; but above all, the recollection I had of it from my earliest voyages up the river, when the house was concealed behind a dense grove of red maples, through which I heard the house-dog bark. I was in haste to buy it, before the proprietor finished getting out some rocks, cutting down the hollow apple trees, and grubbing up some young birches which had sprung up in the pasture, or, in short, had made any more of his improvements. To enjoy these advantages I was ready to carry it on; like Atlas,[3] to take the world on my shoulders,—I never heard what compensation he received for that,—and do all those things which had no other motive or excuse but that I might pay for it and be unmolested in my possession of it; for I knew all the while that it would yield the most abundant crop of the kind I wanted if I could only afford to let it alone. But it turned out as I have said.

All that I could say, then, with respect to farming on a large scale, (I have always cultivated a garden,) was, that I had had my seeds ready. Many think that seeds improve with age. I have no doubt that time discriminates between the good and the bad; and when at last I shall plant, I shall be less likely to be disappointed. But I would say to my fellows, once for all, As long as possible live free and uncommitted. It makes but little difference whether you are committed to a farm or the county jail.

Old Cato,[4] whose "De Re Rusticâ" is my "Cultivator," says, and the only translation I have seen makes sheer nonsense of the passage, "When you think of getting a farm, turn it thus in your mind, not to buy greedily; nor spare your pains to look at it, and do not think it enough to go round it once. The oftener you go there

3. According to Greek mythology, Atlas supported the world on his shoulders.
4. Marcus Porcius Cato (234–149 B.C.), Roman statesman and author of books on agriculture.

the more it will please you, if it is good." I think I shall not buy greedily, but go round and round it as long as I live, and be buried in it first, that it may please me the more at last.

The present was my next experiment of this kind, which I purpose to describe more at length; for convenience, putting the experience of two years into one. As I have said, I do not propose to write an ode to dejection, but to brag as lustily as chanticleer in the morning, standing on his roost, if only to wake my neighbors up.

When first I took up my abode in the woods, that is, began to spend my nights as well as days there, which, by accident, was on Independence day, or the fourth of July, 1845, my house was not finished for winter, but was merely a defence against the rain, without plastering or chimney, the walls being of rough weather-stained boards, with wide chinks, which made it cool at night. The upright white hewn studs and freshly planed door and window casings gave it a clean and airy look, especially in the morning, when its timbers were saturated with dew, so that I fancied that by noon some sweet gum would exude from them. To my imagination it retained throughout the day more or less of this auroral character, reminding me of a certain house on a mountain which I had visited the year before. This was an airy and unplastered cabin, fit to entertain a travelling god, and where a goddess might trail her garments. The winds which passed over my dwelling were such as sweep over the ridges of mountains, bearing the broken strains, or celestial parts only, of terrestrial music. The morning wind forever blows, the poem of creation is uninterrupted; but few are the ears that hear it. Olympus [5] is but the outside of the earth every where.

The only house I had been the owner of before, if I except a boat, was a tent, which I used occasionally when making excursions in the summer, and this is still rolled up in my garret; but the boat, after passing from hand to hand, has gone down the stream of time. With this more substantial shelter about me, I had made some progress toward settling in the world. This frame, so slightly clad, was a sort of crystallization around me, and reacted on the builder. It was suggestive somewhat as a picture in outlines. I did not need to go out doors to take the air, for the atmosphere within had lost none of its freshness. It was not so much within doors as behind a door where I sat, even in the rainiest weather. The Harivansa [6] says, "An abode without birds is like a meat without

5. In ancient Greek mythology, the home of the gods.
6. An epic poem concerning the Hindu god, Krishna, written about the fifth century A.D.

seasoning." Such was not my abode, for I found myself suddenly
neighbor to the birds; not by having imprisoned one, but having
caged myself near them. I was not only nearer to some of those
which commonly frequent the garden and the orchard, but to those
wilder and more thrilling songsters of the forest which never, or
rarely, serenade a villager,—the wood-thrush, the veery, the
scarlet tanager, the field-sparrow, the whippoorwill, and many
others.

I was seated by the shore of a small pond, about a mile and a
half south of the village of Concord and somewhat higher than it,
in the midst of an extensive wood between that town and Lincoln,
and about two miles south of that our only field known to fame,
Concord Battle Ground; [7] but I was so low in the woods that the
opposite shore, half a mile off, like the rest, covered with wood,
was my most distant horizon. For the first week, whenever I
looked out on the pond it impressed me like a tarn high up on the
side of a mountain, its bottom far above the surface of other
lakes, and, as the sun arose, I saw it throwing off its nightly
clothing of mist, and here and there, by degrees, its soft ripples or
its smooth reflecting surface was revealed, while the mists, like
ghosts, were stealthily withdrawing in every direction into the
woods, as at the breaking up of some nocturnal conventicle. The
very dew seemed to hang upon the trees later into the day than
usual, as on the sides of mountains.

This small lake was of most value as a neighbor in the intervals
of a gentle rain storm in August, when, both air and water being
perfectly still, but the sky overcast, mid-afternoon had all the
serenity of evening, and the wood-thrush sang around, and was
heard from shore to shore. A lake like this is never smoother than
at such a time; and the clear portion of the air above it being
shallow and darkened by clouds, the water, full of light and reflections, becomes a lower heaven itself so much the more important. From a hill top near by, where the wood had been recently cut off, there was a pleasing vista southward across the
pond, through a wide indentation in the hills which form the
shore there, where their opposite sides sloping toward each other
suggested a stream flowing out in that direction through a wooded
valley, but stream there was none. That way I looked between and
over the near green hills to some distant and higher ones in the
horizon, tinged with blue. Indeed, by standing on tiptoe I could
catch a glimpse of some of the peaks of the still bluer and more
distant mountain ranges in the north-west, those true-blue coins
from heaven's own mint, and also of some portion of the village.
But in other directions, even from this point, I could not see over

7. Site of the opening battle of the American Revolution, April 19, 1775.

or beyond the woods which surrounded me. It is well to have some water in your neighborhood, to give buoyancy to and float the earth. One value even of the smallest well is, that when you look into it you see that earth is not continent but insular. This is as important as that it keeps butter cool. When I looked across the pond from this peak toward the Sudbury meadows, which in time of flood I distinguished elevated perhaps by a mirage in their seething valley, like a coin in a basin, all the earth beyond the pond appeared like a thin crust insulated and floated even by this small sheet of intervening water, and I was reminded that this on which I dwelt was but *dry land*.

Though the view from my door was still more contracted, I did not feel crowded or confined in the least. There was pasture enough for my imagination. The low shrub-oak plateau to which the opposite shore arose, stretched away toward the prairies of the West and the steppes of Tartary, affording ample room for all the roving families of men. "There are none happy in the world but beings who enjoy freely a vast horizon,"—said Damodara,[8] when his herds required new and larger pastures.

Both place and time were changed, and I dwelt nearer to those parts of the universe and to those eras in history which had most attracted me. Where I lived was as far off as many a region viewed nightly by astronomers. We are wont to imagine rare and delectable places in some remote and more celestial corner of the system, behind the constellation of Cassiopeia's Chair, far from noise and disturbance. I discovered that my house actually had its site in such a withdrawn, but forever new and unprofaned, part of the universe. If it were worth the while to settle in those parts near to the Pleiades or the Hyades, to Aldebaran or Altair,[9] then I was really there, or at an equal remoteness from the life which I had left behind, dwindled and twinkling with as fine a ray to my nearest neighbor, and to be seen only in moonless nights by him. Such was that part of creation where I had squatted;—

> "There was a shepherd that did live,
> And held his thoughts as high
> As were the mounts whereon his flocks
> Did hourly feed him by." [1]

What should we think of the shepherd's life if his flocks always wandered to higher pastures than his thoughts?

Every morning was a cheerful invitation to make my life of equal simplicity, and I may say innocence, with Nature herself. I have been as sincere a worshipper of Aurora as the Greeks. I got

8. Another name for Krishna.
9. Like Cassiopeia's Chair, Pleiades and Aldebaran are constellations of stars.
1. An anonymous poem, first published in 1610.

up early and bathed in the pond; that was a religious exercise, and one of the best things which I did. They say that characters were engraven on the bathing tub of king Tching-thang [2] to this effect: "Renew thyself completely each day; do it again, and again, and forever again." I can understand that. Morning brings back the heroic ages. I was as much affected by the faint hum of a mosquito making its invisible and unimaginable tour through my apartment at earliest dawn, when I was sitting with door and windows open, as I could be by any trumpet that ever sang of fame. It was Homer's requiem; itself an Iliad and Odyssey in the air, singing its own wrath and wanderings. There was something cosmical about it; a standing advertisement, till forbidden, of the everlasting vigor and fertility of the world. The morning, which is the most memorable season of the day, is the awakening hour. Then there is least somnolence in us; and for an hour, at least, some part of us awakes which slumbers all the rest of the day and night. Little is to be expected of that day, if it can be called a day, to which we are not awakened by our Genius, but by the mechanical nudgings of some servitor, are not awakened by our own newly-acquired force and aspirations from within, accompanied by the undulations of celestial music, instead of factory bells, and a fragrance filling the air—to a higher life than we fell asleep from; and thus the darkness bear its fruit, and prove itself to be good, no less than the light. That man who does not believe that each day contains an earlier, more sacred, and auroral hour than he has yet profaned, has despaired of life, and is pursuing a descending and darkening way. After a partial cessation of his sensuous life, the soul of man, or its organs rather, are reinvigorated each day, and his Genius tries again what noble life it can make. All memorable events, I should say, transpire in morning time and in a morning atmosphere. The Vedas [3] say, "All intelligences awake with the morning." Poetry and art, and the fairest and most memorable of the actions of men, date from such an hour. All poets and heroes, like Memnon, are the children of Aurora, and emit their music at sunrise. To him whose elastic and vigorous thought keeps pace with the sun, the day is a perpetual morning. It matters not what the clocks say or the attitudes and labors of men. Morning is when I am awake and there is a dawn in me. Moral reform is the effort to throw off sleep. Why is it that men give so poor an account of their day if they have not been slumbering? They are not such poor calculators. If they had not been overcome with drowsiness they would have performed something. The millions are awake enough for physical labor; but only one in a million is awake enough for effective intellectual exertion, only one in a

2. Another name for Confucius.   3. Ancient Hindu scriptures.

hundred millions to a poetic or divine life. To be awake is to be alive. I have never yet met a man who was quite awake. How could I have looked him in the face?

We must learn to reawaken and keep ourselves awake, not by mechanical aids, but by an infinite expectation of the dawn, which does not forsake us in our soundest sleep. I know of no more encouraging fact than the unquestionable ability of man to elevate his life by a conscious endeavor. It is something to be able to paint a particular picture, or to carve a statue, and so to make a few objects beautiful; but it is far more glorious to carve and paint the very atmosphere and medium through which we look, which morally we can do. To affect the quality of the day, that is the highest of arts. Every man is tasked to make his life, even in its details, worthy of the contemplation of his most elevated and critical hour. If we refused, or rather used up, such paltry information as we get, the oracles would distinctly inform us how this might be done.

I went to the woods because I wished to live deliberately, to front only the essential facts of life, and see if I could not learn what it had to teach, and not, when I came to die, discover that I had not lived. I did not wish to live what was not life, living is so dear; nor did I wish to practise resignation, unless it was quite necessary. I wanted to live deep and suck out all the marrow of life, to live so sturdily and Spartan-like [4] as to put to rout all that was not life, to cut a broad swath and shave close, to drive life into a corner, and reduce it to its lowest terms, and, if it proved to be mean, why then to get the whole and genuine meanness of it, and publish its meanness to the world; or if it were sublime, to know it by experience, and be able to give a true account of it in my next excursion. For most men, it appears to me, are in a strange uncertainty about it, whether it is of the devil or of God, and have *somewhat hastily* concluded that it is the chief end of man here to "glorify God and enjoy him forever."

Still we live meanly, like ants; though the fable tells us that we were long ago changed into men; like pygmies we fight with cranes; it is error upon error, and clout upon clout, and our best virtue has for its occasion a superfluous and evitable wretchedness. Our life is frittered away by detail. An honest man has hardly need to count more than his ten fingers, or in extreme cases he may add his ten toes, and lump the rest. Simplicity, simplicity, simplicity! I say, let your affairs be as two or three, and not a hundred or a thousand; instead of a million count half a dozen, and keep your accounts on your thumb nail. In the midst of this

4. The Spartans of ancient Greece were courageous warriors who lived hardy and rigorous lives.

chopping sea of civilized life, such are the clouds and storms and quicksands and thousand-and-one items to be allowed for, that a man has to live, if he would not founder and go to the bottom and not make his port at all, by dead reckoning, and he must be a great calculator indeed who succeeds. Simplify, simplify. Instead of three meals a day, if it be necessary eat but one; instead of a hundred dishes, five; and reduce other things in proportion. Our life is like a German Confederacy,[5] made up of petty states, with its boundary forever fluctuating, so that even a German cannot tell you how it is bounded at any moment. The nation itself, with all its so called internal improvements, which, by the way, are all external and superficial, is just such an unwieldy and overgrown establishment, cluttered with furniture and tripped up by its own traps, ruined by luxury and heedless expense, by want of calculation and a worthy aim, as the million households in the land; and the only cure for it as for them is in a rigid economy, a stern and more than Spartan simplicity of life and elevation of purpose. It lives too fast. Men think that it is essential that the *Nation* have commerce, and export ice, and talk through a telegraph, and ride thirty miles an hour, without a doubt, whether *they* do or not; but whether we should live like baboons or like men, is a little uncertain. If we do not get out sleepers, and forge rails, and devote days and nights to the work, but go to tinkering upon our *lives* to improve *them*, who will build railroads? And if railroads are not built, how shall we get to heaven in season? But if we stay at home and mind our business, who will want railroads? We do not ride on the railroad; it rides upon us. Did you ever think what those sleepers are that underlie the railroad? Each one is a man, an Irishman, or a Yankee man. The rails are laid on them, and they are covered with sand, and the cars run smoothly over them. They are sound sleepers, I assure you. And every few years a new lot is laid down and run over; so that, if some have the pleasure of riding on a rail, others have the misfortune to be ridden upon. And when they run over a man that is walking in his sleep, a supernumerary sleeper in the wrong position, and wake him up, they suddenly stop the cars, and make a hue and cry about it, as if this were an exception. I am glad to know that it takes a gang of men for every five miles to keep the sleepers down and level in their beds as it is, for this is a sign that they may sometime get up again.

Why should we live with such hurry and waste of life? We are determined to be starved before we are hungry. Men say that a stitch in time saves nine, and so they take a thousand stitches today to save nine to-morrow. As for *work*, we haven't any of any

5. A loose collection of states which existed from 1815 to 1866.

consequence. We have the Saint Vitus' dance,[6] and cannot possibly keep our heads still. If I should only give a few pulls at the parish bell-rope, as for a fire, that is, without setting the bell, there is hardly a man on his farm in the outskirts of Concord, notwithstanding that press of engagements which was his excuse so many times this morning, nor a boy, nor a woman, I might almost say, but would forsake all and follow that sound, not mainly to save property from the flames, but, if we will confess the truth, much more to see it burn, since burn it must, and we, be it known, did not set it on fire,—or to see it put out, and have a hand in it, if that is done as handsomely; yes, even if it were the parish church itself. Hardly a man takes a half hour's nap after dinner, but when he wakes he holds up his head and asks, "What's the news?" as if the rest of mankind had stood his sentinels. Some give directions to be waked every half hour, doubtless for no other purpose; and then, to pay for it, they tell what they have dreamed. After a night's sleep the news is as indispensable as the breakfast. "Pray tell me any thing new that has happened to a man any where on this globe,"—and he reads it over his coffee and rolls, that a man has had his eyes gouged out this morning on the Wachito River;[7] never dreaming the while that he lives in the dark unfathomed mammoth cave of this world, and has but the rudiment of an eye himself.

For my part, I could easily do without the post-office. I think that there are very few important communications made through it. To speak critically, I never received more than one or two letters in my life—I wrote this some years ago—that were worth the postage. The penny-post is, commonly, an institution through which you seriously offer a man that penny for his thoughts which is so often safely offered in jest. And I am sure that I never read any memorable news in a newspaper. If we read of one man robbed, or murdered, or killed by accident, or one house burned, or one vessel wrecked, or one steamboat blown up, or one cow run over on the Western Railroad,[8] or one mad dog killed, or one lot of grasshoppers in the winter,—we never need read of another. One is enough. If you are acquainted with the principle, what do you care for a myriad instances and applications? To a philosopher all *news*, as it is called, is gossip, and they who edit and read it are old women over their tea. Yet not a few are greedy after this gossip. There was such a rush, as I hear, the other day at one of the offices to learn the foreign news by the last arrival, that several large squares of plate glass belonging to the establishment

6. Chorea, a nervous disease accompanied by involuntary movements, depression, and emotional instability.
7. Now called the Ouachita River; it begins in Arkansas and empties into the Red River in Louisiana.
8. Originally running through western Massachusetts into New York State.

were broken by the pressure,—news which I seriously think a
ready wit might write a twelvemonth or twelve years beforehand
with sufficient accuracy. As for Spain, for instance, if you know
how to throw in Don Carlos and the Infanta, and Don Pedro and
Seville and Granada,[9] from time to time in the right proportions,—
they may have changed the names a little since I saw the papers,—
and serve up a bull-fight when other entertainments fail, it will
be true to the letter, and give us as good an idea of the exact
state or ruin of things in Spain as the most succinct and lucid reports under this head in the newspapers: and as for England,
almost the last significant scrap of news from that quarter was the
revolution of 1649; and if you have learned the history of her
crops for an average year, you never need attend to that thing
again, unless your speculations are of a merely pecuniary character. If one may judge who rarely looks into the newspapers,
nothing new does ever happen in foreign parts, a French revolution not excepted.

What news! how much more important to know what that is
which was never old! "Kieou-he-yu [1] (great dignitary of the state
of Wei) sent a man to Khoung-tseu to know his news. Khoung-
tseu caused the messenger to be seated near him, and questioned
him in these terms: What is your master doing? The messenger
answered with respect: My master desires to diminish the number
of his faults, but he cannot accomplish it. The messenger being
gone, the philosopher remarked: What a worthy messenger! What
a worthy messenger!" The preacher, instead of vexing the ears
of drowsy farmers on their day of rest at the end of the week,—for
Sunday is the fit conclusion of an ill-spent week, and not the
fresh and brave beginning of a new one,—with this one other
draggletail of a sermon, should shout with thundering voice,—
"Pause! Avast! Why so seeming fast, but deadly slow?"

Shams and delusions are esteemed for soundest truths, while
reality is fabulous. If men would steadily observe realities only,
and not allow themselves to be deluded, life, to compare it with
such things as we know, would be like a fairy tale and the
Arabian Nights' Entertainments.[2] If we respected only what is
inevitable and has a right to be, music and poetry would resound
along the streets. When we are unhurried and wise, we perceive
that only great and worthy things have any permanent and absolute
existence,—that petty fears and petty pleasures are but the shadow

9. Thoreau names persons involved in
Portuguese and Spanish politics in the
1830s and '40s: Dom Pedro was Emperor of Brazil whose daughter became
Queen of Portugal; Don Carlos con-
nived against his niece, the Infanta,
for the Spanish throne.
1. A character in one of Confucius'
books.
2. A collection of stories from the
Middle East, compiled about the tenth
century.

of the reality. This is always exhilarating and sublime. By closing
the eyes and slumbering, and consenting to be deceived by shows,
men establish and confirm their daily life of routine and habit
every where, which still is built on purely illusory foundations.
Children, who play life, discern its true law and relations more
clearly than men, who fail to live it worthily, but who think that
they are wiser by experience, that is, by failure. I have read in a
Hindoo book, that "there was a king's son, who, being expelled
in infancy from his native city, was brought up by a forester, and,
growing up to maturity in that state, imagined himself to belong
to the barbarous race with which he lived. One of his father's
ministers having discovered him, revealed to him what he was,
and the misconception of his character was removed, and he knew
himself to be a prince. So soul," continues the Hindoo philosopher,
"from the circumstances in which it is placed, mistakes its own
character, until the truth is revealed to it by some holy teacher,
and then it knows itself to be *Brahme*." I perceive that we inhabitants of New England live this mean life that we do because
our vision does not penetrate the surface of things. We think that
that *is* which *appears* to be. If a man should walk through this
town and see only the reality, where, think you, would the "Mill-
dam" [3] go to? If he should give us an account of the realities he
beheld there, we should not recognize the place in his description.
Look at a meeting-house, or a court-house, or a jail, or a shop, or
a dwelling-house, and say what that thing really is before a true
gaze, and they would all go to pieces in your account of them.
Men esteem truth remote, in the outskirts of the system, behind
the farthest star, before Adam and after the last man. In eternity
there is indeed something true and sublime. But all these times and
places and occasions are now and here. God himself culminates
in the present moment, and will never be more divine in the lapse
of all the ages. And we are enabled to apprehend at all what is
sublime and noble only by the perpetual instilling and drenching
of the reality that surrounds us. The universe constantly and
obediently answers to our conceptions; whether we travel fast or
slow, the track is laid for us. Let us spend our lives in conceiving
then. The poet or the artist never yet had so fair and noble a design but some of his posterity at least could accomplish it.

Let us spend one day as deliberately as Nature, and not be
thrown off the track by every nutshell and mosquito's wing that
falls on the rails. Let us rise early and fast, or break fast, gently
and without perturbation; let company come and let company go,
let the bells ring and the children cry,—determined to make a day

3. Concord was originally a mill town; the dam was a general meeting place.

of it. Why should we knock under and go with the stream? Let us not be upset and overwhelmed in that terrible rapid and whirlpool called a dinner, situated in the meridian shallows. Weather this danger and you are safe, for the rest of the way is down hill. With unrelaxed nerves, with morning vigor, sail by it, looking another way, tied to the mast like Ulysses.[4] If the engine whistles, let it whistle till it is hoarse for its pains. If the bell rings, why should we run? We will consider what kind of music they are like. Let us settle ourselves, and work and wedge our feet downward through the mud and slush of opinion, and prejudice, and tradition, and delusion, and appearance, that alluvion which covers the globe, through Paris and London, through New York and Boston and Concord, through church and state, through poetry and philosophy and religion, till we come to a hard bottom and rocks in place, which we can call *reality*, and say, This is, and no mistake; and then begin, having a *point d'appui*,[5] below freshet and frost and fire, a place where you might found a wall or a state, or set a lamp-post safely, or perhaps a gauge, not a Nilometer,[6] but a Realo-meter, that future ages might know how deep a freshet of shams and appearances had gathered from time to time. If you stand right fronting and face to face to a fact, you will see the sun glimmer on both its surfaces, as if it were a cimeter, and feel its sweet edge dividing you through the heart and marrow, and so you will happily conclude your mortal career. Be it life or death, we crave only reality. If we are really dying, let us hear the rattle in our throats and feel cold in the extremities; if we are alive, let us go about our business.

Time is but the stream I go a-fishing in. I drink at it; but while I drink I see the sandy bottom and detect how shallow it is. Its thin current slides away, but eternity remains. I would drink deeper; fish in the sky, whose bottom is pebbly with stars. I cannot count one. I know not the first letter of the alphabet. I have always been regretting that I was not as wise as the day I was born. The intellect is a cleaver; it discerns and rifts its way into the secret of things. I do not wish to be any more busy with my hands than is necessary. My head is hands and feet. I feel all my best faculties concentrated in it. My instinct tells me that my head is an organ for burrowing, as some creatures use their snout and fore-paws, and with it I would mine and burrow my way through these hills. I think that the richest vein is somewhere hereabouts; so by the divining rod [7] and thin rising vapors I judge; and here I will begin to mine.

---

4. The Roman name of Odysseus.
5. A base; a point of support.
6. An ancient instrument for recording the rise and fall of the Nile River in Egypt.
7. A forked twig which is supposed to indicate the presence of underground water.

Reading

With a little more deliberation in the choice of their pursuits, all men would perhaps become essentially students and observers, for certainly their nature and destiny are interesting to all alike. In accumulating property for ourselves or our posterity, in founding a family or a state, or acquiring fame even, we are mortal; but in dealing with truth we are immortal, and need fear no change nor accident. The oldest Egyptian or Hindoo philosopher raised a corner of the veil from the statue of the divinity; and still the trembling robe remains raised, and I gaze upon as fresh a glory as he did, since it was I in him that was then so bold, and it is he in me that now reviews the vision. No dust has settled on that robe; no time has elapsed since that divinity was revealed. That time which we really improve, or which is improvable, is neither past, present, nor future.

My residence was more favorable, not only to thought, but to serious reading, than a university; and though I was beyond the range of the ordinary circulating library, I had more than ever come within the influence of those books which circulate round the world, whose sentences were first written on bark, and are now merely copied from time to time on to linen paper. Says the poet Mîr Camar Uddîn Mast,[1] "Being seated to run through the region of the spiritual world; I have had this advantage in books. To be intoxicated by a single glass of wine; I have experienced this pleasure when I have drunk the liquor of the esoteric doctrines." I kept Homer's Iliad on my table through the summer, though I looked at his page only now and then. Incessant labor with my hands, at first, for I had my house to finish and my beans to hoe at the same time, made more study impossible. Yet I sustained myself by the prospect of such reading in future. I read one or two shallow books of travel in the intervals of my work, till that employment made me ashamed of myself, and I asked where it was then that I lived.

The student may read Homer or Æschylus[2] in the Greek without danger of dissipation or luxuriousness, for it implies that he in some measure emulate their heroes, and consecrate morning hours to their pages. The heroic books, even if printed in the character of our mother tongue, will always be in a language dead to degenerate times; and we must laboriously seek the meaning of each word and line, conjecturing a larger sense than

1. A Persian poet of the eighteenth century. 2. Greek dramatist (525–456 B.C.).

common use permits out of what wisdom and valor and generosity we have. The modern cheap and fertile press, with all its translations, has done little to bring us nearer to the heroic writers of antiquity. They seem as solitary, and the letter in which they are printed as rare and curious, as ever. It is worth the expense of youthful days and costly hours, if you learn only some words of an ancient language, which are raised out of the trivialness of the street, to be perpetual suggestions and provocations. It is not in vain that the farmer remembers and repeats the few Latin words which he has heard. Men sometimes speak as if the study of the classics would at length make way for more modern and practical studies; but the adventurous student will always study classics, in whatever language they may be written and however ancient they may be. For what are the classics but the noblest recorded thoughts of man? They are the only oracles which are not decayed, and there are such answers to the most modern inquiry in them as Delphi and Dodona [3] never gave. We might as well omit to study Nature because she is old. To read well, that is, to read true books in a true spirit, is a noble exercise, and one that will task the reader more than any exercise which the customs of the day esteem. It requires a training such as the athletes underwent, the steady intention almost of the whole life to this object. Books must be read as deliberately and reservedly as they were written. It is not enough even to be able to speak the language of that nation by which they are written, for there is a memorable interval between the spoken and the written language, the language heard and the language read. The one is commonly transitory, a sound, a tongue, a dialect merely, almost brutish, and we learn it unconsciously, like the brutes, of our mothers. The other is the maturity and experience of that; if that is our mother tongue, this is our father tongue, a reserved and select expression, too significant to be heard by the ear, which we must be born again in order to speak. The crowds of men who merely *spoke* the Greek and Latin tongues in the middle ages were not entitled by the accident of birth to *read* the works of genius written in those languages; for these were not written in that Greek or Latin which they knew, but in the select language of literature. They had not learned the nobler dialects of Greece and Rome, but the very materials on which they were written were waste paper to them, and they prized instead a cheap contemporary literature. But when the several nations of Europe had acquired distinct though rude written languages of their own, sufficient for the purposes of their rising literatures, then first learning revived, and scholars were enabled to discern from that remoteness the treas-

3. The most famous oracles of ancient Greece.

ures of antiquity. What the Roman and Grecian multitude could not *hear*, after the lapse of ages a few scholars *read*, and a few scholars only are still reading it.

However much we may admire the orator's occasional bursts of eloquence, the noblest written words are commonly as far behind or above the fleeting spoken language as the firmament with its stars is behind the clouds. *There* are the stars, and they who can may read them. The astronomers forever comment on and observe them. They are not exhalations like our daily colloquies and vaporous breath. What is called eloquence in the forum is commonly found to be rhetoric in the study. The orator yields to the inspiration of a transient occasion, and speaks to the mob before him, to those who can *hear* him; but the writer, whose more equable life is his occasion, and who would be distracted by the event and the crowd which inspire the orator, speaks to the intellect and heart of mankind, to all in any age who can *understand* him.

No wonder that Alexander [4] carried the Iliad with him on his expeditions in a precious casket. A written word is the choicest of relics. It is something at once more intimate with us and more universal than any other work of art. It is the work of art nearest to life itself. It may be translated into every language, and not only be read but actually breathed from all human lips;—not be represented on canvas or in marble only, but be carved out of the breath of life itself. The symbol of an ancient man's thought becomes a modern man's speech. Two thousand summers have imparted to the monuments of Grecian literature, as to her marbles, only a maturer golden and autumnal tint, for they have carried their own serene and celestial atmosphere into all lands to protect them against the corrosion of time. Books are the treasured wealth of the world and the fit inheritance of generations and nations. Books, the oldest and the best, stand naturally and rightfully on the shelves of every cottage. They have no cause of their own to plead, but while they enlighten and sustain the reader his common sense will not refuse them. Their authors are a natural and irresistible aristocracy in every society, and, more than kings or emperors, exert an influence on mankind. When the illiterate and perhaps scornful trader has earned by enterprise and industry his coveted leisure and independence, and is admitted to the circles of wealth and fashion, he turns inevitably at last to those still higher but yet inaccessible circles of intellect and genius, and is sensible only of the imperfection of his culture and the vanity and insufficiency of all his riches, and further proves his good sense by the pains which he

4. Alexander the Great of Macedon (356–323 B.C.), king and conqueror of the Persian empire.

takes to secure for his children that intellectual culture whose want he so keenly feels; and thus it is that he becomes the founder of a family.

Those who have not learned to read the ancient classics in the language in which they were written must have a very imperfect knowledge of the history of the human race; for it is remarkable that no transcript of them has ever been made into any modern tongue, unless our civilization itself may be regarded as such a transcript. Homer has never yet been printed in English, nor Æschylus, nor Virgil [5] even,—works as refined, as solidly done, and as beautiful almost as the morning itself; for later writers, say what we will of their genius, have rarely, if ever, equalled the elaborate beauty and finish and the lifelong and heroic literary labors of the ancients. They only talk of forgetting them who never knew them. It will be soon enough to forget them when we have the learning and the genius which will enable us to attend to and appreciate them. That age will be rich indeed when those relics which we call Classics, and the still older and more than classic but even less known Scriptures of the nations, shall have still further accumulated, when the Vaticans shall be filled with Vedas and Zendavestas [6] and Bibles, with Homers and Dantes [7] and Shakspeares, and all the centuries to come shall have successively deposited their trophies in the forum of the world. By such a pile we may hope to scale heaven at last.

The works of the great poets have never yet been read by mankind, for only great poets can read them. They have only been read as the multitude read the stars, at most astrologically, not astronomically. Most men have learned to read to serve a paltry convenience, as they have learned to cipher in order to keep accounts and not be cheated in trade; but of reading as a noble intellectual exercise they know little or nothing; yet this only is reading, in a high sense, not that which lulls us as a luxury and suffers the nobler faculties to sleep the while, but what we have to stand on tiptoe to read and devote our most alert and wakeful hours to.

I think that having learned our letters we should read the best that is in literature, and not be forever repeating our a b abs, and words of one syllable, in the fourth or fifth classes, sitting on the lowest and foremost form all our lives. Most men are satisfied if they read or hear read, and perchance have been convicted by the wisdom of one good book, the Bible, and for the rest of their lives vegetate and dissipate their faculties in what is called easy

5. The greatest epic poet of ancient Rome, author of the *Aeneid* (70–19 B.C.).
6. The scripture of Zoroastrianism, a religion which began in Iran in the sixth or seventh century B.C.
7. Italian epic poet (1265–1321), author of *The Divine Comedy*.

reading. There is a work in several volumes in our Circulating Library entitled Little Reading, which I thought referred to a town of that name which I had not been to. There are those who, like cormorants and ostriches, can digest all sorts of this, even after the fullest dinner of meats and vegetables, for they suffer nothing to be wasted. If others are the machines to provide this provender, they are the machines to read it. They read the nine thousandth tale about Zebulon and Sephronia,[8] and how they loved as none had ever loved before, and neither did the course of their true love run smooth,—at any rate, how it did run and stumble, and get up again and go on! how some poor unfortunate got up on to a steeple, who had better never have gone up as far as the belfry; and then, having needlessly got him up there, the happy novelist rings the bell for all the world to come together and hear, O dear! how he did get down again! For my part, I think that they had better metamorphose all such aspiring heroes of universal noveldom into man weathercocks, as they used to put heroes among the constellations, and let them swing round there till they are rusty, and not come down at all to bother honest men with their pranks. The next time the novelist rings the bell I will not stir though the meeting-house burn down. "The Skip of the Tip-Toe-Hop, a Romance of the Middle Ages, by the celebrated author of 'Tittle-Tol-Tan,' to appear in monthly parts; a great rush; don't all come together." All this they read with saucer eyes, and erect and primitive curiosity, and with unwearied gizzard, whose corrugations even yet need no sharpening, just as some little four-year-old bencher his two-cent gilt-covered edition of Cinderella,—without any improvement, that I can see, in the pronunciation, or accent, or emphasis, or any more skill in extracting or inserting the moral. The result is dulness of sight, a stagnation of the vital circulations, and a general deliquium and sloughing off of all the intellectual faculties. This sort of gingerbread is baked daily and more sedulously than pure wheat or rye-and-Indian in almost every oven, and finds a surer market.

The best books are not read even by those who are called good readers. What does our Concord culture amount to? There is in this town, with a very few exceptions, no taste for the best or for very good books even in English literature, whose words all can read and spell. Even the college-bred and so called liberally educated men here and elsewhere have really little or no acquaintance with the English classics; and as for the recorded wisdom of mankind, the ancient classics and Bibles, which are accessible to all who will know of them, there are the feeblest efforts any where

8. Probably intended to represent standard characters in highly romantic novels.

made to become acquainted with them. I know a woodchopper, of middle age, who takes a French paper, not for news as he says, for he is above that, but to "keep himself in practice," he being a Canadian by birth; and when I asked him what he considers the best thing he can do in this world, he says, beside this, to keep up and add to his English. This is about as much as the college bred generally do or aspire to do, and they take an English paper for the purpose. One who has just come from reading perhaps one of the best English books will find how many with whom he can converse about it? Or suppose he comes from reading a Greek or Latin classic in the original, whose praises are familiar even to the so called illiterate; he will find nobody at all to speak to, but must keep silence about it. Indeed, there is hardly the professor in our colleges, who, if he has mastered the difficulties of the language, has proportionally mastered the difficulties of the wit and poetry of a Greek poet, and has any sympathy to impart to the alert and heroic reader; and as for the sacred Scriptures, or Bibles of mankind, who in this town can tell me even their titles? Most men do not know that any nation but the Hebrews have had a scripture. A man, any man, will go considerably out of his way to pick up a silver dollar; but here are golden words, which the wisest men of antiquity have uttered, and whose worth the wise of every succeeding age have assured us of; —and yet we learn to read only as far as Easy Reading, the primers and class-books, and when we leave school, the "Little Reading," and story books, which are for boys and beginners; and our reading, our conversation and thinking, are all on a very low level, worthy only of pygmies and manikins.

I aspire to be acquainted with wiser men than this our Concord soil has produced, whose names are hardly known here. Or shall I hear the name of Plato [9] and never read his book? As if Plato were my townsman and I never saw him,—my next neighbor and I never heard him speak or attended to the wisdom of his words. But how actually is it? His Dialogues, which contain what was immortal in him, lie on the next shelf, and yet I never read them. We are under-bred and low-lived and illiterate; and in this respect I confess I do not make any very broad distinction between the illiterateness of my townsman who cannot read at all, and the illiterateness of him who has learned to read only what is for children and feeble intellects. We should be as good as the worthies of antiquity, but partly by first knowing how good they were. We are a race of tit-men, [1] and soar but little higher in our intellectual flights than the columns of the daily paper.

9. Greek philosopher (427?–347? B.C.).
1. Literally, the smallest pig in a litter; figuratively, a physically or mentally small man.

It is not all books that are as dull as their readers. There are probably words addressed to our condition exactly, which, if we could really hear and understand, would be more salutary than the morning or the spring to our lives, and possibly put a new aspect on the face of things for us. How many a man has dated a new era in his life from the reading of a book. The book exists for us perchance which will explain our miracles and reveal new ones. The at present unutterable things we may find somewhere uttered. These same questions that disturb and puzzle and confound us have in their turn occurred to all the wise men; not one has been omitted; and each has answered them, according to his ability, by his words and his life. Moreover, with wisdom we shall learn liberality. The solitary hired man on a farm in the outskirts of Concord, who has had his second birth and peculiar religious experience, and is driven as he believes into silent gravity and exclusiveness by his faith, may think it is not true; but Zoroaster, thousands of years ago, travelled the same road and had the same experience; but he, being wise, knew it to be universal, and treated his neighbors accordingly, and is even said to have invented and established worship among men. Let him humbly commune with Zoroaster then, and, through the liberalizing influence of all the worthies, with Jesus Christ himself, and let "our church" go by the board.

We boast that we belong to the nineteenth century and are making the most rapid strides of any nation. But consider how little this village does for its own culture. I do not wish to flatter my townsmen, nor to be flattered by them, for that will not advance either of us. We need to be provoked,—goaded like oxen, as we are, into a trot. We have a comparatively decent system of common schools, schools for infants only; but excepting the half-starved Lyceum [2] in the winter, and latterly the puny beginning of a library suggested by the state, no school for ourselves. We spend more on almost any article of bodily aliment or ailment than on our mental aliment. It is time that we had uncommon schools, that we did not leave off our education when we begin to be men and women. It is time that villages were universities, and their elder inhabitants the fellows of universities, with leisure—if they are indeed so well off—to pursue liberal studies the rest of their lives. Shall the world be confined to one Paris or one Oxford forever? Cannot students be boarded here and get a liberal education under the skies of Concord? Can we not hire some Abelard [3] to lecture to us? Alas! what with foddering the cattle and tend-

2. In ancient Greece, a grove near Athens in which the philosopher, Aristotle, taught; in Thoreau's time, an organization which sponsored lectures and concerts.

3. Peter Abelard (1079–1142), a French philosopher, theologian, and teacher.

ing the store, we are kept from school too long, and our education is sadly neglected. In this country, the village should in some
respects take the place of the nobleman of Europe. It should be
the patron of the fine arts. It is rich enough. It wants only the
magnanimity and refinement. It can spend money enough on such
things as farmers and traders value, but it is thought Utopian [4]
to propose spending money for things which more intelligent
men know to be of far more worth. This town has spent seventeen
thousand dollars on a town-house, thank fortune or politics, but
probably it will not spend so much on living wit, the true meat to
put into that shell, in a hundred years. The one hundred and
twenty-five dollars annually subscribed for a Lyceum in the winter
is better spent than any other equal sum raised in the town. If we
live in the nineteenth century, why should we not enjoy the
advantages which the nineteenth century offers? Why should our
life be in any respect provincial? If we will read newspapers, why
not skip the gossip of Boston and take the best newspaper in the
world at once?—not be sucking the pap of "neutral family" [5]
papers, or browsing "Olive-Branches" [6] here in New England. Let
the reports of all the learned societies come to us, and we will see
if they know any thing. Why should we leave it to Harper &
Brothers and Redding & Co.[7] to select our reading? As the nobleman of cultivated taste surrounds himself with whatever conduces
to his culture,—genius—learning—wit—books—paintings—statu-
ary—music—philosophical instruments, and the like; so let the
village do,—not stop short at a pedagogue, a parson, a sexton, a
parish library, and three selectmen, because our pilgrim forefathers
got through a cold winter once on a bleak rock with these. To
act collectively is according to the spirit of our institutions; and I
am confident that, as our circumstances are more flourishing, our
means are greater than the nobleman's. New England can hire all
the wise men in the world to come and teach her, and board them
round the while, and not be provincial at all. That is the *uncommon*
school we want. Instead of noblemen, let us have noble villages of
men. If it is necessary, omit one bridge over the river, go round a
little there, and throw one arch at least over the darker gulf of
ignorance which surrounds us.

Sounds

But while we are confined to books, though the most select and
classic, and read only particular written languages, which are

4. Utopia: an imaginary and ideal land.
5. I.e., a newspaper which avoided
political issues in favor of family entertainment.

6. A Methodist weekly newspaper.
7. Book publishers, located in New
York and Boston, respectively.

themselves but dialects and provincial, we are in danger of forgetting the language which all things and events speak without metaphor, which alone is copious and standard. Much is published, but little printed. The rays which stream through the shutter will be no longer remembered when the shutter is wholly removed. No method nor discipline can supersede the necessity of being forever on the alert. What is a course of history, or philosophy, or poetry, no matter how well selected, or the best society, or the most admirable routine of life, compared with the discipline of looking always at what is to be seen? Will you be a reader, a student merely, or a seer? Read your fate, see what is before you, and walk on into futurity.

I did not read books the first summer; I hoed beans. Nay, I often did better than this. There were times when I could not afford to sacrifice the bloom of the present moment to any work, whether of the head or hands. I love a broad margin to my life. Sometimes, in a summer morning, having taken my accustomed bath, I sat in my sunny doorway from sunrise till noon, rapt in a revery, amidst the pines and hickories and sumachs, in undisturbed solitude and stillness, while the birds sang around or flitted noiseless through the house, until by the sun falling in at my west window, or the noise of some traveller's wagon on the distant highway, I was reminded of the lapse of time. I grew in those seasons like corn in the night, and they were far better than any work of the hands would have been. They were not time subtracted from my life, but so much over and above my usual allowance. I realized what the Orientals mean by contemplation and the forsaking of works. For the most part, I minded not how the hours went. The day advanced as if to light some work of mine; it was morning, and lo, now it is evening, and nothing memorable is accomplished. Instead of singing like the birds, I silently smiled at my incessant good fortune. As the sparrow had its trill, sitting on the hickory before my door, so had I my chuckle or suppressed warble which he might hear out of my nest. My days were not days of the week, bearing the stamp of any heathen deity, nor were they minced into hours and fretted by the ticking of a clock; for I lived like the Puri Indians,[1] of whom it is said that "for yesterday, to-day, and to-morrow they have only one word, and they express the variety of meaning by pointing backward for yesterday, forward for to-morrow, and overhead for the passing day." This was sheer idleness to my fellow-townsmen, no doubt; but if the birds and flowers had tried me by their standard, I should not have been found wanting. A man must find his occasions in himself, it is

---

1. A tribe in eastern Brazil; the quotation is from Ida Pfeiffer.

true. The natural day is very calm, and will hardly reprove his indolence.

I had this advantage, at least, in my mode of life, over those who were obliged to look abroad for amusement, to society and the theatre, that my life itself was become my amusement and never ceased to be novel. It was a drama of many scenes and without an end. If we were always indeed getting our living, and regulating our lives according to the last and best mode we had learned, we should never be troubled with ennui. Follow your genius closely enough, and it will not fail to show you a fresh prospect every hour. Housework was a pleasant pastime. When my floor was dirty, I rose early, and, setting all my furniture out of doors on the grass, bed and bedstead making but one budget, dashed water on the floor, and sprinkled white sand from the pond on it, and then with a broom scrubbed it clean and white; and by the time the villagers had broken their fast the morning sun had dried my house sufficiently to allow me to move in again, and my meditations were almost uninterrupted. It was pleasant to see my whole household effects out on the grass, making a little pile like a gypsy's pack, and my three-legged table, from which I did not remove the books and pen and ink, standing amid the pines and hickories. They seemed glad to get out themselves, and as if unwilling to be brought in. I was sometimes tempted to stretch an awning over them and take my seat there. It was worth the while to see the sun shine on these things, and hear the free wind blow on them; so much more interesting most familiar objects look out of doors than in the house. A bird sits on the next bough, life-everlasting grows under the table, and blackberry vines run round its legs; pine cones, chestnut burs, and strawberry leaves are strewn about. It looked as if this was the way these forms came to be transferred to our furniture, to tables, chairs, and bedsteads,—because they once stood in their midst.

My house was on the side of a hill, immediately on the edge of the larger wood, in the midst of a young forest of pitch pines and hickories, and half a dozen rods from the pond, to which a narrow footpath led down the hill. In my front yard grew the strawberry, blackberry, and life-everlasting, johnswort and goldenrod, shrub-oaks and sand-cherry, blueberry and groundnut. Near the end of May, the sand-cherry, (*cerasus pumila,*) adorned the sides of the path with its delicate flowers arranged in umbels cylindrically about its short stems, which last, in the fall, weighed down with good sized and handsome cherries, fell over in wreaths like rays on every side. I tasted them out of compliment to Nature, though they were scarcely palatable. The sumach, (*rhus glabra,*) grew luxuriantly about the house, pushing up through the embankment which I had made, and growing five or six feet the first season. Its broad pinnate tropical leaf was pleasant though strange to look on. The large buds, suddenly pushing out late in the spring from dry sticks which had seemed to be dead, developed themselves as by magic into graceful green and tender boughs, an inch in diameter; and sometimes, as I sat at my window, so heedlessly did they grow and tax their weak joints, I heard a fresh and tender bough suddenly fall like a fan to the ground, when there was not a breath of air stirring, broken off by its own weight. In August, the large masses of berries, which, when in flower, had attracted many wild bees, gradually assumed their bright velvety crimson hue, and by their weight again bent down and broke the tender limbs.

As I sit at my window this summer afternoon, hawks are circling about my clearing; the tantivy of wild pigeons, flying by twos and threes athwart my view, or perching restless on the white-pine boughs behind my house, gives a voice to the air; a fishhawk dimples the glassy surface of the pond and brings up a fish; a mink steals out of the marsh before my door and seizes a frog by the shore; the sedge is bending under the weight of the reed-birds flitting hither and thither; and for the last half hour I have heard the rattle of railroad cars, now dying away and then reviving like the beat of a partridge, conveying travellers from Boston to the country. For I did not live so out of the world as that boy, who, as I hear, was put out to a farmer in the east part of the town, but ere long ran away and came home again, quite down at the heel and homesick. He had never seen such a dull and out-of-the-way place; the folks were all gone off; why, you couldn't even hear the whistle! I doubt if there is such a place in Massachusetts now:—

" In truth, our village has become a butt
  For one of those fleet railroad shafts, and o'er
  Our peaceful plain its soothing sound is—Concord." [2]

The Fitchburg Railroad touches the pond about a hundred rods south of where I dwell. I usually go to the village along its causeway, and am, as it were, related to society by this link. The men on the freight trains, who go over the whole length of the road, bow to me as to an old acquaintance, they pass me so often, and apparently they take me for an employee; and so I am. I too would fain be a track-repairer somewhere in the orbit of the earth.

The whistle of the locomotive penetrates my woods summer and

2. From "Walden Spring" by Ellery Channing (1818–1901), one of Thoreau's closest friends.

winter, sounding like the scream of a hawk sailing over some farmer's yard, informing me that many restless city merchants are arriving within the circle of the town, or adventurous country traders from the other side. As they come under one horizon, they shout their warning to get off the track to the other, heard sometimes through the circles of two towns. Here come your groceries, country; your rations, countrymen! Nor is there any man so independent on his farm that he can say them nay. And here's your pay for them! screams the countryman's whistle; timber like long battering rams going twenty miles an hour against the city's walls, and chairs enough to seat all the weary and heavy laden that dwell within them. With such huge and lumbering civility the country hands a chair to the city. All the Indian huckleberry hills are stripped, all the cranberry meadows are raked into the city. Up comes the cotton, down goes the woven cloth; up comes the silk, down goes the woollen; up come the books, but down goes the wit that writes them.

When I meet the engine with its train of cars moving off with planetary motion,—or, rather, like a comet, for the beholder knows not if with that velocity and with that direction it will ever revisit this system, since its orbit does not look like a returning curve,—with its steam cloud like a banner streaming behind in golden and silver wreaths, like many a downy cloud which I have seen, high in the heavens, unfolding its masses to the light, —as if this travelling demigod, this cloud-compeller, would ere long take the sunset sky for the livery of his train; when I hear the iron horse make the hills echo with his snort like thunder, shaking the earth with his feet, and breathing fire and smoke from his nostrils, (what kind of winged horse or fiery dragon they will put into the new Mythology I don't know,) it seems as if the earth had got a race now worthy to inhabit it. If all were as it seems, and men made the elements their servants for noble ends! If the cloud that hangs over the engine were the perspiration of heroic deeds, or as beneficent as that which floats over the farmer's fields, then the elements and Nature herself would cheerfully accompany men on their errands and be their escort.

I watch the passage of the morning cars with the same feeling that I do the rising of the sun, which is hardly more regular. Their train of clouds stretching far behind and rising higher and higher, going to heaven while the cars are going to Boston, conceals the sun for a minute and casts my distant field into the shade, a celestial train beside which the petty train of cars which hugs the earth is but the barb of the spear. The stabler of the iron horse was up early this winter morning by the light of the stars amid the mountains, to fodder and harness his steed. Fire, too, was awakened thus early to put the vital heat in him and get him off. If the enterprise were as innocent as it is early! If the snow lies deep, they strap on his snow-shoes, and with the giant plough plough a furrow from the mountains to the seaboard, in which the cars, like a following drill-barrow, sprinkle all the restless men and floating merchandise in the country for seed. All day the fire-steed flies over the country, stopping only that his master may rest, and I am awakened by his tramp and defiant snort at midnight, when in some remote glen in the woods he fronts the elements incased in ice and snow; and he will reach his stall only with the morning star, to start once more on his travels without rest or slumber. Or perchance, at evening, I hear him in his stable blowing off the superfluous energy of the day, that he may calm his nerves and cool his liver and brain for a few hours of iron slumber. If the enterprise were as heroic and commanding as it is protracted and unwearied!

Far through unfrequented woods on the confines of towns, where once only the hunter penetrated by day, in the darkest night dart these bright saloons without the knowledge of their inhabitants; this moment stopping at some brilliant station-house in town or city, where a social crowd is gathered, the next in the Dismal Swamp,[3] scaring the owl and fox. The startings and arrivals of the cars are now the epochs in the village day. They go and come with such regularity and precision, and their whistle can be heard so far, that the farmers set their clocks by them, and thus one well conducted institution regulates a whole country. Have not men improved somewhat in punctuality since the railroad was invented? Do they not talk and think faster in the depot than they did in the stage-office? There is something electrifying in the atmosphere of the former place. I have been astonished at the miracles it has wrought; that some of my neighbors, who, I should have prophesied, once for all, would never get to Boston by so prompt a conveyance, were on hand when the bell rang. To do things "railroad fashion" is now the by-word; and it is worth the while to be warned so often and so sincerely by any power to get off its track. There is no stopping to read the riot act, no firing over the heads of the mob, in this case. We have constructed a fate, an *Atropos*,[4] that never turns aside. (Let that be the name of your engine.) Men are advertised that at a certain hour and minute these bolts will be shot toward particular points of the compass; yet it interferes with no man's business, and the children go to school on the other track. We live the steadier for it.

---

3. A coastal swamp in southeastern Virginia and northeastern North Carolina.

4. In Greek mythology, one of the three Fates who determined when a man was to die.

We are all educated thus to be sons of Tell.[5] The air is full of invisible bolts. Every path but your own is the path of fate. Keep on your own track, then.

What recommends commerce to me is its enterprise and bravery. It does not clasp its hands and pray to Jupiter. I see these men every day go about their business with more or less courage and content, doing more even than they suspect, and perchance better employed than they could have consciously devised. I am less affected by their heroism who stood up for half an hour in the front line at Buena Vista,[6] than by the steady and cheerful valor of the men who inhabit the snow-plough for their winter quarters; who have not merely the three-o'-clock in the morning courage, which Bonaparte [7] thought was the rarest, but whose courage does not go to rest so early, who go to sleep only when the storm sleeps or the sinews of their iron steed are frozen. On this morning of the Great Snow,[8] perchance, which is still raging and chilling men's blood, I hear the muffled tone of their engine bell from out the fog bank of their chilled breath, which announces that the cars *are coming*, without long delay, notwithstanding the veto of a New England north-east snow storm, and I behold the ploughmen covered with snow and rime, their heads peering above the mould-board which is turning down other than daisies and the nests of field-mice, like bowlders of the Sierra Nevada, [9] that occupy an outside place in the universe.

Commerce is unexpectedly confident and serene, alert, adventurous, and unwearied. It is very natural in its methods withal, far more so than many fantastic enterprises and sentimental experiments, and hence its singular success. I am refreshed and expanded when the freight train rattles past me, and I smell the stores which go dispensing their odors all the way from Long Wharf to Lake Champlain,[1] reminding me of foreign parts, of coral reefs, and Indian oceans, and tropical climes, and the extent of the globe. I feel more like a citizen of the world at the sight of the palm-leaf which will cover so many flaxen New England heads the next summer, the Manilla hemp and cocoa-nut husks, the old junk, gunny bags, scrap iron, and rusty nails. This car-load of torn sails is more legible and interesting now than if they should be wrought into paper and printed books. Who can write so

5. I.e., one of the sons of William Tell who, according to legend, shot an arrow through an apple which rested on his son's head.
6. One of the battles of the Mexican War (1846–1848).
7. Napoleon Bonaparte (1769–1821), French general and emperor.
8. Several heavy storms have been referred to as "the Great Snow," although Thoreau may have been thinking of the storm of February, 1717.
9. A mountain range in eastern California.
1. The Long Wharf was one of the major piers in Boston; Lake Champlain is in central New York.

graphically the history of the storms they have weathered as these
rents have done? They are proof-sheets which need no correction.
Here goes lumber from the Maine woods, which did not go out
to sea in the last freshet, risen four dollars on the thousand because of what did go out or was split up; pine, spruce, cedar,
—first, second, third and fourth qualities, so lately all of one
quality, to wave over the bear, and moose, and caribou. Next rolls
Thomaston [2] lime, a prime lot, which will get far among the hills
before it gets slacked. These rags in bales, of all hues and qualities,
the lowest condition to which cotton and linen descend, the final
result of dress,—of patterns which are now no longer cried up,
unless it be in Milwaukie, as those splendid articles, English,
French, or American prints, ginghams, muslins, &c., gathered
from all quarters both of fashion and poverty, going to become
paper of one color or a few shades only, on which forsooth will
be written tales of real life, high and low, and founded on fact!
This closed car smells of salt fish, the strong New England and
commercial scent, reminding me of the Grand Banks [3] and the
fisheries. Who has not seen a salt fish, thoroughly cured for this
world, so that nothing can spoil it, and putting the perseverance of
the saints to the blush? with which you may sweep or pave the
streets, and split your kindlings, and the teamster shelter himself
and his lading against sun wind and rain behind it,—and the trader,
as a Concord trader once did, hang it up by his door for a sign
when he commences business, until at last his oldest customer cannot tell surely whether it be animal, vegetable, or mineral, and yet
it shall be as pure as a snowflake, and if it be put into a pot and
boiled, will come out an excellent dun fish for a Saturday's
dinner. Next Spanish hides, with the tails still preserving their
twist and the angle of elevation they had when the oxen that
wore them were careering over the pampas of the Spanish main,
—a type of all obstinacy, and evincing how almost hopeless and
incurable are all constitutional vices. I confess, that practically
speaking, when I have learned a man's real disposition, I have no
hopes of changing it for the better or worse in this state of
existence. As the Orientals say, "A cur's tail may be warmed, and
pressed, and bound round with ligatures, and after a twelve years'
labor bestowed upon it, still it will retain its natural form." The
only effectual cure for such inveteracies as these tails exhibit is to
make glue of them, which I believe is what is usually done with
them, and then they will stay put and stick. Here is a hogshead of
molasses or of brandy directed to John Smith, Cuttingsville, Ver-

2. A town in southern Maine, famous
for its lime deposits.
3. A major fishing ground in the northern Atlantic Ocean, southeast of Newfoundland.

mont, some trader among the Green Mountains, who imports for
the farmers near his clearing, and now perchance stands over
his bulk-head and thinks of the last arrivals on the coast, how
they may affect the price for him, telling his customers this moment, as he has told them twenty times before this morning, that
he expects some by the next train of prime quality. It is advertised
in the Cuttingsville Times.

While these things go up other things come down. Warned by
the whizzing sound, I look up from my book and see some tall
pine, hewn on far northern hills, which has winged its way over
the Green Mountains [4] and the Connecticut, shot like an arrow
through the township within ten minutes, and scarce another eye
beholds it; going

> "to be the mast
> Of some great ammiral." [5]

And hark! here comes the cattle-train bearing the cattle of a
thousand hills, sheepcots, stables, and cowyards in the air, drovers
with their sticks, and shepherd boys in the midst of their flocks, all
but the mountain pastures, whirled along like leaves blown from
the mountains by the September gales. The air is filled with the
bleating of calves and sheep, and the hustling of oxen, as if a
pastoral valley were going by. When the old bell-weather at the
head rattles his bell, the mountains do indeed skip like rams and
the little hills like lambs. A car-load of drovers, too, in the
midst, on a level with their droves now, their vocation gone, but
still clinging to their useless sticks as their badge of office. But
their dogs, where are they? It is a stampede to them; they are
quite thrown out; they have lost the scent. Methinks I hear them
barking behind the Peterboro' Hills,[6] or panting up the western
slope of the Green Mountains. They will not be in at the death.
Their vocation, too, is gone. Their fidelity and sagacity are below par now. They will slink back to their kennels in disgrace, or
perchance run wild and strike a league with the wolf and the
fox. So is your pastoral life whirled past and away. But the bell
rings, and I must get off the track and let the cars go by;—

> What's the railroad to me?
> I never go to see
> Where it ends.
> It fills a few hollows,
> And makes banks for the swallows,
> It sets the sand a-blowing,
> And the blackberries a-growing,

but I cross it like a cart-path in the woods. I will not have my

4. A range of mountains in Vermont.   6. A range in southern New Hamp-
5. From *Paradise Lost* by John Milton.   shire, visible from Concord.

eyes put out and my ears spoiled by its smoke and steam and hissing.

Now that the cars are gone by and all the restless world with them, and the fishes in the pond no longer feel their rumbling, I am more alone than ever. For the rest of the long afternoon, perhaps, my meditations are interrupted only by the faint rattle of a carriage or team along the distant highway.

Sometimes, on Sundays, I heard the bells, the Lincoln, Acton, Bedford,[7] or Concord bell, when the wind was favorable, a faint, sweet, and, as it were, natural melody, worth importing into the wilderness. At a sufficient distance over the woods this sound acquires a certain vibratory hum, as if the pine needles in the horizon were the strings of a harp which it swept. All sound heard at the greatest possible distance produces one and the same effect, a vibration of the universal lyre, just as the intervening atmosphere makes a distant ridge of earth interesting to our eyes by the azure tint it imparts to it. There came to me in this case a melody which the air had strained, and which had conversed with every leaf and needle of the wood, that portion of the sound which the elements had taken up and modulated and echoed from vale to vale. The echo is, to some extent, an original sound, and therein is the magic and charm of it. It is not merely a repetition of what was worth repeating in the bell, but partly the voice of the wood; the same trivial words and notes sung by a wood-nymph.

At evening, the distant lowing of some cow in the horizon beyond the woods sounded sweet and melodious, and at first I would mistake it for the voices of certain minstrels by whom I was sometimes serenaded, who might be straying over hill and dale; but soon I was not unpleasantly disappointed when it was prolonged into the cheap and natural music of the cow. I do not mean to be satirical, but to express my appreciation of those youths' singing, when I state that I perceived clearly that it was akin to the music of the cow, and they were at length one articulation of Nature.

Regularly at half past seven, in one part of the summer, after the evening train had gone by, the whippoorwills chanted their vespers for half an hour, sitting on a stump by my door, or upon the ridge pole of the house. They would begin to sing almost with as much precision as a clock, within five minutes of a particular time, referred to the setting of the sun, every evening. I had a rare opportunity to become acquainted with their habits. Sometimes I heard four or five at once in different parts of the wood, by accident one a bar behind another, and so near me that I

7. Towns near Concord.

distinguished not only the cluck after each note, but often that
singular buzzing sound like a fly in a spider's web, only proportionally louder. Sometimes one would circle round and round me
in the woods a few feet distant as if tethered by a string, when
probably I was near its eggs. They sang at intervals throughout the
night, and were again as musical as ever just before and about
dawn.

When other birds are still the screech owls take up the strain,
like mourning women their ancient u-lu-lu. Their dismal scream is
truly Ben Jonsonian.[8] Wise midnight hags! It is no honest and
blunt tu-whit tu-who of the poets, but, without jesting, a most
solemn graveyard ditty, the mutual consolations of suicide lovers
remembering the pangs and the delights of supernal love in the
infernal groves. Yet I love to hear their wailing, their doleful responses, trilled along the woodside; reminding me sometimes of
music and singing birds; as if it were the dark and tearful side of
music, the regrets and sighs that would fain be sung. They are the
spirits, the low spirits and melancholy forebodings, of fallen souls
that once in human shape night-walked the earth and did the deeds
of darkness, now expiating their sins with their wailing hymns or
threnodies in the scenery of their transgressions. They give me a
new sense of the variety and capacity of that nature which is our
common dwelling. *Oh-o-o-o-o that I never had been bor-r-r-r-n!*
sighs one on this side of the pond, and circles with the restlessness
of despair to some new perch on the gray oaks. Then—*that I
never had been bor-r-r-r-n!* echoes another on the farther side with
tremulous sincerity, and—*bor-r-r-r-n!* comes faintly from far in
the Lincoln woods.

I was also serenaded by a hooting owl. Near at hand you
could fancy it the most melancholy sound in Nature, as if she
meant by this to stereotype and make permanent in her choir the
dying moans of a human being,—some poor weak relic of mortality who has left hope behind, and howls like an animal, yet
with human sobs, on entering the dark valley, made more awful
by a certain gurgling melodiousness,—I find myself beginning with
the letters gl when I try to imitate it,—expressive of a mind which
has reached the gelatinous mildewy stage in the mortification of all
healthy and courageous thought. It reminded me of ghouls and
idiots and insane howlings. But now one answers from far woods
in a strain made really melodious by distance,—*Hoo hoo hoo,
hoorer hoo*; and indeed for the most part it suggested only pleasing
associations, whether heard by day or night, summer or winter.

I rejoice that there are owls. Let them do the idiotic and

8. Ben Jonson (1573?–1637), English dramatist; the reference may be to his
"Witches' Song."

maniacal hooting for men. It is a sound admirably suited to swamps and twilight woods which no day illustrates, suggesting a vast and undeveloped nature which men have not recognized. They represent the stark twilight and unsatisfied thoughts which all have. All day the sun has shone on the surface of some savage swamp, where the double spruce stands hung with usnea lichens, and small hawks circulate above, and the chicadee lisps amid the evergreens, and the partridge and rabbit skulk beneath; but now a more dismal and fitting day dawns, and a different race of creatures awakes to express the meaning of Nature there.

Late in the evening I heard the distant rumbling of wagons over bridges,—a sound heard farther than almost any other at night,— the baying of dogs, and sometimes again the lowing of some disconsolate cow in a distant barn-yard. In the mean while all the shore rang with the trump of bullfrogs, the sturdy spirits of ancient winebibbers and wassailers, still unrepentant, trying to sing a catch in their Stygian lake,[9]—if the Walden nymphs will pardon the comparison, for though there are almost no weeds, there are frogs there,—who would fain keep up the hilarious rules of their old festal tables, though their voices have waxed hoarse and solemnly grave, mocking at mirth, and the wine has lost its flavor, and become only liquor to distend their paunches, and sweet intoxication never comes to drown the memory of the past, but mere saturation and waterloggedness and distention. The most aldermanic, with his chin upon a heart-leaf, which serves for a napkin to his drooling chaps, under this northern shore quaffs a deep draught of the once scorned water, and passes round the cup with the ejaculation *tr-r-r-oonk, tr-r-r-oonk, tr-r-r-oonk!* and straightway comes over the water from some distant cove the same password repeated, where the next in seniority and girth has gulped down to his mark; and when this observance has made the circuit of the shores, then ejaculates the master of ceremonies, with satisfaction, *tr-r-r-oonk!* and each in his turn repeats the same down to the least distended, leakiest, and flabbiest paunched, that there be no mistake; and then the bowl goes round again and again, until the sun disperses the morning mist, and only the patriarch is not under the pond, but vainly bellowing *troonk* from time to time, and pausing for a reply.

I am not sure that I ever heard the sound of cock-crowing from my clearing, and I thought that it might be worth the while to keep a cockerel for his music merely, as a singing bird. The note of this once wild Indian pheasant is certainly the most remarkable of any bird's, and if they could be naturalized without being

9. I.e., any gloomy lake; in Greek mythology, the Styx was one of five rivers surrounding the land of the dead.

domesticated, it would soon become the most famous sound in our woods, surpassing the clangor of the goose and the hooting of the owl; and then imagine the cackling of the hens to fill the pauses when their lords' clarions rested! No wonder that man added this bird to his tame stock,—to say nothing of the eggs and drumsticks. To walk in a winter morning in a wood where these birds abounded, their native woods, and hear the wild cockerels crow on the trees, clear and shrill for miles over the resounding earth, drowning the feebler notes of other birds,—think of it! It would put nations on the alert. Who would not be early to rise, and rise earlier and earlier every successive day of his life, till he became unspeakably healthy, wealthy, and wise? This foreign bird's note is celebrated by the poets of all countries along with the notes of their native songsters. All climates agree with brave Chanticleer. He is more indigenous even than the natives. His health is ever good, his lungs are sound, his spirits never flag. Even the sailor on the Atlantic and Pacific is awakened by his voice; but its shrill sound never roused me from my slumbers. I kept neither dog, cat, cow, pig, nor hens, so that you would have said there was a deficiency of domestic sounds; neither the churn, nor the spinning wheel, nor even the singing of the kettle, nor the hissing of the urn, nor children crying, to comfort one. An old-fashioned man would have lost his senses or died of ennui before this. Not even rats in the wall, for they were starved out, or rather were never baited in,—only squirrels on the roof and under the floor, a whippoorwill on the ridge pole, a blue-jay screaming beneath the window, a hare or woodchuck under the house, a screech-owl or a cat-owl behind it, a flock of wild geese or a laughing loon on the pond, and a fox to bark in the night. Not even a lark or an oriole, those mild plantation birds, ever visited my clearing. No cockerels to crow nor hens to cackle in the yard. No yard! but unfenced Nature reaching up to your very sills. A young forest growing up under your windows, and wild sumachs and blackberry vines breaking through into your cellar; sturdy pitch-pines rubbing and creaking against the shingles for want of room, their roots reaching quite under the house. Instead of a scuttle or a blind blown off in the gale,—a pine tree snapped off or torn up by the roots behind your house for fuel. Instead of no path to the front-yard gate in the Great Snow,—no gate—no front-yard,—and no path to the civilized world!

Solitude

This is a delicious evening, when the whole body is one sense, and imbibes delight through every pore. I go and come with a strange liberty in Nature, a part of herself. As I walk along the stony shore of the pond in my shirt sleeves, though it is cool as well as cloudy and windy, and I see nothing special to attract me, all the elements are unusually congenial to me. The bullfrogs trump to usher in the night, and the note of the whippoorwill is borne on the rippling wind from over the water. Sympathy with the fluttering alder and poplar leaves almost takes away my breath; yet, like the lake, my serenity is rippled but not ruffled. These small waves raised by the evening wind are as remote from storm as the smooth reflecting surface. Though it is now dark, the wind still blows and roars in the wood, the waves still dash, and some creatures lull the rest with their notes. The repose is never complete. The wildest animals do not repose, but seek their prey now; the fox, and skunk, and rabbit, now roam the fields and woods without fear. They are Nature's watchmen,—links which connect the days of animated life.

When I return to my house I find that visitors have been there and left their cards, either a bunch of flowers, or a wreath of evergreen, or a name in pencil on a yellow walnut leaf or a chip. They who come rarely to the woods take some little piece of the forest into their hands to play with by the way, which they leave, either intentionally or accidentally. One has peeled a willow wand, woven it into a ring, and dropped it on my table. I could always tell if visitors had called in my absence, either by the bended twigs or grass, or the print of their shoes, and generally of what sex or age or quality they were by some slight trace left, as a flower dropped, or a bunch of grass plucked and thrown away, even as far off as the railroad, half a mile distant, or by the lingering odor of a cigar or pipe. Nay, I was frequently notified of the passage of a traveller along the highway sixty rods off by the scent of his pipe.

There is commonly sufficient space about us. Our horizon is never quite at our elbows. The thick wood is not just at our door, nor the pond, but somewhat is always clearing, familiar and worn by us, appropriated and fenced in some way, and reclaimed from Nature. For what reason have I this vast range and circuit, some square miles of unfrequented forest, for my privacy, abandoned to me by men? My nearest neighbor is a mile distant, and no house is visible from any place but the hill-tops within half a mile of my own. I have my horizon bounded by woods all to myself; a distant view of the railroad where it touches the pond on the one hand, and of the fence which skirts the woodland road on the other. But for the most part it is as solitary where I live as on the prairies. It is as much Asia or Africa as New England. I have, as it were, my own sun and moon and stars, and a little world all to myself. At night there was never a traveller passed my house, or knocked at my door, more than if I were the first or last man; unless it were in the spring, when at long intervals some came from the village to fish for pouts,—they plainly fished much more in the Walden Pond of their own natures, and baited their hooks with darkness,—but they soon retreated, usually with light baskets, and left "the world to darkness and to me," and the black kernel of the night was never profaned by any human neighborhood. I believe that men are generally still a little afraid of the dark, though the witches are all hung, and Christianity and candles have been introduced.

Yet I experienced sometimes that the most sweet and tender, the most innocent and encouraging society may be found in any natural object, even for the poor misanthrope and most melancholy man. There can be no very black melancholy to him who lives in the midst of Nature and has his senses still. There was never yet such a storm but it was Æolian music [1] to a healthy and innocent ear. Nothing can rightly compel a simple and brave man to a vulgar sadness. While I enjoy the friendship of the seasons I trust that nothing can make life a burden to me. The gentle rain which waters my beans and keeps me in the house to-day is not drear and melancholy, but good for me too. Though it prevents my hoeing them, it is of far more worth than my hoeing. If it should continue so long as to cause the seeds to rot in the ground and destroy the potatoes in the low lands, it would still be good for the grass on the uplands, and, being good for the grass, it would be good for me. Sometimes, when I compare myself with other men, it seems as if I were more favored by the gods than they, beyond any deserts that I am conscious of; as if I had a warrant and surety at their hands which my fellows have not, and were especially guided and guarded. I do not flatter myself, but if it be possible they flatter me. I have never felt lonesome, or in the least oppressed by a sense of solitude, but once, and that was a few weeks after I came to the woods, when, for an hour, I doubted if the near neighborhood of man was not essential to a serene and healthy life. To be alone was something unpleasant. But I was at the same time conscious of a slight insanity in my mood, and seemed to foresee my recovery. In the midst of a gentle rain while these thoughts prevailed, I was suddenly sensible of such sweet and beneficent society in Nature, in the very pattering of the drops, and in every sound and sight around my house, an infinite and unaccountable friendliness all at once like an atmosphere sustaining me, as made the fancied advantages of human

1. Music produced by an Æolian harp, a stringed instrument which produces sounds when exposed to a current of air; in Greek mythology, Æolus was the god of the winds.

neighborhood insignificant, and I have never thought of them since. Every little pine needle expanded and swelled with sympathy and befriended me. I was so distinctly made aware of the presence of something kindred to me, even in scenes which we are accustomed to call wild and dreary, and also that the nearest of blood to me and humanest was not a person nor a villager, that I thought no place could ever be strange to me again.—

> "Mourning untimely consumes the sad;
> Few are their days in the land of the living,
> Beautiful daughter of Toscar." [2]

Some of my pleasantest hours were during the long rain storms in the spring or fall, which confined me to the house for the afternoon as well as the forenoon, soothed by their ceaseless roar and pelting; when an early twilight ushered in a long evening in which many thoughts had time to take root and unfold themselves. In those driving north-east rains which tried the village houses so, when the maids stood ready with mop and pail in front entries to keep the deluge out, I sat behind my door in my little house, which was all entry, and thoroughly enjoyed its protection. In one heavy thunder shower the lightning struck a large pitch-pine across the pond, making a very conspicuous and perfectly regular spiral groove from top to bottom, an inch or more deep, and four or five inches wide, as you would groove a walking-stick. I passed it again the other day, and was struck with awe on looking up and beholding that mark, now more distinct than ever, where a terrific and resistless bolt came down out of the harmless sky eight years ago. Men frequently say to me, "I should think you would feel lonesome down there, and want to be nearer to folks, rainy and snowy days and nights especially." I am tempted to reply to such,—This whole earth which we inhabit is but a point in space. How far apart, think you, dwell the two most distant inhabitants of yonder star, the breadth of whose disk cannot be appreciated by our instruments? Why should I feel lonely? is not our planet in the Milky Way? This which you put seems to me not to be the most important question. What sort of space is that which separates a man from his fellows and makes him solitary? I have found that no exertion of the legs can bring two minds much nearer to one another. What do we want most to dwell near to? Not to many men surely, the depot, the post-office, the bar-room, the meeting-house, the school-house, the grocery, Beacon Hill, or the Five Points,[3] where men most congregate, but to the

---

2. From the pseudo-epic poems of "Ossian"; the poem's hero was attempting to console Malvina, daughter of Toscar, after the death of her lover.

3. Beacon Hill was the fashionable section of Boston; Five Points, in New York City, was known for its crime.

perennial source of our life, whence in all our experience we have found that to issue, as the willow stands near the water and sends out its roots in that direction. This will vary with different natures, but this is the place where a wise man will dig his cellar. . . . I one evening overtook one of my townsmen, who has accumulated what is called "a handsome property,"—though I never got a *fair* view of it,—on the Walden road, driving a pair of cattle to market, who inquired of me how I could bring my mind to give up so many of the comforts of life. I answered that I was very sure I liked it passably well; I was not joking. And so I went home to my bed, and left him to pick his way through the darkness and the mud to Brighton,[4]—or Bright-town,—which place he would reach some time in the morning.

Any prospect of awakening or coming to life to a dead man makes indifferent all times and places. The place where that may occur is always the same, and indescribably pleasant to all our senses. For the most part we allow only outlying and transient circumstances to make our occasions. They are, in fact, the cause of our distraction. Nearest to all things is that power which fashions their being. *Next* to us the grandest laws are continually being executed. *Next* to us is not the workman whom we have hired, with whom we love so well to talk, but the workman whose work we are.

"How vast and profound is the influence of the subtile powers of Heaven and of Earth!"

"We seek to perceive them, and we do not see them; we seek to hear them, and we do not hear them; identified with the substance of things, they cannot be separated from them."

"They cause that in all the universe men purify and sanctify their hearts, and clothe themselves in their holiday garments to offer sacrifices and oblations to their ancestors. It is an ocean of subtile intelligences. They are every where, above us, on our left, on our right; they environ us on all sides." [5]

We are the subjects of an experiment which is not a little interesting to me. Can we not do without the society of our gossips a little while under these circumstances,—have our own thoughts to cheer us? Confucius says truly, "Virtue does not remain as an abandoned orphan; it must of necessity have neighbors."

With thinking we may be beside ourselves in a sane sense. By a conscious effort of the mind we can stand aloof from actions and their consequences; and all things, good and bad, go by us like a torrent. We are not wholly involved in Nature. I may be either

4. A suburb of Boston.
5. Confucius, *The Doctrine of the Mean.*

the driftwood in the stream, or Indra [6] in the sky looking down on it. I *may* be affected by a theatrical exhibition; on the other hand, I *may not* be affected by an actual event which appears to concern me much more. I only know myself as a human entity; the scene, so to speak, of thoughts and affections; and am sensible of a certain doubleness by which I can stand as remote from myself as from another. However intense my experience, I am conscious of the presence and criticism of a part of me, which, as it were, is not a part of me, but spectator, sharing no experience, but taking note of it; and that is no more I than it is you. When the play, it may be the tragedy, of life is over, the spectator goes his way. It was a kind of fiction, a work of the imagination only, so far as he was concerned. This doubleness may easily make us poor neighbors and friends sometimes.

I find it wholesome to be alone the greater part of the time. To be in company, even with the best, is soon wearisome and dissipating. I love to be alone. I never found the companion that was so companionable as solitude. We are for the most part more lonely when we go abroad among men than when we stay in our chambers. A man thinking or working is always alone, let him be where he will. Solitude is not measured by the miles of space that intervene between a man and his fellows. The really diligent student in one of the crowded hives of Cambridge College is as solitary as a dervis in the desert. The farmer can work alone in the field or the woods all day, hoeing or chopping, and not feel lonesome, because he is employed; but when he comes home at night he cannot sit down in a room alone, at the mercy of his thoughts, but must be where he can "see the folks," and recreate, and as he thinks remunerate himself for his day's solitude; and hence he wonders how the student can sit alone in the house all night and most of the day without ennui and "the blues;" but he does not realize that the student, though in the house, is still at work in *his* field, and chopping in *his* woods, as the farmer in his, and in turn seeks the same recreation and society that the latter does, though it may be a more condensed form of it.

Society is commonly too cheap. We meet at very short intervals, not having had time to acquire any new value for each other. We meet at meals three times a day, and give each other a new taste of that old musty cheese that we are. We have had to agree on a certain set of rules, called etiquette and politeness, to make this frequent meeting tolerable and that we need not come to open war. We meet at the post-office, and at the sociable, and about the fireside every night; we live thick and are in each other's way, and stumble over one another, and I think that we thus

6. In early Hindu religion, the god of earth, thunder, and rain.

lose some respect for one another. Certainly less frequency would suffice for all important and hearty communications. Consider the girls in a factory,—never alone, hardly in their dreams. It would be better if there were but one inhabitant to a square mile, as where I live. The value of a man is not in his skin, that we should touch him.

I have heard of a man lost in the woods and dying of famine and exhaustion at the foot of a tree, whose loneliness was relieved by the grotesque visions with which, owing to bodily weakness, his diseased imagination surrounded him, and which he believed to be real. So also, owing to bodily and mental health and strength, we may be continually cheered by a like but more normal and natural society, and come to know that we are never alone.

I have a great deal of company in my house; especially in the morning, when nobody calls. Let me suggest a few comparisons, that some one may convey an idea of my situation. I am no more lonely than the loon in the pond that laughs so loud, or than Walden Pond itself. What company has that lonely lake, I pray? And yet it has not the blue devils, but the blue angels in it, in the azure tint of its waters. The sun is alone, except in thick weather, when there sometimes appear to be two, but one is a mock sun. God is alone,—but the devil, he is far from being alone; he sees a great deal of company; he is legion. I am no more lonely than a single mullein or dandelion in a pasture, or a bean leaf, or sorrel, or a horse-fly, or a humble-bee. I am no more lonely than the Mill Brook, or a weathercock, or the north star, or the south wind, or an April shower, or a January thaw, or the first spider in a new house.

I have occasional visits in the long winter evenings, when the snow falls fast and the wind howls in the wood, from an old settler and original proprietor, who is reported to have dug Walden Pond, and stoned it, and fringed it with pine woods; who tells me stories of old time and of new eternity; and between us we manage to pass a cheerful evening with social mirth and pleasant views of things, even without apples or cider,—a most wise and humorous friend, whom I love much, who keeps himself more secret than ever did Goffe or Whalley; [7] and though he is thought to be dead, none can show where he is buried. An elderly dame, too, dwells in my neighborhood, invisible to most persons, in whose odorous herb garden I love to stroll sometimes, gathering simples and listening to her fables; for she has a genius

7. William Goffe (d. ca. 1679) and Edward Whalley (1615?–1675?), two of the men indicted for killing Charles I of England, fled to America where they lived in hiding.

of unequalled fertility, and her memory runs back farther than mythology, and she can. tell me the original of every fable, and on what fact every one is founded, for the incidents occurred when she was young. A ruddy and lusty old dame, who delights in all weathers and seasons, and is likely to outlive all her children yet.

The indescribable innocence and beneficence of Nature,—of sun and wind and rain, of summer and winter,—such health, such cheer, they afford forever! and such sympathy have they ever with our race, that all Nature would be affected, and the sun's brightness fade, and the winds would sigh humanely, and the clouds rain tears, and the woods shed their leaves and put on mourning in midsummer, if any man should ever for a just cause grieve. Shall I not have intelligence with the earth? Am I not partly leaves and vegetable mould myself?

What is the pill which will keep us well, serene, contented? Not my or thy great-grandfather's, but our great-grandmother Nature's universal, vegetable, botanic medicines, by which she has kept herself young always, outlived so many old Parrs [8] in her day, and fed her health with their decaying fatness. For my panacea, instead of one of those quack vials of a mixture dipped from Acheron and the Dead Sea,[9] which come out of those long shallow black-schooner looking wagons which we sometimes see made to carry bottles, let me have a draught of undiluted morning air. Morning air! If men will not drink of this at the fountainhead of the day, why, then, we must even bottle up some and sell it in the shops, for the benefit of those who have lost their subscription ticket to morning time in this world. But remember, it will not keep quite till noonday even in the coolest cellar, but drive out the stopples long ere that and follow westward the steps of Aurora. I am no worshipper of Hygeia,[1] who was the daughter of that old herb-doctor Æsculapius, and who is represented on monuments holding a serpent in one hand, and in the other a cup out of which the serpent sometimes drinks; but rather of Hebe,[2] cupbearer to Jupiter, who was the daughter of Juno and wild lettuce, and who had the power of restoring gods and men to the vigor of youth. She was probably the only thoroughly sound-conditioned, healthy, and robust young lady that ever walked the globe, and wherever she came it was spring.

---

8. Any long-lived man such as Thomas Parr, an Englishman who reputedly lived 152 years.
9. In Greek mythology, Acheron was one of the five rivers surrounding the land of the dead; the Dead Sea is a large salt lake on the Israel-Jordan border.
1. In Greek mythology, the goddess of health and the daughter of Æsculapius, the god of medical arts.
2. In Greek mythology, Hebe was the goddess of youth, the daughter of Zeus (called "Jupiter" by the Romans) and Hera (called "Juno" by the Romans); according to some legends, Hebe was conceived after Hera ate some wild lettuce.

Visitors

I think that I love society as much as most, and am ready enough to fasten myself like a bloodsucker for the time to any full-blooded man that comes in my way. I am naturally no hermit, but might possibly sit out the sturdiest frequenter of the bar-room, if my business called me thither.

I had three chairs in my house; one for solitude, two for friendship, three for society. When visitors came in larger and unexpected numbers there was but the third chair for them all, but they generally economized the room by standing up. It is surprising how many great men and women a small house will contain. I have had twenty-five or thirty souls, with their bodies, at once under my roof, and yet we often parted without being aware that we had come very near to one another. Many of our houses, both public and private, with their almost innumerable apartments, their huge halls and their cellars for the storage of wines and other munitions of peace, appear to me extravagantly large for their inhabitants. They are so vast and magnificent that the latter seem to be only vermin which infest them. I am surprised when the herald blows his summons before some Tremont or Astor or Middlesex House,[1] to see come creeping out over the piazza for all inhabitants a ridiculous mouse, which soon again slinks into some hole in the pavement.

One inconvenience I sometimes experienced in so small a house, the difficulty of getting to a sufficient distance from my guest when we began to utter the big thoughts in big words. You want room for your thoughts to get into sailing trim and run a course or two before they make their port. The bullet of your thought must have overcome its lateral and ricochet motion and fallen into its last and steady course before it reaches the ear of the hearer, else it may plough out again through the side of his head. Also, our sentences wanted room to unfold and form their columns in the interval. Individuals, like nations, must have suitable broad and natural boundaries, even a considerable neutral ground, between them. I have found it a singular luxury to talk across the pond to a companion on the opposite side. In my house we were so near that we could not begin to hear,—we could not speak low enough to be heard; as when you throw two stones into calm water so near that they break each other's undulations. If we are merely loquacious and loud talkers, then we can afford to stand very near to-

1. Prosperous hotels in Boston, New York, and Concord, respectively.

gether, cheek by jowl, and feel each other's breath; but if we speak reservedly and thoughtfully, we want to be farther apart, that all animal heat and moisture may have a chance to evaporate. If we would enjoy the most intimate society with that in each of us which is without, or above, being spoken to, we must not only be silent, but commonly so far apart bodily that we cannot possibly hear each other's voice in any case. Referred to this standard, speech is for the convenience of those who are hard of hearing; but there are many fine things which we cannot say if we have to shout. As the conversation began to assume a loftier and grander tone, we gradually shoved our chairs farther apart till they touched the wall in opposite corners, and then commonly there was not room enough.

My "best" room, however, my withdrawing room, always ready for company, on whose carpet the sun rarely fell, was the pine wood behind my house. Thither in summer days, when distinguished guests came, I took them, and a priceless domestic swept the floor and dusted the furniture and kept the things in order.

If one guest came he sometimes partook of my frugal meal, and it was no interruption to conversation to be stirring a hastypudding, or watching the rising and maturing of a loaf of bread in the ashes, in the mean while. But if twenty came and sat in my house there was nothing said about dinner, though there might be bread enough for two, more than if eating were a forsaken habit; but we naturally practised abstinence; and this was never felt to be an offence against hospitality, but the most proper and considerate course. The waste and decay of physical life, which so often needs repair, seemed miraculously retarded in such a case, and the vital vigor stood its ground. I could entertain thus a thousand as well as twenty; and if any ever went away disappointed or hungry from my house when they found me at home, they may depend upon it that I sympathized with them at least. So easy is it, though many housekeepers doubt it, to establish new and better customs in the place of the old. You need not rest your reputation on the dinners you give. For my own part, I was never so effectually deterred from frequenting a man's house, by any kind of Cerberus [2] whatever, as by the parade one made about dining me, which I took to be a very polite and roundabout hint never to trouble him so again. I think I shall never revisit those scenes. I should be proud to have for the motto of my cabin those lines of Spenser [3] which one of my visitors inscribed on a yellow walnut leaf for a card:—

2. In classical mythology, a three-headed dog who guarded the entrance to the land of the dead.

3. Edmund Spenser (1552?–1599), English poet; the quotation is from *The Faerie Queene*.

"Arrivéd there, the little house they fill,
    Ne looke for entertainment where none was;
Rest is their feast, and all things at their will:
    The noblest mind the best contentment has."

When Winslow,[4] afterward governor of the Plymouth Colony, went with a companion on a visit of ceremony to Massassoit on foot through the woods, and arrived tired and hungry at his lodge, they were well received by the king, but nothing was said about eating that day. When the night arrived, to quote their own words,—"He laid us on the bed with himself and his wife, they at the one end and we at the other, it being only plank, laid a foot from the ground, and a thin mat upon them. Two more of his chief men, for want of room, pressed by and upon us; so that we were worse weary of our lodging than of our journey." At one o'clock the next day Massassoit "brought two fishes that he had shot," about thrice as big as a bream; "these being boiled, there were at least forty looked for a share in them. The most ate of them. This meal only we had in two nights and a day; and had not one of us bought a partridge, we had taken our journey fasting." Fearing that they would be light-headed for want of food and also sleep, owing to "the savages' barbarous singing, (for they used to sing themselves asleep,)" and that they might get home while they had strength to travel, they departed. As for lodging, it is true they were but poorly entertained, though what they found an inconvenience was no doubt intended for an honor; but as far as eating was concerned, I do not see how the Indians could have done better. They had nothing to eat themselves, and they were wiser than to think that apologies could supply the place of food to their guests; so they drew their belts tighter and said nothing about it. Another time when Winslow visited them, it being a season of plenty with them, there was no deficiency in this respect.

As for men, they will hardly fail one any where. I had more visitors while I lived in the woods than at any other period of my life; I mean that I had some. I met several there under more favorable circumstances than I could any where else. But fewer came to see me upon trivial business. In this respect, my company was winnowed by my mere distance from town. I had withdrawn so far within the great ocean of solitude, into which the rivers of society empty, that for the most part, so far as my needs were concerned, only the finest sediment was deposited around me. Beside, there were wafted to me evidences of unexplored and uncultivated continents on the other side.

4. Edward Winslow (1595–1655); Massassoit was an Indian chief friendly to the Pilgrims.

Who should come to my lodge this morning but a true Homeric or Paphlagonian [5] man,—he had so suitable and poetic a name that I am sorry I cannot print it here,—a Canadian, a wood-chopper and post-maker, who can hole fifty posts in a day, who made his last supper on a woodchuck which his dog caught. He, too, has heard of Homer, and, "if it were not for books," would "not know what to do rainy days," though perhaps he has not read one wholly through for many rainy seasons. Some priest who could pronounce the Greek itself taught him to read his verse in the testament in his native parish far away; and now I must translate to him, while he holds the book, Achilles' reproof to Patroclus [6] for his sad countenance.—"Why are you in tears, Patroclus, like a young girl?"—

"Or have you alone heard some news from Phthia?
They say that Menœtius lives yet, son of Actor,
And Peleus lives, son of Æacus, among the Myrmidons,
Either of whom having died, we should greatly grieve."

He says, "That's good." He has a great bundle of white-oak bark under his arm for a sick man, gathered this Sunday morning. "I suppose there's no harm in going after such a thing to-day," says he. To him Homer was a great writer, though what his writing was about he did not know. A more simple and natural man it would be hard to find. Vice and disease, which cast such a sombre moral hue over the world, seemed to have hardly any existence for him. He was about twenty-eight years old, and had left Canada and his father's house a dozen years before to work in the States, and earn money to buy a farm with at last, perhaps in his native country. He was cast in the coarsest mould; a stout but sluggish body, yet gracefully carried, with a thick sunburnt neck, dark bushy hair, and dull sleepy blue eyes, which were occasionally lit up with expression. He wore a flat gray cloth cap, a dingy wool-colored greatcoat, and cowhide boots. He was a great consumer of meat, usually carrying his dinner to his work a couple of miles past my house,—for he chopped all summer,—in a tin pail; cold meats, often cold woodchucks, and coffee in a stone bottle which dangled by a string from his belt; and sometimes he offered me a drink. He came along early, crossing my bean-field, though without anxiety or haste to get to his work, such as Yankees exhibit. He wasn't a-going to hurt himself. He didn't care if he only earned his board. Frequently he would leave his dinner in the bushes, when his dog had caught a woodchuck by the way, and go

5. Paphlagonia was an ancient country in northern Asia Minor on the Black Sea; the woodchopper was Alex Therien whose name was the equivalent of the French *terrien*, a landowner or farmer.
6. In Homer's *Iliad*, Achilles was the greatest warrior of the Greeks; Patroclus was his closest friend.

back a mile and a half to dress it and leave it in the cellar of the house where he boarded, after deliberating first for half an hour whether he could not sink it in the pond safely till nightfall,— loving to dwell long upon these themes. He would say, as he went by in the morning, "How thick the pigeons are! If working every day were not my trade, I could get all the meat I should want by hunting,—pigeons, woodchucks, rabbits, partridges,—by gosh! I could get all I should want for a week in one day."

He was a skilful chopper, and indulged in some flourishes and ornaments in his art. He cut his trees level and close to the ground, that the sprouts which came up afterward might be more vigorous and a sled might slide over the stumps; and instead of leaving a whole tree to support his corded wood, he would pare it away to a slender stake or splinter which you could break off with your hand at last.

He interested me because he was so quiet and solitary and so happy withal; a well of good humor and contentment which overflowed at his eyes. His mirth was without alloy. Sometimes I saw him at his work in the woods, felling trees, and he would greet me with a laugh of inexpressible satisfaction, and a salutation in Canadian French, though he spoke English as well. When I approached him he would suspend his work, and with half-suppressed mirth lie along the trunk of a pine which he had felled, and, peeling off the inner bark, roll it up into a ball and chew it while he laughed and talked. Such an exuberance of animal spirits had he that he sometimes tumbled down and rolled on the ground with laughter at any thing which made him think and tickled him. Looking round upon the trees he would exclaim,— "By George! I can enjoy myself well enough here chopping; I want no better sport." Sometimes, when at leisure, he amused himself all day in the woods with a pocket pistol, firing salutes to himself at regular intervals as he walked. In the winter he had a fire by which at noon he warmed his coffee in a kettle; and as he sat on a log to eat his dinner the chicadees would sometimes come round and alight on his arm and peck at the potato in his fingers; and he said that he "liked to have the little *fellers* about him."

In him the animal man chiefly was developed. In physical endurance and contentment he was cousin to the pine and the rock. I asked him once if he was not sometimes tired at night, after working all day; and he answered, with a sincere and serious look, "Gorrappit, I never was tired in my life." But the intellectual and what is called spiritual man in him were slumbering as in an infant. He had been instructed only in that innocent and ineffectual way in which the Catholic priests teach the aborigines, by which the pupil is never educated to the degree of consciousness, but only to the degree of trust and reverence, and a child is not made a man, but kept a child. When Nature made him, she gave him a strong body and contentment for his portion, and propped him on every side with reverence and reliance, that he might live out his threescore years and ten a child. He was so genuine and unsophisticated that no introduction would serve to introduce him, more than if you introduced a woodchuck to your neighbor. He had got to find him out as you did. He would not play any part. Men paid him wages for work, and so helped to feed and clothe him; but he never exchanged opinions with them. He was so simply and naturally humble—if he can be called humble who never aspires—that humility was no distinct quality in him, nor could he conceive of it. Wiser men were demigods to him. If you told him that such a one was coming, he did as if he thought that any thing so grand would expect nothing of himself, but take all the responsibility on itself, and let him be forgotten still. He never heard the sound of praise. He particularly reverenced the writer and the preacher. Their performances were miracles. When I told him that I wrote considerably, he thought for a long time that it was merely the handwriting which I meant, for he could write a remarkably good hand himself. I sometimes found the name of his native parish handsomely written in the snow by the highway, with the proper French accent, and knew that he had passed. I asked him if he ever wished to write his thoughts. He said that he had read and written letters for those who could not, but he never tried to write thoughts,—no, he could not, he could not tell what to put first, it would kill him, and then there was spelling to be attended to at the same time!

I heard that a distinguished wise man and reformer asked him if he did not want the world to be changed; but he answered with a chuckle of surprise in his Canadian accent, not knowing that the question had ever been entertained before, "No, I like it well enough." It would have suggested many things to a philosopher to have dealings with him. To a stranger he appeared to know nothing of things in general; yet I sometimes saw in him a man whom I had not seen before, and I did not know whether he was as wise as Shakspeare or as simply ignorant as a child, whether to suspect him of a fine poetic consciousness or of stupidity. A townsman told me that when he met him sauntering through the village in his small close-fitting cap, and whistling to himself, he reminded him of a prince in disguise.

His only books were an almanac and an arithmetic, in which last he was considerably expert. The former was a sort of cyclopædia to him, which he supposed to contain an abstract of human knowledge, as indeed it does to a considerable extent. I loved to

sound him on the various reforms of the day, and he never failed
to look at them in the most simple and practical light. He had
never heard of such things before. Could he do without factories?
I asked. He had worn the home-made Vermont gray, he said, and
that was good. Could he dispense with tea and coffee? Did this
country afford any beverage beside water? He had soaked hemlock
leaves in water and drank it, and thought that was better than
water in warm weather. When I asked him if he could do without
money, he showed the convenience of money in such a way as to
suggest and coincide with the most philosophical accounts of the
origin of this institution, and the very derivation of the word
pecunia.[7] If an ox were his property, and he wished to get needles
and thread at the store, he thought it would be inconvenient and
impossible soon to go on mortgaging some portion of the creature
each time to that amount. He could defend many institutions better
than any philosopher, because, in describing them as they concerned him, he gave the true reason for their prevalence, and
speculation had not suggested to him any other. At another time,
hearing Plato's definition of a man,—a biped without feathers,—
and that one exhibited a cock plucked and called it Plato's man,
he thought it an important difference that the *knees* bent the
wrong way. He would sometimes exclaim, "How I love to talk!
By George, I could talk all day!" I asked him once, when I had
not seen him for many months, if he had got a new idea this
summer. "Good Lord," said he, "a man that has to work as I do,
if he does not forget the ideas he has had, he will do well. May be
the man you hoe with is inclined to race; then, by gorry, your
mind must be there; you think of weeds." He would sometimes
ask me first on such occasions, if I had made any improvement.
One winter day I asked him if he was always satisfied with himself, wishing to suggest a substitute within him for the priest without, and some higher motive for living. "Satisfied!" said he;
"some men are satisfied with one thing, and some with another.
One man, perhaps, if he has got enough, will be satisfied to sit
all day with his back to the fire and his belly to the table, by
George!" Yet I never, by any manœuvring, could get him to take
the spiritual view of things; the highest that he appeared to conceive of was a simple expediency, such as you might expect an
animal to appreciate; and this, practically, is true of most men. If
I suggested any improvement in his mode of life, he merely
answered, without expressing any regret, that it was too late. Yet
he thoroughly believed in honesty and the like virtues.

There was a certain positive originality, however slight, to be

7. Latin for "money"; derived from *pecus*, "cattle."

detected in him, and I occasionally observed that he was thinking for himself and expressing his own opinion, a phenomenon so rare that I would any day walk ten miles to observe it, and it amounted to the re-origination of many of the institutions of society. Though he hesitated, and perhaps failed to express himself distinctly, he always had a presentable thought behind. Yet his thinking was so primitive and immersed in his animal life, that, though more promising than a merely learned man's, it rarely ripened to any thing which can be reported. He suggested that there might be men of genius in the lowest grades of life, however permanently humble and illiterate, who take their own view always, or do not pretend to see at all; who are as bottomless even as Walden Pond was thought to be, though they may be dark and muddy.

Many a traveller came out of his way to see me and the inside of my house, and, as an excuse for calling, asked for a glass of water. I told them that I drank at the pond, and pointed thither, offering to lend them a dipper. Far off as I lived, I was not exempted from that annual visitation which occurs, methinks, about the first of April, when every body is on the move; and I had my share of good luck, though there were some curious specimens among my visitors. Half-witted men from the almshouse and elsewhere came to see me; but I endeavored to make them exercise all the wit they had, and make their confessions to me; in such cases making wit the theme of our conversation; and so was compensated. Indeed, I found some of them to be wiser than the so called *overseers* of the poor and selectmen of the town, and thought it was time that the tables were turned. With respect to wit, I learned that there was not much difference between the half and the whole. One day, in particular, an inoffensive, simple-minded pauper, whom with others I had often seen used as fencing stuff, standing or sitting on a bushel in the fields to keep cattle and himself from straying, visited me, and expressed a wish to live as I did. He told me, with the utmost simplicity and truth, quite superior, or rather *inferior*, to any thing that is called humility, that he was "deficient in intellect." These were his words. The Lord had made him so, yet he supposed the Lord cared as much for him as for another. "I have always been so," said he, "from my childhood; I never had much mind; I was not like other children; I am weak in the head. It was the Lord's will, I suppose." And there he was to prove the truth of his words. He was a metaphysical puzzle to me. I have rarely met a fellow-man on such promising ground,—it was so simple and sincere and so true all that he said. And, true enough, in proportion as he appeared to humble himself was he exalted. I did not know at first but it was

the result of a wise policy. It seemed that from such a basis of
truth and frankness as the poor weak-headed pauper had laid, our
intercourse might go forward to something better than the intercourse of sages.

I had some guests from those not reckoned commonly among
the town's poor, but who should be; who are among the world's
poor, at any rate; guests who appeal, not to your hospitality, but
to your *hospitalality*; who earnestly wish to be helped, and preface
their appeal with the information that they are resolved, for one
thing, never to help themselves. I require of a visitor that he be
not actually starving, though he may have the very best appetite
in the world, however he got it. Objects of charity are not guests.
Men who did not know when their visit had terminated, though I
went about my business again, answering them from greater and
greater remoteness. Men of almost every degree of wit called on
me in the migrating season. Some who had more wits than they
knew what to do with; runaway slaves with plantation manners,
who listened from time to time, like the fox in the fable, as if they
heard the hounds a-baying on their track, and looked at me
beseechingly, as much as to say,—

"O Christian, will you send me back?"

One real runaway slave, among the rest, whom I helped to forward
toward the northstar. Men of one idea, like a hen with one
chicken, and that a duckling; men of a thousand ideas, and un-
kempt heads, like those hens which are made to take charge of a
hundred chickens, all in pursuit of one bug, a score of them lost
in every morning's dew,—and become frizzled and mangy in consequence; men of ideas instead of legs, a sort of intellectual centi-
pede that made you crawl all over. One man proposed a book in
which visitors should write their names, as at the White Mountains; but, alas! I have too good a memory to make that necessary.

I could not but notice some of the peculiarities of my visitors.
Girls and boys and young women generally seemed glad to be in
the woods. They looked in the pond and at the flowers, and improved their time. Men of business, even farmers, thought only of
solitude and employment, and of the great distance at which I
dwelt from something or other; and though they said that they
loved a ramble in the woods occasionally, it was obvious that they
did not. Restless committed men, whose time was all taken up in
getting a living or keeping it; ministers who spoke of God as if
they enjoyed a monopoly of the subject, who could not bear all
kinds of opinions; doctors, lawyers, uneasy housekeepers who pried
into my cupboard and bed when I was out,—how came Mrs. ——
to know that my sheets were not as clean as hers?—young men who

had ceased to be young, and had concluded that it was safest to follow the beaten track of the professions,—all these generally said that it was not possible to do so much good in my position. Ay! there was the rub. The old and infirm and the timid, of whatever age or sex, thought most of sickness, and sudden accident and death; to them life seemed full of danger,—what danger is there if you don't think of any?—and they thought that a prudent man would carefully select the safest position, where Dr. B.[8] might be on hand at a moment's warning. To them the village was literally a *com-munity*, a league for mutual defence, and you would suppose that they would not go a-huckleberrying without a medicine chest. The amount of it is, if a man is alive, there is always *danger* that he may die, though the danger must be allowed to be less in proportion as he is dead-and-alive to begin with. A man sits as many risks as he runs. Finally, there were the self-styled reformers, the greatest bores of all, who thought that I was forever singing,—

> This is the house that I built;
> This is the man that lives in the house that I built;

but they did not know that the third line was,—

> These are the folks that worry the man
> That lives in the house that I built.

I did not fear the hen-harriers, for I kept no chickens; but I feared the men-harriers rather.

I had more cheering visitors than the last. Children come a-berrying, railroad men taking a Sunday morning walk in clean shirts, fishermen and hunters, poets and philosophers, in short, all honest pilgrims, who came out to the woods for freedom's sake, and really left the village behind, I was ready to greet with,— "Welcome, Englishmen! welcome, Englishmen!"[9] for I had had communication with that race.

The Bean-Field

Meanwhile my beans, the length of whose rows, added together, was seven miles already planted, were impatient to be hoed, for the earliest had grown considerably before the latest were in the ground; indeed they were not easily to be put off. What was the meaning of this so steady and self-respecting, this small Herculean labor, I knew not. I came to love my rows, my beans,

---

8. Josiah Bartlett II, a physician from Concord.
9. Reputedly the greeting of the Indian, Samoset, to the Pilgrims who landed at Plymouth.

though so many more than I wanted. They attached me to the earth, and so I got strength like Antæus.[1] But why should I raise them? Only Heaven knows. This was my curious labor all summer, —to make this portion of the earth's surface, which had yielded only cinquefoil, blackberries, johnswort, and the like, before, sweet wild fruits and pleasant flowers, produce instead this pulse. What shall I learn of beans or beans of me? I cherish them, I hoe them, early and late I have an eye to them; and this is my day's work. It is a fine broad leaf to look on. My auxiliaries are the dews and rains which water this dry soil, and what fertility is in the soil itself, which for the most part is lean and effete. My enemies are worms, cool days, and most of all woodchucks. The last have nibbled for me a quarter of an acre clean. But what right had I to oust johnswort and the rest, and break up their ancient herb garden? Soon, however, the remaining beans will be too tough for them, and go forward to meet new foes.

When I was four years old, as I well remember, I was brought from Boston to this my native town, through these very woods and this field, to the pond. It is one of the oldest scenes stamped on my memory. And now to-night my flute has waked the echoes over that very water. The pines still stand here older than I; or, if some have fallen, I have cooked my supper with their stumps, and a new growth is rising all around, preparing another aspect for new infant eyes. Almost the same johnswort springs from the same perennial root in this pasture, and even I have at length helped to clothe that fabulous landscape of my infant dreams, and one of the results of my presence and influence is seen in these bean leaves, corn blades, and potato vines.

I planted about two acres and a half of upland; and as it was only about fifteen years since the land was cleared, and I myself had got out two or three cords of stumps, I did not give it any manure; but in the course of the summer it appeared by the arrow-heads which I turned up in hoeing, that an extinct nation had anciently dwelt here and planted corn and beans ere white men came to clear the land, and so, to some extent, had exhausted the soil for this very crop.

Before yet any woodchuck or squirrel had run across the road, or the sun had got above the shrub-oaks, while all the dew was on, though the farmers warned me against it,—I would advise you to do all your work if possible while the dew is on,—I began to level the ranks of haughty weeds in my bean-field and throw dust upon their heads. Early in the morning I worked barefooted, dabbling like a plastic artist in the dewy and crumbling sand, but later in

1. A mythical giant who got his strength from touching the earth; he was strangled by Hercules, who held him off the ground.

the day the sun blistered my feet. There the sun lighted me to hoe beans, pacing slowly backward and forward over that yellow gravelly upland, between the long green rows, fifteen rods, the one end terminating in a shrub oak copse where I could rest in the shade, the other in a blackberry field where the green berries deepened their tints by the time I had made another bout. Removing the weeds, putting fresh soil about the bean stems, and encouraging this weed which I had sown, making the yellow soil express its summer thought in bean leaves and blossoms rather than in wormwood and piper and millet grass, making the earth say beans instead of grass,—this was my daily work. As I had little aid from horses or cattle, or hired men or boys, or improved implements of husbandry, I was much slower, and became much more intimate with my beans than usual. But labor of the hands, even when pursued to the verge of drudgery, is perhaps never the worst form of idleness. It has a constant and imperishable moral, and to the scholar it yields a classic result. A very *agricola laboriosus* [2] was I to travellers bound westward through Lincoln and Wayland to nobody knows where; they sitting at their ease in gigs, with elbows on knees, and reins loosely hanging in festoons; I the home-staying, laborious native of the soil. But soon my homestead was out of their sight and thought. It was the only open and cultivated field for a great distance on either side of the road; so they made the most of it; and sometimes the man in the field heard more of travellers' gossip and comment than was meant for his ear: "Beans so late! peas so late!"—for I continued to plant when others had began to hoe,—the ministerial husbandman had not suspected it. "Corn, my boy, for fodder; corn for fodder." "Does he *live* there?" asks the black bonnet of the gray coat; and the hard-featured farmer reins up his grateful dobbin to inquire what you are doing where he sees no manure in the furrow, and recommends a little chip dirt, or any little waste stuff, or it may be ashes or plaster. But here were two acres and a half of furrows, and only a hoe for cart and two hands to draw it,—there being an aversion to other carts and horses,—and chip dirt far away. Fellow-travellers as they rattled by compared it aloud with the fields which they had passed, so that I came to know how I stood in the agricultural world. This was one field not in Mr. Coleman's report.[3] And, by the way, who estimates the value of the crop which Nature yields in the still wilder fields unimproved by man? The crop of *English* hay is carefully weighed, the moisture calculated, the silicates and the potash; but in all

2. "Hard-working farmer"; Lincoln and Wayland are towns near Concord.
3. Henry Coleman (1785–1849), State Commissioner for the Agricultural Survey of Massachusetts.

dells and pond holes in the woods and pastures and swamps grows a rich and various crop only unreaped by man. Mine was, as it were, the connecting link between wild and cultivated fields; as some states are civilized, and others half-civilized, and others savage or barbarous, so my field was, though not in a bad sense, a half-cultivated field. They were beans cheerfully returning to their wild and primitive state that I cultivated, and my hoe played the *Rans des Vaches* [4] for them.

Near at hand, upon the topmost spray of a birch, sings the brown-thrasher—or red mavis, as some love to call him—all the morning, glad of your society, that would find out another farmer's field if yours were not here. While you are planting the seed, he cries,—"Drop it, drop it,—cover it up, cover it up,—pull it up, pull it up, pull it up." But this was not corn, and so it was safe from such enemies as he. You may wonder what his rigmarole his amateur Paganini [5] performances on one string or on twenty, have to do with your planting, and yet prefer it to leached ashes or plaster. It was a cheap sort of top dressing in which I had entire faith.

As I drew a still fresher soil about the rows with my hoe, I disturbed the ashes of unchronicled nations who in primeval years lived under these heavens, and their small implements of war and hunting were brought to the light of this modern day. They lay mingled with other natural stones, some of which bore the marks of having been burned by Indian fires, and some by the sun, and also bits of pottery and glass brought hither by the recent cultivators of the soil. When my hoe tinkled against the stones, that music echoed to the woods and the sky, and was an accompaniment to my labor which yielded an instant and immeasurable crop. It was no longer beans that I hoed, nor I that hoed beans; and I remembered with as much pity as pride, if I remembered at all, my acquaintances who had gone to the city to attend the oratorios. The night-hawk circled overhead in the sunny afternoons—for I sometimes made a day of it—like a mote in the eye, or in heaven's eye, falling from time to time with a swoop and a sound as if the heavens were rent, torn at last to very rags and tatters, and yet a seamless cope remained; small imps that fill the air and lay their eggs on the ground on bare sand or rocks on the tops of hills, where few have found them; graceful and slender like ripples caught up from the pond, as leaves are raised by the wind to float in the heavens; such kindredship is in Nature. The hawk is aerial brother of the wave which he sails over and surveys, those his perfect air-inflated wings answering to the elemental unfledged

4. A song for calling cattle, sung or played by Swiss cowherds.

5. Nicolo Paganini (1782–1840), Italian violinist and composer.

pinions of the sea. Or sometimes I watched a pair of hen-hawks circling high in the sky, alternately soaring and descending, approaching and leaving one another, as if they were the imbodiment of my own thoughts. Or I was attracted by the passage of wild pigeons from this wood to that, with a slight quivering winnowing sound and carrier haste; or from under a rotten stump my hoe turned up a sluggish portentous and outlandish spotted salamander, a trace of Egypt and the Nile, yet our contemporary. When I paused to lean on my hoe, these sounds and sights I heard and saw any where in the row, a part of the inexhaustible entertainment which the country offers.

On gala days the town fires its great guns, which echo like popguns to these woods, and some waifs of martial music occasionally penetrate thus far. To me, away there in my bean-field at the other end of the town, the big guns sounded as if a puff ball had burst; and when there was a military turnout of which I was ignorant, I have sometimes had a vague sense all the day of some sort of itching and disease in the horizon, as if some eruption would break out there soon, either scarlatina or canker-rash, until at length some more favorable puff of wind, making haste over the fields and up the Wayland road, brought me information of the "trainers." It seemed by the distant hum as if somebody's bees had swarmed, and that the neighbors, according to Virgil's advice, by a faint *tintinnabulum* upon the most sonorous of their domestic utensils, were endeavoring to call them down into the hive again. And when the sound died quite away, and the hum had ceased, and the most favorable breezes told no tale, I knew that they had got the last drone of them all safely into the Middlesex hive, and that now their minds were bent on the honey with which it was smeared.

I felt proud to know that the liberties of Massachusetts and of our fatherland were in such safe keeping; and as I turned to my hoeing again I was filled with an inexpressible confidence, and pursued my labor cheerfully with a calm trust in the future.

When there were several bands of musicians, it sounded as if all the village was a vast bellows, and all the buildings expanded and collapsed alternately with a din. But sometimes it was a really noble and inspiring strain that reached these woods, and the trumpet that sings of fame, and I felt as if I could spit a Mexican with a good relish,—for why should we always stand for trifles?—and looked round for a woodchuck or a skunk to exercise my chivalry upon. These martial strains seemed as far away as Palestine, and reminded me of a march of crusaders in the horizon, with a slight tantivy and tremulous motion of the elm-tree tops which overhang the village. This was one of the *great* days; though the sky had from my clearing only the same everlastingly great look that it wears daily, and I saw no difference in it.

It was a singular experience that long acquaintance which I cultivated with beans, what with planting, and hoeing, and harvesting, and threshing, and picking over, and selling them,—the last was the hardest of all,—I might add eating, for I did taste. I was determined to know beans. When they were growing, I used to hoe from five o'clock in the morning till noon, and commonly spent the rest of the day about other affairs. Consider the intimate and curious acquaintance one makes with various kinds of weeds,—it will bear some iteration in the account, for there was no little iteration in the labor,—disturbing their delicate organizations so ruthlessly, and making such invidious distinctions with his hoe, levelling whole ranks of one species, and sedulously cultivating another. That's Roman wormwood,—that's pigweed,—that's sorrel,—that's piper-grass,—have at him, chop him up, turn his roots upward to the sun, don't let him have a fibre in the shade, if you do he'll turn himself t'other side up and be as green as a leek in two days. A long war, not with cranes, but with weeds, those Trojans who had sun and rain and dews on their side. Daily the beans saw me come to their rescue armed with a hoe, and thin the ranks of their enemies, filling up the trenches with weedy dead. Many a lusty crest-waving Hector,[6] that towered a whole foot above his crowding comrades, fell before my weapon and rolled in the dust.

Those summer days which some of my contemporaries devoted to the fine arts in Boston or Rome, and others to contemplation in India, and others to trade in London or New York, I thus, with the other farmers of New England, devoted to husbandry. Not that I wanted beans to eat, for I am by nature a Pythagorean,[7] so far as beans are concerned, whether they mean porridge or voting, and exchanged them for rice; but, perchance, as some must work in fields if only for the sake of tropes and expression, to serve a parable-maker one day. It was on the whole a rare amusement, which continued too long, might have become a dissipation. Though I gave them no manure, and did not hoe them all once, I hoed them unusually well as far as I went, and was paid for it in the end, "there being in truth," as Evelyn says, "no compost or lætation whatsoever comparable to this continual motion, repastination, and turning of the mould with the spade." "The earth," he adds elsewhere, "especially if fresh, has a certain magnetism in it, by which it attracts the salt, power, or virtue (call it

---

6. In Homer's *Iliad*, the bravest of the Trojan warriors.
7. A follower of the Greek philosopher and mathematician, Pythagoras (582–507? B.C.), who reputedly forbade his disciples to eat beans.

either) which gives it life, and is the logic of all the labor and stir we keep about it, to sustain us; all dungings and other sordid temperings being but the vicars succedaneous to this improvement." Moreover, this being one of those "worn-out and exhausted lay fields which enjoy their sabbath," had perchance, as Sir Kenelm Digby [8] thinks likely, attracted "vital spirits" from the air. I harvested twelve bushels of beans.

But to be more particular, for it is complained that Mr. Coleman has reported chiefly the expensive experiments of gentlemen farmers, my outgoes were,—

For a hoe, ...	$ 0 54	
Ploughing, harrowing, and furrowing, . . .	7 50,	Too much.
Beans for seed, ...	3 12½	
Potatoes "	1 33	
Peas "	0 40	
Turnip seed, ...	0 06	
White line for crow fence, ...	0 02	
Horse cultivator and boy three hours, . . .	1 00	
Horse and cart to get crop, ...	0 75	
In all, ...	$14 72½	

My income was, (patrem familias vendacem, non emacem esse oportet,) [9] from

Nine bushels and twelve quarts of beans sold, . .	$16 94
Five " large potatoes, ...	2 50
Nine " small, ...	2 25
Grass, ...	1 00
Stalks, ...	0 75
In all, ...	$23 44

Leaving a pecuniary profit, as I have elsewhere said, of $8 71½.

This is the result of my experience in raising beans. Plant the common small white bush bean about the first of June, in rows three feet by eighteen inches apart, being careful to select fresh round and unmixed seed. First look out for worms, and supply vacancies by planting anew. Then look out for woodchucks, if it is an exposed place, for they will nibble off the earliest tender leaves almost clean as they go; and again, when the young tendrils make their appearance, they have notice of it, and will shear them off with both buds and young pods, sitting erect like a squirrel. But above all harvest as early as possible, if you would escape frosts and have a fair and salable crop; you may save much loss by this means.

8. English author (1603–1661) who combined a study of nature with an interest in pseudo-science.

9. "A householder should be one who sells, not one who buys" (from Cato, *De Agri Cultura*).

This further experience also I gained. I said to myself, I will not plant beans and corn with so much industry another summer, but such seeds, if the seed is not lost, as sincerity, truth, simplicity, faith, innocence, and the like, and see if they will not grow in this soil, even with less toil and manurance, and sustain me, for surely it has not been exhausted for these crops. Alas! I said this to myself; but now another summer is gone, and another, and another, and I am obliged to say to you, Reader, that the seeds which I planted, if indeed they *were* the seeds of those virtues, were wormeaten or had lost their vitality, and so did not come up. Commonly men will only be brave as their fathers were brave, or timid. This generation is very sure to plant corn and beans each new year precisely as the Indians did centuries ago and taught the first settlers to do, as if there were a fate in it. I saw an old man the other day, to my astonishment, making the holes with a hoe for the seventieth time at least, and not for himself to lie down in! But why should not the New Englander try new adventures, and not lay so much stress on his grain, his potato and grass crop, and his orchards,—raise other crops than these? Why concern ourselves so much about our beans for seed, and not be concerned at all about a new generation of men? We should really be fed and cheered if when we met a man we were sure to see that some of the qualities which I have named, which we all prize more than those other productions, but which are for the most part broadcast and floating in the air, had taken root and grown in him. Here comes such a subtle and ineffable quality, for instance, as truth or justice, though the slightest amount or new variety of it, along the road. Our ambassadors should be instructed to send home such seeds as these, and Congress help to distribute them over all the land. We should never stand upon ceremony with sincerity. We should never cheat and insult and banish one another by our meanness, if there were present the kernel of worth and friendliness. We should not meet thus in haste. Most men I do not meet at all, for they seem not to have time; they are busy about their beans. We would not deal with a man thus plodding ever, leaning on a hoe or a spade as a staff between his work, not as a mushroom, but partially risen out of the earth, something more than erect, like swallows alighted and walking on the ground:—

> "And as he spake, his wings would now and then
> Spread, as he meant to fly, then close again," [1]

so that we should suspect that we might be conversing with an angel. Bread may not always nourish us; but it always does us good, it even takes stiffness out of our joints, and makes us supple

1. Francis Quarles (1592–1644), English poet: "The Shepheard's Oracles," Ec. V.

and buoyant, when we knew not what ailed us, to recognize any generosity in man or Nature, to share any unmixed and heroic joy.

Ancient poetry and mythology suggest, at least, that husbandry was once a sacred art; but it is pursued with irreverent haste and heedlessness by us, our object being to have large farms and large crops merely. We have no festival, nor procession, nor ceremony, not excepting our Cattle-shows and so called Thanksgivings, by which the farmer expresses a sense of the sacredness of his calling, or is reminded of its sacred origin. It is the premium and the feast which tempt him. He sacrifices not to Ceres[2] and the Terrestrial Jove, but to the infernal Plutus rather. By avarice and selfishness, and a grovelling habit, from which none of us is free, of regarding the soil as property, or the means of acquiring property chiefly, the landscape is deformed, husbandry is degraded with us, and the farmer leads the meanest of lives. He knows Nature but as a robber. Cato says that the profits of agriculture are particularly pious or just, (*maximeque pius quæstus,*) and according to Varro[3] the old Romans "called the same earth Mother and Ceres, and thought that they who cultivated it led a pious and useful life, and that they alone were left of the race of King Saturn." [4]

We are wont to forget that the sun looks on our cultivated fields and on the prairies and forests without distinction. They all reflect and absorb his rays alike, and the former make but a small part of the glorious picture which he beholds in his daily course. In his view the earth is all equally cultivated like a garden. Therefore we should receive the benefit of his light and heat with a corresponding trust and magnanimity. What though I value the seed of these beans, and harvest that in the fall of the year? This broad field which I have looked at so long looks not to me as the principal cultivator, but away from me to influences more genial to it, which water and make it green. These beans have results which are not harvested by me. Do they not grow for woodchucks partly? The ear of wheat, (in Latin *spica*, obsoletely *speca*, from *spe*, hope,) should not be the only hope of the husbandman; its kernel or grain (*granum*, from *gerendo*, bearing,) is not all that it bears. How, then, can our harvest fail? Shall I not rejoice also at the abundance of the weeds whose seeds are the granary of the birds? It matters little comparatively whether the fields fill the farmer's barns. The true husbandman will cease from anxiety, as the squirrels manifest no concern whether the woods will bear

2. In Roman mythology, the goddess of corn and harvests; "Jove" is another name for the Roman "Jupiter"; Plutus is the god of riches (who should not be confused with Pluto, the god of hell).

3. Marcus Terrentius Varro (116–27? B.C.), Roman author.
4. In Roman mythology, the god of agriculture (called "Cronus" by the Greeks).

chestnuts this year or not, and finish his labor with every day, relinquishing all claim to the produce of his fields, and sacrificing in his mind not only his first but his last fruits also.

The Village

After hoeing, or perhaps reading and writing, in the forenoon, I usually bathed again in the pond, swimming across one of its coves for a stint, and washed the dust of labor from my person, or smoothed out the last wrinkle which study had made, and for the afternoon was absolutely free. Every day or two I strolled to the village to hear some of the gossip which is incessantly going on there, circulating either from mouth to mouth, or from newspaper to newspaper, and which, taken in homœopathic doses, was really as refreshing in its way as the rustle of leaves and the peeping of frogs. As I walked in the woods to see the birds and squirrels, so I walked in the village to see the men and boys; instead of the wind among the pines I heard the carts rattle. In one direction from my house there was a colony of muskrats in the river meadows; under the grove of elms and buttonwoods in the other horizon was a village of busy men, as curious to me as if they had been prairie dogs, each sitting at the mouth of its burrow, or running over to a neighbor's to gossip. I went there frequently to observe their habits. The village appeared to me a great news room; and on one side, to support it, as once at Redding & Company's on State Street, they kept nuts and raisins, or salt and meal and other groceries. Some have such a vast appetite for the former commodity, that is, the news, and such sound digestive organs, that they can sit forever in public avenues without stirring, and let it simmer and whisper through them like the Etesian winds,[1] or as if inhaling ether, it only producing numbness and insensibility to pain,—otherwise it would often be painful to hear,—without affecting the consciousness. I hardly ever failed, when I rambled through the village, to see a row of such worthies, either sitting on a ladder sunning themselves, with their bodies inclined forward and their eyes glancing along the line this way and that, from time to time, with a voluptuous expression, or else leaning against a barn with their hands in their pockets, like caryatides, as if to prop it up. They, being commonly out of doors, heard whatever was in the wind. These are the coarsest mills, in which all gossip is first rudely digested or cracked up before it is emptied into finer and more delicate hoppers within doors. I observed that the vitals of the village were the grocery,

---

1. Northerly Mediterranean summer winds which recur annually.

the bar-room, the post-office, and the bank; and, as a necessary part of the machinery, they kept a bell, a big gun, and a fire-engine, at convenient places; and the houses were so arranged as to make the most of mankind, in lanes and fronting one another, so that every traveller had to run the gantlet, and every man, woman, and child might get a lick at him. Of course, those who were stationed nearest to the head of the line, where they could most see and be seen, and have the first blow at him, paid the highest prices for their places; and the few straggling inhabitants in the outskirts, where long gaps in the line began to occur, and the traveller could get over walls or turn aside into cow paths, and so escape, paid a very slight ground or window tax. Signs were hung out on all sides to allure him; some to catch him by the appetite, as the tavern and victualling cellar; some by the fancy, as the dry goods store and the jeweller's; and others by the hair or the feet or the skirts, as the barber, the shoemaker, or the tailor. Besides, there was a still more terrible standing invitation to call at every one of these houses, and company expected about these times. For the most part I escaped wonderfully from these dangers, either by proceeding at once boldly and without deliberation to the goal, as is recommended to those who run the gantlet, or by keeping my thoughts on high things, like Orpheus,[2] who, "loudly singing the praises of the gods to his lyre, drowned the voices of the Sirens, and kept out of danger." Sometimes I bolted suddenly, and nobody could tell my whereabouts, for I did not stand much about gracefulness, and never hesitated at a gap in a fence. I was even accustomed to make an irruption into some houses, where I was well entertained, and after learning the kernels and very last sieve-ful of news, what had subsided, the prospects of war and peace, and whether the world was likely to hold together much longer, I was let out through the rear avenues, and so escaped to the woods again.

It was very pleasant, when I staid late in town, to launch myself into the night, especially if it was dark and tempestuous, and set sail from some bright village parlor or lecture room, with a bag of rye or Indian meal upon my shoulder, for my snug harbor in the woods, having made all tight without and withdrawn under hatches with a merry crew of thoughts, leaving only my outer man at the helm, or even tying up the helm when it was plain sailing. I had many a genial thought by the cabin fire "as I sailed." I was never cast away nor distressed in any weather, though I encountered some severe storms. It is darker in the woods, even in common nights, than most suppose. I frequently had to look up at

2. In Greek mythology, the son of a Muse whose music had supernatural powers and whose singing could charm animals and inanimate objects.

the opening between the trees above the path in order to learn my route, and, where there was no cart-path, to feel with my feet the faint track which I had worn, or steer by the known relation of particular trees which I felt with my hands, passing between two pines for instance, not more than eighteen inches apart, in the midst of the woods, invariably, in the darkest night. Sometimes, after coming home thus late in a dark and muggy night, when my feet felt the path which my eyes could not see, dreaming and absent-minded all the way, until I was aroused by having to raise my hand to lift the latch, I have not been able to recall a single step of my walk, and I have thought that perhaps my body would find its way home if its master should forsake it, as the hand finds its way to the mouth without assistance. Several times, when a visitor chanced to stay into evening, and it proved a dark night, I was obliged to conduct him to the cart-path in the rear of the house, and then point out to him the direction he was to pursue, and in keeping which he was to be guided rather by his feet than his eyes. One very dark night I directed thus on their way two young men who had been fishing in the pond. They lived about a mile off through the woods, and were quite used to the route. A day or two after one of them told me that they wandered about the greater part of the night, close by their own premises, and did not get home till toward morning, by which time, as there had been several heavy showers in the mean while, and the leaves were very wet, they were drenched to their skins. I have heard of many going astray even in the village streets, when the darkness was so thick that you could cut it with a knife, as the saying is. Some who live in the outskirts, having come to town a-shopping in their wagons, have been obliged to put up for the night; and gentlemen and ladies making a call have gone half a mile out of their way, feeling the sidewalk only with their feet, and not knowing when they turned. It is a surprising and memorable, as well as valuable experience, to be lost in the woods any time. Often in a snow storm, even by day, one will come out upon a well-known road and yet find it impossible to tell which way leads to the village. Though he knows that he has travelled it a thousand times, he cannot recognize a feature in it, but it is as strange to him as if it were a road in Siberia. By night, of course, the perplexity is infinitely greater. In our most trivial walks, we are constantly, though unconsciously, steering like pilots by certain well-known beacons and headlands, and if we go beyond our usual course we still carry in our minds the bearing of some neighboring cape; and not till we are completely lost, or turned round,—for a man needs only to be turned round once with his eyes shut in this world to be lost,—do we appreciate the vastness and strangeness of

Nature. Every man has to learn the points of compass again as often as he awakes, whether from sleep or any abstraction. Not till we are lost, in other words, not till we have lost the world, do we begin to find ourselves, and realize where we are and the infinite extent of our relations.

One afternoon, near the end of the first summer, when I went to the village to get a shoe from the cobbler's, I was seized and put into jail, because, as I have elsewhere related,[3] I did not pay a tax to, or recognize the authority of, the state which buys and sells men, women, and children, like cattle at the door of its senate-house. I had gone down to the woods for other purposes. But, wherever a man goes, men will pursue and paw him with their dirty institutions, and, if they can, constrain him to belong to their desperate odd-fellow society. It is true, I might have resisted forcibly with more or less effect, might have run "amok" against society; but I preferred that society should run "amok" against me, it being the desperate party. However, I was released the next day, obtained my mended shoe, and returned to the woods in season to get my dinner of huckleberries on Fair-Haven Hill. I was never molested by any person but those who represented the state. I had no lock nor bolt but for the desk which held my papers, not even a nail to put over my latch or windows. I never fastened my door night or day, though I was to be absent several days; not even when the next fall I spent a fortnight in the woods of Maine. And yet my house was more respected than if it had been surrounded by a file of soldiers. The tired rambler could rest and warm himself by my fire, the literary amuse himself with the few books on my table, or the curious, by opening my closet door, see what was left of my dinner, and what prospect I had of a supper. Yet, though many people of every class came this way to the pond, I suffered no serious inconvenience from these sources, and I never missed any thing but one small book, a volume of Homer, which perhaps was improperly gilded, and this I trust a soldier of our camp has found by this time. I am convinced, that if all men were to live as simply as I then did, thieving and robbery would be unknown. These take place only in communities where some have got more than is sufficient while others have not enough. The Pope's Homers[4] would soon get properly distributed.—

> "Nec bella fuerunt,
> Faginus astabat dum scyphus ante dapes."
> "Nor wars did men molest,
> When only beechen bowls were in request."

3. I.e., in "Civil Disobedience."
4. Alexander Pope (1688–1744) translated Homer's *Iliad* and *Odyssey* into
English.

"You who govern public affairs, what need have you to employ punishments? Love virtue, and the people will be virtuous. The virtues of a superior man are like the wind; the virtues of a common man are like the grass; the grass, when the wind passes over it, bends."[5]

The Ponds

Sometimes, having had a surfeit of human society and gossip, and worn out all my village friends, I rambled still farther westward than I habitually dwell, into yet more unfrequented parts of the town, "to fresh woods and pastures new," or, while the sun was setting, made my supper of huckleberries and blueberries on Fair Haven Hill, and laid up a store for several days. The fruits do not yield their true flavor to the purchaser of them, nor to him who raises them for the market. There is but one way to obtain it, yet few take that way. If you would know the flavor of huckleberries, ask the cow-boy or the partridge. It is a vulgar error to suppose that you have tasted huckleberries who never plucked them. A huckleberry never reaches Boston; they have not been known there since they grew on her three hills. The ambrosial and essential part of the fruit is lost with the bloom which is rubbed off in the market cart, and they become mere provender. As long as Eternal Justice reigns, not one innocent huckleberry can be transported thither from the country's hills.

Occasionally, after my hoeing was done for the day, I joined some impatient companion who had been fishing on the pond since morning, as silent and motionless as a duck or a floating leaf, and, after practising various kinds of philosophy, had concluded commonly, by the time I arrived, that he belonged to the ancient sect of Cœnobites.[1] There was one older man, an excellent fisher and skilled in all kinds of woodcraft, who was pleased to look upon my house as a building erected for the convenience of fishermen; and I was equally pleased when he sat in my doorway to arrange his lines. Once in a while we sat together on the pond, he at one end of the boat, and I at the other; but not many words passed between us, for he had grown deaf in his later years, but he occasionally hummed a psalm, which harmonized well enough with my philosophy. Our intercourse was thus altogether one of unbroken harmony, far more pleasing to remember than if it had been carried on by speech. When, as was commonly the case, I had none to commune with, I used to raise the echoes by strik-

5. From Confucius' *Analects*.   1. A member of a religious community.

ing with a paddle on the side of my boat, filling the surrounding woods with circling and dilating sound, stirring them up as the keeper of a menagerie his wild beasts, until I elicited a growl from every wooded vale and hill-side.

In warm evenings I frequently sat in the boat playing the flute, and saw the perch, which I seemed to have charmed, hovering around me, and the moon travelling over the ribbed bottom, which was strewed with the wrecks of the forest. Formerly I had come to this pond adventurously, from time to time, in dark summer nights, with a companion, and making a fire close to the water's edge, which we thought attracted the fishes, we caught pouts with a bunch of worms strung on a thread; and when we had done, far in the night, threw the burning brands high into the air like skyrockets, which, coming down into the pond, were quenched with a loud hissing, and we were suddenly groping in total darkness. Through this, whistling a tune, we took our way to the haunts of men again. But now I had made my home by the shore.

Sometimes, after staying in a village parlor till the family had all retired, I have returned to the woods, and, partly with a view to the next day's dinner, spent the hours of midnight fishing from a boat by moonlight, serenaded by owls and foxes, and hearing, from time to time, the creaking note of some unknown bird close at hand. These experiences were very memorable and valuable to me, —anchored in forty feet of water, and twenty or thirty rods from the shore, surrounded sometimes by thousands of small perch and shiners, dimpling the surface with their tails in the moonlight, and communicating by a long flaxen line with mysterious nocturnal fishes which had their dwelling forty feet below, or sometimes dragging sixty feet of line about the pond as I drifted in the gentle night breeze, now and then feeling a slight vibration along it, indicative of some life prowling about its extremity, of dull uncertain blundering purpose there, and slow to make up its mind. At length you slowly raise, pulling hand over hand, some horned pout squeaking and squirming to the upper air. It was very queer, especially in dark nights, when your thoughts had wandered to vast and cosmogonal themes in other spheres, to feel this faint jerk, which came to interrupt your dreams and link you to Nature again. It seemed as if I might next cast my line upward into the air, as well as downward into this element which was scarcely more dense. Thus I caught two fishes as it were with one hook.

The scenery of Walden is on a humble scale, and, though very beautiful, does not approach to grandeur, nor can it much concern one who has not long frequented it or lived by its shore; yet this pond is so remarkable for its depth and purity as to merit a particular description. It is a clear and deep green well, half a mile long and a mile and three quarters in circumference, and contains about sixty-one and a half acres; a perennial spring in the midst of pine and oak woods, without any visible inlet or outlet except by the clouds and evaporation. The surrounding hills rise abruptly from the water to the height of forty to eighty feet, though on the south-east and east they attain to about one hundred and one hundred and fifty feet respectively, within a quarter and a third of a mile. They are exclusively woodland. All our Concord waters have two colors at least, one when viewed at a distance, and another, more proper, close at hand. The first depends more on the light, and follows the sky. In clear weather, in summer, they appear blue at a little distance, especially if agitated, and at a great distance all appear alike. In stormy weather they are sometimes of a dark slate color. The sea, however, is said to be blue one day and green another without any perceptible change in the atmosphere. I have seen our river, when, the landscape being covered with snow, both water and ice were almost as green as grass. Some consider blue "to be the color of pure water, whether liquid or solid." But, looking directly down into our waters from a boat, they are seen to be of very different colors. Walden is blue at one time and green at another, even from the same point of view. Lying between the earth and the heavens, it partakes of the color of both. Viewed from a hill-top it reflects the color of the sky, but near at hand it is of a yellowish tint next the shore where you can see the sand, then a light green, which gradually deepens to a uniform dark green in the body of the pond. In some lights, viewed even from a hill-top, it is of a vivid green next the shore. Some have referred this to the reflection of the verdure; but it is equally green there against the railroad sand-bank, and in the spring, before the leaves are expanded, and it may be simply the result of the prevailing blue mixed with the yellow of the sand. Such is the color of its iris. This is that portion, also, where in the spring, the ice being warmed by the heat of the sun reflected from the bottom, and also transmitted through the earth, melts first and forms a narrow canal about the still frozen middle. Like the rest of our waters, when much agitated, in clear weather, so that the surface of the waves may reflect the sky at the right angle, or because there is more light mixed with it, it appears at a little distance of a darker blue than the sky itself; and at such a time, being on its surface, and looking with divided vision, so as to see the reflection, I have discerned a matchless and indescribable light blue, such as watered or changeable silks and sword blades suggest, more cerulean than the sky itself, alternating with the original dark green on the opposite sides of the waves, which last appeared but muddy in comparison. It is a vitreous greenish blue, as I remember it, like those patches of the winter sky seen through cloud vistas in the west before sundown. Yet a single glass of its water held up to the light is as colorless as an equal quantity of air. It is well known that a large plate of glass will have a green tint, owing, as the makers say, to its "body," but a small piece of the same will be colorless. How large a body of Walden water would be required to reflect a green tint I have never proved. The water of our river is black or a very dark brown to one looking directly down on it, and, like that of most ponds, imparts to the body of one bathing in it a yellowish tinge; but this water is of such crystalline purity that the body of the bather appears of an alabaster whiteness, still more unnatural, which, as the limbs are magnified and distorted withal, produces a monstrous effect, making fit studies for a Michael Angelo.[2]

The water is so transparent that the bottom can easily be discerned at the depth of twenty-five or thirty feet. Paddling over it, you may see many feet beneath the surface the schools of perch and shiners, perhaps only an inch long, yet the former easily distinguished by their transverse bars, and you think that they must be ascetic fish that find a subsistence there. Once, in the winter, many years ago, when I had been cutting holes through the ice in order to catch pickerel, as I stepped ashore I tossed my axe back on to the ice, but, as if some evil genius had directed it, it slid four or five rods directly into one of the holes, where the water was twenty-five feet deep. Out of curiosity, I lay down on the ice and looked through the hole, until I saw the axe a little on one side, standing on its head, with its helve erect and gently swaying to and fro with the pulse of the pond; and there it might have stood erect and swaying till in the course of time the handle rotted off, if I had not disturbed it. Making another hole directly over it with an ice chisel which I had, and cutting down the longest birch which I could find in the neighborhood with my knife, I made a slip-noose, which I attached to its end, and, letting it down carefully, passed it over the knob of the handle, and drew it by a line along the birch, and so pulled the axe out again.

The shore is composed of a belt of smooth rounded white stones like paving stones, excepting one or two short sand beaches, and is so steep that in many places a single leap will carry you into water over your head; and were it not for its remarkable transparency, that would be the last to be seen of its bottom till it rose on the opposite side. Some think it is bottomless. It is no-

2. Italian painter, sculptor, and architect (1475–1564).

where muddy, and a casual observer would say that there were no weeds at all in it; and of noticeable plants, except in the little meadows recently overflowed, which do not properly belong to it, a closer scrutiny does not detect a flag nor a bulrush, nor even a lily, yellow or white, but only a few small heart-leaves and pota-mogetons, and perhaps a water-target or two; all which however a bather might not perceive; and these plants are clean and bright like the element they grow in. The stones extend a rod or two into the water, and then the bottom is pure sand, except in the deepest parts, where there is usually a little sediment, probably from the decay of the leaves which have been wafted on to it so many successive falls, and a bright green weed is brought up on anchors even in midwinter.

We have one other pond just like this, White Pond in Nine Acre Corner, about two and a half miles westerly; but, though I am acquainted with most of the ponds within a dozen miles of this centre, I do not know a third of this pure and well-like character. Successive nations perchance have drank at, admired, and fathomed it, and passed away, and still its water is green and pellucid as ever. Not an intermitting spring! Perhaps on that spring morning when Adam and Eve were driven out of Eden Walden Pond was already in existence, and even then breaking up in a gentle spring rain accompanied with mist and a southerly wind, and covered with myriads of ducks and geese, which had not heard of the fall, when still such pure lakes sufficed them. Even then it had commenced to rise and fall, and had clarified its waters and colored them of the hue they now wear, and obtained a patent of heaven to be the only Walden Pond in the world and distiller of celestial dews. Who knows in how many unremembered nations' literatures this has been the Castalian Fountain? [3] or what nymphs presided over it in the Golden Age? [4] It is a gem of the first water which Concord wears in her coronet.

Yet perchance the first who came to this well have left some trace of their footsteps. I have been surprised to detect encircling the pond, even where a thick wood has just been cut down on the shore, a narrow shelf-like path in the steep hill-side, alternately rising and falling, approaching and receding from the water's edge, as old probably as the race of man here, worn by the feet of aboriginal hunters, and still from time to time unwittingly trodden by the present occupants of the land. This is particularly distinct to one standing on the middle of the pond in winter, just after a light snow has fallen, appearing as a clear undulating white line, unobscured by weeds and twigs, and very obvious a quarter of

3. In Greek mythology, a fountain on Mount Parnassus, the source of poetic inspiration.

4. In classical mythology, an early and ideal period of civilization.

a mile off in many places where in summer it is hardly distinguishable close at hand. The snow reprints it, as it were, in clear white type alto-relievo.[5] The ornamented grounds of villas which will one day be built here may still preserve some trace of this.

The pond rises and falls, but whether regularly or not, and within what period, nobody knows, though, as usual, many pretend to know. It is commonly higher in the winter and lower in the summer, though not corresponding to the general wet and dryness. I can remember when it was a foot or two lower, and also when it was at least five feet higher, than when I lived by it. There is a narrow sand-bar running into it, with very deep water on one side, on which I helped boil a kettle of chowder, some six rods from the main shore, about the year 1824, which it has not been possible to do for twenty-five years; and on the other hand, my friends used to listen with incredulity when I told them, that a few years later I was accustomed to fish from a boat in a secluded cove in the woods, fifteen rods from the only shore they knew, which place was long since converted into a meadow. But the pond has risen steadily for two years, and now, in the summer of '52, is just five feet higher than when I lived there, or as high as it was thirty years ago, and fishing goes on again in the meadow. This makes a difference of level, at the outside, of six or seven feet; and yet the water shed by the surrounding hills is insignificant in amount, and this overflow must be referred to causes which affect the deep springs. This same summer the pond has begun to fall again. It is remarkable that this fluctuation, whether periodical or not, appears thus to require many years for its accomplishment. I have observed one rise and a part of two falls, and I expect that a dozen or fifteen years hence the water will again be as low as I have ever known it. Flints' Pond, a mile eastward, allowing for the disturbance occasioned by its inlets and outlets, and the smaller intermediate ponds also, sympathize with Walden, and recently attained their greatest height at the same time with the latter. The same is true, as far as my observation goes, of White Pond.

This rise and fall of Walden at long intervals serves this use at least; the water standing at this great height for a year or more, though it makes it difficult to walk round it, kills the shrubs and trees which have sprung up about its edge since the last rise, pitch-pines, birches, alders, aspens, and others, and, falling again, leaves an unobstructed shore; for, unlike many ponds and all waters which are subject to a daily tide, its shore is cleanest when

5. A sculptural term referring to the projection of a figure from the background; also called "high relief."

the water is lowest. On the side of the pond next my house, a row of pitch pines fifteen feet high has been killed and tipped over as if by a lever, and thus a stop put to their encroachments; and their size indicates how many years have elapsed since the last rise to this height. By this fluctuation the pond asserts its title to a shore, and thus the *shore* is *shorn*, and the trees cannot hold it by right of possession. These are the lips of the lake on which no beard grows. It licks its chaps from time to time. When the water is at its height, the alders, willows, and maples send forth a mass of fibrous red roots several feet long from all sides of their stems in the water, and to the height of three or four feet from the ground, in the effort to maintain themselves; and I have known the high-blueberry bushes about the shore, which commonly produce no fruit, bear an abundant crop under these circumstances.

Some have been puzzled to tell how the shore became so regularly paved. My townsmen have all heard the tradition, the oldest people tell me that they heard it in their youth, that anciently the Indians were holding a pow-wow upon a hill here, which rose as high into the heavens as the pond now sinks deep into the earth, and they used much profanity, as the story goes, though this vice is one of which the Indians were never guilty, and while they were thus engaged the hill shook and suddenly sank, and only one old squaw, named Walden, escaped, and from her the pond was named.[6] It has been conjectured that when the hill shook these stones rolled down its side and became the present shore. It is very certain, at any rate, that once there was no pond here, and now there is one; and this Indian fable does not in any respect conflict with the account of that ancient settler whom I have mentioned, who remembers so well when he first came here with his divining rod, saw a thin vapor rising from the sward, and the hazel pointed steadily downward, and he concluded to dig a well here. As for the stones, many still think that they are hardly to be accounted for by the action of the waves on these hills; but I observe that the surrounding hills are remarkably full of the same kind of stones, so that they have been obliged to pile them up in walls on both sides of the railroad cut nearest the pond; and, moreover, there are most stones where the shore is most abrupt; so that, unfortunately, it is no longer a mystery to me. I detect the paver. If the name was not derived from that of some English locality,—Saffron Walden,[7] for instance,—one might suppose that it was called, originally, *Walled-in* Pond.

6. This is told of Alexander's Lake in Killingly Ct. by Barber v. *his* Con. Hist. Coll. [Thoreau's note].
7. Evelyn in his Diary (1654) mentions "the parish of Saffron Walden, famous for the abundance of Saffron there cultivated, and esteemed the best of any foreign country." [Thoreau's note.] Saffron Walden is a town forty miles from London, England.

The pond was my well ready dug. For four months in the year its water is as cold as it is pure at all times; and I think that it is then as good as any, if not the best, in the town. In the winter, all water which is exposed to the air is colder than springs and wells which are protected from it. The temperature of the pond water which had stood in the room where I sat from five o'clock in the afternoon till noon the next day, the sixth of March, 1846, the thermometer having been up to 65° or 70° some of the time, owing partly to the sun on the roof, was 42°, or one degree colder than the water of one of the coldest wells in the village just drawn. The temperature of the Boiling Spring [8] the same day was 45°, or the warmest of any water tried, though it is the coldest that I know of in summer, when, beside, shallow and stagnant surface water is not mingled with it. Moreover, in summer, Walden never becomes so warm as most water which is exposed to the sun, on account of its depth. In the warmest weather I usually placed a pailful in my cellar, where it became cool in the night, and remained so during the day; though I also resorted to a spring in the neighborhood. It was as good when a week old as the day it was dipped, and had no taste of the pump. Whoever camps for a week in summer by the shore of a pond, needs only bury a pail of water a few feet deep in the shade of his camp to be independent on the luxury of ice.

There have been caught in Walden, pickerel, one weighing seven pounds, to say nothing of another which carried off a reel with great velocity, which the fisherman safely set down at eight pounds because he did not see him, perch and pouts, some of each weighing over two pounds, shiners, chivins or roach, (*Leuciscus pulchellus*,) a very few breams,[9] and a couple of eels, one weighing four pounds,—I am thus particular because the weight of a fish is commonly its only title to fame, and these are the only eels I have heard of here;—also, I have a faint recollection of a little fish some five inches long, with silvery sides and a greenish back, somewhat dace-like in its character, which I mention here chiefly to link my facts to fable. Nevertheless, this pond is not very fertile in fish. Its pickerel, though not abundant, are its chief boast. I have seen at one time lying on the ice pickerel of at least three different kinds; a long and shallow one, steel-colored, most like those caught in the river; a bright golden kind, with greenish reflections and remarkably deep, which is the most common here; and another, golden-colored, and shaped like the last, but peppered on the sides with small dark brown or black spots,

8. A "bubbling" spring (not a "hot spring") located half a mile west of Walden Pond.

9. Pomotis obesus [Nov. 26–58] one trout weighing a little over 5 lbs— (Nov. 14–57) [Thoreau's note].

intermixed with a few faint blood-red ones, very much like a trout. The specific name *reticulatus* would not apply to this; it should be *guttatus* rather. These are all very firm fish, and weigh more than their size promises. The shiners, pouts, and perch also, and indeed all the fishes which inhabit this pond, are much cleaner, handsomer, and firmer fleshed than those in the river and most other ponds, as the water is purer, and they can easily be distinguished from them. Probably many ichthyologists would make new varieties of some of them. There are also a clean race of frogs and tortoises, and a few muscles in it; muskrats and minks leave their traces about it, and occasionally a travelling mud-turtle visits it. Sometimes, when I pushed off my boat in the morning, I disturbed a great mud-turtle which had secreted himself under the boat in the night. Ducks and geese frequent it in the spring and fall, the white-bellied swallows (*Hirundo bicolor*) skim over it, kingfisher dart away from its cover, and the peet-weets (*Totanus macularius*) "teter" along its stony shores all summer. I have sometimes disturbed a fishhawk sitting on a white-pine over the water; but I doubt if it is ever profaned by the wing of a gull, like Fair Haven.[1] At most, it tolerates one annual loon. These are all the animals of consequence which frequent it now.

You may see from a boat, in calm weather, near the sandy eastern shore, where the water is eight or ten feet deep, and also in some other parts of the pond, some circular heaps half a dozen feet in diameter by a foot in height, consisting of small stones less than a hen's egg in size, where all around is bare sand. At first you wonder if the Indians could have formed them on the ice for any purpose, and so, when the ice melted, they sank to the bottom; but they are too regular and some of them plainly too fresh for that. They are similar to those found in rivers; but as there are no suckers nor lampreys here, I know not by what fish they could be made. Perhaps they are the nests of the chivin. These lend a pleasing mystery to the bottom.

The shore is irregular enough not to be monotonous. I have in my mind's eye the western indented with deep bays, the bolder northern, and the beautifully scolloped southern shore, where successive capes overlap each other and suggest unexplored coves between. The forest has never so good a setting, nor is so distinctly beautiful, as when seen from the middle of a small lake amid hills which rise from the water's edge; for the water in which it is reflected not only makes the best foreground in such a case, but, with its winding shore, the most natural and agreeable

1. A wide bay in the Sudbury River about a mile south of Walden Pond.

boundary to it. There is no rawness nor imperfection in its edge there, as where the axe has cleared a part, or a cultivated field abuts on it. The trees have ample room to expand on the water side, and each sends forth its most vigorous branch in that direction. There Nature has woven a natural selvage, and the eye rises by just gradations from the low shrubs of the shore to the highest trees. There are few traces of man's hand to be seen. The water laves the shore as it did a thousand years ago.

A lake is the landscape's most beautiful and expressive feature. It is earth's eye; looking into which the beholder measures the depth of his own nature. The fluviatile trees next the shore are the slender eyelashes which fringe it, and the wooded hills and cliffs around are its overhanging brows.

Standing on the smooth sandy beach at the east end of the pond, in a calm September afternoon, when a slight haze makes the opposite shore line indistinct, I have seen whence came the expression, "the glassy surface of a lake." When you invert your head, it looks like a thread of finest gossamer stretched across the valley, and gleaming against the distant pine woods, separating one stratum of the atmosphere from another. You would think that you could walk dry under it to the opposite hills, and that the swallows which skim over might perch on it. Indeed, they sometimes dive below the line, as it were by mistake, and are undeceived. As you look over the pond westward you are obliged to employ both your hands to defend your eyes against the reflected as well as the true sun, for they are equally bright; and if, between the two, you survey its surface critically, it is literally as smooth as glass, except where the skater insects (Hydrometer), at equal intervals scattered over its whole extent, by their motions in the sun produce the finest imaginable sparkle on it, or, perchance, a duck plumes itself, or, as I have said, a swallow skims so low as to touch it. It may be that in the distance a fish describes an arc of three or four feet in the air, and there is one bright flash where it emerges, and another where it strikes the water; sometimes the whole silvery arc is revealed; or here and there, perhaps, is a thistle-down floating on its surface, which the fishes dart at and so dimple it again. It is like molten glass cooled but not congealed, and the few motes in it are pure and beautiful like the imperfections in glass. You may often detect a yet smoother and darker water, separated from the rest as if by an invisible cobweb, boom of the water nymphs, resting on it. From a hill-top you can see a fish leap in almost any part; for not a pickerel or shiner picks an insect from this smooth surface but it manifestly disturbs the equilibrium of the whole lake. It is wonderful with what elaborateness this simple fact is advertised,—this piscine murder will out,—and from my distant perch I 'distinguish the circling undulations when they are half a dozen rods in diameter. You can even detect a water-bug (*Gyrinus*) ceaselessly progressing over the smooth surface a quarter of a mile off; for they furrow the water slightly, making a conspicuous ripple bounded by two diverging lines, but the skaters glide over it without rippling it perceptibly. When the surface is considerably agitated there are no skaters nor water-bugs on it, but apparently, in calm days, they leave their havens and adventurously glide forth from the shore by short impulses till they completely cover it. It is a soothing employment, on one of those fine days in the fall when all the warmth of the sun is fully appreciated, to sit on a stump on such a height as this, overlooking the pond, and study the dimpling circles which are incessantly inscribed on its otherwise invisible surface amid the reflected skies and trees. Over this great expanse there is no disturbance but it is thus at once gently smoothed away and assuaged, as, when a vase of water is jarred, the trembling circles seek the shore and all is smooth again. Not a fish can leap or an insect fall on the pond but it is thus reported in circling dimples, in lines of beauty, as it were the constant welling up of its fountain, the gentle pulsing of its life, the heaving of its breast. The thrills of joy and thrills of pain are undistinguishable. How peaceful the phenomena of the lake! Again the works of man shine as in the spring. Ay, every leaf and twig and stone and cob-web sparkles now at mid-afternoon as when covered with dew in a spring morning. Every motion of an oar or an insect produces a flash of light; and if an oar falls, how sweet the echo!

In such a day, in September or October, Walden is a perfect forest mirror, set round with stones as precious to my eye as if fewer or rarer. Nothing so fair, so pure, and at the same time so large, as a lake, perchance, lies on the surface of the earth. Sky water. It needs no fence. Nations come and go without defiling it. It is a mirror which no stone can crack, whose quick-silver will never wear off, whose gilding Nature continually repairs; no storms, no dust, can dim its surface ever fresh;—a mirror in which all impurity presented to it sinks, swept and dusted by the sun's hazy brush,—this the light dust-cloth,—which retains no breath that is breathed on it, but sends its own to float as clouds high above its surface, and be reflected in its bosom still.

A field of water betrays the spirit that is in the air. It is continually receiving new life and motion from above. It is intermediate in its nature between land and sky. On land only the grass and trees wave, but the water itself is rippled by the wind. I see where the breeze dashes across it by the streaks or flakes of light. It is remarkable that we can look down on its surface. We shall, perhaps, look down thus on the surface of air at length, and mark where a still subtler spirit sweeps over it.

The skaters and water-bugs finally disappear in the latter part of October, when the severe frosts have come; and then and in November, usually, in a calm day, there is absolutely nothing to ripple the surface. One November afternoon, in the calm at the end of a rain storm of several days' duration, when the sky was still completely overcast and the air was full of mist, I observed that the pond was remarkably smooth, so that it was difficult to distinguish its surface; though it no longer reflected the bright tints of October, but the sombre November colors of the surrounding hills. Though I passed over it as gently as possible, the slight undulations produced by my boat extended almost as far as I could see, and gave a ribbed appearance to the reflections. But, as I was looking over the surface, I saw here and there at a distance a faint glimmer, as if some skater insects which had escaped the frosts might be collected there, or, perchance, the surface, being so smooth, betrayed where a spring welled up from the bottom. Paddling gently to one of these places, I was surprised to find myself surrounded by myriads of small perch, about five inches long, of a rich bronze color in the green water, sporting there and constantly rising to the surface and dimpling it, sometimes leaving bubbles on it. In such transparent and seemingly bottomless water, reflecting the clouds, I seemed to be floating through the air as in a balloon, and their swimming impressed me as a kind of flight or hovering, as if they were a compact flock of birds passing just beneath my level on the right or left, their fins, like sails, set all around them. There were many such schools in the pond, apparently improving the short season before winter would draw an icy shutter over their broad skylight, sometimes giving to the surface an appearance as if a slight breeze struck it, or a few rain-drops fell there. When I approached carelessly and alarmed them, they made a sudden plash and rippling with their tails, as if one had struck the water with a brushy bough, and instantly took refuge in the depths. At length the wind rose, the mist increased, and the waves began to run, and the perch leaped much higher than before, half out of water, a hundred black points, three inches long, at once above the surface. Even as late as the fifth of December, one year, I saw some dimples on the surface, and thinking it was going to rain hard immediately, the air being full of mist, I made haste to take my place at the oars and row homeward; already the rain seemed rapidly increasing, though I felt none on my cheek, and I anticipated a thorough soaking. But suddenly the dimples ceased, for they were produced by the perch, which the noise of my oars had scared into the depths, and I saw their schools dimly disappearing; so I spent a dry afternoon after all.

An old man who used to frequent this pond nearly sixty years ago, when it was dark with surrounding forests, tells me that in those days he sometimes saw it all alive with ducks and other water fowl, and that there were many eagles about it. He came here a-fishing, and used an old log canoe which he found on the shore. It was made of two white-pine logs dug out and pinned together, and was cut off square at the ends. It was very clumsy, but lasted a great many years before it became water-logged and perhaps sank to the bottom. He did not know whose it was; it belonged to the pond. He used to make a cable for his anchor of strips of hickory bark tied together. An old man, a potter, who lived by the pond before the Revolution, told him once that there was an iron chest at the bottom, and that he had seen it. Sometimes it would come floating up to the shore; but when you went toward it, it would go back into deep water and disappear. I was pleased to hear of the old log canoe, which took the place of an Indian one of the same material but more graceful construction, which perchance had first been a tree on the bank, and then, as it were, fell into the water, to float there for a generation, the most proper vessel for the lake. I remember that when I first looked into these depths there were many large trunks to be seen indistinctly lying on the bottom, which had either been blown over formerly, or left on the ice at the last cutting, when wood was cheaper; but now they have mostly disappeared.

When I first paddled a boat on Walden, it was completely surrounded by thick and lofty pine and oak woods, and in some of its coves grape vines had run over the trees next the water and formed bowers under which a boat could pass. The hills which form its shores are so steep, and the woods on them were then so high, that, as you looked down from the west end, it had the appearance of an amphitheatre for some kind of sylvan spectacle. I have spent many an hour, when I was younger, floating over its surface as the zephyr willed, having paddled my boat to the middle, and lying on my back across the seats, in a summer forenoon, dreaming awake, until I was aroused by the boat touching the sand, and I arose to see what shore my fates had impelled me to; days when idleness was the most attractive and productive industry. Many a forenoon have I stolen away, preferring to spend thus the most valued part of the day; for I was rich, if not in money, in sunny hours and summer days, and spent them lavishly; nor do I regret that I did not waste more of them in the workshop or the teacher's desk. But since I left those shores the wood-choppers have still further laid them waste, and now for many a year there will be no more rambling through the aisles of the wood, with occasional vistas through which you see the water. My Muse may be excused if she is silent henceforth. How can you expect the birds to sing when their groves are cut down?

Now the trunks of trees on the bottom, and the old log canoe, and the dark surrounding woods, are gone, and the villagers, who scarcely know where it lies, instead of going to the pond to bathe or drink, are thinking to bring its water, which should be as sacred as the Ganges [2] at least, to the village in a pipe, to wash their dishes with!—to earn their Walden by the turning of a cock or drawing of a plug! That devilish Iron Horse, whose ear-rending neigh is heard throughout the town, has muddied the Boiling Spring with his foot, and he it is that has browsed off all the woods on Walden shore; that Trojan horse, with a thousand men in his belly, introduced by mercenary Greeks! Where is the country's champion, the Moore of Moore Hall,[3] to meet him at the Deep Cut and thrust an avenging lance between the ribs of the bloated pest?

Nevertheless, of all the characters I have known, perhaps Walden wears best, and best preserves its purity. Many men have been likened to it, but few deserve that honor. Though the woodchoppers have laid bare first this shore and then that, and the Irish have built their sties by it, and the railroad has infringed on its border, and the ice-men have skimmed it once, it is itself unchanged, the same water which my youthful eyes fell on; all the change is in me. It has not acquired one permanent wrinkle after all its ripples. It is perennially young, and I may stand and see a swallow dip apparently to pick an insect from its surface as of yore. It struck me again to-night, as if I had not seen it almost daily for more than twenty years,—Why, here is Walden, the same woodland lake that I discovered so many years ago; where a forest was cut down last winter another is springing up by its shore as lustily as ever; the same thought is welling up to its surface that was then; it is the same liquid joy and happiness to itself and its Maker, ay, and it *may* be to me. It is the work of a brave man surely, in whom there was no guile! He rounded this water with his hand, deepened and clarified it in his thought, and in his will bequeathed it to Concord. I see by its face that it is visited by the same reflection; and I can almost say, Walden, is it you?

> It is no dream of mine,
> To ornament a line;
> I cannot come nearer to God and Heaven

---

2. A river in northern India, believed to be sacred by the Hindus.

3. According to an old English ballad, a hero who killed a dragon.

Than I live to Walden even.
I am its stony shore,
And the breeze that passes o'er;
In the hollow of my hand
Are its water and its sand,
And its deepest resort
Lies high in my thought.

The cars never pause to look at it; yet I fancy that the engineers
and firemen and brakemen, and those passengers who have a
season ticket and see it often, are better men for the sight. The
engineer does not forget at night, or his nature does not, that he
has beheld this vision of serenity and purity once at least during
the day. Though seen but once, it helps to wash out State-street [4]
and the engine's soot. One proposes that it be called "God's
Drop." [5]

I have said that Walden has no visible inlet nor outlet, but it
is on the one hand distantly and indirectly related to Flints' Pond,
which is more elevated, by a chain of small ponds coming from
that quarter, and on the other directly and manifestly to Concord
River, which is lower, by a similar chain of ponds through which
in some other geological period it may have flowed, and by a
little digging, which God forbid, it can be made to flow thither
again. If by living thus reserved and austere, like a hermit in
the woods, so long, it has acquired such wonderful purity, who
would not regret that the comparatively impure waters of Flints'
Pond should be mingled with it, or itself should ever go to waste
its sweetness in the ocean wave?

Flints', or Sandy Pond, in Lincoln, our greatest lake and inland
sea, lies about a mile east of Walden. It is much larger, being said
to contain one hundred and ninety-seven acres, and is more fertile
in fish; but it is comparatively shallow, and not remarkably pure.
A walk through the woods thither was often my recreation. It was
worth the while, if only to feel the wind blow on your cheek
freely, and see the waves run, and remember the life of mariners.
I went a-chestnutting there in the fall, on windy days, when the
nuts were dropping into the water and were washed to my feet;
and one day, as I crept along its sedgy shore, the fresh spray blowing in my face, I came upon the mouldering wreck of a boat,
the sides gone, and hardly more than the impression of its flat
bottom left amid the rushes; yet its model was sharply defined, as
if it were a large decayed pad, with its veins. It was as impressive
a wreck as one could imagine on the sea-shore, and had as good

4. The financial district of Boston.
5. "God's medicine," so-called by Emerson.

a moral. It is by this time mere vegetable mould and undistinguishable pond shore, through which rushes and flags have pushed up.
I used to admire the ripple marks on the sandy bottom, at the
north end of this pond, made firm and hard to the feet of the
wader by the pressure of the water, and the rushes which grew in
Indian file, in waving lines, corresponding to these marks, rank
behind rank, as if the waves had planted them. There also I have
found, in considerable quantities, curious balls, composed apparently of fine grass or roots, of pipewort perhaps, from half an
inch to four inches in diameter, and perfectly spherical. These
wash back and forth in shallow water on a sandy bottom, and are
sometimes cast on the shore. They are either solid grass, or have a
little sand in the middle. At first you would say that they were
formed by the action of the waves, like a pebble; yet the smallest
are made of equally coarse materials, half an inch long, and they
are produced only at one season of the year. Moreover, the waves,
I suspect, do not so much construct as wear down a material which
has already acquired consistency. They preserve their form when
dry for an indefinite period.

Flints' Pond! Such is the poverty of our nomenclature. What
right had the unclean and stupid farmer, whose farm abutted on
this sky water, whose shores he has ruthlessly laid bare, to give his
name to it? Some skin-flint, who loved better the reflecting surface
of a dollar, or a bright cent, in which he could see his own brazen
face; who regarded even the wild ducks which settled in it as
trespassers; his fingers grown into crooked and horny talons
from the long habit of grasping harpy-like;—so it is not named
for me. I go not there to see him nor to hear of him; who never
saw it, who never bathed in it, who never loved it, who never
protected it, who never spoke a good word for it, nor thanked God
that he had made it. Rather let it be named from the fishes that
swim in it, the wild fowl or quadrupeds which frequent it, the
wild flowers which grow by its shores, or some wild man or child
the thread of whose history is interwoven with its own; not from
him who could show no title to it but the deed which a like-
minded neighbor or legislature gave him,—him who thought only
of its money value; whose presence perchance cursed all the shore;
who exhausted the land around it, and would fain have exhausted
the waters within it; who regretted only that it was not English
hay or cranberry meadow,—there was nothing to redeem it, forsooth, in his eyes,—and would have drained and sold it for the
mud at its bottom. It did not turn his mill, and it was no *privilege*
to him to behold it. I respect not his labors, his farm where every
thing has its price; who would carry the landscape, who would
carry his God, to market, if he could get any thing for him; who

goes to market *for* his god as it is; on whose farm nothing grows
free, whose fields bear no crops, whose meadows no flowers, whose
trees no fruits, but dollars; who loves not the beauty of his fruits,
whose fruits are not ripe for him till they are turned to dollars.
Give me the poverty that enjoys true wealth. Farmers are respectable and interesting to me in proportion as they are poor,—
poor farmers. A model farm! where the house stands like a fungus in a muck-heap, chambers for men, horses, oxen, and swine,
cleansed and uncleansed, all contiguous to one another! Stocked
with men! A great grease-spot, redolent of manures and butter-
milk! Under a high state of cultivation, being manured with the
hearts and brains of men! As if you were to raise your potatoes
in the church-yard! Such is a model farm.

No, no; if the fairest features of the landscape are to be named
after men, let them be the noblest and worthiest men alone. Let
our lakes receive as true names at least as the Icarian Sea,[6] where
"still the shore" a "brave attempt resounds."

Goose Pond, of small extent, is on my way to Flints'; Fair-
Haven, an expansion of Concord River, said to contain some
seventy acres, is a mile south-west; and White Pond, of about
forty acres, is a mile and a half beyond Fair-Haven. This is my
lake country. These, with Concord River, are my water privileges;
and night and day, year in year out, they grind such grist as I
carry to them.

Since the woodcutters, and the railroad, and I myself have
profaned Walden, perhaps the most attractive, if not the most
beautiful, of all our lakes, the gem of the woods, is White Pond;
—a poor name from its commonness, whether derived from the
remarkable purity of its waters or the color of its sands. In these
as in other respects, however, it is a lesser twin of Walden. They
are so much alike that you would say they must be connected
under ground. It has the same stony shore, and its waters are of
the same hue. As at Walden, in sultry dog-day weather, looking
down through the woods on some of its bays which are not so
deep but that the reflection from the bottom tinges them, its
waters are of a misty bluish-green or glaucous color. Many years
since I used to go there to collect the sand by cart-loads, to make
sand-paper with, and I have continued to visit it ever since. One
who frequents it proposes to call it Virid Lake. Perhaps it might
be called Yellow-Pine Lake, from the following circumstance.
About fifteen years ago you could see the top of a pitch-pine, of
the kind called yellow-pine hereabouts, though it is not a distinct
species, projecting above the surface in deep water, many rods

6. The island of Icarus is located in the Ægean sea, east of Greece.

from the shore. It was even supposed by some that the pond had sunk, and this was one of the primitive forest that formerly stood there. I find that even so long ago as 1792, in a "Topographical Description of the Town of Concord," by one of its citizens, in the Collections of the Massachusetts Historical Society, the author, after speaking of Walden and White Ponds, adds: "In the middle of the latter may be seen, when the water is very low, a tree which appears as if it grew in the place where it now stands, although the roots are fifty feet below the surface of the water; the top of this tree is broken off, and at that place measures fourteen inches in diameter." In the spring of '49 I talked with the man who lives nearest the pond in Sudbury, who told me that it was he who got out this tree ten or fifteen years before. As near as he could remember, it stood twelve or fifteen rods from the shore, where the water was thirty or forty feet deep. It was in the winter, and he had been getting out ice in the forenoon, and had resolved that in the afternoon, with the aid of his neighbors, he would take out the old yellow-pine. He sawed a channel in the ice toward the shore, and hauled it over and along and out on to the ice with oxen; but, before he had gone far in his work, he was surprised to find that it was wrong end upward, with the stumps of the branches pointing down, and the small end firmly fastened in the sandy bottom. It was about a foot in diameter at the big end, and he had expected to get a good saw-log, but it was so rotten as to be fit only for fuel, if for that. He had some of it in his shed then. There were marks of an axe and of woodpeckers on the but. He thought that it might have been a dead tree on the shore, but was finally blown over into the pond, and after the top had become water-logged, while the but-end was still dry and light, had drifted out and sunk wrong end up. His father, eighty years old, could not remember when it was not there. Several pretty large logs may still be seen lying on the bottom, where, owing to the undulation of the surface, they look like huge water snakes in motion.

This pond has rarely been profaned by a boat, for there is little in it to tempt a fisherman. Instead of the white lily, which requires mud, or the common sweet flag, the blue flag (*Iris versicolor*) grows thinly in the pure water, rising from the stony bottom all around the shore, where it is visited by humming birds in June, and the color both of its bluish blades and its flowers, and especially their reflections, are in singular harmony with the glaucous water.

White Pond and Walden are great crystals on the surface of the earth, Lakes of Light. If they were permanently congealed, and small enough to be clutched, they would, perchance, be carried off by slaves, like precious stones, to adorn the heads of emperors; but being liquid, and ample, and secured to us and our successors forever, we disregard them, and run after the diamond of Kohinoor.[7] They are too pure to have a market value; they contain no muck. How much more beautiful than our lives, how much more transparent than our characters, are they! We never learned meanness of them. How much fairer than the pool before the farmer's door, in which his ducks swim! Hither the clean wild ducks come. Nature has no human inhabitant who appreciates her. The birds with their plumage and their notes are in harmony with the flowers, but what youth or maiden conspires with the wild luxuriant beauty of Nature? She flourishes most alone, far from the towns where they reside. Talk of heaven! ye disgrace earth.

Baker Farm

Sometimes I rambled to pine groves, standing like temples, or like fleets at sea, full-rigged, with wavy boughs, and rippling with light, so soft and green and shady that the Druids [1] would have forsaken their oaks to worship in them; or to the cedar wood beyond Flints' Pond, where the trees, covered with hoary blue berries, spiring higher and higher, are fit to stand before Valhalla,[2] and the creeping juniper covers the ground with wreaths full of fruit; or to swamps where the usnea lichen hangs in festoons from the black-spruce trees, and toad-stools, round tables of the swamp gods, cover the ground, and more beautiful fungi adorn the stumps, like butterflies or shells, vegetable winkles; where the swamp-pink and dogwood grow, the red alder-berry glows like eyes of imps, the waxwork grooves and crushes the hardest woods in its folds, and the wild-holly berries make the beholder forget his home with their beauty, and he is dazzled and tempted by nameless other wild forbidden fruits, too fair for mortal taste. Instead of calling on some scholar, I paid many a visit to particular trees, of kinds which are rare in this neighborhood, standing far away in the middle of some pasture, or in the depths of a wood or swamp, or on a hill-top; such as the black-birch, of which we have some handsome specimens two feet in diameter; its cousin the yellow-birch, with its loose golden vest, perfumed like the first; the beech, which has so neat a bole and beautifully lichen-painted, perfect in all its details, of which, excepting scattered specimens, I know but one small grove of sizable trees left in the township, supposed by some to have been planted by the

7. A famous diamond from India, weighing 106 carats, now part of the British crown jewels.
1. A priest of an ancient Celtic re-
ligion.
2. In Norse mythology, a great hall in which the souls of dead warriors live.

pigeons that were once baited with beech nuts near by; it is worth the while to see the silver grain sparkle when you split this wood; the bass; the hornbeam; the *celtis occidentalis*, or false elm, of which we have but one well-grown; some taller mast of a pine, a shingle tree, or a more perfect hemlock than usual, standing like a pagoda in the midst of the woods; and many others I could mention. These were the shrines I visited both summer and winter.

Once it chanced that I stood in the very abutment of a rainbow's arch, which filled the lower stratum of the atmosphere, tinging the grass and leaves around, and dazzling me as if I looked through colored crystal. It was a lake of rainbow light, in which, for a short while, I lived like a dolphin. If it had lasted longer it might have tinged my employments and life. As I walked on the railroad causeway, I used to wonder at the halo of light around my shadow, and would fain fancy myself one of the elect. One who visited me declared that the shadows of some Irishmen before him had no halo about them, that it was only natives that were so distinguished. Benvenuto Cellini [3] tells us in his memoirs, that, after a certain terrible dream or vision which he had during his confinement in the castle of St. Angelo, a resplendent light appeared over the shadow of his head at morning and evening, whether he was in Italy or France, and it was particularly conspicuous when the grass was moist with dew. This was probably the same phenomenon to which I have referred, which is especially observed in the morning, but also at other times, and even by moonlight. Though a constant one, it is not commonly noticed, and, in the case of an excitable imagination like Cellini's, it would be basis enough for superstition. Beside, he tells us that he showed it to very few. But are they not indeed distinguished who are conscious that they are regarded at all?

I set out one afternoon to go a-fishing to Fair-Haven, through the woods, to eke out my scanty fare of vegetables. My way led through Pleasant Meadow, an adjunct of the Baker Farm, that retreat of which a poet has since sung, beginning,—[4]

> "Thy entry is a pleasant field,
>   Which some mossy fruit trees yield
>   Partly to a ruddy brook,
>   By gliding musquash undertook,
>   And mercurial trout,
>   Darting about."

I thought of living there before I went to Walden. I "hooked" the

3. Italian sculptor and goldsmith, known for his autobiography.
4. All the poetic excerpts in this chapter are from "Baker Farm" by Ellery Channing.

apples, leaped the brook, and scared the musquash and the trout.
It was one of those afternoons which seem indefinitely long before one, in which many events may happen, a large portion of
our natural life, though it was already half spent when I started.
By the way there came up a shower, which compelled me to stand
half an hour under a pine, piling boughs over my head, and wearing my handkerchief for a shed; and when at length I had made
one cast over the pickerel-weed, standing up to my middle in
water, I found myself suddenly in the shadow of a cloud, and the
thunder began to rumble with such emphasis that I could do no
more than listen to it. The gods must be proud, thought I, with such
forked flashes to rout a poor unarmed fisherman. So I made haste
for shelter to the nearest hut, which stood half a mile from any
road, but so much the nearer to the pond, and had long been
uninhabited:—

> "And here a poet builded,
>   In the completed years,
> For behold a trival cabin
>   That to destruction steers."

So the Muse fables. But therein, as I found, dwelt now John
Field, an Irishman, and his wife, and several children, from the
broad-faced boy who assisted his father at his work, and now
came running by his side from the bog to escape the rain, to the
wrinkled, sibyl-like,[5] cone-headed infant that sat upon its father's
knee as in the palaces of nobles, and looked out from its home in
the midst of wet and hunger inquisitively upon the stranger, with
the privilege of infancy, not knowing but it was the last of a noble
line, and the hope and cynosure of the world, instead of John
Field's poor starveling brat. There we sat together under that part
of the roof which leaked the least, while it showered and thundered
without. I had sat there many times of old before the ship was
built that floated this family to America. An honest, hard-working,
but shiftless man plainly was John Field; and his wife, she too was
brave to cook so many successive dinners in the recesses of that
lofty stove; with round greasy face and bare breast, still thinking
to improve her condition one day; with the never absent mop in
one hand, and yet no effects of it visible any where. The chickens,
which had also taken shelter here from the rain, stalked about
the room like members of the family, too humanized methought
to roast well. They stood and looked in my eye or pecked at my
shoe significantly. Meanwhile my host told me his story, how hard
he worked "bogging" for a neighboring farmer, turning up a
meadow with a spade or bog hoe at the rate of ten dollars an

5. In ancient Greece, a sibyl was a fortune-teller who lived to be very old.

acre and the use of the land with manure for one year, and his little broad-faced son worked cheerfully at his father's side the while, not knowing how poor a bargain the latter had made. I tried to help him with my experience, telling him that he was one of my nearest neighbors, and that I too, who came a-fishing here, and looked like a loafer, was getting my living like himself; that I lived in a tight, light, and clean house, which hardly cost more than the annual rent of such a ruin as his commonly amounts to; and how, if he chose, he might in a month or two build himself a palace of his own; that I did not use tea, nor coffee, nor butter, nor milk, nor fresh meat, and so did not have to work to get them; again, as I did not work hard, I did not have to eat hard, and it cost me but a trifle for my food; but as he began with tea, and coffee, and butter, and milk, and beef, he had to work hard to pay for them, and when he had worked hard he had to eat hard again to repair the waste of his system,—and so it was as broad as it was long, indeed it was broader than it was long, for he was discontented and wasted his life into the bargain; and yet he had rated it as a gain in coming to America, that here you could get tea, and coffee, and meat every day. But the only true America is that country where you are at liberty to pursue such a mode of life as may enable you to do without these, and where the state does not endeavor to compel you to sustain the slavery and war and other superfluous expenses which directly or indirectly result from the use of such things. For I purposely talked to him as if he were a philosopher, or desired to be one. I should be glad if all the meadows on the earth were left in a wild state, if that were the consequence of men's beginning to redeem themselves. A man will not need to study history to find out what is best for his own culture. But alas! the culture of an Irishman is an enterprise to be undertaken with a sort of moral bog hoe. I told him, that as he worked so hard at bogging, he required thick boots and stout clothing, which yet were soon soiled and worn out, but I wore light shoes and thin clothing, which cost not half so much, though he might think that I was dressed like a gentleman, (which, however, was not the case,) and in an hour or two, without labor, but as a recreation, I could, if I wished, catch as many fish as I should want for two days, or earn enough money to support me a week. If he and his family would live simply, they might all go a-huckleberrying in the summer for their amusement. John heaved a sigh at this, and his wife stared with arms a-kimbo, and both appeared to be wondering if they had capital enough to begin such a course with, or arithmetic enough to carry it through. It was sailing by dead reckoning to them, and they saw not clearly how to make their port so; therefore I suppose they still take life bravely, after

their fashion, face to face, giving it tooth and nail, not having skill
to split its massive columns with any fine entering wedge, and rout
it in detail;—thinking to deal with it roughly, as one should
handle a thistle. But they fight at an overwhelming disadvantage,—
living, John Field, alas! without arithmetic, and failing so.

"Do you ever fish?" I asked. "O yes, I catch a mess now and
then when I am lying by; good perch I catch." "What's your bait?"
"I catch shiners with fish-worms, and bait the perch with them."
"You'd better go now, John," said his wife with glistening and
hopeful face; but John demurred.

The shower was now over, and a rainbow above the eastern
woods promised a fair evening; so I took my departure. When I
had got without I asked for a dish, hoping to get a sight of the well
bottom, to complete my survey of the premises; but there, alas!
are shallows and quicksands, and rope broken withal, and bucket
irrecoverable. Meanwhile the right culinary vessel was selected,
water was seemingly distilled, and after consultation and long delay passed out to the thirsty one,—not yet suffered to cool, not
yet to settle. Such gruel sustains life here, I thought; so, shutting
my eyes, and excluding the motes by a skilfully directed under-
current, I drank to genuine hospitality the heartiest draught I
could. I am not squeamish in such cases when manners are
concerned.

As I was leaving the Irishman's roof after the rain, bending my
steps again to the pond, my haste to catch pickerel, wading in
retired meadows, in sloughs and bog-holes, in forlorn and savage
places, appeared for an instant trivial to me who had been sent to
school and college; but as I ran down the hill toward the redden-
ing west, with the rainbow over my shoulder, and some faint
tinkling sounds borne to my ear through the cleansed air, from I
know not what quarter, my Good Genius seemed to say,—Go
fish and hunt far and wide day by day,—farther and wider,—and
rest thee by many brooks and hearth-sides without misgiving.
Remember thy Creator in the days of thy youth. Rise free from
care before the dawn, and seek adventures. Let the noon find
thee by other lakes, and the night overtake thee every where at
home. There are no larger fields than these, no worthier games
than may here be played. Grow wild according to thy nature,
like these sedges and brakes, which will never become English
hay. Let the thunder rumble; what if it threaten ruin to farmers
crops? that is not its errand to thee. Take shelter under the cloud,
while they flee to carts and sheds. Let not to get a living be thy
trade, but thy sport. Enjoy the land, but own it not. Through
want of enterprise and faith men are where they are, buying and
selling, and spending their lives like serfs.

O Baker Farm!

> "Landscape where the richest element
> Is a little sunshine innocent." * *

> "No one runs to revel
> On thy rail-fenced lea." * *

> "Debate with no man hast thou,
>   With questions art never perplexed,
> As tame at the first sight as now,
>   In thy plain russet gabardine dressed." * *

> "Come ye who love,
>   And ye who hate,
> Children of the Holy Dove,
>   And Guy Faux of the state,
> And hang conspiracies
> From the tough rafters of the trees!"

Men come tamely home at night only from the next field or street, where their household echoes haunt, and their life pines because it breathes its own breath over again; their shadows morning and evening reach farther than their daily steps. We should come home from far, from adventures, and perils, and discoveries every day, with new experience and character.

Before I had reached the pond some fresh impulse had brought out John Field, with altered mind, letting go "bogging" ere this sunset. But he, poor man, disturbed only a couple of fins while I was catching a fair string, and he said it was his luck; but when we changed seats in the boat luck changed seats too. Poor John Field!—I trust he does not read this, unless he will improve by it, —thinking to live by some derivative old country mode in this primitive new country,—to catch perch with shiners. It is good bait sometimes, I allow. With his horizon all his own, yet he a poor man, born to be poor, with his inherited Irish poverty or poor life, his Adam's grandmother and boggy ways, not to rise in this world, he nor his posterity, till their wading webbed bog-trotting feet get *talaria* 6 to their heels.

Higher Laws

As I came home through the woods with my string of fish, trailing my pole, it being now quite dark, I caught a glimpse of a woodchuck stealing across my path, and felt a strange thrill of

6. Winged sandals, or wings growing directly from the ankles.

savage delight, and was strongly tempted to seize and devour him raw; not that I was hungry then, except for that wildness which he represented. Once or twice, however, while I lived at the pond, I found myself ranging the woods, like a half-starved hound, with a strange abandonment, seeking some kind of venison which I might devour, and no morsel could have been too savage for me. The wildest scenes had become unaccountably familiar. I found in myself, and still find, an instinct toward a higher, or, as it is named, spiritual life, as do most men, and another toward a primitive rank and savage one, and I reverence them both. I love the wild not less than the good. The wildness and adventure that are in fishing still recommended it to me. I like sometimes to take rank hold on life and spend my day more as the animals do. Perhaps I have owed to this employment and to hunting, when quite young, my closest acquaintance with Nature. They early introduce us to and detain us in scenery with which otherwise, at that age, we should have little acquaintance. Fishermen, hunters, wood-choppers, and others, spending their lives in the fields and woods, in a peculiar sense a part of Nature themselves, are often in a more favorable mood for observing her, in the intervals of their pursuits, than philosophers or poets even, who approach her with expectation. She is not afraid to exhibit herself to them. The traveller on the prairie is naturally a hunter, on the head waters of the Missouri and Columbia a trapper, and at the Falls of St. Mary [1] a fisherman. He who is only a traveller learns things at second-hand and by the halves, and is poor authority. We are most interested when science reports what those men already know practically or instinctively, for that alone is a true *humanity*, or account of human experience.

They mistake who assert that the Yankee has few amusements, because he has not so many public holidays, and men and boys do not play so many games as they do in England, for here the more primitive but solitary amusements of hunting fishing and the like have not yet given place to the former. Almost every New England boy among my contemporaries shouldered a fowling piece between the ages of ten and fourteen; and his hunting and fishing grounds were not limited like the preserves of an English nobleman, but were more boundless even than those of a savage. No wonder, then, that he did not oftener stay to play on the common. But already a change is taking place, owing, not to an increased humanity, but to an increased scarcity of game, for perhaps the hunter is the greatest friend of the animals hunted, not

1. St. Marys River forms part of the boundary between Michigan and Ontario; the Sault Sainte Marie Canals now permit ships to circumvent the falls and the rapids.

excepting the Humane Society.

Moreover, when at the pond, I wished sometimes to add fish to my fare for variety. I have actually fished from the same kind of necessity that the first fishers did. Whatever humanity I might conjure up against it was all factitious, and concerned my philosophy more than my feelings. I speak of fishing only now, for I had long felt differently about fowling, and sold my gun before I went to the woods. Not that I am less humane than others, but I did not perceive that my feelings were much affected. I did not pity the fishes nor the worms. This was habit. As for fowling, during the last years that I carried a gun my excuse was that I was studying ornithology, and sought only new or rare birds. But I confess that I am now inclined to think that there is a finer way of studying ornithology than this. It requires so much closer attention to the habits of the birds, that, if for that reason only, I have been willing to omit the gun. Yet notwithstanding the objection on the score of humanity, I am compelled to doubt if equally valuable sports are ever substituted for these; and when some of my friends have asked me anxiously about their boys, whether they should let them hunt, I have answered, yes,—remembering that it was one of the best parts of my education,—*make* them hunters, though sportsmen only at first, if possible, mighty hunters at last, so that they shall not find game large enough for them in this or any vegetable wilderness,—hunters as well as fishers of men. Thus far I am of the opinion of Chaucer's nun,[2] who

> "yave not of the text a pulled hen
> That saith that hunters ben not holy men."

There is a period in the history of the individual, as of the race, when the hunters are the "best men," as the Algonquins [3] called them. We cannot but pity the boy who has never fired a gun; he is no more humane, while his education has been sadly neglected. This was my answer with respect to those youths who were bent on this pursuit, trusting that they would soon outgrow it. No humane being, past the thoughtless age of boyhood, will wantonly murder any creature, which holds its life by the same tenure that he does. The hare in its extremity cries like a child. I warn you, mothers, that my sympathies do not always make the usual phil-*anthropic* distinctions.

Such is oftenest the young man's introduction to the forest, and the most original part of himself. He goes thither at first as a hunter and fisher, until at last, if he has the seeds of a better life

2. A character in the *Canterbury Tales* by Geoffrey Chaucer (1340?–1400); the line describes the Monk, however, and not the Nun.

3. A tribe of Indians formerly inhabiting the area north of the St. Lawrence River in Canada.

in him, he distinguishes his proper objects, as a poet or naturalist it may be, and leaves the gun and fish-pole behind. The mass of men are still and always young in this respect. In some countries a hunting parson is no uncommon sight. Such a one might make a good shepherd's dog, but is far from being the Good Shepherd. I have been surprised to consider that the only obvious employment, except wood-chopping, ice-cutting, or the like business, which ever to my knowledge detained at Walden Pond for a whole half day any of my fellow-citizens, whether fathers or children of the town, with just one exception, was fishing. Commonly they did not think that they were lucky, or well paid for their time, unless they got a long string of fish, though they had the opportunity of seeing the pond all the while. They might go there a thousand times before the sediment of fishing would sink to the bottom and leave their purpose pure; but no doubt such a clarifying process would be going on all the while. The governor and his council faintly remember the pond, for they went a-fishing there when they were boys; but now they are too old and dignified to go a-fishing, and so they know it no more forever. Yet even they expect to go to heaven at last. If the legislature regards it, it is chiefly to regulate the number of hooks to be used there; but they know nothing about the hook of hooks with which to angle for the pond itself, impaling the legislature for a bait. Thus, even in civilized communities, the embryo man passes through the hunter stage of development.

I have found repeatedly, of late years, that I cannot fish without falling a little in self-respect. I have tried it again and again. I have skill at it, and, like many of my fellows, a certain instinct for it, which revives from time to time, but always when I have done I feel that it would have been better if I had not fished. I think that I do not mistake. It is a faint intimation, yet so are the first streaks of morning. There is unquestionably this instinct in me which belongs to the lower orders of creation; yet with every year I am less a fisherman, though without more humanity or even wisdom; at present I am no fisherman at all. But I see that if I were to live in a wilderness I should again be tempted to become a fisher and hunter in earnest. Beside, there is something essentially unclean about this diet and all flesh, and I began to see where housework commences, and whence the endeavor, which costs so much, to wear a tidy and respectable appearance each day, to keep the house sweet and free from all ill odors and sights. Having been my own butcher and scullion and cook, as well as the gentleman for whom the dishes were served up, I can speak from an unusually complete experience. The practical objection to animal food in my case was its uncleanness; and, besides, when I had caught and cleaned and cooked and eaten my fish, they seemed not to have fed me essentially. It was insignificant and unnecessary, and cost more than it came to. A little bread or a few potatoes would have done as well, with less trouble and filth. Like many of my contemporaries, I had rarely for many years used animal food, or tea, or coffee, &c.; not so much because of any ill effects which I had traced to them, as because they were not agreeable to my imagination. The repugnance to animal food is not the effect of experience, but is an instinct. It appeared more beautiful to live low and fare hard in many respects; and though I never did so, I went far enough to please my imagination. I believe that every man who has ever been earnest to preserve his higher or poetic faculties in the best condition has been particularly inclined to abstain from animal food, and from much food of any kind. It is a significant fact, stated by entomologists, I find it in Kirby and Spence,[4] that "some insects in their perfect state, though furnished with organs of feeding, make no use of them;" and they lay it down as "a general rule, that almost all insects in this state eat much less than in that of larvæ. The voracious caterpillar when transformed into a butterfly," . . "and the gluttonous maggot when become a fly," content themselves with a drop or two of honey or some other sweet liquid. The abdomen under the wings of the butterfly still represents the larva. This is the tid-bit which tempts his insectivorous fate. The gross feeder is a man in the larva state; and there are whole nations in that condition, nations without fancy or imagination, whose vast abdomens betray them.

It is hard to provide and cook so simple and clean a diet as will not offend the imagination; but this, I think, is to be fed when we feed the body; they should both sit down at the same table. Yet perhaps this may be done. The fruits eaten temperately need not make us ashamed of our appetites, nor interrupt the worthiest pursuits. But put an extra condiment into your dish, and it will poison you. It is not worth the while to live by rich cookery. Most men would feel shame if caught preparing with their own hands precisely such a dinner, whether of animal or vegetable food, as is every day prepared for them by others. Yet till this is otherwise we are not civilized, and, if gentlemen and ladies, are not true men and women. This certainly suggests what change is to be made. It may be vain to ask why the imagination will not be reconciled to flesh and fat. I am satisfied that it is not. Is it not a reproach that man is a carniverous animal? True, he can and does live, in a great measure, by preying on other animals; but this is a miserable way,—as any one who will go to snaring rabbits, or

4. William Kirby and William Spence, *An Introduction to Entomology*, origin- ally published in London, later re- printed in Philadelphia (1846).

slaughtering lambs, may learn,—and he will be regarded as a benefactor of his race who shall teach man to confine himself to a
more innocent and wholesome diet. Whatever my own practice
may be, I have no doubt that it is a part of the destiny of the
human race, in its gradual improvement, to leave off eating animals, as surely as the savage tribes have left off eating each other
when they came in contact with the more civilized.

If one listens to the faintest but constant suggestions of his
genius, which are certainly true, he sees not to what extremes, or
even insanity, it may lead him; and yet that way, as he grows
more resolute and faithful, his road lies. The faintest assured
objection which one healthy man feels will at length prevail over
the arguments and customs of mankind. No man ever followed his
genius till it misled him. Though the result were bodily weakness,
yet perhaps no one can say that the consequences were to be regretted, for these were a life in conformity to higher principles.
If the day and the night are such that you greet them with joy,
and life emits a fragrance like flowers and sweet-scented herbs,
is more elastic, more starry, more immortal,—that is your success.
All nature is your congratulation, and you have cause momentarily
to bless yourself. The greatest gains and values are farthest from
being appreciated. We easily come to doubt if they exist. We soon
forget them. They are the highest reality. Perhaps the facts most
astounding and most real are never communicated by man to man.
The true harvest of my daily life is somewhat as intangible and
indescribable as the tints of morning or evening. It is a little star-
dust caught, a segment of the rainbow which I have clutched.

Yet, for my part, I was never unusually squeamish; I could
sometimes eat a fried rat with a good relish, if it were necessary.
I am glad to have drunk water so long, for the same reason that
I prefer the natural sky to an opium-eater's heaven. I would fain
keep sober always; and there are infinite degrees of drunkenness.
I believe that water is the only drink for a wise man; wine is not
so noble a liquor; and think of dashing the hopes of a morning with
a cup of warm coffee, or of an evening with a dish of tea! Ah, how
low I fall when I am tempted by them! Even music may be intoxi-
cating. Such apparently slight causes destroyed Greece and Rome,
and will destroy England and America. Of all ebriosity, who does
not prefer to be intoxicated by the air he breathes? I have found
it to be the most serious objection to coarse labors long continued,
that they compelled me to eat and drink coarsely also. But to tell
the truth, I find myself at present somewhat less particular in
these respects. I carry less religion to the table, ask no blessing;
not because I am wiser than I was, but, I am obliged to confess,
because, however much it is to be regretted, with years I have

grown more coarse and indifferent. Perhaps these questions are entertained only in youth, as most believe of poetry. My practice is "nowhere," my opinion is here. Nevertheless I am far from regarding myself as one of those privileged ones to whom the Ved[5] refers when it says, that "he who has true faith in the Omnipresent Supreme Being may eat all that exists," that is, is not bound to inquire what is his food, or who prepares it; and even in their case it is to be observed, as a Hindoo commentator has remarked, that the Vedant limits this privilege to "the time of distress."

Who has not sometimes derived an inexpressible satisfaction from his food in which appetite had no share? I have been thrilled to think that I owed a mental perception to the commonly gross sense of taste, that I have been inspired through the palate, that some berries which I had eaten on a hill-side had fed my genius. "The soul not being mistress of herself," says Thseng-tseu,[6] "one looks, and one does not see; one listens, and one does not hear; one eats, and one does not know the savor of food." He who distinguishes the true savor of his food can never be a glutton; he who does not cannot be otherwise. A puritan may go to his brown-bread crust with as gross an appetite as ever an alderman to his turtle. Not that food which entereth into the mouth defileth a man, but the appetite with which it is eaten. It is neither the quality nor the quantity, but the devotion to sensual savors; when that which is eaten is not a viand to sustain our animal, or inspire our spiritual life, but food for the worms that possess us. If the hunter has a taste for mud-turtles, muskrats, and other such savage tid-bits, the fine lady indulges a taste for jelly made of a calf's foot, or for sardines from over the sea, and they are even. He goes to the mill-pond, she to her preserve-pot. The wonder is how they, how you and I, can live this slimy beastly life, eating and drinking.

Our whole life is startlingly moral. There is never an instant's truce between virtue and vice. Goodness is the only investment that never fails. In the music of the harp which trembles round the world it is the insisting on this which thrills us. The harp is the travelling patterer for the Universe's Insurance Company, recommending its laws, and our little goodness is all the assessment that we pay. Though the youth at last grows indifferent, the laws of the universe are not indifferent, but are forever on the side of the most sensitive. Listen to every zephyr for some reproof, for it is surely there, and he is unfortunate who does not hear it. We cannot touch a string or move a stop but the charming moral transfixes us. Many an irksome noise, go a long way off, is heard as music,

5. More commonly, "Veda."   6. Confucius.

a proud sweet satire on the meanness of our lives.

We are conscious of an animal in us, which awakens in proportion as our higher nature slumbers. It is reptile and sensual, and perhaps cannot be wholly expelled; like the worms which, even in life and health, occupy our bodies. Possibly we may withdraw from it, but never change its nature. I fear that it may enjoy a certain health of its own; that we may be well, yet not pure. The other day I picked up the lower jaw of a hog, with white and sound teeth and tusks, which suggested that there was an animal health and vigor distinct from the spiritual. This creature succeeded by other means than temperance and purity. "That in which men differ from brute beasts," says Mencius,[7] "is a thing very inconsiderable; the common herd lose it very soon; superior men preserve it carefully." Who knows what sort of life would result if we had attained to purity? If I knew so wise a man as could teach me purity I would go to seek him forthwith. "A command over our passions, and over the external senses of the body, and good acts, are declared by the Ved to be indispensable in the mind's approximation to God." Yet the spirit can for the time pervade and control every member and function of the body, and transmute what in form is the grossest sensuality into purity and devotion. The generative energy, which, when we are loose, dissipates and makes us unclean, when we are continent invigorates and inspires us. Chastity is the flowering of man; and what are called Genius, Heroism, Holiness, and the like, are but various fruits which succeed it. Man flows at once to God when the channel of purity is open. By turns our purity inspires and our impurity casts us down. He is blessed who is assured that the animal is dying out in him day by day, and the divine being established. Perhaps there is none but has cause for shame on account of the inferior and brutish nature to which he is allied. I fear that we are such gods or demigods only as fauns and satyrs, the divine allied to beasts, the creatures of appetite, and that, to some extent, our very life is our disgrace.—

> "How happy's he who hath due place assigned
> To his beasts and disaforested his mind!
>
>   *   *   *   *   *
>
> Can use his horse, goat, wolf, and ev'ry beast,
> And is not ass himself to all the rest!
> Else man not only is the herd of swine,
> But he's those devils too which did incline
> Them to a headlong rage, and made them worse."[8]

---

7. Latinized name of Meng-tse, Chinese philosopher (d. 289? B.C.).

8. "To Sir Edward Herbert," by John Donne (1573–1631).

All sensuality is one, though it takes many forms; all purity is one. It is the same whether a man eat, or drink, or cohabit, or sleep sensually. They are but one appetite, and we only need to see a person do any one of these things to know how great a sensualist he is. The impure can neither stand nor sit with purity. When the reptile is attacked at one mouth of his burrow, he shows himself at another. If you would be chaste, you must be temperate. What is chastity? How shall a man know if he is chaste? He shall not know it. We have heard of this virtue, but we know not what it is. We speak conformably to the rumor which we have heard. From exertion come wisdom and purity; from sloth ignorance and sensuality. In the student sensuality is a sluggish habit of mind. An unclean person is universally a slothful one, one who sits by a stove, whom the sun shines on prostrate, who reposes without being fatigued. If you would avoid uncleanness, and all the sins, work earnestly, though it be at cleaning a stable. Nature is hard to be overcome, but she must be overcome. What avails it that you are Christian, if you are not purer than the heathen, if you deny yourself no more, if you are not more religious? I know of many systems of religion esteemed heathenish whose precepts fill the reader with shame, and provoke him to new endeavors, though it be to the performance of rites merely.

I hesitate to say these things, but it is not because of the subject,— I care not how obscene my *words* are,—but because I cannot speak of them without betraying my impurity. We discourse freely without shame of one form of sensuality, and are silent about another. We are so degraded that we cannot speak simply of the necessary functions of human nature. In earlier ages, in some countries, every function was reverently spoken of and regulated by law. Nothing was too trivial for the Hindoo lawgiver, however offensive it may be to modern taste. He teaches how to eat, drink, cohabit, void excrement and urine, and the like, elevating what is mean, and does not falsely excuse himself by calling these things trifles.

Every man is the builder of a temple, called his body, to the god he worships, after a style purely his own, nor can he get off by hammering marble instead. We are all sculptors and painters, and our material is our own flesh and blood and bones. Any nobleness begins at once to refine a man's features, any meanness or sensuality to imbrute them.

John Farmer sat at his door one September evening, after a hard day's work, his mind still running on his labor more or less. Having bathed he sat down to recreate his intellectual man. It was a rather cool evening, and some of his neighbors were apprehending a frost. He had not attended to the train of his thoughts long when he heard some one playing on a flute, and that sound harmonized with his mood. Still he thought of his work; but the burden of his thought was, that though this kept running in his head, and he found himself planning and contriving it against his will, yet it concerned him very little. It was no more than the scurf of his skin, which was constantly shuffled off. But the notes of the flute came home to his ears out of a different sphere from that he worked in, and suggested work for certain faculties which slumbered in him. They gently did away with the street, and the village, and the state in which he lived. A voice said to him,—Why do you stay here and live this mean moiling life, when a glorious existence is possible for you? Those same stars twinkle over other fields than these.—But how to come out of this condition and actually migrate thither? All that he could think of was to practise some new austerity, to let his mind descend into his body and redeem it, and treat himself with ever increasing respect.

Brute Neighbors

Sometimes I had a companion in my fishing,[1] who came through the village to my house from the other side of the town, and the catching of the dinner was as much a social exercise as the eating of it.

Hermit. I wonder what the world is doing now. I have not heard so much as a locust over the sweet-fern these three hours. The pigeons are all asleep upon their roosts,—no flutter from them. Was that a farmer's noon horn which sounded from beyond the woods just now? The hands are coming in to boiled salt beef and cider and Indian bread. Why will men worry themselves so? He that does not eat need not work. I wonder how much they have reaped. Who would live there where a body can never think for the barking of Bose?[2] And O, the housekeeping! to keep bright the devil's door-knobs, and scour his tubs this bright day! Better not keep a house. Say, some hollow tree; and then for morning calls and dinner-parties! Only a wood-pecker tapping. O, they swarm; the sun is too warm there; they are born too far into life for me. I have water from the spring, and a loaf of brown bread on the shelf.—Hark! I hear a rustling of the leaves. Is it some ill-fed village hound yielding to the instinct of the chase? or the lost pig which is said to be in these woods, whose tracks I saw after the rain? It comes on apace; my sumachs and sweet-briers tremble.—Eh, Mr. Poet, is it you? How do you like the world to-day?

1. The companion, and the poet of the following dialogue, was Ellery Channing.

2. In Thoreau's time, a generic name for any dog.

Poet. See those clouds; how they hang! That's the greatest thing I have seen to-day. There's nothing like it in old paintings, nothing like it in foreign lands,—unless when we were off the coast of Spain. That's a true Mediterranean sky. I thought, as I have my living to get, and have not eaten to-day, that I might go a-fishing. That's the true industry for poets. It is the only trade I have learned. Come, let's along.

Hermit. I cannot resist. My brown bread will soon be gone. I will go with you gladly soon, but I am just concluding a serious meditation. I think that I am near the end of it. Leave me alone, then, for a while. But that we may not be delayed, you shall be digging the bait meanwhile. Angle-worms are rarely to be met with in these parts, where the soil was never fattened with manure; the race is nearly extinct. The sport of digging the bait is nearly equal to that of catching the fish, when one's appetite is not too keen; and this you may have all to yourself to-day. I would advise you to set in the spade down yonder among the ground-nuts, where you see the johnswort waving. I think that I may warrant you one worm to every three sods you turn up, if you look well in among the roots of the grass, as if you were weeding. Or, if you choose to go farther, it will not be unwise, for I have found the increase of fair bait to be very nearly as the squares of the distances.

Hermit alone. Let me see; where was I? Methinks I was nearly in this frame of mind; the world lay about at this angle. Shall I go to heaven or a-fishing? If I should soon bring this meditation to an end, would another so sweet occasion be likely to offer? I was as near being resolved into the essence of things as ever I was in my life. I fear my thoughts will not come back to me. If it would do any good, I would whistle for them. When they make us an offer, is it wise to say, We will think of it? My thoughts have left no track, and I cannot find the path again. What was it that I was thinking of? It was a very hazy day. I will just try these three sentences of Con-fut-see;[3] they may fetch that state about again. I know not whether it was the dumps or a budding ecstasy. Mem.[4] There never is but one opportunity of a kind.

Poet. How now, Hermit, is it too soon? I have got just thirteen whole ones, beside several which are imperfect or under-sized; but they will do for the smaller fry; they do not cover up the hook so much. Those village worms are quite too large; a shiner may make a meal off one without finding the skewer.

Hermit. Well, then, let's be off. Shall we to the Concord? There's good sport there if the water be not too high.

3. Confucius.   4. Memorandum.

Why do precisely these objects which we behold make a world? Why has man just these species of animals for his neighbors; as if nothing but a mouse could have filled this crevice? I suspect that Pilpay & Co.[5] have put animals to their best use, for they are all beasts of burden, in a sense, made to carry some portion of our thoughts.

The mice which haunted my house were not the common ones, which are said to have been introduced into the country, but a wild native kind (*mus leucopus*) not found in the village. I sent one to a distinguished naturalist, and it interested him much. When I was building, one of these had its nest underneath the house, and before I had laid the second floor, and swept out the shavings, would come out regularly at lunch time and pick up the crums at my feet. It probably had never seen a man before; and it soon became quite familiar, and would run over my shoes and up my clothes. It could readily ascend the sides of the room by short impulses, like a squirrel, which it resembled in its motions. At length, as I leaned with my elbow on the bench one day, it ran up my clothes, and along my sleeve, and round and round the paper which held my dinner, while I kept the latter close, and dodged and played at bo-peep with it; and when at last I held still a piece of cheese between my thumb and finger, it came and nibbled it, sitting in my hand, and afterward cleaned its face and paws, like a fly, and walked away.

A phœbe soon built in my shed, and a robin for protection in a pine which grew against the house. In June the partridge, (*Tetrao umbellus*,) which is so shy a bird, led her brood past my windows, from the woods in the rear to the front of my house, clucking and calling to them like a hen, and in all her behavior proving herself the hen of the woods. The young suddenly disperse on your approach, at a signal from the mother, as if a whirlwind had swept them away, and they so exactly resemble the dried leaves and twigs that many a traveller has placed his foot in the midst of a brood, and heard the whir of the old bird as she flew off, and her anxious calls and mewing, or seen her trail her wings to attract his attention, without suspecting their neighborhood. The parent will sometimes roll and spin round before you in such a dishabille, that you cannot, for a few moments, detect what kind of creature it is. The young squat still and flat, often running their heads under a leaf, and mind only their mother's directions given from a distance, nor will your approach make them run again and betray themselves. You may even tread on them, or have your eyes on them for a minute, without dis-

5. Pilpay, sometimes spelled "Bidpai," was a collector of ancient Sanskrit fables.

covering them. I have held them in my open hand at such a time, and still their only care, obedient to their mother and their instinct, was to squat there without fear or trembling. So perfect is this instinct, that once, when I had laid them on the leaves again, and one accidentally fell on its side, it was found with the rest in exactly the same position ten minutes afterward. They are not callow like the young of most birds, but more perfectly developed and precocious even than chickens. The remarkably adult yet innocent expression of their open and serene eyes is very memorable. All intelligence seems reflected in them. They suggest not merely the purity of infancy, but a wisdom clarified by experience. Such an eye was not born when the bird was, but is coeval with the sky it reflects. The woods do not yield another such a gem. The traveller does not often look into such a limpid well. The ignorant or reckless sportsman often shoots the parent at such a time, and leaves these innocents to fall a prey to some prowling beast or bird, or gradually mingle with the decaying leaves which they so much resemble. It is said that when hatched by a hen they will directly disperse on some alarm, and so are lost, for they never hear the mother's call which gathers them again. These were my hens and chickens.

It is remarkable how many creatures live wild and free though secret in the woods, and still sustain themselves in the neighborhood of towns, suspected by hunters only. How retired the otter manages to live here! He grows to be four feet long, as big as a small boy, perhaps without any human being getting a glimpse of him. I formerly saw the raccoon in the woods behind where my house is built, and probably still heard their whinnering at night. Commonly I rested an hour or two in the shade at noon, after planting, and ate my lunch, and read a little by a spring which was the source of a swamp and of a brook, oozing from under Brister's Hill, half a mile from my field. The approach to this was through a succession of descending grassy hollows, full of young pitch-pines, into a larger wood about the swamp. There, in a very secluded and shaded spot, under a spreading white-pine, there was yet a clean firm sward to sit on. I had dug out the spring and made a well of clear gray water, where I could dip up a pailful without roiling it, and thither I went for this purpose almost every day in midsummer, when the pond was warmest. Thither too the wood-cock led her brood, to probe the mud for worms, flying but a foot above them down the bank, while they ran in a troop beneath; but at last, spying me, she would leave her young and circle round and round me, nearer and nearer till within four or five feet, pretending broken wings and legs, to attract my attention, and get off her young, who would already have taken up their march, with faint wiry peep, single file through the swamp, as she directed. Or I heard the peep of the young when I could not see the parent bird. There too the turtle-doves sat over the spring, or fluttered from bough to bough of the soft white-pines over my head; or the red squirrel, coursing down the nearest bough, was particularly familiar and inquisitive. You only need sit still long enough in some attractive spot in the woods that all its inhabitants may exhibit themselves to you by turns.

I was witness to events of a less peaceful character. One day when I went out to my wood-pile, or rather my pile of stumps, I observed two large ants, the one red, the other much larger, nearly half an inch long, and black, fiercely contending with one another. Having once got hold they never let go, but struggled and wrestled and rolled on the chips incessantly. Looking farther, I was surprised to find that the chips were covered with such combatants, that it was not a *duellum*, but a *bellum*,[6] a war between two races of ants, the red always pitted against the black, and frequently two red ones to one black. The legions of these Myrmidons [7] covered all the hills and vales in my wood-yard, and the ground was already strewn with the dead and dying, both red and black. It was the only battle which I have ever witnessed, the only battle-field I ever trod while the battle was raging; internecine war; the red republicans on the one hand, and the black imperialists on the other. On every side they were engaged in deadly combat, yet without any noise that I could hear, and human soldiers never fought so resolutely. I watched a couple that were fast locked in each other's embraces, in a little sunny valley amid the chips, now at noon-day prepared to fight till the sun went down, or life went out. The smaller red champion had fastened himself like a vice to his adversary's front, and through all the tumblings on that field never for an instant ceased to gnaw at one of his feelers near the root, having already caused the other to go by the board; while the stronger black one dashed him from side to side, and, as I saw on looking nearer, had already divested him of several of his members. They fought with more pertinacity than bull-dogs. Neither manifested the least disposition to retreat. It was evident that their battle-cry was Conquer or die. In the mean while there came along a single red ant on the hill-side of this valley, evidently full of excitement, who either had despatched his foe, or had not yet taken part in the battle; probably the latter, for he had lost none of his limbs; whose mother

6. Not a duel, "a combat between two," but a war.
7. In Greek legend, a warlike people who fought with Achilles in the Trojan War.

had charged him to return with his shield or upon it. Or perchance he was some Achilles, who had nourished his wrath apart, and had now come to avenge or rescue his Patroclus. He saw this unequal combat from afar,—for the blacks were nearly twice the size of the red,—he drew near with rapid pace till he stood on his guard within half an inch of the combatants; then, watching his opportunity, he sprang upon the black warrior, and commenced his operations near the root of his right fore-leg, leaving the foe to select among his own members; and so there were three united for life, as if a new kind of attraction had been invented which put all other locks and cements to shame. I should not have wondered by this time to find that they had their respective musical bands stationed on some eminent chip, and playing their national airs the while, to excite the slow and cheer the dying combatants. I was myself excited somewhat even as if they had been men. The more you think of it, the less the difference. And certainly there is not the fight recorded in Concord history, at least, if in the history of America, that will bear a moment's comparison with this, whether for the numbers engaged in it, or for the patriotism and heroism displayed. For numbers and for carnage it was an Austerlitz or Dresden.[8] Concord Fight! [9] Two killed on the patriots' side, and Luther Blanchard wounded! Why here every ant was a Buttrick,—"Fire! for God's sake fire!"—and thousands shared the fate of Davis and Hosmer. There was not one hireling there. I have no doubt that it was a principle they fought for, as much as our ancestors, and not to avoid a three-penny tax on their tea; and the results of this battle will be as important and memorable to those whom it concerns as those of the battle of Bunker Hill, at least.

I took up the chip on which the three I have particularly described were struggling, carried it into my house, and placed it under a tumbler on my window-sill, in order to see the issue. Holding a microscope to the first-mentioned red ant, I saw that, though he was assiduously gnawing at the near fore-leg of his enemy, having severed his remaining feeler, his own breast was all torn away, exposing what vitals he had there to the jaws of the black warrior, whose breast-plate was apparently too thick for him to pierce; and the dark carbuncles of the sufferer's eyes shone with ferocity such as war only could excite. They struggled half an hour longer under the tumbler, and when I looked again the black soldier had severed the heads of his foes from their bodies, and the still living heads were hanging on either side of him like ghastly trophies

8. Two battles fought by Napoleon.
9. The first major battle of the American Revolution. The five hundred "minutemen" were under the command of Major John Buttrick; Isaac Davis and David Hosmer were the only two Americans killed.

at his saddle-bow, still apparently as firmly fastened as ever, and he was endeavoring with feeble struggles, being without feelers and with only the remnant of a leg, and I know not how many other wounds, to divest himself of them; which at length, after half an hour more, he accomplished. I raised the glass, and he went off over the window-sill in that crippled state. Whether he finally survived that combat, and spent the remainder of his days in some Hotel des Invalides,[1] I do not know; but I thought that his industry would not be worth much thereafter. I never learned which party was victorious, nor the cause of the war; but I felt for the rest of that day as if I had had my feelings excited and harrowed by witnessing the struggle, the ferocity and carnage, of a human battle before my door.

Kirby and Spence tell us that the battles of ants have long been celebrated and the date of them recorded, though they say that Huber [2] is the only modern author who appears to have witnessed them. "Æneas Sylvius," [3] say they, "after giving a very circumstantial account of one contested with great obstinacy by a great and small species on the trunk of a pear tree," adds that " 'This action was fought in the pontificate of Eugenius the Fourth,[4] in the presence of Nicholas Pistoriensis, an eminent lawyer, who related the whole history of the battle with the greatest fidelity.' A similar engagement between great and small ants is recorded by Olaus Magnus,[5] in which the small ones, being victorious, are said to have buried the bodies of their own soldiers, but left those of their giant enemies a prey to the birds. This event happened previous to the expulsion of the tyrant Christiern the Second from Sweden." The battle which I witnessed took place in the Presidency of Polk,[6] five years before the passage of Webster's Fugitive-Slave Bill.

Many a village Bose, fit only to course a mud-turtle in a victualling cellar, sported his heavy quarters in the woods, without the knowledge of his master, and ineffectually smelled at old fox burrows and woodchucks' holes; led perchance by some slight cur which nimbly threaded the wood, and might still inspire a natural terror in its denizens;—now far behind his guide, barking like a canine bull toward some small squirrel which had treed itself for scrutiny, then, cantering off, bending the bushes with his weight, imagining that he is on the track of some stray member of the jerbilla family. Once I was surprised to see a cat walking along the

---

1. A veterans' hospital in Paris.
2. Francois Huber (1750–1831), a blind Swiss entomologist.
3. The pen name of Pope Pius II (1405–1464), poet and historian.
4. Pope from 1431 to 1437.
5. Swedish historian (1490–1558).

6. James K. Polk (1795–1849), president from 1845 to 1849. Daniel Webster (1782–1852), senator from Massachusetts; he did not introduce the Fugitive Slave Bill, but he assisted in its passage.

stony shore of the pond, for they rarely wander so far from home. The surprise was mutual. Nevertheless the most domestic cat, which has lain on a rug all her days, appears quite at home in the woods, and, by her sly and stealthy behavior, proves herself more native there than the regular inhabitants. Once, when berrying, I met with a cat with young kittens in the woods, quite wild, and they all, like their mother, had their backs up and were fiercely spitting at me. A few years before I lived in the woods there was what was called a "winged cat" in one of the farm-houses in Lincoln nearest the pond, Mr. Gilian Baker's. When I called to see her in June, 1842, she was gone a-hunting in the woods, as was her wont, (I am not sure whether it was a male or female, and so use the more common pronoun,) but her mistress told me that she came into the neighborhood a little more than a year before, in April, and was finally taken into their house; that she was of a dark brownish-gray color, with a white spot on her throat, and white feet, and had a large bushy tail like a fox; that in the winter the fur grew thick and flatted out along her sides, forming strips ten or twelve inches long by two and a half wide, and under her chin like a muff, the upper side loose, the under matted like felt, and in the spring these appendages dropped off. They gave me a pair of her "wings," which I keep still. There is no appearance of a membrane about them. Some thought it was part flying-squirrel or some other wild animal, which is not impossible, for, according to naturalists, prolific hybrids have been produced by the union of the marten and domestic cat. This would have been the right kind of cat for me to keep, if I had kept any; for why should not a poet's cat be winged as well as his horse?

In the fall the loon (*Colymbus glacialis*) came, as usual, to moult and bathe in the pond, making the woods ring with his wild laughter before I had risen. At rumor of his arrival all the Mill-dam sportsmen are on the alert, in gigs and on foot, two by two and three by three, with patent rifles and conical balls and spy-glasses. They come rustling through the woods like autumn leaves, at least ten men to one loon. Some station themselves on this side of the pond, some on that, for the poor bird cannot be omnipresent; if he dive here he must come up there. But now the kind October wind rises, rustling the leaves and rippling the surface of the water, so that no loon can be heard or seen, though his foes sweep the pond with spy-glasses, and make the woods resound with their discharges. The waves generously rise and dash angrily, taking sides with all waterfowl, and our sportsmen must beat a retreat to town and shop and unfinished jobs. But they were too often successful. When I went to get a pail of water

early in the morning I frequently saw this stately bird sailing out
of my cove within a few rods. If I endeavored to overtake him
in a boat, in order to see how he would manœuvre, he would dive
and be completely lost, so that I did not discover him again,
sometimes, till the latter part of the day. But I was more than a
match for him on the surface. He commonly went off in a rain.

As I was paddling along the north shore one very calm October
afternoon, for such days especially they settle on to the lakes, like
the milkweed down, having looked in vain over the pond for a
loon, suddenly one, sailing out from the shore toward the middle
a few rods in front of me, set up his wild laugh and betrayed
himself. I pursued with a paddle and he dived, but when he came
up I was nearer than before. He dived again, but I miscalculated
the direction he would take, and we were fifty rods apart when
he came to the surface this time, for I had helped to widen the
interval; and again he laughed long and loud, and with more
reason than before. He manœuvred so cunningly that I could not
get within half a dozen rods of him. Each time, when he came
to the surface, turning his head this way and that, he coolly
surveyed the water and the land, and apparently chose his course
so that he might come up where there was the widest expanse
of water and at the greatest distance from the boat. It was surprising how quickly he made up his mind and put his resolve into
execution. He led me at once to the widest part of the pond, and
could not be driven from it. While he was thinking one thing in
his brain, I was endeavoring to divine his thought in mine. It was a
pretty game, played on the smooth surface of the pond, a man
against a loon. Suddenly your adversary's checker disappears beneath
the board, and the problem is to place yours nearest to where his
will appear again. Sometimes he would come up unexpectedly on
the opposite side of me, having apparently passed directly under
the boat. So long-winded was he and so unweariable, that when he
had swum farthest he would immediately plunge again, nevertheless; and then no wit could divine where in the deep pond,
beneath the smooth surface, he might be speeding his way like a
fish, for he had time and ability to visit the bottom of the pond
in its deepest part. It is said that loons have been caught in
the New York lakes eighty feet beneath the surface, with hooks
set for trout,—though Walden is deeper than that. How surprised must the fishes be to see this ungainly visitor from
another sphere speeding his way amid their schools! Yet he appeared to know his course as surely under water as on the
surface, and swam much faster there. Once or twice I saw a ripple
where he approached the surface, just put his head out to recon-

noitre, and instantly dived again. I found that it was as well for me to rest on my oars and wait his reappearing as to endeavor to calculate where he would rise; for again and again, when I was straining my eyes over the surface one way, I would suddenly be startled by his unearthly laugh behind me. But why, after displaying so much cunning, did he invariably betray himself the moment he came up by that loud laugh? Did not his white breast enough betray him? He was indeed a silly loon, I thought. I could commonly hear the plash of the water when he came up, and so also detected him. But after an hour he seemed as fresh as ever, dived as willingly and swam yet farther than at first. It was surprising to see how serenely he sailed off with unruffled breast when he came to the surface, doing all the work with his webbed feet beneath. His usual note was this demoniac laughter, yet somewhat like that of a water-fowl; but occasionally, when he had balked me most successfully and come up a long way off, he uttered a long-drawn unearthly howl, probably more like that of a wolf than any bird; as when a beast puts his muzzle to the ground and deliberately howls. This was his looning,—perhaps the wildest sound that is ever heard here, making the woods ring far and wide. I concluded that he laughed in derision of my efforts, confident of his own resources. Though the sky was by this time overcast, the pond was so smooth that I could see where he broke the surface when I did not hear him. His white breast, the stillness of the air, and the smoothness of the water were all against him. At length, having come up fifty rods off, he uttered one of those prolonged howls, as if calling on the god of loons to aid him, and immediately there came a wind from the east and rippled the surface, and filled the whole air with misty rain, and I was impressed as if it were the prayer of the loon answered, and his god was angry with me; and so I left him disappearing far away on the tumultuous surface.

For hours, in fall days, I watched the ducks cunningly tack and veer and hold the middle of the pond, far from the sportsman; tricks which they will have less need to practise in Louisiana bayous. When compelled to rise they would sometimes circle round and round and over the pond at a considerable height, from which they could easily see to other ponds and the river, like black motes in the sky; and, when I thought they had gone off thither long since, they would settle down by a slanting flight of a quarter of a mile on to a distant part which was left free; but what beside safety they got by sailing in the middle of Walden I do not know, unless they love its water for the same reason that I do.

House-Warming

In October I went a-graping to the river meadows, and loaded myself with clusters more precious for their beauty and fragrance than for food. There too I admired, though I did not gather, the cranberries, small waxen gems, pendants of the meadow grass, pearly and red, which the farmer plucks with an ugly rake, leaving the smooth meadow in a snarl, heedlessly measuring them by the bushel and the dollar only, and sells the spoils of the meads to Boston and New York; destined to be *jammed*, to satisfy the tastes of lovers of Nature there. So butchers rake the tongues of bison out of the prairie grass, regardless of the torn and drooping plant. The barberry's brilliant fruit was likewise food for my eyes merely; but I collected a small store of wild apples for coddling, which the proprietor and travellers had overlooked. When chestnuts were ripe I laid up half a bushel for winter. It was very exciting at that season to roam the then boundless chestnut woods of Lincoln,— they now sleep their long sleep under the railroad,—with a bag on my shoulder, and a stick to open burrs with in my hand, for I did not always wait for the frost, amid the rustling of leaves and the loud reproofs of the red-squirrels and the jays, whose half-consumed nuts I sometimes stole, for the burrs which they had selected were sure to contain sound ones. Occasionally I climbed and shook the trees. They grew also behind my house, and one large tree which almost overshadowed it, was, when in flower, a bouquet which scented the whole neighborhood, but the squirrels and the jays got most of its fruit; the last coming in flocks early in the morning and picking the nuts out of the burrs before they fell. I relinquished these trees to them and visited the more distant woods composed wholly of chestnut. These nuts, as far as they went, were a good substitute for bread. Many other substitutes might, perhaps, be found. Digging one day for fish-worms I discovered the ground-nut (*Apios tuberosa*) on its string, the potato of the aborigines, a sort of fabulous fruit, which I had begun to doubt if I had ever dug and eaten in childhood, as I had told, and had not dreamed it. I had often since seen its crimpled red velvety blossom supported by the stems of other plants without knowing it to be the same. Cultivation has well nigh exterminated it. It has a sweetish taste, much like that of a frostbitten potato, and I found it better boiled than roasted. This tuber seemed like a faint promise of Nature to rear her own children and feed them simply here at some future period. In these days of fatted cattle and waving grain-fields, this humble root, which was once the *totem* of an Indian tribe,[1] is quite forgotten, or known only by its flowering vine; but let wild Nature reign here once more, and the tender and luxurious English grains will probably disappear before a myriad of foes, and without the care of man the crow may carry back even the last seed of corn to the great corn-field of the Indian's God in the south-west, whence he is said to have brought it; but the now almost exterminated ground-nut will perhaps revive and flourish in spite of frosts and wildness, prove itself indigenous, and resume its ancient importance and dignity as the diet of the hunter tribe. Some Indian Ceres or Minerva [2] must have been the inventor and bestower of it; and when the reign of poetry commences here, its leaves and string of nuts may be represented on our works of art.

Already, by the first of September, I had seen two or three small maples turned scarlet across the pond, beneath where the white stems of three aspens diverged, at the point of a promontory, next the water. Ah, many a tale their color told! And gradually from week to week the character of each tree came out, and it admired itself reflected in the smooth mirror of the lake. Each morning the manager of this gallery substituted some new picture, distinguished by more brilliant or harmonious coloring, for the old upon the walls.

The wasps came by thousands to my lodge in October, as to winter quarters, and settled on my windows within and on the walls over-head, sometimes deterring visitors from entering. Each morning, when they were numbed with cold, I swept some of them out, but I did not trouble myself much to get rid of them; I even felt complimented by their regarding my house as a desirable shelter. They never molested me seriously, though they bedded with me; and they gradually disappeared, into what crevices I do not know, avoiding winter and unspeakable cold.

Like the wasps, before I finally went into winter quarters in November, I used to resort to the north-east side of Walden, which the sun, reflected from the pitch-pine woods and the stony shore, made the fire-side of the pond; it is so much pleasanter and wholesomer to be warmed by the sun while you can be, than by an artificial fire. I thus warmed myself by the still glowing embers which the summer, like a departed hunter, had left.

When I came to build my chimney I studied masonry. My bricks being second-hand ones required to be cleaned with a trowel, so

---

1. According to some authorities, the potato was believed by some Indians to bear a spiritual relation to their tribe.
2. In Roman mythology, Minerva was the goddess of wisdom and invention.

that I learned more than usual of the qualities of bricks and trowels. The mortar on them was fifty years old, and was said to be still growing harder; but this is one of those sayings which men love to repeat whether they are true or not. Such sayings themselves grow harder and adhere more firmly with age, and it would take many blows with a trowel to clean an old wiseacre of them. Many of the villages of Mesopotamia [3] are built of second-hand bricks of a very good quality, obtained from the ruins of Babylon, and the cement on them is older and probably harder still. However that may be, I was struck by the peculiar toughness of the steel which bore so many violent blows without being worn out. As my bricks had been in a chimney before, though I did not read the name of Nebuchadnezzar [4] on them, I picked out as many fireplace bricks as I could find, to save work and waste, and I filled the spaces between the bricks about the fireplace with stones from the pond shore, and also made my mortar with the white sand from the same place. I lingered most about the fireplace, as the most vital part of the house. Indeed, I worked so deliberately, that though I commenced at the ground in the morning, a course of bricks raised a few inches above the floor served for my pillow at night; yet I did not get a stiff neck for it that I remember; my stiff neck is of older date. I took a poet [5] to board for a fortnight about those times, which caused me to be put to it for room. He brought his own knife, though I had two, and we used to scour them by thrusting them into the earth. He shared with me the labors of cooking. I was pleased to see my work rising so square and solid by degrees, and reflected, that, if it proceeded slowly, it was calculated to endure a long time. The chimney is to some extent an independent structure, standing on the ground and rising through the house to the heavens; even after the house is burned it still stands sometimes, and its importance and independence are apparent. This was toward the end of summer. It was now November.

The north wind had already begun to cool the pond, though it took many weeks of steady blowing to accomplish it, it is so deep. When I began to have a fire at evening, before I plastered my house, the chimney carried smoke particularly well, because of the numerous chinks between the boards. Yet I passed some cheerful evenings in that cool and airy apartment, surrounded by the rough brown boards full of knots, and rafters with the bark on high over-head. My house never pleased my eye so much after it was

3. An ancient country in southwestern Asia.
4. King of ancient Babylonia (604–561 B.C.).
5. Ellery Channing.

plastered, though I was obliged to confess that it was more comfortable. Should not every apartment in which man dwells be lofty enough to create some obscurity over-head, where flickering shadows may play at evening about the rafters? These forms are more agreeable to the fancy and imagination than fresco paintings or other the most expensive furniture. I now first began to inhabit my house, I may say, when I began to use it for warmth as well as shelter. I had got a couple of old fire-dogs to keep the wood from the hearth, and it did me good to see the soot form on the back of the chimney which I had built, and I poked the fire with more right and more satisfaction than usual. My dwelling was small, and I could hardly entertain an echo in it; but it seemed larger for being a single apartment and remote from neighbors. All the attractions of a house were concentrated in one room; it was kitchen, chamber, parlor, and keeping-room; [6] and whatever satisfaction parent or child, master or servant, derive from living in a house, I enjoyed it all. Cato says, the master of a family (*patremfamilias*) must have in his rustic villa "cellam oleariam, vinariam, dolia multa, uti lubeat caritatem expectare, et rei, et virtuti, et gloriæ erit," that is, "an oil and wine cellar, many casks, so that it may be pleasant to expect hard times; it will be for his advantage, and virtue, and glory." I had in my cellar a firkin of potatoes, about two quarts of peas with the weevil in them, and on my shelf a little rice, a jug of molasses, and of rye and Indian meal a peck each.

I sometimes dream of a larger and more populous house, standing in a golden age, of enduring materials, and without gingerbread work, which shall still consist of only one room, a vast, rude, substantial, primitive hall, without ceiling or plastering, with bare rafters and purlins supporting a sort of lower heaven over one's head,—useful to keep off rain and snow; where the king and queen posts stand out to receive your homage, when you have done reverence to the prostrate Saturn [7] of an older dynasty on stepping over the sill; a cavernous house, wherein you must reach up a torch upon a pole to see the roof; where some may live in the fire-place, some in the recess of a window, and some on settles, some at one end of the hall, some at another, and some aloft on rafters with the spiders, if they choose; a house which you have got into when you have opened the outside door, and the ceremony is over; where the weary traveller may wash, and eat, and converse, and sleep, without further journey; such a shelter as you would be glad to reach in a tempestuous night, containing

6. A New England dialect term for a sitting-room.
7. A Roman god (known to the Greeks as "Cronus"), overthrown by Jupiter (Greek: "Zeus").

all the essentials of a house, and nothing for house-keeping; where you can see all the treasures of the house at one view, and every thing hangs upon its peg that a man should use; at once kitchen, pantry, parlor, chamber, store-house, and garret; where you can see so necessary a thing as a barrel or a ladder, so convenient a thing as a cupboard, and hear the pot boil, and pay your respects to the fire that cooks your dinner and the oven that bakes your bread, and the necessary furniture and utensils are the chief ornaments; where the washing is not put out, nor the fire, nor the mistress, and perhaps you are sometimes requested to move from off the trap-door, when the cook would descend into the cellar, and so learn whether the ground is solid or hollow beneath you without stamping. A house whose inside is as open and manifest as a bird's nest, and you cannot go in at the front door and out at the back without seeing some of its inhabitants; where to be a guest is to be presented with the freedom of the house, and not to be carefully excluded from seven eighths of it, shut up in a particular cell, and told to make yourself at home there,—in solitary confinement. Nowadays the host does not admit you to *his* hearth, but has got the mason to build one for yourself somewhere in his alley, and hospitality is the art of *keeping* you at the greatest distance. There is as much secrecy about the cooking as if he had a design to poison you. I am aware that I have been on many a man's premises, and might have been legally ordered off, but I am not aware that I have been in many men's houses. I might visit in my old clothes a king and queen who lived simply in such a house as I have described, if I were going their way; but backing out of a modern palace will be all that I shall desire to learn, if ever I am caught in one.

It would seem as if the very language of our parlors would lose all its nerve and degenerate into *parlaver* [8] wholly, our lives pass at such remoteness from its symbols, and its metaphors and tropes are necessarily so far fetched, through slides and dumb-waiters, as it were; in other words, the parlor is so far from the kitchen and workshop. The dinner even is only the parable of a dinner, commonly. As if only the savage dwelt near enough to Nature and Truth to borrow a trope from them. How can the scholar, who dwells away in the North West Territory [9] or the Isle of Man,[1] tell what is parliamentary in the kitchen?

However, only one or two of my guests were ever bold enough to stay and eat a hasty-pudding with me; but when they saw that crisis approaching they beat a hasty retreat rather, as if it would

8. A punning combination of "parlor" and "palaver," i.e., "empty, profuse talk."
9. The area included within the current states of Ohio, Indiana, Illinois, Michigan, Wisconsin, and Minnesota.
1. An island in the Irish sea.

shake the house to its foundations. Nevertheless, it stood through a great many hasty-puddings.

I did not plaster till it was freezing weather. I brought over some whiter and cleaner sand for this purpose from the opposite shore of the pond in a boat, a sort of conveyance which would have tempted me to go much farther if necessary. My house had in the mean while been shingled down to the ground on every side. In lathing I was pleased to be able to send home each nail with a single blow of the hammer, and it was my ambition to transfer the plaster from the board to the wall neatly and rapidly. I remembered the story of a conceited fellow, who, in fine clothes, was wont to lounge about the village once, giving advice to workmen. Venturing one day to substitute deeds for words, he turned up his cuffs, seized a plasterer's board, and having loaded his trowel without mishap, with a complacent look toward the lathing overhead, made a bold gesture thitherward; and straightway, to his complete discomfiture, received the whole contents in his ruffled bosom. I admired anew the economy and convenience of plastering, which so effectually shuts out the cold and takes a handsome finish, and I learned the various casualties to which the plasterer is liable. I was surprised to see how thirsty the bricks were which drank up all the moisture in my plaster before I had smoothed it, and how many pailfuls of water it takes to christen a new hearth. I had the previous winter made a small quantity of lime by burning the shells of the *Unio fluviatilis*, which our river affords, for the sake of the experiment; so that I knew where my materials came from. I might have got good limestone within a mile or two and burned it myself, if I had cared to do so.

The pond had in the mean while skimmed over in the shadiest and shallowest coves, some days or even weeks before the general freezing. The first ice is especially interesting and perfect, being hard, dark, and transparent, and affords the best opportunity that ever offers for examining the bottom where it is shallow; for you can lie at your length on ice only an inch thick, like a skater insect on the surface of the water, and study the bottom at your leisure, only two or three inches distant, like a picture behind a glass, and the water is necessarily always smooth then. There are many furrows in the sand where some creature has travelled about and doubled on its tracks; and, for wrecks, it is strewn with the cases of cadis worms made of minute grains of white quartz. Perhaps these have creased it, for you find some of their cases in the furrows, though they are deep and broad for them to make. But the ice itself is the object of most interest, though you must improve the earliest opportunity to study it. If you examine it closely

the morning after it freezes, you find that the greater part of the
bubbles, which at first appeared to be within it, are against its
under surface, and that more are continually rising from the
bottom; while the ice is as yet comparatively solid and dark, that
is, you see the water through it. These bubbles are from an
eightieth to an eighth of an inch in diameter, very clear and
beautiful, and you see your face reflected in them through the ice.
There may be thirty or forty of them to a square inch. There are
also already within the ice narrow oblong perpendicular bubbles
about half an inch long, sharp cones with the apex upward; or
oftener, if the ice is quite fresh, minute spherical bubbles one directly above another, like a string of beads. But these within the
ice are not so numerous nor obvious as those beneath. I sometimes used to cast on stones to try the strength of the ice, and
those which broke through carried in air with them, which formed
very large and conspicuous white bubbles beneath. One day when
I came to the same place forty-eight hours afterward, I found
that those large bubbles were still perfect, though an inch more
of ice had formed, as I could see distinctly by the seam in the edge
of a cake. But as the last two days had been very warm, like an
Indian summer, the ice was not now transparent, showing the
dark green color of the water, and the bottom, but opaque and
whitish or gray, and though twice as thick was hardly stronger
than before, for the air bubbles had greatly expanded under this
heat and run together, and lost their regularity; they were no
longer one directly over another, but often like silvery coins
poured from a bag, one overlapping another, or in thin flakes, as if
occupying slight cleavages. The beauty of the ice was gone, and
it was too late to study the bottom. Being curious to know what
position my great bubbles occupied with regard to the new ice, I
broke out a cake containing a middling sized one, and turned it
bottom upward. The new ice had formed around and under the
bubble, so that it was included between the two ices. It was wholly
in the lower ice, but close against the upper, and was flattish, or
perhaps slightly lenticular, with a rounded edge, a quarter of an
inch deep by four inches in diameter; and I was surprised to find
that directly under the bubble the ice was melted with great
regularity in the form of a saucer reversed, to the height of five
eighths of an inch in the middle, leaving a thin partition there between the water and the bubble, hardly an eighth of an inch thick;
and in many places the small bubbles in this partition had burst
out downward, and probably there was no ice at all under the
largest bubbles, which were a foot in diameter. I inferred that the
infinite number of minute bubbles which I had first seen against the
under surface of the ice were now frozen in likewise, and that

each, in its degree, had operated like a burning glass on the ice beneath to melt and rot it. These are the little air-guns which contribute to make the ice crack and whoop.

At length the winter set in in good earnest, just as I had finished plastering, and the wind began to howl around the house as it had not had permission to do so till then. Night after night the geese came lumbering in in the dark with a clangor and a whistling of wings, even after the ground was covered with snow, some to alight in Walden, and some flying low over the woods toward Fair Haven, bound for Mexico. Several times, when returning from the village at ten or eleven o'clock at night, I heard the tread of a flock of geese, or else ducks, on the dry leaves in the woods by a pond-hole behind my dwelling, where they had come up to feed, and the faint honk or quack of their leader as they hurried off. In 1845 Walden froze entirely over for the first time on the night of the 22d of December, Flints' and other shallower ponds and the river having been frozen ten days or more; in '46, the 16th; in '49, about the 31st; and in '50, about the 27th of December; in '52, the 5th of January; in '53, the 31st of December. The snow had already covered the ground since the 25th of November, and surrounded me suddenly with the scenery of winter. I withdrew yet farther into my shell, and endeavored to keep a bright fire both within my house and within my breast. My employment out of doors now was to collect the dead wood in the forest, bringing it in my hands or on my shoulders, or sometimes trailing a dead pine tree under each arm to my shed. An old forest fence which had seen its best days was a great haul for me. I sacrificed it to Vulcan,[2] for it was past serving the god Terminus.[3] How much more interesting an event is that man's supper who has just been forth in the snow to hunt, nay, you might say, steal, the fuel to cook it with! His bread and meat are sweet. There are enough fagots and waste wood of all kinds in the forests of most of our towns to support many fires, but which at present warm none, and, some think, hinder the growth of the young wood. There was also the drift-wood of the pond. In the course of the summer I had discovered a raft of pitch-pine logs with the bark on, pinned together by the Irish when the railroad was built. This I hauled up partly on the shore. After soaking two years and then lying high six months it was perfectly sound, though waterlogged past drying. I amused myself one winter day with sliding this piece-meal across the pond, nearly half a mile, skating behind with one end of a log fifteen feet long on my shoulder, and the other on the ice; or I

2. In Roman mythology, the god of fire.

3. In Roman mythology, the god of boundaries.

tied several logs together with a birch withe, and then, with a
longer birch or alder which had a hook at the end, dragged them
across. Though completely waterlogged and almost as heavy as
lead, they not only burned long, but made a very hot fire; nay, I
thought that they burned better for the soaking, as if the pitch,
being confined by the water, burned longer as in a lamp.

Gilpin,[4] in his account of the forest borderers of England, says
that "the encroachments of trespassers, and the houses and fences
thus raised on the borders of the forest," were "considered as
great nuisances by the old forest law, and were severely punished
under the name of *purprestures,* as tending *ad terrorem ferarum—
ad nocumentum forestæ,* &c.," to the frightening of the game and
the detriment of the forest. But I was interested in the preserva-
tion of the venison and the vert more than the hunters or wood-
choppers, and as much as though I had been the Lord Warden [5]
himself; and if any part was burned, though I burned it myself by
accident, I grieved with a grief that lasted longer and was more
inconsolable than that of the proprietors; nay, I grieved when it
was cut down by the proprietors themselves. I would that our
farmers when they cut down a forest felt some of that awe which
the old Romans did when they came to thin, or let in the light to,
a consecrated grove, (*lucum conlucare,*) that is, would believe that
it is sacred to some god. The Roman made an expiatory offering,
and prayed, Whatever god or goddess thou art to whom this grove
is sacred, be propitious to me, my family, and children, &c.

It is remarkable what a value is still put upon wood even in this
age and in this new country, a value more permanent and universal
than that of gold. After all our discoveries and inventions no man
will go by a pile of wood. It is as precious to us as it was to our
Saxon and Norman [6] ancestors. If they made their bows of it, we
make our gun-stocks of it. Michaux,[7] more than thirty years ago,
says that the price of wood for fuel in New York and Philadelphia
"nearly equals, and sometimes exceeds, that of the best wood in
Paris, though this immense capital annually requires more than
three hundred thousand cords, and is surrounded to the distance of
three hundred miles by cultivated plains." In this town the price
of wood rises almost steadily, and the only question is, how much
higher it is to be this year than it was the last. Mechanics and
tradesmen who come in person to the forest on no other errand,
are sure to attend the wood auction, and even pay a high price for

---

4. William Gilpin (1724–1804), English author and naturalist.
5. A person who has the responsibility
of protecting the wildlife and preserving
the greenery of a forest.
6. The Saxons invaded England in the
fifth century, the Normans in the
eleventh century.
7. Probably Francois Michaux, whom
Thoreau mentions in his *Journal;* he
was the author of *North American
Sylva.*

the privilege of gleaning after the wood-chopper. It is now many years that men have resorted to the forest for fuel and the materials of the arts; the New Englander and the New Hollander, the Parisian and the Celt, the farmer and Robinhood, Goody Blake and Harry Gill,[8] in most parts of the world the prince and the peasant, the scholar and the savage, equally require still a few sticks from the forest to warm them and cook their food. Neither could I do without them.

Every man looks at his wood-pile with a kind of affection. I loved to have mine before my window, and the more chips the better to remind me of my pleasing work. I had an old axe which nobody claimed, with which by spells in winter days, on the sunny side of the house, I played about the stumps which I had got out of my bean-field. As my driver prophesied when I was ploughing, they warmed me twice, once while I was splitting them, and again when they were on the fire, so that no fuel could give out more heat. As for the axe, I was advised to get the village blacksmith to "jump" it;[9] but I jumped him, and, putting a hickory helve from the woods into it, made it do. If it was dull, it was at least hung true.

A few pieces of fat pine were a great treasure. It is interesting to remember how much of this food for fire is still concealed in the bowels of the earth. In previous years I had often gone "prospecting" over some bare hill-side, where a pitch-pine wood had formerly stood, and got out the fat pine roots. They are almost indestructible. Stumps thirty or forty years old, at least, will still be sound at the core, though the sap-wood has all become vegetable mould, as appears by the scales of the thick bark forming a ring level with the earth four or five inches distant from the heart. With axe and shovel you explore this mine, and follow the marrowy store, yellow as beef tallow, or as if you had struck on a vein of gold, deep into the earth. But commonly I kindled my fire with the dry leaves of the forest, which I had stored up in my shed before the snow came. Green hickory finely split makes the wood-chopper's kindlings, when he has a camp in the woods. Once in a while I got a little of this. When the villagers were lighting their fires beyond the horizon, I too gave notice to the various wild inhabitants of Walden vale, by a smoky streamer from my chimney, that I was awake.—

> Light-winged Smoke, Icarian bird,
> Melting thy pinions in thy upward flight,
> Lark without song, and messenger of dawn,

8. In a poem by William Wordsworth (1770–1850), Harry Gill denies fuel to Goody Blake, whereupon she curses him to eternal cold.

9. To flatten or lengthen the end of a piece of metal by hammering it.

Circling above the hamlets as thy nest;
Or else, departing dream, and shadowy form
Of midnight vision, gathering up thy skirts;
By night star-veiling, and by day
Darkening the light and blotting out the sun;
Go thou my incense upward from this hearth,
And ask the gods to pardon this clear flame.

Hard green wood just cut, though I used but little of that, answered my purpose better than any other. I sometimes left a good fire when I went to take a walk in a winter afternoon; and when I returned, three or four hours afterward, it would be still alive and glowing. My house was not empty though I was gone. It was as if I had left a cheerful housekeeper behind. It was I and Fire that lived there; and commonly my housekeeper proved trustworthy. One day, however, as I was splitting wood, I thought that I would just look in at the window and see if the house was not on fire; it was the only time I remember to have been particularly anxious on this score; so I looked and saw that a spark had caught my bed, and I went in and extinguished it when it had burned a place as big as my hand. But my house occupied so sunny and sheltered a position, and its roof was so low, that I could afford to let the fire go out in the middle of almost any winter day.

The moles nested in my cellar, nibbling every third potato, and making a snug bed even there of some hair left after plastering and of brown paper; for even the wildest animals love comfort and warmth as well as man, and they survive the winter only because they are so careful to secure them. Some of my friends spoke as if I was coming to the woods on purpose to freeze myself. The animal merely makes a bed, which he warms with his body in a sheltered place; but man, having discovered fire, boxes up some air in a spacious apartment, and warms that, instead of robbing himself, makes that his bed, in which he can move about divested of more cumbrous clothing, maintain a kind of summer in the midst of winter, and by means of windows even admit the light, and with a lamp lengthen out the day. Thus he goes a step or two beyond instinct, and saves a little time for the fine arts. Though, when I had been exposed to the rudest blasts a long time, my whole body began to grow torpid, when I reached the genial atmosphere of my house I soon recovered my faculties and prolonged my life. But the most luxuriously housed has little to boast of in this respect, nor need we trouble ourselves to speculate how the human race may be at last destroyed. It would be easy to cut their threads any time with a little sharper blast from the north. We go on dating from Cold Fridays and Great Snows; but a little colder Friday, or greater snow, would put a period to man's existence on the globe.

The next winter I used a small cooking-stove for economy, since I did not own the forest; but it did not keep fire so well as the open fire-place. Cooking was then, for the most part, no longer a poetic, but merely a chemic process. It will soon be forgotten, in these days of stoves, that we used to roast potatoes in the ashes, after the Indian fashion. The stove not only took up room and scented the house, but it concealed the fire, and I felt as if I had lost a companion. You can always see a face in the fire. The laborer, looking into it at evening, purifies his thoughts of the dross and earthiness which they have accumulated during the day. But I could no longer sit and look into the fire, and the pertinent words of a poet [1] recurred to me with new force.—

> "Never, bright flame, may be denied to me
> Thy dear, life imaging, close sympathy.
> What but my hopes shot upward e'er so bright?
> What but my fortunes sunk so low in night?
>
> Why art thou banished from our hearth and hall,
> Thou who art welcomed and beloved by all?
> Was thy existence then too fanciful
> For our life's common light, who are so dull?
> Did thy bright gleam mysterious converse hold
> With our congenial souls? secrets too bold?
> Well, we are safe and strong, for now we sit
> Beside a hearth where no dim shadows flit,
> Where nothing cheers nor saddens, but a fire
> Warms feet and hands—nor does to more aspire;
> By whose compact utilitarian heap
> The present may sit down and go to sleep,
> Nor fear the ghosts who from the dim past walked,
> And with us by the unequal light of the old wood fire
>   talked."
>
> (Mrs. Hooper)

Former Inhabitants; and Winter Visitors

I weathered some merry snow storms, and spent some cheerful winter evenings by my fire-side, while the snow whirled wildly without, and even the hooting of the owl was hushed. For many weeks I met no one in my walks but those who came occasionally to cut wood and sled it to the village. The elements, however,

1. Ellen Sturgis Hooper (1812–1848), a minor American poet widely admired by the Transcendentalists. The excerpt is from "The Wood-Fire."

abetted me in making a path through the deepest snow in the woods, for when I had once gone through the wind blew the oak leaves into my tracks, where they lodged, and by absorbing the rays of the sun melted the snow, and so not only made a dry bed for my feet, but in the night their dark line was my guide. For human society I was obliged to conjure up the former occupants of these woods. Within the memory of many of my townsmen the road near which my house stands resounded with the laugh and gossip of inhabitants, and the woods which border it were notched and dotted here and there with their little gardens and dwellings, though it was then much more shut in by the forest than now. In some places, within my own remembrance, the pines would scrape both sides of a chaise at once, and women and children who were compelled to go this way to Lincoln alone and on foot did it with fear, and often ran a good part of the distance. Though mainly but a humble route to neighboring villages, or for the woodman's team, it once amused the traveller more than now by its variety, and lingered longer in his memory. Where now firm open fields stretch from the village to the woods, it then ran through a maple swamp on a foundation of logs, the remnants of which, doubtless, still underlie the present dusty highway, from the Stratten, now the Alms House, Farm, to Brister's Hill.

East of my bean-field, across the road, lived Cato Ingraham, slave of Duncan Ingraham, Esquire, gentleman of Concord village; who built his slave a house, and gave him permission to live in Walden Woods;—Cato, not Uticensis, but Concordiensis.[1] Some say that he was a Guinea Negro. There are a few who remember his little patch among the walnuts, which he let grow up till he should be old and need them; but a younger and whiter speculator got them at last. He too, however, occupies an equally narrow house at present. Cato's half-obliterated cellar hole still remains, though known to few, being concealed from the traveller by a fringe of pines. It is now filled with the smooth sumach, (*Rhus glabra,*) and one of the earliest species of goldenrod (*Solidago stricta*) grows there luxuriantly.

Here, by the very corner of my field, still nearer to town, Zilpha, a colored woman, had her little house, where she spun linen for the townsfolk, making the Walden Woods ring with her shrill singing, for she had a loud and notable voice. At length, in the war of 1812, her dwelling was set on fire by English soldiers, prisoners on parole, when she was away, and her cat and dog and hens were all burned up together. She led a hard

1. I.e., not the Roman statesman, Marcus Porcius Cato (95–46 B.C.), who died in the town of Utica in north Africa, but Cato of Concord.

life, and somewhat inhumane. One old frequenter of these woods remembers, that as he passed her house one noon he heard her muttering to herself over her gurgling pot,—"Ye are all bones, bones!" I have seen bricks amid the oak copse there.

Down the road, on the right hand, on Brister's Hill, lived Brister Freeman, "a handy Negro," slave of Squire Cummings once,—there where grow still the apple-trees which Brister planted and tended; large old trees now, but their fruit still wild and ciderish to my taste. Not long since I read his epitaph in the old Lincoln burying-ground, a little on one side, near the unmarked graves of some British grenadiers who fell in the retreat from Concord,—where he is styled "Sippio Brister,"—Scipio Africanus [2] he had some title to be called,—"a man of color," as if he were discolored. It also told me, with staring emphasis, when he died; which was but an indirect way of informing me that he ever lived. With him dwelt Fenda, his hospitable wife, who told fortunes, yet pleasantly,—large, round, and black, blacker than any of the children of night, such a dusky orb as never rose on Concord before or since.

Farther down the hill, on the left, on the old road in the woods, are marks of some homestead of the Stratton family; whose orchard once covered all the slope of Brister's Hill, but was long since killed out by pitch-pines, excepting a few stumps, whose old roots furnish still the wild stocks of many a thrifty village tree.[3]

Nearer yet to town, you come to Breed's location, on the other side of the way, just on the edge of the wood; ground famous for the pranks of a demon not distinctly named in old mythology, who has acted a prominent and astounding part in our New England life, and deserves, as much as any mythological character, to have his biography written one day; who first comes in the guise of a friend or hired man, and then robs and murders the whole family,—New-England Rum. But history must not yet tell the tragedies enacted here; let time intervene in some measure to assuage and lend an azure tint to them. Here the most indistinct and dubious tradition says that once a tavern stood; the well the same, which tempered the traveller's beverage and refreshed his steed. Here then men saluted one another, and heard and told the news, and went their ways again.

Breed's hut was standing only a dozen years ago, though it had long been unoccupied. It was about the size of mine. It was

2. Roman general (236?–183? B.C.) who was awarded the honorary name, "Africanus," after he defeated the Carthaginian general, Hannibal.
3. Surveying for Cyrus Jarvis Dec. 23 '56—he shows me a deed of this lot containing 6 A. 52 rods all on the W. of the Wayland Road—& "consisting of plowland, orcharding & woodland"— sold by Joseph Stratton to Samuel Swan of Concord In holder Aug. 11th 1777 [Thoreau's note].

set on fire by mischievous boys, one Election night, if I do not mistake. I lived on the edge of the village then, and had just lost myself over Davenant's Gondibert,[4] that winter that I labored with a lethargy,—which, by the way, I never knew whether to regard as a family complaint, having an uncle who goes to sleep shaving himself, and is obliged to sprout potatoes in a cellar Sundays, in order to keep awake and keep the Sabbath, or as the consequence of my attempt to read Chalmers' collection of English poetry[5] without skipping. It fairly overcame my Nervii.[6] I had just sunk my head on this when the bells rung fire, and in hot haste the engines rolled that way, led by a straggling troop of men and boys, and I among the foremost, for I had leaped the brook. We thought it was far south over the woods,—we who had run to fires before,—barn, shop, or dwelling-house, or all together. "It's Baker's barn," cried one. "It is the Codman Place," affirmed another. And then fresh sparks went up above the wood, as if the roof fell in, and we all shouted "Concord to the rescue!" Wagons shot past with furious speed and crushing loads, bearing, perchance, among the rest, the agent of the Insurance Company, who was bound to go however far; and ever and anon the engine bell tinkled behind, more slow and sure, and rearmost of all, as it was afterward whispered, came they who set the fire and gave the alarm. Thus we kept on like true idealists, rejecting the evidence of our senses, until at a turn in the road we heard the crackling and actually felt the heat of the fire from over the wall, and realized, alas! that we were there. The very nearness of the fire but cooled our ardor. At first we thought to throw a frog-pond on to it; but concluded to let it burn, it was so far gone and so worthless. So we stood round our engine, jostled one another, expressed our sentiments through speaking trumpets, or in lower tone referred to the great conflagrations which the world has witnessed, including Bascom's shop, and, between ourselves, we thought that, were we there in season with our "tub," [7] and a full frog-pond by, we could turn that threatened last and universal one into another flood. We finally retreated without doing any mischief,—returned to sleep and Gondibert. But as for Gondibert, I would except that passage in the preface about wit being the soul's powder,—"but most of mankind are strangers to wit, as Indians are to powder."

It chanced that I walked that way across the fields the follow-

---

4. William D'Avenant (1606–1668), English dramatist and poet; *Gondibert* is an unfinished romantic epic of chivalry.
5. Alexander Chalmers, *The Works of the English Poets from Chaucer to* *Cowper* (London, 1810), 21 vols.
6. A punning reference to a northern European tribe which was defeated by Julius Caesar in 57 B.C.
7. A hand-drawn fire engine.

ing night, about the same hour, and hearing a low moaning at this spot, I drew near in the dark, and discovered the only survivor of the family that I know, the heir of both its virtues and its vices, who alone was interested in this burning, lying on his stomach and looking over the cellar wall at the still smouldering cinders beneath, muttering to himself, as is his wont. He had been working far off in the river meadows all day, and had improved the first moments that he could call his own to visit the home of his fathers and his youth. He gazed into the cellar from all sides and points of view by turns, always lying down to it, as if there was some treasure, which he remembered, concealed between the stones, where there was absolutely nothing but a heap of bricks and ashes. The house being gone, he looked at what there was left. He was soothed by the sympathy which my mere presence implied, and showed me, as well as the darkness permitted, where the well was covered up; which, thank Heaven, could never be burned; and he groped long about the wall to find the well-sweep which his father had cut and mounted, feeling for the iron hook or staple by which a burden had been fastened to the heavy end,—all that he could now cling to,—to convince me that it was no common "rider." [8] I felt it, and still remark it almost daily in my walks, for by it hangs the history of a family.

Once more, on the left, where are seen the well and lilac bushes by the wall, in the now open field, lived Nutting and Le Grosse. But to return toward Lincoln.

Farther in the woods than any of these, where the road approaches nearest to the pond, Wyman the potter squatted, and furnished his townsmen with earthen ware, and left descendants to succeed him. Neither were they rich in worldly goods, holding the land by sufferance while they lived; and there often the sheriff came in vain to collect the taxes, and "attached a chip," [9] for form's sake, as I have read in his accounts, there being nothing else that he could lay his hands on. One day in midsummer, when I was hoeing, a man who was carrying a load of pottery to market stopped his horse against my field and inquired concerning Wyman the younger. He had long ago bought a potter's wheel of him, and wished to know what had become of him. I had read of the potter's clay and wheel in Scripture, but it had never occurred to me that the pots we use were not such as had come down unbroken from those days, or grown on trees like gourds somewhere, and I was pleased to hear that so fictile an art was ever practised in my neighborhood.

The last inhabitant of these woods before me was an Irishman, Hugh Quoil, (if I have spelt his name with coil enough,)

8. The top rail of a fence.　　　　9. Confiscated a worthless item.

who occupied Wyman's tenement,—Col. Quoil, he was called. Rumor said that he had been a soldier at Waterloo.[1] If he had lived I should have made him fight his battles over again. His trade here was that of a ditcher. Napoleon went to St. Helena; Quoil came to Walden Woods. All I know of him is tragic. He was a man of manners, like one who had seen the world, and was capable of more civil speech than you could well attend to. He wore a great coat in mid-summer, being affected with the trembling delirium, and his face was the color of carmine. He died in the road at the foot of Brister's Hill shortly after I came to the woods, so that I have not remembered him as a neighbor. Before his house was pulled down, when his comrades avoided it as "an unlucky castle," I visited it. There lay his old clothes curled up by use, as if they were himself, upon his raised plank bed. His pipe lay broken on the hearth, instead of a bowl broken at the fountain. The last could never have been the symbol of his death, for he confessed to me that, though he had heard of Brister's Spring, he had never seen it; and soiled cards, kings of diamonds spades and hearts, were scattered over the floor. One black chicken which the administrator could not catch, black as night and as silent, not even croaking, awaiting Reynard, still went to roost in the next apartment. In the rear there was the dim outline of a garden, which had been planted but had never received its first hoeing, owing to those terrible shaking fits, though it was now harvest time. It was over-run with Roman wormwood and beggar-ticks, which last stuck to my clothes for all fruit. The skin of a woodchuck was freshly stretched upon the back of the house, a trophy of his last Waterloo; but no warm cap or mittens would he want more.

Now only a dent in the earth marks the site of these dwellings, with buried cellar stones, and strawberries, raspberries, thimbleberries, hazel-bushes, and sumachs growing in the sunny sward there; some pitch-pine or gnarled oak occupies what was the chimney nook, and a sweet-scented black-birch, perhaps, waves where the door-stone was. Sometimes the well dent is visible, where once a spring oozed; now dry and tearless grass; or it was covered deep,— not to be discovered till some late day,—with a flat stone under the sod, when the last of the race departed. What a sorrowful act must that be,—the covering up of wells! coincident with the opening of wells of tears. These cellar dents, like deserted fox burrows, old holes, are all that is left where once were the stir and bustle of human life, and "fate, free-will, foreknowledge absolute," [2] in some form and dialect or other were by turns discussed. But all I can learn of their conclusions amounts to just this, that

---

1. A Belgian village, scene of Napoleon's defeat, June 18, 1815. 2. Milton, *Paradise Lost*, II, 560.

"Cato and Brister pulled wool;" [3] which is about as edifying as the history of more famous schools of philosophy.

Still grows the vivacious lilac a generation after the door and lintel and the sill are gone, unfolding its sweet-scented flowers each spring, to be plucked by the musing traveller; planted and tended once by children's hands, in front-yard plots,—now standing by wall-sides in retired pastures, and giving place to new-rising forests; —the last of that stirp, sole survivor of that family. Little did the dusky children think that the puny slip with its two eyes only, which they stuck in the ground in the shadow of the house and daily watered, would root itself so, and outlive them, and house itself in the rear that shaded it, and grown man's garden and orchard, and tell their story faintly to the lone wanderer a half century after they had grown up and died,—blossoming as fair, and smelling as sweet, as in that first spring. I mark its still tender, civil, cheerful, lilac colors.

But this small village, germ of something more, why did it fail while Concord keeps its ground? Were there no natural advantages,—no water privileges, forsooth? Ay, the deep Walden Pond and cool Brister's Spring,—privilege to drink long and healthy draughts at these, all unimproved by these men but to dilute their glass. They were universally a thirsty race. Might not the basket, stable-broom, mat-making, corn-parching, linen-spinning, and pottery business have thrived here, making the wilderness to blossom like the rose, and a numerous posterity have inherited the land of their fathers? The sterile soil would at least have been proof against a low-land degeneracy. Alas! how little does the memory of these human inhabitants enhance the beauty of the landscape! Again, perhaps, Nature will try, with me for a first settler, and my house raised last spring to be the oldest in the hamlet.

I am not aware that any man has ever built on the spot which I occupy. Deliver me from a city built on the site of a more ancient city, whose materials are ruins, whose gardens cemeteries. The soil is blanched and accursed there, and before that becomes necessary the earth itself will be destroyed. With such reminiscences I repeopled the woods and lulled myself asleep.

At this season I seldom had a visitor. When the snow lay deepest no wanderer ventured near my house for a week or fortnight at a time, but there I lived as snug as a meadow mouse, or as cattle and poultry which are said to have survived for a long time buried in drifts, even without food; or like that early settler's family in the town of Sutton, in this state, whose cottage was

3. I.e., performed menial tasks.

completely covered by the great snow of 1717 when he was absent, and an Indian found it only by the hole which the chimney's breath made in the drift, and so relieved the family. But no friendly Indian concerned himself about me; nor needed he, for the master of the house was at home. The Great Snow! How cheerful it is to hear of! When the farmers could not get to the woods and swamps with their teams, and were obliged to cut down the shade trees before their houses, and when the crust was harder cut off the trees in the swamps ten feet from the ground, as it appeared the next spring.

In the deepest snows, the path which I used from the highway to my house, about half a mile long, might have been represented by a meandering dotted line, with wide intervals between the dots. For a week of even weather I took exactly the same number of steps, and of the same length, coming and going, stepping deliberately and with the precision of a pair of dividers in my own deep tracks,—to such routine the winter reduces us,—yet often they were filled with heaven's own blue. But no weather interfered fatally with my walks, or rather my going abroad, for I frequently tramped eight or ten miles through the deepest snow to keep an appointment with a beech-tree, or a yellow-birch, or an old acquaintance among the pines; when the ice and snow causing their limbs to droop, and so sharpening their tops, had changed the pines into fir-trees; wading to the tops of the highest hills when the snow was nearly two feet deep on a level, and shaking down another snow-storm on my head at every step; or sometimes creeping and floundering thither on my hands and knees, when the hunters had gone into winter quarters. One afternoon I amused myself by watching a barred owl (*Strix nebulosa*) sitting on one of the lower dead limbs of a white-pine, close to the trunk, in broad daylight, I standing within a rod of him. He could hear me when I moved and cronched the snow with my feet, but could not plainly see me. When I made most noise he would stretch out his neck, and erect his neck feathers, and open his eyes wide; but their lids soon fell again, and he began to nod. I too felt a slumberous influence after watching him half an hour, as he sat thus with his eyes half open, like a cat, winged brother of the cat. There was only a narrow slit left between their lids, by which he preserved a peninsular relation to me; thus, with half-shut eyes, looking out from the land of dreams, and endeavoring to realize me, vague object or mote that interrupted his visions. At length, on some louder noise or my nearer approach, he would grow uneasy and sluggishly turn about on his perch, as if impatient at having his dreams disturbed; and when he launched himself off and flapped through the pines, spreading his wings to unexpected breadth, I

could not hear the slightest sound from them. Thus, guided amid
the pine boughs rather by a delicate sense of their neighborhood
than by sight, feeling his twilight way as it were with his sensitive
pinions, he found a new perch, where he might in peace await the
dawning of his day.

As I walked over the long causeway made for the railroad
through the meadows, I encountered many a blustering and nipping
wind, for nowhere has it freer play; and when the frost had
smitten me on one cheek, heathen as I was, I turned to it the
other also. Nor was it much better by the carriage road from
Brister's Hill. For I came to town still, like a friendly Indian,
when the contents of the broad open fields were all piled up
between the walls of the Walden road, and half an hour sufficed
to obliterate the tracks of the last traveller. And when I returned
new drifts would have formed, through which I floundered, where
the busy north-west wind had been depositing the powdery snow
round a sharp angle in the road, and not a rabbit's track, nor even
the fine print, the small type, of a meadow (deer) mouse was to be
seen. Yet I rarely failed to find, even in mid-winter, some warm and
springy swamp where the grass and the skunk-cabbage still put
forth with perennial verdure, and some hardier bird occasionally
awaited the return of spring.

Sometimes, notwithstanding the snow, when I returned from my
walk at evening I crossed the deep tracks of a woodchopper leading
from my door, and found his pile of whittlings on the hearth, and
my house filled with the odor of his pipe. Or on a Sunday
afternoon, if I chanced to be at home, I heard the cronching of
the snow made by the step of a long-headed farmer, who from
far through the woods sought my house, to have a social "crack;"
one of the few of his vocation who are "men on their farms;" who
donned a frock instead of a professor's gown, and is as ready to
extract the moral out of church or state as to haul a load of
manure from his barn-yard. We talked of rude and simple times, when
men sat about large fires in cold bracing weather, with clear heads;
and when other dessert failed, we tried our teeth on many a nut
which wise squirrels have long since abandoned, for those which
have the thickest shells are commonly empty.

The one who came from farthest to my lodge, through deepest
snows and most dismal tempests, was a poet.[4] A farmer, a hunter, a
soldier, a reporter, even a philosopher, may be daunted; but nothing can deter a poet, for he is actuated by pure love. Who can
predict his comings and goings? His business calls him out at all
hours, even when doctors sleep. We made that small house ring
with boisterous mirth and resound with the murmur of much sober

4. Ellery Channing.

talk, making amends then to Walden vale for the long silences. Broadway was still and deserted in comparison. At suitable intervals there were regular salutes of laughter, which might have been referred indifferently to the last uttered or the forth-coming jest. We made many a "bran new" theory of life over a thin dish of gruel, which combined the advantages of conviviality with the clear-headedness which philosophy requires.

I should not forget that during my last winter at the pond there was another welcome visitor,[5] who at one time came through the village, through snow and rain and darkness, till he saw my lamp through the trees, and shared with me some long winter evenings. One of the last of the philosophers,—Connecticut gave him to the world,—he peddled first her wares, afterwards, as he declares, his brains. These he peddles still, prompting God and disgracing man, bearing for fruit his brain only, like the nut its kernel. I think that he must be the man of the most faith of any alive. His words and attitude always suppose a better state of things than other men are acquainted with, and he will be the last man to be disappointed as the ages revolve. He has no venture in the present. But though comparatively disregarded now, when his day comes, laws unsuspected by most will take effect, and masters of families and rulers will come to him for advice.—

"How blind that cannot see serenity!"

A true friend of man; almost the only friend of human progress. An Old Mortality,[6] say rather an Immortality, with unwearied patience and faith making plain the image engraven in men's bodies, the God of whom they are but defaced and leaning monuments. With his hospitable intellect he embraces children, beggars, insane, and scholars, and entertains the thought of all, adding to it commonly some breadth and elegance. I think that he should keep a caravansary on the world's highway, where philosophers of all nations might put up, and on his sign should be printed, "Entertainment for man, but not for his beast. Enter ye that have leisure and a quiet mind, who earnestly seek the right road." He is perhaps the sanest man and has the fewest crotchets of any I chance to know; the same yesterday and to-morrow. Of yore we had sauntered and talked, and effectually put the world behind us; for he was pledged to no institution in it, freeborn, *ingenuus*.[7] Whichever way we turned, it seemed that the heavens and the earth had met together, since he enhanced the beauty of the landscape. A blue-robed man, whose fittest roof is the overarching

5. Amos Bronson Alcott (1799–1888), Transcendentalist and educator.
6. The title of a novel by Sir Walter Scott (1771–1832); the leading char-acter wanders through Scotland repairing and cleaning gravestones.
7. Freeborn, noble.

sky which reflects his serenity. I do not see how he can ever die; Nature cannot spare him.

Having each some shingles of thought well dried, we sat and whittled them, trying our knives, and admiring the clear yellowish grain of the pumpkin pine. We waded so gently and reverently, or we pulled together so smoothly, that the fishes of thought were not scared from the stream, nor feared any angler on the bank, but came and went grandly, like the clouds which float through the western sky, and the mother-o'-pearl flocks which sometimes form and dissolve there. There we worked, revising mythology, rounding a fable here and there, and building castles in the air for which earth offered no worthy foundation. Great Looker! Great Expecter! to converse with whom was a New England Night's Entertainment. Ah! such discourse we had, hermit and philosopher, and the old settler I have spoken of,—we three,— it expanded and racked my little house; I should not dare to say how many pounds' weight there was above the atmospheric pressure on every circular inch; it opened its seams so that they had to be calked with much dulness thereafter to stop the consequent leak;—but I had enough of that kind of oakum already picked.

There was one other [8] with whom I had "solid seasons," long to be remembered, at his house in the village, and who looked in upon me from time to time; but I had no more for society there.

There too, as every where, I sometimes expected the Visitor who never comes. The Vishnu Purana [9] says, "The house-holder is to remain at eventide in his court-yard as long as it takes to milk a cow, or longer if he pleases, to await the arrival of a guest." I often performed this duty of hospitality, waited long enough to milk a whole herd of cows, but did not see the man approaching from the town.

Winter Animals

When the ponds were firmly frozen, they afforded not only new and shorter routes to many points, but new views from their surfaces of the familiar landscape around them. When I crossed Flints' Pond, after it was covered with snow, though I had often paddled about and skated over it, it was so unexpectedly wide and so strange that I could think of nothing but Baffin's Bay.[1] The Lincoln hills rose up around me at the extremity of a snowy plain, in which I did not remember to have stood before; and the fishermen, at an indeterminable distance over the ice, moving slowly

---

8. Ralph Waldo Emerson (1803–1882), a leading Transcendentalist and a close friend of Thoreau.

9. A Hindu scripture.
1. A part of the north Atlantic Ocean between Greenland and Canada.

about with their wolfish dogs, passed for sealers or Esquimaux, or in misty weather loomed like fabulous creatures, and I did not know whether they were giants or pygmies. I took this course when I went to lecture in Lincoln in the evening, travelling in no road and passing no house between my own hut and the lecture room. In Goose Pond, which lay in my way, a colony of musk-rats dwelt, and raised their cabins high above the ice, though none could be seen abroad when I crossed it. Walden, being like the rest usually bare of snow, or with only shallow and interrupted drifts on it, was my yard, where I could walk freely when the snow was nearly two feet deep on a level elsewhere and the villagers were confined to their streets. There, far from the village street, and except at very long intervals, from the jingle of sleigh-bells, I slid and skated, as in a vast moose-yard well trodden, overhung by oak woods and solemn pines bent down with snow or bristling with icicles.

For sounds in winter nights, and often in winter days, I heard the forlorn but melodious note of a hooting owl indefinitely far; such a sound as the frozen earth would yield if struck with a suitable plectrum, the very *lingua vernacula*[2] of Walden Wood, and quite familiar to me at last, though I never saw the bird while it was making it. I seldom opened my door in a winter evening without hearing it; *Hoo hoo hoo, hoorer hoo,* sounded sonorously, and the first three syllables accented somewhat like *how der do;* or sometimes *hoo hoo* only. One night in the beginning of winter, before the pond froze over, about nine o'clock, I was startled by the loud honking of a goose, and, stepping to the door, heard the sound of their wings like a tempest in the woods as they flew low over my house. They passed over the pond toward Fair Haven, seemingly deterred from settling by my light, their commodore honking all the while with a regular beat. Suddenly an un-mistakable cat-owl from very near me, with the most harsh and tremendous voice I ever heard from any inhabitant of the woods, responded at regular intervals to the goose, as if determined to expose and disgrace this intruder from Hudson's Bay[3] by exhibiting a greater compass and volume of voice in a native, and *boo-hoo* him out of Concord horizon. What do you mean by alarming the citadel at this time of night consecrated to me? Do you think I am ever caught napping at such an hour, and that I have not got lungs and a larynx as well as yourself? *Boo-hoo, boo-hoo, boo-hoo!* It was one of the most thrilling discords I ever heard. And yet, if you had a discriminating ear, there were in it the elements of a concord such as these plains never saw nor heard.

2. The native language of a locality.   3. An inland sea in north central Canada.

I also heard the whooping of the ice in the pond, my great bed-fellow in that part of Concord, as if it were restless in its bed and would fain turn over, were troubled with flatulency and bad dreams; or I was waked by the cracking of the ground by the frost, as if some one had driven a team against my door, and in the morning would find a crack in the earth a quarter of a mile long and a third of an inch wide.

Sometimes I heard the foxes as they ranged over the snow crust, in moonlight nights, in search of a partridge or other game, barking raggedly and demoniacally like forest dogs, as if laboring with some anxiety, or seeking expression, struggling for light and to be dogs outright and run freely in the streets; for if we take the ages into our account, may there not be a civilization going on among brutes as well as men? They seemed to me to be rudimental, burrowing men, still standing on their defence, awaiting their transformation. Sometimes one came near to my window, attracted by my light, barked a vulpine curse at me, and then retreated.

Usually the red squirrel (*Sciurus Hudsonius*) waked me in the dawn, coursing over the roof and up and down the sides of the house, as if sent out of the woods for this purpose. In the course of the winter I threw out half a bushel of ears of sweet-corn, which had not got ripe, on to the snow crust by my door, and was amused by watching the motions of the various animals which were baited by it. In the twilight and the night the rabbits came regularly and made a hearty meal. All day long the red squirrels came and went, and afforded me much entertainment by their manœuvres. One would approach at first warily through the shrub-oaks, running over the snow crust by fits and starts like a leaf blown by the wind, now a few paces this way, with wonderful speed and waste of energy, making inconceivable haste with his "trotters," as if it were for a wager, and now as many paces that way, but never getting on more than half a rod at a time; and then suddenly pausing with a ludicrous expression and a gratuitous somerset, as if all the eyes in the universe were fixed on him,—for all the motions of a squirrel, even in the most solitary recesses of the forest, imply spectators as much as those of a dancing girl,—wasting more time in delay and circumspection than would have sufficed to walk the whole distance,—I never saw one walk,—and then suddenly, before you could say Jack Robinson, he would be in the top of a young pitch-pine, winding up his clock and chiding all imaginary spectators, soliloquizing and talking to all the universe at the same time,—for no reason that I could ever detect, or he himself was aware of, I suspect. At length he would reach the corn, and selecting a suitable ear, frisk about in the same uncertain trigonometrical way to the top-most stick of my wood-pile, before my window, where he looked me in the face, and there sit for hours, supplying himself with a new ear from time to time, nibbling at first voraciously and throwing the half-naked cobs about; till at length he grew more dainty still and played with his food, tasting only the inside of the kernel, and the ear, which was held balanced over the stick by one paw, slipped from his careless grasp and fell to the ground, when he would look over at it with a ludicrous expression of uncertainty, as if suspecting that it had life, with a mind not made up whether to get it again, or a new one, or be off; now thinking of corn, then listening to hear what was in the wind. So the little impudent fellow would waste many an ear in a forenoon; till at last, seizing some longer and plumper one, considerably bigger than himself, and skilfully balancing it, he would set out with it to the woods, like a tiger with a buffalo, by the same zig-zag course and frequent pauses, scratching along with it as if it were too heavy for him and falling all the while, making its fall a diagonal between a perpendicular and horizontal, being determined to put it through at any rate;—a singularly frivolous and whimsical fellow;—and so he would get off with it to where he lived, perhaps carry it to the top of a pine tree forty or fifty rods distant, and I would afterwards find the cobs strewn about the woods in various directions.

At length the jays arrive, whose discordant screams were heard long before, as they were warily making their approach an eighth of a mile off, and in a stealthy and sneaking manner they flit from tree to tree, nearer and nearer, and pick up the kernels which the squirrels have dropped. Then, sitting on a pitch-pine bough, they attempt to swallow in their haste a kernel which is too big for their throats and chokes them; and after great labor they disgorge it, and spend an hour in the endeavor to crack it by repeated blows with their bills. They were manifestly thieves, and I had not much respect for them; but the squirrels, though at first shy, went to work as if they were taking what was their own.

Meanwhile also came the chicadees in flocks, which, picking up the crums the squirrels had dropped, flew to the nearest twig, and, placing them under their claws, hammered away at them with their little bills, as if it were an insect in the bark, till they were sufficiently reduced for their slender throats. A little flock of these tit-mice came daily to pick a dinner out of my wood-pile, or the crums at my door, with faint flitting lisping notes, like the tinkling of icicles in the grass, or else with sprightly *day day day*, or more rarely, in spring-like days, a wiry summery *phe-be* from the woodside. They were so familiar that at length one alighted on an armful of wood which I was carrying in, and pecked at the sticks without fear. I once had a sparrow alight upon my shoulder for a moment while I was hoeing in a village garden, and I felt that I was more distinguished by that circumstance than I should have been by any epaulet I could have worn. The squirrels also grew at last to be quite familiar, and occasionally stepped upon my shoe, when that was the nearest way.

When the ground was not yet quite covered, and again near the end of winter, when the snow was melted on my south hill-side and about my wood-pile, the partridges came out of the woods morning and evening to feed there. Whichever side you walk in the woods the partridge bursts away on whirring wings, jarring the snow from the dry leaves and twigs on high, which comes sifting down in the sun-beams like golden dust; for this brave bird is not to be scared by winter. It is frequently covered up by drifts, and, it is said, "sometimes plunges from on wing into the soft snow, where it remains concealed for a day or two." I used to start them in the open land also, where they had come out of the woods at sunset to "bud" the wild apple-trees. They will come regularly every evening to particular trees, where the cunning sportsman lies in wait for them, and the distant orchards next the woods suffer thus not a little. I am glad that the partridge gets fed, at any rate. It is Nature's own bird which lives on buds and diet-drink.

In dark winter mornings, or in short winter afternoons, I sometimes heard a pack of hounds threading all the woods with hounding cry and yelp, unable to resist the instinct of the chase, and the note of the hunting horn at intervals, proving that man was in the rear. The woods ring again, and yet no fox bursts forth on to the open level of the pond, nor following pack pursuing their Actæon.[4] And perhaps at evening I see the hunters returning with a single brush trailing from their sleigh for a trophy, seeking their inn. They tell me that if the fox would remain in the bosom of the frozen earth he would be safe, or if he would run in a straight line away no fox-hound could overtake him; but, having left his pursuers far behind, he stops to rest and listen till they come up, and when he runs he circles round to his old haunts, where the hunters await him. Sometimes, however, he will run upon a wall many rods, and then leap off far to one side, and he appears to know that water will not retain his scent. A hunter told me that he once saw a fox pursued by hounds burst out on to Walden when the ice was covered with shallow puddles, run part way across, and then return to the

4. In classical mythology, a hunter who was transformed into a stag and killed by his own dogs.

same shore. Ere long the hounds arrived, but here they lost the scent. Sometimes a pack hunting by themselves would pass my door, and circle round my house, and yelp and hound without regarding me, as if afflicted by a species of madness, so that nothing could divert them from the pursuit. Thus they circle until they fall upon the recent trail of a fox, for a wise hound will forsake every thing else for this. One day a man came to my hut from Lexington to inquire after his hound that made a large track, and had been hunting for a week by himself. But I fear that he was not the wiser for all I told him, for every time I attempted to answer his questions he interrupted me by asking, "What do you do here?" He had lost a dog, but found a man.

One old hunter who has a dry tongue, who used to come to bathe in Walden once every year when the water was warmest, and at such times looked in upon me, told me, that many years ago he took his gun one afternoon and went out for a cruise in Walden Wood; and as he walked the Wayland road he heard the cry of hounds approaching, and ere long a fox leaped the wall into the road, and as quick as thought leaped the other wall out of the road, and his swift bullet had not touched him. Some way behind came an old hound and her three pups in full pursuit, hunting on their own account, and disappeared again in the woods. Late in the afternoon, as he was resting in the thick woods south of Walden, he heard the voice of the hounds far over toward Fair Haven still pursuing the fox; and on they came, their hounding cry which made all the woods ring sounding nearer and nearer, now from Well-Meadow, now from the Baker Farm. For a long time he stood still and listened to their music, so sweet to a hunter's ear, when suddenly the fox appeared, threading the solemn aisles with an easy coursing pace, whose sound was concealed by a sympathetic rustle of the leaves, swift and still, keeping the ground, leaving his pursuers far behind; and, leaping upon a rock amid the woods, he sat erect and listening, with his back to the hunter. For a moment compassion restrained the latter's arm; but that was a short-lived mood, and as quick as thought can follow thought his piece was levelled, and *whang!*—the fox rolling over the rock lay dead on the ground. The hunter still kept his place and listened to the hounds. Still on they came, and now the near woods resounded through all their aisles with their demoniac cry. At length the old hound burst into view with muzzle to the ground, and snapping the air as if possessed, and ran directly to the rock; but spying the dead fox she suddenly ceased her hounding, as if struck dumb with amazement, and walked round and round him in silence; and one by one her pups arrived, and, like their mother, were sobered into silence by the mystery. Then the hunter came forward and stood in their midst, and the mystery was solved. They waited in silence while he skinned the fox, then followed the brush a while, and at length turned off into the woods again. That evening a Weston [5] Squire came to the Concord hunter's cottage to inquire for his hounds, and told how for a week they had been hunting on their own account from Weston woods. The Concord hunter told him what he knew and offered him the skin; but the other declined it and departed. He did not find his hounds that night, but the next day learned that they had crossed the river and put up at a farm-house for the night, whence, having been well fed, they took their departure early in the morning.

The hunter who told me this could remember one Sam Nutting, who used to hunt bears on Fair Haven Ledges, and exchange their skins for rum in Concord village; who told him, even, that he had seen a moose there. Nutting had a famous fox-hound named Burgoyne,—he pronounced it Bugine,—which my informant used to borrow. In the "Wast Book" [6] of an old trader of this town, who was also a captain, town-clerk, and representative, I find the following entry. Jan. 18th, 1742–3, "John Melven Cr. by 1 Grey Fox 0—2—3;" they are not now found here; and in his leger, Feb. 7th, 1743, Hezekiah Stratton has credit "by ½ a Catt [7] skin 0—1—4½;" of course, a wild-cat, for Stratton was a sergeant in the old French war, and would not have got credit for hunting less noble game. Credit is given for deer skins also, and they were daily sold. One man still preserves the horns of the last deer that was killed in this vicinity, and another has told me the particulars of the hunt in which his uncle was engaged. The hunters were formerly a numerous and merry crew here. I remember well one gaunt Nimrod [8] who would catch up a leaf by the road-side and play a strain on it wilder and more melodious, if my memory serves me, than any hunting horn.

At midnight, when there was a moon, I sometimes met with hounds in my path prowling about the woods, which would skulk out of my way, as if afraid, and stand silent amid the bushes till I had passed.

Squirrels and wild mice disputed for my store of nuts. There were scores of pitch-pines around my house, from one to four inches in diameter, which had been gnawed by mice the previous winter,—a Norwegian winter for them, for the snow lay long and deep, and they were obliged to mix a large proportion of pine bark with their other diet. These trees were alive and apparently

5. A town near Concord.
6. A daybook, a diary.
7. (can it be Calf? v. Mott ledger near beginning) [Thoreau's note]. Thoreau also underlined the word "Catt" in the text.
8. Described in the Bible as "a mighty hunter."

flourishing at mid-summer, and many of them had grown a foot, though completely girdled; but after another winter such were without exception dead. It is remarkable that a single mouse should thus be allowed a whole pine tree for its dinner, gnawing round instead of up and down it; but perhaps it is necessary in order to thin these trees, which are wont to grow up densely.

The hares (*Lepus Americanus*) were very familiar. One had her form under my house all winter, separated from me only by the flooring, and she startled me each morning by her hasty departure when I began to stir,—thump, thump, thump, striking her head against the floor timbers in her hurry. They used to come round my door at dusk to nibble the potato parings which I had thrown out, and were so nearly the color of the ground that they could hardly be distinguished when still. Sometimes in the twilight I alternately lost and recovered sight of one sitting motionless under my window. When I opened my door in the evening, off they would go with a squeak and a bounce. Near at hand they only excited my pity. One evening one sat by my door two paces from me, at first trembling with fear, yet unwilling to move; a poor wee thing, lean and bony, with ragged ears and sharp nose, scant tail and slender paws. It looked as if Nature no longer contained the breed of nobler bloods, but stood on her last toes. Its large eyes appeared young and unhealthy, almost dropsical. I took a step, and lo, away it scud with an elastic spring over the snow crust, straightening its body and its limbs into graceful length, and soon put the forest between me and itself,—the wild free venison, asserting its vigor and the dignity of Nature. Not without reason was its slenderness. Such then was its nature. (*Lepus*, *levipes*, light-foot, some think.)

What is a country without rabbits and partridges? They are among the most simple and indigenous animal products; ancient and venerable families known to antiquity as to modern times; of the very hue and substance of Nature, nearest allied to leaves and to the ground,—and to one another; it is either winged or it is legged. It is hardly as if you had seen a wild creature when a rabbit or a partridge bursts away, only a natural one, as much to be expected as rustling leaves. The partridge and the rabbit are still sure to thrive, like true natives of the soil, whatever revolutions occur. If the forest is cut off, the sprouts and bushes which spring up afford them concealment, and they become more numerous than ever. That must be a poor country indeed that does not support a hare. Our woods teem with them both, and around every swamp may be seen the partridge or rabbit walk, beset with twiggy fences and horse-hair snares, which some cow-boy tends.

The Pond in Winter

After a still winter night I awoke with the impression that some question had been put to me, which I had been endeavoring in vain to answer in my sleep, as what—how—when—where? But there was dawning Nature, in whom all creatures live, looking in at my broad windows with serene and satisfied face, and no question on *her* lips. I awoke to an answered question, to Nature and daylight. The snow lying deep on the earth dotted with young pines, and the very slope of the hill on which my house is placed, seemed to say, Forward! Nature puts no question and answers none which we mortals ask. She has long ago taken her resolution. "O Prince, our eyes contemplate with admiration and transmit to the soul the wonderful and varied spectacle of this universe. The night veils without doubt a part of this glorious creation; but day comes to reveal to us this great work, which extends from earth even into the plains of the ether."

Then to my morning work. First I take an axe and pail and go in search of water, if that be not a dream. After a cold and snowy night it needed a divining rod to find it. Every winter the liquid and trembling surface of the pond, which was so sensitive to every breath, and reflected every light and shadow, becomes solid to the depth of a foot or a foot and a half, so that it will support the heaviest teams, and perchance the snow covers it to an equal depth, and it is not to be distinguished from any level field. Like the marmots in the surrounding hills, it closes its eye-lids and becomes dormant for three months or more. Standing on the snow-covered plain, as if in a pasture amid the hills, I cut my way first through a foot of snow, and then a foot of ice, and open a window under my feet, where, kneeling to drink, I look down into the quiet parlor of the fishes, pervaded by a softened light as through a window of ground glass, with its bright sanded floor the same as in summer; there a perennial waveless serenity reigns as in the amber twilight sky, corresponding to the cool and even temperament of the inhabitants. Heaven is under our feet as well as over our heads.

Early in the morning, while all things are crisp with frost, men come with fishing reels and slender lunch, and let down their fine lines through the snowy field to take pickerel and perch; wild men, who instinctively follow other fashions and trust other authorities than their townsmen, and by their goings and comings stitch towns together in parts where else they would be ripped.

They sit and eat their luncheon in stout fear-naughts [1] on the dry
oak leaves on the shore, as wise in natural lore as the citizen is in
artificial. They never consulted with books, and know and can
tell much less than they have done. The things which they practise
are said not yet to be known. Here is one fishing for pickerel with
grown perch for bait. You look into his pail with wonder as into
a summer pond, as if he kept summer locked up at home, or knew
where she had retreated. How, pray, did he get these in mid-
winter? O, he got worms out of rotten logs since the ground
froze, and so he caught them. His life itself passes deeper in
Nature than the studies of the naturalist penetrate; himself a
subject for the naturalist. The latter raises the moss and bark
gently with his knife in search of insects; the former lays open logs
to their core with his axe, and moss and bark fly far and wide. He
gets his living by barking trees. Such a man has some right to
fish, and I love to see Nature carried out in him. The perch
swallows the grub-worm, the pickerel swallows the perch, and
the fisherman swallows the pickerel; and so all the chinks in the
scale of being are filled.

When I strolled around the pond in misty weather I was sometimes amused by the primitive mode which some ruder fisherman
had adopted. He would perhaps have placed alder branches over
the narrow holes in the ice, which were four or five rods apart and
an equal distance from the shore, and having fastened the end of
the line to a stick to prevent its being pulled through, have
passed the slack line over a twig of the alder, a foot or more
above the ice, and tied a dry oak leaf to it, which, being pulled
down, would show when he had a bite. These alders loomed
through the mist at regular intervals as you walked half way
round the pond.

Ah, the pickerel of Walden! when I see them lying on the ice,
or in the well which the fisherman cuts in the ice, making a
little hole to admit the water, I am always surprised by their
rare beauty, as if they were fabulous fishes, they are so foreign to
the streets, even to the woods, foreign as Arabia to our Concord
life. They possess a quite dazzling and transcendent beauty which
separates them by a wide interval from the cadaverous cod and
haddock whose fame is trumpeted [2] in our streets. They are not
green like the pines, nor gray like the stones, nor blue like the
sky; but they have, to my eyes, if possible, yet rarer colors, like
flowers and precious stones, as if they were the pearls, the animal-
ized *nuclei* [3] or crystals of the Walden water. They, of course,

---

1. A coat made of heavy woolen material.
2. In the nineteenth century, fish sellers
blew horns as they went through the
streets.
3. The core; an essential central element.

are Walden all over and all through; are themselves small Waldens in the animal kingdom, Waldenses.[4] It is surprising that they are caught here,—that in this deep and capacious spring, far beneath the rattling teams and chaises and tinkling sleighs that travel the Walden road, this great gold and emerald fish swims. I never chanced to see its kind in any market; it would be the cynosure of all eyes there. Easily, with a few convulsive quirks, they give up their watery ghosts, like a mortal translated before his time to the thin air of heaven.

As I was desirous to recover the long lost bottom of Walden Pond, I surveyed it carefully, before the ice broke up, early in '46, with compass and chain and sounding line. There have been many stories told about the bottom, or rather no bottom, of this pond, which certainly had no foundation for themselves. It is remarkable how long men will believe in the bottomlessness of a pond without taking the trouble to sound it. I have visited two such Bottomless Ponds in one walk in this neighborhood. Many have believed that Walden reached quite through to the other side of the globe. Some who have lain flat on the ice for a long time, looking down through the illusive medium, perchance with watery eyes into the bargain, and driven to hasty conclusions by the fear of catching cold in their breasts, have seen vast holes "into which a load of hay might be driven," if there were any body to drive it, the undoubted source of the Styx and entrance to the Infernal Regions from these parts. Others have gone down from the village with a "fifty-six" [5] and a wagon load of inch rope, but yet have failed to find any bottom; for while the "fifty-six" was resting by the way, they were paying out the rope in the vain attempt to fathom their truly immeasurable capacity for marvellousness. But I can assure my readers that Walden has a reasonably tight bottom at a not unreasonable, though at an unusual, depth. I fathomed it easily with a cod-line and a stone weighing about a pound and a half, and could tell accurately when the stone left the bottom, by having to pull so much harder before the water got underneath to help me. The greatest depth was exactly one hundred and two feet; to which may be added the five feet which it has risen since, making one hundred and seven. This is a remarkable depth for so small an area; yet not an inch of it can be spared by the imagination. What if all ponds were shallow? Would it not react on the minds of men? I am thankful that this pond was made deep and pure for a symbol. While men believe in the infinite some ponds will be thought to be bottomless.

4. A sect of religious dissenters founded about 1170 by Peter Waldo in France.

5. A 56-pound iron weight.

A factory owner, hearing what depth I had found, thought that it could not be true, for, judging from his acquaintance with dams, sand would not lie at so steep an angle. But the deepest ponds are not so deep in proportion to their area as most suppose, and, if drained, would not leave very remarkable valleys. They are not like cups between the hills; for this one, which is so unusually deep for its area, appears in a vertical section through its centre not deeper than a shallow plate. Most ponds, emptied, would leave a meadow no more hollow than we frequently see. William Gilpin, who is so admirable in all that relates to landscapes, and usually so correct, standing at the head of Loch Fyne, in Scotland, which he describes as "a bay of salt water, sixty or seventy fathoms deep, four miles in breadth," and about fifty miles long, surrounded by mountains, observes, "If we could have seen it immediately after the diluvian crash, or whatever convulsion of Nature occasioned it, before the waters gushed in, what a horrid chasm it must have appeared!

> So high as heaved the tumid hills, so low
> Down sunk a hollow bottom, broad, and deep,
> Capacious bed of waters—." [6]

But if, using the shortest diameter of Loch Fyne, we apply these proportions to Walden, which, as we have seen, appears already in a vertical section only like a shallow plate, it will appear four times as shallow. So much for the *increased* horrors of the chasm of Loch Fyne when emptied. No doubt many a smiling valley with its stretching cornfields occupies exactly such a "horrid chasm," from which the waters have receded, though it requires the insight and the far sight of the geologist to convince the unsuspecting inhabitants of this fact. Often an inquisitive eye may detect the shores of a primitive lake in the low horizon hills, and no subsequent elevation of the plain have been necessary to conceal their history. But it is easiest, as they who work on the highways know, to find the hollows by the puddles after a shower. The amount of it is, the imagination, give it the least license, dives deeper and soars higher than Nature goes. So, probably, the depth of the ocean will be found to be very inconsiderable compared with its breadth.

As I sounded through the ice I could determine the shape of the bottom with greater accuracy than is possible in surveying harbors which do not freeze over, and I was surprised at its general regularity. In the deepest part there are several acres more level than almost any field which is exposed to the sun wind and plough. In one instance, on a line arbitrarily chosen, the depth did

6. Milton, *Paradise Lost*, VII, 288–290.

not vary more than one foot in thirty rods; and generally, near the middle, I could calculate the variation for each one hundred feet in any direction beforehand within three or four inches. Some are accustomed to speak of deep and dangerous holes even in quiet sandy ponds like this, but the effect of water under these circumstances is to level all inequalities. The regularity of the bottom and its conformity to the shores and the range of the neighboring hills were so perfect that a distant promontory betrayed itself in the soundings quite across the pond, and its direction could be determined by observing the opposite shore. Cape becomes bar, and plain shoal, and valley and gorge deep water and channel.

When I had mapped the pond by the scale of ten rods to an inch, and put down the soundings, more than a hundred in all, I observed this remarkable coincidence. Having noticed that the number indicating the greatest depth was apparently in the centre of the map, I laid a rule on the map lengthwise, and then breadthwise, and found, to my surprise, that the line of greatest length intersected the line of greatest breadth *exactly* at the point of greatest depth, notwithstanding that the middle is so nearly level, the outline of the pond far from regular, and the extreme length and breadth were got by measuring into the coves; and I said to myself, Who knows but this hint would conduct to the deepest part of the ocean as well as of a pond or puddle? Is not this the rule also for the height of mountains, regarded as the opposite of valleys? We know that a hill is not highest at its narrowest part.

Of five coves, three, or all which had been sounded, were observed to have a bar quite across their mouths and deeper water within, so that the bay tended to be an expansion of water within the land not only horizontally but vertically, and to form a basin or independent pond, the direction of the two capes showing the course of the bar. Every harbor on the sea-coast, also, has its bar at its entrance. In proportion as the mouth of the cove was wider compared with its length, the water over the bar was deeper compared with that in the basin. Given, then, the length and breadth of the cove, and the character of the surrounding shore, and you have almost elements enough to make out a formula for all cases.

In order to see how nearly I could guess, with this experience, at the deepest point in a pond, by observing the outlines of its surface and the character of its shores alone, I made a plan of White Pond, which contains about forty-one acres, and, like this, has no island in it, nor any visible inlet or outlet; and as the line of greatest breadth fell very near the line of least breadth, where two opposite capes approached each other and two opposite bays receded, I ventured to mark a point a short distance from the latter line, but still on the line of greatest length, as the deepest. The deepest part was found to be within one hundred feet of this, still farther in the direction to which I had inclined, and was only one foot deeper, namely, sixty feet. Of course, a stream running through, or an island in the pond, would make the problem much more complicated.

If we knew all the laws of Nature, we should need only one fact, or the description of one actual phenomenon, to infer all the particular results at that point. Now we know only a few laws, and our result is vitiated, not, of course, by any confusion or irregularity in Nature, but by our ignorance of essential elements in the calculation. Our notions of law and harmony are commonly confined to those instances which we detect; but the harmony which results from a far greater number of seemingly conflicting, but really concurring, laws, which we have not detected, is still more wonderful. The particular laws are as our points of view, as, to the traveller, a mountain outline varies with every step, and it has an infinite number of profiles, though absolutely but one form. Even when cleft or bored through it is not comprehended in its entireness.

What I have observed of the pond is no less true in ethics. It is the law of average. Such a rule of the two diameters not only guides us toward the sun in the system and the heart in man, but draw lines through the length and breadth of the aggregate of a man's particular daily behaviors and waves of life into his coves and inlets, and where they intersect will be the height or depth of his character. Perhaps we need only to know how his shores trend and his adjacent country or circumstances, to infer his depth and concealed bottom. If he is surrounded by mountainous circumstances, an Achillean shore,[7] whose peaks overshadow and are reflected in his bosom, they suggest a corresponding depth in him. But a low and smooth shore proves him shallow on that side. In our bodies, a bold projecting brow falls off to and indicates a corresponding depth of thought. Also there is a bar across the entrance of our every cove, or particular inclination; each is our harbor for a season, in which we are detained and partially land-locked. These inclinations are not whimsical usually, but their form, size, and direction are determined by the promontories of the shore, the ancient axes of elevation. When this bar is gradually increased by storms, tides, or currents, or there is a subsidence of the waters, so that it reaches to the surface, that which was at first but an inclination in the shore in which a thought was harbored becomes an individual lake, cut off from the ocean, wherein the

7. The Greek hero, Achilles, was reportedly born in Thessaly, a mountainous region in northeastern Greece.

thought secures its own conditions, changes, perhaps, from salt to fresh, becomes a sweet sea, dead sea, or a marsh. At the advent of each individual into this life, may we not suppose that such a bar has risen to the surface somewhere? It is true, we are such poor navigators that our thoughts, for the most part, stand off and on upon a harborless coast, are conversant only with the bights of the bays of poesy, or steer for the public ports of entry, and go into the dry docks of science, where they merely refit for this world, and no natural currents concur to individualize them.

As for the inlet or outlet of Walden, I have not discovered any but rain and snow and evaporation, though perhaps, with a thermometer and a line, such places may be found, for where the water flows into the pond it will probably be coldest in summer and warmest in winter. When the ice-men were at work here in '46–7, the cakes sent to the shore were one day rejected by those who were stacking them up there, not being thick enough to lie side by side with the rest; and the cutters thus discovered that the ice over a small space was two or three inches thinner than elsewhere, which made them think that there was an inlet there. They also showed me in another place what they thought was a "leach hole," [8] through which the pond leaked out under a hill into a neighboring meadow, pushing me out on a cake of ice to see it. It was a small cavity under ten feet of water; but I think that I can warrant the pond not to need soldering till they find a worse leak than that. One has suggested, that if such a "leach hole" should be found, its connection with the meadow, if any existed, might be proved by conveying some colored powder or sawdust to the mouth of the hole, and then putting a strainer over the spring in the meadow, which would catch some of the particles carried through by the current.

While I was surveying, the ice, which was sixteen inches thick, undulated under a slight wind like water. It is well known that a level cannot be used on ice. At one rod from the shore its greatest fluctuation, when observed by means of a level on land directed toward a graduated staff on the ice, was three quarters of an inch, though the ice appeared firmly attached to the shore. It was probably greater in the middle. Who knows but if our instruments were delicate enough we might detect an undulation in the crust of the earth? When two legs of my level were on the shore and the third on the ice, and the sights were directed over the latter, a rise or fall of the ice of an almost infinitesimal amount made a difference of several feet on a tree across the pond. When I began to cut holes for sounding, there were three or four inches of water

8. A hole through which water percolates or filters.

on the ice under a deep snow which had sunk it thus far; but the water began immediately to run into these holes, and continued to run for two days in deep streams, which wore away the ice on every side, and contributed essentially, if not mainly, to dry the surface of the pond; for, as the water ran in, it raised and floated the ice. This was somewhat like cutting a hole in the bottom of a ship to let the water out. When such holes freeze, and a rain succeeds, and finally a new freezing forms a fresh smooth ice over all, it is beautifully mottled internally by dark figures, shaped somewhat like a spider's web, what you may call ice rosettes, produced by the channels worn by the water flowing from all sides to a centre. Sometimes, also, when the ice was covered with shallow puddles, I saw a double shadow of myself, one standing on the head of the other, one on the ice, the other on the trees or hill-side.

While yet it is cold January, and snow and ice are thick and solid, the prudent landlord comes from the village to get ice to cool his summer drink; impressively, even pathetically wise, to foresee the heat and thirst of July now in January,—wearing a thick coat and mittens! when so many things are not provided for. It may be that he lays up no treasures in this world which will cool his summer drink in the next. He cuts and saws the solid pond, unroofs the house of fishes, and carts off their very element and air, held fast by chains and stakes like corded wood, through the favoring winter air, to wintry cellars, to underlie the summer there. It looks like solidified azure, as, far off, it is drawn through the streets. These ice-cutters are a merry race, full of jest and sport, and when I went among them they were wont to invite me to saw pit-fashion with them, I standing underneath.

In the winter of '46–7 there came a hundred men of Hyperborean [9] extraction swoop down on to our pond one morning, with many car-loads of ungainly-looking farming tools, sleds, ploughs, drill-barrows, turf-knives, spades, saws, rakes, and each man was armed with a double-pointed pike-staff, such as is not described in the New-England Farmer or the Cultivator.[1] I did not know whether they had come to sow a crop of winter rye, or some other kind of grain recently introduced from Iceland. As I saw no manure, I judged that they meant to skim the land, as I had done, thinking the soil was deep and had lain fallow long enough. They said that a gentleman farmer, who was behind the scenes, wanted to double his money, which, as I understood, amounted to half a

9. According to classical legend, a tribe which lived far north of Greece in a land of continual sunshine and happiness.
1. Nineteenth-century farm journals.

million already; but in order to cover each one of his dollars with another, he took off the only coat, ay, the skin itself, of Walden Pond in the midst of a hard winter. They went to work at once, ploughing, harrowing, rolling, furrowing, in admirable order, as if they were bent on making this a model farm; but when I was looking sharp to see what kind of seed they dropped into the furrow, a gang of fellows by my side suddenly began to hook up the virgin mould itself, with a peculiar jerk, clean down to the sand, or rather the water,—for it was a very springy soil,—indeed all the *terra firma* [2] there was,—and haul it away on sleds, and then I guessed that they must be cutting peat in a bog. So they came and went every day, with a peculiar shriek from the locomotive, from and to some point of the polar regions, as it seemed to me, like a flock of arctic snow-birds. But sometimes Squaw Walden had her revenge, and a hired man, walking behind his team, slipped through a crack in the ground down toward Tartarus, [3] and he who was so brave before suddenly became but the ninth part of a man, almost gave up his animal heat, and was glad to take refuge in my house, and acknowledge that there was some virtue in a stove; or sometimes the frozen soil took a piece of steel out of a ploughshare, or a plough got set in the furrow and had to be cut out.

To speak literally, a hundred Irishmen, with Yankee overseers, came from Cambridge every day to get out the ice. They divided it into cakes by methods too well known to require description, and these, being sledded to the shore, were rapidly hauled off on to an ice platform, and raised by grappling irons and block and tackle, worked by horses, on to a stack, as surely as so many barrels of flour, and there placed evenly side by side, and row upon row, as if they formed the solid base of an obelisk designed to pierce the clouds. They told me that in a good day they could get out a thousand tons, which was the yield of about one acre. Deep ruts and "cradle holes" were worn in the ice, as on *terra firma*, by the passage of the sleds over the same track, and the horses invariably ate their oats out of cakes of ice hollowed out like buckets. They stacked up the cakes thus in the open air in a pile thirty-five feet high on one side and six or seven rods square, putting hay between the outside layers to exclude the air; for when the wind, though never so cold, finds a passage through, it will wear large cavities, leaving slight supports or studs only here and there, and finally topple it down. At first it looked like a vast blue fort or Valhalla; but when they began to tuck the coarse meadow hay into the crevices, and this became covered with rime and icicles, it looked like a venerable moss-grown and hoary ruin, built

2. Solid ground.

3. In Greek mythology, a region in the land of the dead.

of azure-tinted marble, the abode of Winter, that old man we see in the almanac,—his shanty, as if he had a design to estivate with us. They calculated that not twenty-five per cent. of this would reach its destination, and that two or three per cent. would be wasted in the cars. However, a still greater part of this heap had a different destiny from what was intended; for, either because the ice was found not to keep so well as was expected, containing more air than usual, or for some other reason, it never got to market. This heap, made in the winter of '46-7 and estimated to contain ten thousand tons, was finally covered with hay and boards; and though it was unroofed the following July, and a part of it carried off, the rest remaining exposed to the sun, it stood over that summer and the next winter, and was not quite melted till September 1848. Thus the pond recovered the greater part.

Like the water, the Walden ice, seen near at hand, has a green tint, but at a distance is beautifully blue, and you can easily tell it from the white ice of the river, or the merely greenish ice of some ponds, a quarter of a mile off. Sometimes one of those great cakes slips from the ice-man's sled into the village street, and lies there for a week like a great emerald, an object of interest to all passers. I have noticed that a portion of Walden which in the state of water was green will often, when frozen, appear from the same point of view blue. So the hollows about this pond will, sometimes, in the winter, be filled with a greenish water somewhat like its own, but the next day will have frozen blue. Perhaps the blue color of water and ice is due to the light and air they contain, and the most transparent is the bluest. Ice is an interesting subject for contemplation. They told me that they had some in the ice-houses at Fresh Pond five years old which was as good as ever. Why is it that a bucket of water soon becomes putrid, but frozen remains sweet forever? It is commonly said that this is the difference between the affections and the intellect.

Thus for sixteen days I saw from my window a hundred men at work like busy husbandmen, with teams and horses and apparently all the implements of farming, such a picture as we see on the first page of the almanac; and as often as I looked out I was reminded of the fable of the lark and the reapers, or the parable of the sower, and the like; and now they are all gone, and in thirty days more, probably, I shall look from the same window on the pure sea-green Walden water there, reflecting the clouds and the trees, and sending up its evaporations in solitude, and no traces will appear that a man has ever stood there. Perhaps I shall hear a solitary loon laugh as he dives and plumes himself, or shall see a lonely fisher in his boat, like a floating leaf, beholding his form reflected in the waves, where lately a hundred men securely labored.

Thus it appears that the sweltering inhabitants of Charleston and New Orleans, of Madras and Bombay and Calcutta,[4] drink at my well. In the morning I bathe my intellect in the stupendous and cosmogonal philosophy of the Bhagvat Geeta, since whose composition years of the gods have elapsed, and in comparison with which our modern world and its literature seem puny and trivial; and I doubt if that philosophy is not to be referred to a previous state of existence, so remote is its sublimity from our conceptions. I lay down the book and go to my well for water, and lo! there I meet the servant of the Bramin, priest of Brahma and Vishnu and Indra,[5] who still sits in his temple on the Ganges reading the Vedas, or dwells at the root of a tree with his crust and water jug. I meet his servant come to draw water for his master, and our buckets as it were grate together in the same well. The pure Walden water is mingled with the sacred water of the Ganges. With favoring winds it is wafted past the site of the fabulous islands of Atlantis [6] and the Hesperides,[7] makes the periplus of Hanno,[8] and, floating by Ternate and Tidore [9] and the mouth of the Persian Gulf, melts in the tropic gales of the Indian seas, and is landed in ports of which Alexander [1] only heard the names.

Spring

The opening of large tracts by the ice-cutters commonly causes a pond to break up earlier; for the water, agitated by the wind, even in cold weather, wears away the surrounding ice. But such was not the effect on Walden that year, for she had soon got a thick new garment to take the place of the old. This pond never breaks up so soon as the others in this neighborhood, on account both of its greater depth and its having no stream passing through it to melt or wear away the ice. I never knew it to open in the course of a winter, not excepting that of '52–3, which gave the ponds so severe a trial. It commonly opens about the first of April, a week or ten days later than Flints' Pond and Fair-Haven, beginning to melt on the north side and in the shallower parts where it began to freeze. It indicates better than any water here-

4. Madras, Bombay, and Calcutta, all major cities in India, were three of the many places that bought ice from New England merchants.
5. The three major Hindu deities.
6. A mythical island west of Gibraltar.
7. In Greek mythology, the so-called "daughters of the Evening" who lived near the Atlas mountains of northwest Africa.
8. Follows the route of the Carthaginian explorer, Hanno, who traveled to west Africa.
9. Islands in the Molucca Sea, south of the Philippine Islands.
1. Alexander the Great.

abouts the absolute progress of the season, being least affected
by transient changes of temperature. A severe cold of a few days'
duration in March may very much retard the opening of the
former ponds, while the temperature of Walden increases almost
uninterruptedly. A thermometer thrust into the middle of Walden
on the 6th of March, 1847, stood at 32°, or freezing point; near
the shore at 33°; in the middle of Flints' Pond, the same day, at
32½°; at a dozen rods from the shore, in shallow water, under ice
a foot thick, at 36°. This difference of three and a half degrees
between the temperature of the deep water and the shallow in the
latter pond, and the fact that a great proportion of it is comparatively shallow, show why it should break up so much sooner than
Walden. The ice in the shallowest part was at this time several
inches thinner than in the middle. In mid-winter the middle had
been the warmest and the ice thinnest there. So, also, every one
who has waded about the shores of a pond in summer must have
perceived how much warmer the water is close to the shore, where
only three or four inches deep, than a little distance out, and on
the surface where it is deep, than near the bottom. In spring the
sun not only exerts an influence through the increased temperature
of the air and earth, but its heat passes through ice a foot or more
thick, and is reflected from the bottom in shallow water, and so
also warms the water and melts the under side of the ice, at the
same time that it is melting it more directly above, making it uneven, and causing the air bubbles which it contains to extend
themselves upward and downward until it is completely honey-
combed, and at last disappears suddenly in a single spring rain.
Ice has its grain as well as wood, and when a cake begins to rot
or "comb," that is, assume the appearance of honey-comb, whatever may be its position, the air cells are at right angles with
what was the water surface. Where there is a rock or a log rising
near to the surface the ice over it is much thinner, and is frequently
quite dissolved by this reflected heat; and I have been told that in
the experiment at Cambridge to freeze water in a shallow wooden
pond, though the cold air circulated underneath, and so had
access to both sides, the reflection of the sun from the bottom more
than counterbalanced this advantage. When a warm rain in the
middle of the winter melts off the snow-ice from Walden, and
leaves a hard dark or transparent ice on the middle, there will
be a strip of rotten though thicker white ice, a rod or more wide,
about the shores, created by this reflected heat. Also, as I have
said, the bubbles themselves within the ice operate as burning
glasses to melt the ice beneath.

The phenomena of the year take place every day in a pond on
a small scale. Every morning, generally speaking, the shallow water

is being warmed more rapidly than the deep, though it may not be made so warm after all, and every evening it is being cooled more rapidly until the morning. The day is an epitome of the year. The night is the winter, the morning and evening are the spring and fall, and the noon is the summer. The cracking and booming of the ice indicate a change of temperature. One pleasant morning after a cold night, February 24th, 1850, having gone to Flints' Pond to spend the day, I noticed with surprise, that when I struck the ice with the head of my axe, it resounded like a gong for many rods around, or as if I had struck on a tight drum-head. The pond began to boom about an hour after sunrise, when it felt the influence of the sun's rays slanted upon it from over the hills; it stretched itself and yawned like a waking man with a gradually increasing tumult, which was kept up three or four hours. It took a short siesta at noon, and boomed once more toward night, as the sun was withdrawing his influence. In the right stage of the weather a pond fires its evening gun with great regularity. But in the middle of the day, being full of cracks, and the air also being less elastic, it had completely lost its resonance, and probably fishes and muskrats could not then have been stunned by a blow on it. The fishermen say that the "thundering of the pond" scares the fishes and prevents their biting. The pond does not thunder every evening, and I cannot tell surely when to expect its thundering; but though I may perceive no difference in the weather, it does. Who would have suspected so large and cold and thick-skinned a thing to be so sensitive? Yet it has its law to which it thunders obedience when it should as surely as the buds expand in the spring. The earth is all alive and covered with papillæ. The largest pond is as sensitive to atmospheric changes as the globule of mercury in its tube.

One attraction in coming to the woods to live was that I should have leisure and opportunity to see the spring come in. The ice in the pond at length begins to be honey-combed, and I can set my heel in it as I walk. Fogs and rains and warmer suns are gradually melting the snow; the days have grown sensibly longer; and I see how I shall get through the winter without adding to my wood-pile, for large fires are no longer necessary. I am on the alert for the first signs of spring, to hear the chance note of some arriving bird, or the striped squirrel's chirp, for his stores must be now nearly exhausted, or see the woodchuck venture out of his winter quarters. On the 13th of March, after I had heard the bluebird, song-sparrow, and red-wing, the ice was still nearly a foot thick. As the weather grew warmer, it was not sensibly worn away by the water, nor broken up and floated off as in rivers, but, though it was completely melted for half a rod in width about the shore, the middle was merely honey-combed and saturated with water, so that you could put your foot through it when six inches thick; but by the next day evening, perhaps, after a warm rain followed by fog, it would have wholly disappeared, all gone off with the fog, spirited away. One year I went across the middle only five days before it disappeared entirely. In 1845 Walden was first completely open on the 1st of April; in '46, the 25th of March; in '47, the 8th of April; in '51, the 28th of March; in '52, the 18th of April; in '53, the 23d of March; in '54, about the 7th of April.

Every incident connected with the breaking up of the rivers and ponds and the settling of the weather is particularly interesting to us who live in a climate of so great extremes. When the warmer days come, they who dwell near the river hear the ice crack at night with a startling whoop as loud as artillery, as if its icy fetters were rent from end to end, and within a few days see it rapidly going out. So the alligator comes out of the mud with quakings of the earth. One old man, who has been a close observer of Nature, and seems as thoroughly wise in regard to all her operations as if she had been put upon the stocks when he was a boy, and he had helped to lay her keel,—who has come to his growth, and can hardly acquire more of natural lore if he should live to the age of Methuselah,[1]—told me, and I was surprised to hear him express wonder at any of Nature's operations, for I thought that there were no secrets between them, that one spring day he took his gun and boat, and thought that he would have a little sport with the ducks. There was ice still on the meadows, but it was all gone out of the river, and he dropped down without obstruction from Sudbury, where he lived, to Fair-Haven Pond, which he found, unexpectedly, covered for the most part with a firm field of ice. It was a warm day, and he was surprised to see so great a body of ice remaining. Not seeing any ducks, he hid his boat on the north or back side of an island in the pond, and then concealed himself in the bushes on the south side, to await them. The ice was melted for three or four rods from the shore, and there was a smooth and warm sheet of water, with a muddy bottom, such as the ducks love, within, and he thought it likely that some would be along pretty soon. After he had lain still there about an hour he heard a low and seemingly very distant sound, but singularly grand and impressive, unlike any thing he had ever heard, gradually swelling and increasing as if it would have a universal and memorable ending, a sullen rush and roar, which seemed to him all at once like the sound of a vast body of fowl

---

1. As recorded in the *Bible*, Methuselah lived to be 969 years old.

coming in to settle there, and, seizing his gun, he started up in haste and excited; but he found, to his surprise, that the whole body of the ice had started while he lay there, and drifted in to the shore, and the sound he had heard was made by its edge grating on the shore,—at first gently nibbled and crumbled off, but at length heaving up and scattering its wrecks along the island to a considerable height before it came to a stand still.

At length the sun's rays have attained the right angle, and warm winds blow up mist and rain and melt the snow banks, and the sun dispersing the mist smiles on a checkered landscape of russet and white smoking with incense, through which the traveller picks his way from islet to islet, cheered by the music of a thousand tinkling rills and rivulets whose veins are filled with the blood of winter which they are bearing off.

Few phenomena gave me more delight than to observe the forms which thawing sand and clay assume in flowing down the sides of a deep cut on the railroad through which I passed on my way to the village, a phenomenon not very common on so large a scale, though the number of freshly exposed banks of the right material must have been greatly multiplied since railroads were invented. The material was sand of every degree of fineness and of various rich colors, commonly mixed with a little clay. When the frost comes out in the spring, and even in a thawing day in the winter, the sand begins to flow down the slopes like lava, sometimes bursting out through the snow and overflowing it where no sand was to be seen before. Innumerable little streams overlap and interlace one with another, exhibiting a sort of hybrid product, which obeys half way the law of currents, and half way that of vegetation. As it flows it takes the forms of sappy leaves or vines, making heaps of pulpy sprays a foot or more in depth, and resembling, as you look down on them, the laciniated lobed and imbricated thalluses of some lichens; or you are reminded of coral, of leopards' paws or birds' feet, of brains or lungs or bowels, and excrements of all kinds. It is a truly *grotesque* vegetation, whose forms and color we see imitated in bronze, a sort of architectural foliage more ancient and typical than acanthus, chiccory, ivy, vine, or any vegetable leaves; destined perhaps, under some circumstances, to become a puzzle to future geologists. The whole cut impressed me as if it were a cave with its stalactites laid open to the light. The various shades of the sand are singularly rich and agreeable, embracing the different iron colors, brown, gray, yellowish, and reddish. When the flowing mass reaches the drain at the foot of the bank it spreads out flatter into *strands*, the separate streams losing their semi-cylindrical form and gradually becoming more flat and broad, running together as they are more moist, till they form an almost flat *sand*, still variously and beautifully shaded, but in which you can trace the original forms of vegetation; till at length, in the water itself, they are converted into *banks*, like those formed off the mouths of rivers, and the forms of vegetation are lost in the ripple marks on the bottom.

The whole bank, which is from twenty to forty feet high, is sometimes overlaid with a mass of this kind of foliage, or sandy rupture, for a quarter of a mile on one or both sides, the produce of one spring day. What makes this sand foliage remarkable is its springing into existence thus suddenly. When I see on the one side the inert bank,—for the sun acts on one side first,—and on the other this luxuriant foliage, the creation of an hour, I am affected as if in a peculiar sense I stood in the laboratory of the Artist who made the world and me,—had come to where he was still at work, sporting on this bank, and with excess of energy strewing his fresh designs about. I feel as if I were nearer to the vitals of the globe, for this sandy overflow is something such a foliaceous mass as the vitals of the animal body. You find thus in the very sands an anticipation of the vegetable leaf. No wonder that the earth expresses itself outwardly in leaves, it so labors with the idea inwardly. The atoms have already learned this law, and are pregnant by it. The overhanging leaf sees here its prototype. *Internally*, whether in the globe or animal body, it is a moist thick *lobe*, a word especially applicable to the liver and lungs and the *leaves* of fat, (λείβω, *labor, lapsus*, to flow or slip downward, a lapsing; λοβος, *globus*, lobe, globe; also lap, flap, and many other words,) *externally* a dry thin *leaf*, even as the *f* and *v* are a pressed and dried *b*. The radicals of lobe are *lb*, the soft mass of the *b* (single lobed, or B, double lobed,) with a liquid *l* behind it pressing it forward. In globe, *glb*, the guttural *g* adds to the meaning the capacity of the throat. The feathers and wings of birds are still drier and thinner leaves. Thus, also, you pass from the lumpish grub in the earth to the airy and fluttering butterfly. The very globe continually transcends and translates itself, and becomes winged in its orbit. Even ice begins with delicate crystal leaves, as if it had flowed into moulds which the fronds of water plants have impressed on the watery mirror. The whole tree itself is but one leaf, and rivers are still vaster leaves whose pulp is intervening earth, and towns and cities are the ova of insects in their axils.

When the sun withdraws the sand ceases to flow, but in the morning the streams will start once more and branch and branch again into a myriad of others. You here see perchance how blood vessels are formed. If you look closely you observe that first there pushes forward from the thawing mass a stream of softened sand with a drop-like point, like the ball of the finger, feeling its way slowly and blindly downward, until at last with more heat and moisture, as the sun gets higher, the most fluid portion, in its effort to obey the law to which the most inert also yields, separates from the latter and forms for itself a meandering channel or artery within that, in which is seen a little silvery stream glancing like lightning from one stage of pulpy leaves or branches to another, and ever and anon swallowed up in the sand. It is wonderful how rapidly yet perfectly the sand organizes itself as it flows, using the best material its mass affords to form the sharp edges of its channel. Such are the sources of rivers. In the silicious matter which the water deposits is perhaps the bony system, and in the still finer soil and organic matter the fleshy fibre or cellular tissue. What is man but a mass of thawing clay? The ball of the human finger is but a drop congealed. The fingers and toes flow to their extent from the thawing mass of the body. Who knows what the human body would expand and flow out to under a more genial heaven? Is not the hand a spreading *palm* leaf with its lobes and veins? The ear may be regarded, fancifully, as a lichen, *umbilicaria*, on the side of the head, with its lobe or drop. The lip—*labium*, from *labor* (?)—laps or lapses from the sides of the cavernous mouth. The nose is a manifest congealed drop or stalactite. The chin is a still larger drop, the confluent dripping of the face. The cheeks are a slide from the brows into the valley of the face, opposed and diffused by the cheek bones. Each rounded lobe of the vegetable leaf, too, is a thick and now loitering drop, larger or smaller; the lobes are the fingers of the leaf; and as many lobes as it has, in so many directions it tends to flow, and more heat or other genial influences would have caused it to flow yet farther.

Thus it seemed that this one hillside illustrated the principle of all the operations of Nature. The Maker of this earth but patented a leaf. What Champollion [2] will decipher this hieroglyphic for us, that we may turn over a new leaf at last? This phenomenon is more exhilarating to me than the luxuriance and fertility of vineyards. True, it is somewhat excrementitious in its character, and there is no end to the heaps of liver lights and bowels, as if the globe were turned wrong side outward; but this suggests at least that Nature has some bowels, and there again is mother of humanity. This is the frost coming out of the ground; this is Spring. It precedes the green and flowery spring, as mythology precedes regular poetry. I know of nothing more purgative of winter fumes and indigestions. It convinces me that Earth is still in her swaddling

2. Jean Francois Champollion (1790–1832), French Egyptologist, deciphered the Rosetta stone which provided a key to the ancient inscriptions of Egypt.

clothes, and stretches forth baby fingers on every side. Fresh curls spring from the baldest brow. There is nothing inorganic. These foliaceous heaps lie along the bank like the slag of a furnace, showing that Nature is "in full blast" within. The earth is not a mere fragment of dead history, stratum upon stratum like the leaves of a book, to be studied by geologists and antiquaries chiefly, but living poetry like the leaves of a tree, which precede flowers and fruit,—not a fossil earth, but a living earth; compared with whose great central life all animal and vegetable life is merely parasitic. Its throes will heave our exuviæ from their graves. You may melt your metals and cast them into the most beautiful moulds you can; they will never excite me like the forms which this molten earth flows out into. And not only it, but the institutions upon it, are plastic like clay in the hands of the potter.

Ere long, not only on these banks, but on every hill and plain and in every hollow, the frost comes out of the ground like a dormant quadruped from its burrow, and seeks the sea with music, or migrates to other climes in clouds. Thaw with his gentle persuasion is more powerful than Thor [3] with his hammer. The one melts, the other but breaks in pieces.

When the ground was partially bare of snow, and a few warm days had dried its surface somewhat, it was pleasant to compare the first tender signs of the infant year just peeping forth with the stately beauty of the withered vegetation which had withstood the winter,—life-everlasting, golden-rods, pinweeds, and graceful wild grasses, more obvious and interesting frequently than in summer even, as if their beauty was not ripe till then; even cotton-grass, cat-tails, mulleins, johns-wort, hard-hack, meadow-sweet, and other strong stemmed plants, those unexhausted granaries which entertain the earliest birds,—decent weeds, at least, which widowed Nature wears. I am particularly attracted by the arching and sheaf-like top of the wool-grass; it brings back the summer to our winter memories, and is among the forms which art loves to copy, and which, in the vegetable kingdom, have the same relation to types already in the mind of man that astronomy has. It is an antique style older than Greek or Egyptian. Many of the phenomena of Winter are suggestive of an inexpressible tenderness and fragile delicacy. We are accustomed to hear this king described as a rude and boisterous tyrant; but with the gentleness of a lover he adorns the tresses of Summer.

At the approach of spring the red-squirrels got under my house,

3. In Norse mythology, the god of war and thunder.

two at a time, directly under my feet as I sat reading or writing, and kept up the queerest chuckling and chirruping and vocal pirouetting and gurgling sounds that ever were heard; and when I stamped they only chirruped the louder, as if past all fear and respect in their mad pranks, defying humanity to stop them. No you don't—chickaree—chickaree. They were wholly deaf to my arguments, or failed to perceive their force, and fell into a strain of invective that was irresistible.

The first sparrow of spring! The year beginning with younger hope than ever! The faint silvery warblings heard over the partially bare and moist fields from the blue-bird, the song-sparrow, and the red-wing, as if the last flakes of winter tinkled as they fell! What at such a time are histories, chronologies, traditions, and all written revelations? The brooks sing carols and glees to the spring. The marsh-hawk sailing low over the meadow is already seeking the first slimy life that awakes. The sinking sound of melting snow is heard in all dells, and the ice dissolves apace in the ponds. The grass flames up on the hillsides like a spring fire,—"et primitus oritur herba imbribus primoribus evocata," [4]—as if the earth sent forth an inward heat to greet the returning sun; not yellow but green is the color of its flame;—the symbol of perpetual youth, the grass-blade, like a long green ribbon, streams from the sod into the summer, checked indeed by the frost, but anon pushing on again, lifting its spear of last year's hay with the fresh life below. It grows as steadily as the rill oozes out of the ground. It is almost identical with that, for in the growing days of June, when the rills are dry, the grass blades are their channels, and from year to year the herds drink at this perennial green stream, and the mower draws from it betimes their winter supply. So our human life but dies down to its root, and still puts forth its green blade to eternity.

Walden is melting apace. There is a canal two rods wide along the northerly and westerly sides, and wider still at the east end. A great field of ice has cracked off from the main body. I hear a song-sparrow singing from the bushes on the shore,—*olit, olit, olit,—chip, chip, chip, che char,—che wiss, wiss, wiss.* He too is helping to crack it. How handsome the great sweeping curves in the edge of the ice, answering somewhat to those of the shore, but more regular! It is unusually hard, owing to the recent severe but transient cold, and all watered or waved like a palace floor. But the wind slides eastward over its opaque surface in vain, till it reaches the living surface beyond. It is glorious to behold this ribbon of water sparkling in the sun, the bare face of the pond full

4. "And for the first time, the grass rises, called forth by the first rains."

of glee and youth, as if it spoke the joy of the fishes within it, and of the sands on its shore,—a silvery sheen as from the scales of a *leuciscus*,[5] as it were all one active fish. Such is the contrast between winter and spring. Walden was dead and is alive again. But this spring it broke up more steadily, as I have said.

The change from storm and winter to serene and mild weather, from dark and sluggish hours to bright and elastic ones, is a memorable crisis which all things proclaim. It is seemingly instantaneous at last. Suddenly an influx of light filled my house, though the evening was at hand, and the clouds of winter still overhung it, and the eaves were dripping with sleety rain. I looked out the window, and lo! where yesterday was cold gray ice there lay the transparent pond already calm and full of hope as in a summer evening, reflecting a summer evening sky in its bosom, though none was visible overhead, as if it had intelligence with some remote horizon. I heard a robin in the distance, the first I had heard for many a thousand years, methought, whose note I shall not forget for many a thousand more,—the same sweet and powerful song as of yore. O the evening robin, at the end of a New England summer day! If I could ever find the twig he sits upon! I mean *he*; I mean *the twig*. This at least is not the *Turdus migratorius*.[6] The pitch-pines and shrub-oaks about my house, which had so long drooped, suddenly resumed their several characters, looked brighter, greener, and more erect and alive, as if effectually cleansed and restored by the rain. I knew that it would not rain any more. You may tell by looking at any twig of the forest, ay, at your very wood-pile, whether its winter is past or not. As it grew darker, I was startled by the *honking* of geese flying low over the woods, like weary travellers getting in late from southern lakes, and indulging at last in unrestrained complaint and mutual consolation. Standing at my door, I could hear the rush of their wings; when, driving toward my house, they suddenly spied my light, and with hushed clamor wheeled and settled in the pond. So I came in, and shut the door, and passed my first spring night in the woods.

In the morning I watched the geese from the door through the mist, sailing in the middle of the pond, fifty rods off, so large and tumultuous that Walden appeared like an artificial pond for their amusement. But when I stood on the shore they at once rose up with a great flapping of wings at the signal of their commander, and when they had got into rank circled about over my head, twenty-nine of them, and then steered straight to Canada, with a regular *honk* from the leader at intervals, trusting to break their

5. A small fresh-water fish.   6. Migratory thrush.

fast in muddier pools. A "plump" of ducks rose at the same time and took the route to the north in the wake of their noisier cousins.

For a week I heard the circling groping clangor of some solitary goose in the foggy mornings, seeking its companion, and still peopling the woods with the sound of a larger life than they could sustain. In April the pigeons were seen again flying express in small flocks, and in due time I heard the martins twittering over my clearing, though it had not seemed that the township contained so many that it could afford me any, and I fancied that they were peculiarly of the ancient race that dwelt in hollow trees ere white men came. In almost all climes the tortoise and the frog are among the precursors and heralds of this season, and birds fly with song and glancing plumage, and plants spring and bloom, and winds blow, to correct this slight oscillation of the poles and preserve the equilibrium of Nature.

As every season seems best to us in its turn, so the coming in of spring is like the creation of Cosmos out of Chaos and the realization of the Golden Age.—[7]

> "Eurus ad Auroram, Nabathacaque regna recessit,
>   Persidaque, et radiis juga subdita matutinis."

> "The East-Wind withdrew to Aurora and the Nabathæan
>   kingdom,
> And the Persian, and the ridges placed under the morning rays.

> *   *   *   *

> Man was born. Whether that Artificer of things,
> The origin of a better world, made him from the divine seed;
> Or the earth being recent and lately sundered from the high
> Ether, retained some seeds of cognate heaven." [8]

A single gentle rain makes the grass many shades greener. So our prospects brighten on the influx of better thoughts. We should be blessed if we lived in the present always, and took advantage of every accident that befell us, like the grass which confesses the influence of the slightest dew that falls on it; and did not spend our time in atoning for the neglect of past opportunities, which we call doing our duty. We loiter in winter while it is already spring. In a pleasant spring morning all men's sins are forgiven. Such a day is a truce to vice. While such a sun holds out to burn, the vilest sinner may return. Through our own recovered innocence we discern the innocence of our neighbors. You may have known your

---

7. According to Greek mythology, the universe ("Cosmos") was created from some unformed original state ("Chaos"); the Golden Age of innocence, peace, and happiness occurred soon after creation.
8. Ovid's *Metamorphoses*, Book I, lines 61–62, 78–81.

neighbor yesterday for a thief, a drunkard, or a sensualist, and merely pitied or despised him, and despaired of the world; but the sun shines bright and warm this first spring morning, recreating the world, and you meet him at some serene work, and see how his exhausted and debauched veins expand with still joy and bless the new day, feel the spring influence with the innocence of infancy, and all his faults are forgotten. There is not only an atmosphere of good will about him, but even a savor of holiness groping for expression, blindly and ineffectually perhaps, like a new-born instinct, and for a short hour the south hill-side echoes to no vulgar jest. You see some innocent fair shoots preparing to burst from his gnarled rind and try another year's life, tender and fresh as the youngest plant. Even he has entered into the joy of his Lord. Why the jailer does not leave open his prison doors,—why the judge does not dismiss his case,—why the preacher does not dismiss his congregation! It is because they do not obey the hint which God gives them, nor accept the pardon which he freely offers to all.

"A return to goodness produced each day in the tranquil and beneficent breath of the morning, causes that in respect to the love of virtue and the hatred of vice, one approaches a little the primitive nature of man, as the sprouts of the forest which has been felled. In like manner the evil which one does in the interval of a day prevents the germs of virtues which began to spring up again from developing themselves and destroys them.

"After the germs of virtue have thus been prevented many times from developing themselves, then the beneficent breath of evening does not suffice to preserve them. As soon as the breath of evening does not suffice longer to preserve them, then the nature of man does not differ much from that of the brute. Men seeing the nature of this man like that of the brute, think that he has never possessed the innate faculty of reason. Are those the true and natural sentiments of man?" [9]

> "The Golden Age was first created, which without any avenger
> Spontaneously without law cherished fidelity and rectitude.
> Punishment and fear were not; nor were threatening words read
> On suspended brass; nor did the suppliant crowd fear
> The words of their judge; but were safe without an avenger.
> Not yet the pine felled on its mountains had descended
> To the liquid waves that it might see a foreign world,
> And mortals knew no shores but their own.
>
>   *   *   *   *
>
> There was eternal spring, and placid zephyrs with warm
> Blasts soothed the flowers born without seed." [1]

9. From the Chinese philosopher, Meng-tse.

1. Ovid's *Metamorphoses*, Book I, lines 89–96, 107–8.

On the 29th of April, as I was fishing from the bank of the river near the Nine-Acre-Corner bridge, standing on the quaking grass and willow roots, where the muskrats lurk, I heard a singular rattling sound, somewhat like that of the sticks which boys play with their fingers, when, looking up, I observed a very slight and graceful hawk, like a night-hawk, alternately soaring like a ripple and tumbling a rod or two over and over, showing the underside of its wings, which gleamed like a satin ribbon in the sun, or like the pearly inside of a shell. This sight reminded me of falconry and what nobleness and poetry are associated with that sport. The Merlin it seemed to me it might be called: but I care not for its name. It was the most ethereal flight I had ever witnessed. It did not simply flutter like a butterfly, nor soar like the larger hawks, but it sported with proud reliance in the fields of air; mounting again and again with its strange chuckle, it repeated its free and beautiful fall, turning over and over like a kite, and then recovering from its lofty tumbling, as if it had never set its foot on *terra firma*. It appeared to have no companion in the universe,— sporting there alone,—and to need none but the morning and the ether with which it played. It was not lonely, but made all the earth lonely beneath it. Where was the parent which hatched it, its kindred, and its father in the heavens? The tenant of the air, it seemed related to the earth but by an egg hatched some time in the crevice of a crag;—or was its native nest made in the angle of a cloud, woven of the rainbow's trimmings and the sunset sky, and lined with some soft midsummer haze caught up from earth? Its eyry now some cliffy cloud.

Beside this I got a rare mess of golden and silver and bright cupreous fishes, which looked like a string of jewels. Ah! I have penetrated to those meadows on the morning of many a first spring day, jumping from hummock to hummock, from willow root to willow root, when the wild river valley and the woods were bathed in so pure and bright a light as would have waked the dead, if they had been slumbering in their graves, as some suppose. There needs no stronger proof of immortality. All things must live in such a light. O Death, where was thy sting? O Grave, where was thy victory, then?

Our village life would stagnate if it were not for the unexplored forests and meadows which surround it. We need the tonic of wildness,—to wade sometimes in marshes where the bittern and the meadow-hen lurk, and hear the booming of the snipe; to smell the whispering sedge where only some wilder and more solitary fowl builds her nest, and the mink crawls with its belly close to the ground. At the same time that we are earnest to explore and learn all things, we require that all things be mysterious and unexplorable, that land and sea be infinitely wild, unsurveyed and unfathomed by us because unfathomable. We can never have enough of Nature. We must be refreshed by the sight of inexhaustible vigor, vast and Titanic features, the sea-coast with its wrecks, the wilderness with its living and its decaying trees, the thunder cloud, and the rain which lasts three weeks and produces freshets. We need to witness our own limits transgressed, and some life pasturing freely where we never wander. We are cheered when we observe the vulture feeding on the carrion which disgusts and disheartens us and deriving health and strength from the repast. There was a dead horse in the hollow by the path to my house, which compelled me sometimes to go out of my way, especially in the night when the air was heavy, but the assurance it gave me of the strong appetite and inviolable health of Nature was my compensation for this. I love to see that Nature is so rife with life that myriads can be afforded to be sacrificed and suffered to prey on one another; that tender organizations can be so serenely squashed out of existence like pulp,—tadpoles which herons gobble up, and tortoises and toads run over in the road; and that sometimes it has rained flesh and blood! With the liability to accident, we must see how little account is to be made of it. The impression made on a wise man is that of universal innocence. Poison is not poisonous after all, nor are any wounds fatal. Compassion is a very untenable ground. It must be expeditious. Its pleadings will not bear to be stereotyped.

Early in May, the oaks, hickories, maples, and other trees, just putting out amidst the pine woods around the pond, imparted a brightness like sunshine to the landscape, especially in cloudy days, as if the sun were breaking through mists and shining faintly on the hill-sides here and there. On the third or fourth of May I saw a loon in the pond, and during the first week of the month I heard the whippoorwill, the brown-thrasher, the veery, the wood-pewee, the chewink, and other birds. I had heard the wood-thrush long before. The phœbe had already come once more and looked in at my door and window, to see if my house was cavern-like enough for her, sustaining herself on humming wings with clinched talons, as if she held by the air, while she surveyed the premises. The sulphur-like pollen of the pitch-pine soon covered the pond and the stones and rotten wood along the shore, so that you could have collected a barrel-ful. This is the "sulphur showers" we hear of. Even in Calidas' [2] drama of Sacontala, we read of "rills dyed yellow with the golden dust of the lotus." And so the seasons went rolling on into summer, as one rambles into higher and higher

---

2. Fifth-century Hindu poet and dramatist; also spelled "Kalidasa."

grass.

Thus was my first year's life in the woods completed; and the second year was similar to it. I finally left Walden September 6th, 1847.

Conclusion

To the sick the doctors wisely recommend a change of air and scenery. Thank Heaven, here is not all the world. The buckeye does not grow in New England, and the mocking-bird is rarely heard here. The wild-goose is more of a cosmopolite than we; he breaks his fast in Canada, takes a luncheon in the Ohio, and plumes himself for the night in a southern bayou. Even the bison, to some extent, keeps pace with the seasons, cropping the pastures of the Colorado only till a greener and sweeter grass awaits him by the Yellowstone. Yet we think that if rail-fences are pulled down, and stone-walls piled up on our farms, bounds are henceforth set to our lives and our fates decided. If you are chosen town-clerk, forsooth, you cannot go to Tierra del Fuego this summer: but you may go to the land of infernal fire nevertheless. The universe is wider than our views of it.

Yet we should oftener look over the tafferel of our craft, like curious passengers, and not make the voyage like stupid sailors picking oakum.[1] The other side of the globe is but the home of our correspondent. Our voyaging is only great-circle sailing,[2] and the doctors prescribe for diseases of the skin merely. One hastens to Southern Africa to chase the giraffe; but surely that is not the game he would be after. How long, pray, would a man hunt giraffes if he could? Snipes and woodcocks also may afford rare sport; but I trust it would be nobler game to shoot one's self.—

> "Direct your eye right inward, and you'll find
> A thousand regions in your mind
> Yet undiscovered. Travel them, and be
> Expert in home-cosmography." [3]

What does Africa,—what does the West stand for? Is not our own interior white on the chart? black though it may prove, like the coast, when discovered. Is it the source of the Nile,[4] or the

1. Oakum, a hemp fiber obtained by untwisting and picking out the fibers of old rope, is used for caulking seams in a ship; picking oakum is a dull and monotonous job.
2. In geometry, a great circle is a circle formed on the surface of a sphere by a plane which passes through the center of the sphere; great-circle sailing is navigation along the arc of any great circle on the earth's surface.
3. William Habbington (1605–1664), "To My Honoured Friend Sir Ed. P. Knight." Thoreau modernized the spelling and changed "eye-sight" to "eye right."
4. The longest river in Africa. In Thoreau's day, geographers were attempting to discover the sources of many major rivers.

Niger,[5] or the Mississippi, or a North-West Passage [6] around this continent, that we would find? Are these the problems which most concern mankind? Is Franklin [7] the only man who is lost, that his wife should be so earnest to find him? Does Mr. Grinnell [8] know where he himself is? Be rather the Mungo Park,[9] the Lewis and Clarke [1] and Frobisher,[2] of your own streams and oceans; explore your own higher latitudes,—with shiploads of preserved meats to support you, if they be necessary; and pile the empty cans sky-high for a sign. Were preserved meats invented to preserve meat merely? Nay, be a Columbus to whole new continents and worlds within you, opening new channels, not of trade, but of thought. Every man is the lord of a realm beside which the earthly empire of the Czar is but a petty state, a hummock left by the ice. Yet some can be patriotic who have no *self*-respect, and sacrifice the greater to the less. They love the soil which makes their graves, but have no sympathy with the spirit which may still animate their clay. Patriotism is a maggot in their heads. What was the meaning of that South-Sea Exploring Expedition,[3] with all its parade and expense, but an indirect recognition of the fact, that there are continents and seas in the moral world, to which every man is an isthmus or an inlet, yet unexplored by him, but that it is easier to sail many thousand miles through cold and storm and cannibals, in a government ship, with five hundred men and boys to assist one, than it is to explore the private sea, the Atlantic and Pacific Ocean of one's being alone.—

> "Erret, et extremos alter scrutetur Iberos.
> Plus habet hic vitæ, plus habet ille viæ." [4]

Let them wander and scrutinize the outlandish Australians.
I have more of God, they more of the road.

It is not worth the while to go round the world to count the cats in Zanzibar.[5] Yet do this even till you can do better, and

---

5. A river in western Africa.
6. A water route between the Atlantic and Pacific along the northern coast of North America.
7. John Franklin (1786–1847), English explorer who died in an attempt to find the Northwest Passage.
8. Henry Grinnell (1799–1874), an American, organized an expedition to search for John Franklin.
9. Scottish explorer (1771–1806?) who traced the course of the Niger River.
1. Meriwether Lewis (1774–1809) and William Clark (1770–1838) led an expedition to discover a land route to the Pacific Ocean (1804–1806).

2. Martin Frobisher (1535?–1594), English explorer who attempted three times to find the Northwest Passage.
3. An expedition sponsored by the U.S. Navy and led by Charles Wilkes (1798–1877) which explored the South Pacific and Antarctic Oceans in 1838–1842.
4. From Claudian (fl. 400 A.D.), "The Old Man of Verona." In his translation, Thoreau substitutes "Australians" for "Iberians" (i.e., those living in the part of Europe now comprising Spain and Portugal).
5. An island off the coast of eastern Africa.

you may perhaps find some "Symmes' Hole" [6] by which to get at the inside at last. England and France, Spain and Portugal, Gold Coast and Slave Coast,[7] all front on this private sea; but no bark from them has ventured out of sight of land, though it is without doubt the direct way to India. If you would learn to speak all tongues and conform to the customs of all nations, if you would travel farther than all travellers, be naturalized in all climes, and cause the Sphinx [8] to dash her head against a stone, even obey the precept of the old philospher,[9] and Explore thyself. Herein are demanded the eye and the nerve. Only the defeated and deserters go to the wars, cowards that run away and enlist. Start now on that farthest western way, which does not pause at the Mississippi or the Pacific, nor conduct toward a worn-out China or Japan, but leads on direct a tangent to this sphere, summer and winter, day and night, sun down, moon down, and at last earth down too.

It is said that Mirabeau [1] took to highway robbery "to ascertain what degree of resolution was necessary in order to place one's self in formal opposition to the most sacred laws of society." He declared that "a soldier who fights in the ranks does not require half so much courage as a foot-pad,"—"that honor and religion have never stood in the way of a well-considered and a firm resolve." This was manly, as the world goes; and yet it was idle, if not desperate. A saner man would have found himself often enough "in formal opposition" to what are deemed "the most sacred laws of society," through obedience to yet more sacred laws, and so have tested his resolution without going out of his way. It is not for a man to put himself in such an attitude to society, but to maintain himself in whatever attitude he find himself through obedience to the laws of his being, which will never be one of opposition to a just government, if he should chance to meet with such.

I left the woods for as good a reason as I went there. Perhaps it seemed to me that I had several more lives to live, and could not spare any more time for that one. It is remarkable how easily and insensibly we fall into a particular route, and make a beaten track for ourselves. I had not lived there a week before

6. According to John Symmes, a retired Army officer, "the earth is hollow and habitable within"; from 1818 until his death in 1829, he tried to raise support for an expedition.
7. The Ivory, Gold, and Slave Coasts are regions located along the Gulf of Guinea on the western coast of Africa.
8. In Greek mythology, a winged monster with a woman's head and a lion's body that destroyed anyone unable to guess her riddle; according to legend, Oedipus guessed the riddle, and the Sphinx killed herself.
9. The Greek philosopher, Socrates (469?–399 B.C.), was noted for his dictum "Know thyself."
1. Honore Riqueti, Count de Mirabeau (1749–1791), French Revolutionary statesman.

my feet wore a path from my door to the pond-side; and though it is five or six years since I trod it, it is still quite distinct. It is true, I fear that others may have fallen into it, and so helped to keep it open. The surface of the earth is soft and impressible by the feet of men; and so with the paths which the mind travels. How worn and dusty, then, must be the highways of the world, how deep the ruts of tradition and conformity! I did not wish to take a cabin passage, but rather to go before the mast and on the deck of the world, for there I could best see the moonlight amid the mountains. I do not wish to go below now.

I learned this, at least, by my experiment; that if one advances confidently in the direction of his dreams, and endeavors to live the life which he has imagined, he will meet with a success unexpected in common hours. He will put some things behind, will pass an invisible boundary; new, universal, and more liberal laws will begin to establish themselves around and within him; or the old laws be expanded, and interpreted in his favor in a more liberal sense, and he will live with the license of a higher order of beings. In proportion as he simplifies his life, the laws of the universe will appear less complex, and solitude will not be solitude, nor poverty poverty, nor weakness weakness. If you have built castles in the air, your work need not be lost; that is where they should be. Now put the foundations under them.

It is a ridiculous demand which England and America make, that you shall speak so that they can understand you. Neither men nor toad-stools grow so. As if that were important, and there were not enough to understand you without them. As if Nature could support but one order of understandings, could not sustain birds as well as quadrupeds, flying as well as creeping things, and *hush* and *who*, which Bright [2] can understand, were the best English. As if there were safety in stupidity alone. I fear chiefly lest my expression may not be *extra- vagant* enough, may not wander far enough beyond the narrow limits of my daily experience, so as to be adequate to the truth of which I have been convinced. *Extra vagance!* it depends on how you are yarded. The migrating buffalo, which seeks new pastures in another latitude, is not extravagant like the cow which kicks over the pail, leaps the cow-yard fence, and runs after her calf, in milking time. I desire to speak somewhere *without* bounds; like a man in a waking moment, to men in their waking moments; for I am convinced that I cannot exaggerate enough even to lay the foundation of a true expression. Who that has heard a strain of music feared

2. A common name for an ox.

then lest he should speak extravagantly any more forever? In view of the future or possible, we should live quite laxly and undefined in front, our outlines dim and misty on that side; as our shadows reveal an insensible perspiration toward the sun. The volatile truth of our words should continually betray the inadequacy of the residual statement. Their truth is instantly *translated*; its literal monument alone remains. The words which express our faith and piety are not definite; yet they are significant and fragrant like frankincense to superior natures.

Why level downward to our dullest perception always, and praise that as common sense? The commonest sense is the sense of men asleep, which they express by snoring. Sometimes we are inclined to class those who are once-and-a-half witted with the half-witted, because we appreciate only a third part of their wit. Some would find fault with the morning-red, if they ever got up early enough. "They pretend," as I hear, "that the verses of Kabir [3] have four different senses; illusion, spirit, intellect, and the exoteric doctrine of the Vedas;" but in this part of the world it is considered a ground for complaint if a man's writings admit of more than one interpretation. While England endeavors to cure the potato-rot, will not any endeavor to cure the brain-rot, which prevails so much more widely and fatally?

I do not suppose that I have attained to obscurity, but I should be proud if no more fatal fault were found with my pages on this score than was found with the Walden ice. Southern customers objected to its blue color, which is the evidence of its purity, as if it were muddy, and preferred the Cambridge ice, which is white, but tastes of weeds. The purity men love is like the mists which envelop the earth, and not like the azure ether beyond.

Some are dinning in our ears that we Americans, and moderns generally, are intellectual dwarfs compared with the ancients, or even the Elizabethan men. But what is that to the purpose? A living dog is better than a dead lion. Shall a man go and hang himself because he belongs to the race of pygmies, and not be the biggest pygmy that he can? Let every one mind his own business, and endeavor to be what he was made.

Why should we be in such desperate haste to succeed, and in such desperate enterprises? If a man does not keep pace with his companions, perhaps it is because he hears a different drummer. Let him step to the music which he hears, however measured or far away. It is not important that he should mature as soon

3. An Indian mystic of the fifteenth century who tried to reconcile the religions of the Hindus and Moslems; the quotation is from Garcin de Tassy, *History of Hindu Literature* (Paris, 1839).

as an apple-tree or an oak. Shall he turn his spring into summer? If the condition of things which we were made for is not yet, what were any reality which we can substitute? We will not be shipwrecked on a vain reality. Shall we with pains erect a heaven of blue glass over ourselves, though when it is done we shall be sure to gaze still at the true ethereal heaven far above, as if the former were not?

There was an artist [4] in the city of Kouroo who was disposed to strive after perfection. One day it came into his mind to make a staff. Having considered that in an imperfect work time is an ingredient, but into a perfect work time does not enter, he said to himself, It shall be perfect in all respects, though I should do nothing else in my life. He proceeded instantly to the forest for wood, being resolved that it should not be made of unsuitable material; and as he searched for and rejected stick after stick, his friends gradually deserted him, for they grew old in their works and died, but he grew not older by a moment. His singleness of purpose and resolution, and his elevated piety, endowed him, without his knowledge, with perennial youth. As he made no compromise with Time, Time kept out of his way, and only sighed at a distance because he could not overcome him. Before he had found a stock in all respects suitable the city of Kouroo was a hoary ruin, and he sat on one of its mounds to peel the stick. Before he had given it the proper shape the dynasty of the Candahars was at an end, and with the point of the stick he wrote the name of the last of that race in the sand, and then resumed his work. By the time he had smoothed and polished the staff Kalpa was no longer the pole-star; and ere he had put on the ferule and the head adorned with precious stones, Brahma had awoke and slumbered many times. But why do I stay to mention these things? When the finishing stroke was put to his work, it suddenly expanded before the eyes of the astonished artist into the fairest of all the creations of Brahma. He had made a new system in making a staff, a world with full and fair proportions; in which, though the old cities and dynasties had passed away, fairer and more glorious ones had taken their places. And now he saw by the heap of shavings still fresh at his feet, that, for him and his work, the former lapse of time had been an illusion, and that no more time had elapsed than is required for

4. Scholars generally agree that this "legend" was probably composed by Thoreau. In the Hindu scripture, Bha-gavad-Gita, there is a nation of Kooroo; Kalpa is not a star but the period of time between the creation and destruc-tion of the world, said to be more than four billion years; Brahma, the supreme Hindu deity, reputedly has a day and night equal to one Kalpa: at the end of every kalpa, the world is absorbed into Brahma and then re-created.

a single scintillation from the brain of Brahma to fall on and inflame the tinder of a mortal brain. The material was pure, and his art was pure; how could the result be other than wonderful?

No face which we can give to a matter will stead us so well at last as the truth. This alone wears well. For the most part, we are not where we are, but in a false position. Through an infirmity of our natures, we suppose a case, and put ourselves into it, and hence are in two cases at the same time, and it is doubly difficult to get out. In sane moments we regard only the facts, the case that is. Say what you have to say, not what you ought. Any truth is better than make-believe. Tom Hyde, the tinker, standing on the gallows, was asked if he had any thing to say. "Tell the tailors," said he, "to remember to make a knot in their thread before they take the first stitch." His companion's prayer is forgotten.

However mean your life is, meet it and live it; do not shun it and call it hard names. It is not so bad as you are. It looks poorest when you are richest. The fault-finder will find faults even in paradise. Love your life, poor as it is. You may perhaps have some pleasant, thrilling, glorious hours, even in a poorhouse. The setting sun is reflected from the windows of the almshouse as brightly as from the rich man's abode; the snow melts before its door as early in the spring. I do not see but a quiet mind may live as contentedly there, and have as cheering thoughts, as in a palace. The town's poor seem to me often to live the most independent lives of any. May be they are simply great enough to receive without misgiving. Most think that they are above being supported by the town; but it oftener happens that they are not above supporting themselves by dishonest means, which should be more disreputable. Cultivate poverty like a garden herb, like sage. Do not trouble yourself much to get new things, whether clothes or friends. Turn the old; return to them. Things do not change; we change. Sell your clothes and keep your thoughts. God will see that you do not want society. If I were confined to a corner of a garret all my days, like a spider, the world would be just as large to me while I had my thoughts about me. The philosopher [5] said: "From an army of three divisions one can take away its general, and put it in disorder; from the man the most abject and vulgar one cannot take away his thought." Do not seek so anxiously to be developed, to subject yourself to many influences to be played on; it is all dissipation. Humility like darkness reveals the heavenly lights. The shadows of poverty and meanness gather around us, "and lo! creation widens to our

5. Confucius.

view." [6] We are often reminded that if there were bestowed on us the wealth of Crœsus,[7] our aims must still be the same, and our means essentially the same. Moreover, if you are restricted in your range by poverty, if you cannot buy books and newspapers, for instance, you are but confined to the most significant and vital experiences; you are compelled to deal with the material which yields the most sugar and the most starch. It is life near the bone where it is sweetest. You are defended from being a trifler. No man loses ever on a lower level by magnanimity on a higher. Superfluous wealth can buy superfluities only. Money is not required to buy one necessary of the soul.

I live in the angle of a leaden wall, into whose composition was poured a little alloy of bell metal. Often, in the repose of my mid-day, there reaches my ears a confused *tintinnabulum* [8] from without. It is the noise of my contemporaries. My neighbors tell me of their adventures with famous gentlemen and ladies, what notabilities they met at the dinner-table; but I am no more interested in such things than in the contents of the Daily Times. The interest and the conversation are about costume and manners chiefly; but a goose is a goose still, dress it as you will. They tell me of California and Texas, of England and the Indies, of the Hon. Mr. —— of Georgia or of Massachusetts, all transient and fleeting phenomena, till I am ready to leap from their court-yard like the Mameluke bey.[9] I delight to come to my bearings,—not walk in procession with pomp and parade, in a conspicuous place, but to walk even with the Builder of the universe, if I may,—not to live in this restless, nervous, bustling, trivial Nineteenth Century, but stand or sit thoughtfully while it goes by. What are men celebrating? They are all on a committee of arrangements, and hourly expect a speech from somebody. God is only the president of the day, and Webster [1] is his orator. I love to weigh, to settle, to gravitate toward that which most strongly and rightfully attracts me;—not hang by the beam of the scale and try to weigh less,—not suppose a case, but take the case that is; to travel the only path I can, and that on which no power can resist me. It affords me no satisfaction to commence to spring an arch before I have got a solid foundation. Let us not play

6. From "Night and Death," by Joseph Blanco White, English ecclesiastic and poet (1775–1841). According to White, both night and death reveal knowledge of a wider universe to us. In the poem, the line is: "lo! creation widened in man's view."
7. King of Lydia, in western Asia Minor, in the sixth century B.C., noted for his wealth.
8. Literally, a small tinkling bell; here, a widespread ringing of several discordant bells.
9. The Mamelukes, a military caste in Egypt, were massacred in 1811 by Mehemet Ali, viceroy of Egypt; a disputed story holds that one man leaped from a wall to his horse and escaped. "Bey" is a term of respect.
1. Daniel Webster, senator from Massachusetts and a noted orator.

at kittlybenders.[2] There is a solid bottom every where. We read that the traveller asked the boy if the swamp before him had a hard bottom. The boy replied that it had. But presently the traveller's horse sank in up to the girths, and he observed to the boy, "I thought you said that this bog had a hard bottom." "So it has," answered the latter, "but you have not got half way to it yet." So it is with the bogs and quicksands of society; but he is an old boy that knows it. Only what is thought said or done at a certain rare coincidence is good. I would not be one of those who will foolishly drive a nail into mere lath and plastering; such a deed would keep me awake nights. Give me a hammer, and let me feel for the furrowing. Do not depend on the putty. Drive a nail home and clinch it so faithfully that you can wake up in the night and think of your work with satisfaction,—a work at which you would not be ashamed to invoke the Muse.[3] So will help you God, and so only. Every nail driven should be as another rivet in the machine of the universe, you carrying on the work.

Rather than love, than money, than fame, give me truth. I sat at a table where were rich food and wine in abundance, and obsequious attendance, but sincerity and truth were not; and I went away hungry from the inhospitable board. The hospitality was as cold as the ices. I thought that there was no need of ice to freeze them. They talked to me of the age of the wine and the fame of the vintage; but I thought of an older, a newer, and purer wine, of a more glorious vintage, which they had not got, and could not buy. The style, the house and grounds and "entertainment" pass for nothing with me. I called on the king, but he made me wait in his hall, and conducted like a man incapacitated for hospitality. There was a man in my neighborhood who lived in a hollow tree. His manners were truly regal. I should have done better had I called on him.

How long shall we sit in our porticoes practising idle and musty virtues, which any work would make impertinent? As if one were to begin the day with long-suffering, and hire a man to hoe his potatoes; and in the afternoon go forth to practise Christian meekness and charity with goodness aforethought! Consider the China pride [4] and stagnant self-complacency of mankind. This generation reclines a little to congratulate itself on being the last of an illustrious line; and in Boston and London and Paris and Rome, thinking of its long descent, it speaks of its progress in art and science and literature with satisfaction. There

2. A game in which children attempt to run or skate on thin ice without breaking it.
3. In Greek mythology, one of the nine goddesses of poetry, music, dance, and so forth; epic poems traditionally begin with an invocation to the Muses.
4. The Chinese empire was commonly believed to be smug and self-satisfied.

are the Records of the Philosophical Societies, and the public Eulogies of *Great Men!* It is the good Adam contemplating his own virtue. "Yes, we have done great deeds, and sung divine songs, which shall never die,"—that is, as long as *we* can remember them. The learned societies and great men of Assyria,[5]—where are they? What youthful philosophers and experimentalists we are! There is not one of my readers who has yet lived a whole human life. These may be but the spring months in the life of the race. If we have had the seven-years' itch, we have not seen the seventeen-year locust yet in Concord. We are acquainted with a mere pellicle of the globe on which we live. Most have not delved six feet beneath the surface, nor leaped as many above it. We know not where we are. Beside, we are sound asleep nearly half our time. Yet we esteem ourselves wise, and have an established order on the surface. Truly, we are deep thinkers, we are ambitious spirits! As I stand over the insect crawling amid the pine needles on the forest floor, and endeavoring to conceal itself from my sight, and ask myself why it will cherish those humble thoughts, and hide its head from me who might, perhaps, be its benefactor, and impart to its race some cheering information, I am reminded of the greater Benefactor and Intelligence that stands over me the human insect.

There is an incessant influx of novelty into the world, and yet we tolerate incredible dulness. I need only suggest what kind of sermons are still listened to in the most enlightened countries. There are such words as joy and sorrow, but they are only the burden of a psalm, sung with a nasal twang, while we believe in the ordinary and mean. We think that we can change our clothes only. It is said that the British Empire is very large and respectable, and that the United States are a first-rate power. We do not believe that a tide rises and falls behind every man which can float the British Empire like a chip, if he should ever harbor it in his mind. Who knows what sort of seventeen-year locust will next come out of the ground? The government of the world I live in was not framed, like that of Britain, in after-dinner conversations over the wine.

The life in us is like the water in the river. It may rise this year higher than man has ever known it, and flood the parched uplands; even this may be the eventful year, which will drown out all our muskrats. It was not always dry land where we dwell. I see far inland the banks which the stream anciently washed, before science began to record its freshets. Every one has heard the story which has gone the rounds of New England, of a strong and

5. An ancient empire in western Asia.

beautiful bug which came out of the dry leaf of an old table of apple-tree wood, which had stood in a farmer's kitchen for sixty years, first in Connecticut, and afterward in Massachusetts,— from an egg deposited in the living tree many years earlier still, as appeared by counting the annual layers beyond it; which was heard gnawing out for several weeks, hatched perchance by the heat of an urn. Who does not feel his faith in a resurrection and immortality strengthened by hearing of this? Who knows what beautiful and winged life, whose egg has been buried for ages under many concentric layers of woodenness in the dead dry life of society, deposited at first in the alburnum of the green and living tree, which has been gradually converted into the semblance of its well-seasoned tomb,—heard perchance gnawing out now for years by the astonished family of man, as they sat round the festive board,—may unexpectedly come forth from amidst society's most trivial and handselled furniture, to enjoy its perfect summer life at last!

I do not say that John or Jonathan [6] will realize all this; but such is the character of that morrow which mere lapse of time can never make to dawn. The light which puts out our eyes is darkness to us. Only that day dawns to which we are awake. There is more day to dawn. The sun is but a morning star.

THE END.

6. Common mid-nineteenth century names for an Englishman and an American, respectively.

A TEXTUAL NOTE ON *WALDEN*

After *Walden* was published, Thoreau went carefully through one copy and made a number of corrections and annotations, a complete list of which was compiled by Reginald L. Cook and published in the *Thoreau Society Bulletin*, no. 42 (Winter, 1953). With the exceptions noted below, these are incorporated in the present edition. Where possible, they are included in the text; where the annotations are long and obviously not intended as part of the text, they are included among the footnotes and are followed by the bracketed statement: [Thoreau's note]. The following is a list of the included corrections and annotations:

First Edition	Thoreau's correction or annotation
page 14, line 3: post	port
page 17, line 10: wheat was handed	wheat is said to have been handed
page 64, line 24: come to the end of them	accomplish it
page 79, line 33: are	were
page 79, line 33: rings	rang
page 85, line 6: single	double
page 91, line 29: remunerate,	remunerate
page 114, line 6: invariably	invariably,
page 122, line 24:	This is told of Alexander's Lake in Killingly Ct. by Barber v. *his* Con. Hist. Coll. [Written in the margin.]
page 122, bottom of page	Evelyn in his Diary (1654) mentions "the parish of Saffron Walden, famous for the abundance of Saffron there cultivated, and esteemed the best of any foreign country."
page 123, line 29: breams	breams, Pomotis obesus [Nov. 26–58] one trout weighing a little over 5 lbs—(Nov. 14–57)
page 124, line 16: it,	it, kingfisher dart away from its cover,
page 125, line 30: insects,	insects (Hydrometer),
page 134, line 23: white	black
page 150, line 9: kind	kind (*mus leucopus*)
page 169, line 32:	(Mrs. Hooper)
page 171, line 21: Stratten	Stratton
page 171, line 25:	[Thoreau inserted an "X" at the end of the line and, at the bottom of the page, wrote:] X Surveying for Cyrus Jarvis Dec. 23 '56—he shows me a deed of this lot containing 6 A. 52 rods all on the W. of the Wayland Road—& "consisting of plowland, orcharding & woodland"—sold by Joseph Stratton to Samuel Swan of Concord In holder Aug. 11th 1777
page 177, line 18: meadow	meadow (deer)
page 181, line 44: brisk	frisk
page 185, line 24: Catt	*Catt* [In the margin opposite Thoreau has written:] (can it be Calf? v. Mott ledger near beginning)

Not included in the text of the present edition are the marks of interrogation (?) which Thoreau inserted in the margins opposite four separate passages in the first edition. If these marks were included, they would occur in the margins opposite the following passages:

page 23, line 43   page 179, line 15
page 173, line 39   page 193, line 8

Additionally, while every effort has been made to reproduce the words of Thoreau's text, including the annotations which he made in his "correction copy," there are nonetheless some consistent and non-substantive differences between the present text and the first edition of *Walden*. Thus, the present edition does not follow the first edition in the kind or variety of type styles. In the first edition, the chapter titles and so-called "running heads" all ended with a period, and there was a long dash below each chapter title; the present edition omits the periods and dashes in these instances.

Moreover, since the present edition has been completely reset, the hyphens which indicate breaks in words at the ends of line generally do not conform in placement to those found in the first edition, and one place where the printer of the first edition inadvertently omitted a line-ending hyphen has been ignored since in the present edition the word ("gratuitous," p. 181, l. 34) does not end a line. Two obvious misspellings not noted by Thoreau or his printer have been silently corrected ("occasionally," p. 107, l. 38, corrected from "occcasionally"; "neighborhood," p. 119, l. 34, corrected from "neighhorhood"); other possible misspellings have been preserved since they might reflect Thoreau's own preferences. A period inadvertently omitted in the first edition has been restored (p. 159, l. 39).

Finally, the title of the first edition was: *Walden; or, Life in the Woods*. After the first edition appeared, Thoreau wrote to his publisher and requested that, in all future printings, the title be shortened to: *Walden*.

Civil Disobedience

I heartily accept the motto,—"That government is best which governs least;"[1] and I should like to see it acted up to more rapidly and systematically. Carried out, it finally amounts to this, which also I believe,—"That government is best which governs not at all;" and when men are prepared for it, that will be the kind of government which they will have. Government is at best but an expedient; but most governments are usually, and all governments are sometimes, inexpedient. The objections which have been brought against a standing army, and they are many and weighty, and deserve to prevail, may also at last be brought against a standing government. The standing army is only an arm of the standing government. The government itself, which is only the mode which the people have chosen to execute their will, is equally liable to be abused and perverted before the people can act through it. Witness the present Mexican war,[2] the work of comparatively a few individuals using the standing government as their tool; for, in the outset, the people would not have consented to this measure.

This American government,—what is it but a tradition, though a recent one, endeavoring to transmit itself unimpaired to posterity, but each instant losing some of its integrity? It has not the vitality and force of a single living man; for a single man can bend it to his will. It is a sort of wooden gun to the people themselves; and, if ever they should use it in earnest as a real one against each other, it will surely split. But it is not the less necessary for this; for the people must have some complicated machinery or other, and hear its din, to satisfy that idea of government which they have. Governments show thus how successfully men can be imposed on, even impose on themselves, for their own advantage. It is excellent, we must all allow; yet this government never of itself furthered any enterprise, but by the alacrity with which it got out of its way. It does not keep the country free. It does not settle the West. It does not educate. The

1. The motto of the *United States Magazine and Democratic Review*, a monthly literary-political journal; a similar statement occurs in Emerson's essay, "Politics."

2. Between Mexico and the United States (1846–1848); the issues included slavery and the annexation of Texas.

character inherent in the American people has done all that has been accomplished; and it would have done somewhat more, if the government had not sometimes got in its way. For government is an expedient by which men would fain succeed in letting one another alone; and, as has been said, when it is most expedient, the governed are most let alone by it. Trade and commerce, if they were not made of India rubber,[3] would never manage to bounce over the obstacles which legislators are continually putting in their way; and, if one were to judge these men wholly by the effects of their actions, and not partly by their intentions, they would deserve to be classed and punished with those mischievous persons who put obstructions on the railroads.

But, to speak practically and as a citizen, unlike those who call themselves no-government men, I ask for, not at once no government, but *at once* a better government. Let every man make known what kind of government would command his respect, and that will be one step toward obtaining it.

After all, the practical reason why, when the power is once in the hands of the people, a majority are permitted, and for a long period continue, to rule, is not because they are most likely to be in the right, nor because this seems fairest to the minority, but because they are physically the strongest. But a government in which the majority rule in all cases cannot be based on justice, even as far as men understand it. Can there not be a government in which majorities do not virtually decide right and wrong, but conscience?—in which majorities decide only those questions to which the rule of expediency is applicable? Must the citizen ever for a moment, or in the least degree, resign his conscience to the legislator? Why has every man a conscience, then? I think that we should be men first, and subjects afterward. It is not desirable to cultivate a respect for the law, so much as for the right. The only obligation which I have a right to assume, is to do at any time what I think right. It is truly enough said, that a corporation has no conscience; but a corporation of conscientious men is a corporation *with* a conscience. Law never made men a whit more just; and, by means of their respect for it, even the well-disposed are daily made the agents of injustice. A common and natural result of an undue respect for law is, that you may see a file of soldiers, colonel, captain, corporal, privates, powder-monkeys[4] and all, marching in admirable order over hill and dale to the wars, against their wills, aye, against their common sense and consciences, which makes it very steep

3. A form of crude rubber made from latex.

4. A young boy in military service who carries gunpowder from a storehouse to the guns.

marching indeed, and produces a palpitation of the heart. They
have no doubt that it is a damnable business in which they are
concerned; they are all peaceably inclined. Now, what are they?
Men at all? or small moveable forts and magazines, at the service
of some unscrupulous man in power? Visit the Navy Yard,[5]
and behold a marine, such a man as an American government
can make, or such as it can make a man with its black arts, a
mere shadow and reminiscence of humanity, a man laid out
alive and standing, and already, as one may say, buried under
arms with funeral accompaniments, though it may be

> "Not a drum was heard, nor a funeral note,
>   As his corse to the ramparts we hurried;
> Not a soldier discharged his farewell shot
>   O'er the grave where our hero we buried." [6]

The mass of men serve the State thus, not as men mainly,
but as machines, with their bodies. They are the standing army,
and the militia, jailers, constables, *posse comitatus*,[7] &c. In
most cases there is no free exercise whatever of the judgment
or of the moral sense; but they put themselves on a level with
wood and earth and stones; and wooden men can perhaps be
manufactured that will serve the purpose as well. Such command
no more respect than men of straw, or a lump of dirt. They have
the same sort of worth only as horses and dogs. Yet such as these
even are commonly esteemed good citizens. Others, as most
legislators, politicians, lawyers, ministers, and office-holders, serve
the State chiefly with their heads; and, as they rarely make
any moral distinctions, they are as likely to serve the devil, without
intending it, as God. A very few, as heroes, patriots, martyrs,
reformers in the great sense, and *men*, serve the State with their
consciences also, and so necessarily resist it for the most part;
and they are commonly treated by it as enemies. A wise man
will only be useful as a man, and will not submit to be "clay,"
and "stop a hole to keep the wind away," [8] but leave that office
to his dust at least:—

> "I am too high-born to be propertied,
>   To be a secondary at control,
> Or useful serving-man and instrument
>   To any sovereign state throughout the world." [9]

He who gives himself entirely to his fellow-men appears to
them useless and selfish; but he who gives himself partially to

5. Probably the U.S. Navy Yard in
Boston, Massachusetts.
6. Charles Wolfe (1791–1823), "The
Burial of Sir John Moore at Corunna."
7. A body of men summoned by a
sheriff to assist in keeping peace.
8. Shakespeare, *Hamlet*, V, i, 236-7.
9. Shakespeare, *King John*, V, ii,
79–82.

them is pronounced a benefactor and philanthropist.

How does it become a man to behave toward this American government to-day? I answer that he cannot without disgrace be associated with it. I cannot for an instant recognize that political organization as *my* government which is the *slave's* government also.

All men recognize the right of revolution; that is, the right to refuse allegiance to and to resist the government, when its tyranny or its inefficiency are great and unendurable. But almost all say that such is not the case now. But such was the case, they think, in the Revolution of '75.[1] If one were to tell me that this was a bad government because it taxed certain foreign commodities brought to its ports, it is most probable that I should not make an ado about it, for I can do without them: all machines have their friction; and possibly this does enough good to counterbalance the evil. At any rate, it is a great evil to make a stir about it. But when the friction comes to have its machine, and oppression and robbery are organized, I say, let us not have such a machine any longer. In other words, when a sixth of the population of a nation which has undertaken to be the refuge of liberty are slaves, and a whole country is unjustly overrun and conquered by a foreign army, and subjected to military law, I think that it is not too soon for honest men to rebel and revolutionize. What makes this duty the more urgent is the fact, that the country so overrun is not our own, but ours is the invading army.

Paley,[2] a common authority with many on moral questions, in his chapter on the "Duty of Submission to Civil Government," resolves all civil obligation into expediency; and he proceeds to say, "that so long as the interest of the whole society requires it, that is, so long as the established government cannot be resisted or changed without public inconveniency, it is the will of God that the established government be obeyed, and no longer."—"This principle being admitted, the justice of every particular case of resistance is reduced to a computation of the quantity of the danger and grievance on the one side, and of the probability and expense of redressing it on the other." Of this, he says, every man shall judge for himself. But Paley appears never to have contemplated those cases to which the rule of expediency does not apply, in which a people, as well as an individual, must do justice, cost what it may. If I have unjustly wrested a plank from a drowning man, I must restore it to him though I drown myself. This, according to Paley, would be inconvenient. But he that

1. The American Revolution.
2. William Paley (1743–1805), British philosopher; the quotation is from his *Principles of Moral and Political Philosophy*.

would save his life, in such a case, shall lose it. This people must cease to hold slaves, and to make war on Mexico, though it cost them their existence as a people.

In their practice, nations agree with Paley; but does any one think that Massachusetts does exactly what is right at the present crisis?

"A drab of state, a cloth-o'-silver slut,
    To have her train borne up, and her soul trail in the dirt." [3]

Practically speaking, the opponents to a reform in Massachusetts are not a hundred thousand politicians at the South, but a hundred thousand merchants and farmers here, who are more interested in commerce and agriculture than they are in humanity, and are not prepared to do justice to the slave and to Mexico, *cost what it may*. I quarrel not with far-off foes, but with those who, near at home, co-operate with, and do the bidding of those far away, and without whom the latter would be harmless. We are accustomed to say, that the mass of men are unprepared; but improvement is slow, because the few are not materially wiser or better than the many. It is not so important that many should be as good as you, as that there be some absolute goodness somewhere; for that will leaven the whole lump. There are thousands who are *in opinion* opposed to slavery and to the war, who yet in effect do nothing to put an end to them; who, esteeming themselves children of Washington and Franklin, sit down with their hands in their pockets, and say that they know not what to do, and do nothing; who even postpone the question of freedom to the question of free-trade, and quietly read the prices-current along with the latest advices from Mexico, after dinner, and, it may be, fall asleep over them both. What is the price-current of an honest man and patriot to-day? They hesitate, and they regret, and sometimes they petition; but they do nothing in earnest and with effect. They will wait, well disposed, for others to remedy the evil, that they may no longer have it to regret. At most, they give only a cheap vote, and a feeble countenance and God-speed, to the right, as it goes by them. There are nine hundred and ninety-nine patrons of virtue to one virtuous man; but it is easier to deal with the real possessor of a thing than with the temporary guardian of it.

All voting is a sort of gaming, like chequers or backgammon, with a slight moral tinge to it, a playing with right and wrong, with moral questions; and betting naturally accompanies it. The character of the voters is not staked. I cast my vote, perchance, as I think right; but I am not vitally concerned that that right

3. Cyril Tourneur (1575?–1626), *The Revengers Tragœdie*, IV, iv.

should prevail. I am willing to leave it to the majority. Its obligation, therefore, never exceeds that of expediency. Even voting *for the right* is *doing* nothing for it. It is only expressing to men feebly your desire that it should prevail. A wise man will not leave the right to the mercy of chance, nor wish it to prevail through the power of the majority. There is but little virtue in the action of masses of men. When the majority shall at length vote for the abolition of slavery, it will be because they are indifferent to slavery, or because there is but little slavery left to be abolished by their vote. *They* will then be the only slaves. Only *his* vote can hasten the abolition of slavery who asserts his own freedom by his vote.

I hear of a convention to be held at Baltimore, or elsewhere, for the selection of a candidate for the Presidency, made up chiefly of editors, and men who are politicians by profession; but I think, what is it to any independent, intelligent, and respectable man what decision they may come to, shall we not have the advantage of his wisdom and honesty, nevertheless? Can we not count upon some independent votes? Are there not many individuals in the country who do not attend conventions? But no: I find that the respectable man, so called, has immediately drifted from his position, and despairs of his country, when his country has more reason to despair of him. He forthwith adopts one of the candidates thus selected as the only *available* one, thus proving that he is himself *available* for any purposes of the demagogue. His vote is of no more worth than that of any unprincipled foreigner or hireling native, who may have been bought. Oh for a man who is a *man*, and, as my neighbor says, has a bone in his back which you cannot pass your hand through! Our statistics are at fault: the population has been returned too large. How many *men* are there to a square thousand miles in this country? Hardly one. Does not America offer any inducement for men to settle here? The American has dwindled into an Odd Fellow,[4]—one who may be known by the development of his organ of gregariousness, and a manifest lack of intellect and cheerful self-reliance; whose first and chief concern, on coming into the world, is to see that the alms-houses are in good repair; and, before yet he has lawfully donned the virile garb, to collect a fund for the support of the widows and orphans that may be; who, in short, ventures to live only by the aid of the mutual insurance company, which has promised to bury him decently.

It is not a man's duty, as a matter of course, to devote himself to the eradication of any, even the most enormous wrong; he

---

4. A member of the Independent Order of Odd Fellows, a secret fraternal organization.

may still properly have other concerns to engage him; but it is his duty, at least, to wash his hands of it, and, if he gives it no thought longer, not to give it practically his support. If I devote myself to other pursuits and contemplations, I must first see, at least, that I do not pursue them sitting upon another man's shoulders. I must get off him first, that he may pursue his contemplations too. See what gross inconsistency is tolerated. I have heard some of my townsmen say, "I should like to have them order me out to help put down an insurrection of the slaves, or to march to Mexico,—see if I would go;" and yet these very men have each, directly by their allegiance, and so indirectly, at least, by their money, furnished a substitute. The soldier is applauded who refuses to serve in an unjust war by those who do not refuse to sustain the unjust government which makes the war; is applauded by those whose own act and authority he disregards and sets at nought; as if the State were penitent to that degree that it hired one to scourge it while it sinned, but not to that degree that it left off sinning for a moment. Thus, under the name of order and civil government, we are all made at last to pay homage to and support our own meanness. After the first blush of sin, comes its indifference; and from immoral it becomes, as it were, *un*moral, and not quite unnecessary to that life which we have made.

The broadest and most prevalent error requires the most disinterested virtue to sustain it. The slight reproach to which the virtue of patriotism is commonly liable, the noble are most likely to incur. Those who, while they disapprove of the character and measures of a government, yield to it their allegiance and support, are undoubtedly its most conscientious supporters, and so frequently the most serious obstacles to reform. Some are petitioning the State to dissolve the Union, to disregard the requisitions of the President. Why do they not dissolve it themselves,—the union between themselves and the State,—and refuse to pay their quota into its treasury? Do not they stand in the same relation to the State, that the State does to the Union? And have not the same reasons prevented the State from resisting the Union, which have prevented them from resisting the State?

How can a man be satisfied to entertain an opinion merely, and enjoy *it*? Is there any enjoyment in it, if his opinion is that he is aggrieved? If you are cheated out of a single dollar by your neighbor, you do not rest satisfied with knowing that you are cheated, or with saying that you are cheated, or even with petitioning him to pay you your due; but you take effectual steps at once to obtain the full amount, and see that you are never cheated again. Action from principle,—the perception and the performance of right,—changes things and relations; it is essentially revolutionary, and does not consist wholly with any thing which was. It not only divides states and churches, it divides families; aye, it divides the *individual*, separating the diabolical in him from the divine.

Unjust laws exist: shall we be content to obey them, or shall we endeavor to amend them, and obey them until we have succeeded, or shall we transgress them at once? Men generally, under such a government as this, think that they ought to wait until they have persuaded the majority to alter them. They think that, if they should resist, the remedy would be worse than the evil. But it is the fault of the government itself that the remedy *is* worse than the evil. *It* makes it worse. Why is it not more apt to anticipate and provide for reform? Why does it not cherish its wise minority? Why does it cry and resist before it is hurt? Why does it not encourage its citizens to be on the alert to point out its faults, and *do* better than it would have them? Why does it always crucify Christ, and excommunicate Copernicus [5] and Luther,[6] and pronounce Washington and Franklin rebels?

One would think, that a deliberate and practical denial of its authority was the only offence never contemplated by government; else, why has it not assigned its definite, its suitable and proportionate penalty? If a man who has no property refuses but once to earn nine shillings [7] for the State, he is put in prison for a period unlimited by any law that I know, and determined only by the discretion of those who placed him there; but if he should steal ninety times nine shillings from the State, he is soon permitted to go at large again.

If the injustice is part of the necessary friction of the machine of government, let it go, let it go: perchance it will wear smooth, —certainly the machine will wear out. If the injustice has a spring, or a pulley, or a rope, or a crank, exclusively for itself, then perhaps you may consider whether the remedy will not be worse than the evil; but if it is of such a nature that it requires you to be the agent of injustice to another, then, I say, break the law. Let your life be a counter friction to stop the machine. What I have to do is to see, at any rate, that I do not lend myself to the wrong which I condemn.

As for adopting the ways which the State has provided for remedying the evil, I know not of such ways. They take too

5. Nicolaus Copernicus (1473–1543), Polish astronomer; he was not excommunicated, but his dissertation on the solar system was banned by the Roman Catholic Church.
6. Martin Luther (1483–1546), German theologian, leader of the German Reformation.
7. A shilling is a British coin, the twentieth part of a pound, worth about twenty-three cents in Thoreau's time.

much time, and a man's life will be gone. I have other affairs to attend to. I came into this world, not chiefly to make this a good place to live in, but to live in it, be it good or bad. A man has not every thing to do, but something; and because he cannot do *every thing*, it is not necessary that he should do *something* wrong. It is not my business to be petitioning the governor or the legislature any more than it is theirs to petition me; and, if they should not hear my petition, what should I do then? But in this case the State has provided no way: its very Constitution is the evil. This may seem to be harsh and stubborn and unconciliatory; but it is to treat with the utmost kindness and consideration the only spirit that can appreciate or deserves it. So is all change for the better, like birth and death which convulse the body.

I do not hesitate to say, that those who call themselves abolitionists should at once effectually withdraw their support, both in person and property, from the government of Massachusetts, and not wait till they constitute a majority of one, before they suffer the right to prevail through them. I think that it is enough if they have God on their side, without waiting for that other one. Moreover, any man more right than his neighbors, constitutes a majority of one already.

I meet this American government, or its representative the State government, directly, and face to face, once a year, no more, in the person of its tax-gatherer; this is the only mode in which a man situated as I am necessarily meets it; and it then says distinctly, Recognize me; and the simplest, the most effectual, and, in the present posture of affairs, the indispensablest mode of treating with it on this head, of expressing your little satisfaction with and love for it, is to deny it then. My civil neighbor, the tax-gatherer, is the very man I have to deal with,—for it is, after all, with men and not with parchment that I quarrel,—and he has voluntarily chosen to be an agent of the government. How shall he ever know well what he is and does as an officer of the government, or as a man, until he is obliged to consider whether he shall treat me, his neighbor, for whom he has respect, as a neighbor and well-disposed man, or as a maniac and disturber of the peace, and see if he can get over this obstruction to his neighborliness without a ruder and more impetuous thought or speech corresponding with his action? I know this well, that if one thousand, if one hundred, if ten men whom I could name, —if ten *honest* men only,—aye, if *one* HONEST man, in this State of Massachusetts, *ceasing to hold slaves*, were actually to withdraw from this copartnership, and be locked up in the county jail therefor, it would be the abolition of slavery in America.

For it matters not how small the beginning may seem to be: what is once well done is done for ever. But we love better to talk about it: that we say is our mission. Reform keeps many scores of newspapers in its service, but not one man. If my esteemed neighbor, the State's ambassador,[8] who will devote his days to the settlement of the question of human rights in the Council Chamber, instead of being threatened with the prisons of Carolina, were to sit down the prisoner of Massachusetts, that State which is so anxious to foist the sin of slavery upon her sister,—though at present she can discover only an act of inhospitality to be the ground of a quarrel with her,—the Legislature would not wholly waive the subject the following winter.

Under a government which imprisons any unjustly, the true place for a just man is also a prison. The proper place to-day, the only place which Massachusetts has provided for her freer and less desponding spirits, is in her prisons, to be put out and locked out of the State by her own act, as they have already put themselves out by their principles. It is there that the fugitive slave, and the Mexican prisoner on parole, and the Indian come to plead the wrongs of his race, should find them; on that separate, but more free and honorable ground, where the State places those who are not *with* her but *against* her,—the only house in a slave-state in which a free man can abide with honor. If any think that their influence would be lost there, and their voices no longer afflict the ear of the State, that they would not be as an enemy within its walls, they do not know by how much truth is stronger than error, nor how much more eloquently and effectively he can combat injustice who has experienced a little in his own person. Cast your whole vote, not a strip of paper merely, but your whole influence. A minority is powerless while it conforms to the majority; it is not even a minority then; but it is irresistible when it clogs by its whole weight. If the alternative is to keep all just men in prison, or give up war and slavery, the State will not hesitate which to choose. If a thousand men were not to pay their tax-bills this year, that would not be a violent and bloody measure, as it would be to pay them, and enable the State to commit violence and shed innocent blood. This is, in fact, the definition of a peaceable revolution, if any such is possible. If the tax-gatherer, or any other public officer, asks me, as one has done, "But what shall I do?" my answer is, "If you really wish to do any thing, resign your office." When

8. Samuel Hoar (1778–1856), a Congressman from Concord, was sent to Charleston, South Carolina, to protest the treatment accorded Negro seamen from Massachusetts. Hoar was expelled from Charleston by the legislature of South Carolina.

the subject has refused allegiance, and the officer has resigned his office, then the revolution is accomplished. But even suppose blood should flow. Is there not a sort of blood shed when the conscience is wounded? Through this wound a man's real manhood and immortality flow out, and he bleeds to an everlasting death. I see this blood flowing now.

I have contemplated the imprisonment of the offender, rather than the seizure of his goods,—though both will serve the same purpose,—because they who assert the purest right, and consequently are most dangerous to a corrupt State, commonly have not spent much time in accumulating property. To such the State renders comparatively small service, and a slight tax is wont to appear exorbitant, particularly if they are obliged to earn it by special labor with their hands. If there were one who lived wholly without the use of money, the State itself would hesitate to demand it of him. But the rich man—not to make any invidious comparison—is always sold to the institution which makes him rich. Absolutely speaking, the more money, the less virtue; for money comes between a man and his objects, and obtains them for him; and it was certainly no great virtue to obtain it. It puts to rest many questions which he would otherwise be taxed to answer; while the only new question which it puts is the hard but superfluous one, how to spend it. Thus his moral ground is taken from under his feet. The opportunities of living are diminished in proportion as what are called the "means" are increased. The best thing a man can do for his culture when he is rich is to endeavour to carry out those schemes which he entertained when he was poor. Christ answered the Herodians [9] according to their condition. "Show me the tribute-money," said he;—and one took a penny out of his pocket;—If you use money which has the image of Cæsar on it, and which he has made current and valuable, that is, *if you are men of the State,* and gladly enjoy the advantages of Cæsar's government, then pay him back some of his own when he demands it; "Render therefore to Cæsar that which is Cæsar's, and to God those things which are God's,"—leaving them no wiser than before as to which was which; for they did not wish to know.

When I converse with the freest of my neighbors, I perceive that, whatever they may say about the magnitude and seriousness of the question, and their regard for the public tranquillity, the long and the short of the matter is, that they cannot spare the

9. A follower of Herod Antipas, tetrarch of Galilee from 4 B.C. to 39 A.D. Tiberius Caesar was the Roman emperor from 14 to 37 A.D. The story is told in Matthew, xxii.

protection of the existing government, and they dread the consequences of disobedience to it to their property and families. For my own part, I should not like to think that I ever rely on the protection of the State. But, if I deny the authority of the State when it presents its tax-bill, it will soon take and waste all my property, and so harass me and my children without end. This is hard. This makes it impossible for a man to live honestly and at the same time confortably in outward respects. It will not be worth the while to accumulate property; that would be sure to go again. You must hire or squat somewhere, and raise but a small crop, and eat that soon. You must live within yourself, and depend upon yourself, always tucked up and ready for a start, and not have many affairs. A man may grow rich in Turkey even, if he will be in all respects a good subject of the Turkish government. Confucius [1] said,—"If a State is governed by the principles of reason, poverty and misery are subjects of shame; if a State is not governed by the principles of reason, riches and honors are the subjects of shame." No: until I want the protection of Massachusetts to be extended to me in some distant southern port, where my liberty is endangered, or until I am bent solely on building up an estate at home by peaceful enterprise, I can afford to refuse allegiance to Massachusetts, and her right to my property and life. It costs me less in every sense to incur the penalty of disobedience to the State, than it would to obey. I should feel as if I were worth less in that case.

Some years ago, the State met me in behalf of the church, and commanded me to pay a certain sum toward the support of a clergyman whose preaching my father attended, but never I myself. "Pay it," it said, "or be locked up in the jail." I declined to pay. But, unfortunately, another man saw fit to pay it. I did not see why the schoolmaster should be taxed to support the priest, and not the priest the schoolmaster; for I was not the State's schoolmaster, but I supported myself by voluntary subscription. I did not see why the lyceum should not present its tax-bill, and have the State to back its demand, as well as the church. However, at the request of the selectmen, I condescended to make some such statement as this in writing:—"Know all men by these presents, that I, Henry Thoreau, do not wish to be regarded as a member of any incorporated society which I have not joined." This I gave to the town-clerk; and he has it. The State, having thus learned that I did not wish to be regarded as a member of that church, has never made a like demand

1. *The Analects,* VIII, xiii.

on me since; though it said that it must adhere to its original presumption that time. If I had known how to name them, I should then have signed off in detail from all the societies which I never signed on to; but I did not know where to find a complete list.

I have paid no poll-tax for six years. I was put into a jail once on this account, for one night; and, as I stood considering the walls of solid stone, two or three feet thick, the door of wood and iron, a foot thick, and the iron grating which strained the light, I could not help being struck with the foolishness of that institution which treated me as if I were mere flesh and blood and bones, to be locked up. I wondered that it should have concluded at length that this was the best use it could put me to, and had never thought to avail itself of my services in some way. I saw that, if there was a wall of stone between me and my townsmen, there was a still more difficult one to climb or break through, before they could get to be as free as I was. I did not for a moment feel confined, and the walls seemed a great waste of stone and mortar. I felt as if I alone of all my townsmen had paid my tax. They plainly did not know how to treat me, but behaved like persons who are underbred. In every threat and in every compliment there was a blunder; for they thought that my chief desire was to stand the other side of that stone wall. I could not but smile to see how industriously they locked the door on my meditations, which followed them out again without let or hinderance, and *they* were really all that was dangerous. As they could not reach me, they had resolved to punish my body; just as boys, if they cannot come at some person against whom they have a spite, will abuse his dog. I saw that the State was half-witted, that it was timid as a lone woman with her silver spoons, and that it did not know its friends from its foes, and I lost all my remaining respect for it, and pitied it.

Thus the State never intentionally confronts a man's sense, intellectual or moral, but only his body, his senses. It is not armed with superior wit or honesty, but with superior physical strength. I was not born to be forced. I will breathe after my own fashion. Let us see who is the strongest. What force has a multitude? They only can force me who obey a higher law than I. They force me to become like themselves. I do not hear of *men* being *forced* to live this way or that by masses of men. What sort of life were that to live? When I meet a government which says to me, "Your money or your life," why should I be in haste to give it my money? It may be in a great strait, and not know what to do: I cannot help that. It must help itself; do as I do. It is not worth the while to snivel about it. I am not responsible for the successful working of the machinery of society. I am not the son of the engineer. I perceive that, when an acorn and a chestnut fall side by side, the one does not remain inert to make way for the other, but both obey their own laws, and spring and grow and flourish as best they can, till one, perchance, overshadows and destroys the other. If a plant cannot live according to its nature, it dies; and so a man.

The night in prison was novel and interesting enough. The prisoners in their shirt-sleeves were enjoying a chat and the evening air in the door-way, when I entered. But the jailer said, "Come, boys, it is time to lock up;" and so they dispersed, and I heard the sound of their steps returning into the hollow apartments. My room-mate was introduced to me by the jailer, as "a first-rate fellow and a clever man." When the door was locked, he showed me where to hang my hat, and how he managed matters there. The rooms were whitewashed once a month; and this one, at least, was the whitest, most simply furnished, and probably the neatest apartment in the town. He naturally wanted to know where I came from, and what brought me there; and, when I had told him, I asked him in my turn how he came there, presuming him to be an honest man, of course; and, as the world goes, I believe he was. "Why," said he, "they accuse me of burning a barn; but I never did it." As near as I could discover, he had probably gone to bed in a barn when drunk, and smoked his pipe there; and so a barn was burnt. He had the reputation of being a clever man, had been there some three months waiting for his trial to come on, and would have to wait as much longer; but he was quite domesticated and contented, since he got his board for nothing, and thought that he was well treated.

He occupied one window, and I the other; and I saw, that if one stayed there long, his principal business would be to look out the window. I had soon read all the tracts that were left there, and examined where former prisoners had broken out, and where a grate had been sawed off, and heard the history of the various occupants of that room; for I found that even here there was a history and a gossip which never circulated beyond the walls of the jail. Probably this is the only house in the town where verses are composed, which are afterward printed in a circular form, but not published. I was shown quite a long list of verses which were composed by some young men who had been detected in an attempt to escape, who avenged themselves by singing them.

I pumped my fellow-prisoner as dry as I could, for fear I should never see him again; but at length he showed me which was my bed, and left me to blow out the lamp.

It was like travelling into a far country, such as I had never expected to behold, to lie there for one night. It seemed to me that I never had heard the town-clock strike before, nor the evening sounds of the village; for we slept with the windows open, which were inside the grating. It was to see my native village in the light of the middle ages, and our Concord was turned into a Rhine [2] stream, and visions of knights and castles passed before me. They were the voices of old burghers that I heard in the streets. I was an involuntary spectator and auditor of whatever was done and said in the kitchen of the adjacent village-inn,—a wholly new and rare experience to me. It was a closer view of my native town. I was fairly inside of it. I never had seen its institutions before. This is one of its peculiar institutions; for it is a shire [3] town. I began to comprehend what its inhabitants were about.

In the morning, our breakfasts were put through the hole in the door, in small oblong-square tin pans, made to fit, and holding a pint of chocolate, with brown bread, and an iron spoon. When they called for the vessels again, I was green enough to return what bread I had left; but my comrade seized it, and said that I should lay that up for lunch or dinner. Soon after, he was let out to work at haying in a neighboring field, whither he went every day, and would not be back till noon; so he bade me good-day, saying that he doubted if he should see me again.

When I came out of prison,—for some one [4] interfered, and paid the tax,—I did not perceive that great changes had taken place on the common, such as he observed who went in a youth, and emerged a tottering and gray-headed man; and yet a change had to my eyes come over the scene,— the town, and State, and country,—greater than any that mere time could effect. I saw yet more distinctly the State in which I lived. I saw to what extent the people among whom I lived could be trusted as good neighbors and friends; that their friendship was for summer weather only; that they did not greatly purpose to do right; that they were a distinct race from me by their prejudices and superstitions, as the Chinamen and Malays are; that, in their sacrifices to humanity, they ran no risks, not even to their property; that, after all, they were not so noble but they treated the thief as he had treated them, and hoped, by a certain outward observance and a few prayers, and by walking in a particular straight though useless path from time to time, to save their souls. This may be to judge my neighbors harshly; for I believe that most of them are not aware that they have such an institution as the jail in their village.

It was formerly the custom in our village, when a poor debtor came out of jail, for his acquaintances to salute him, looking through their fingers, which were crossed to represent the grating

2. A river in central Europe flowing north from Switzerland through Germany and the Netherlands into the North Sea.

3. The seat of government in a county.
4. Probably Thoreau's aunt, Maria Thoreau.

of a jail window, "How do ye do?" My neighbors did not thus salute me, but first looked at me, and then at one another, as if I had returned from a long journey. I was put into jail as I was going to the shoemaker's to get a shoe which was mended. When I was let out the next morning, I proceeded to finish my errand, and, having put on my mended shoe, joined a huckleberry party, who were impatient to put themselves under my conduct; and in half an hour,—for the horse was soon tackled,[5] —was in the midst of a huckleberry field, on one of our highest hills, two miles off; and then the State was nowhere to be seen. This is the whole history of "My Prisons." [6]

I have never declined paying the highway tax, because I am as desirous of being a good neighbor as I am of being a bad subject; and, as for supporting schools, I am doing my part to educate my fellow-countrymen now. It is for no particular item in the tax-bill that I refuse to pay it. I simply wish to refuse allegiance to the State, to withdraw and stand aloof from it effectually. I do not care to trace the course of my dollar, if I could, till it buys a man, or a musket to shoot one with,—the dollar is innocent,—but I am concerned to trace the effects of my allegiance. In fact, I quietly declare war with the State, after my fashion, though I will still make what use and get what advantage of her I can, as is usual in such cases.

If others pay the tax which is demanded of me, from a sympathy with the State, they do but what they have already done in their own case, or rather they abet injustice to a greater extent than the State requires. If they pay the tax from a mistaken interest in the individual taxed, to save his property or prevent his going to jail, it is because they have not considered wisely how far they let their private feelings interfere with the public good.

This, then, is my position at present. But one cannot be too much on his guard in such a case, lest his action be biassed by obstinacy, or an undue regard for the opinions of men. Let him see that he does only what belongs to himself and to the hour.

I think sometimes, Why, this people mean well; they are only ignorant; they would do better if they knew how: why give your neighbors this pain to treat you as they are not inclined to? But I think, again, this is no reason why I should do as they do, or permit others to suffer much greater pain of a different kind. Again, I sometimes say to myself, When many millions of men, without heat, without ill-will, without personal feeling of any kind, demand of you a few shillings only, without the possibility, such is their constitution, of retracting or altering

5. Harnessed.
6. A reference to *Le Mie Prigioni*, the memoirs of the Italian patriot, Silvio Pellico (1789–1854).

their present demand, and without the possibility, on your side, of appeal to any other millions, why expose yourself to this overwhelming brute force? You do not resist cold and hunger, the winds and the waves, thus obstinately; you quietly submit to a thousand similar necessities. You do not put your head into the fire. But just in proportion as I regard this as not wholly a brute force, but partly a human force, and consider that I have relations to those millions as to so many millions of men, and not of mere brute or inanimate things, I see that appeal is possible, first and instantaneously, from them to the Maker of them, and, secondly, from them to themselves. But, if I put my head deliberately into the fire, there is no appeal to fire or to the Maker of fire, and I have only myself to blame. If I could convince myself that I have any right to be satisfied with men as they are, and to treat them accordingly, and not according, in some respects, to my requisitions and expectations of what they and I ought to be, then, like a good Mussulman [7] and fatalist, I should endeavor to be satisfied with things as they are, and say it is the will of God. And, above all, there is this difference between resisting this and a purely brute or natural force, that I can resist this with some effect; but I cannot expect, like Orpheus, to change the nature of the rocks and trees and beasts.

I do not wish to quarrel with any man or nation. I do not wish to split hairs, to make fine distinctions, or set myself up as better than my neighbors. I seek rather, I may say, even an excuse for conforming to the laws of the land. I am but too ready to conform to them. Indeed I have reason to suspect myself on this head; and each year, as the tax-gatherer comes round, I find myself disposed to review the acts and position of the general and state governments, and the spirit of the people, to discover a pretext for conformity. I believe that the State will soon be able to take all my work of this sort out of my hands, and then I shall be no better a patriot than my fellow-countrymen. Seen from a lower point of view, the Constitution, with all its faults, is very good; the law and the courts are very respectable; even this State and this American government are, in many respects, very admirable and rare things, to be thankful for, such as a great many have described them; but seen from a point of view a little higher, they are what I have described them; seen from a higher still, and the highest, who shall say what they are, or that they are worth looking at or thinking of at all?

---

7. A Moslem, a Mohammedan; generally spelled "Musselman."

However, the government does not concern me much, and I shall bestow the fewest possible thoughts on it. It is not many moments that I live under a government, even in this world. If a man is thought-free, fancy-free, imagination-free, that which *is not* never for a long time appearing *to be* to him, unwise rulers or reformers cannot fatally interrupt him.

I know that most men think differently from myself; but those whose lives are by profession devoted to the study of these or kindred subjects, content me as little as any. Statesmen and legislators, standing so completely within the institution, never distinctly and nakedly behold it. They speak of moving society, but have no resting-place without it. They may be men of a certain experience and discrimination, and have no doubt invented ingenious and even useful systems, for which we sincerely thank them; but all their wit and usefulness lie within certain not very wide limits. They are wont to forget that the world is not governed by policy and expediency. Webster never goes behind government, and so cannot speak with authority about it. His words are wisdom to those legislators who contemplate no essential reform in the existing government; but for thinkers, and those who legislate for all time, he never once glances at the subject. I know of those whose serene and wise speculations on this theme would soon reveal the limits of his mind's range and hospitality. Yet, compared with the cheap professions of most reformers, and the still cheaper wisdom and eloquence of politicians in general, his are almost the only sensible and valuable words, and we thank Heaven for him. Comparatively, he is always strong, original, and, above all, practical. Still his quality is not wisdom, but prudence. The lawyer's truth is not Truth, but consistency, or a consistent expediency. Truth is always in harmony with herself, and is not concerned chiefly to reveal the justice that may consist with wrong-doing. He well deserves to be called, as he has been called, the Defender of the Constitution. There are really no blows to be given by him but defensive ones. He is not a leader, but a follower. His leaders are the men of '87.[8] "I have never made an effort," he says, "and never propose to make an effort; I have never countenanced an effort, and never mean to countenance an effort, to disturb the arrangement as originally made, by which the various States came into the Union." Still thinking of the sanction which the Constitution gives to slavery, he says, "Because it was a part of the original

8. Members of the Federal Constitutional Convention, held in Philadelphia in 1787 and presided over by George Washington. The quotations which follow are from Webster's speech in the Senate on the admission of Texas as a state.

compact,—let it stand." Notwithstanding his special acuteness and ability, he is unable to take a fact out of its merely political relations, and behold it as it lies absolutely to be disposed of by the intellect,—what, for instance, it behoves a man to do here in America to-day with regard to slavery, but ventures, or is driven, to make some such desperate answer as the following, while professing to speak absolutely, and as a private man,—from which what new and singular code of social duties might be inferred?—"The manner," says he, "in which the government of those States where slavery exists are to regulate it, is for their own consideration, under their responsibility to their constituents, to the general laws of propriety, humanity, and justice, and to God. Associations formed elsewhere, springing from a feeling of humanity, or any other cause, have nothing whatever to do with it. They have never received any encouragement from me, and they never will." [9]

They who know of no purer sources of truth, who have traced up its stream no higher, stand, and wisely stand, by the Bible and the Constitution, and drink at it there with reverence and humility; but they who behold where it comes trickling into this lake or that pool, gird up their loins once more, and continue their pilgrimage toward its fountain-head.

No man with a genius for legislation has appeared in America. They are rare in the history of the world. There are orators, politicians, and eloquent men, by the thousand; but the speaker has not yet opened his mouth to speak, who is capable of settling the much-vexed questions of the day. We love eloquence for its own sake, and not for any truth which it may utter, or any heroism it may inspire. Our legislators have not yet learned the comparative value of free-trade and of freedom, of union, and of rectitude, to a nation. They have no genius or talent for comparatively humble questions of taxation and finance, commerce and manufactures and agriculture. If we were left solely to the wordy wit of legislators in Congress for our guidance, uncorrected by the seasonable experience and the effectual complaints of the people, America would not long retain her rank among the nations. For eighteen hundred years, though perchance I have no right to say it, the New Testament has been written; yet where is the legislator who has wisdom and practical talent enough to avail himself of the light which it sheds on the science of legislation?

The authority of government, even such as I am willing to submit to,—for I will cheerfully obey those who know and can do better

9. These extracts have been inserted since the Lecture was read. [Thoreau's note.]

than I, and in many things even those who neither know nor
can do so well,—is still an impure one: to be strictly just, it
must have the sanction and consent of the governed. It can
have no pure right over my person and property but what I
concede to it. The progress from an absolute to a limited monarchy, from a limited monarchy to a democracy, is a progress
toward a true respect for the individual. Is a democracy, such
as we know it, the last improvement possible in government?
Is it not possible to take a step further towards recognizing and
organizing the rights of man? There will never be a really free
and enlightened State, until the State comes to recognize the
individual as a higher and independent power, from which all
its own power and authority are derived, and treats him accordingly. I please myself with imagining a State at last which can
afford to be just to all men, and to treat the individual with
respect as a neighbor; which even would not think it inconsistent
with its own repose, if a few were to live aloof from it, not
meddling with it, nor embraced by it, who fulfilled all the duties
of neighbors and fellow-men. A State which bore this kind of
fruit, and suffered it to drop off as fast as it ripened, would prepare
the way for a still more perfect and glorious State, which also
I have imagined, but not yet anywhere seen.

A TEXTUAL NOTE ON "CIVIL DISOBEDIENCE"

Thoreau first wrote "Civil Disobedience" as a lecture, which he delivered at the Concord Lyceum in February, 1848. It first appeared in print under the title of "Resistance to Civil Government" in a collection of essays called *Æsthetic Papers*, edited by Elizabeth P. Peabody and published by her in Boston in 1849. The text included in the present volume is taken from this first published version. The essay was not reprinted during Thoreau's lifetime.

It was first reprinted in *A Yankee in Canada, with Anti-Slavery and Reform Papers* (Boston: Ticknor and Fields, 1866) and then in the "Riverside" (1893) and "Walden" (1906) editions of Thoreau's works. One interesting feature of these latter editions is the presence of an unidentified poem which occurs in the middle of the paragraph beginning, "I do not wish to quarrel . . ." (p. 240 in the present edition), between the sentence which ends, "pretext for conformity" and the one which begins, "I believe that the State. . . ." The poem, as it occurs in the 1866 edition, is as follows:

> "We must affect our country as our parents,
> And if at any time we alienate
> Our love or industry from doing it honor,
> We must respect effects and teach the soul
> Matter of conscience and religion,
> And not desire of rule or benefit."

The poem is from *Battle of Alcazar* (1594), II, ii, 425–430, by the English dramatist George Peele. The version in the 1866 edition of "Civil Disobedience" is slightly misquoted.

In the first edition, "he" (p. 232, l. 4) is misprinted as "be."

Background

The following excerpts are taken from *The Journal of Henry David Thoreau*, edited by Bradford Torrey and Francis H. Allen. The first five entries were dated by Thoreau. The last three entries, which are separated by three asterisks centered on the page (* * *), are undated but were all written while Thoreau was residing at Walden Pond. The footnotes have been supplied by the editor of the present edition.

From Thoreau's Journal

[December 15, 1841]

[*Dec.*] 15. *Wednesday*. A mild summer sun shines over forest and lake. The earth looks as fair this morning as the Valhalla of the gods. Indeed our spirits never go beyond nature. In the woods there is an inexpressible happiness. Their mirth is but just repressed. In winter, when there is but one green leaf for many rods, what warm content is in them! They are not rude, but tender, even in the severest cold. Their nakedness is their defense. All their sounds and sights are elixir to my spirit. They possess a divine health. God is not more well. Every sound is inspiriting and fraught with the same mysterious assurance, from the creaking of the boughs in January to the soft sough of the wind in July.

How much of my well-being, think you, depends on the condition of my lungs and stomach,—such cheap pieces of Nature as they, which, indeed, she is every day reproducing with prodigality. Is the arrow indeed fatal which rankles in the breast of the bird on the bough, in whose eye all this fair landscape is reflected, and whose voice still echoes through the wood?

The trees have come down to the bank to see the river go by. This old, familiar river is renewed each instant; only the channel is the same. The water which so calmly reflects the fleeting clouds and the primeval trees I have never seen before. It may have washed some distant shore, or framed a glacier or iceberg at the north, when I last stood here. Seen through a mild atmosphere, the works of the husbandman, his plowing and reaping, have a beauty to the beholder which the laborer never sees.

I seem to see somewhat more of my own kith and kin in the lichens on the rocks than in any books. It does seem as if mine were a peculiarly wild nature, which so yearns toward all wildness. I know of no redeeming qualities in me but a sincere love for some things, and when I am reproved I have to fall back on to this ground. This is my argument in reserve for all cases. My love is invulnerable. Meet me on that ground, and you will find me strong. When I am condemned, and condemn myself utterly, I think straightway, "But I rely on my love for some things." Therein I am whole and entire. Therein I am God-propped.

When I see the smoke curling up through the woods from some farmhouse invisible, it is more suggestive of the poetry of rural and domestic life than a nearer inspection can be. Up goes the smoke as quietly as the dew exhales in vapor from these pine leaves and oaks; as busy, disposing itself in circles and in wreaths, as the housewife on the hearth below. It is cotemporary with a piece of human biography, and waves as a feather in some *man's* cap. Under that rod of sky there is some plot a-brewing, some ingenuity has planted itself, and we shall see what it will do. It tattles of more things than the boiling of the pot. It is but one of man's breaths. All that is interesting in history or fiction is transpiring beneath that cloud. The subject of all life and death, of happiness and grief, goes thereunder.

When the traveller in the forest, attaining to some eminence, descries a column of smoke in the distance, it is a very gentle hint to him of the presence of man. It seems as if it would establish friendly relations between them without more ado.

[January 5, 1842]

Jan. 5. Wednesday. I find that whatever hindrances may occur I write just about the same amount of truth in my Journal; for the record is more concentrated, and usually it is some very real and earnest life, after all, that interrupts. All flourishes are omitted. If I saw wood from morning to night, though I grieve that I could not observe the train of my thoughts during that time, yet, in the evening, the few scrannel lines which describe my day's occupations will make the creaking of the saw more musical than my freest fancies could have been. I find incessant labor with the hands, which engrosses the attention also, the best method to remove palaver out of one's style. One will not dance at his work who has wood to cut and cord before the night falls in the short days of winter; but every stroke will be husbanded, and ring soberly through the wood; and so will his lines ring and tell on the ear, when at evening he settles the accounts of the day. I have often been astonished at the force and precision of style to which busy laboring men, unpracticed in writing, easily attain when they are required to make the effort. It seems as if their sincerity and plainness were the main thing to be taught in schools,—and yet not in the schools, but in the fields, in actual service, I should say. The scholar not unfrequently envies the propriety and emphasis with which the farmer calls to his team, and confesses that if that lingo were written it would surpass his labored sentences.

Who is not tired of the weak and flowing periods of the politician and scholar, and resorts not even to the Farmer's Almanac,[1] to read the simple account of the month's labor, to restore his tone again? I want to see a sentence run clear through to the end, as deep and fertile as a well-drawn furrow which shows that the plow was pressed down to the beam. If our scholars would lead more earnest lives, we should not witness those lame conclusions to their ill-sown discourses, but their sentences would pass over the ground like loaded rollers, and not mere hollow and wooden ones, to press in the seed and make it germinate.

A well-built sentence, in the rapidity and force with which it works, may be compared to a modern corn-planter, which furrows out, drops the seed, and covers it up at one movement.

The scholar requires hard labor as an impetus to his pen. He will learn to grasp it as firmly and wield it as gracefully and effectually as an axe or a sword. When I consider the labored periods of some gentleman scholar, who perchance in feet and inches comes up to the standard of his race, and is nowise deficient in girth, I am amazed at the immense sacrifice of thews and sinews. What! these proportions and these bones, and this their work! How these hands hewed this fragile matter, mere filagree or embroidery fit for ladies' fingers! Can this be a stalwart man's work, who has marrow in his backbone and a tendon Achilles[2] in his heel? They who set up Stonehenge[3] did somewhat,—much in comparison,—if it were only their strength was once fairly laid out, and they stretched themselves.

[July 5, 1846]

July 5. Saturday. Walden.—Yesterday I came here to live. My house makes me think of some mountain houses I have seen, which seemed to have a fresher auroral atmosphere about them, as I fancy of the halls of Olympus. I lodged at the house of a saw-miller last summer, on the Caatskill Mountains,[4] high up as Pine Orchard, in the blueberry and raspberry region, where the quiet and cleanliness and coolness seemed to be all one,— which had their ambrosial character. He was the miller of the Kaaterskill Falls. They were a clean and wholesome family, inside and out, like their house. The latter was not plastered, only

1. A book containing information on phases of the moon, weather forecasts, and other useful data.
2. In Greek mythology, a great warrior whose only vulnerable spot was in the tendon which connects the heel to the calf of the leg.
3. A prehistoric structure in England.
4. A group of mountains in southern New York; generally spelled "Catskill."

lathed, and the inner doors were not hung. The house seemed high-placed, airy, and perfumed, fit to entertain a travelling god. It was so high, indeed, that all the music, the broken strains, the waifs and accompaniments of tunes, that swept over the ridge of the Caatskills, passed through its aisles. Could not man be man in such an abode? And would he ever find out this grovelling life? It was the very light and atmosphere in which the works of Grecian art were composed, and in which they rest. They have appropriated to themselves a loftier hall than mortals ever occupy, at least on a level with the mountain-brows of the world. There was wanting a little of the glare of the lower vales, and in its place a pure twilight as became the precincts of heaven. Yet so equable and calm was the season there that you could not tell whether it was morning or noon or evening. Always there was the sound of the morning cricket.

[July 6, 1846]

July 6. I wish to meet the facts of life—the vital facts, which are the phenomena or actuality the gods meant to show us—face to face, and so I came down here. Life! who knows what it is, what it does? If I am not quite right here, I am less wrong than before; and now let us see what they will have. The preacher, instead of vexing the ears of drowsy farmers on their day of rest, at the end of the week,—for Sunday always seemed to me like a fit conclusion of an ill-spent week and not the fresh and brave beginning of a new one,—with this one other draggletail and postponed affair of a sermon, from thirdly to fifteenthly, should teach them with a thundering voice pause and simplicity. "Stop! Avast! Why so fast?" In all studies we go not forward but rather backward with redoubled pauses. We always study *antiques* with silence and reflection. Even time has a depth, and below its surface the waves do not lapse and roar. I wonder men can be so frivolous almost as to attend to the gross form of negro slavery, there are so many keen and subtle masters who subject us both. Self-emancipation in the West Indies of a man's thinking and imagining provinces, which should be more than his island territory,—one emancipated heart and intellect! It would knock off the fetters from a million slaves.

[July 7, 1846]

July 7. I am glad to remember to-night, as I sit by my door, that I too am at least a remote descendant of that heroic race of men of whom there is tradition. I too sit here on the shore of my Ithaca,[5] a fellow-wanderer and survivor of Ulysses. How symbolical, significant of I know not what, the pitch pine stands here before my door! Unlike any glyph I have seen sculptured or painted yet, one of Nature's later designs, yet perfect as her Grecian art. There it is, a done tree. Who can mend it? And now where is the generation of heroes whose lives are to pass amid these our northern pines, whose exploits shall appear to posterity pictured amid these strong and shaggy forms? Shall there be only arrows and bows to go with these pines on some pipe-stone quarry at length? There is something more respectable than railroads in these simple relics of the Indian race. What hieroglyphs shall we add to the pipe-stone quarry?

If we can forget, we have done somewhat; if we can remember, we have done somewhat. Let us remember this.

The Great Spirit makes indifferent all times and places. The place where he is seen is always the same, and indescribably pleasant to all our senses. We had allowed only neighboring and transient circumstances to make our occasions. They were, in fact, the causes of our distractions. But nearest to all things is that power which fashions their being. Next to us the grandest laws are being enacted and administered. Next to us is not the workman whom we have hired, but ever the workman whose work we are. He is at work, not in my backyard, but inconceivably nearer than that. We are the subjects of an experiment how singular! Can we not dispense with the society of our gossips a little while under these circumstances?

My auxiliaries are the dews and rains,—to water this dry soil,—and genial fatness in the soil itself, which for the most part is lean and effete. My enemies are worms, cool days, and most of all woodchucks. They have nibbled for me an eighth of an acre clean. I plant in faith, and they reap. This is the tax I pay for ousting johnswort and the rest. But soon the surviving beans will be too tough for woodchucks, and then they will go forward to meet new foes.

[From Volume I (undated)]

All nature is classic and akin to art. The sumach and pine and hickory which surround my house remind me of the most graceful sculpture. Sometimes their tops, or a single limb or leaf,

5. An island off the coast of Greece; according to legend, the home of Odysseus (who was called "Ulysses" by the Romans).

seems to have grown to a distinct expression as if it were a symbol for me to interpret. Poetry, painting, and sculpture claim at once and associate with themselves those perfect specimens of the art of nature,—leaves, vines, acorns, pine cones, etc. The critic must at last stand as mute though contented before a true poem as before an acorn or a vine leaf. The perfect work of art is received again into the bosom of nature whence its material proceeded, and that criticism which can only detect its unnaturalness has no longer any office to fulfill. The choicest maxims that have come down to us are more beautiful or integrally wise than they are wise to our understandings. This wisdom which we are inclined to pluck from their stalk is the point only of a single association. Every natural form—palm leaves and acorns, oak leaves and sumach and dodder—are untranslatable aphorisms.

Twenty-three years since, when I was five years old, I was brought from Boston to this pond, away in the country,—which was then but another name for the extended world for me,—one of the most ancient scenes stamped on the tablets of my memory, the oriental Asiatic valley of my world, whence so many races and inventions have gone forth in recent times. That woodland vision for a long time made the drapery of my dreams. That sweet solitude my spirit seemed so early to require that I might have room to entertain my thronging guests, and that speaking silence that my ears might distinguish the significant sounds. Somehow or other it at once gave the preference to this recess among the pines, where almost sunshine and shadow were the only inhabitants that varied the scene, over that tumultuous and varied city, as if it had found its proper nursery.

Well, now, to-night my flute awakes the echoes over this very water, but one generation of pines has fallen, and with their stumps I have cooked my supper, and a lusty growth of oaks and pines is rising all around its brim and preparing its wilder aspect for new infant eyes. Almost the same johnswort springs from the same perennial root in this pasture. Even I have at length helped to clothe that fabulous landscape of my imagination, and one result of my presence and influence is seen in these bean leaves and corn blades and potato vines.

* * *

Emerson does not consider things in respect to their essential utility, but an important partial and relative one, as works of art perhaps. His probes pass one side of their centre of gravity. His exaggeration is of a part, not of the whole.

How many an afternoon has been stolen from more profitable,

if not more attractive, industry,—afternoons when a good run of custom might have been expected on the main street, such as tempt the ladies out a-shopping,—spent, I say, by me away in the meadows, in the well-nigh hopeless attempt to set the river on fire or be set on fire by it, with such tinder as I had, with such flint as I was. Trying at least to make it flow with milk and honey, as I had heard of, or liquid gold, and drown myself without getting wet,—a laudable enterprise, though I have not much to show for it.

So many autumn days spent outside the town, trying to hear what was in the wind, to hear it and carry it express. I well-nigh sunk all my capital in it, and lost my own breath into the bargain, by running in the face of it. Depend upon it, if it had concerned either of the parties, it would have appeared in the yeoman's gazette, the *Freeman*,[6] with other earliest intelligence.

For many years I was self-appointed inspector of snow-storms and rain-storms, and did my duty faithfully, though I never received one cent for it.

Surveyor, if not of higher ways, then of forest paths and all across-lot routes, keeping many open ravines bridged and passable at all seasons, where the public heel had testified to the importance of the same, all not only without charge, but even at considerable risk and inconvenience. Many a mower would have forborne to complain had he been aware of the invisible public good that was in jeopardy.

So I went on, I may say without boasting, I trust, faithfully minding my business without a partner, till it became more and more evident that my townsmen would not, after all, admit me into the list of town officers, nor make the place a sinecure with moderate allowance.

I have looked after the wild stock of the town, which pastures in common, and every one knows that these cattle give you a good deal of trouble in the way of leaping fences. I have counted and registered all the eggs I could find at least, and have had an eye to all nooks and corners of the farm, though I did n't always know whether Jonas or Solomon [7] worked in a particular field to-day; that was none of my business. I only knew him for one of the men, and trusted that he was as well employed as I was. I had to make my daily entries in the general farm book, and my duties may sometimes have made me a little stubborn and unyielding.

Many a day spent on the hilltops waiting for the sky to fall,

6. A common name for a newspaper. 7. Common given names in mid-nineteenth century New England.

that I might catch something, though I never caught much, only a little, manna-wise, that would dissolve again in the sun.

My accounts, indeed, which I can swear to have been faithfully kept, I have never got audited, still less accepted, still less paid and settled. However, I have n't set my heart upon *that*.

I have watered the red huckleberry and the sand cherry and the hoopwood tree, and the cornel and spoonhunt and yellow violet, which might have withered else in dry seasons. The white grape.

To find the bottom of Walden Pond, and what inlet and outlet it might have.

* * *

We can afford to lend a willing ear occasionally to those earnest reformers of the age. Let us treat them hospitably. Shall we be charitable only to the poor? What though they are fanatics? Their errors are likely to be generous errors, and these may be they who will put to rest the American Church and the American government, and awaken better ones in their stead.

Let us not meanly seek to maintain our delicate lives in chambers or in legislative halls by a timid watchfulness of the rude mobs that threaten to pull down our baby-houses. Let us not think to raise a revenue which shall maintain our domestic quiet by an impost on the liberty of speech. Let us not think to live by the principle of self-defense. Have we survived our accidents hitherto, think you, by virtue of our good swords,—that three-foot lath that dangles by your side, or those brazen-mouthed pieces under the burying hill which the trainers keep to hurrah with in the April and July mornings? Do our protectors burrow under the burying-ground hill, on the edge of the bean-field which you all know, gorging themselves once a year with powder and smoke, and kept bright and in condition by a chafing of oiled rags and rotten stone? Have we resigned the protection of our hearts and civil liberties to that feathered race of wading birds and marching men who drill but once a month?—and I mean no reproach to our Concord train-bands,[8] who certainly make a handsome appearance—and dance well. Do we enjoy the sweets of domestic life undisturbed, because the naughty boys are all shut up in that whitewashed "stone-yard," as it is called, and see the Concord meadows only through a grating.

No, let us live amid the free play of the elements. Let the dogs bark, let the cocks crow, and the sun shine, and the winds blow!

8. A militia.

Reviews and Essays
in Criticism

Note

With a few exceptions, the following reviews and essays are printed in their entirety. The exceptions occur in those cases where, for the sake of space, long quotations from *Walden* have been omitted; each omission is marked by three asterisks: * * * . In the essays by Drinnon, Emerson, and Lowell, and in the chapters from the books by Lewis, Matthiessen, and Shanley, the footnotes have been slightly revised, primarily to facilitate reference to the present edition. In all other cases, the footnotes are those of the authors of the essays. Titles enclosed within brackets have been supplied by the present editor.

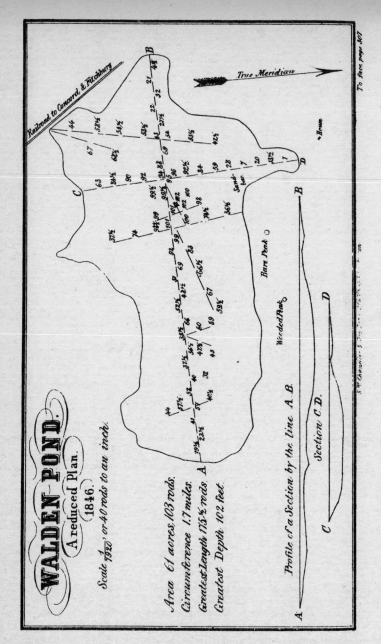

The map, overleaf, was drawn by Thoreau and lithographed for the first edition by S. W. Chandler & Bro. of Boston. It faced p. 307 of the first edition, a page which contained substantially the same material as p. 189 of the present edition.

DANIEL RICKETSON †

[Letter to Thoreau]

Brooklawn, near New Bedford Mass. Aug. 12th, 1854

Dear Sir,

I have just finished reading "Walden" and hasten to thank you for the great degree of satisfaction it has afforded me. Having always been a lover of Nature, in man, as well as in the material universe, I hail with pleasure every original production in literature which bears the stamp of a genuine and earnest love for the true philosophy of human life.—Such I assure you I esteem your book to be. To many, and to most, it will appear to be the wild musings of an eccentric and strange mind, though all must recognize your affectionate regard for the gentle denizens of the woods and pond as well as the great love you have shewn for what are familiarly called the beauties of Nature. But to me the book appears to evince a mind most thoroughly self possessed, highly cultivated with a strong vein of common sense. The whole book is a prose poem (pardon the solecism) and at the same time as simple as a running brook.

I have always loved ponds of pure translucent water, and some of my happiest and most memorable days have been passed on and around the beautiful Middleboro' Ponds, particularly the largest, Assawampset—here King Philip frequently came, and a beautiful round hill near by, is still known as "King Philip's look-out." I have often felt an inclination when tired of the noise and strife of society, to retire to the shores of this noble old pond, or rather lake, for it is some 5 or 6 miles in length and 2 broad. But I have a wife and four children, & besides have got a *little* too far along, being in my forty-second year, to undertake a new mode of life. I strive however, and have striven during the whole of my life, to live as free from the restraint of mere forms & ceremonies as I possibly can. I love a quiet, peaceful rural retirement; but it was not my fate to realize this until a little past thirty years of age—since then I have been a sort of rustic, genteel perhaps, rustic. Not so very genteel you might reply, if you saw the place where I am writing. It is a rough board shanty 12 x 14 three miles from New Bedford in a quiet &

† From W. Harding and Carl Bode, eds., *The Correspondence of Henry David Thoreau* (New York, 1958). Pp. 332–35. Published by New York University Press.

secluded spot—here for the present I eat, & sleep, read, write, receive visitors &c. My house is now *undergoing* repairs &c and my family are in town. A short time since a whip-poor-will serenaded me, and later at night I hear the cuckoos near my windows. It has long been my delight to observe the feathered tribes, and earlier in life I was quite an ornithologist. The coming of the first Blue bird in early Spring is to me still a delightful circumstance. But more particularly soothing to me is the insect hum so multitudinous at this season.—Now as I write the crickets & other little companions are sweetly & soothingly singing around my dwelling, & occasionally in my room. I am quite at home with partridges, Quails, rabbits skunks & woodchucks. But Winter is my best time, then I am a great tramper through the woods. O how I love the woods. I have walked thousands of miles in the woods hereabouts. I recognize many of my own experiences in your "Walden." Still I am not altogether given up to these matters—they are my pastimes. I have a farm to attend to, fruit trees & a garden & a little business occasionally in town to look after, but much leisure nevertheless. In fact I am the only man of leisure I know of, every body here as well as elsewhere is upon the stir. I love quiet, this you know friend Thoreau dont necessarily imply that the body should be still all the time. I am often quietest, arn't you, when walking among the still haunts of Nature or hoeing perhaps beans as I have oftentimes done as well as corn & potatoes &c &c.

Poetry has been to me a great consolation amid the jarring elements of this life. The English poets some of them at least, and one Latin, our good old Virgil, have been like household gods to me.—Cowper's Task, my greatest favorite now lies before me in which I had been reading & alternately looking at the western sky just after sunset before I commenced this letter. Cowper was a true lover of the country. How often have I felt the force of these lines upon the country in my own experience

> "I never framed a wish or formed a plan,
>   That flattered me with hopes of earthly bliss
>   But there I laid the scene."

All through my boyhood, *the country* haunted my thoughts. Though blessed with a good home, books & teachers, the latter however with one exception were not blessings, I would have exchanged all for the life of a rustic. I envied as I then thought the freedom of the farmer boy. But I have long thought that the life of the farmer, that is most farmers, possessed but little of the poetry of labour. How we accumulate cares around us. The very repairs I am now making upon my

house will to some considerable extent increase my cares. A rough
board shanty, rye & indian bread, water from the spring, or as in
your case, from the pond, and other things in keeping, do not
burden the body & mind. It is fine houses, fine furniture, sumptuous
fare, fine clothes, and many in number, horses & carriages, servants
&c &c &c, there are the harpies, that so disturb our real happiness.

My next move in life I hope will be into a much more simple
mode of living. I should like to live in a small house, with my
family, uncarpeted white washed walls, simple old fashioned
furniture & plain wholesome old fashioned fare. Though I
have always been inclined to be a vegetarian in diet & once lived
in capital health two years on the Graham system.

Well this will do for myself. Now for you friend Thoreau.
Why return to the world again? a life such as you spent at Walden
was too true & beautiful to be abandoned for any slight reason.

The ponds I allude to are much more secluded than Walden,
and really delightful places—Should you ever incline again to
try your "philosophy of living" I would introduce you into haunts,
that your very soul would leap to behold. Well I thought I
would just write you a few lines to thank you for the pleasure
I have received from the reading of your "Walden," but I
have found myself running on till now. I feel that you are a
kindred spirit and so fear not. I was pleased to find a kind word
or two in your book for the poor down trodden slave. Wilberforce,
Clarkson and John Woolman & Anthony Benezet were household
words in my father's house.—I early became acquainted with
the subject of slavery for my parents were Quakers, & Quakers
were then all Abolitionists. My love of Nature, absolute, undefiled
Nature makes me an abolitionist. How could I listen to the
woodland songs—or gaze upon the outstretched landscape, or
look at the great clouds & the starry heavens and be aught but
a friend of the poor and oppressed coloured race of our land
But why do I write—it is in vain to portray these things—they
can only be felt and lived, and to you of all others I would refrain
from being prolix.

I have outlived, or nearly so, all ambition for notoriety. I
wish only to be a simple, good man & so live that when I
come to surrender up my spirit to the Great Father, I may depart
in peace.

I wrote the above last evening. It is now Sunday afternoon,
and alone in my Shanty I sit down at my desk to add a little
more. A great white cloud which I have been watching for
the past half hour is now majestically moving off to the north
east before the fine S.W. breeze which sets in here nearly every

summer afternoon from the ocean. We have here the best climate in New England—sheltered on the north & east by dense pine woods from the cold winds which so cut up the healths of eastern folks, or rather are suffered to—but I think if the habits of our people were right the north easters would do but little harm. I never heard that the Indians were troubled by them—but they were nature's philosophers and lived in the woods. I *love* to go by my instincts, inspiration rather. O how much we lose by civilization! In the eyes of the world you & I are demi savages—But I rather think we could stand our hand at the dinner table or in the drawing room with most of folks. I would risk you anywhere, and as for myself I have about done with the follies of "society." I never was trump'd yet.

I have lived out all the experiences of idle youth—some gentle, & some savage experiences but my heart was not made of the stuff for a sportsman or angler—early in life I ranged the woods, fields & shores with my gun, or rod, but I found that all I sought could be obtained much better without the death dealing implements. So now my rustic staff is all the companion I usually take, unless my old dog joins me—taking no track as he often does, and bounding upon me in some distant thicket. My favorite books are—Cowper's task, Thomson's Seasons Milton, Shakespeare, &c &c— Goldsmith Gray's Elegy— Beattie's Minstrel (parts) Howitt, Gil. White, (Selbourne) Bewick (wood-engraver) moderns—Wordsworth Ch. Lamb—De Quincy, Macauly, Kit. North, &c &c

These and others are more my companions than men. I like talented women & swear lustily by May Wolstoncroft, &c &c—Roland, Joan d'arc & somewhat by dear Margaret Fuller.

The smaller fry, let go by—

Again permit me to thank you for the pleasure & strength I have found in reading "Walden."

Dear Mr Walden good bye for the present.

> Yours most respectfully
> Daniel Ricketson

Henry D. Thoreau Esq

A. P. PEABODY †

Critical Notice

The economical details and calculations in this book are more curious than useful; for the author's life in the woods was on too narrow a scale to find imitators. But in describing his hermitage and his forest life, he says so many pithy and brilliant things, and offers so many piquant, and, we may add, so many just, comments on society as it is, that his book is well worth the reading, both for its actual contents and its suggestive capacity.

CHARLES FREDERICK BRIGGS ‡

A Yankee Diogenes

The New England character is essentially anti-Diogenic; the Yankee is too shrewd not to comprehend the advantages of living in what we call the world; there are no bargains to be made in the desert, nobody to be taken advantage of in the woods, while the dwellers in tubs and shanties have slender opportunities of bettering their condition by barter. When the New Englander leaves his home, it is not for the pleasure of living by himself; if he is migratory in his habits, it is not from his fondness for solitude, nor from any impatience he feels at living in a crowd. Where there are most men, there is, generally, most money, and there is where the strongest attractions exist for the genuine New Englander. A Yankee Diogenes is a *lusus,* and we feel a peculiar interest in reading the account which an oddity of that kind gives of himself. The name of Thoreau has not a New England sound; but we believe that the author of *Walden* is a genuine New Englander, and of New England antecedents and education. Although he plainly gives the reasons for publishing his book, at the outset, he does not clearly state the causes that led him to live the life of a hermit on the shore of Walden Pond. But we infer from his volume that his aim was the very remarkable one of trying to be something, while he lived upon nothing; in opposition to the general rule of striving to live upon something, while doing nothing. Mr. Thoreau probably tried the experiment

† From *North American Review,* 79 (October, 1854), 536. ‡ From *Putnam's Monthly Magazine,* 4 (October, 1854), 443–48.

long enough to test its success, and then fell back again into his normal condition. But he does not tell us that such was the case. He was happy enough to get back among the good people of Concord, we have no doubt; for although he paints his shanty-life in rose-colored tints, we do not believe he liked it, else why not stick to it? We have a mistrust of the sincerity of the St. Simon Sylites', and suspect that they come down from their pillars in the night-time, when nobody is looking at them. Diogenes placed his tub where Alexander would be sure of seeing it, and Mr. Thoreau ingenuously confesses that he occasionally went out to dine, and when the society of woodchucks and chipping-squirrels were insufficient for his amusement, he liked to go into Concord and listen to the village gossips in the stores and taverns. Mr. Thoreau informs us that he lived alone in the woods, by the shore of Walden Pond, in a shanty built by his own hands, a mile from any neighbor, two years and a half. What he did there besides writing the book before us, cultivating beans, sounding Walden Pond, reading Homer, baking johnny-cakes, studying Brahminical theology, listening to chipping-squirrels, receiving visits, and having high imaginations, we do not know. He gives us the results of his bean cultivation with great particularity, and the cost of his shanty; but the actual results of his two years and a half of hermit life he does not give. But there have been a good many lives spent and a good deal of noise made about them, too, from the sum total of whose results not half so much good could be extracted as may be found in this little volume. Many a man will find pleasure in reading it, and many a one, we hope, will be profited by its counsels. A tour in Europe would have cost a good deal more, and not have produced half as much. As a matter of curiosity, to show how cheaply a gentleman of refined tastes, lofty aspirations and cultivated intellect may live, even in these days of high prices, we copy Mr. Thoreau's account of his first year's operations; he did better, he informs us, the second year. The entire cost of his house, which answered all his purposes, and was as comfortable and showy as he desired, was $28 12½. But one cannot live on a house unless he rents it to somebody else, even though he be a philosopher and a believer in Vishnu. Mr. Thoreau felt the need of a little ready money, one of the most convenient things in the world to have by one, even before his house was finished.

"Wishing to earn ten or twelve dollars by some agreeable and honest method," he observes, "I planted about two acres and a half of light and sandy soil, chiefly with beans, but also a small part with potatoes and corn, peas and turnips." As he was a squatter, he paid nothing for rent, and as he was making no calculation for future crops, he expended nothing for manure so that the results of his farming will not be highly instructive to young agriculturists, nor be likely to be held up as excitements to farming pursuits by agricultural periodicals.

According to his figures it cost him twenty-seven cents a week to live, clothes included; and for this sum he lived healthily and happily, received a good many distinguished visitors, who, to humor his style, used to leave their names on a leaf or a chip, when they did not happen to find him at home. But, it strikes us that all the knowledge which the "Hermit of Walden" gained by his singular experiment in living might have been done just as well, and as satisfactorily, without any experiment at all. We know what it costs to feed prisoners, paupers and soldiers; we know what the cheapest and most nutritious food costs, and how little it requires to keep up the bodily health of a full-grown man. A very simple calculation will enable any one to satisfy himself in regard to such points. and those who wish to live upon twenty-seven cents a week, may indulge in that pleasure. The great Abernethy's prescription for the attainment of perfect bodily health was, "live on sixpence a day and earn it." But that would be Sybaritic indulgence compared with Mr. Thoreau's experience, whose daily expenditure hardly amounted to a quarter of that sum. And he lived happily, too, though it don't exactly speak volumes in favor of his system to announce that he only continued his economical mode of life two years. If it was "the thing," why did he not continue it? But, if he did not always live like a hermit, squatting on other people's property, and depending upon chance perch and pickerel for his dinner, he lived long enough by his own labor, and carried his system of economy to such a degree of perfection, that he tells us:

> "More than five years I maintained myself thus solely by the labor of my hands, and I found that by working about six weeks in a year, I could meet all the expenses of living."

* * *

There is nothing of the mean or sordid in the economy of Mr. Thoreau, though to some his simplicity and abstemiousness may appear trivial and affected; he does not live cheaply for the sake of saving, nor idly to avoid labor; but, that he may live independently and enjoy his great thoughts; that he may read the Hindoo scriptures and commune with the visible forms of nature. We must do him the credit to admit that there is no mock sentiment, nor simulation of piety or philanthropy in his volume. He is not much of a cynic, and though we have called him a Yankee Diogenes, the only personage to whom he bears a decided resemblance is that good humored creation of Dickens, Mark Tapley, whose delight was in being jolly under difficulties. The following passage might have been written by Mr. Tapley if that person had ever turned author, for the sake of testing the provocatives to jollity, which may be found in the literary profession:

"Sometimes, when I compare myself with other men, it seems as if I were more favored by the gods than they, beyond any deserts that I am conscious of; as if I had a warrant and a surety at their hands which my fellows have not, and especially guided and guarded. I do not flatter myself, but if it be possible they flatter me. I have never felt lonesome, or in the least oppressed by a sense of solitude, but once, and that was a few weeks after I came to the woods, when, for an hour, I doubted if the near neighborhood of man was not essential to a serene and healthy life. To be alone was something unpleasant. But I was at the same time conscious of a slight insanity in my mood, and seemed to foresee my recovery. In the midst of a gentle rain, while these thoughts prevailed, I was suddenly sensible of such sweet and beneficent society in Nature, in the very pattering of the drops, and in every sound and sight around my house, an infinite and unaccountable friendlyness all at once like an atmosphere sustaining me, as made the fancied advantages of human neighborhood insignificant, and I have never thought of them since."

* * *

There is much excellent good sense delivered in a very comprehensive and by no means unpleasant style in Mr. Thoreau's book, and let people think as they may of the wisdom or propriety of living after his fashion, denying oneself all the luxuries which the earth can afford, for the sake of leading a life of lawless vagabondage, and freedom from starched collars, there are but few readers who will fail to find profit and refreshment in his pages. Perhaps some practical people will think that a philosopher like Mr. Thoreau might have done the world a better service by purchasing a piece of land, and showing how much it might be made to produce, instead of squatting on another man's premises, and proving how little will suffice to keep body and soul together. But we must allow philosophers, and all other men, to fulfil their missions in their own way. If Mr. Thoreau had been a practical farmer, we should not have been favored with his volume; his corn and cabbage would have done but little towards profiting us, and we might never have been the better for his labors. As it is, we see how much more valuable to mankind is our philosophical vagabond than a hundred sturdy agriculturists; any plodder may raise beans, but it is only one in a million who can write a readable volume.

GEORGE ELIOT

[An Early British Review]†

In a volume called *Walden; or, Life in the Woods,* published last year, but quite interesting enough to make it worth while for us to break our rule by a retrospective notice—we have a bit of pure American life (not the 'go a-head' species, but its opposite pole), animated by that energetic, yet calm spirit of innovation, that practical as well as theoretic independence of formulæ, which is peculiar to some of the finer American minds. The writer tells us how he chose, for some years, to be a stoic of the woods; how he built his house; how he earned the necessaries of his simple life by cultivating a bit of ground. He tells his system of diet, his studies, his reflections, and his observations of natural phenomena. These last are not only made by a keen eye, but have their interest enhanced by passing through the medium of a deep poetic sensibility; and, indeed, we feel throughout the book the presence of a refined as well as a hardy mind. People—very wise in their own eyes—who would have every man's life ordered according to a particular pattern, and who are intolerant of every existence the utility of which is not palpable to them, may pooh-pooh Mr. Thoreau and this episode in his history, as unpractical and dreamy. Instead of contesting their opinion ourselves, we will let Mr. Thoreau speak for himself. There is plenty of sturdy sense mingled with his unworldliness.

† *Westminster Review,* 65 (9 N.S.) (January 1856), 302–303.

RALPH WALDO EMERSON

Thoreau †

IT seemed as if the breezes brought him,
It seemed as if the sparrows taught him,
As if by secret sign he knew
Where in far fields the orchis grew.

Henry David Thoreau was the last male descendant of a French ancestor who came to this country from the Isle of Guernsey. His character exhibited occasional traits drawn from this blood, in singular combination with a very strong Saxon genius.

He was born in Concord, Massachusetts, on the 12th of July, 1817. He was graduated at Harvard College in 1837, but without any literary distinction. An iconoclast in literature, he seldom thanked colleges for their service to him, holding them in small esteem, whilst yet his debt to them was important. After leaving the University, he joined his brother in teaching a private school, which he soon renounced. His father was a manufacturer of lead-pencils, and Henry applied himself for a time to this craft, believing he could make a better pencil than was then in use. After completing his experiments, he exhibited his work to chemists and artists in Boston, and having obtained their certificates to its excellence and to it equality with the best London manufacture, he returned home contented. His friends congratulated him that he had now opened his way to fortune. But he replied, that he should never make another pencil. "Why should I? I would not do again what I have done once." He resumed his endless walks and miscellaneous studies, making every day some new acquaintance with Nature, though as yet never speaking of zoölogy or botany, since, though very studious of natural facts, he was incurious of technical and textual science.

At this time, a strong, healthy youth, fresh from college, whilst all his companions were choosing their profession, or eager to begin some lucrative employment, it was inevitable that his thoughts should be exercised on the same question, and it required rare decision to refuse all the accustomed paths and keep his solitary freedom at the cost of disappointing the natural expectations of his family and friends: all the more difficult that he had a perfect probity, was exact in securing his own independence, and in holding every man to the like duty. But Thoreau never faltered. He was a born protestant. He declined to give up his

† From *Atlantic Monthly*, August, 1862.

large ambition of knowledge and action for any narrow craft or profession, aiming at a much more comprehensive calling, the art of living well. If he slighted and defied the opinions of others, it was only that he was more intent to reconcile his practice with his own belief. Never idle or self-indulgent, he preferred, when he wanted money, earning it by some piece of manual labor agreeable to him, as building a boat or a fence, planting, grafting, surveying, or other short work, to any long engagements. With his hardy habits and few wants, his skill in wood-craft, and his powerful arithmetic, he was very competent to live in any part of the world. It would cost him less time to supply his wants than another. He was therefore secure of his leisure.

A natural skill for mensuration, growing out of his mathematical knowledge and his habit of ascertaining the measures and distances of objects which interested him, the size of trees, the depth and extent of ponds and rivers, the height of mountains, and the air-line distance of his favorite summits,—this, and his intimate knowledge of the territory about Concord, made him drift into the profession of land-surveyor. It had the advantage for him that it led him continually into new and secluded grounds, and helped his studies of Nature. His accuracy and skill in this work were readily appreciated, and he found all the employment he wanted.

He could easily solve the problems of the surveyor, but he was daily beset with graver questions, which he manfully confronted. He interrogated every custom, and wished to settle all his practice on an ideal foundation. He was a protestant à *outrance*, and few lives contain so many renunciations. He was bred to no profession; he never married; he lived alone; he never went to church; he never voted; he refused to pay a tax to the State; he ate no flesh, he drank no wine, he never knew the use of tobacco; and, though a naturalist, he used neither trap nor gun. He chose, wisely no doubt for himself, to be the bachelor of thought and Nature. He had no talent for wealth, and knew how to be poor without the least hint of squalor or inelegance. Perhaps he fell into his way of living without forecasting it much, but approved it with later wisdom. "I am often reminded," he wrote in his journal, "that if I had bestowed on me the wealth of Crœsus, my aims must be still the same, and my means essentially the same." He had no temptations to fight against,—no appetites, no passions, no taste for elegant trifles. A fine house, dress, the manners and talk of highly cultivated people were all thrown away on him. He much preferred a good Indian, and considered these refinements as impediments to conversation, wishing to meet his companion on the simplest terms. He declined invitations to dinner-parties, because there each was in every one's way, and he could not meet the individuals to any purpose. "They make their pride," he said, "in making their dinner cost much; I make my pride in making my dinner cost little." When asked at table what dish he preferred, he answered, "The nearest." He did not like the taste of wine, and never had a vice in his life. He said,—"I have a faint recollection of pleasure derived from smoking dried lily-stems, before I was a man. I had commonly a supply of these. I have never smoked anything more noxious."

He chose to be rich by making his wants few, and supplying them himself. In his travels, he used the railroad only to get over so much country as was unimportant to the present purpose, walking hundreds of miles, avoiding taverns, buying a lodging in farmers' and fishermen's houses, as cheaper, and more agreeable to him, and because there he could better find the men and the information he wanted.

There was somewhat military in his nature, not to be subdued, always manly and able, but rarely tender, as if he did not feel himself except in opposition. He wanted a fallacy to expose, a blunder to pillory, I may say required a little sense of victory, a roll of the drum, to call his powers into full exercise. It cost him nothing to say No; indeed he found it much easier than to say Yes. It seemed as if his first instinct on hearing a proposition was to controvert it, so impatient was he of the limitations of our daily thought. This habit, of course, is a little chilling to the social affections; and though the companion would in the end acquit him of any malice or untruth, yet it mars conversation. Hence, no equal companion stood in affectionate relations with one so pure and guileless. "I love Henry," said one of his friends "but I cannot like him; and as for taking his arm, I should as soon think of taking the arm of an elm-tree."

Yet, hermit and stoic as he was, he was really fond of sympathy, and threw himself heartily and childlike into the company of young people whom he loved, and whom he delighted to entertain, as he only could, with the varied and endless anecdotes of his experiences by field and river: and he was always ready to lead a huckleberry-party or a search for chestnuts or grapes. Talking, one day, of a public discourse, Henry remarked, that whatever succeeded with the audience was bad. I said, "Who would not like to write something which all can read, like Robinson Crusoe? and who does not see with regret that his page is not solid with a right materialistic treatment, which delights everybody?" Henry objected, of course, and vaunted the better lectures which reached only a few persons. But, at supper, a young girl, understanding that he was to lecture at the Lyceum, sharply asked him, "Whether his lecture would be a nice, interesting story, such as she wished to hear, or whether it was one of those old philosophical things that she did not care about." Henry turned to her, and bethought himself, and, I saw, was trying to believe that he had matter that might fit her and her brother, who were to sit up and go to the lecture, if it was a good one for them.

He was a speaker and actor of the truth, born such, and was ever running into dramatic situations from this cause. In any circumstance it interested all bystanders to know what part Henry would take, and what he would say; and he did not disappoint expectation, but used an original judgment on each emergency. In 1845 he built himself a small framed house on the shores of Walden Pond, and lived there two years alone, a life of labor and study. This action was quite native and fit for him. No one who knew him would tax him with affectation. He was more unlike his neighbors in his thought than in his action. As soon as he had exhausted the advantages of that solitude, he abandoned it. In 1847, not approving some uses to which the public expenditure was applied, he refused to pay his town tax, and was put in jail. A friend paid the tax for him, and he was released. The like annoyance was threatened the next year. But, as his friends paid the tax, notwithstanding his protest, I believe he ceased to resist. No opposition or ridicule had any weight with him. He coldly and fully stated his opinion without affecting to believe that it was the opinion of the company. It was of no consequence if every one present held the opposite opinion. On one occasion he went to the University Library to procure some books. The librarian refused to lend them. Mr. Thoreau repaired to the President, who stated to him the rules and usages, which permitted the loan of books to resident graduates, to clergymen who were alumni, and to some others resident within a circle of ten miles' radius from the College. Mr. Thoreau explained to the President that the railroad had destroyed the old scale of distances,—that the library was useless, yes, and President and College useless, on the terms of his rules,—that the one benefit he owed to the College was its library,—that, at this moment, not only his want of books was imperative but he wanted a large number of books, and assured him that he, Throeau, and not the librarian, was the proper custodian of these. In short, the President found the petitioner so formidable, and the rules getting to look so ridiculous, that he ended by giving him a privilege which in his hands proved unlimited thereafter.

No truer American existed than Thoreau. His preference of his country and condition was genuine, and his aversation from

English and European manners and tastes almost reached contempt. He listened impatiently to news or *bonmots* gleaned from London circles; and though he tried to be civil, these anecdotes fatigued him. The men were all imitating each other, and on a small mould. Why can they not live as far apart as possible, and each be a man by himself? What he sought was the most energetic nature; and he wished to go to Oregon, not to London. "In every part of Great Britain," he wrote in his diary, "are discovered traces of the Romans, their funereal urns, their camps, their roads, their dwellings. But New England, at least is not based on any Roman ruins. We have not to lay the foundations of our houses on the ashes of a former civilization."

But, idealist as he was, standing for abolition of slavery, abolition of tariffs, almost for abolition of government, it is needless to say he found himself not only unrepresented in actual politics, but almost equally opposed to every class of reformers. Yet he paid the tribute of his uniform respect to the Anti-Slavery party. One man, whose personal acquaintance he had formed, he honored with exceptional regard. Before the first friendly word had been spoken for Captain John Brown, he sent notices to most houses in Concord that he would speak in a public hall on the condition and character of John Brown, on Sunday evening, and invited all people to come. The Republican Committee, the Abolitionist Committee, sent him word that it was premature and not advisable. He replied,—"I did not send to you for advice, but to announce that I am to speak." The hall was filled at an early hour by people of all parties, and his earnest eulogy of the hero was heard by all respectfully, by many with a sympathy that surprised themselves.

It was said of Plotinus that he was ashamed of his body, and 't is very likely he had good reason for it,—that his body was a bad servant, and he had not skill in dealing with the material world, as happens often to men of abstract intellect. But Mr. Thoreau was equipped with a most adapted and serviceable body. He was of short stature, firmly built, of light complexion, with strong, serious blue eyes, and a grave aspect,—his face covered in the late years with a becoming beard. His senses were acute, his frame well-knit and hardy, his hands strong and skilful in the use of tools. And there was a wonderful fitness of body and mind. He could pace sixteen rods more accurately than another man could measure them with rod and chain. He could find his path in the woods at night, he said, better by his feet than his eyes. He could estimate the measure of a tree very well by his eye; he could estimate the weight of a calf or a pig, like a dealer. From a box containing a bushel or more of loose pencils, he could take up with his hands fast enough just a dozen pencils at every grasp. He was a good swimmer, runner, skater, boatman, and would probably outwalk most countrymen in a day's journey. And the relation of body to mind was still finer than we have indicated. He said he wanted every stride his legs made. The length of his walk uniformly made the length of his writing. If shut up in the house he did not write at all.

He had a strong common-sense, like that which Rose Flammock the weaver's daughter in Scott's romance commends in her father, as resembling a yardstick, which, whilst it measures dowlas and diaper, can equally well measure tapestry and cloth of gold. He had always a new resource. When I was planting forest trees, and had procured half a peck of acorns, he said that only a small portion of them would be sound, and proceeded to examine them and select the sound ones. But finding this took time, he said, "I think if you put them all into water the good ones will sink;" which experiment we tried with success. He could plan a garden or a house or a barn; would have been competent to lead a "Pacific Exploring Expedition;" could give judicious counsel in the gravest private or public affairs.

He lived for the day, not cumbered and mortified by his memory. If he brought you yesterday a new proposition, he would bring you to-day another not less revolutionary. A very industrious man, and setting, like all highly organized men, a high value on his time, he seemed the only man of leisure in town, always ready for any excursion that promised well, or for conversation prolonged into late hours. His trenchant sense was never stopped by his rules of daily prudence, but was always up to the new occasion. He liked and used the simplest food, yet, when some one urged a vegetable diet, Thoreau thought all diets a very small matter, saying that "the man who shoots the buffalo lives better than the man who boards at the Graham House." He said,—"You can sleep near the railroad, and never be disturbed: Nature knows very well what sounds are worth attending to, and has made up her mind not to hear the railroad-whistle. But things respect the devout mind, and a mental ecstacy was never interrupted." He noted what repeatedly befell him, that, after receiving from a distance a rare plant, he would presently find the same in his own haunts. And those pieces of luck which happen only to good players happened to him. One day, walking with a stranger, who inquired where Indian arrow-heads could be found, he replied, "Everywhere," and, stooping forward, picked one on the instant from the ground. At Mount Washington, in Tuckerman's Ravine, Thoreau had a bad fall, and sprained his foot. As he was in the act of getting up from his fall, he saw for the first time the leaves of the *Arnica mollis*.

His robust common sense, armed with stout hands, keen perceptions and strong will, cannot yet account for the superiority which shone in his simple and hidden life. I must add the cardinal fact, that there was an excellent wisdom in him, proper to a rare class of men, which showed him the material world as a means and symbol. This discovery, which sometimes yields to poets a certain casual and interrupted light, serving for the ornament of their writing, was in him an unsleeping insight; and whatever faults or obstructions of temperament might cloud it, he was not disobedient to the heavenly vision. In his youth, he said, one day, "The other world is all my art; my pencils will draw no other; my jack-knife will cut nothing else; I do not use it as a means." This was the muse and genius that ruled his opinions, conversation, studies, work and course of life. This made him a searching judge of men. At first glance he measured his companion, and, though insensible to some fine traits of culture, could very well report his weight and calibre. And this made the impression of genius which his conversation sometimes gave.

He understood the matter in hand at a glance, and saw the limitations and poverty of those he talked with, so that nothing seemed concealed from such terrible eyes. I have repeatedly known young men of sensibility converted in a moment to the belief that this was the man they were in search of, the man of men, who could tell them all they should do. His own dealing with them was never affectionate, but superior, didactic, scorning their petty ways,—very slowly conceding, or not conceding at all, the promise of his society at their houses, or even at his own. "Would he not walk with them?" "He did not know. There was nothing so important to him as his walk; he had no walks to throw away on company." Visits were offered him from respectful parties, but he declined them. Admiring friends offered to carry him at their own cost to the Yellowstone River,—to the West Indies,—to South America. But though nothing could be more grave or considered than his refusals, they remind one, in quite new relations, of that fop Brummel's reply to the gentleman who offered him his carriage in a shower, "But where will *you* ride, then?"—and what accusing silences, and what searching and irresistible speeches, battering down all defenses, his companions can remember!

Mr. Thoreau dedicated his genius with such entire love to the fields, hills and waters of his native town, that he made them known and interesting to all reading Americans, and to people over the sea. The river on whose banks he was born and died he knew from its springs to its confluence with the Merrimack. He had made summer and winter observtaions on it for many years, and at every hour of the day ana night. The result of the recent survey of the Water Commissioners appointed by the State of Massachusetts he had reached by his private experiments, several years earlier. Every fact which occurs in the bed, on the banks, or in the air over it; the fishes, and their spawning and nests, their manners, their food; the shad-flies which fill the air on a certain evening once a year, and which are snapped at by the fishes so ravenously that many of these die of repletion; the conical heaps of small stones on the river-shallows, the huge nests of small fishes, one of which will sometimes overfill a cart; the birds which frequent the stream, heron, duck, sheldrake, loon, osprey; the snake, muskrat, otter, woodchuck and fox, on the banks; the turtle, frog, hyla and cricket, which make the banks vocal,—were all know to him, and, as it were, townsmen and fellow-creatures; so that he felt an absurdity or violence in any narrative of one of these by itself apart, and still more of it dimensions on an inch-rule, or in the exhibition of its skeleton, or the specimen of a squirrel or a bird in brandy. He liked to speak of the manners of the river, as itself a lawful creature, yet with exactness, and always to an observed fact. As he knew the river, so the ponds in this region.

One of the weapons he used, more important to him than microscope or alcohol-receiver to other investigators, was a whim which grew on him by indulgence, yet appeared in gravest statement, namely, of extolling his own town and neighborhood as the most favored centre for natural observation. He remarked that the Flora of Massachusetts embraced almost all the important plants of America,—most of the oaks, most of the willows, the best pines, the ash, the maple, the beech, the nuts. He returned Kane's "Arctic Voyage" to a friend of whom he had borrowed it, with the remark, that "Most of the phenomena noted might be observed in Concord." He seemed a little envious of the Pole, for the coincident sunrise and sunset, or five minutes' day after six months: a splendid fact, which Annursnuc had never afforded him. He found red snow in one of his walks, and told me that he expected to find yet the *Victoria regia* in Concord. He was the attorney of the indigenous plants, and owned to a preference of the weeds to the imported plants as of the Indian to the civilized man, and noticed, with pleasure, that the willow bean-poles of his neighbor had grown more than his beans. "See these weeds," he said, "which have been hoed at by a million farmers all spring and summer, and yet have prevailed, and just now come out triumphant over all lanes, pastures, fields and gardens, such is their vigor. We have insulted them with low names, too,—as Pigweed, Wormwood, Chick-weed, Shad-blossom." He says, "They have brave names, too,—Ambrosia, Stellaria, Amelanchier, Amaranth, etc."

I think his fancy for referring everything to the meridian of Concord did not grow out of any ignorance or depreciation of other longitudes or latitudes, but was rather a playful expression of his conviction of the indifference of all places, and that the best place for each is where he stands. He expressed it once in this wise:—"I think nothing is to be hoped from you, if this bit of mould under your feet is not sweeter to you to eat than any other in this world, or in any world."

The other weapon with which he conquered all obstacles in science was patience. He knew how to sit immovable, a part of the rock he rested on, until the bird, the reptile, the fish, which had retired from him, should come back and resume its habits, nay, moved by curiosity, should come to him and watch him.

It was a pleasure and a privilege to walk with him. He knew the country like a fox or a bird, and passed through it as freely by paths of his own. He knew every track in the snow or on the ground, and what creature had taken this path before him. One must submit abjectly to such a guide, and the reward was great. Under his arm he carried an old music-book to press plants; in his pocket, his diary and pencil, a spy-glass for birds, microscope, jack-knife, and twine. He wore a straw hat, stout shoes, strong gray trousers, to brave scrub-oaks and smilax, and to climb a tree for a hawk's or a squirrel's nest. He waded into the pool for the water-plants, and his strong legs were no insignificant part of his armor. On the day I speak of he looked for the Menyanthes, detected it across the wide pool, and, on examination of the florets, decided that it had been in flower five days. He drew out of his breast-pocket his diary, and read the names of all the plants that should bloom on this day, whereof he kept account as a banker when his notes fall due. The Cypripedium not due till to-morrow. He thought that, if waked up from a trance, in this swamp, he could tell by the plants what time of the year it was within two days. The redstart was flying about, and presently the fine grosbeaks, whose brilliant scarlet "makes the rash gazer wipe his eye," and whose fine clear note Thoreau compared to that of a tanager which has got rid of its hoarseness. Presently he heard a note which he called that of the night-warbler, a bird he had never identified, had been in search of twelve years, which always, when he saw it, was in the act of diving down into a tree or bush, and which

it was vain to seek; the only bird which sings indifferently by
night and by day. I told him he must beware of finding and
booking it, lest life should have nothing more to show him. He
said, "What you seek in vain for, half your life, one day you
come full upon, all the family at dinner. You seek it like a dream,
and as soon as you find it you become its prey."

His interest in the flower or the bird lay very deep in his
mind, was connected with Nature,—and the meaning of Nature
was never attempted to be defined by him. He would not offer
a memoir of his observations to the Natural History Society.
"Why should I? To detach the description from its connections
in my mind would make it no longer true or valuable to me:
and they do not wish what belongs to it." His power of observation
seemed to indicate additional senses. He saw as with microscope,
heard as with ear-trumpet, and his memory was a photographic
register of all he saw and heard. And yet none knew better than
he that it is not the fact that imports, but the impression
or effect of the fact on your mind. Every fact lay in glory in
his mind, a type of the order and beauty of the whole.

His determination on Natural History was organic. He confessed
that he sometimes felt like a hound or a panther, and, if born
among Indians, would have been a fell hunter. But, restrained
by his Massachusetts culture, he played out the game in this
mild form of botany and ichthyology. His intimacy with animals
suggested what Thomas Fuller records of Butler the apiologist,
that "either he had told the bees things or the bees had told
him." Snakes coiled round his leg; the fishes swam into his hand,
and he took them out of the water; he pulled the woodchuck
out of its hole by the tail and took the foxes under his protection
from the hunters. Our naturalist had perfect magnanimity;
he had no secrets: he would carry you to the heron's haunt,
or even to his most prized botanical swamp,—possibly knowing
that you could never find it again, yet willing to take his risks.

No college ever offered him a diploma, or a professor's chair;
no academy made him its corresponding secretary, its discoverer,
or even its member. Perhaps these learned bodies feared the
satire of his presence. Yet so much knowledge of Nature's secret
and genius few others possessed; none in a more large and religious synthesis. For not a particle of respect had he to the
opinions of any man or body of men, but homage solely to the
truth itself; and as he discovered everywhere among doctors some
leaning of courtesy, it discredited them. He grew to be revered
and admired by his townsmen, who had at first known him only
as an oddity. The farmers who employed him as a surveyor soon
discovered his rare accuracy and skill, his knowledge of their

lands, of trees, of birds, of Indian remains and the like, which enabled him to tell every farmer more than he knew before of his own farm; so that he began to feel a little as if Mr. Thoreau had better rights in his land than he. They felt, too, the superiority of character which addressed all men with a native authority.

Indian relics abound in Concord,—arrow-heads, stone chisels, pestles, and fragments of pottery; and on the river-bank, large heaps of clam-shells and ashes mark spots which the savages frequented. These, and every circumstance touching the Indian, were important in his eyes. His visits to Maine were chiefly for love of the Indian. He had the satisfaction of seeing the manufacture of the bark-canoe, as well as of trying his hand in its management on the rapids. He was inquisitive about the making of the stone arrow-head, and in his last days charged a youth setting out for the Rocky Mountains to find an Indian who could tell him that: "It was well worth a visit to California to learn it." Occasionally, a small party of Penobscot Indians would visit Concord, and pitch their tents for a few weeks in summer on the river-bank. He failed not to make acquaintance with the best of them; though he well knew that asking questions of Indians is like catechizing beavers and rabbits. In his last visit to Maine he had great satisfaction from Joseph Polis, an intelligent Indian of Oldtown, who was his guide for some weeks.

He was equally interested in every natural fact. The depth of his perception found likeness of law throughout Nature, and I know not any genius who so swiftly inferred universal law from the single fact. He was no pedant of a department. His eye was open to beauty, and his ear to music. He found these, not in rare conditions, but wheresoever he went. He thought the best of music was in single strains; and he found poetic suggestion in the humming of the telegraph-wire.

His poetry might be bad or good; he no doubt wanted a lyric facility and technical skill, but he had the source of poetry in his spiritual perception. He was a good reader and critic, and his judgment on poetry was to the ground of it. He could not be deceived as to the presence or absence of the poetic element in any composition, and his thirst for this made him negligent and perhaps scornful of superficial graces. He would pass by many delicate rhythms, but he would have detected every live stanza or line in a volume, and knew very well where to find an equal poetic charm in prose. He was so enamored of the spiritual beauty that he held all actual written poems in very light esteem in the comparison. He admired Æschylus and Pindar; but, when some one was commending them, he said that Æschylus and the Greeks, in describing Apollo and Orpheus, had given no song, or no good one. "They ought not to have moved trees, but to have chanted to the gods such a hymn as would have sung all their old ideas out of their heads, and new ones in." His own verses are often rude and defective. The gold does not yet run pure, is drossy and crude. The thyme and marjoram are not yet honey. But if he want lyric fineness and technical merits, if he have not the poetic temperament, he never lacks the causal thought, showing that his genius was better than his talent. He knew the worth of the Imagination for the uplifting and consolation of human life, and liked to throw every thought into a symbol. The fact you tell is of no value, but only the impression. For this reason his presence was poetic, always piqued the curiosity to know more deeply the secrets of his mind. He had many reserves, an unwillingness to exhibit to profane eyes what was still sacred in his own, and knew well how to throw a poetic veil over his experience. All readers of "Walden" will remember his mythical record of his disappointments:—

"I long ago lost a hound, a bay horse and a turtle-dove, and am still on their trail. Many are the travellers I have spoken concerning them, describing their tracks, and what calls they answered to. I have met one or two who have heard the hound, and the tramp of the horse, and even seen the dove disappear behind a cloud; and they seemed as anxious to recover them as if they had lost them themselves." [1]

His riddles were worth the reading, and I confide that if at any time I do not understand the expression, it is yet just. Such was the wealth of his truth that it was not worth his while to use words in vain. His poem entitled "Sympathy" reveals the tenderness under that triple steel of stoicism, and the intellectual subtilty it could animate. His classic poem on "Smoke" suggests Simonides, but is better than any poem of Simonides. His biography is in his verses. His habitual thought makes all his poetry a hymn to the Cause of causes, the Spirit which vivifies and controls his own:—

> "I hearing get, who had but ears,
> And sight, who had but eyes before;
> I moments live, who lived but years,
> And truth discern, who knew but learning's lore."

And still more in these religious lines:—

> "Now chiefly is my natal hour,
> And only now my prime of life;
> I will not doubt the love untold,

1. *Walden*: p. 11.

Which not my worth nor want have bought,
Which wooed me young, and wooes me old,
And to this evening hath me brought."

Whilst he used in his writings a certain petulance of remark in reference to churches or churchmen, he was a person of a rare, tender and absolute religion, a person incapable of any profanation, by act or by thought. Of course, the same isolation which belonged to his original thinking and living detached him from the social religious forms. This is neither to be censured nor regretted. Aristotle long ago explained it, when he said, "One who surpasses his fellow-citizens in virtue is no longer a part of the city. Their law is not for him, since he is a law to himself."

Thoreau was sincerity itself, and might fortify the convictions of prophets in the ethical laws by his holy living. It was a affirmative experience which refused to be set aside. A truth-speaker he, capable of the most deep and strict conversation; a physician to the wounds of any soul; a friend, knowing not only the secret of friendship, but almost worshipped by those few persons who resorted to him as their confessor and prophet, and knew the deep value of his mind and great heart. He thought that without religion or devotion of some kind nothing great was ever accomplished: and he thought that the bigoted sectarian had better bear this in mind.

His virtues, of course, sometimes ran into extremes. It was easy to trace to the inexorable demand on all for exact truth that austerity which made this willing hermit more solitary even than he wished. Himself of a perfect probity, he required not less of others. He had a disgust at crime, and no worldly success would cover it. He detected paltering as readily in dignified and prosperous persons as in beggars, and with equal scorn. Such dangerous frankness was in his dealing that his admirers called him "that terrible Thoreau," as if he spoke when silent, and was still present when he had departed. I think the severity of his ideal interfered to deprive him of a healthy sufficiency of human society.

The habit of a realist to find things the reverse of their appearance inclined him to put every statement in a paradox. A certain habit of antagonism defaced his earlier writings,—a trick of rhetoric not quite outgrown in his later, of substituting for the obvious word and thought its diametrical opposite. He praised wild mountains and winter forests for their domestic air, in snow and ice he would find sultriness, and commended the wilderness for resembling Rome and Paris. "It was so dry, that you might call it wet."

The tendency to magnify the moment, to read all the laws

of Nature in the one object or one combination under your eye, is of course comic to those who do not share the philosopher's perception of identity. To him there was no such thing as size. The pond was a small ocean; the Atlantic, a large Walden Pond. He referred every minute fact to cosmical laws. Though he meant to be just, he seemed haunted by a certain chronic assumption that the science of the day pretended completeness, and he had just found out that the *savans* had neglected to discriminate a particular botanical variety, had failed to describe the seeds or count the sepals. "That is to say," we replied, "the blockheads were not born in Concord; but who said they were? It was their unspeakable misfortune to be born in London, or Paris, or Rome; but, poor fellows, they did what they could, considering that they never saw Bateman's Pond, or Nine-Acre Corner, or Becky Stow's Swamp; besides, what were you sent into the world for, but to add this observation?"

Had his genius been only contemplative, he had been fitted to his life, but with his energy and practical ability he seemed born for great enterprise and for command; and I so much regret the loss of his rare powers of action, that I cannot help counting it a fault in him that he had no ambition. Wanting this, instead of engineering for all America, he was the captain of a huckleberry-party. Pounding beans is good to the end of pounding empires one of these days; but if, at the end of years, it is still only beans!

But these foibles, real or apparent, were fast vanishing in the incessant growth of a spirit so robust and wise, and which effaced its defeats with new triumphs. His study of Nature was a perpetual ornament to him, and inspired his friends with curiosity to see the world through his eyes, and to hear his adventures. They possessed every kind of interest.

He had many elegancies of his own, whilst he scoffed at conventional elegance. Thus, he could not bear to hear the sound of his own steps, the grit of gravel; and therefore never willingly walked in the road, but in the grass, on mountains and in woods. His senses were acute, and he remarked that by night every dwelling-house gives out bad air, like a slaughter-house. He liked the pure fragrance of melilot. He honored certain plants with special regard, and, over all, the pond-lily,—then, the gentian, and the *Mikania scandens*, and "life-everlasting," and a bass-tree which he visited every year when it bloomed, in the middle of July. He thought the scent a more oracular inquisition than the sight,—more oracular and trustworthy. The scent, of course, reveals what is concealed from the other senses. By it he detected earthiness. He delighted in echoes, and said they were almost the only kind of kindred voices that he heard. He loved Nature so well, was so happy in her solitude, that he became very jealous of cities and the sad work which their refinements and artifices made with man and his dwelling. The axe was always destroying his forest. "Thank God," he said, "they cannot cut down the clouds!" "All kinds of figures are drawn on the blue ground with this fibrous white paint."

I subjoin a few sentences taken from his unpublished manuscripts, not only as records of his thought and feeling, but for their power of description and literary excellence:—

"Some circumstantial evidence is very strong, as when you find a trout in the milk."

"The chub is a soft fish, and tastes like boiled brown paper salted."

"The youth gets together his materials to build a bridge to the moon, or, perchance, a palace or temple on the earth, and, at length the middle-aged man concludes to build a wood-shed with them."

"The locust z-ing."

"Devil's-needles zigzagging along the Nut-Meadow brook."

"Sugar is not so sweet to the palate as sound to the healthy ear."

"I put on some hemlock-boughs, and the rich salt crackling of their leaves was like mustard to the ear, the crackling of uncountable regiments. Dead trees love the fire."

"The bluebird carries the sky on his back."

"The tanager flies through the green foliage as if it would ignite the leaves."

"If I wish for a horse-hair for my compass-sight I must go to the stable; but the hair-bird, with her sharp eyes, goes to the road."

"Immortal water, alive even to the superficies."

"Fire is the most tolerable third party."

"Nature made ferns for pure leaves, to show what she could do in that line."

"No tree has so fair a bole and so handsome an instep as the beech."

"How did these beautiful rainbow-tints get into the shell of the fresh-water clam, buried in the mud at the bottom of our dark river?"

"Hard are the times when the infant's shoes are second-foot."

"We are strictly confined to our men to whom we give liberty."

"Nothing is so much to be feared as fear. Atheism may comparatively be popular with God himself."

"Of what significance the things you can forget? A little thought is sexton to all the world."

"How can we expect a harvest of thought who have not had a seed-time of character?"

"Only he can be trusted with gifts who can present a face of bronze to expectations."

"I ask to be melted. You can only ask of the metals that they be tender to the fire that melts them. To nought else can they be tender."

There is a flower known to botanists, one of the same genus with our summer plant called "Life-Everlasting," a *Gnaphalium* like that, which grows on the most inaccessible cliffs of the Tyrolese mountains, where the chamois dare hardly venture, and which the hunter, tempted by its beauty, and by his love (for it is immensely valued by the Swiss maidens), climbs the cliffs to gather, and is sometimes found dead at the foot, with the flower in his hand. It is called by botanists the *Gnaphalium leontopodium*, but by the Swiss *Edelweisse*, which signifies *Noble Purity*. Thoreau seemed to me living in the hope to gather this plant, which belonged to him of right. The scale on which his studies proceeded was so large as to require longevity, and we were the less prepared for his sudden disappearance. The country knows not yet, or in the least part, how great a son it has lost. It seems an injury that he should leave in the midst his broken task which none else can finish, a kind of indignity to so noble a soul that he should depart out of Nature before yet he has been really shown to his peers for what he is. But he, at least, is content. His soul was made for the noblest society; he had in a short life exhausted the capabilities of this world; wherever there is knowledge, wherever there is virtue, wherever there is beauty, he will find a home.

JAMES RUSSELL LOWELL†

Thoreau

What contemporary, if he was in the fighting period of his life, (since Nature sets limits about her conscription for spiritual fields, as the state does in physical warfare), will ever forget what was somewhat vaguely called the "Transcendental Movement" of thirty years ago? Apparently set astir by Carlyle's essays on the "Signs of the Times," and on "History," the final and more immediate impulse seemed to be given by "Sartor Resartus." At least the republication in Boston of that wonderful

† Written in 1865. From the Riverside Edition of The Writings of James Russell Lowell (Boston, 1890), Vol. I, *Literary Essays*, pp. 361–81.

Abraham à Sancta Clara sermon on Falstaff's text of the miserable forked radish gave the signal for a sudden mental and moral mutiny. *Ecce nunc tempus acceptabile!* was shouted on all hands with every variety of emphasis, and by voices of every conceivable pitch, representing the three sexes of men, women, and Lady Mary Wortley Montagues. The nameless eagle of the tree Ygdrasil was about to sit at last, and wild-eyed enthusiasts rushed from all sides, each eager to thrust under the mystic bird that chalk egg from which the new and fairer Creation was to be hatched in due time. *Redeunt Saturnia regna,*—so far was certain, though in what shape, or by what methods, was still a matter of debate. Every possible form of intellectual and physical dyspepsia brought forth its gospel. Bran had its prophets, and the presartorial simplicity of Adam its martyrs, tailored impromptu from the tar-pot by incensed neighbors, and sent forth to illustrate the "feathered Mercury," as defined by Webster and Worcester. Plainness of speech was carried to a pitch that would have taken away the breath of George Fox; and even swearing had its evangelists, who answered a simple inquiry after their health with an elaborate ingenuity of imprecation that might have been honorably mentioned by Marlborough in general orders. Everybody had a mission (with a capital M) to attend to everybody-else's business. No brain but had its private maggot, which must have found pitiably short commons sometimes. Not a few impecunious zealots abjured the use of money (unless earned by other people), professing to live on the internal revenues of the spirit. Some had an assurance of instant millennium so soon as hooks and eyes should be substituted for buttons. Communities were established where everything was to be common but common-sense. Men renounced their old gods, and hesitated only whether to bestow their furloughed allegiance on Thor or Budh. Conventions were held for every hitherto inconceivable purpose. The belated gift of tongues, as among the Fifth Monarchy men, spread like a contagion, rendering its victims incomprehensible to all Christian men; whether equally so to the most distant possible heathen or not was unexperimented, though many would have subscribed liberally that a fair trial might be made. It was the pentecost of Shinar. The day of utterances reproduced the day of rebuses and anagrams, and there was nothing so simple that uncial letters and the style of Diphilus the Labyrinth could not turn it into a riddle. Many foreign revolutionists out of work added to the general misunderstanding their contribution of broken English in every most ingenious form of fracture. All stood ready at a moment's notice to reform everything but themselves. The general motto was:—

"And we'll *talk* with them, too,
And take upon's the mystery of things
As if we were God's spies."

Nature is always kind enough to give even her clouds a humorous lining. I have barely hinted at the comic side of the affair, for the material was endless. This was the whistle and trailing fuse of the shell, but there was a very solid and serious kernel, full of the most deadly explosiveness. Thoughtful men divined it, but the generality suspected nothing. The word "transcendental" then was the maid of all work for those who could not think, as "Pre-Raphaelite" has been more recently for people of the same limited housekeeping. The truth is, that there was a much nearer metaphysical relation and a much more distant æsthetic and literary relation between Carlyle and the Apostles of the Newness, as they were called in New England, than has commonly been supposed. Both represented the reaction and revolt against *Philisterei*, a renewal of the old battle begun in modern times by Erasmus and Reuchlin, and continued by Lessing, Goethe, and, in a far narrower sense, by Heine in Germany, and of which Fielding, Sterne, and Wordsworth in different ways have been the leaders in England. It was simply a struggle for fresh air, in which, if the windows could not be opened, there was danger that panes would be broken, though painted with images of saints and martyrs. Light, colored by these reverend effigies, was none the more respirable for being picturesque. There is only one thing better than tradition, and that is the original and eternal life out of which all tradition takes its rise. It was this life which the reformers demanded, with more or less clearness of consciousness and expression, life in politics, life in literature, life in religion. Of what use to import a gospel from Judæa, if we leave behind the soul that made it possible, the God who keeps it forever real and present? Surely Abana and Pharpar *are* better than Jordan, if a living faith be mixed with those waters and none with these.

Scotch Presbyterianism as a motive of spiritual progress was dead; New England Puritanism was in like manner dead; in other words, Protestantism had made its fortune and no longer protested; but till Carlyle spoke out in the Old World and Emerson in the New, no one had dared to proclaim, *Le roi est mort: vive le roi!* The meaning of which proclamation was essentially this: the vital spirit has long since departed out of this form once so kingly, and the great seal has been in commission long enough; but meanwhile the soul of man, from which all power emanates and to which it reverts, still survives in undiminished royalty; God still survives, little as you gentlemen of the Commission seem to be aware of it,—nay, will possibly outlive the whole of you, incredible as it may appear. The truth is, that both Scotch Presbyterianism and New England ˙Puritanism made their new avatar in Carlyle and Emerson, the heralds of their formal decease, and the tendency of the one toward Authority and of the other toward Independency might have been prophesied by whoever had studied history. The necessity was not so much in the men as in the principles they represented and the traditions which overruled them. The Puritanism of the past found its unwilling poet in Hawthorne, the rarest creative imagination of the century, the rarest in some ideal respects since Shakespeare; but the Puritanism that cannot die, the Puritanism that made New England what it is, and is destined to make America what it should be, found its voice in Emerson. Though holding himself aloof from all active partnership in movements of reform, he has been the sleeping partner who has supplied a great part of their capital.

The artistic range of Emerson is narrow, as every well-read critic must feel at once; and so is that of Æschylus, so is that of Dante, so is that of Montaigne, so is that of Schiller, so is that of nearly every one except Shakespeare; but there is a gauge of height no less than of breadth, of individuality as well as of comprehensiveness, and, above all, there is the standard of genetic power, the test of the masculine as distinguished from the receptive minds. There are staminate plants in literature, that make no fine show of fruit, but without whose pollen, quintessence of fructifying gold, the garden had been barren. Emerson's mind is emphatically one of these, and there is no man to whom our æsthetic culture owes so much. The Puritan revolt had made us ecclesiastically and the Revolution politically independent, but we were still socially and intellectually moored to English thought, till Emerson cut the cable and gave us a chance at the dangers and the glories of blue water. No man young enough to have felt it can forget or cease to be grateful for the mental and moral *nudge* which he received from the writings of his high-minded and brave-spirited countryman. That we agree with him, or that he always agrees with himself, is aside from the question; but that he arouses in us something that we are the better for having awakened, whether that something be of opposition or assent, that he speaks always to what is highest and least selfish in us, few Americans of the generation younger than his own would be disposed to deny. His oration before the Phi Beta Kappa Society at Cambridge, some thirty years ago, was an event without any former parallel in our literary annals, a scene to be always treasured in the memory for its picturesqueness and its inspiration. What crowded and breathless aisles, what windows clustering with eager heads, what enthusiasm of approval, what grim silence of foregone dissent! It was our Yankee version of a lecture by Abelard, our Harvard parallel to the last public appearances of Schelling.

I said that the Transcendental Movement was the protestant spirit of Puritanism seeking a new outlet and an escape from forms and creeds which compressed rather than expressed it. In its motives, its preaching, and its results, it differed radically from the doctrine of Carlyle. The Scotchman, with all his genius, and his humor gigantesque as that of Rabelais, has grown shriller and shriller with years, degenerating sometimes into a common scold, and emptying very unsavory vials of wrath on the head of the sturdy British Socrates of worldly common-sense. The teaching of Emerson tended much more exclusively to self-culture and the independent development of the individual man. It seemed to many almost Pythagorean in its voluntary seclusion from commonwealth affairs. Both Carlyle and Emerson were disciples of Goethe, but Emerson in a far truer sense; and while the one, from his bias toward the eccentric, has degenerated more and more into mannerism, the other has clarified steadily toward perfection of style,—exquisite fineness of material, unobtrusive lowness of tone and simplicity of fashion, the most high-bred garb of expression. Whatever may be said of his thought, nothing can be finer than the delicious limpidness of his phrase. If it was ever questionable whether democracy could develop a gentleman, the problem has been affirmatively solved at last. Carlyle, in his cynicism and his admiration of force in and for itself, has become at last positively inhuman; Emerson, reverencing strength, seeking the highest outcome of the individual, has found that society and politics are also main elements in the attainment of the desired end, and has drawn steadily manward and worldward. The two men represent respectively those grand personifications in the drama of Æschylus, Βία and Κράτος.

Among the pistillate plants kindled to fruitage by the Emersonian pollen, Thoreau is thus far the most remarkable; and it is something eminently fitting that his posthumous works should be offered us by Emerson, for they are strawberries from his own garden. A singular mixture of varieties, indeed, there is;—alpine, some of them, with the flavor of rare mountain air; others wood, tasting of sunny roadside banks or shy openings in the forest; and not a few seedlings swollen hugely by culture, but lacking the fine natural aroma of the more modest kinds. Strange books these are of his, and interesting in many ways,—instructive chiefly as showing how considerable a crop may be raised on a comparatively narrow close of mind, and how much a man may make of his life if he will assiduously follow it, though perhaps never truly finding it at last.

I have just been renewing my recollection of Mr. Thoreau's writings, and have read through his six volumes in the order of their production. I shall try to give an adequate report of their impression upon me both as critic and as mere reader. He seems to me to have been a man with so high a conceit of himself that he accepted without questioning, and insisted on our accepting, his defects and weaknesses of character as virtues and powers peculiar to himself. Was he indolent, he finds none of the activities which attract or employ the rest of mankind worthy of him. Was he wanting in the qualities that make success, it is success that is contemptible, and not himself that lacks persistency and purpose. Was he poor, money was an unmixed evil. Did his life seem a selfish one, he condemns doing good as one of the weakest of superstitions. To be of use was with him the most killing bait of the wily tempter Uselessness. He had no faculty of generalization from outside of himself, or at least no experience which would supply the material of such, and he makes his own whim the law, his own range the horizon of the universe. He condemns a world, the hollowness of whose satisfactions he had never had the means of testing, and we recognize Apemantus behind the mask of Timon. He had little active imagination; of the receptive he had much. His appreciation is of the highest quality; his critical power, from want of continuity of mind, very limited and inadequate. He somewhere cites a simile from Ossian, as an example of the superiority of the old poetry to the new, though, even were the historic evidence less convincing, the sentimental melancholy of those poems should be conclusive of their modernness. He had none of the artistic mastery which controls a great work to the serene balance of completeness, but exquisite mechanical skill in the shaping of sentences and paragraphs, or (more rarely) short bits of verse for the expression of a detached thought, sentiment, or image. His works give one the feeling of a sky full of stars,—something impressive and exhilarating certainly, something high overhead and freckled thickly with spots of isolated brightness; but whether these have any mutual relation with each other, or have any concern with our mundane matters, is for the most part matter of conjecture,—astrology as yet, and not astronomy.

It is curious, considering what Thoreau afterwards became, that he was not by nature an observer. He only saw the things he looked for, and was less poet than naturalist. Till he built his Walden shanty, he did not know that the hickory grew in Concord. Till he went to Maine, he had never seen phosphorescent wood, a phenomenon early familiar to most country boys. At forty he speaks of the seeding of the pine as a new discovery, though one should have thought that its gold-dust of blowing pollen might have earlier drawn his eye. Neither his attention nor his genius was of the spontaneous kind. He discovered nothing. He thought everything a discovery of his own, from moonlight to the planting of acorns and nuts by squirrels. This is a defect in his character, but one of his chief charms as a writer. Everything grows fresh under his hand. He delved in his mind and nature; he planted them with all manner of native and foreign seeds, and reaped assiduously. He was not merely solitary, he would be isolated, and succeeded at last in almost persuading himself that he was autochthonous. He valued everything in proportion as he fancied it to be exclusively his own. He complains in "Walden" that there is no one in Concord with whom he could talk of Oriental literature, though the man was living within two miles of his hut who had introduced him to it. This intellectual selfishness becomes sometimes almost painful in reading him. He lacked that generosity of "communication" which Johnson admired in Burke. De Quincey tells us that Wordsworth was impatient when any one else spoke of mountains, as if he had a peculiar property in them. And we can readily understand why it should be so: no one is satisfied with another's appreciation of his mistress. But Thoreau seems to have prized a lofty way of thinking (often we should be inclined to call it a remote one) not so much because it was good in itself as because he wished few to share it with him. It seems now and then as if he did not seek to lure others up "above our lower region of turmoil," but to leave his own name cut on the mountain peak as the first climber. This itch of originality infects his thought and style. To be misty is not to be mystic. He turns commonplaces end for end, and fancies it makes something new of them. As we walk down Park Street, our eye is caught by Dr. Winship's dumb-bells, one of which bears an inscription testifying that it is the heaviest ever put up at arm's length by any athlete; and in reading Mr. Thoreau's books we cannot help feeling as if he sometimes invited our attention to a particular sophism or paradox as the biggest yet maintained by any single writer. He seeks, at all risks, for perversity of thought, and revives the age of *concetti* while he fancies himself going back to a pre-classical nature. "A day," he says, "passed in the society of those Greek sages, such as described in the Banquet of Xenophon, would not be comparable with the dry wit of decayed cranberry-vines and the fresh Attic salt of the moss-beds." It is not so much the True that he loves as the Out-of-the-Way. As the

Brazen Age shows itself in other men by exaggeration of phrase, so in him by extravagance of statement. He wishes always to trump your suit and to *ruff* when you least expect it. Do you love Nature because she is beautiful? He will find a better argument in her ugliness. Are you tired of the artificial man? He instantly dresses you up an ideal in a Penobscot Indian, and attributes to this creature of his otherwise-mindedness as peculiarities things that are common to all woodsmen, white or red, and this simply because he has not studied the pale-faced variety.

This notion of an absolute originality, as if one could have a patent-right in it, is an absurdity. A man cannot escape in thought, any more than he can in language, from the past and the present. As no one ever invents a word, and yet language somehow grows by general contribution and necessity, so it is with thought. Mr. Thoreau seems to me to insist in public on going back to flint and steel, when there is a match-box in his pocket which he knows very well how to use at a pinch. Originality consists in power of digesting and assimilating thoughts, so that they become part of our life and substance. Montaigne, for example, is one of the most original of authors, though he helped himself to ideas in every direction. But they turn to blood and coloring in his style, and give a freshness of complexion that is forever charming. In Thoreau much seems yet to be foreign and unassimilated, showing itself in symptoms of indigestion. A preacher-up of Nature, we now and then detect under the surly and stoic garb something of the sophist and the sentimentalizer. I am far from implying that this was conscious on his part. But it is much easier for a man to impose on himself when he measures only with himself. A greater familiarity with ordinary men would have done Thoreau good, by showing him how many fine qualities are common to the race. The radical vice of his theory of life was that he confounded physical with spiritual remoteness from men. A man is far enough withdrawn from his fellows if he keep himself clear of their weaknesses. He is not so truly withdrawn as exiled, if he refuse to share in their strength. "Solitude," says Cowley, "can be well fitted and set right but upon a very few persons. They must have enough knowledge of the world to see the vanity of it, and enough virtue to despise all vanity." It is a morbid self-consciousness that pronounces the world of men empty and worthless before trying it, the instinctive evasion of one who is sensible of some innate weakness, and retorts the accusation of it before any has made it but himself. To a healthy mind, the world is a constant challenge of opportunity. Mr. Thoreau had not a healthy mind, or he would not have been so fond of prescribing. His whole life was a search for the doctor. The old mystics had a wiser sense of what the world was worth. They ordained a severe apprenticeship to law, and even ceremonial, in order to the gaining of freedom and mastery over these. Seven years of service for Rachel were to be rewarded at last with Leah. Seven other years of faithfulness with her were to win them at last the true bride of their souls. Active Life was with them the only path to the Contemplative.

Thoreau had no humor, and this implies that he was a sorry logician. Himself an artist in rhetoric, he confounds thought with style when he undertakes to speak of the latter. He was forever talking of getting away from the world, but he must be always near enough to it, nay, to the Concord corner of it, to feel the impression he makes there. He verifies the shrewd remark of Sainte-Beuve, "On touche encore à son temps et très-fort, même quand on le repousse." This egotism of his is a Stylites pillar after all, a seclusion which keeps him in the public eye. The dignity of man is an excellent thing, but therefore to hold one's self too sacred and precious is the reverse of excellent. There is something delightfully absurd in six volumes addressed to a world of such "vulgar fellows" as Thoreau affirmed his fellowmen to be. I once had a glimpse of a genuine solitary who spent his winters one hundred and fifty miles beyond all human communication, and there dwelt with his rifle as his only confidant. Compared with this, the shanty on Walden Pond has something the air, it must be confessed, of the Hermitage of La Chevrette. I do not believe that the way to a true cosmopolitanism carries one into the woods or the society of musquashes. Perhaps the narrowest provincialism is that of Self; that of Kleinwinkel is nothing to it. The natural man, like the singing birds, comes out of the forest as inevitably as the natural bear and the wildcat stick there. To seek to be natural implies a consciousness that forbids all naturalness forever. It is as easy—and no easier—to be natural in a *salon* as in a swamp, if one do not aim at it, for what we call unnaturalness always has its spring in a man's thinking too much about himself. "It is impossible," said Turgot, "for a vulgar man to be simple."

I look upon a great deal of the modern sentimentalism about Nature as a mark of disease. It is one more symptom of the general liver-complaint. To a man of wholesome constitution the wilderness is well enough for a mood or a vacation, but not for a habit of life. Those who have most loudly advertised their passion for seclusion and their intimacy with nature, from Petrarch down, have been mostly sentimentalists, unreal men, misanthropes on the spindle side, solacing an uneasy suspicion of themselves by professing contempt for their kind. They make demands on the world in advance proportioned to their inward measure of their own merit, and are angry that the world pays only by the visible measure of performance. It is true of Rousseau, the modern founder of the sect, true of Saint Pierre, his intellectual child, and of Châteaubriand, his grandchild, the inventor, we might almost say, of the primitive forest, and who first was touched by the solemn falling of a tree from natural decay in the windless silence of the woods. It is a very shallow view that affirms trees and rocks to be healthy, and cannot see that men in communities are just as true to the laws of their organization and destiny; that can tolerate the puffin and the fox, but not the fool and the knave; that would shun politics because of its demagogues, and snuff up the stench of the obscene fungus. The divine life of Nature is more wonderful, more various, more sublime in man than in any other of her works, and the wisdom that is gained by commerce with men, as Montaigne and Shakespeare gained it, or with one's own soul among men, as Dante, is the most delightful, as it is the most precious, of all. In outward nature it is still man that interests us, and we care far less for the things seen than the way in which they are seen by poetic eyes like Wordsworth's or Thoreau's, and the reflections they cast there. To hear the to-do that is often made over the simple fact that a man sees the image of himself in the outward world, one is reminded of a savage when he for the first time catches a glimpse of himself in a looking-glass. "Venerable child of Nature," we are tempted to say, "to whose science in the invention of the tobacco-pipe, to whose art in the tattooing of thine undegenerate hide not yet enslaved by tailors, we are slowly striving to climb back, the miracle thou beholdest is sold in my unhappy country for a shilling!" If matters go on as they have done, and everybody must needs blab of all the favors that have been done him by roadside and river-brink and woodland walk, as if to kiss and tell were no longer treachery, it will be a positive refreshment to meet a man who is as superbly indifferent to Nature as she is to him. By and by we shall have John Smith, of No. –12–12th. Street, advertising that he is not the J. S. who saw a cow-lily on Thursday last, as he never saw one in his life, would not see one if he could, and is prepared to prove an alibi on the day in question.

Solitary communion with Nature does not seem to have been sanitary or sweetening in its influence on Thoreau's character. On the contrary, his letters show him more cynical as he grew older. While he studied with respectful attention the minks and woodchucks, his neighbors, he looked with utter contempt on the august drama of destiny of which his country was the

scene, and on which the curtain had already risen. He was convert-
ing us back to a state of nature "so eloquently," as Voltaire
said of Rousseau, "that he almost persuaded us to go on all
fours," while the wiser fates were making it possible for us to
walk erect for the first time. Had he conversed more with his
fellows, his sympathies would have widened with the assurance
that his peculiar genius had more appreciation, and his writings
a larger circle of readers, or at least a warmer one, than he dreamed
of. We have the highest testimony [1] to the natural sweetness,
sincerity, and nobleness of his temper, and in his books an equally
irrefragable one to the rare quality of his mind. He was not
a strong thinker, but a sensitive feeler. Yet his mind strikes us
as cold and wintry in its purity. A light snow has fallen everywhere
in which he seems to come on the track of the shier sensations
that would elsewhere leave no trace. We think greater compression
would have done more for his fame. A feeling of sameness
comes over us as we read so much. Trifles are recorded with
an over-minute punctuality and conscientiousness of detail.
He registers the state of his personal thermometer thirteen times
a day. We cannot help thinking sometimes of the man who

> "Watches, starves, freezes, and sweats
> To learn but catechisms and alphabets
> Of unconcerning things, matters of fact,"

and sometimes of the saying of the Persian poet, that "when the
owl would boast, he boasts of catching mice at the edge of a
hole." We could readily part with some of his affectations. It
was well enough for Pythagoras to say, once for all, "When I
was Euphorbus at the siege of Troy"; not so well for Thoreau
to travesty it into "When I was a shepherd on the plains of
Assyria." A naïve thing said over again is anything but naïve. But
with every exception, there is no writing comparable with Thoreau's
in kind, that is comparable with it in degree where it is best;
where it disengages itself, that is, from the tangled roots and dead
leaves of a second-hand Orientalism, and runs limpid and smooth
and broadening as it runs, a mirror for whatever is grand and
lovely in both worlds.

George Sand says neatly, that "Art is not a study of positive
reality," (*actuality* were the fitter word,) "but a seeking after
ideal truth." It would be doing very inadequate justice to Thoreau
if we left it to be inferred that this ideal element did not exist
in him, and that too in larger proportion, if less obtrusive, than
his nature-worship. He took nature as the mountain-path to
an ideal world. If the path wind a good deal, if he record too

1. Mr. Emerson, in his Biographical Sketch.

faithfully every trip over a root, if he botanize somewhat wearisomely, he gives us now and then superb outlooks from some jutting crag, and brings us out at last into an illimitable ether, where the breathing is not difficult for those who have any true touch of the climbing spirit. His shanty-life was a mere impossibility, so far as his own conception of it goes, as an entire independency of mankind. The tub of Diogenes had a sounder bottom. Thoreau's experiment actually presupposed all that complicated civilization which it theoretically abjured. He squatted on another man's land; he borrows an axe; his boards, his nails, his bricks, his mortar, his books, his lamp, his fish-hooks, his plough, his hoe, all turn state's evidence against him as an accomplice in the sin of that artificial civilization which rendered it possible that such a person as Henry D. Thoreau should exist at all. *Magnis tamen excidit ausis.* His aim was a noble and useful one, in the direction of "plain living and high thinking." It was a practical sermon on Emerson's text that "things are in the saddle and ride mankind," an attempt to solve Carlyle's problem (condensed from Johnson) of "lessening your denominator." His whole life was a rebuke of the waste and aimlessness of our American luxury, which is an abject enslavement to tawdry upholstery. He had "fine translunary things" in him. His better style as a writer is in keeping with the simplicity and purity of his life. We have said that his range was narrow, but to be a master is to be a master. He had caught his English at its living source, among the poets and prose-writers of its best days; his literature was extensive and recondite; his quotations are always nuggets of the purest ore: there are sentences of his as perfect as anything in the language, and thoughts as clearly crystallized; his metaphors and images are always fresh from the soil; he had watched Nature like a detective who is to go upon the stand; as we read him, it seems as if all-out-of-doors had kept a diary and become its own Montaigne; we look at the landscape as in a Claude Lorraine glass; compared with his, all other books of similar aim, even White's "Selborne," seem dry as a country clergyman's meteorological journal in an old almanac. He belongs with Donne and Browne and Novalis; if not with the originally creative men, with the scarcely smaller class who are peculiar, and whose leaves shed their invisible thought-seed like ferns.

VAN WYCK BROOKS

Thoreau†

In Emerson's white house on the Boston turnpike, Henry Thoreau had taken up his quarters. He occupied the room at the head of the stairs, a little room, but he was a little man: his nose and his thoughts were the biggest things about him. Emerson, and especially Emerson's children, had formed a warm affection for their difficult Henry, difficult, that is, for the rest of Concord but a treasure for the household of a sage. He was short, lean, frail, although nobody guessed it, he was so tough and muscular, with a meagre chest, long arms falling from the collar-bone, a workman's hands and feet, a huge Emersonian beak, rather like Julius Caesar's, bright blue eyes and flaxen hair. He walked with the swinging stride of an old campaigner. His manners were of the homespun sort, different indeed from Emerson's. But, after the first encounter, one perceived that, if Henry Thoreau was a thorn-bush, he was the kind that bears the fragrant flowers.

He was the son of the pencil-maker, who had his little house and shop on Main Street: "J. Thoreau and Sons." The Thoreaus were a mercantile family of small pretensions who had seen better days. They were well-connected in the Channel Islands, where the French Thoreaus were prosperous wine-merchants. Their forbears in Maine, the Scottish Dunbars, had taken the royalist side in the Revolution. As a barefoot village boy, Henry had driven the turkeys and the cow to pasture, and Emerson had vaguely heard of him as a poor student at Harvard. He had written to President Quincy, suggesting Henry's name for a scholarship. Later, Henry walked in to Boston, eighteen miles from Concord, to hear Emerson speak, and walked home again after the lecture. Emerson, touched by this, was still more touched when, after one of his Concord lectures, his sister-in-law, who was boarding with Mrs. Thoreau, said to him, "Henry Thoreau has a thought very like that in his journal." A friendship had soon sprung up between them, and when, one day, the Emersons went on a picnic, to the Cliffs on the Concord river, they asked Henry to

† From Van Wyck Brooks, *The Flowering of New England*, New York, 1936. Pp. 286–302. Copyright, 1936, 1952 by Van Wyck Brooks; renewal © 1964 by Gladys Brooks. Reprinted by permission of E. P. Dutton & Co., Inc. and J. M. Dent & Sons, Ltd.

join them and bring his flute. The village people looked askance at him because he was so pugnacious. He had queer ideas about teaching school, refusing to use the ferule; for with children and simple folk he was always gentle. With others, he was obstinate and harsh. He liked to administer doses of moral quinine, and he never thought of sugaring his pills. He had withdrawn from Dr. Ripley's church with a thesis more defiant than Martin Luther's. He liked to speak of a cold spot as "sultry," and he had a way of calling the woods "domestic." But at boating and camping he was a master-woodsman, skilled as Ulysses, shrewd as any fox. The redskins had forgotten the arts he knew. Arrowheads and Indian fireplaces sprang from the ground when he touched it. He charmed the snakes and fishes. Wild birds perched on his shoulder. His fingers seemed to have more wisdom in them than many a scholar's head.

This young Briareus of the hundred hands was something more than Emerson's factotum. There was nothing he could not do in the matter of painting and papering, building walls, repairing chicken-houses, pruning and grafting fruit-trees, surveying, tinkering, gardening. But these were trifles in his bag of tricks, useful to pay his way in the world and justify his creed of self-reliance. He was a master of other arts that Emerson also knew, and a scholar of unusual distinction; and he wished to be a philosopher, not a mere thinker of subtle thoughts but one who, loving wisdom, lived a life that was simple, magnanimous, free. In fact, he recalled those ancient sages who, when an enemy took the town, walked out of the gate empty-handed, without a care for the morrow. Why should one be burdened with impedimenta? Henry liked the soldier's life, always on the stretch and always ready for a battle. Each of his mornings brought its strenuous sortie. He lived "for to admire and for to see." He had spoken his mind in his college themes about the "blind and unmanly love of wealth" that actuated most of his fellow-beings. The order of things, he said, should be reversed. The seventh should be man's day of toil, wherein to earn his living by the sweat of his brow; he should keep the rest of the week for his joy and wonder.

These views delighted Emerson. In fact, the two agreed on so many subjects, always with an edge of difference, that one might well have supposed the relation between them was that of master and pupil. Emerson was fourteen years the elder; and it was true that Henry had acquired some of his traits and mannerisms: his handwriting, his voice, even his nose seemed to have gone to school to Emerson. There was something contagious in Emerson's aura; everyone was affected by it, nobody seemed able to resist it. Alcott was more than a little Emersonized; and as for Ellery Channing, what did the lady say who heard him lecture?—that his gait, his inflections, the very turn of his eyebrow were Emerson to the life. Henry Thoreau had felt this influence, as he had felt the influence of Carlyle. He had his own form, none the less. Emerson and he had grown in Concord, as two flowers grow in a common bed, one of them larger and more luxuriant, the other with a much more pungent odour; but they stood in different corners of the bed, with an ample space between them, so that the breeze could blow upon each of them freely. They were different enough in temperament, as in their personalities; and Henry phrased their common points of view with a sort of acidulous accent that was never heard on Emerson's lips.

They were of one mind in a dozen matters, not least in regard to the reformers. "As for these communities," said Henry, expressing their joint opinion, "I had rather keep bachelor's hall in hell than go to board in heaven." Much as he liked Alcott, the "best-natured man" he had ever met,—"the rats and mice make their nests in him,"—he turned up his nose at Fruitlands as well as at Brook Farm. He meant to bake his own bread in heaven, and wash his own clothes there. And suppose, he said, these grievances do exist? So do you and I. And the universal soul prefers the man who sets his own house in order first. A foul thing, this "doing good," observed the contemptuous Henry, instead of looking after one's own life, which ought to be one's business, taking care to flourish, and taste and smell sweet, refreshing all mankind. He had had encounters with reformers that filled him with abhorrence. They would not keep their distance. They tried to cover him with a slimy kindness that fairly took the starch out of his clothes. These "lovers" of their kind were almost more injurious to their kind than the feeble souls that met in drawing-rooms, fabulating and paddling in the social slush, and going to their beds unashamed, to take on a new layer of sloth.

Henry had plenty of acid in his composition. He had taken a few suggestions from Zeno the Stoic,—for one, that he had two ears and a single mouth, in order to hear more and speak less,—as Alcott had followed Pythagoras and Emerson, largely, Plato. Emerson, older and riper, with a fund of sunny benevolence, the fruit of a happier culture and a fortunate bringing-up,— Emerson deplored this hedgehog's posture, the spikes, the spines, the quills that made his Henry a John Quincy Adams of the village. But time would certainly soothe and rectify him. Meanwhile, he was a living illustration of all his own ideas, endowed with hands and feet. Henry described himself, or his hope for

himself,—"stuttering, blundering clodhopper" that he said he
was,—in words that seemed to have their truth already. He was
prepared for a glorious life; he had laid out an avenue through
his head, eight rods wide; he had got the world,—much more,
the flesh and the devil,—as it were by the nape of the neck,
and held it under the tide of its own events, and let it go down
stream like a dead dog, till he heard the hollow chambers of
silence stretching away on every side and his own soul expanded
and filled them. He could not help taunting his fellow-Yankees.
Seek first the kingdom of heaven! Lay not up for yourselves
treasures on earth! What does it profit a man! Think of this,
Yankees, think twice, ye who drone these words on the Sabbath
day and spend the other six denying them! "Doing a good business!"—words more profane than any oath, words of death and
sin. The children should not be allowed to hear them. If most
of the merchants had not failed, and most of the banks as well,
Henry's faith in the laws of the world would have been sadly
staggered; for what was the sweetest sight his eyes could see
but a man who was really fulfilling the ends of his being?—maintaining himself, as he could, if he wished to do so, paying the
price in terms of simplification, by a few hours a day at manual
labour. Was he a little impatient and a little narrow? If there
was anything wrong with his angle of vision, there would always
be plenty of others to correct it. For himself, he wished to live
deep. He wished to suck out all the marrow of life, to cut a
broad swath and shave close, to put to rout all that was not
living. If the days and the nights were such that he greeted them
with joy, if life emitted a fragrance like herbs and flowers, if
it was more elastic and more starry, that was his success and
all he asked for.

No use to pretend that, for Emerson, he was a balm, however
much a blessing. No, but he was medicinal,—as a gadfly, good;
as a goad for an indolent writer, who felt that he ought to dig
in his own garden, Henry was even better. As a teacher of natural
history, for a lover of nature who, as a matter of fact, scarcely
knew a robin from a crow, Henry was better still. Best of all,
as a fellow-seeker of wisdom and a man of impeccable taste,
competent to help him with *The Dial*, which Margaret Fuller
could not wrestle with and had asker her Concord friends to
carry on. Henry was a capital editor. He had a sharp eye for
the faults of *The Dial*, the phrases,—well one knew them,—that
had to be pulled open, as one opens the petals of a flower that
cannot open itself. The style of *The Dial* annoyed him as much
as the weak and flowing periods of the politicians. He liked
to see a sentence run clear through to the end, as deep and fertile

as a well-drawn furrow. If only writers lived more earnest lives, their minds would pass over the ground like ploughs, pressed down to the beam, like rollers that were loaded, not hollow and wooden, driving in the seed to germinate. It was the height of art, in his opinion, that, on the first perusal, plain common sense should appear,—a law that gave short shrift to much of *The Dial*; truth on the second perusal, beauty on the third. One had to pay for beauty.

The two friends had much in common, in spite of all their differences. Emerson had never built a boat, nor had he shared the Argonautic life that Henry had enjoyed with his brother John,—the John who had built Emerson's bluebird-box,—rounding the capes and sailing before the wind on the Concord and Merrimac rivers, with their cotton tents and buffalo-skins, bringing back their unexpected news of the foreign folk who lived on the upper reaches. Nor had he roamed over the moors and meadows, with the fishing-rod and gun that Henry loved, before he perceived that it was not for him, as a follower of the Brahmins, to "effect the transmigration of a woodchuck." He was not at home in the wilderness. He could never have whittled a wooden spoon, better than the factories made, to eat his rice with. He could not make a fork from an alder-twig, or a Wedgwood plate out of a strip of birch-bark. Nor, in the matter of teaching school, had he known such good fortune as Henry, who had kept the Concord Academy with his brother John, profiting by Bronson Alcott's methods, taking the children walking, rowing, swimming. But they both liked to lecture at the Lyceum, where Henry acted as secretary, and every citizen who had something to say was expected to give his lecture. Moreover, they loved the same authors. Henry had a preference of his own for works of a local kind, ancient gazetteers, State and county histories, histories of New England towns, farmers' almanacs, agricultural pamphlets, out-of-the-way books on birds and flowers, chronicles of old explorers, the Jesuit Relations, reports on Indian tribes. His mind bristled with antiquarian lore. But when it came to Froissart's bold beauty or Bacon's bolder terseness, to the voyages of Drake and Purchase, to Raleigh and the earlier English poets, there they were both at home. Nothing had attracted Emerson more than Henry's manifest knowledge of Drayton, Daniel, the Fletchers, Cowley, Donne, poets, little known in the eighteen-forties, whose naturalness and vigour Emerson cherished, and who, as Henry said, were as verdurous as evergreen and flowers, rooted in fact and experience, unlike so many florid modern poets who had the tints of flowers without their sap.

They agreed that in literature only the wild was attractive,

and that dullness was only another name for tameness,—the
wildness of the Iliad or of *Hamlet*, with something fresh and
primitive about it, something ambrosial and fertile. All the
Greek poets had this trait, wild in their elegance, wild in their
conciseness. Henry had studied Greek with Jones Very, for
a time his tutor at Harvard, as he had studied German with
Orestes Brownson, with whom he had spent a winter in a Boston
suburb, tutoring Brownson's sons. Greek was his second language.
He had translated *Prometheus Bound* and *The Seven against
Thebes*, with many pieces of the minor poets, Anacreon, Simonides, ivory gems of an ethereal beauty like that of summer
evenings. One could perceive them only with the flower of the
mind. How still and serene life seemed amid these classical studies!
Often, walking along the railway tracks, he listened to the harp
of the telegraph-wires, putting his ear to the posts. Every pore
of the wood was filled with music, and he could find a name
for every strain, every swell and change or inflection of tone in
one of the Greek poets. Often he heard Mimnermus, often
Menander. Emerson had the same impressions when he listened
to his ice-harp at Walden; and Henry, as much as Emerson, delighted in the Oriental scriptures, which he read in the French
and German versions. The Bible had lost its bloom for both;
but the Vedas, the Bhagavad-Gita came to Henry like desert
winds, blown from some Eastern summit. They fell on him like
the light of the moon when the stars are out, in the furthest
reaches of the sky,—free from particulars, simple, universal, uttered
with a morning prescience in the dawn of time. What rhythms,
what a tidal flow! Beside these ancient Asiatic books, with their
truths like fossil truths, clean and dry, true without reference
to persons, true as the truths of science, the literatures of the
European countries seemed to him partial and clannish, pre-
sumptuous in speaking for the world when they spoke only for
corners of it. Henry liked to remember that the barnyard cock
was originally the wild Indian pheasant, such as the poets of
the Upanishads knew.

As they worked over *The Dial*, Emerson, with Henry's concur-
rence, took pains to include some of these Eastern writings.
Emerson chose a group of passages which he called *Ethnical
Scriptures*. Henry, who had translated for his own amusement
The Transmigration of the Seven Brahmins, selected some of
the Laws of Manu. Emerson also insisted on printing some of
Henry's own writings, which Margaret Fuller had had doubts
about. Henry was indifferent to publication. The only audience
he really cared for was his own taste and judgment. He wished
to write well, to warrant every statement and each remark, till

the earth seemed to rest on its axle in order to back it up. Hold the bow tight! was his motto. He longed to write sentences that would lie like boulders on the page, as durable as Roman aqueducts. Sentences kinked and knotted into something hard and significant, which one might swallow like diamonds, without digesting. Sentences nervous and tough as the roots of the pine, like hardened thongs, the sinews of the deer. He wrote best when his knees were strong, when the juices of the fruits that he had eaten, ascending to the brain, gave him a heady force. Margaret Fuller had not liked *The Service*, his manual for the spiritual soldier, suggested by the talk about non-resistance of the mealier-mouthed reformers. But his essay, *The Natural History of Massachusetts*, was beyond cavil or praise. Into *The Dial* it went, with *A Winter Walk*. Henry revised and revised, until his page was a mass of blots and blackness.

Into *The Dial* went also some of his poems, the verses that he had ceased to write. These poems were of a homespun kind, well-woven, but indifferently cut, like Henry's raiment, not intended to please. They were sound and scholarly doggerel, for the most part. The smoke obscured the flame, but now and then a jet rose out of the smoke and Henry wrote a line or two that shivered its way up the spinal marrow. Sometimes the smoke itself, in a handful of lines, suggested by the Greek Anthology, suddenly turned to incense, and the incense became an Icarian bird, melting its pinions in its upward flight. *Smoke, Mist, Haze* were lyrics not to be forgotten. Nor could one forget *A Winter Scene*, not Greek but Anglo-Saxon,—

> The rabbit leaps,
> The mouse out-creeps,
> The flag out-peeps
> Beside the brook,—

or, for the iron strings, the lines called *Inspiration*,—

> If with light head erect I sing,—

to the end of the third stanza, or, if one insisted, to the end of the seventh, but not a syllable further. There spoke the poet who, for the rest, wrote his poetry in his prose journal, in blank-books bought on those rare occasions when he could find a book with clean white pages, not ruled, as most of them were, for records of dollars and cents. If his poems were often disjointed, like his prose, it was because of this habit of journalizing. He jotted down his paragraphs and verses, a thought or a stanza at a time, and waited for a cooler moment to patch them together,—a good way for epigrams, a good way for the gnomic style, but fatal for the poetry of feeling, and none too good for prose. He was a methodical journalizer, much more so than Emerson. He kept his notes as his father and his father's father, the old French merchant from the Channel Islands, had kept their business-ledgers. He had inherited their plodding habits, akin to the sod as he also was, partaking largely of its dull patience. He sometimes felt that he was in danger of living for his journal, instead of living in it for the gods, his regular correspondents, to whom he sent off daily bulletins. His journal was a calendar of the ebbs and flows of the soul. It was a beach on which the waves might cast their pearls and seaweed.

These were happy months for the seekers of Brahma, not to be repeated. From Emerson's house, in 1843, Henry went to Staten Island. Later, in 1848, when Emerson went abroad again, Henry installed himself for a second visit, as counsellor and helper of the household, in the little room at the head of the stairs. But, later still, a shadow fell on the glowing intercourse of the two crusaders. Through whose fault but Henry's? His journal teemed with innuendoes against the friend who "patronized" him. Emerson was too "grand" for him. Emerson belonged to the upper classes and wore their cloak and manners. He was attracted to Plato, but he would not have cared for Socrates, whose life and associations were too humble. Emerson would never have been seen trundling a wheelbarrow through the streets. He would have thought it out of character. Henry was a commoner, as he liked to say. He thought there was something devilish in manners,—and Emerson had had no right to praise him.[1] "One man lies in his words," Henry wrote, "and gets a bad reputation; another in his manners, and enjoys a good one." But what about Alcott's manners, so gracious and courtly, consisting with such artlessness of soul, such frank, open, unaffected goodness? Alcott had no reputation, surely. Was there nothing in beautiful manners but foppery, prudery, starch and affectation, with false pride overtopping all? Was the noble merely the genteel? Henry's notion of the art of living was not too comprehensive. Nor his notion of friendship, either, exacting all and giving back so little.

What he gave was solid. As for the rest, the less cared he. When people spoke of the social virtues, he asked about the virtues of pigs in a litter, lying close together to keep on another warm. As for friends, what were they, for the most part? Bubbles on the water, flowing together. Very few were ever as instructive as the silence which they shattered with their talk. When it

---

1. "Praise begins when things are seen partially. We begin to praise when we begin to see that a thing needs our assistance."—Thoreau's *Journal*.

came to sharing his walks, Henry was rather particular. Alcott served for a stroll, but the real art of walking was beyond him. He always wished to perch on the nearest stump. Hawthorne was even more annoying. One led him to one's loveliest swamp, and Hawthorne stood on the brink, disconsolate. "Let us get out of this dreadful hole," he said. He never even noticed the naked biburnum rising above the dwarf andromeda. Besides, he said that company was a "damnable bore." After all deductions, Emerson was still one's best companion, best but one, Henry's only crony, the moody, witty, generous Ellery Channing, riding his whims like broomsticks, as naturally capricious as a cow is brindled, tender and rough by turns, another social antinomian, even a social outlaw, by his own desire. He was always teasing Henry about his legs, double legs, not cork but steel, which ought to be shown at the World's Fair, he said; and he had a Rabelaisian streak and took pains to shock the sober Henry. There were strange, cold pockets in the air of his mind into which one swam unwittingly. One never knew where one stood with him. But he was crammed with poetry that glittered through the darkness of his reserve like gems in a mine revealed by the gleams of a lantern, or flashed, in his happier moods, like gems in the sunlight. Some of his moods, moreover, were much like Henry's. He wished to be let alone. "If you go to the post-office once," he said, "you are damned."—"No," said Henry, "you are only damned if you get a letter." For Ellery loved solitude. He would sit on the Cliffs by the hour, among the lichens. Then, in the dusk of evening, one saw him flitting past on noiseless pinion, like the barred owl, as wise as unobserved.

Henry, to be sure, had other friends, with whom he exchanged a few words, perhaps on his way to look for mud-turtles in Heywood's luxuriant meadow. There was old Haines, the fisherman, for one, wearing his patched coat of many colours, who represented the Indian still, "Polyphemus" Goodwin, of dubious fame, the one-eyed sportsman of the Concord river, and the crooked old curmudgeon Ebby Hubbard, dressed in his blue frock. There were the musquash-hunters, poets of the wild, up and out early in the wet and cold, ready for any risk at the call of their muse. They were gods of the river and woods, with sparkling faces,—late from the House of Correction, as often as not,—with mystic bottles under their oilskin jackets. How good of George Melvin to follow his bent and not spend all his days in Sunday School! Henry thanked his stars for George Melvin and thought of him with gratitude as he fell asleep. The gawky, loose-hung Melvin, dragging his feet as he walked, who was such a trial to his mother, pleased Henry like an oak-tree on the hill-side.

He was one tribe, and Henry was another; and they were not at war. Henry could not deny that hunting and fishing, in spite of his brahmanic preferences, were as ancient and honourable trades as the sun and the winds pursue, coeval with the faculties of man. As for his friends, he had some who were wilder than Melvin, the breams, who nibbled from his fingers, while he stroked them gently and lifted them out of the river, the muskrat that emerged from the hole in the ice. The muskrat looked at Henry, and Henry looked at the muskrat, wondering what the muskrat thought of him,—safe, low, moderate thoughts, of course. Muskrats never got on stilts, like some of the Transcendentalists. Once he conversed with a woodchuck, three feet away, over a fence. They sat for half an hour, looking into each other's eyes, until they felt mesmeric influences at work over them both. Then Henry moved closer and spoke to the woodchuck, in a quasi-forest lingo, a sort of sylvan baby-talk. The woodchuck ceased to grit his teeth. Henry, with a little stick, lifted up his paw and examined it; then he turned the woodchuck over and studied him underneath. He had a rather mild look. Henry spoke kindly to him and offered him some checkerberry-leaves. The woodchuck was one of the natives. His family had certainly lived in Concord longer than the Emersons or even the Hoars.

For the sort of friends who never hurt one's feelings, one did not have to look far. Sometimes, in the midst of a gentle rain, Henry felt an influence about him that was suddenly sweet and beneficent. Every sight and sound, the very pattering of the drops, was filled with an unaccountable friendliness. It was to seek this, and all it meant, that he went for his daily walk, with note-book and spyglass in his pocket, and the hat with its lining gathered in the middle to make a little shelf, a botany-box. He was another Linnæus, setting out for Lapland, though he did not wish to be a "naturalist." Looking at nature straight in the eye was as fatal as to look at the head of Medusa. The man of science always turned to stone. Henry wished to look at nature sidewise, or to look through nature and beyond it. Too many observations were dissipating. One had to be the magnet, in the midst of all this dust and all these filings. Sometimes he rose at two o'clock, for a walk to the Cliffs, to wait there till sunrise, or to watch the fog on the river. He loved those valleys in the fog in which the trees appeared as if at the bottom of the sea. Sometimes he spent the whole of a moonlight night roaming the lonely pastures, where the cattle were silently feeding, to the croaking of the frogs, the intenser dream of the crickets, the half-throttled note of a cuckoo flying over. The bushes loomed, the potato-vines stood upright, the corn grew apace. One's eyes were partially closed then; the other senses took the lead. Every plant emitted its odour, the swamp-pink in the meadow, the tansy in the road. One caught the peculiar dry scent of the corn, which was just beginning to show its tassels. One heard the tinkling of rills one had never detected before. The moonlight over the village, as one stole into the street, seemed to bring antiquity back again. The church, with its fluted columns, reminded one of the Parthenon. The houses had a classical elegance.

Sometimes, even in the morning, usually sacred to reading and writing, the wind fairly blew him out of doors. The elements were so lively and active, and he felt so sympathetic with them, that he could not sit while the wind went by. His regular time was the afternoon, from two-thirty to five-thirty, the hour for a voyage to the Leaning Hemlocks, along the Assabet river, or perhaps to examine an ant-hill, nearer home. He had observed it the day before, with its little galleries, wide as a match, covered with the sluggish, crawling ants. In the early spring, the stalks and grasses, left from last year, were steeped in rain and snow, and all the brooks flowed with meadow-tea. Then came the May-days of the warm west wind, the dream-frog, leaping, willowy haze-days, when anything might happen and one thought that next year, perhaps, one might be a postman in Peru, or a South African planter, or a Greenland whaler, or a Canton merchant. Better still, a Robinson Crusoe on some far-off isle of the Pacific. Henry sometimes stood under a tree half a day at a time, in a drenching rain, prying with microscopic eyes into the swarming crevices of the bark, or studying the leaves at his feet, or the spreading fungi. He would watch for an hour a battle of ants, struggling on a chip, a black ant with two red adversaries, till the black ant severed the heads of the others, losing its own feelers and most of its legs,—a second Concord fight, no doubt with as just a cause. Or, catching sight of a fox, in some woodland clearing, he yielded to the instinct of the chase, tossed his head aloft and bounded away, snuffing the air like a fox-hound, spurning the humanitarians and the Brahmins. For he felt as wild, at times,—he who preferred a vegetarian diet,—as if he lived on antelope-marrow, devoured without benefit of fire.

The midsummer days came, when the yellow lilies reigned in the river. The painted tortoises dropped from the willow-stumps as he walked over the bridge. The pickerel-weed sent up its blue and the vireo sang incessantly; the poison-sumach showed its green berries, all unconscious of guilt, the breeze displayed the white sides of the oak-leaves and gave the woods a fresh and flowing look, the rush-sparrow jingled her silver change on the broad counter of the pasture. Henry sometimes felt, on days like this, as if he were nature itself, looking into nature, as the blue-eyed grass in the meadow looks in the face of the sky. He would stand for hours, up to his chin, in some retired swamp, scenting the wild honeysuckle, lulled by the minstrel mosquitoes: for he like to subject his body to rougher usage than a grenadier could endure, and he dreamed of still remoter retirements and still more rugged paths. He walked to Second Division Brook and watched the yellow pebbles gleaming under the watercress,— the whole brook as busy as a loom, a woof and warp of ripples, with fairy fingers throwing the shuttle, and the long, waving stream as the fine result. Just the place for a hut, with a footpath to the water. Or he strolled over to Boon's Pond in Stow, when the haze seemed to concentrate the sunlight, and he walked as if in a halo, while the song-sparrow set the day to music, as if the sparrow were itself the music of the mossy rail or fence-post. Or perhaps along the Price Farm Road, with its endless green-grass borders, with room on each side for the berries and birches, where the walls indulged in freaks, not bothering to run parallel with the ruts, and goldenrod yellowed the path. On these old, meandering, uninhabited roads, leading away from towns, these everlasting roads where the sun played truant, one forgot what country one was in. One waved adieu to the village and travelled like a pilgrim, going whither? Whither, indeed? On the promenade deck of the world.

Days to sit in one's boat, looking over the side, when the river-bottom was covered with plants, springing up in the yellowish water, and little sparkling silvery beads of air clung to the axils of the submerged leaves. Days to watch the pout in his flurry struggling to escape from the turtle that held him. In these few inches of mud and water, what ironies, what tragedies, what growth and beauty! In one's ears sounded the roll-call of the harvest-fly, just as it sounded in Greece, in Anacreon's ode. Henry was amphibious, he felt. He could see himself swimming in the brooks and pools, with perch and bream and pout, and dozing with the stately pickerel, under the pads of the river, amid the winding aisles and corridors that were formed by the stems of the plants. And what a luxury, in a warm September, to muse by a wall-side in the sunshine, cuddling under a grey stone, to the siren-song of the cricket. He could always hear in the atmosphere a fine Æolian harp-music, like the mellow sound of distant horns in the hollow mansions of the upper air. The critics seemed to think that music was intermittent. They had to wait for a Mozart or a Paganini. Music was perpetual for Henry. He heard it in the softened air, the wind, the rain, the running water. To his expanded ear what a harp the world was!—even if another sound reached his unwilling sense in the midday stillness, a tintinnabulation from afar, the rumour of his contemporaries. It was of little moment, in these autumn days, when a young man's limbs were full of vigour, when his thoughts were like a flowing morning light, and the stream of his life stretched out before him, with long reaches of serene ripples. Thoughts like wild apples, food for walkers.

F. O. MATTHIESSEN

Walden: Craftsmanship vs. Technique†

'You can't read any genuine history—as that of Herodotus or the Venerable Bede—without perceiving that our interest depends not on the subject but on the man,—on the manner in which he treats the subject and the importance he gives it. A feeble writer . . . must have what he thinks a great theme, which we are already interested in through the accounts of others, but a genius—a Shakespeare, for instance—would make the history of his parish more interesting than another's history of the world.'
—THOREAU's *Journal* (March 1861)

The real test of whether Thoreau mastered organic form can hardly be made on the basis of accounting for the differences in body and flavor between his portrayal of the natural world and Emerson's, revelatory as these differences are. Nor can it be made by considering one of the rare occasions when his verse was redeemed by virtue of his discipline in translating from the Greek Anthology. Nor is it enough to reckon with the excellence of individual passages of prose, since the frequent charge is that whereas Emerson was master of the sentence, Thoreau was master of the paragraph, but that he was unable to go farther and attain 'the highest or structural achievements of form in a whole book.' The only adequate way of answering that is by considering the structure of *Walden* as a whole, by asking to what extent it meets Coleridge's demand of shaping, 'as it develops, itself from within.'

On one level *Walden* is the record of a personal experience, yet even in making that remark we are aware that this book does not go rightfully into the category of *Two Years Before the Mast* or *The Oregon Trail*. Why it presents a richer accumulation than either of those vigorous pieces of contemporary history is explained by its process of composition. Although Thoreau said

† From F. O. Matthiessen, *American Renaissance*, New York, 1948. Pp. 166-175. Copyright 1948 by Oxford University Press. Reprinted by permission of the publishers.

that the bulk of its pages were written during his two years of sojourn by the pond (1845-7), it was not ready for publication until seven years later, and ultimately included a distillation from his journals over the whole period from 1838. A similar process had helped to transform his week's boat trip with his brother from a private to a symbolical event, since the record was bathed in memory for a decade (1839-49) before it found its final shape in words. But the flow of the *Week* is as leisurely and discursive as the bends in the Concord river, and the casual pouring in of miscellaneous poems and essays that Thoreau had previously printed in *The Dial* tends to obscure the cyclical movement. Yet each day advances from dawn to the varied sounds of night, and Thoreau uses an effective device for putting a period to the whole by the shift of the final morning from lazy August to the first sharp forebodings of transforming frost.

The sequence of *Walden* is arranged a good deal more subtly, perhaps because its subject constituted a more central symbol for Thoreau's accruing knowledge of life. He remarked on how the pond itself was one of the earliest scenes in his recollection, dating from the occasion when he had been brought out there one day when he was four, and how thereafter 'that woodland vision for a long time made the drapery of my dreams.' By 1841 he had already announced, "I want to go soon and live away by the pond,' and when pressed by friends about what he would do when he got there, he had asked in turn if it would not be employment enough 'to watch the progress of the seasons'? In that same year he had said: 'I think I could write a poem to be called "Concord." For argument I should have the River, the Woods, the Ponds, the Hills, the Fields, the Swamps and Meadows, the Streets and Buildings, and the Villagers.' In his completed 'poem' these last elements had receded into the background. What had come squarely to the fore, and made the opening chapter by far the longest of all, was the desire to record an experiment in 'Economy' as an antidote to the 'lives of quiet desperation' that he saw the mass of men leading. This essay on how he solved his basic needs of food and shelter might stand by itself, but also carries naturally forward to the more poignant condensation of the same theme in 'Where I lived, and What I lived for,' which reaches its conclusion in the passage on wedging down to reality.

At this point the skill with which Thoreau evolved his composition begins to come into play. On the one hand, the treatment of his material might simply have followed the chronological outline; on the other, it might have drifted into being loosely topical. At first glance it may appear that the latter is what happened, that there is no real cogency in the order of the chapters. That would have been Lowell's complaint, that Thoreau 'had no artistic power such as controls a great work to the serene balance of completeness.' [1] But so far as the opposite can be proved by the effective arrangement of his entire material, the firmness with which Thoreau binds his successive links is worth examining. The student and observer that he has settled himself to be at the end of his second chapter leads easily into his discussion of 'Reading,' but that in turn gives way to his concern with the more fundamental language, which all things speak, in the chapter on 'Sounds.' Then, after he has passed from the tantivy of wild pigeons to the whistle of the locomotive, he reflects that once the cars have gone by and the restless world with them, he is more alone than ever. That starts the transition to the chapter on 'Solitude,' in which the source of his joy is to live by himself in the midst of nature with his senses unimpaired. The natural contrast is made in the next chapter on 'Visitors,' which he opens by saying how he believes he loves society as much as most, and is ready enough to fasten himself 'like a bloodsucker for the time to any full-blooded man' who comes his way. But after he has talked enthusiastically about the French woodchopper, and other welcome friends from the village, he remembers 'restless committed men,' the self-styled reformers who felt it their duty to give him advice. At that he breaks away with 'Meanwhile my beans . . . were impatient to be hoed'; and that opening carries him back to the earlier transition to the chapter on 'Sounds': 'I did not read books the first summer; I hoed beans.'

The effect of that repetition is to remind the reader of the time sequence that is knitting together all these chapters after the building of the cabin in the spring. From 'The Bean Field' as the sphere of his main occupation, he moves on, in 'The Village,' to his strolls for gossip, which, 'taken in homeopathic doses, was really as refreshing in its way as the rustle of leaves and the peeping of frogs.' Whether designedly or not, this chapter is the shortest in the book, and yields to rambles even farther

1. The don of Harvard was not entirely blind to the man of Concord. Even in his notorious essay on *Walden* in *My Study Windows* he perceived that Thoreau 'had caught his English at its living source, among the poets and prose-writers of its best days,' and compared him with Donne and Browne. When Lowell tried to dismiss Thoreau as a crank, he was really bothered, as Henry Canby has pointed out, by Thoreau's attack upon his own ideals of genteel living. How different from Emerson's is Lowell's tone when he says that while Thoreau 'studied with respectful attention the minks and woodchucks, his neighbors, he looked with utter contempt on the august drama of destiny of which his country was the scene, and on which the curtain had already risen.' As Mr. Canby has added: 'By destiny, Lowell clearly means the "manifest destiny" of the exploitation of the West, whose more sordid and unfortunate aspects Thoreau had prophesied two generations before their time of realization.'

away from the community than Walden, to 'The Ponds' and to fishing beyond 'Baker Farm.' As he was returning through the woods with his catch, and glimpsed in the near dark a wood-chuck stealing across his path, then came the moment when he 'felt a strange thrill of savage delight, and was strongly tempted to seize and devour him raw.' And in the flash of his realization of his double instinct towards the spiritual and the wild, he has the starting point for the next two contrasting chapters, 'Higher Laws' and 'Brute Neighbors,' in considering both of which he follows his rule of going far enough to please his imagination.

From here on the structure becomes cyclical, his poem of the seasons or myth of the year. The accounts of his varied ex-cursions have brought him to the day when he felt that he could no longer warm himself by the embers of the sun, which 'summer, like a departed hunter, had left.' Consequently he set about finishing his cabin by building a chimney, and called that act 'House-Warming.' There follows a solid block of winter in the three chapters, 'Winter Visitors,' 'Winter Animals,' and 'The Pond in Winter,' that order suggesting the way in which the radius of his experience contracted then more and more to his immediate surroundings. However, the last pages on the pond deal with the cutting of the ice, and end with that sudden ex-traordinary expansion of his thought which annihilates space and time.

The last movement is the advance to 'Spring.' The activity of the ice company in opening its large tracts has hastened the break-up of the rest of the pond; and, listening to its booming, he recalls that one attraction that brought him to the woods was the opportunity and leisure to watch this renewal of the world. He has long felt in his observations that a day is an epitome of a year, and now he knows that a year is likewise symbolical of a life; and so, in presenting his experience by the pond, he fore-shortens and condenses the twenty-six months to the interval from the beginning of one summer to the next. In the melting season he feels more than ever the mood of expanding promise, and he catches the reader up into this rich forward course by one of his most successful kinesthetic images, which serves to round out his cycle: 'And so the seasons went rolling on into summer, as one rambles into higher and higher grass.' To that he adds only the bare statement of when he left the woods, and a 'Conclusion,' which explains that he did so for as good a reason as he had gone there. He had other lives to live, and he knew now that he could find for himself 'a solid bottom every-where.' That discovery gave him his final serene assurance that 'There is more day to dawn,' and consequently he was not to be disturbed by the 'confused *tintinnabulum*' that sometimes reached his midday repose. He recognized it for the noise of his contemporaries.

The construction of the book involved deliberate rearrangement of material. For instance, a single afternoon's return to the pond in the fall of 1852 was capable of furnishing details that were woven into half a dozen passages of the finished work, two of them separated by seventy pages. Nevertheless, since no invention was demanded, since all the material was a *donnée* of Thoreau's memory, my assertion that *Walden* does not belong with the simple records of experience may require more establishing. The chief clue to how it was transformed into something else lies in Thoreau's extension of his remark that he did not believe himself to be 'wholly involved in Nature.' He went on to say that in being aware of himself as a human entity, he was 'sensible of a certain doubleness' that made him both participant and spectator in any event. This ability to stand 'as remote from myself as from another' is the indispensable attribute of the dramatist. Thoreau makes you share in the excitement of his private scenes, for example, by the kind of generalized significance he can give to his purchase and demolishment of an old shanty for its boards:

> I was informed treacherously by a young Patrick that neighbor Seeley, an Irishman, in the intervals of the carting, transferred the still tolerable, straight, and drivable nails, staples, and spikes to his pocket, and then stood when I came back to pass the time of day, and look freshly up, unconcerned, with spring thoughts, at the devastation; there being a dearth of work, as he said. He was there to represent spectatordom, and help make this seemingly insignificant event one with the removal of the gods of Troy.

The demands he made of great books are significant of his own intentions: 'They have no cause of their own to plead, but while they enlighten and sustain the reader his common sense will not refuse them.' Propaganda is not the source of the inner freedom they offer to the reader, for their relation to life is more inclusive than argument; or, as Thoreau described it, they are at once 'intimate' and 'universal.' He aimed unerringly to reconcile these two extremes in his own writing. His experience had been fundamental in that it had sprung from his determination to start from obedience to the rudimentary needs of a man who wanted to be free. Greenough had seen how, in that sense, 'Obedience is worship,' for by discerning and following the functional patterns of daily behavior, you could discover the proportions of beauty that would express and complete them. It was Thoreau's conviction that by reducing life to its primitive conditions, he had come to the roots from which healthy art must flower, whether in Thessaly or Concord. It was not just a figure of speech when he said that 'Olympus is but the outside of the earth everywhere.' The light touch of his detachment allows the comparison of his small things with great, and throughout the book enables him to possess the universe at home.

As a result *Walden* has spoken to men of widely differing convictions, who have in common only the intensity of their devotion to life. It became a bible for many of the leaders of the British labor movement after Morris. When the sound of a little fountain in a shop window in Fleet Street made him think suddenly of lake water, Yeats remembered also his boyhood enthusiasm for Thoreau. He did not leave London then and go and live on Innisfree. But out of his loneliness in the foreign city he did write the first of his poems that met with a wide response, and 'The Lake Isle'—despite its Pre-Raphaelite flavor—was reminiscent of *Walden* even to 'the small cabin' Yeats built and the 'bean rows' he planted in his imagination. *Walden* was also one of our books that bulked largest for Tolstoy when he addressed his brief message to America (1901) and urged us to rediscover the greatness of our writers of the fifties: 'And I should like to ask the American people why they do not pay more attention to these voices (hardly to be replaced by those of financial and industrial millionaires, or successful generals and admirals), and continue the good work in which they made such hopeful progress.' In 1904 Proust wrote to the Comtesse de Noailles: 'Lisez . . . les pages admirables de *Walden*. Il me semble qu'on les lise en soi-même tant elles sortent du fond de notre expérience intime.'

In his full utilization of his immediate resources Thoreau was the kind of native craftsman whom Greenough recognized as the harbinger of power for our arts. Craftsmanship in this sense involves the mastery of traditional modes and skills; it has been thought of more often in connection with Indian baskets or Yankee tankards and hearth-tools than with the so-called fine arts. In fact, until fairly lately, despite Greenough's pioneering, it has hardly been consistently thought of in relation to American products of any kind. The march of our experience has been so dominantly expansive, from one rapid disequilibrium to the next, that we have neglected to see what Constance Rourke, among others, has now pointed out so effectively: that notwithstanding the inevitable restlessness of our long era of pioneering, at many stages within that process the strong counter-effort of the settlers was for communal security and permanence. From such islands of realiztion and fulfilment within the onrushing torrent have come the objects, the order and balance of which now, when we most need them, we can recognize as among the most valuable possessions of our continent. The conspicuous manifestation of these qualities, as Greenough already knew, has been in architecture as the most social of forms, whether in the clipper, or on the New England green, or in the Shaker communities. But the artifacts of the cabinet maker, the potter and the founder, or whatever other utensils have been shaped patiently and devotedly for common service, are likewise a testimony of what Miss Rourke has called our classic art, recognizing that this term 'has nothing to do with grandeur, that it cannot be copied or imported, but is the outgrowth of a special mode of life and feeling.'

Thoreau's deep obligation to such traditional ways has been obscured by our thinking of him only as the extreme protestant. It is now clear that his revolt was bound up with a determination to do all he could to prevent the dignity of common labor from being degraded by the idle tastes of the rich. When he objected that 'the mason who finishes the cornice of the palace returns at night perchance to a hut not so good as a wigwam,' he showed the identity of his social and aesthetic foundations. Although he did not use Greenough's terms, he was always requiring a functional relationship. What he responded to as beauty was the application of trained skill to the exigencies of existence. He made no arbitrary separation between arts, and admired the Indian's woodcraft or the farmer's thorough care in building a barn on the same grounds that he admired the workmanship of Homer.[2] The depth to which his ideals for fitness and beauty in writing were shaped, half unconsciously, by the modes of productive labor with which he was surrounded, or, in fact, by the work of his own hands in carpentry or pencil-making or gardening, can be read in his instinctive analogies. He knew that the only discipline for Channing's 'sublimo-slipshod style' would be to try to carve some truths as roundly and solidly as a stonecutter. He knew it was no good to write, 'unless you feel strong in the knees.' Or—a more unexpected example to find in him—he believed he had learned an important lesson in design from the fidelity with which the operative in the textile-factory had woven his piece of cloth.

The structural wholeness of *Walden* makes it stand as the firmest product in our literature of such life-giving analogies be-

2. Emerson also said, 'I like a man who likes to see a fine barn as well as a good tragedy.' And Whitman added, as his reaction to the union of work and culture, 'I know that pleasure filters in and oozes out of me at the opera, but I know too that subtly and unaccountably my mind is sweet and odorous within while I clean up my boots and grease the pair that I reserve for stormy weather.'

tween the processes of art and daily work. Moreover, Thoreau's very lack of invention brings him closer to the essential attributes of craftsmanship, if by that term we mean the strict, even spare, almost impersonal 'revelation of the object,' in contrast to the 'elaborated skill,' the combinations of more variegated resources that we describe as technique. This contrast of terms is still Miss Rourke's, in distinguishing between kinds of painting, but it can serve equally to demonstrate why Thoreau's book possesses such solidity in contrast, say, with *Hiawatha* or *Evangeline*. Longfellow was much the more obviously gifted in his available range of forms and subject matters. But his graceful derivations from his models—the versification and gentle tone of Goethe's *Hermann und Dorothea* for *Evangeline*, or the metre of the *Kalevala* for *Hiawatha*—were not brought into fusion with his native themes.[3] Any indigenous strength was lessened by the reader's always being conscious of the metrical dexterity as an ornamental exercise. It is certainly not to be argued that technical proficiency must result in such dilutions, but merely that, as Greenough saw, it was very hard for American artists of that day, who had no developed tradition of their own, not to be thus swamped by their contact with European influences. Their very aspiration for higher standards of art than those with which they were surrounded tended to make them think of form as a decorative refinement which could be imported.

The particular value of the organic principle for a provincial society thus comes into full relief. Thoreau's literal acceptance of Emerson's proposition that vital form 'is only discovered and executed by the artist, not arbitrarily composed by him,' impelled him to minute inspection of his own existence and of the intuitions that rose from it. Although this involved the restriction of his art to parochial limits, to the portrayal of man in terms only of the immediate nature that drew him out, his study of this interaction also brought him to fundamental human patterns unsuspected by Longfellow. Thoreau demonstrated what Emerson had merely observed, that the function of the artist in society is always to renew the primitive experience of the race, that he 'still goes back for materials and begins again on the most advanced stage.' Thoreau's scent for wildness ferreted beneath the merely conscious levels of cultivated man. It served him, in several pages of notes about a debauched muskrat hunter (1859), to uncover and unite once more the chief sources for his own art. He had found himself heartened by the seemingly inexhaustible vitality of this battered character, 'not despairing of life, but keeping the same

3. And as F. L. Pattee has said of *Hiawatha*, in *The Feminine Fifties* (1940): 'The only really Indian thing about the poem is the Indian summer haze that softens all its outlines, but even this atmosphere is Indian only in name: it was borrowed from German romantic poets.'

rank and savage hold on it that his predecessors have for so many generations, while so many are sick and despairing.' Thoreau went on, therefore, half-playfully to speculate what it was that made this man become excited, indeed inspired by the January freshet in the meadows:

There are poets of all kinds and degrees, little known to each other. The Lake School is not the only or the principal one. They love various things. Some love beauty, and some love rum. Some go to Rome, and some go a-fishing, and are sent to the house of correction once a month . . . I meet these gods of the river and woods with sparkling faces (like Apollo's) late from the house of correction, it may be carrying whatever mystic and forbidden bottles or other vessels concealed, while the dull regular priests are steering their parish rafts in a prose mood. What care I to see galleries full of representatives of heathen gods, when I can see natural living ones by an infinitely superior artist, without perspective tube? If you read the Rig Veda, oldest of books, as it were, describing a very primitive people and condition of things, you hear in their prayers of a still older, more primitive and aboriginal race in their midst and round about, warring on them and seizing their flocks and herds, infesting their pastures. Thus is it in another sense in all communities, and hence the prisons and police.

The meandering course of Thoreau's reflections here should not obscure his full discovery that the uneradicated wildness of man is the anarchical basis both of all that is most dangerous and most valuable in him. That he could dig down to the roots of primitive poetry without going a mile from Concord accounts for his ability to create 'a true Homeric or Paphlagonian man' in the likeness of of the French woodchopper. It also helps account for the fact that by following to its uncompromising conclusion his belief that great art can grow from the center of the simplest life, he was able to be universal. He had understood that in the act of expression a man's whole being, and his natural and social background as well, function organically together. He had mastered a definition of art akin to what Maritain has extracted from scholasticism: *Recta ratio factibilium*, the right ordering of the thing to be made, the right revelation of the material.

STANLEY EDGAR HYMAN

Henry Thoreau in Our Time†

In July, 1945, we celebrated the centennial of Henry David Thoreau's retirement to Walden Pond. Almost twice as many old ladies as usual made the pilgrimage to Concord, to see the shrine containing his furniture, and to Walden, where they had the privilege of adding a rock to the cairn where his hut once stood and of opening a box lunch in the picnic ground that stands as his monument. The American Museum of Natural History staged a Walden Pond exhibit. The *Saturday Evening Post* ran an illustrated article. And to add the final mortuary touch, a professor of English published a slim volume called *Walden Revisited*. All in all, it was a typical American literary centennial. Henry Thoreau would probably not have enjoyed it.

A more significant Thoreau centenary would have been July, 1946, the hundredth anniversary of his going to jail. Every reader of *Walden* knows the story. Thoreau had not paid a poll tax for several years, as a sign that he had renounced his allegiance to a government that protected slavery and made war on Mexico, and one day when he walked into Concord to get a mended shoe from the cobbler he was seized and put into jail. That night the tax was paid for him, and the next morning he was freed, obtained his mended shoe, and went back to the woods to pick some berries for dinner. While he was in jail, placidly meditating on the nature of state coercion, Emerson is supposed to have come by and asked: "Henry, what are you doing in *there?*" to which Thoreau is supposed to have replied: "Waldo, what are *you* doing *out there?*"

It takes not much investigation into the story to discover that the actual details of Thoreau's first great political gesture were largely ridiculous. For one thing, the act itself was both safe and imitative, Bronson Alcott having given Thoreau the idea three years before by refusing to pay his taxes and going to jail, where he was treated quite well. For another, Thoreau in jail seems to have been not at all the philosophic muser he makes himself out to be, but, as the jailer later reported, "mad as the devil." For a third, Emerson certainly engaged in no such pat dialogue with him, for the jailer

† From Stanley Edgar Hyman, "Henry Thoreau in Our Times," *The Promised End*, Cleveland Ohio, 1963. Pp. 23–39. Copyright 1963 by Stanley Edgar Hyman. Published by the World Publishing Company. Reprinted by permission of the author.

allowed no visitors, and Emerson's actual reaction to the event was to tell Alcott he thought it was "mean and skulking, and in bad taste." Finally, the person who "interfered" and paid his tax was Thoreau's old Aunt Maria, disguised with a shawl over her head so that Henry would not be angry with her for spoiling his gesture.

Why, then, celebrate the centenary of this absurd event? For only one reason. As a political warrior, Thoreau was a comic little figure with a receding chin, and not enough high style to carry off a gesture. As a political writer, he was the most ringing and magnificent polemicist America has ever produced. Three years later he made an essay called "Civil Disobedience" out of his prison experience, fusing the soft coal of his night in jail into solid diamond. "Civil Disobedience" has all the power and dignity that Thoreau's political act so signally lacked. "Under a government which imprisons any unjustly, the true place for a just man is also a prison," he writes in a line Debs later echoed, ". . . the only home in a slave state in which a free man can abide with honor." "I saw that the State was half-witted, that it was timid as a lone woman with her silver spoons, and that it did not know its friends from its foes, and I lost all my remaining respect for it, and pitied it." He summarizes his position, coolly, reasonably, even humorously, but with utter finality:

> I have never declined paying the highway tax, because I am as desirous of being a good neighbor as I am of being a bad subject; and as for supporting schools, I am doing my part to educate my fellow-countrymen now. It is for no particular item in the tax-bill that I refuse to pay it. I simply wish to refuse allegiance to the State, to withdraw and stand aloof from it effectually. I do not care to trace the course of my dollar, if I could, till it buys a man or a musket to shoot with,—the dollar is innocent,—but I am concerned to trace the effects of my allegiance. In fact, I quietly declare war with the State, after my fashion, though I will still make what use and get what advantage of her I can, as is usual in such cases.

"Civil Disobedience" has been tremendously influential. It powerfully marked the mind of Tolstoy, and changed the direction of his movement. It was the solitary source book on which Gandhi based his campaign of Civil Resistance in India, and Thoreau's ideas multiplied by millions of Indians came fairly close to shattering the power of the British Empire. It has been the bible of countless thousands in totalitarian concentration camps and democratic jails, of partisans and fighters in resistance movements, of men wherever they have found no weapon but principle with which to oppose tyranny. In the relative futility of Thoreau's political act and the real importance of his political essay based on it, we have an allegory for our time on the artist as politician: the artist as strong and serviceable in the earnest practice of his art as he is weak and faintly comic in direct political action. In a day when the pressure on the artist to forsake his art for his duties as a citizen is almost irresistible, when every painter is making posters on nutrition, when every composer is founding a society devoted to doing something about the atom bomb, when every writer is spending more time on committees than on the typewriter, we can use Henry Thoreau's example.

Our first task in creating a Thoreau we can use is distinguishing the real man, or the part of him we want, from the various cardboard Thoreaus commentators have created to fit their wishes or fears. To Emerson, who should have known him better than anyone and certainly didn't, he was a bloodless character distinguished for his ascetic renunciations, a cross between Zeno the Stoic and a cigarstore Indian. Emerson wrote:

> He was bred to no profession; he never married; he lived alone; he never went to church; he never voted; he refused to pay a tax to the State; he ate no flesh; he drank no wine; he never knew the use of tobacco; and, though a naturalist, he used neither trap nor gun.

To his poet-friend and biographer Ellery Channing, Thoreau was the Poet-Naturalist, a sweet singer of woodland beauty, and to his young Abolitionist friend and biographer Frank Sanborn, he was a Concord warrior, a later embattled farmer. To Lowell, an embattled Cambridge gentleman, he was a Transcendentalist crackpot and phony who insisted on going back to flint and steel when he had a matchbox in his pocket, a fellow to the loonies who thought bran or swearing or the substitution of hooks and eyes for buttons would save the world. To Stevenson, full of Victorian vigor and beans, Thoreau was a simple skulker.

In our century Thoreau has fared little better. To Paul Elmer More he was one of Rousseau's wild men, but moving toward the higher self-restraint of neo-Humanism's "inner check." John Macy, one of our early Socialist critics, found him a powerful literary radical, but a little too selfish and aloof to be a good Socialist. To Lewis Mumford he was the Father of our National and State Parks, and to Léon Bazalgette, a French biographer, he was a savage, one of Chateaubriand's noble redmen in the virgin forest. Parrington makes him a researcher in economics, and *Walden* a handbook of economy to refute Adam Smith. To Constance Rourke he is the slick Yankee peddler out of vaudeville, who turns the tables on smart alecks, and to Gilbert Seldes he is an Antinomian.

Ludwig Lewisohn, an amateur sexologist and the Peeping Tom

of our criticism, assures us that Thoreau was a clammy prig, the result of being hopelessly inhibited to the point of psychical impotence, or else hopelessly undersexed. The mechanical Marxists of the thirties are about as useful. V. F. Calverton conceded that he was "the best individual product of the petty bourgeois ideology" of his period, but hopelessly distorted by "Anarcho-individualism" and a probable sexual abnormality. Granville Hicks dismisses him with an epigram: "Nothing in American literature is more admirable than Henry Thoreau's devotion to his principles, but the principles are, unfortunately, less significant than the devotion." Van Wyck Brooks gives us Thoreau as a quirky, rather charming New England eccentric, his only vigorous feature an entirely fictitous hostility to the Irish, projected from Brooks's own discreet xenophobia. To Edward Dahlberg, a philosophic anarchist and disciple of D. H. Lawrence, Thoreau is a philosophic anarchist and earlier Lawrence. And Henry Seidel Canby, who manages to be one of the best biographers in America and almost the worst critic, sums up his excellent, definitive biography with the revelation that Thoreau was a neurotic, sublimating his passions in a loving study of nature.

From these cockeyed and contradictory extractions of Thoreau's "essence" we can reach two conclusions. One is that he is probably a subtler and more ambiguous character than anyone seems to have noticed. The other is that he must somehow still retain a powerful magic, or there would not be such a need to capture or destroy him, to canonize the shade or weight it down in the earth under a cairn of rocks. It seems obvious that we shall have to create a Thoreau for ourselves.

The first thing we should insist on is that Thoreau was a writer, not a man who lived in the woods or didn't pay taxes or went to jail. Other men did all these before him with more distinction. At his best Thoreau wrote the only really first-rate prose ever written by an American, with the possible exception of Abraham Lincoln. The "Plea for Captain John Brown," his most sustained lyric work, rings like *Areopagitica*, and like *Areopagitica* is the product of passion combined with complete technical mastery. Here are two sentences:

> The momentary charge at Balaklava, in obedience to a blundering command, proving what a perfect machine the soldier is, has, properly enough, been celebrated by a poet laureate; but the steady, and for the most part successful, charge of this man, for some years, against the legions of Slavery, in obedience to an infinitely higher command, is as much more memorable than that as an intelligent and conscientious man is superior to a machine. Do you think that that will go unsung?

Thoreau was not only a writer, but a writer in the great stream of the American tradition, the mythic and nonrealist writers, Hawthorne and Melville, Twain and James, and, in our own day, as Malcolm Cowley has been most insistent in pointing out, Hemingway and Faulkner. In pointing out Hemingway's kinship, not to our relatively barren realists and naturalists, but to our "haunted and nocturnal writers, the men who dealt in images that were symbols of an inner world," Cowley demonstrates that the idyllic fishing landscape of such a story as "Big Two-Hearted River" is not a real landscape setting for a real fishing trip, but an enchanted landscape full of rituals and taboos, a metaphor or projection of an inner state. It would not be hard to demonstrate the same thing for the landscape in *Walden*. One defender of such a view would be Henry Thoreau, who writes in his *Journals*, along with innumerable tributes to the power of mythology, that the richest function of nature is to symbolize human life, to become fable and myth for man's inward experience. F. O. Matthiessen, probably the best critic we have devoting himself to American literature, has claimed that Thoreau's power lies precisely in his re-creation of basic myth, in his role as the protagonist in a great cyclic ritual drama.

Central to any interpretation of Thoreau is Walden, both the experience of living by the pond and the book that reported it. As he explains it in the book, it was an experiment in human ecology (and if Thoreau was a scientist in any field, it was ecology, though he preceded the term), an attempt to work out a satisfactory relationship between man and his environment. He writes:

I went to the woods because I wished to live deliberately, to front only the essential facts of life, and see if I could not learn what it had to teach, and not, when I came to die, discover that I had not lived. I did not wish to live what was not life, living is so dear; nor did I wish to practice resignation, unless it was quite necessary. I wanted to live deep and suck out all the marrow of life, to live so sturdily and Spartan-like as to put to rout all that was not life, to cut a broad swath and shave close, to drive life into a corner, and reduce it to its lowest terms, and, if it proved to be mean, why then to get the whole and genuine meanness of it, and publish its meanness to the world; or if it were sublime, to know it by experience, and be able to give a true account of it in my next excursion.

And of his leaving:

I left the woods for as good a reason as I went there. Perhaps it seemed to me that I had several more lives to live, and could not spare any more time for that one.

At Walden, Thoreau reports the experience of awakening one morning with the sense that some question had been put to him, which he had been endeavoring in vain to answer in his sleep. In his terms, that question would be the problem with which he begins "Life Without Principle": "Let us consider the way in which we spend our lives." His obsessive image, running through everything he ever wrote, is the myth of Apollo, glorious god of the sun, forced to labor on earth tending the flocks of King Admetus. In one sense, of course, the picture of Henry Thoreau forced to tend anyone's flocks is ironic, and Stevenson is right when he notes sarcastically: "Admetus never got less work out of any servant since the world began." In another sense the myth has a basic rightness, and is, like the Pied Piper of Hamelin, an archetypal allegory of the artist in a society that gives him no worthy function and no commensurate reward.

The sun is Thoreau's key symbol, and all of *Walden* is a development in the ambiguities of sun imagery. The book begins with the theme: "But alert and healthy natures remember that the sun rose clear," and ends: "There is more day to dawn. The sun is but a morning star." Thoreau's movement from an egocentric to a sociocentric view is the movement from "I have, as it were, my own sun, and moon, and stars, and a little world all to myself" to "The same sun which ripens my beans illumines at once a system of earths like ours." The sun is an old Platonist like Emerson that must set before Thoreau's true sun can rise, it is menaced by every variety of mist, haze, smoke, and darkness, it is Thoreau's brother, it is both his own cold affection and the threat of sensuality that would corrupt goodness as it taints meat, it is himself in a pun on s-o-n, s-u-n. When Abolitionism becomes a nagging demand Thoreau can no longer resist, a Negro woman is a dusky orb rising on Concord, and, when John Brown finally strikes his blow, for Thoreau the sun shines on him, and he works "in the clearest light that shines on the land." The final announcement of Thoreau's triumphant rebirth at Walden is the sun breaking through mists. It is not to our purpose here to explore the deep and complex ambiguities of Thoreau's sun symbol, or in fact to do more than note a few of many contexts, but no one can study the sun references in *Walden* without realizing that Thoreau is a deeper and more complicated writer than we have been told, and that the book is essentially dynamic rather than static, a movement *from* something *to* something, rather than the simple reporting of an experience.

Walden is, in fact, a vast rebirth ritual, the purest and most complete in our literature. We know rebirth rituals to operate characteristically by means of fire, ice, or decay, mountains and pits, but we are staggered by the amount and variety of these in the book. We see Thoreau build his shanty of boards he has first purified in the sun, record approvingly an Indian purification ritual of burning all the tribe's old belongings and provisions, and later go off into a description of the way he is cleansed and renewed by his own fireplace. We see him note the magic purity of the ice on Walden Pond, the fact that frozen water never turns stale, and the rebirth involved when the ice breaks up, all sins are forgiven, and "Walden was dead and is alive again." We see him exploring every phase and type of decay: rotting ice, decaying trees, moldy pitch pine and rotten wood, excrement, maggots, a vulture feeding on a dead horse, carrion, tainted meat, and putrid water. The whole of Walden runs to symbols of graves and coffins, with consequent rising from them, to wombs and emergence from them, and ends on the fable of a live insect resurrected from an egg long buried in wood. Each day at Walden Thoreau was reborn by his bath in the pond, a religious exercise he says he took for purification and renewal, and the whole two years and two months he compresses into the cycle of a year, to frame the book on the archetypal rebirth pattern of the death and renewal of vegetation, ending it with the magical emergence of spring.

On the thread of decay and rebirth Thoreau strings all his preoccupations. Meat is a symbol of evil, sensuality; its tainting symbolized goodness and affection corrupted: the shameful defilement of chastity smells like carrion (in which he agreed with Shakespeare); the eating of meat causes slavery and unjust war. (Thoreau, who was a vegetarian, sometimes felt so wild he was tempted to seize and devour a woodchuck raw, or yearned like a savage for the raw marrow of kudus—those were the periods when he wanted to seize the world by the neck and hold it under water like a dog until it drowned.) But even slavery and injustice are a decaying and death, and Thoreau concludes *Slavery in Massachusetts* with: "We do not complain that they *live*, but that they do not *get buried*. Let the living bury them; even they are good for manure." Always, in Thoreau's imagery, what this rotting meat will fertilize is fruit, ripe fruit. It is his chief good. He wanted "the flower and fruit of man," the "ripeness." The perfect and glorious state he forsees will bear men as fruit, suffering them to drop off as they ripen; John Brown's heroism is a good seed that will bear good fruit, a future crop of heroes. Ultimately Brown, in one of the most terrifying puns ever written, was "ripe" for the gallows. On the metaphor of the organic process of birth, growth, decay, and rebirth out of decay, Thoreau organizes his whole life and experience.

I have maintained that Walden is a dynamic process, a job of symbolic action, a moving *from* something *to* something. From what to what? On an abstract level, from individual isolation to collective identification, from, in Macaulay's terms, a Platonic philosophy of pure truth to a Baconian philosophy of use. It is interesting to note that the term Bacon used for the utilitarian ends of knowledge, for the relief of man's estate, is "fruit." The Thoreau who went to Walden was a pure Platonist, a man who could review a Utopian book and announce that it was too practical, that its chief fault was aiming "to secure the greatest degree of gross comfort and pleasure merely." The man who left Walden was the man who thought it was less important for John Brown to right a Greek accent slanting the wrong way than to right a falling slave. Early in the book Thoreau gives us his famous Platonic myth of having long ago lost a hound, a bay horse, and a turtle dove. Before his is through his symbolic quest is for a human being, and near the end of the book he reports of a hunter: "He had lost a dog but found a man." All through *Walden* Thoreau weighs Platonic and Baconian values: men keep chickens for the glorious sound of a crowing cock "to say nothing of the eggs and drumsticks"; a well reminds a man of the insignificance of his dry pursuits on a surface largely water, and also keeps the butter cool. By the end of the book he has brought Transcendentalism down to earth, has taken Emerson's castles in the air, to use his own figure, and built foundations under them.

Thoreau's political value, for us, is largely in terms of this transition from philosophic aloofness. We see in him the honest artist struggling for terms on which he can adjust to society *in his capacity as artist*. As might be expected from such a process, Thoreau's social statements are full of contradictions, and quotations can be amputated from the context of his work to bolster any position from absolute anarchism to ultimate Toryism, if indeed they are very far apart. At his worst, he is simply a nut reformer, one of the horde in his period, attempting to "improve" an Irish neighbor by lecturing him on abstinence from tea, coffee, and meat as the solution to all his problems, and the passage in *Walden* describing the experience is the most condescending and offensive in a sometimes infuriating book. At his best, Thoreau is the clearest voice for social ethics that ever spoke out in America.

One of the inevitable consequences of Emersonian idealism was the ease with which it could be used to sugar-coat social injustice, as a later generation was to discover when it saw robber barons piling up fortunes while intoning Emersonian slogans of Self-Reliance and Compensation. If the Lowell factory owner was more enslaved than one of his child laborers, there was little point in seeking to improve the lot of the child laborer, and frequently Emerson seemed to be preaching a principle that would forbid

both the rich and the poor to sleep under bridges. Thoreau begins
Walden in these terms, remarking that it is frivolous to attend "to
the gross but somewhat foreign form of servitude called Negro
Slavery when there are so many keen and subtle masters that enslave"; that the rich are a "seemingly wealthy, but most terribly
impoverished class of all" since they are fettered by their gold and
silver; that the day laborer is more independent than his employer,
since his day ends with sundown, while his employer has no respite
from one year to another; even that if you give a ragged man
money he will perhaps buy more rags with it, since he is frequently
gross, with a taste for rags.

Against this ingenious and certainly unintentioned social palli-
ation, *Walden* works through to sharp social criticism: of the
New England textile factory system, whose object is "not that mankind may be well and honestly clad, but, unquestionably, that the
corporations may be enriched"; of the degradation of the laboring
class of his time, "living in sties," shrunken in mind and body; of
the worse condition of the Southern slaves; of the lack of dignity
and privacy in the lives of factory girls, "never alone, hardly in
their dreams"; of the human consequences of commerce and tech-
nology; of the greed and corruption of the money-mad New England
of his day, seeing the whole world in the bright reflecting surface
of a dollar.

As his bitterness and awareness increased, Thoreau's direct action
became transmuted. He had always, like his friends and family,
helped the Underground Railway run escaped slaves to Canada.
He devotes a sentence to one such experience in *Walden*, and
amplifies it in his *Journal*, turning a quiet and terrible irony on
the man's attempt to buy his freedom from his master, who was
his father, and exercised paternal love by holding out for more
than the slave could pay. These actions, however, in a man who
disliked Abolitionism, seem to have been simple reflexes of common decency, against his principles, which would free the slave
first by striking off his spiritual chains. From this view, Thoreau
works tortuously through to his final identification of John Brown,
the quintessence of direct social action, with all beauty, music,
poetry, philosophy, and Christianity. Finally Brown becomes
Christ, an indignant militant who cleansed the temple, preached
radical doctrines, and was crucified by the slave owners. In what
amounts almost to worship of Brown, Thoreau both deifies the
action he had tried to avoid and transcends it in passion. Brown
died for him, thus he need free no more slaves.

At the same time, Thoreau fought his way through the Emersonian doctrine that a man might wash his hands of wrong, providing he did not himself commit it. He writes in "Civil
Disobedience":

It is not a man's duty, as a matter of course, to devote himself to the eradication of any, even the most enormous wrong; he may still properly have other concerns to engage him; but it is his duty, at least, to wash his hands of it, and, if he gives it no thought longer, not to give it practically his support. If I devote myself to other pursuits and contemplations, I must first see, at least, that I do not pursue them sitting upon another man's shoulders. I must get off him first, that he may pursue his contemplations too.

Here he has recognized the fallacy of the Greek philosopher, free because he is supported by the labor of slaves, and the logic of this realization was to drive him, through the superiority and smugness of "God does not sympathize with the popular movements," and "I came into this world, not chiefly to make this a good place to live in, but to live in it, be it good or bad," to the militant fury of "My thoughts are murder to the State, and involuntarily go plotting against her."

Thoreau's progress also involved transcending his economics. The first chapter of *Walden*, entitled "Economy," is an elaborate attempt to justify his life and views in the money terms of New England commerce. He speaks of going to the woods as "going into business" on "slender capital," of his "enterprise"; gives the reader his "accounts," even to the halfpenny, of what he spends and what he takes in; talks of "buying dear," of "paying compound interest," etc. Thoreau accepts the ledger principle, though he sneaks into the Credit category such unusual profits on his investment as "leisure and independence and health." His money metaphor begins to break down when he writes of the Massachusetts citizens who read of the unjust war against Mexico as sleepily as they read the prices current, and he cries out: "What is the price current of an honest man and patriot today?" By the time of the John Brown affair he has evolved two absolutely independent economies, a money economy and a moral economy. He writes:

> "But he won't gain anything by it." Well, no, I don't suppose he could get four-and-sixpence a day for being hung, take the year round; but then he stands a chance to save a considerable part of his soul,—and *such* a soul!—when *you* do not. No doubt you can get more in your market for a quart of milk than for a quart of blood, but that is not the market that heroes carry their blood to.

What, then, can we make of this complicated social pattern to our purposes? Following Emerson's doctrine and example, Thoreau was frequently freely inconsistent. (He was able to write in *Walden*, "I would rather sit on a pumpkin and have it all to myself, than to be crowded on a velvet cushion," and a few pages later, "None is so poor that he need sit on a pumpkin.") One of his chief contradictions was on the matter of reforming the world through his example. He could disclaim hoping to influence anyone with "I do not mean to prescribe rules to strong and valiant natures" and then take it back immediately with "I foresee that all men will at length establish their lives on that basis." Certainly to us his hatred of technological progress, of the division of labor, even of farming with draft animals and fertilizer, is backward-looking and reactionary. Certainly he distrusted co-operative action and all organization. But the example of Jefferson reminds us that a man may be economically backward-looking and still be our noblest spokesman just as Hamilton reminds us that a man may bring us reaction and injustice tied up in the bright issue of economic progress.

To the doctrine of naked expediency so tempting to our time, the worship of power and success for which the James Burnhams among us speak so plausibly, Thoreau opposes only one weapon —*principle*. Not policy or expediency must be the test, but justice and principle. "Read not the Times, read the Eternities." *Walden* has been a bible for the British labor movement since the days of William Morris. We might wonder what the British Labour Party, now that it is in power, or the rest of us, in and out of power, who claim to speak for principle, would make of Thoreau's doctrine: "If I have unjustly wrested a plank from a drowning man, I must restore it to him though I drown myself."

All of this takes us far afield from what must be Thoreau's chief importance to us, his writing. The resources of his craft warrant our study. One of his most eloquent devices, typified by the crack about the Times and Eternities, is a root use of words—resulting from his lifelong interest in language and etymology—fresh, shocking, and very close to the pun. We can see the etymological passion developing in the *Journal* notes that a "wild" man is actually a "willed" man, that our "fields" are "felled" woods. His early writings keep reminding us that a "saunterer" is going to a "Sainte Terre," a Holy Land; that three roads can make a village "trivial"; that when our center is outside us we are "eccentric"; that a "landlord" is literally a "lord of the land"; that he has been "breaking" silence for years and has hardly made a "rent" in it. By the time he wrote *Walden* this habit had developed into one of his most characteristic ironic devices: the insistence that telling his townsmen about his life is not "impertinent" but "pertinent," that professors of philosophy are not philosophers, but people who "profess" it, that the "bent" of his genius is a very "crooked" one. In the "Plea for Captain John Brown" the device achieves a whiplash power. He says that Brown's "humanities" were the freeing of slaves, not the study of grammar; that a Board of Commissions is lumber of which he had only lately heard; of the Governor of Massachusetts: "He was no Governor of mine. He did not govern me." Sometimes these puns double and triple to permit him to pack a number of complex meanings into a single word, like the "dear" in "Living is so dear." The discord of goose-honk and owl-cry he hears by the pond becomes a "concord" that is at once musical harmony, his native town, and concord as "peace."

Closely related to these serious puns in Thoreau is a serious epigrammatic humor, wry quotable lines which pack a good deal of meaning and tend to make their point by shifting linguistic levels. "Some circumstantial evidence is very strong, as when you find a trout in the milk." To a man who threatened to plumb his depths: "I trust you will not strike your head against the bottom." "The partridge loves peas, but not those that go with her into the pot." On his habit of exaggeration: "You must speak loud to those who are hard of hearing." He reported that the question he feared was not "How much wood did you burn?" but "What did you do while you were warm?" Dying, he said to someone who wanted to talk about the next world: "One world at a time"; and to another, who asked whether he had made his peace with God: "We have never quarrelled." When Emerson remarked that they taught all branches of learning at Harvard: "All of the branches and none of the roots." Refusing to pay a dollar for his Harvard diploma: "Let every sheep keep but his own skin." Asked to write for *The Ladies' Companion:* "I could not write anything companionable." Many of these are variants of the same joke, and in a few cases, the humor is sour and forced, like the definition of a pearl as "the hardened tear of a diseased clam, murdered in its old age," or a soldier as "a fool made conspicuous by a painted coat." But these are penalties any man who works for humor must occasionally pay, and Thoreau believed this "indispensable pledge of sanity" to be so important that without some leaven of it "the abstruse thinker may justly be suspected of mysticism, fanaticism or insanity." "Especially the transcendental philosophy needs the leaven of humor," he wrote, in what must go down as an understatement.

Thoreau was perhaps more precise about his own style and more preoccupied generally with literary craft than any American writer except Henry James. He rewrote endlessly, not only, like James, for greater precision, but unlike James, for greater simplicity. "Simplify, Simplify, Simplify," he gave as the three cardinal principles of both life and art. Emerson had said of Montaigne: "Cut these words and they would bleed" and Thoreau's is perhaps the only American style in his century of which this is true. Criticizing De Quincey, he stated his own prose aesthetic, "the *art* of writing," demanding sentences that are concentrated and nutty, that suggest far more than they say, that are kinked and knotted into something hard and significant, to be swallowed like a diamond without digesting. "Sentences which are expensive, towards which so many volumes, so much life, went; which lie like boulders on the page, up and down or across; which contain the seed of other sentences, not mere repetition, but creation; which a man might sell his grounds and castles to build." In another place he notes that writing must be done with gusto, must be vascular. A sense of Thoreau's preoccupation with craft comes with noting that when he lists "My faults" in the *Journal*, all seven of them turn out to be of his prose style. Writing for Thoreau was so obsessive, so vital a physical process, that at various times he describes it in the imagery of eating, procreation, excretion, mystic trance, and even his old favorite, the tree bearing ripe fruit. An anthology of Thoreau's passages on the art of writing would be as worth compiling as Henry James's *Prefaces*, and certainly as useful to both the writer and the reader.

Thoreau's somewhat granite pride and aloofness are at their most appealing, and very like James Joyce's, when he is defending his manuscripts against editorial bowdlerizing, when he stands as the embattled writer against the phalanx of cowardice and stupidity. He fought Emerson and Margaret Fuller on a line in one of his poems they printed in *The Dial*, and won. When the editor of *Putnam's Monthly* cut passages from an article, Thoreau wrote to a friend: "The editor requires the liberty to omit the heresies without consulting me, a privilege California is not rich enough to bid for" and he withdrew the series. His letter to Lowell, the editor of *The Atlantic*, when Lowell cut a "pantheistic" sentence out of cowardice, is a masterpiece of bitter fury, withering Lowell like a premature bud in a blast.

Henry Thoreau's and John Brown's personalities were as different as any two personalities can be; one the gentle, rather shy scholar who took children huckleberrying; the other the harsh military Puritan who could murder the children of slavers in cold blood on the Pottawatomie, making the fearful statement, "Nits grow to be lice." Almost the only things they had in common—that made Thoreau perceive that Brown was his man, his ideas in action, almost his Redeemer—were principle and literary style. Just as writers in our own day were drawn to Sacco and Vanzetti perhaps as much for the majesty of Vanzetti's untutored prose as for the obvious justice of their case, Thoreau somehow found the most convincing thing about Brown to be his speech to the court. At the end of his "Plea" he quotes Brown's "sweet and noble strain":

> I pity the poor in bondage that have none to help them; that is why I am here; not to gratify any personal animosity, revenge, or vindictive spirit. It is my sympathy with the oppressed and the wronged, that are as good as you, and as precious as the sight of God.

adding only: "You don't know your testament when you see it."

"This unlettered man's speaking and writing are standard English" he writes in another paper on Brown. "It suggests that the one great rule of composition—and if I were a professor of rhetoric I should insist on this—is, to *speak the truth*." It was certainly Thoreau's great rule of composition. "He was a speaker and actor of the truth," Emerson said in his obituary of Thoreau. We have never had too many of those. He was also, perhaps as a consequence, a very great writer. We have never had too many of those, either.

JOSEPH WOOD KRUTCH

Paradise Found†

The retirement to Walden is the central feature in the legend of Thoreau. It is the one thing about him which everybody knows, and the prominence which must be given it in any account of his life is justified by the fact that the experience unquestionably served to release his creative powers. But even if it had not actually had any such demonstrable effect, it would still be so artistically right that it would assume, willy-nilly, a very prominent place in his story. A philosopher should pass his forty days in the wilderness, and Thoreau, to whom the enduring legends were the only interesting form of fiction, would have been pleased to realize —whether or not he ever actually did realize—that he was following a pattern consecrated by eternal repetition.

From 1840 on, good reasons for withdrawing from social life had begun to accumulate in the *Journal*. The "garret" motif recurs, along with the determination to wipe his hands of life; to see how mean it is and to have nothing to do with it. He was deter-

† From Joseph Wood Krutch, *Henry David Thoreau*, New York, 1948. Pp. 69-82. Copyright 1948 by William Sloane Associates. Reprinted by permission of the publishers.

mined to "move away from public opinion, from government, from religion, from education, from society." "There are certain current expressions and blasphemous moods of viewing things, as when we say 'he is doing a good business' more profane than cursing and swearing. There is death and sin in such words. Let not the children hear them." And he was also willing to go even further. "No true and brave person will be content to live on such a footing with his fellows and himself as the laws of every household require. The house is the very haunt and lair of our vice. I am impatient to withdraw myself from under its roof as an unclean spot. There is no circulation there; it is full of stagnant and mephitic vapors." He determines "to meet myself face to face sooner or later" and on a visit to Cambridge he is suddenly overwhelmed with distaste for the collection of English poets he had come to seek. "When looking over dry and dusty volumes of the English poets, I cannot believe that those fresh and fair creations I had imagined are contained in them. English poetry from Gower down, collected into one alcove, and so from the library window compared with the commonest nature, seems very mean. Poetry cannot breathe in the scholar's atmosphere. I can hardly be serious with myself when I remember that I have come to Cambridge after poetry; and while I am running over the catalogue and selecting, I think it would be a shorter way to a complete volume to step at once into the field or wood, with a very low reverence to students and librarians. Milton did not see what company he was to fall into."

For all this, Thoreau did not—pleasant as it would be to imagine it so—go arrowlike from Staten Island and its fiasco to Walden pond. Instead he returned to his parents' home, and helped them in building the new house called "Texas" because of its remoteness from the Milldam which was regarded as the center of Concord. It may even have been about this time that he devised an improved method of producing graphite which was to lift the financial state of the family. But no discovery of Yankee ingenuity in himself was likely to divert him into the cultivation of so dubious a gift.

To Emerson he complained that he found it impossible to do more than one thing at a time and that, though his evenings were nominally free for study, "if he was in the day inventing machines for sawing his plumbago, he invents wheels all the evening and night also." The fear that he might develop into what his neighbors would call a useful citizen merely added urgency to a long-recognized desire to retire somehow from the village into the country. Once he had considered even the possibility of becoming a farmer, until he asked himself the all-sufficient question: "What have I to do with plows?" and made the proper comment: "I plow another furrow." And, as early as December 24, 1841, he had written: "I want to go soon and live away by the pond, where I shall hear only the wind whispering among the reeds. It will be a success if I shall have left myself behind."

Three years and a half were to elapse between the time when that last passage was written (presumably in Emerson's house) and the time when Thoreau actually took up his residence "by the pond." The whole of the Staten Island episode intervened and so did his unhappy concern with machines for sawing plumbago. But it is obvious that he had not really accepted any of the ways of living he had tried. There seemed no way of making a living— teaching, writing, or pencil-making—which did not take up more precious time than he was willing to give to it, and the solution of the problem, very obvious to him though few other men have ever been able to accept it, was simply to need less rather than to get more. Teetotaler though he was, he might have echoed Omar's wonder what the vintners buy one half so precious as the stuff they sell. The wine of life was ill exchanged for cake and he was sure that bread could be got for very little.

All the region round about Concord through which he had wandered as boy and as man seemed to him sacred through intimacy, but Walden pond had long had for him a special significance. At the age of five, when he was living with his parents in Boston during his father's school-teaching period, and when he had, no doubt, all but forgot what the country was like, he was brought back to Concord for a visit and was taken to Walden pond. It became at once, so he said, somewhat incoherently, "one of the most ancient scenes stamped on the tablets of my memory, the oriental Asiatic valley of my world, whence so many races and inventions have gone forth in recent times. That woodland vision for a long time made a drapery of my dreams. That sweet solitude my spirit seemed so early to require that I might have room to entertain my thronging guests, and that speaking silence that my ears might distinguish the significant sounds. Somehow or other it at once gave the preference to this recess among the pines, where almost sunshine and shadow were the only inhabitants that varied the scene, over that tumultuous and varied city, as if it had found its proper nursery."

He had returned there many times, and fortunately for him Emerson now owned a most suitable spot on the pond side where a garret might be built without any troublesome house beneath it. In exchange for the privilege of putting up a hut there, Thoreau would clear the brier patch and be, besides, as grateful as an anarchist with scant respect for property rights was likely to be. In March 1845, he began to prepare his site and during the rest of the spring he was busy with the aid of several friends constructing the solidly built one-room cabin which Ellery Channing, whom Thoreau had met through Emerson a few years before, described as no more than "a larger coat and hat—a sentry box on the shore . . . ready to walk into in rain or snow or cold."

In an ecstasy of enthusiasm over his discovery of just how little one could get along with and just how absurd it was for a man to invest ten to fifteen years of his life earning shelter, Thoreau was later to suggest, somewhat less than seriously, that the large boxes for tools which he had seen by the railroad might serve the purpose. "Every man who was hard-pushed might get such a one for a dollar, and, having bored a few auger holes in it, to admit the air at least, get into it when it rained and at night, and hook down the lid, and so have freedom in his love, and in his soul be free. . . . You could sit up as late as you pleased, and, whenever you got up, go abroad without any landlord or houselord dogging you for rent. Many a man is harassed to death to pay the rent of a larger and more luxurious box who would not have frozen to death in such a box as this."

The cabin by Walden pond went one step, if hardly more than one step, beyond this. It was, so he tells us, tight-shingled and plastered, ten feet wide by fifteen long, with a garret, a closet, two windows, two trap doors, one door to the outside, and one fireplace. It cost him in materials exactly twenty-eight dollars, twelve and one-half cents, and it was certainly worth the money, though the jocose Channing must have his little fun: "As for its being in the ordinary meaning a house, it was so superior to the common domestic contrivances that I do not associate it with them. By standing on a chair you could reach into the garret, and a corn broom fathomed the depth of the cellar. It had no lock to the door, no curtain to the window, and belonged to nature nearly as much as to man." When visitors came they got a chair outside, and no superfluous furniture was allowed to accumulate. There was, besides the simplest utensils, a bed, a table, a desk, and a lookingglass three inches in diameter. There were also three chairs—just to show, as Thoreau remarked, that there was no use going to extremes. "None is so poor that he need sit on a pumpkin." A lady once offered to present him with a mat for wiping his feet, but he preferred the sod before the door which would need no shaking. "It is best to avoid the beginnings of evil."

On July 4, 1845, he officially took up residence and within a few days he was not only recalling in the *Journal* his boyhood visit but also congratulating himself upon having found his way back again:

Now, to-night my flute awakes the echoes over this very water, but one generation of pines has fallen, and with their stumps I have cooked my supper, and a lusty growth of oaks and pines is rising all around its brim and preparing its wilder aspect for new infant eyes. Almost the same johnswort springs from the same perennial root in this pasture. Even I have at length helped to clothe that fabulous landscape of my imagination, and one result of my presence and influence is seen in these bean leaves and corn blades and potato vines.

Outwardly there was nothing sensational in what Thoreau had undertaken to do. In one of its aspects the enterprise was merely a practical, if somewhat eccentric, solution of the problem of a man already past the first flush of youth who had found no trade or profession which pleased him, and who wished to live as cheaply as possible. There was not, as there was in the Fruitlands or Brook Farm experiments, any element of the merely lunatic. If we can divest ourselves of the knowledge that the hero of the story is now—as indisputably as any American writer—a world figure, and if we can remember that to his fellow townsmen he was not even, as he was to Emerson, a promising if still unfruitful thinker, we can realize that to many who heard of his retirement to the near-by woods, it was hardly more than the mean shift of a ne'er-do-well.

It was also, outwardly, not an adventure, but a gesture, at most. The woods were not very wild and not very remote; Thoreau's hut was within easy walking distance of the village; friends or acquaintances often dropped in to see him, and he often walked into the village for a dinner with some townsman, or to collect a bit of gossip. Thousands now living in cities are more isolated from other human beings than he ever was; thousands of others in thinly populated regions of the earth are physically more alone without thinking of themselves as being especially isolated. In the account which he gave of his experience he notes derisively that conventional fellow townsmen asked "if I did not feel lonesome; if I was not afraid, and the like"; but physically his taking to the woods was less hazardous than a week-end camping expedition in Bear Mountain Park and his surroundings were considerably less wild. If the one-hundredth anniversary of his retirement was extensively noted in newspapers a few years ago and if it was appropriately celebrated by nature lovers and amateur woodsmen, this was not because Thoreau had exhibited any especially adventurous spirit so far as the facing of any physical hardships is concerned. He scarcely belongs among the adventurous explorers, for whom in truth he had little respect since he thought of them as men perversely unaware of the fact that undiscovered country enough to occupy any man lay both within and just around us all. Indeed, on one of the last pages of *Walden* he was to ask derisively about an adventurer and about a patron of adventurers then in the public eye: "Is Franklin the only man who is lost, that his wife should be so earnest to find him? Does Mr. Grinnell know where he himself is?" Already he felt, as he was much later to note in the *Journal*: "It is in vain to dream of a wildness distant from ourselves. . . . I shall never find in the wilds of Labrador any greater wildness than in some recess in Concord, *i.e.* than I import into it."

But if Thoreau's retirement was rather a gesture than an adventure, it was also what gestures at their most striking must become—namely, a symbol, and to his often very downright mind the importance of the symbol lay in part in the fact that it involved certain acts which, however unspectacular, were nevertheless visible and concrete attempts to put into some sort of actual practice theories which could not honorably be allowed to remain merely theories. Emerson might talk about plain living and about breaking with convention, but there was nothing in his outward way of life capable of shocking the most conventional. He did not *do* anything. He did not take even a first step. He was, as a matter of fact, always to hold himself aloof from the experiments in which other Transcendentalists, even finally Hawthorne, were to become involved. Thoreau wanted to begin to live some special kind of life, not merely to think about one. He was determined to take some step, and among the various attempts which he makes in *Walden* to imply or state what his life in the woods had accomplished for him, perhaps the most significant is: "I learned this, at least, by my experiment; that if one advances confidently in the direction of his dreams, and endeavors to live the life which he has imagined, he will meet with a success unexpected in common hours."

Undoubtedly Thoreau was conscious that he was making his contribution to the series of experiments with which so many New Englanders were, or were soon to be, busy. Being an individualist it was inevitable that he should set up a kind of one-man Brook Farm, and for him, the only one concerned, it was a success from the start. Something of that happy confidence, that sense of being right and of having found the true path which was to inform *Walden*, the book, begins immediately to inform the pages of the deeply contented *Journal* from which the book was quarried. He was to lose some of that confidence again in later years, perhaps inevitably to lose it as he endeavored to reconcile and to think out to the end various paradoxes, each one of which seemed by itself so absolute and incontrovertible a revelation. But for the moment each was sufficient unto itself as each, somewhat obscurely and almost irascibly perceived before, took on its clear outline now. It was, he had proved, possible to simplify, not merely to talk about simplifying; possible to renounce those errors which, as he wrote, had made men the slaves of their own tools. If a man could not ride everywhere in next to no time and for next to nothing, he could live somewhere for almost as little. "And the cost of a thing is the amount of life it requires to be exchanged for it, immediately or in the long run."

Some part of his delight was merely from the gratification of what some more recent psychologist might dub the Robinson Crusoe complex, and that complex, though no doubt more or less consciously present in every man's mental make-up, was very highly developed in Thoreau. "It is worth the while," he wrote while still at Walden, "to have lived a primitive wilderness life at some time, to know what are, after all, the necessaries of life and what methods society has taken to supply them. I have looked over the old day-books of the merchants with the same view—to see what it was shopmen bought. They are the grossest groceries. Salt is perhaps the most important article in such a list, and most commonly bought at the stores, of articles commonly thought to be necessaries . . . by the farmer. . . . Here's the rub then. I see how I could supply every other article I need, without using the shops, and to obtain this might be the fit occasion for a visit to the seashore. Yet even salt cannot strictly speaking be called a necessary of human life, since many tribes do not use it."

But simple, self-sustaining existence was not an end in itself. "I wish," he wrote, on his third day beside the pond, "to meet the facts of life—the vital facts which are the phenomena or actuality the Gods meant to show us—face to face, and so I came down here." But even that was not quite all. Thoreau was still, and always remained, enough of a Transcendentalist to believe that there was also some ultimate truth beyond "phenomena" and "actuality" which could be caught only, if at all, by grace of a direct, superrational communication from nature to man. And one thing was certain: at Walden one saw more of the significant "phenomena" and "actualities" than one saw of them in a city or even in a village, and on the basis of that fact it was reasonable to suppose that, living more naturally, one was also more nearly attuned to the truth which might some day be communicated.

To a mouse which ran over his shoes and up the inside of his pantaloons he fed a bit of cheese from his fingers, feeling the comfortable assurance that "There is not much danger of the mouse tribe becoming extinct in hard winters, for their granary is a cheap and extensive one." "And then the frogs, bullfrogs; they are the more sturdy spirits of ancient wine-bibbers and wassailers, still unrepentant, trying to sing a catch in their Stygian lakes." He was sure that he was more nearly of the frogs' fellowship than he was of any fellowship gathered in towns; more a part of their ancient world than of that newer one which had created needs to which it was now enslaved. "If I am not quite right here," he wrote, "I am less wrong than before." And he was supremely happy. "Sometimes, when I compare myself with other men, methinks I am favored by the gods. They seem to whisper joy to me beyond my deserts, and that I do have a solid warrant and surety at their hands, which my fellows do not. I do not flatter myself, but if it were possible, they flatter me. I am especially guided and guarded." And again: "Every natural form—palm leaves and acorns, oak leaves and sumach and dodder—are [sic] untranslatable aphorisms."

Despite such sentiments as this last, Thoreau was nevertheless beginning to free himself from the naïve Transcendentalist assumption that the lessons of nature are merely little allegories confirming the prejudices of the human moralists. Ultimately, indeed, he was to go so far in the other direction as to be all but forced into a pantheism which left little place for merely human concerns. But at the perfect Walden moment he had gone to nature to learn a lesson which he thought would be new and which he still assumed would be humanly comprehensible. "Dictates," which seemed to carry the authority of divine suggestion, came to him from beyond himself. What, he asked, if we were to obey them? What if, for example, we were to refuse, as they seemed to suggest we ought, either to eat meat or to buy and sell? And for the moment he did not ask the question which was later to trouble him much even though he never quite put it into words—the question how the divine in man, which forbids him to eat his fellows, is related to the natural which bids other natural creatures eat their own kind.

Poetry, which had seemed so dusty in the library alcove, came to life again. "There are," he realized afresh, "no monuments of antiquity comparable to the classics for interest and importance. . . . Books, the oldest and the best, stand rightfully on the shelves of every cottage." But "Books must be read as deliberately and reservedly as they were written." Men, too, once one is out from under their roofs, once one can see them by choice rather than by necessity, once they stand on their own legs, once—above all—one can meet them without being entangled in what he called "their dirty institutions," were often interesting and, sometimes, in certain of their aspects, attractive creatures. Ten days after he had installed himself, Therien, the French Canadian wood chopper who had made his dinner on woodchuck the night before, passed by. He was, said Thoreau, a true Paphlagonian man though he too had heard of Homer. Soon Henry and he were fast, self-reliant friends. Therien was a well of good humor and contentment. "By George!" he would say. "I can enjoy myself well enough here chopping; I want no better sport." "In him," Thoreau wrote, "the animal man chiefly was developed. In physical endurance and contentment he was cousin to the pine and the rock." But, as Thoreau remembered when he came to give the wood chopper his due place in the public record of the Walden adventure, "the intellectual and what is called the spiritual man in him were slumbering as in an infant."

Perhaps the association with Therien helped to prevent Thoreau from ever falling into the delusion that he wished actually to return to the merely primitive man, or that wildness, for all that he cherished a strain of it in himself and others, was sufficient in itself. It was not long after he had first met Therien that he wrote into the *Journal*: "Though the race is not so degenerated but a man might possibly live in a cave to-day and keep himself warm by furs, yet, as caves and wild beasts are not plenty enough to accommodate all at the present day, it were certainly better to accept the advantages which the invention and industry of mankind offer." He never proposed, as flippant critics seem usually to assume, that we should dispense with all the material inventions of civilization, much less with its intellectual refinements. Neither did he ever seriously believe that all the latter could be maintained without any of the former. What he did wish to find out was how many tools and conveniences were really necessary and at what point they began to cost more in time and effort than they were worth—an inquiry which, by the way, has never been satisfactorily concluded by Thoreau or anyone else. Even at Walden, where he was admittedly conducting a somewhat extreme experiment, he was seeking not so much to get away from either men or the things they had surrounded themselves with as from the demands which they and their kind of society made upon him.

* * *

SHERMAN PAUL

Resolution at Walden†

I

Walden was published in 1854, eight years before Thoreau died, some seven years after his life in the woods. His journal shows that he had proposed such a "poem" for himself as early as 1841, that its argument would be "the River, the Woods, the Ponds, the Hills, the Fields, the Swamps and Meadows, the Streets and Buildings, and the Villagers. Then Morning, Noon, and Evening, Spring, Summer, Autumn, and Winter, Night, Indian Summer, and the Mountains in the Horizon." Like *A Week on the Concord and Merrimack Rivers* (1849)—"If one would reflect," Thoreau had written in 1837, "let him embark on some placid stream, and float with the current"—*Walden* took a long time maturing, a longer time, because it was more than the stream of his reflections. The *Week* had been written out of joyousness and to memorialize his most perfect excursion in nature. *Walden*, however, was Thoreau's recollected experience, recollected not in tranquillity, but in the years of what he himself called his "decay." Although one need only search the journals to find many of the events of *Walden* freshly put down. *Walden* itself reveals that Thoreau was now looking at these events with more experienced eyes: his long quarrel with society has intervened, his youthful inspiration had become more difficult to summon, the harvest of the *Week* he had hoped to bestow on the public lay in his attic, and, growing older, he was still without a vocation that others would recognize. In *Walden*, at once his victorious hymn to Nature, to her perpetual forces of life, inspiration and renewal, Thoreau defended his vocation by creating its eternal symbol.

The common moral of *Walden* is that of the virtue of simplicity; and simplicity is usually taken on the prudential level of economy with which Thoreau seemingly began the book. In terms of Thoreau's spiritual economy, however, simplicity was more than freedom from the burdens of a mortgaged life: it was an ascetic, a severe discipline, like solitude for Emerson, by which Thoreau concentrated his forces and was able to confront the facts of life without the intervening barriers of society or possessions. For sim-

† From *Accent*, XII (1953), 101–13. Reprinted by permission of Sherman Paul.

plicity, Thoreau often substituted poverty, a word which both set him apart from his materialistic neighbors and hallowed his vocation with its religious associations of renunciation and higher dedication. It was the suitable condition for the spiritual crusader: the sign in a land of traders of his profession. But it also signified his inner condition. "By poverty," he said, "*i.e.* simplicity of life and fewness of incidents, I am solidified and crystallized, as a vapor or liquid by cold. It is a singular concentration of strength and energy and flavor. Chastity is perpetual acquaintance with the All. My diffuse and vaporous life becomes as frost leaves and spiculae radiant as gems on the weeds and stubble in a winter morning." Such poverty or purity was a necessity of *his* economy. "You think," he continued, "that I am impoverishing myself by withdrawing from men, but in my solitude I have woven for myself a silken web or *chrysalis*, and, nymph-like, shall ere long burst forth a more perfect creature, fitted for a higher society. By simplicity, commonly called poverty, my life is concentrated and so becomes organized, or a κόσμος, which before was inorganic and lumpish."

This was also the hope of his paean to spring in *Walden*, to "pass from the lumpish grub in the earth to the airy and fluttering butterfly." The purpose of his experiment at Walden Pond, begun near the end of his years of undisciplined rapture— Emerson said that the vital heat of the poet begins to ebb at thirty—was to build an organic life as consciously as he built his hut (and his book), and so retain his vital heat. "May I never," he had recorded in his journal, "let the vestal fire go out in my recesses." But there was desperation in his attempt to keep his vital heat, because it was only *vital* (or rather he felt it so) when he was maturing beyond the lumpish, grub-like existence. As well as the advocacy of the organic life which promised renewal and growth, *Walden* for Thoreau filled the immediate need of self-therapy. In the serenity and joy of his art this is often overlooked, but it is there in the journals behind the book. And the greatness of *Walden*, from this perspective at least, is the resolution Thoreau was able to fulfill through art. By creating an organic form he effected his own resolution for rebirth: by conscious endeavor he recaptured, if not the youthful ecstasy of his golden age, a mature serenity.

This serenity, however, is still alert, wakeful, tense. It was a victory of discipline. "That aim in life is highest," Thoreau noted during the composition of *Walden*, "which requires the highest and finest discipline." That aim was highest, that discipline the highest vocation, because the goal and fulfillment of all transcendental callings was purity—a oneness with Nature in which the untarnished mirror of the soul reflected the fullness of being. The cost of doing without conventional life was not too great for Thoreau, considering his desire to "perceive things truly and simply." He believed that "a fatal coarseness is the result of mixing in the trivial affairs of men." And to justify his devotion to purity he wrote *Walden*, a promise of the higher society a man can make when he finds his *natural* center, a record of things and events so simple and fundamental that all lives less courageous and principled are shamed by the *realometer* it provides. Like other masterworks of its time, it has the unique strain of American romanticism: behind its insistent individualism and desire for experience, there is still more earnest conviction of the necessity of virtue.

II

In the concluding pages of *Walden*, Thoreau remarked that "in this part of the world it is considered a ground for complaint if a man's writings admit of more than one interpretation." With his contemporaries, Emerson, Hawthorne, Melville, he wanted the "volatile truth" of his words to "betray the inadequacy of the residual statement." He would have considered *Walden* a failure if it served only to communicate an eccentric's refusal to go along with society, if, taken literally, its spiritual courage was thinned to pap for tired businessmen long since beyond the point of no return. For *Walden* was *his* myth: "A fact truly and absolutely stated," he said, "is taken out of the region of common sense and acquires a mythologic or universal significance." This was the extravagance he sought—this going beyond the bounds. For him, only the fact stated without reference to convention or institution, with only reference to the self which has tasted the world and digested it, which has been "drenched" and "saturated" with truth, is properly humanized—is properly myth. Primarily to immerse himself in truth, to merge himself with the law of Nature, and to humanize this experience by the alchemy of language, Thoreau went to Walden. There, free from external references, he could purify himself and live a sympathetic existence, alive to the currents of being. What he reported, then, would be the experience of the self in its unfolding and exploration of the "not-me." The literal record would merely remain the residual statement —no one knew better the need for concrete fact; but it would also yield a *translated* meaning.

The whole of *Walden* is an experience of the microcosmic and cosmic travels of the self. At Walden Pond, Thoreau wrote, "I have, as it were, my own sun and moon and stars, and a little world all to myself." Thoreau, of course, was a great traveller, if only a saunterer. The profession of traveller appealed to his imagination; it was, he said, the "best symbol of our life." And "Walking" was the best short statement of his way of life, of his journey to the holy land. He yearned, he wrote in 1851, "for one of those old, meandering, dry, uninhabited roads, which lead away from towns. . . ." He wanted to find a place "where you can walk and think with least obstruction, there being nothing to measure progress by; where you can pace when your breast is full, and cherish your moodiness; where you are not in false relations with men. . . ." He wanted "a road where I can travel," where "I can walk, and recover the lost child that I am without any ringing of a bell." The road he wanted led to Walden. There he regained the primal world, and lived the pristine initiation into consciousness over again. "Both place and time were changed," he said in *Walden*, "and I dwelt nearer to those parts of the universe and to those eras in history which had most attracted me."

In this effort to live out of time and space or to live in all times and places, *Walden* immediately suggests Melville's *Moby-Dick*. Melville had written another voyage of the self on which he explored reality, charted the constituents of a chaos, and raised his discovery to the universal level of archetypal experience. He had elaborated the myth of the hunter which Thoreau also employed in the chapter on "Higher Laws." "There is a period in the history of the individual, as of the race," he wrote, "when hunters are the 'best men'. . . ." Hunting, he added, "is oftenest the young man's introduction to the forest [Melville's sea], and the most original part of himself. He goes thither at first as a hunter and fisher, until at last, if he has the seeds of a better life in him, he distinguishes his proper objects. . . ." It was in these "wild" employments of his youth that Thoreau acknowledged his "closest acquaintance with Nature." For Nature revealed herself to the hunter more readily than to "philosophers or poets even, who approach her with expectation"—or, as Melville knew, to the participant and not the observer of life. If Thoreau had long since given up hunting, he still found a sustaining link with the wild in his bean field.

There are obvious differences, of course, in the quality of these travels—each author had his spiritual torment, Melville the need for belief, Thoreau the need for recommunion. But both were projecting the drama of their selves, a drama that in both instances ended in rebirth; and the methods both employed were remarkably similar. Each abstracted himself from the conventional world, established a microcosm by which to test the conventions, and worked at a basic and heroic occupation. For example, the village stands in the same symbolic relation to Thoreau at Walden that the land does to Melville's sea; and it is the occupation in both that supplies

the residual statement. In Thoreau's case, it is also a primitive concern with essentials: building his hut, planting, hoeing and harvesting his beans, fishing and naturalizing. And the nature of the
occupation gives each its spiritual quality, because whaling (but-
chery) and colonizing (building from scratch) are projections of
different visions of the universe of which only the central similarity
remains—the exploration of self.

But this similarity is a sufficient signature for both; one recog-
nizes the existential kinship. At the conclusion of *Walden* Thoreau
declared: "Explore thyself . . . Be . . . the Mungo Park, the
Lewis and Clark and Frobisher, of your own streams and
oceans. . . ."—

> ". . . . . be
> Expert in home-cosmography."

For "there are continents and seas in the moral world to which
every man is an isthmus or an inlet, yet unexplored by him, . . .
[and] it is easier to sail many thousand miles through cold and
storm and cannibals, in a government ship, with five hundred men
and boys to assist one, than it is to explore the private sea, the
Atlantic and Pacific Ocean of one's being alone." Melville at
Pittsfield would have agreed that "herein are demanded the eye and
the nerve." But if Melville needed the watery two-thirds of the
world and the great whale for this quest, Thoreau, who had the
gift of enlarging the small, needed only the pond and its pickerel.
And where Melville needed the destructive forces of the sea to
mirror himself, Thoreau, who had seen the place of violence
in the total economy of nature, needed only the recurrence of
the seasons.

III

Walden was Thoreau's quest for a reality he had lost, and
for this reason it was a quest for purity. Purity meant a return to
the spring (and springtime) of life, to the golden age of his youth
and active senses, when the mirror of his self was not clouded by
self-consciousness. *Walden*, accordingly, follows the cycle of developing consciousness, a cycle that parallels the change of the seasons.
It is a recapitulation of Thoreau's development (and the artistic
reason he put the experience of two years into one)—a development from the sensuous, active, external (unconscious *and* out-of-
doors) summer of life, through the stages of autumnal consciousness
and the withdrawal inward to the self-reflection of winter, to the
promise of ecstatic rebirth in the spring. It was a matter of
purification because Thoreau had reached the winter of decay at
the time *Walden* was being revised for the press. With consciousness had come the knowledge of the "reptile" and "sensual"

which he knew could not "be wholly expelled." "I fear," he
wrote, "that it [the sensual] may enjoy a certain health of its own;
that we may be well, yet not pure." For the mind's approach to
God, he knew that the severest discipline was necessary: his chapter
on "Higher Laws" is concerned almost entirely with the regimen
of the appetites because "man flows at once to God when the
channel of purity is open." The undeniable sensual energy—
the "generative energy"—he had unconsciously enjoyed in the
ecstasy of youth, now needed control. "The generative energy,"
he wrote, "which, when we are loose, dissipates and makes us
unclean, when we are continent invigorates and inspires us." He
was consciously using instinct for higher ends, seeking chasity by
control.

In Walden Pond he saw the image of his purified self—that
pristine, eternal self he hoped to possess. In 1853, while he was
working on his book, he noted in his journal: "How watchful
we must be to keep the crystal well that we were made, clear!—
that it be not make turbid by our contact with the world, so that
it will not reflect objects." The pond, he recalled, was one of
the "oldest scenes stamped on my memory." He had been taken to
see it when he was four years old. Now, playing his flute beside
its waters, his beans, corn and potatoes replacing the damage of the
years, he felt that another aspect was being prepared "for new infant
eyes," that "even I have at length helped to clothe that fabulous
landscape of my infant dreams. . . ." Later, he recalled his
youthful reveries on its waters: "I have spent many an hour,
when I was younger, floating over its surface as the zephyr
willed . . . dreaming awake. . . ." But time (and wood-choppers)
had ravished its shores: "My Muse may be excused," he explained, "if she is silent henceforth. How can you expect the
birds to sing when their groves are cut down?" It was the confession of the Apollo who had had to serve Admetus, a confession
he made again in "Walking." Visited by fewer thoughts each
year, he said that "the grove in our minds is laid waste—sold to
feed unnecessary fires of ambition. . . ."

But Thoreau discovered at Walden that even though the
groves were cut down, the pond itself remained the same—it
"best preserves its purity." "It is itself unchanged," he learns,
"the same water my youthful eyes fell on; all the change is in
me. . . . It is perennially young. . . ." Catching sight of his eternal
self and realizing that the waste of years had only touched his
shore, his empirical self, he exclaimed, "Why, here is Walden, the
same woodland lake that I discovered so many years ago . . . it is
the same liquid joy and happiness to itself and its Maker, ay,
and it *may* be to me." The pond, so constant, clear and pure,

was truly the *Walled in* pond, the undefiled soul of which the Thoreau-in-decay said, "I am its stony shore. . . ."

If Thoreau spent his youth drifting with the inspiring zephyrs on Walden's surface, he now plumbed its depths, angled for its pickerel and its bottom. For it was the purpose of *Walden* to find bottom, to affirm reality; and the reality Thoreau discovered in the soul and in the whole economy of Nature he found at the bottom of the pond. What renewed his faith was the sign of the never-dying, all-promising generative force which he symbolized when he wrote: ". . . a bright green weed is brought up on anchors even in midwinter." The hope of a renewed life, rhapsodized in the concluding chapters of *Walden* and there symbolized in the hardy blade of grass—the green flame of life—, was the assurance he now had that "there is nothing inorganic."

And by sounding the bottom Thoreau also discovered the law of the universe and of the intellect that made possible his organic participation in the process of renewal and provided him the guarantee of its expression in natural objects. "The regularity of the bottom and its conformity to the shores and the range of the neighboring hills were so perfect," he wrote, "that a distant promontory betrayed itself in the soundings quite across the pond, and its direction could be determined by observing the opposite shore." He found, too, that the intersection of the lines of greatest length and breadth coincided with the point of greatest depth; and he suggested that this physical law might be applied to ethics. "Draw lines through the length and breadth of the aggregate of a man's particular daily behaviors and waves of life into his coves and inlets, and where they intersect will be the height or depth of his character. Perhaps we need only to know how his shores tend and his adjacent country or circumstances, to infer his depth and concealed bottom." *Walden* was just such an account of Thoreau's moral topography, and if the lines were drawn, the pond itself would be his center. For wasn't the eternal self, like the pond, " 'God's Drop' "?

The search for the bottom was conscious exploration. Here, and in the passages on fishing for pickerel and chasing the loon, Thoreau was not a naturalist but a natural historian of the intellect, using the natural facts as symbols for his quest for inspiration and thought. In "Brute Neighbors" he had asked, "Why do precisely these objects which we behold make a world?" And he had answered that "they are all beasts of burden . . . made to carry some portion of our thoughts." The natural world merely reflects ourselves. Having overcome his doubts of this central article of transcendental faith by assuring himself of the regularity of Walden's depth—that the hidden reality corresponded to its visible shores, that "Heaven is under our feet as well as over our heads"—he could trust once more his own projection of mood and thought to be reflected in its proper and corresponding object. He had noted in his journal that the poet "sees a flower or other object, and it is beautiful or affecting to him because it is a symbol of his thought, and what he indistinctly feels or perceives is matured in some other organization. The objects I behold correspond to my mood." His concern with the pond and the seasons, then, was symbolic of his soul's preoccupation. "Our moulting season . . . must be the crisis in our lives," he said; and like the loon he retired to a solitary pond to spend it. There, like the caterpillar—to use another symbol—, "by an internal industry and expansion" he cast off his "wormy coat."

IV

Thoreau went to Walden to become an unaccommodated man, to shed his lendings and to find his naked and sufficient self. Of this, the pond was the symbol. He also went to clothe himself in response to his inner needs. Building an organic life was again a conscious endeavor which was chastened by the necessity of maintaining his vital heat—the heat of body and spirit; for his purpose was not to return to nature, but to combine "the hardiness of . . . savages with the intellectualness of the civilized man." "The civilized man," he said, "is a more experienced and wiser savage," meaning, of course, that the instinctive life was most rewarding when channeled by intellectual principles. "What was *enthusiasm* in the young man," he wrote during the crisis of his life, "must become *temperament* in the mature man." The woodchopper, the animal man, must be educated to consciousness, and still retain his innocence. Properly seen in the total economy of Nature the once freely taken gift of inspiration must be earned by perceiving the law of Nature, by the tragic awareness that inspiration, like its source, has its seasons. The villagers, Thoreau wrote indignantly, "instead of going to the pond to bathe or drink, are thinking to bring its waters, which should be as sacred as the Ganges at least, to the village in a pipe, to wash their dishes with!—to earn their Walden by the turning of a cock or drawing of a plug!" The spiritual soldier had learned that after laying siege to Nature, only passivity would bring victory.

Thoreau earned his Walden by awaiting the return of spring, by sharing the organic process. Of this his hut and his bean-field became the symbols. The latter, as we have seen, helped to renew the aspect of the pond; as the work of the active self, it was rightly an alteration of the shore. And the pond, as the pure, eternal self—the "perfect forest mirror"—, was the calm surface on which these purifying activities were reflected. Thoreau labored in his bean-field because he took seriously Emerson's injunction to action in *The American Scholar*. He knew that the higher ends of the activity of the empirical self were self-consciousness, that the eternal self, the passive center, only acquired consciousness by observing the empirical self at work on the circumference. He recognized "a certain doubleness by which I can stand as remote from myself as from another." "However intense my experience," he wrote, "I am conscious of the presence of and criticism of a part of me, which, as it were, is not part of me, but spectator, sharing no experience, but taking note of it. . . ." The reward of activity, the result of this drama of selves, was self-reflection, insight. "All perception of truth is the detection of an analogy," Thoreau noted in the journal; "we reason from our hands to our head." And so through the labor of the hands, even to the point of drudgery, he was "determined to know beans." He did not need the beans for food but for sympathy with Nature; he needed to work them because, as he said, "They attached me to the earth, and so I got strength like Antaeus." His fields were also symbolic of his attempt to link the wild and the cultivated. And the "immeasurable crop" his devoted hoeing yielded came from the penetration of the earth's crust—a knowledge of the depths similar in significance to Melville's descent to the unwarped primal world. "I disturbed," Thoreau wrote, "the ashes of unchronicled nations who in primeval times lived under these heavens. . . ." In his bean-field beside Walden he was not serving Admetus, for he had found a way to delve beneath the "established order on the surface."

The prudential value of this labor came to $16.94, but the spiritual value was the realization that the Massachusetts soil could sustain the seeds of virtue—that in Thoreau's case at least, the seed had not lost its vitality and that the harvest of his example might be "a new generation of men." Later on, in the chapter on "Former Inhabitants," he again disturbed the surface by delving into the past, comparing his life at Walden to the defeated lives of its previous occupants. Here, Thoreau expressed his desire for the higher society, the ideal community in which he could wholly participate and which he hoped he was beginning. "Again, perhaps, Nature will try," he wrote, "with me for the first settler. . . . I am not aware that any man has ever built on the spot which I occupy." Like Joyce's Finnegan, he was to be the father of cities, not those reared on ancient sites, but cities growing out of the union with the earth. Looking back to Concord from the distances of past and future, Thoreau felt that *Walden* was not so much his quarrel with society, but an expiation. "Through our recovered innocence," he confessed, "we discern the

innocence of our neighbors." He was willing to share his regeneration, for above the constant interplay of Walden and village, there
hovered a vision of an ideal village that transcended both. In the
radical sense of the word, Thoreau, who had given up the wilder
pursuit of hunting for farming, was a civilizer.

When he came to build his hut—the container of his vital
heat—Thoreau used second-hand materials and borrowed tools and
showed his dependence on civilization. He did not abandon collective wisdom: his intention was to practice philosophy, to come
directly at a conduct of life, that is, to simplify, or experience the
solid satisfaction of knowing immediately the materials that made
his life. He scrupulously accounts for these materials, he tells their
history—where he got the boards, who used them and under what
conditions. And James Collins' life in the shanty is implicitly
contrasted with Thoreau's, especially in Thoreau's remark that he
purified the boards by bleaching and warping them in the sun. He
also acknowledged his debt for tools. He did not push his economy
too far, to the verge of self-sufficiency that some believe necessary to
a defense of *Walden* as social gospel. He said—and this is the
only way of repaying one's social indebtedness—that he sharp-
ened the tools by use. In a similar way, he applied the funded
wisdom of man to his experiment on life. Individualist that he
was, he often confirmed his experience by the experience of others:
he made his use of the classics and scriptures, Indian lore and
colonial history, pay their way. He was starting from scratch,
but he knew that the materials were old.

The building of the hut is so thoroughly described because on
the symbolic level it is the description of the building of the
body for his soul. A generation that was read in Swedenborg
might have been expected to see this correspondence. "It would
be worth the while," Thoreau suggested, "to build still more
deliberately than I did, considering, for instance, what foundation
a door, a window, a cellar, a garret, have in the nature of man,
and perchance never raising any superstructure until we found a
better reason for it than our temporal necessities even." He was
speaking the language of functionalism that Swedenborgianism had
popularized; and after listing his previous shelters, he remarked that
"this frame, so slightly clad, was a sort of crystallization around
me, and reacted on the builder."

Thoreau built his hut as he needed it, to meet the progressing
seasons of developing consciousness, a development which was as
organic as the seasons. He subscribed to Emerson's use of the cycle
of day and night as the symbol of the ebb and flow of inspiration
and extended it to the seasons: "The day is an epitome of the year.
The night is the winter, the morning and evenings are spring and

fall, and the noon is the summer." In this way he also followed
Emerson's "history" of consciousness. "The Greek," Emerson wrote,
"was the age of observation; the Middle Age, that of fact and
thought; ours, that of reflection and ideas." In *Walden*, Thoreau's
development began in the summer, the season of the senses and
of delicious out-of-door life. This was the period when he was in
sympathetic communion with Nature, refreshed by the tonic of
wildness. The chapters on "Sounds" and "Solitude" belong to
this period, during which he enjoyed the atmospheric presence of
Nature so essential to his inspiration. And the hut, which he
began in the spring and first occupied at this time, was merely
a frame through which Nature readily passed.

When the "north wind had already begun to cool the pond,"
Thoreau said that he first began to "inhabit my house." During
the autumn season of harvest and preparation for winter, he
lathed and plastered; and finally as winter approached he built
his fireplace and chimney, "the most vital part of the house. . . ."
By the fireside, in the period of reflection and inner life, he
lingered most, communing with his self.[1] It was the time of soul-
searching, when he cut through the pond's ice and saw that "its
bright sanded floor [was] the same as in the summer"; and before
the ice broke up he surveyed its bottom. Even in this desolate
season Thoreau looked for all the signs of spring's organic promise,
and in the representative anecdote of his despair, he told of Nature's
sustaining power: "After a still winter night I awoke with the
impression that some question had been put to me, which I had
been endeavoring in vain to answer in my sleep, as what—how—
when—where? But there was dawning Nature, in whom all creatures live, looking in at my broad windows with serene and
satisfied face, and no questions on *her* lips. I awoke to an answered question, to Nature and daylight." Even in the winter of
his discontent, Nature seemed to him to say " 'Forward' " and he
could calmly await the inevitable golden age of spring.

V

Rebirth came with spring. In one of the best sustained analogies
in transcendental writing, the chapter "Spring," Thoreau reported
ecstatically the translation of the frozen sand and clay of the railroad
cut into the thawing streams of life. Looking at the sand foliage—
the work of an hour—he said that "I am affected as if . . . I stood
in the laboratory of the Artist who made the world and me. . . ."
The Artist of the world, like Thoreau and like Goethe whom he
had in mind, labored "with the idea inwardly" and its correspondence, its flowering, was the leaf. Everywhere Thoreau per-

1. Hawthorne in "Peter Goldthwaite's Treasure" and Melville in "I and My
Chimney" also made imaginative use of the house and the chimney.

ceived this symbol of creation, and in ascending forms from the sand, the animal body, the feathers and wings of birds, to the "airy" butterfly. "Thus it seemed," he wrote, "that this one hillside illustrated the principle of all the operations of Nature. The Maker of this earth but patented a leaf." And the moral Thoreau drew from this illustration was the central law of his life, for it was the law of renewal: "This earth is not a mere fragment of dead history, stratum upon stratum like the leaves of a book, to be studied by geologists and antiquarians chiefly, but living poetry like the leaves of a tree, which precede flowers and fruit,—not a fossil earth, but a living earth; compared with whose great central life all animal and vegetable life is merely parasitic. Its throes will heave our exuviae from their graves." And furthermore the law applied to man and the higher society: ". . . the institutions upon it [the earth] are plastic like clay in the hands of the potter."

For Thoreau, who had found that the law of his life was the law of Life, these perceptions were the stuff of ecstasy. Reveling in the sound of the first sparrow, Thoreau wrote, "What at such a time are histories, chronologies, traditions, and all written revelations?" The spring had brought forth "the symbol of perpetual youth," the grass-blade; human life, having died down to its root, now put forth "its green blade to eternity." Walden Pond had begun to melt—"Walden was dead and is alive again." The change in the flowing sand, from excremental to spiritual, had also been accomplished in him by the discipline of purity: "The change from storm and winter to serene and mild weather, from dark and sluggish hours to bright and elastic ones." Like the dawning of inspiration this "memorable crisis" was "seemingly instantaneous at last." "Suddenly," Thoreau recorded that change, "an influx of light filled my house, though evening was at hand, and the clouds of winter still overhung it, and the eaves were dripping with sleety rain. I looked out of the window, and lo! where yesterday was cold grey ice there lay the transparent pond already calm and full of hope as in a summer evening, reflecting a summer evening sky in its bosom, though none was visible overhead, as if it had intelligence with some remote horizon. I heard a robin in the distance, the first I had heard for many a thousand years, methought, whose note I shall not forget for many a thousand more,—the same sweet and powerful song as of yore. . . . So I came in, and shut the door, and passed my first spring night in the woods."

With the coming of spring had come "the creation of Cosmos out of Chaos and the realization of the Golden Age." And with his renewal had come the vindication of his life of purity. He had recorded what he felt was nowhere recorded, "a simple and ir-

repressible satisfaction with the gift of life. . . ." He had suggested what the eye of the partridge symbolized to him, not merely
"the purity of infancy, but a wisdom clarified by experience." He
had recounted the experience of his purification so well that even
the reader who accepts only the residual statement feels purified.
"I do not say," he wisely wrote at the end of *Walden*, "that John
or Jonathan will realize all this [the perfect summer life]; but
such is the character of that morrow which mere lapse of time can
never make to dawn." To affirm this eternal present, to restore,
as he said in "The Service," the original of which Nature is the
reflection, he fashioned *Walden* as he himself lived, after the
example of the artist of the city of Kouroo. This parable unlocks
the largest meaning of the book. The artist of Kouroo "was
disposed to strive after perfection," Thoreau wrote; and striving,
he lived in the eternity of inspiration which made the passing of
dynasties, even eras, an illusion. In fashioning his staff, merely by
minding his destiny and his art, he had made a new world
"with full and fair proportions." The result, Thoreau knew,
could not be "other than wonderful," because "the material was
pure, and his art was pure. . . ."

E. B. WHITE

Walden—1954 †

In his journal for July 10–12, 1841, Thoreau wrote: "A slight
sound at evening lifts me up by the ears, and makes life seem
inexpressibly serene and grand. It may be in Uranus, or it may be
in the shutter." The book into which he later managed to
pack both Uranus and the shutter was published in 1854, and
now, a hundred years having gone by, "Walden," its serenity and
grandeur unimpaired, still lifts us up by the ears, still translates
for us that language we are in danger of forgetting, "which all
things and events speak without metaphor, which alone is copious
and standard."

"Walden" is an oddity in American letters. It may very well be
the oddest of our distinguished oddities. For many it is a great
deal too odd, and for many it is a particular bore. I have not
found it to be a well-liked book among my acquaintances, although

† From *The Points of My Compass* (Harper & Row, 1962), in which this essay is titled "A Slight Sound at Evening" and dated "Allen Cove, 1954." Pp. 15–25. Copyright 1954, by E. B. White. Originally published in *The Yale Review* under the title "Walden—1954", and reprinted with the permission of Harper & Row, Publishers and Hamish Hamilton, Ltd.

usually spoken of with respect, and one literary critic for whom I have the highest regard can find no reason why anyone gives "Walden" a second thought. To admire the book is, in fact, something of an embarrassment, for the mass of men have an indistinct notion that its author was a sort of Nature Boy.

I think, it is of some advantage to encounter the book at a period in one's life when the normal anxieties and enthusiasms and rebellions of youth closely resemble those of Thoreau in that spring of 1845 when he borrowed an axe, went out to the woods, and began to whack down some trees for timber. Received at such a juncture, the book is like an invitation to life's dance, assuring the troubled recipient that no matter what befalls him in the way of success or failure he will always be welcome at the party—that the music is played for him, too, if he will but listen and move his feet. In effect, that is what the book is—an invitation, unengraved; and it stirs one as a young girl is stirred by her first big party bid. Many think it a sermon; many set it down as an attempt to rearrange society; some think it an exercise in natureloving; some find it a rather irritating collection of inspirational puffballs by an eccentric show-off. I think it none of these. It still seems to me the best youth's companion yet written by an American, for it carries a solemn warning against the loss of one's valuables, it advances a good argument for traveling light and trying new adventures, it rings with the power of positive adoration, it contains religious feeling without religious images, and it steadfastly refuses to record bad news. Even its pantheistic note is so pure as to be noncorrupting—pure as the flute-note blown across the pond on those faraway summer nights. If our colleges and universities were alert, they would present a cheap pocket edition of the book to every senior upon graduating, along with his sheepskin, or instead of it. Even if some senior were to take it literally and start felling trees, there could be worse mishaps: the axe is older than the Dictaphone and it is just as well for a young man to see what kind of chips he leaves before listening to the sound of his own voice. And even if some were to get no farther than the table of contents, they would learn how to name eighteen chapters by the use of only thirty-nine words and would see how sweet are the uses of brevity.

If Thoreau had merely left us an account of a man's life in the woods, or if he had simply retreated to the woods and there recorded his complaints about society, or even if he had contrived to include both records in one essay, "Walden" would probably not have lived a hundred years. As things turned out, Thoreau, very likely without knowing quite what he was up to, took man's relation to nature and man's dilemma in society and man's capacity for elevating his spirit and he beat all these matters together, in a wild free interval of self-justification and delight, and produced an original omelette from which people can draw nourishment in a hungry day. "Walden" is one of the first of the vitamin-enriched American dishes. If it were a little less good than it is, or even a little less queer, it would be an abominable book. Even as it is, it will continue to baffle and annoy the literal mind and all those who are unable to stomach its caprices and imbibe its theme. Certainly the plodding economist will continue to have rough going if he hopes to emerge from the book with a clear system of economic thought. Thoreau's assault on the Concord society of the mid-nineteenth century has the quality of a modern Western: he rides into the subject at top speed, shooting in all directions. Many of his shots ricochet and nick him on the rebound, and throughout the melee there is a horrendous cloud of inconsistencies and contradictions, and when the shooting dies down and the air clears, one is impressed chiefly by the courage of the rider and by how splendid it was that somebody should have ridden in there and raised all that ruckus.

When he went to the pond, Thoreau struck an attitude and did so deliberately, but his posturing was not to draw the attention of others to him but rather to draw his own attention more closely to himself. "I learned this at least by my experiment: that if one advances confidently in the direction of his dreams, and endeavors to live the life which he has imagined, he will meet with a success unexpected in common hours." The sentence has the power to resuscitate the youth drowning in his sea of doubt. I recall my exhilaration upon reading it, many years ago, in a time of hesitation and despair. It restored me to health. And now in 1954 when I salute Henry Thoreau on the hundredth birthday of his book, I am merely paying off an old score—or an installment on it.

In his journal for May 3–4, 1838—Boston to Portland—he wrote: "Midnight—head over the boat's side—between sleeping and waking—with glimpses of one or more lights in the vicinity of Cape Ann. Bright moonlight—the effect heightened by seasickness." The entry illuminates the man, as the moon the sea on that night in May. In Thoreau the natural scene was heightened, not depressed, by a disturbance of the stomach, and nausea met its match at last. There was a steadiness in at least one passenger if there was none in the boat. Such steadiness (which in some would be called intoxication) is at the heart of "Walden"—confidence, faith, the discipline of looking always at what is to be seen, undeviating gratitude for the life-everlasting that he found growing in his front yard. "There is nowhere recorded a simple and irrepressible satisfaction with the gift of life, any memorable praise of God." He worked to correct that deficiency. "Walden" is his acknowledgment of the gift of life. It is the testament of a man in a high state of indignation because (it seemed to him) so few ears heard the uninterrupted poem of creation, the morning wind that forever blows. If the man sometimes wrote as though all his readers were male, unmarried, and well-connected, it is because he gave his testimony during the callow years, and, for that matter, never really grew up. To reject the book because of the immaturity of the author and the bugs in the logic is to throw away a bottle of good wine because it contains bits of the cork.

Thoreau said he required of every writer, first and last, a simple and sincere account of his own life. Having delivered himself of this chesty dictum, he proceeded to ignore it. In his books and even in his enormous journal, he withheld or disguised most of the facts from which an understanding of his life could be drawn. "Walden," subtitled "Life in the Woods," is not a simple and sincere account of a man's life, either in or out of the woods; it is an account of a man's journey into the mind, a toot on the trumpet to alert the neighbors. Thoreau was well aware that no one can alert his neighbors who is not wide awake himself, and he went to the woods (among other reasons) to make sure that he would stay awake during his broadcast. What actually took place during the years 1845–47 is largely unrecorded, and the reader is excluded from the private life of the author, who supplies almost no gossip about himself, a great deal about his neighbors and about the universe.

As for me, I cannot in this short ramble give a simple and sincere account of my own life, but I think Thoreau might find it instructive to know that this memorial essay is being written in a house that, through no intent on my part, is the same size and shape as his own domicile on the pond—about ten by fifteen, tight, plainly finished, and at a little distance from my Concord. The house in which I sit this morning was built to accommodate a boat, not a man, but by long experience I have learned that in most respects it shelters me better than the larger dwelling where my bed is, and which, by design, is a manhouse not a boathouse. Here in the boathouse I am a wilder and, it would appear, a healthier man, by a safe margin. I have a chair, a bench, a table, and I can walk into the water if I tire of the land. My house fronts a cove. Two fishermen have just arrived to spot fish from the air—an osprey and a man in a small yellow plane who works for the fish company. The man, I have noticed, is less well equipped than the hawk, who can dive directly on his fish and carry it away, without telephoning. A mouse and a squirrel share the house with me. The building is, in fact, a multiple dwelling, a semidetached affair. It is because I am semidetached while here that I find it possible to transact this private business with the fewest obstacles.

There is also a woodchuck here, living forty feet away under the wharf. When the wind is right, he can smell my house; and when the wind is contrary, I can smell his. We both use the wharf for sunning, taking turns, each adjusting his schedule to the other's convenience. Thoreau once ate a woodchuck. I think he felt he owed it to his readers, and that it was little enough, considering the indignities they were suffering at his hands and the dressing-down they were taking. (Parts of "Walden" are pure scold.) Or perhaps he ate the woodchuck because he believed every man should acquire strict business habits, and the woodchuck was destroying his market beans. I do not know. Thoreau had a strong experimental streak in him. It is probably no harder to eat a woodchuck than to construct a sentence that lasts a hundred years. At any rate, Thoreau is the only writer I know who prepared himself for his great ordeal by eating a woodchuck; also the only one who got a hangover from drinking too much water. (He was drunk the whole time, though he seldom touched wine or coffee or tea.)

Here in this compact house where I would spend one day as deliberately as Nature if I were not being pressed by *The Yale Review*, and with a woodchuck (as yet uneaten) for neighbor, I can feel the companionship of the occupant of the pondside cabin in Walden woods, a mile from the village, near the Fitchburg right of way. Even my immediate business is no barrier between us: Thoreau occasionally batted out a magazine piece, but was always suspicious of any sort of purposeful work that cut into his time. A man, he said, should take care not to be thrown off the track by every nutshell and mosquito's wing that falls on the rails.

There has been much guessing as to why he went to the pond. To set it down to escapism is, of course, to misconstrue what happened. Henry went forth to battle when he took to the woods, and "Walden" is the report of a man torn by two powerful and opposing drives—the desire to enjoy the world (and not be derailed by a mosquito wing) and the urge to set the world straight. One cannot join these two successfully, but sometimes, in rare cases, something good or even great results from the attempt of the tormented spirit to reconcile them. Henry went forth to battle, and if he set the stage himself, if he fought on his own terms and with his own weapons, it was because it was his nature to do things differently from most men, and to act in a cocky fashion. If the pond and the woods seemed a more plausible site for a house than an in-town location, it was because a cowbell made for him a sweeter sound than a churchbell. "Walden," the book, makes the sound of a cowbell, more than a churchbell, and proves the point, although both sounds are in it, and both remarkably clear and sweet. He simply preferred his churchbell at a little distance.

I think one reason he went to the woods was a perfectly simple and commonplace one—and apparently he thought so, too. "At a certain season of our life," he wrote, "we are accustomed to consider every spot as the possible site of a house." There spoke the young man, a few years out of college, who had not yet broken away from home. He hadn't married, and he had found no job that measured up to his rigid standards of employment, and like any young man, or young animal, he felt uneasy and on the defensive until he had fixed himself a den. Most young men, of course, casting about for a site, are content merely to draw apart from their kinfolks. Thoreau, convinced that the greater part of what his neighbors called good was bad, withdrew from a great deal more than family: he pulled out of everything for a while, to serve everybody right for being so stuffy, and to try his own prejudices on the dog.

The house-hunting sentence above, which starts the Chapter called "Where I Lived, and What I Lived For," is followed by another passage that is worth quoting here because it so beautifully illustrates the offbeat prose that Thoreau was master of, a prose at once strictly disciplined and wildly abandoned. "I have surveyed the country on every side within a dozen miles of where I live," continued this delirious young man. "In imagination I have bought all the farms in succession, for all were to be bought, and I knew their price. I walked over each farmer's premises, tasted his wild apples, discoursed on husbandry with him, took his farm at his price, at any price, mortgaging it to him in my mind; even put a higher price on it—took everything but a deed of it—took his word for his deed, for I dearly love to talk—cultivated it, and him too to some extent, I trust, and withdrew when I had enjoyed it long enough, leaving him to carry it on." A copydesk man would get a double hernia trying to clean up that sentence for the management, but the sentence needs no fixing, for it perfectly captures the meaning of the writer and the quality of the ramble.

"Wherever I sat, there I might live, and the landscape radiated from me accordingly." Thoreau, the home-seeker, sitting on his hummock with the entire State of Massachusetts radiating from him, is to me the most humorous of the New England figures, and "Walden" the most humorous of the books, though its humor is almost continuously subsurface and there is nothing funny anywhere, except a few weak jokes and bad puns that rise to the surface like the perch in the pond that rose to the sound of the maestro's flute. Thoreau tended to write in sentences, a feat not every writer is capable of, and "Walden" is, rhetorically speaking, a collection of certified sentences, some of them, it would now appear, as indestructible as they are errant. The book is distilled from the vast journals, and this accounts for its intensity: he picked out bright particles that pleased his eye, whirled them in the kaleidoscope of his content, and produced the pattern that has endured—the color, the form, the light.

On this its hundredth birthday, Thoreau's "Walden" is pertinent and timely. In our uneasy season, when all men unconsciously seek a retreat from a world that has got almost completely out of hand, his house in the Concord woods is a haven. In our culture of gadgetry and the multiplicity of convenience, his cry "Simplicity, simplicity, simplicity!" has the insistence of a fire alarm. In the brooding atmosphere of war and the gathering radioactive storm, the innocence and serenity of his summer afternoons are enough to burst the remembering heart, and one gazes back upon that pleasing interlude—its confidence, its purity, its deliberateness—with awe and wonder, as one would look upon the face of a child asleep.

"This small lake was of most value as a neighbor in the intervals of a gentle rain-storm in August, when, both air and water being perfectly still, but the sky overcast, midafternoon had all the serenity of evening, and the wood-thrush sang around, and was heard from shore to shore." Now, in the perpetual overcast in which our days are spent, we hear with extra perception and deep gratitude that song, tying century to century.

I sometimes amuse myself by bringing Henry Thoreau back to life and showing him the sights. I escort him into a phone booth and let him dial Weather. "This is a delicious evening," the girl's voice says, "when the whole body is one sense, and imbibes delight through every pore." I show him the spot in the Pacific where an island used to be, before some magician made it vanish. "We know not where we are," I murmur. "The light which puts out our eyes is darkness to us. Only that day dawns to which we are awake." I thumb through the latest copy of "Vogue" with him. "Of two patterns which differ only by a few threads more or less of a particular color," I read, "the one will be sold readily, the other lie on the shelf, though it frequently happens that, after the lapse of a season, the latter becomes the most fashionable."

Together we go outboarding on the Assabet, looking for what we've lost—a hound, a bay horse, a turtledove. I show him a distracted farmer who is trying to repair a hay baler before the thunder shower breaks. "This farmer," I remark, "is endeavoring to solve the problem of a livelihood by a formula more complicated than the problem itself. To get his shoe strings he speculates in herds of cattle."

I take the celebrated author to Twenty-One for lunch, so the waiters may study his shoes. The proprietor welcomes us. "The gross feeder," remarks the proprietor, sweeping the room with his arm, "is a man in the larva stage." After lunch we visit a classroom in one of those schools conducted by big corporations to teach their superannuated executives how to retire from business without serious injury to their health. (The shock to men's systems these days when relieved of the exacting routine of amassing wealth is very great and must be cushioned.) "It is not necessary," says the teacher to his pupils, "that a man should earn his living by the sweat of his brow, unless he sweats easier than I do. We are determined to be starved before we are hungry."

I turn on the radio and let Thoreau hear Winchell beat the red hand around the clock. "Time is but the stream I go a-fishing in," shouts Mr. Winchell, rattling his telegraph key. "Hardly a man takes a half hour's nap after dinner, but when he wakes he holds up his head and asks, 'What's the news?' If we read of one man robbed, or murdered, or killed by accident, or one house burned, or one vessel wrecked, or one steamboat blown up, or one cow run over on the Western Railroad, or one mad dog killed, or one lot of grasshoppers in the winter—we need never read of another. One is enough."

I doubt that Thoreau would be thrown off balance by the fantastic sights and sounds of the twentieth century. "The Concord nights," he once wrote, "are stranger than the Arabian nights." A four-engined air liner would merely serve to confirm his early views on travel. Everywhere he would observe, in new shapes and sizes, the old predicaments and follies of men—the desperation, the impedimenta, the meanness—along with the visible capacity for elevation of the mind and soul. "This curious world which we inhabit is more wonderful than it is convenient; more beautiful than it is useful; it is more to be admired and enjoyed than used." He would see that today ten thousand engineers are busy making sure that the world shall be convenient if they bust doing it, and others are determined to increase its usefulness even though its beauty is lost somewhere along the way.

At any rate, I'd like to stroll about the countryside in Thoreau's company for a day, observing the modern scene, inspecting today's snowstorm, pointing out the sights, and offering belated apologies for my sins. Thoreau is unique among writers in that those who admire him find him uncomfortable to live with—a regular hairshirt of a man. A little band of dedicated Thoreauvians would be a sorry sight indeed: fellows who hate compromise and have compromised, fellows who love wildness and have lived tamely, and at their side, censuring them and chiding them, the ghostly figure of this upright man, who long ago gave corroboration to impulses they perceived were right and issued warnings against the things they instinctively knew to be their enemies. I should hate to be called a Thoreauvian, yet I wince every time I walk into the barn I'm pushing before me, seventy-five feet by forty, and the author of "Walden" has served as my conscience through the long stretches of my trivial days.

Hairshirt or no, he is a better companion than most, and I would not swap him for a soberer or more reasonable friend even if I could. I can reread his famous invitation with undiminished excitement. The sad thing is that not more acceptances have been received, that so many decline for one reason or another, pleading some previous engagement or ill health. But the invitation stands. It will beckon as long as this remarkable book stays in print— which will be as long as there are August afternoons in the intervals of a gentle rainstorm, as long as there are ears to catch the faint sounds of the orchestra. I find it agreeable to sit here this morning, in a house of correct proportions, and hear across a century of time his flute, his frogs, and his seductive summons to the wildest revels of them all.

R. W. B. LEWIS

[One Kind of Adam] †

"We have the Saint Vitus dance." This was Thoreau's view of the diversion of energies to material expansion and of the enthusiastic arithmetic by which expansion was constantly being measured. Miles of post roads and millions of tons of domestic export did not convince Thoreau that first principles ought to be overhauled; but a close interest in these matters did convince him that

† From R. W. B. Lewis, *The American Adam*, Chicago, Illinois 1955. Section III of Chapter I, pp 20-27. Copyright 1955 by The University of Chicago Press. Reprinted by permission of the publishers.

first principles had been abandoned. Probably nobody of his generation had a richer sense of the potentiality for a fresh, free, and uncluttered existence; certainly no one projected the need for the ritual burning of the past in more varied and captivating metaphors. This is what W*alden* is about; it is the most searching contemporary account of the desire for a new kind of life. But Thoreau's announcement of a spiritual molting season (one of his favorite images) did not arise from a belief that the building of railroads was proof of the irrelevance of too-well-remembered doctrines. Long before Whitman, himself a devotee of the dazzling sum, attacked the extremes of commercialism in *Democratic Vistas,* Thoreau was insisting that the obsession with railroads did not demonstrate the hope for humanity, but tended to smother it. "Men think it is essential that the *Nation* have commerce, and export ice, and talk through a telegraph and ride thirty miles an hour, without a doubt, whether *they* do or not; but whether we should live like baboons or men is a little uncertain."

Watching the local railroad train as it passed near Walden Pond on the recently laid track between Fitchburg and Boston, Thoreau noticed that while the narrow little cars moved eastward along the ground, the engine smoke drifted skyward, broadening out as it rose. The picture (it occurs in the chapter called "Sounds") provided him with a meaningful glimpse of that wholeness, of interrelated doubleness, which was for Thoreau the required shape of the life that was genuinely lived. The trouble with railroads—he said it, in fancy, to the scores of workmen he saw starting up in protest against him—was that so few persons who rode on them were heading in any definite direction or were aware of a better direction than Boston; quite a few persons were simply run over, while the building of railroads crushed the heart and life out of the builders. The trouble, in general, with expending one's strength on "internal improvements" was that the achievement, like the aim, was partial: there was nothing internal about them. The opportunity that Thoreau looked out upon from his hut at Walden was for no such superficial accomplishment, but for a wholeness of spirit realized in a direct experience of the whole of nature. The words "nature" and "wholeness" have been overworked and devitalized (Thoreau and Emerson are partly to blame), and now they are suspect; but they glow with health in the imaginatively ordered prose of Henry Thoreau.

The narrator of W*alden* is a witness to a truly new world which the speaker alone has visited, from which he has just returned, and which he is sure every individual ought to visit at least once—not the visible world around Walden Pond, but an inner world which the Walden experience allowed him to explore.

Thoreau like to pretend that his book was a purely personal act of private communion. But that was part of his rhetoric, and *Walden* is a profoundly rhetorical book, emerging unmistakably from the long New England preaching tradition; though here the trumpet call announces the best imaginable news rather than apocalyptic warnings. Thoreau, in *Walden*, is a man who has come back down into the cave to tell the residents there that they are really in chains, suffering fantastic punishments they have imposed on themselves, seeing by a light that is reflected and derivative. A major test of the visionary hero must always be the way he can put his experience to work for the benefit of mankind; he demonstrates his freedom in the liberation of others. Thoreau prescribes the following cure: the total renunciation of the traditional, the conventional, the socially acceptable, the well-worn paths of conduct, and the total immersion in nature.

Everything associated with the past should be burned away. The past should be cast off like dead skin. Thoreau remembered with sympathetic humor the pitiful efforts of one John Field, an Irishman living at near-by Baker Farm, to catch perch with shiners: "thinking to live by some derivative old-country mode in this primitive new country." "I look on England today," he wrote, "as an old gentleman who is travelling with a great deal of baggage, trumpery which has accumulated from long housekeeping, which he has not the courage to burn." Thoreau recorded with approval and some envy a Mexican purification rite practiced every fifty-two years; and he added, "I have scarcely heard of a truer sacrament." These periodic symbolic acts of refreshment, which whole societies ought to perform in each generation ("One generation abandons the enterprises of another like stranded vessels"), were valid exactly because they were images of fundamental reality itself. Individuals and groups should enact the rhythmic death and rebirth reflected in the change of season from winter to spring, in the sequence of night and day. "The phenomena of the year take place every day in a pond on a small scale." These were some of the essential facts discovered by Thoreau when he fronted them at Walden; and the experience to which he was to become a witness took its shape, in act and in description, from a desire to live in accordance with these facts. So it was that he refused the offer of a door-mat, lest he should form the habit of shaking it every morning; and, instead, every morning "I got up early and bathed in the pond; that was a religious exercise, and one of the best things which I did."

The language tells us everything, as Thoreau meant it to. He had his own sacramental system, his own rite of baptism. But his use of the word "nature" indicates that the function of sacraments was to expose the individual again to the currents flowing through nature, rather than to the grace flowing down from supernature. The ritual of purification was no less for Thoreau than for St. Paul a dying into life; but Thoreau marched to the music he heard; it was the music of the age; and he marched in a direction *opposite* to St. Paul. His familiar witticism, "One world at a time" (made on his deathbed to an eager abolitionist named Pillsbury, who looked for some illumination of the future life from the dying seer) was a fair summary of his position: with this addition, that poetry traditionally taken as hints about what could be seen through a glass darkly about the next world was taken by Thoreau as what had been seen by genius, face to face with this one. He was among the first to see Christian literature as only the purest and most inspiring of the fables about the relation of man to nature and about the infinite capacities of the unaided human spirit. The Bible (Thoreau referred to it simply as "an old book") was the finest poem which had ever been written; it was the same in substance as Homeric or Hindu mythology, but it was richer in metaphor. The Bible spoke more sharply to the human condition. This was why Thoreau, like Whitman, could employ the most traditional of religious phrases and invest them with an unexpected and dynamic new life.

It is not surprising that transcendentalism was Puritanism turned upside down, as a number of critics have pointed out; historically, it could hardly have been anything else. Transcendentalism drew on the vocabularies of European romanticism and Oriental mysticism; but the only available local vocabulary was the one that the hopeful were so anxious to escape from, and a very effective way to discredit its inherited meaning was to serve it up in an unfamiliar context. There was something gratifyingly shocking in such a use of words: "What demon possessed me that I behaved so well?" Thoreau spoke as frequently as he could, therefore, about a *sacrament*, a sacred mystery, such as baptism: in order to define the cleansing, not of St. Paul's natural man, but of the conventional or traditional man; in order, precisely, to bring into being the natural man. For the new tensions out of which insights were drawn and moral choices provoked were no longer the relation of nature and grace, of man and God, but of the natural and the artificial, the new and the old, the individual and the social or conventional. Thoreau had, as he remarked in his other deathbed witticism, no quarrel with God; his concern was simply other.

His concern was with the strangulation of nature by convention. The trouble with conventions and traditions in the New World was that they had come first; they had come from abroad and from a very long way back; and they had been superimposed upon nature. They had to be washed away, like sin, so that the natural could reveal itself again and could be permitted to create its own organic conventions. They had to be renounced, as the first phase of the ritual; and if renunciation was, as Emily Dickinson thought, a piercing virtue, it was not because it made possible an experience of God in an infusion of grace, but because it made possible an experience of self in a bath of nature.

Thoreau had, of course, learned a good deal from Emerson, whose early energy was largely directed toward constructing "an original relation with the universe" and who reverted time and again to the same theme: "beware of tradition"; "forget historical Christianity"; "lop off all superfluity and tradition, and fall back on the nature of things." And what was this nature of things which men were enjoined to fall back on? Lowell understood some of it, in one of the better sentences of his querulous and uneven essay on Thoreau (1865): "There is only one thing better than tradition, and that is the original and eternal life out of which all tradition takes its rise. It was this life which the reformers demanded, with more or less clearness of consciousness and expression, life in politics, life in literature, life in religion." But even in this moment of qualified approval, Lowell makes it sound too pallid, soft, and ethereal. Nature was not merely the mountains and the prairie, any more than it was merely the bees and the flowers; but it was all of those things too, and it must always include them. If nature was partly represented by "Higher Laws," as the title of one chapter in *Walden* tells us, it was represented also by "Brute Neighbors," "Winter Animals," and a "Bean-Field," as we know from the titles of other chapters. Thoreau's nature is bounded by an irony which applies the phrase "Higher Laws" to a chapter that, for all its idealism, talks at some length about fried rats.

Irony too—the doubleness of things—Thoreau could learn from Emerson, as each of them had learned from Coleridge and Plato. "All the universe over," Emerson wrote in his journal (1842), "there is just one thing, this old double." The old double, the ideal and the actual, the higher law and the fried rat, required a double consciousness and found expression in a double criticism; nature could be satisfied with nothing else. Emerson tramped in mud puddles, and Thoreau, more adventurously, swam in Walden Pond; the puddle and the pond were instances of unimpeded nature; but both men searched, in their separate ways, for the spiritual analogues which completed the doubleness of nature. Their ability to address themselves with very nearly equal fluency to both dimensions of consciousness gave later comfort to idealists and nominalists alike, though neither group understood the Emersonian principle that only the whole truth could be true at all. Bronson Alcott was the most high-minded of the contemporary idealists, but Emerson chided him for neglecting the value of the many in his rapture for the one, and thought he had genius but no talent. "The philosophers of Fruitlands," Emerson said in 1843, naming Alcott's experimental community, "have such an image of virtue before their eyes, that the poetry of man and nature they never see; the poetry that is man's life, the poorest pastoral clownish life; the light that shines on a man's hat, in a child's spoon." He was harder, of course, on those who saw only the hat and the spoon: the materialists and the tradesmen whom he excoriated in many essays, and writers who stuck too obstinately to the ordinary (Emerson would say, the "vulgar") aspects of the visible world.

Thoreau's personal purification rite began with the renunciation of old hats and old spoons and went forward to the moment—as he describes himself in the opening paragragh of "Higher Laws" —when the initiate stood fully alive in the midst of nature, eating a woodchuck with his fingers, and supremely aware, at the same instant, of the higher law of virtue. "I love the wild not less than the good," Thoreau admitted, announcing duplicity in his own peculiar accent. The structure of *Walden* has a similar beginning and a similar motion forward. The book starts amid the punishing conventions of Concord, departs from them to the pond and the forest, explores the natural surroundings, and exposes the natural myth of the yearly cycle, to conclude with the arrival of spring, the full possession of life, and a representative anecdote about the sudden bursting into life of a winged insect long buried in an old table of apple-tree wood.[1]

Individual chapters are sometimes carried along to the same rhythm. "Sounds," for example, starts with conventional signs and then looks to nature for more authentic ones; it picks up the cycle of the day, as Thoreau listens to sounds around the clock; and it concludes with a total surrender to the vitalizing power of unbounded nature. Thoreau had been talking about his reading in the previous chapter; now he reminds us: "While we are confined to books . . . we are in danger of forgetting the language which all things and events speak without metaphor." Sounds are elements of this natural language: the sound of the trains passing in the morning; the church bells from Lincoln, Bedford, or Concord; the lowing of cows in the evening; "regularly at half-past seven," the vesper chant of the whip-poor-wills; the "maniacal hooting of

1. I am indebted here to the analysis of *Walden* as a rebirth ritual by Stanley Hyman, "Henry Thoreau in Our Time." * * *

owls," which "represent the stark twilight and unsatisfied thoughts which all have"; "late in the evening . . . the distant rumbling of wagons over bridges,—a sound heard farther than almost any other at night,—the baying of dogs . . . the trump of bull-frogs"; and then at dawn the morning song of the cockerel, the lusty call to awaken of the chanticleer which Thoreau offered on the title-page as the symbol of the book. "To walk in a winter morning, in a wood where these birds abounded . . . think of it! It would put nations on the alert." Finally, in a morning mood, Thoreau closes his chapter rejoicing that his hut has no yard, no fence, but is part of unfenced nature itself.

It was with the ultimate aim of making such an experience possible—a life determined by nature and enriched by a total awareness—that Thoreau insisted so eloquently upon the baptismal or rebirth rite. What he was demanding was that individuals start life all over again, and that in the new world a fresh start was literally and immediately possible to anyone wide enough awake to attempt it. It was in this way that the experience could also appear as a return to childhood, to the scenes and the wonder of that time. In a particularly revealing moment, Thoreau reflected, while adrift on the lake in the moonlight and playing the flute for the fishes, on a boyhood adventure at that very place. "But now," he said, "I made my home by the shore." Thoreau reflected the curious but logical reverence of his age for children: "Children, who play life, discern its true law and relations more clearly than men, who fail to live it worthily." Children seemed for Thoreau to possess some secret which had been lost in the deadening process of growing up, some intimation (like Wordsworth's child) which had faded under the routine pressure of everyday life. Emerson found the new attitude of adults toward children the appropriate symbol with which to introduce his retrospective summary of the times (1867): "Children had been repressed and kept in the background; now they were considered, cosseted and pampered." Thoreau thought he knew why: because "every child begins the world again"; every child managed to achieve without conscious effort what the adult could achieve only by the strenuous, periodic act of refreshment. In this sense, the renewal of life was a kind of homecoming; the busks and the burnings were preparatory to recapturing the outlook of children.

Psychologists who have followed Jung's poetic elaboration and doctrinaire schematizing of the guarded suggestions of Freud could make a good deal of the impulse. They might describe it as an impulse to return to the womb; and some support could doubtless be found in the image-clusters of Walden: water, caves, shipwrecks, and the like. This approach might persuasively maintain that the end of the experience narrated by Thoreau was the re-integration of the personality. And since, according to Jung, "the lake in the valley is the unconscious," it is possible to hold that *Walden* enacts and urges the escape from the convention-ridden conscious and the release of the spontaneous energies of personality lying beneath the surface, toward a reuniting of the psychic "old double." An analysis of this sort can be helpful and even illuminating, and it could be applied to the entire program of the party of Hope, substituting terms associated with the unconscious for all the terms associated with Emerson's "Reason." A certain warrant for the psychological interpretation can be found in the novels of Dr. Holmes, and the methodological issue arises more sharply in that discussion. But we may also remind ourselves that the psychological vocabulary simply manipulates a set of metaphors other than those we normally use. Probably we do not need to go so far afield to grasp what Thoreau was seeking to explain; we may even suspect that he meant what he said. And what he said was that he went to the woods in order to live deliberately, "to front only the essential facts of life"; because human life and human expression were so burdened with unexamined habits, the voice of experience so muffled by an uninvestigated inheritance, that only by a total rejection of those habits and that inheritance and by a recovery of a childlike wonder and directness could anyone find out whether life were worth living at all.

Thoreau, like most other members of the hopeful party, understood dawn and birth better than he did night and death. He responded at once to the cockerel in the morning; the screech owls at night made him bookish and sentimental. And though their wailing spoke to him about "the low spirits and melancholy forebodings of fallen souls," the whole dark side of the world was no more than another guaranty of the inexhaustible variety of nature.[2] Thoreau knew not evil; his American busk would have fallen short, like the bonfire in Hawthorne's fantasy, of the profounder need for the purification of the human heart. He would have burned away the past as the accumulation of artifice, in the name of the natural and the essential. But if the natural looked to him so much more wholesome and so much more dependable than others have since thought it, his account of the recovery of nature was never less than noble: the noblest expression, in fact and in language, of the first great aspiration of the age.

2. Thoreau goes on to say that the hooting of owls "is a sound admirably suited to swamps and twilight woods which no day illustrates, suggesting a vast and undeveloped nature which men have not yet recognized." The figurative language here is suggestive and may be surprising to anyone who supposes Thoreau unaware of the very existence of the cloacal regions of mind and nature.

GEORGE HENDRICK

The Influence of Thoreau's "Civil Disobedience" on Gandhi's *Satyagraha* †

The influence of Henry Thoreau upon Mahatma Gandhi, now universally recognized, is generally treated perfunctorily; almost all popular articles on Thoreau usually devote at least one sentence to Gandhi's indebtedness to "Civil Disobedience." Since *Indian Opinion*, the South African newspaper published by Gandhi from 1903 to 1914, is now available for study, much new material on Gandhi's knowledge of Thoreau has come to light. Before *Indian Opinion* could be studied, information about Gandhi's indebtedness to Thoreau was scattered and fragmentary. For example, Gandhi, in his 1942 appeal "To American Friends," wrote, "You have given me a teacher in Thoreau, who furnished me through his essay on the 'Duty of Civil Disobedience' scientific confirmation of what I was doing in South Africa." [1]

Similarly, Gandhi had written to Franklin Delano Roosevelt in 1942, "I have profited greatly by the writings of Thoreau and Emerson." [2] Roger Baldwin, chairman of the American Civil Liberties Union, rode with Gandhi on a train trip through France in 1931 and noticed that the only visible book was Thoreau's "Civil Disobedience." Baldwin remarked on the extremeness of Thoreau's doctrine, and Gandhi replied that the essay "contained the essence of his political philosophy, not only as India's struggle related to the British, but as to his own views of the relation of citizens to government." [3]

At the Second Round Table Conference in London that same year, the American reporter Webb Miller, a long-time admirer of Thoreau, asked Gandhi, "Did you ever read an American named Henry D. Thoreau?" Gandhi replied, "Why, of course I read Thoreau. I read *Walden* first in Johannesburg in South Africa in 1906 and his ideas influenced me greatly. I adopted some of them and recommended the study of Thoreau to all my friends who were helping me in the cause of Indian independence. Why, I actually took the name of my movement from Thoreau's essay,

† From *The New England Quarterly*, XXIX, 462–71 (December, 1956). Reprinted by permission of the editors of NEQ.
1. D. G. Tendulkar, *Mahatma: Life*

of Mohandas Karamchand Gandhi (Bombay, 1951–1954), VI, 177.
2. Tendulkar, *Mahatma* . . . , VI, 144.
3. *Thoreau Society Bulletin*, XI, 2 (April, 1945).

'On the Duty of Civil Disobedience,' written about eighty years ago." [4] Miller noticed that Gandhi, a "Hindu mystic," adopted from Thoreau the philosophy which was to affect millions of Indians and inspire them to defy the powerful British Empire. "It would seem," Miller concluded, "that Gandhi received back from America what was fundamentally the philosophy of India after it had been distilled and crystallized in the mind of Thoreau." [5]

Because of lack of information, however, inaccuracies have been perpetuated. Henry Seidel Canby wrote in the *Yale Review* that "Civil Disobedience" came to Gandhi's attention while he was studying law in London in 1907.[6] The New York *Evening Post* used this information in an editorial and then received a letter of correction and amplification from Henry S. L. Polak, Gandhi's co-worker in South Africa, stating,

I cannot recall whether, early in 1907, he or I first came across the volume of Thoreau's Essays (published, I believe, in Scott's Library) but we were both of us enormously impressed by the confirmation of the rightness of the principle of passive resistence and civil disobedience that had already been started against the objectionable laws, contained in the essay 'On the Duty of Civil Disobedience.' [7]

Gandhi's letter to Henry S. Salt on Thoreau's influence contradicts some of Polak's statement. Salt, one of Thoreau's earliest biographers, was interested in writing the life of Gandhi and undoubtedly would have studied Gandhi's indebtedness to Thoreau but was discouraged from writing by G. B. Shaw, who said that there was nothing more to be said about saints after his play on Joan.[8] Salt, however, did write to Gandhi, whom he had first met in London in the 1890's, asking about the influence of Thoreau. Gandhi replied, in a letter which has often been reprinted, that "Civil Disobedience" had "left a deep impression" upon him and that he had

. . . translated a portion for the readers of *Indian Opinion* in South Africa, which I was then editing, and I made copious extracts for the English part of the paper. The essay seemed to be so convincing and truthful that I felt the need of knowing more of Thoreau, and I came across your Life of him, his 'Walden,' and other essays, all of which I read with great pleasure and equal profit.[9]

4. Webb Miller, *I Found No Peace* (Garden City, 1938), 238–239.
5. Miller, *I Found No Peace*, 238–239.
6. Henry Seidel Canby, "Thoreau and the Machine Age," *Yale Review*, xx, 517 (March, 1931).
7. New York *Evening Post*, May 11, 1931, p. 8.
8. Stephen Winsten, *Salt and His Circle* (London, 1951), 170.
9. Henry S. Salt, *Company I Have Kept* (London, 1930), 100–101.

The extracts were made, not from the volume from Scott's Library, but from Arthur C Fifield's "Simple Life" edition of the essay and presented under the headline, "For Passive Resisters."

The extracts began with a quotation from Tolstoy, "The principle of State necessity can bind only those men to disobey God's law, who, for the sake of worldly advantages try to reconcile the irreconcileable; but a Christian, who sincerely believes that the fulfilment of Jesus' teaching shall bring him salvation, cannot attach any importance to this principle," and then gave a short biographical sketch of Thoreau who "taught nothing he was not prepared to practice in himself." Thoreau was extolled as one who went to jail "for the sake of his principles and suffering humanity." The five columns of extracts from "Civil Disobedience" present Thoreau's argument forcefully and accurately, emphasizing that the essay's "incisive logic is unanswerable." [1]

The extracts present in brief the main ideas of Thoreau's closely argued essay; the following passage fundamental in Gandhi's philosophy of *Satyagraha*, as many other sections of "Civil Disobedience" were, well demonstrates Gandhi's method of extracting the heart of an idea from essays:

> Under a government which imprisons any unjustly, the true place for a just man is also prison.
>
> If any think that their influence would be lost there, and their voices no longer afflict the ear of the State, that they would not be as an enemy without its walls, they do not know by how much truth is stronger than error, nor how much more eloquently and effectively he can combat injustice who has experienced a little in his own person.
>
> Cast your whole vote, not a strip of paper merely, but your whole influence. A minority is powerless while it conforms to the majority; it is not even a minority then; but it is irresistible when it clogs by its whole weight.
>
> If the alternative is to keep all just men in prison, or give up war and slavery, the State will not hesitate which to choose. If a thousand men were not to pay their tax-bills this year, that would not be a violent and bloody measure as it would be to pay them, and enable the State to commit violence and shed innocent blood. [2]

There can be no doubt about the appeal of Thoreau's essay which Gandhi read at a crucial phase of his life. He was then fighting the Asiatic Registration Act ("Black Act") which required all Asiatics over eight years of age residing in the Trans-

1. *Indian Opinion*, October 26, 1907,   2. *Indian Opinion*, October 26, 1907,
p. 438.   pp. 439–440.

vaal to register and, as if they were criminals, give their finger-prints. Failure to register would result in a fine, a prison term, or deportation. "I have never known legislation of this nature," Gandhi wrote, "being directed against free men in any part of the world." [3]

Indian Opinion helped awaken the Indians to the effects of the "Black Act," and when a protest meeting was called for September 11, 1907, in Johannesburg, delegates representing all segments of the 13,000 Indians in the Transvaal were present. The Fourth Resolution passed that day declared that Indians would not submit to the Ordinance and would suffer all the penalties of their disobedience. Sheth Haji Habib while seconding the resolution declared that it should be passed with God as witness; Gandhi, sensing the effectiveness of a religious vow, made an impassioned speech of support ending, "Every one should fully realize his responsibility, then only pledge himself independently of others and understand that he himself must be true to his pledge even unto death, no matter what others do." [4]

Gandhi entitled the chapter describing the meeting of September 11, 1907, "The Advent of Satyagraha." Although this meeting was held five weeks before the extract from "Civil Disobedience" were published in *Indian Opinion*, he undoubtedly already knew Thoreau's philosophy. On September 7, 1907, four days before the meeting in the Imperial Theatre, *Indian Opinion*, in an unsigned article, quoted Thoreau:

'. . . All machines have friction, and possibly this does enough good to counter-balance the evil. At any rate, it is a great evil to make a stir about it. But, when the friction comes to have its machine, and oppression and robbery are paramount, I say, let us not have such a machine any longer.' In the Asiatic Registration Act, British Indians have not only a law which has some evil in it, that is to say, using Thoreau's words, a machine with friction in it, but it is evil legalised, or it represents friction with machinery provided for it. Resistance to such an evil is a divine duty. . . .[5]

If Gandhi did not write all of the articles which mention Thoreau, he certainly read them, as his newspaper received his constant attention. "During ten years," he wrote, "that is, until 1914, . . . there was hardly an issue of *Indian Opinion* without an article from me." [6]

Gandhi may well have read *Walden* as early as 1906; before

3. M. K. Gandhi, *Satyagraha in South Africa* (Madras, 1928), 157–158.
4. M. K. Gandhi, *Satyagraha in South Africa*, 169.
5. *Indian Opinion*, September 7, 1907, p. 363.
6. M. K. Gandhi, *Autobiography* (Washington, 1948), 348.

the first *Satyagraha* movement he dispensed with servants, acted as his own scavenger, and attempted to be independent of machinery. His views were seemingly influenced by *Walden*, but since he was using the London *Times* as a pattern for *Indian Opinion*, his journalistic endeavors did not reflect his personal interests as his later papers in India did, and his reactions to *Walden* were not discussed in the paper. It was rather the Thoreau who went to jail "for the sake of his principles and suffering humanity" who was emphasized in *Indian Opinion* because he confirmed the non-coöperation campaign.

Readers of *Indian Opinion* were frequently reminded of Thoreau's essay on civil disobedience. Thoreau had opposed the enslavement of man; Indians, being enslaved themselves, needed encouragement in their struggle. The Indian community was openly defying the registration act, and the resistances of Thoreau, Tolstoy, Jesus, and Socrates seemed vital confirmations to Gandhi. On November 9, 1907, *Indian Opinion* announced an essay contest on "The Ethics of Passive Resistance." The terms of the competition stated that the essay should contain an examination "of Thoreau's classic, 'On the Duty of Civil Disobedience,' Tolstoi's works—more especially 'The Kingdom of Heaven is within You,' . . . and also the application of the 'Apology of Socrates' to the question." [7] Those who entered the essay competition had access to "Civil Disobedience," as it had been reprinted in pamphlet form for sale at 3*d*. and issued in time to be used by contestants not familiar with the essay. [8]

Only four essays were eventually to be entered in the contest, and before the essays were judged, Gandhi, who had refused to register, was arrested. He was sentenced on January 10, 1908, to two months of simple imprisonment. Gandhi remembered that there was a "slight feeling of awkwardness due to the fact that I was standing as an accused in the very Court where I had often appeared as counsel." He then added a Thoreauvian comment: "But I well remember that I considered the former role as far more honourable than the latter, and did not feel the slightest hesitation in entering the prisoner's box." [9]

During this first incarceration, Gandhi read Tolstoy, Ruskin, Socrates, Huxley, Bacon, and the *Gita*—the work which greatly influenced him, as it did Thoreau, according to Arthur C. Christy in his *The Orient in American Transcendentalism*. Since his days in London when he had first studied the *Gita*, Gandhi had rejected the fundamentalist interpretation that this Hindu Bible was a historical work justifying violence. Gandhi felt

7. *Indian Opinion*, November 9, 1907, p. 465.
8. *Indian Opinion*, November 23, 1907,
9. Gandhi, *Satyagraha in South Africa*, 231.
p. 494.

that "under the guise of physical warfare, it described the duel that perpetually went on in the hearts of mankind, and that physical warfare was brought in merely to make the description of the internal duel more alluring." [1] Thoreau, in his criticism of the *Gita* in *A Week on the Concord and Merrimack Rivers*, had protested the seeming justification of violence; Gandhi undoubtedly knew of Thoreau's interest in Oriental literature through reading of *Walden* and Salt's *Life of Henry David Thoreau*, although Gandhi seemingly never saw *A Week* with its extended comments on the *Gita*.

A settlement calling for voluntary rather than compulsory registration for Indians was arrived at, and Gandhi's days of reading were cut short. Thoreau's essay on civil disobedience was again brought to the attention of *Indian Opinion* readers when on April 18, 1908, the prize essay, "The Ethics of Passive Resistance," was printed. Reverend J. J. Doke read the first four essays submitted, and awarded the first prize to M. S. Maurice. *Indian Opinion* carefully pointed out that the essay which won did not reach the level which they had anticipated; it was indeed a pedestrian production; the section on Thoreau was largely a reproduction of the extracts which *Indian Opinion* had printed, and the sections on Tolstoy, Ruskin, and Jesus were uninspired.[2]

The continued interest in civil disobedience was justified, as General Smuts refused to keep his bargain to repeal the compulsory registration act after the Indians had voluntarily registered. Gandhi was unwilling to tolerate Smuts's breach of faith; an Indian ultimatum was sent stating that if the Asiatic Registration Act were not repealed the registration certificates of the Indians would be burned. Gandhi's inspiration may well have come from reading Salt's biography of Thoreau. Salt noted that Thoreau's essay on "Slavery in Massachusetts," ". . . was delivered as an address at the anti-slavery celebration at Framingham in 1854, on which occasion the Constitution of the United States was publicly burned by Lloyd Garrison, an incident which may explain the passionate tone of Thoreau's paper." [3]

The certificates were burned on August 16, 1908, and Gandhi was arrested and sentenced to the Volksrust prison on October 10, 1908. He worked all during the day, but in the mornings and evenings and on Sundays he read "the two famous books of Ruskin, Essays of Thoreau," and parts of the Bible, the

1. Gandhi, *The Gita According to Gandhi* (Ahmedabad, 1951), 127.
2. *Indian Opinion*, April 18, 1908, pp. 175–177.
3. Salt, *Life of Henry David Thoreau* (London, 1896), 114. I have been unable to date Gandhi's reading of the Salt biography; there was interest in Garrison among the workers of *Indian Opinion* at this time, however, as the paper ran extracts from Garrison's works on March 19, 1910.

Essays of Bacon, and several books in Gujarati. "From Thoreau and Ruskin," he wrote, "I could find out arguments in favor of our fight." [4]

Gandhi believed that it was the "height of one's good fortune to be in jail in the interests and good name of one's country and religion." In jail the necessities of life were provided and the soul was left free; the body was restrained, but not the soul. A malevolent warden merely taught self-control to the prisoner. Gandhi trusted "that the readers of this my second experience of life in the Transvaal jail will be convinced that the real road to ultimate happiness lies in going to jail and undergoing sufferings and privations there in the interest of one's country and religion." [5]

He ended his account of his second jailing by adding, "Placed in a similar position for refusing his poll-tax, the American citizen, Thoreau, expressed similar thoughts in 1849. Seeing the walls of the cell in which he was confined, made of solid stone two or three feet thick and the door of wood and iron a foot thick, he said to himself thus:

> I saw that, if there was a wall of stone between me and my townsmen, there was a still more difficult one to climb or break through before they could get to be as free as I was. . . . I saw that the State was half-witted, that it was as timid as a lone woman with her silver spoons, and that it did not know its friends from its foes, and I lost all my remaining respect for it and pitied it.[6]

Gandhi's transformation from a respectable lawyer to a radical political leader was completed.

Thoreau was not ignored during the years after *Satyagraha* was first tried; for several years after 1908 passive resistance was offered on a small scale, and Gandhi himself did not court arrest. Two years after *Indian Opinion* had printed extracts from "Civil Disobedience," it printed selections from Mazzini with the comment: "We believe that when the first stage of passive resistance was at its height, the extracts we gave from Thoreau's essay 'On the Duty of Civil Disobedience' were very greatly appreciated by Indian passive resisters." [7] Gandhi himself was still reading Thoreau; by 1909 he considered that "railways, machineries, and the corresponding increase of indulgent habits are

4. Gandhi, *Speeches and Writings* (Madras, 1933), 226.
5. Gandhi, *Speeches and Writings*, 227.
6. Gandhi, *Speeches and Writings*, 227–228. Only the first and last sentences of Gandhi's quotation from Thoreau are reproduced here.
7. *Indian Opinion*, February 20, 1909, pp. 89–90.

the true badge of slavery of the Indian people, as they are of Europeans." [8] Thoreau and Tolstoy had said the same thing, and their influence is particularly strong in Gandhi's *Hind Swaraj* (Indian Home Rule), a severe castigation of the evils of Western imperialism which enslaved colonial peoples and brought material prosperity to the governing nations. Works by Tolstoy, Ruskin, Edward Carpenter, and Thoreau's "On the Duty of Civil Disobedience" and "Life Without Principle" were among the sources listed in the bibliography; and in a Preface to *Hind Swaraj* printed in *Indian Opinion*, Gandhi stated, "Whilst the views expressed in 'Hind Swaraj' are held by me, I have but endeavoured humbly to follow Tolstoy, Ruskin, Thoreau, Emerson and other writers, besides the masters of Indian philosophy." [9] *Hind Swaraj*, banned in India, was a call for individual, Thoreauvian regeneration and shows that in 1909, six years before he was to leave South Africa, Gandhi was beginning to think of Indian affairs. One year after the publication of *Hind Swaraj*, *Indian Opinion* published excerpts from "Life Without Principle," under the title "Thoughts from Thoreau." [1]

These extracts, condemning commerce, government, and intellectual stagnation, must have delighted Gandhi. The middle-class lawyer Gandhi underwent a conversion in South Africa which made him discard almost all aspects of his old life and beliefs and made him turn to writers who probed the meaning of civilization. Once Gandhi adopted and modified Thoreauvian-Tolstoyan-Ruskinian principles, he acted without hesitation and with determination.

Gandhi found in Thoreau a practical man willing to practice his beliefs. It is a mistake, however, to overestimate Thoreau's influence upon Gandhi and the *Satyagraha* movement—to maintain that Gandhi did nothing original and merely applied Thoreauvian teachings. Gandhi himself protested to P. Kodanda Rao in 1935, "The statement that I derived my idea of Civil Disobedience from the writings of Thoreau is wrong. The resistance to authority . . . was well advanced before I got the essay. . . ." [2] The Passive Resistance movement, however, had not been tested when Gandhi first read "Civil Disobedience," and the essay offered confirmation of the effectiveness of deliberate resistance to unjust laws. There can be no doubt that Gandhi was deeply indebted to the Thoreau who defied society and government to follow his conscience.

8. Tendulkar, *Mahatma* . . . , I, 127.
9. *Indian Opinion*, April 2, 1910, p. 110.
1. *Indian Opinion*, June 10, 1911, pp. 230–231; July 22, 1911, p. 287.
2. Louis Fischer, *The Life of Mahatma Gandhi* (New York, 1950), 87.

J. LYNDON SHANLEY

The Successive Versions of *Walden* †

The immediate beginning of *Walden* was in 1846 when Thoreau learned that the audience at one of his Lyceum lectures—probably the one on Carlyle on February 4, 1846—had expected to hear about his life in the woods. People on the streets and in stores and parlors had asked him, "What's it like there?" "What do you eat?" "Aren't you lonesome?" They seemed incredulous concerning his life; some were clearly bewildered, like the man who came to the hut looking for his dog but was incapable of listening to Thoreau's attempts to help him; he kept repeating, "What do you do here?" [1] Thoreau discovered that all this was more than idle curiosity and that people did want answers and enlightenment if they could be had. Sometime before March 13, 1846, he wrote in his journal in preparation for a lecture, "After I lectured here before, this winter, I heard that some of my townsmen had expected of me some account of my life at the pond. This I will endeavor to give to-night." [2]

This was no encouragement for Thoreau to let pass; he wanted to lecture and write for money, and his journal already contained the beginnings of the two major elements in *Walden*: the story of how he lived at the pond, and the comparison of what he lived for with what many people of New England lived for. From the time he went to the pond, he had noted in his journal the events and thoughts of his days, undoubtedly with the idea of using the notes for lectures and essays as he was even then using earlier ones in writing *A Week*. And he was also thinking of a lecture on the mean and sneaking lives led by many people in Concord and New England. Sometime between

† From J. Lyndon Shanley, *The Making of Walden*, Chicago, Illinois, 1957. Pp. 18–33. Copyright 1957 by the University of Chicago Press. Reprinted by permission of the publishers.
1. *The Writings of Henry David Thoreau* (20 vols.; Boston: Houghton Mifflin Co., 1906), *Journal*, I, 398; entry is undated; whenever possible, journal entries are referred to by date. Unless otherwise indicated, all references to Thoreau's published writings are to this edition. [Shanley uses Arabic numbers to refer to paragraphs in particular chapters. *Editor*]
2. I, 485; entry is undated; it precedes by several pages an entry dated March 13, 1846. In slightly revised form it is the second paragraph of the first version. The reference is probably to his lecture on Carlyle, on February 4, 1846, at the Concord Lyceum; see Walter Harding, "A Checklist of Thoreau's Lectures," *Bulletin of the New York Public Library*, LII (1948), 80.

December 23, 1845, and March 26, 1846, he wrote the opening lines of the lecture in his journal; they consisted of the first sentence of "Economy," 3, and all of "Economy," 7, and they began: "I wish to say something to-night not of and concerning the Chinese and Sandwich-Islanders, but *to* and concerning you who hear me." [3] With the stimulus of his townsmen's questions, he set out to develop and combine the two elements.

His first step in writing the first version was to gather the material which lay everywhere in his journals, not only those written at the pond but also the ones he had kept in earlier years. From notes of 1840 and 1841 he took items for his comments on clothes; [4] and from the journal he had kept while living at William Emerson's on Staten Island in 1843 [5] he took the lyrical passage on the coming of spring, "Spring," 13. He used the material of successive entries or even the parts of a single entry at widely scattered points in the first and later versions of *Walden*. For example, eleven consecutive journal paragraphs written on or near July 16, 1845, dealt with Alek Therien and other visitors, the advantages of a frontier or primitive life, and the mice at Walden; in the first version Thoreau used them in "Visitors," in two places in "Economy," and in the section on animals. Frequently, as a comparison of journal entries and the text shows, he adopted material from the journal with little change. Often, however, a journal entry was only the germ of a longer passage. He developed the following unpublished inter-lineation as the first draft of "Economy," 56, in I; later he interlined the rest of the paragraph in III: "There is no place in the village for a work of art, or statue for instance if one had come down to us—for our lives our houses furnish no proper pedestal for it. It is more beautiful out of doors where there is no house—no man." [6]

In the cases just given, Thoreau took what he wanted from various journal entries and did not go back to them when he revised his work; in other cases, however, he used only some of the material at hand and later returned for more. In the first version he took over from his journal the material for "Economy," 7, but not until the third version did he take over the first sentence of "Economy," 3, which immediately preceded 7 in the

3. I, 395; entry is undated. The journal entry immediately preceding it is dated December 23, 1845, but many pages were torn out between the two entries. The first dated entry after the one quoted is for March 26, 1846; it is considerably farther on in the journal.
4. See * * * the journal for July 12, 1840, February 5, and April 5, 1841. He did not use earlier journal items of April 8, 1839, and March 21, 1840, until later versions.
5. HM 13182 in the Huntington Library; printed in *The First and Last Journeys of Thoreau*, ed. F. B. Sanborn (Boston: Bibliophile Society, 1905).
6. See * * * the manuscript journal, Vol. VII, in the Morgan Library, New York, N.Y.

journal.[7] He drew on the following journal entry of his third day at the pond, July 6, 1845, at five different times. He used three items in three widely separated places in the first version, and after writing the second version, he interlined two other items from this entry, again at some distance from one another:

July 6. [Version I. Cf. "Where I Lived," 16:] I wish to meet the facts of life—the vital facts, which are the phenomena or actuality the gods meant to show us—face to face, and so I came down here. Life! who knows what it is, what it does? If I am not quite right here, I am less wrong than before; and now let us see what they will have. [Interlined in version II. Cf. "Where I Lived," 20:] The preacher, instead of vexing the ears of drowsy farmers on their day of rest, at the end of the week,—for Sunday always seemed to me like a fit conclusion of an ill-spent week and not the fresh and brave beginning of a new one,—with this one other draggletail and postponed affair of a sermon, from thirdly to fifteenthly, should teach them with a thundering voice pause and simplicity. "Stop! Avast! Why so fast?" [At the beginning of "Reading" in version I, but not in text:] In all studies we go not forward but rather backward with redoubled pauses. We always study *antiques* [Thoreau's italics] with silence and reflection. Even time has a depth, and below its surface the waves do not lapse and roar. [Version I, "Economy," 8:] I wonder men can be so frivolous almost as to attend to the gross form of negro slavery, there are so many keen and subtle masters who subject us both. [Interlined in version II, "Economy," 8:] Self-emancipation in the West Indies of a man's thinking and imagining provinces, which should be more than his island territory,—one emancipated heart and intellect! It would knock off the fetters from a million slaves.

He did not always lift separable items and use them in more or less developed form. Sometimes he found suggestions for two or three different points in a single note. An unpublished leaf (HM 924), torn from a journal or notebook, contains a series of brief notes that Thoreau developed in "Visitors," "The Ponds," "House-Warming," and "The Pond in Winter"; one of the notes reads (unless otherwise noted, italics here and in subsequent quotations from manuscripts indicate material interlined by Thoreau):

A place of pines—of forest scenes and events visited by successive nations of men all of whom have successively *admired* & fathomed it—but still its water is green and pellucid, not an intermittent spring—somewhat perennial in it—while the nations

7. I, 395–96; entry is undated.

pass away *offering its perennial well to the animal nations.* A true well—a gem of the first water—which Concord wears in her coronet.

looking blue as amethyst or solidified azure far off as it is drawn through the streets. Green in the deeps—blue in the shallows. Perhaps the grass is a denser deeper heaven.

He used "a place of pines," the "perennial" quality of the spring-well, and the observation on the green and blue of Walden's water in "The Ponds," 5, the color of the ice in "The Pond in Winter," 16, and the major part of the note in "The Ponds." [8]

When he was actually writing out the first version, Thoreau did not simply leaf through his journals and take what he wanted as he found it. He first gathered his material and ordered it. The evidence for this is clear, even though not extensive. In the back of one of his journals of 1845–47 he wrote out a preliminary list of topics for the later part of the first version, and then he numbered the topics in the order in which he first intended to use them in *Walden*.[9] In the margin of the manuscript journal of July, 1845, he marked the order of the items on the advantages of a primitive and frontier life before he copied them in the first version.[1] In other cases, as with the following notes on clothing, he wrote out his material with the intention of working it over later. The phrase at the end indicates that he had previously assembled or written out other material on clothing.

Comparatively speaking tattooing is not necessarily the hideous custom it is described to be. It is the same taste that prints the calico which the wearer put off and on, and the consistent objection is rather to the fashion of the print than to the practice itself. It is not therefore barbarous because it is skin deep. [Compare "Economy," 40.]

When I meet a fine lady or gentleman dressed at the top of the fashion I wonder what they would do if there should be an earthquake or a fire should suddenly break out; for they appear to have counted on fine weather & a smooth course only. Our dress should to some extent be such as will fit equally well in good & in bad fortune. [Compare "Economy," 37.]

When our garments are worn out we hang them up in the fields to scare crows with, as if the reason why men scare crows was in their clothes. I have often experienced the difficulty of getting within gunshot of a crow. It is not because they

8. Neither "an intermittent spring" nor "a gem . . . in her coronet" is in "The Ponds," 8, in version I; how much of paragraph 5 was in I is not certain because some of it was on a missing leaf.

9. Volume VI of the manuscript journals in the Morgan Library.
1. Compare *Journal*, I, 367–68, undated entry.

smell powder. [This appears in the first and other versions but not in text.]

It is true all costume off a man is grotesque. It is only the serious eye & the sincere life passed within it, which restrain laughter, and consecrate the costume of any people. Let Harlequin be taken with a fit of the colic in the midst of his buffoonery, and his trappings will have to serve that mood too. When the soldier is hit with a cannon ball rags are as becoming as purple. As soon in short as a man engages to eat walk work & sit & meet all the contingencies of life therein, his costume is hallowed, and may be the theme of poetry. [Compare "Economy," 39.]

I have little hesitation in saying & [in the first version this phrase introduces material that is in "Economy," 41].[2]

In some cases he assembled notes on a topic by tearing pages out of his journals; hence the mutilation of the early manuscript journals and the presence of torn-out journal pages in the *Walden* manuscript and in miscellaneous manuscript gatherings.

As he took over his raw material, Thoreau broke it up, changed it in detail, developed it, and finally ordered it so that he might offer his hearers and readers, not the immediate, random, and intermittent notes of a journal, but a reflected-on and consciously shaped re-creation of his experience. A torn leaf in the *Walden* manuscript gives us a glimpse of how he roughed out such a piece as the story of investigating, wrecking, and removing James Collins' shanty. He went over it at least twice, for he made one set of interlineations in ink and another in pencil (here and elsewhere, angle brackets < > indicate canceled material in manuscripts):

[Torn; two words not clear] became a dead cat—and buried at last. Lintel none but perennial passage for hens *under the door board*. I threw down this dwelling <next day> [pencil:] *this morning*—drawing the nails—and removed it to the pond side in small cart loads *one early thrush gave me a note or two by the way—which was encouraging* [second interlining in pencil:] *as I drove along the woodland path*. Penurious [?] Seeley neighbor Irishman—as I was informed *by young Patrick treacherously* transferring in the intervals the still tolerable straight driveable nails—staples spikes to his pocket—and then stood to look on unconcerned *in the sun* and pass the time of day. <There by the ponside [*sic*] they bleached—warped> [pencil:] *& then spread the boards on the grass to bleach and warp* back again in the sun <upon the grass> Seeley *with his spring thoughts* gazing freshly up at the devastation seeking [for "seeing"?] there is a dearth of work—he *there* to

2. HM 924, on the verso of a leaf discarded from *A Week*.

represent spectatordom jingling his pockets lowly—a transaction of singular quietness.

Thoreau must have begun to write out the first version of *Walden* late in 1846 or early in 1847. He had finished part of it by February 10 and 17, 1847, when he lectured at the Concord Lyceum on his life at the pond;[3] but he was still at work later in the winter and spring, for in this version he wrote of the ice-cutters of the winter of 1846–47: "This winter [later changed to 'In the winter of 46 & 47'] as you all know there came a hundred men"; and "They have not been able to break up our pond any earlier than usual this year as they expected to—for she has got a thick new garment to replace the old." Speaking of his house-keeping earlier, he had said: "I trust that none of my hearers will be so uncharitable as to look into my house now—after hearing this, at the end of an unusually dirty winter, with critical housewife's eyes, for I intend to celebrate the first bright & unquestionable spring morning by scrubbing my house with sand until it is as white as a lily—or, at any rate, as the washerwoman said of her clothes, as white as a 'wiolet.'" He wrote these passages with the possibility of reading them in lectures in 1847. They were not written, as were some later additions, merely as if he were at Walden.

There is no conclusive evidence that he completed this version before he left the pond in September, 1847, but since he was writing about the ice-cutters of "The Pond in Winter" by early spring,[4] it seems reasonable to conclude that he would have written the remaining twenty-seven pages of version I by September, or even earlier. The fact that he later interlined "Left Walden Sept. 6, 1847" at the end of this version also suggests that he had finished before that date.

Thoreau's own statements seem to imply that the first version was longer than it actually was. The first draft of the first paragraph of *Walden* (in version III, 1849) begins: "At the time the following pages were written I lived alone in the woods." Late in 1853 or very early in 1854 he changed this to read as it does in the published text, "the following pages, or rather the bulk of them." In the unpublished preface of version VII, 1854, he said: "Nearly all of this volume was written eight or nine years ago in the scenery & under the circumstances which it describes, and a considerable part was read at that time as lectures before the Concord Lyceum. In what is now added

3. Harding, "A Checklist of Thoreau's Lectures," p. 80.
4. On p. 209 of the 236 pages in the second sequence of Thoreau's numbering.

the object has been chiefly to make it a completer & truer account of that portion of the author's life." By the phrases "the bulk of them" and "nearly all of this volume" Thoreau may have meant that he had written more of *Walden* at the pond than at any other one time; certainly, the version of *Walden* he wrote at the pond was only about half as long as the final text.

* * *

The first version has the spirit and the style of *Walden,* but the spirit is not so strongly developed and the style is not so finished. Mark Van Doren said of *Walden,* "it was written in bounding spirits, with eyes twinkling and tongue in cheek." [5] So it was, and Thoreau wrote with the same joy and humor and challenging assurance at the beginning. There is a considerable difference, however, between the first and the last versions; the flavor is the same, but at the end it is much richer, since, as time went on, Thoreau added more and more of every element: for example, by far the greater part of the description of his immediate surroundings in "The Ponds," all the account of the friends who came to see him in "Winter Visitors," and the gay satire and poetry of all of "Conclusion." And he added the learning and authority of most of his quotations and specific references to earlier writers. Of fifty such items in the first half of *Walden* [6] only seven are in the first version; Thoreau added the others at various times in all the later versions.[7] He also improved the flavor significantly by cutting out the mediocre verse which bulks large in the first version.

The style of this version is recognizably that of the published text—homely and elaborate, witty and humorous, reflective and argumentative, scornful and gentle. And narrative, anecdote, lyric description, character sketch, satire, exposition—all kinds are here. But, understandably enough, in many places the writing does not have the clarity, force, and rhythms that we find in *Walden* itself; only by a long and untiring pursuit was Thoreau to win that perfection. A number of passages in the first version, if taken by themselves, may be superior in some respects to the revisions of them in the final text. The description of his partially finished house, "Where I Lived," 8, and the advice of his

---

5. *Henry David Thoreau,* p. 11.
6. Counting separately the quotations from the Bible in "Economy," 47 and 48; and those (from Confucius?) in "Solitude," 7, 8, 9. Because of the leaves missing in the later part of the first version of *Walden,* it is not possible to tell what quotations were in it.
7. In the first half of *Walden* he added quotations and specific references to authorities thus: he interlined two in version I; twelve in II; three in III; he wrote six in IV and interlined one; wrote three in V and interlined three; wrote six in VI and interlined one; wrote three in VII. Three quotations and references are not in the manuscript; either Thoreau added them in the copy for the printer, or they were on leaves missing from versions later than the first.

"Good Genius," "Baker Farm," 6, for example, have a greater spontaneity and immediacy in the first version. But the later versions of such passages are more in keeping with the movement and tone of the final text. Thoreau inevitably sacrificed some liveliness and directness as he developed his lectures into a book which would give a fuller account of his experience.

Thoreau's quarrel with the ways of his contemporaries and the general outline as well as a large part of his story are in the first version, but it is by no means a "scale model" of *Walden* in either content or form. The major points of his criticism in "Economy" are laid out, but many illustrations and some reflections are missing, and there is little of "Higher Laws" and nothing of "Conclusion." As for his story, this version contains the greater part of his account of what he did in the summer and the description in the earlier chapters of the general quality of his life, but the account of the rest of the year is thin. Various parts of the final text are very unevenly represented, and the order and relations of the parts are quite different in many places, particularly in the second half, where the sequence of topics and of the events of the year is by no means so carefully worked out. Much was to be changed by later work.

When Thoreau left Walden Pond and returned to the village in September, 1847, he probably had a draft of *A Week* as well as the first version of *Walden*, and he also had material for several articles. If he was to realize his hopes of a career as a writer, he had to finish some of his pieces and publish them. At first, in the last months of 1847 and well into 1848, he seems to have been engaged on things other than *Walden*. By January 12, 1848, he lectured on the trip he had made to Ktaadn in the summer of 1846, and he sent off the completed essay "Ktaadn" to Horace Greeley by the end of March.[8] He had also prepared at least part of "Civil Disobedience" by January and February, 1848, when he lectured on the relation of the individual to the state.[9] And he worked on *A Week* in the spring and part of the summer of 1848, for in March he told Elliot Cabot that since he had not yet found a publisher for it, he was going to "mend it" and would "look at it again directly" when he had finished some other things; and in May he wrote to Greeley, "My book grows in bulk as I work on it." [1]

In view of all this, Thoreau probably did not return to any extended work on *Walden* until sometime after the middle of 1848. When he did so, he revised the first version in great

8. *Familiar Letters*, p. 150; *The Maine Woods*, p. ix.   9. Harding, "A Checklist," pp. 80–81.   1. *Familiar Letters*, pp. 156, 172.

detail not only to improve it for lectures such as those he gave in 1848–49 in Salem, Portland, and Worcester, as well as in Concord [2] but also with an eye toward publication. He crowded in at the top of the first page of the first version: "Walden or Life in / the woods by Henry Thoreau / Addressed to my Townsmen;" and later he put in a motto: "Where I have been / There was none seen." In a number of places he changed "lecture" to "book," "audience" to "readers," and "hear" to "read."

Having worked over the first version, Thoreau wrote version II.[3] He revised it and then wrote version III so close upon II that they almost seem one piece. At one point, a passage of II is on one side of a leaf and a passage of III on the other; at a second point, a passage of III that runs for five pages begins on the bottom of a page that has material of II on it. Furthermore, the pagination of the two versions runs in one series where Thoreau fitted the material of III into II. It is certain, however, that there are two versions here and that Thoreau wrote III after II: not only are the ink and handwriting different, but also III contains revisions of parts of II.

Neither version II nor III is much longer than I. The effect and apparent intention of his work in these versions was to tidy up and to increase the clarity and force of the first version, which he had written at the pond. And so he could properly write in III: "At the time the following pages were written I lived alone, in the woods." [4] There is no direct evidence as to when he wrote II and III, but all the circumstances indicate conclusively that he did so in 1848–49 and that he was preparing for early publication. Version II is essentially a fair copy of much of I with its corrections; the handwriting in II is the most carefully formed in the whole manuscript. In III, which consists almost entirely of rewriting of parts of I and II, the first page has in its upper half both title and author written out in a large hand, and it contains the first draft of the explanatory first paragraph of *Walden*.[5]

2. Harding, "A Checklist," pp. 81–82.

3. Thoreau made most of the revisions in version I before writing II and III, but he went over I at later times too; for example, he interlined material from the journal for November 3, 1852, in "Winter Animals," 3, in I.

4. The nature of his additions, cancellations, and rearrangements of material from version to version makes it impossible to give descriptions of the contents of the various versions that would be accurate and at the same time clear. The Table of Additions on pp. 70–73 shows in summary fashion what each new version contributed to the building up of *Walden;* chap. iv gives a full account of the way in which Thoreau made the additions.

5. Thoreau thriftily thought of lectures even as he wrote versions II and III for publication; the manuscript of both versions has "book," "readers," etc.; but at several points it has "lecture" where version I had been revised to read "book." In version III in the first sentence of "Economy," 3, Thoreau wrote of his lecture in "this city" (later changed to "town"), probably Portland in March, 1849, or Worcester on April 20, 1849.

The external evidence has been mentioned already: early in 1849 Thoreau asked Ticknor and Company about the possibility of their publishing *Walden;* on February 28, 1849, his Aunt Maria wrote that he was preparing *Walden* for the press; [6] and some copies of the first edition of *A Week* included a notice in the advertising pages that *Walden* would be published soon.

In 1849 Thoreau had a version of *Walden,* consisting of material in I, II, and III, which members of his family read and of which he could have made a fair copy; but there is no evidence in the manuscript that he made such a copy, although a letter of February 8, 1849, to Thoreau from Ticknor's might suggest that he had sent the publisher a manuscript of *Walden.* They wrote: "We find on looking over publishing matters that we cannot well undertake anything more at present. If however you feel inclined, we will publish 'Walden or Life in the Woods' on our own a/c, say One Thousand copies, allowing you 10 pr. ct. copyright on the Retail Price on all that are sold. The style of printing & binding to be like Emersons Essays." [7] On the other hand, there is no copy in the *Walden* manuscript that Thoreau could have sent to the publishers at this time; and in view of all that is there, it seems most unlikely that, if there had been such a copy, it would not be in the manuscript.

I think the situation in February, 1849, was this. Thoreau had completed his work on *A Week* and was probably not very far from being able to complete a publishable version of *Walden.* We know that he had finished *A Week* and that he sent a fair copy of it to Ticknor's, for in a letter of February 16, 1849, they told him that they would publish the book at his expense, 1,000 copies in sheets for an estimated $381.24.[8] But it seems likely that he only inquired in advance about the possibility of their publishing *Walden.* Apparently the price quoted for *A Week,* and perhaps the terms offered for *Walden,* led Thoreau to seek another publisher, James Munroe, who published *A Week* in May, 1849, and at the same time announced in the advertising pages of *A Week* that *Walden* would "be published soon." But Thoreau never finished preparing *Walden* for publication at this time because *A Week* did not sell.

A publisher would hardly have risked Thoreau's second book immediately, and Thoreau could not put out a second book at his own expense—he did not settle his account with Munroe for publishing *A Week* until November 28, 1853.[9] Even had he had the money, perhaps Thoreau would not have finished *Walden* and

6. *The Cost Books of Ticknor and Fields,* ed. W. S. Tryon and William Charvat (New York, 1949), p. 289; Canby, *Thoreau,* p. 248.

7. *The Cost Books,* p. 289.
8. *Ibid.,* p. 289.
9. *Journal,* V, 521.

published it at this time after seeing the reception given to A Week. How much the failure of A Week affected the course of Thoreau's life is a matter for conjecture, but the results for *Walden* are plain. William Charvat points out how the work of Poe, Melville, Hawthorne, Emerson, and others benefited in some respects because of "the pressures which contemporary readers and the booktrade exerted upon them." [1] The much-lamented plight of the artist in America may have its good effects. Indirectly, the public's lack of appreciation of A Week had a great deal to do with *Walden's* being the masterpiece it is. The financial failure of A Week kept Thoreau from publishing *Walden* when he first wanted to, and when he did publish it five years later, he had enlarged and improved it almost beyond compare.

From 1849 until late 1851 or the beginning of 1852, Thoreau's work on *Walden* consisted only of revisions in the copy of versions I, II, and III. It is not possible to determine exactly when he made various corrections, but it was undoubtedly during 1850–51 that he put in all or most of the quotations from Chinese and Hindu writings that are interlined in II and III, for he commented in the journal for May 6, 1851: "Like some other preachers, I have added my texts—derived from the Chinese and Hindoo scriptures—long after my discourse was written." A few other scattered items in the journals of 1850–51 suggest that he thought of *Walden* from time to time, but it is certain that he did not write any significant amount of new material in the manuscript until January or February of 1852. [2] By January 17, 1852, he was engrossed in *Walden* once more. On that day he wrote in his journal two items on visitors and a short paragraph on the date and manner of his moving to the hut, and he clearly intended to use them in his book. [3] Then in the journal for January 21 he wrote the draft of the battle of the ants which he was soon to add to "Brute Neighbors" in version IV; and more *Walden* material appears frequently in the journals of succeding weeks and months.

Once Thoreau had taken up his work again, he wrote and rewrote and continually added to his book until he sent the final copy to the printer in 1854. There are four distinct groups of leaves in the manuscript marking four distinct stages of work (the

1. "Literary Economics and Literary History," *English Institute Essays, 1949* (New York: Columbia University Press, 1950), pp. 73–91.
2. For example, see journal for November 8, 1850, and "House-Warming," 3 and 4. And such an item as "Economy," 31, on the Indian selling baskets, may have been written up before 1852; it depends on undated journal material of 1850 (II, 84), and Thoreau wrote

it out on a separate leaf for inclusion in *Walden*.
3. "Visitors," 15; "Where I Lived," 8. On the same day he also wrote his comment on Madame Pfeiffer's clothes, "Economy," 35, and on January 11 he had written much of the passage on architecture, "Economy," 67, but he was not necessarily thinking of *Walden* as he put these two items in the journal.

lost copy for the printer was a fifth) between the beginning of 1852 and the late spring of 1854. The period during which Thoreau wrote each version can be determined by the dates of the journal material he used in it and by its relation to the versions preceding and following it, but we cannot tell exactly when he began or stopped working on any of them.

He wrote version IV at various times during 1852. He drew much of the new material for it from his journals for 1850, 1851, and the first half of 1852; there are also a few items from September, October, and November, 1852. He published two considerable pieces of this version in *Sartain's Magazine* of July, 1852: "A Poet Buys a Farm" and "The Iron Horse." [4] Late in 1852 or early in 1853 Thoreau dropped IV and fairly soon afterward began version V. In view of the extent of the new manuscript, Thoreau must have worked on V well into 1853, but it contains practically no material from the journals of 1853. Late in that year he began VI, and he probably did not complete it until the beginning of 1854. As he finished this version he wrote "The End," but he still had considerable work before him.

He undoubtedly wrote VII in February or March, immediately after finishing VI. The title page, table of contents, and preface in this version might suggest that its leaves were the remnants of a rewriting Thoreau prepared for the printer, but they were not. All the passages in VII are short, and Thoreau fitted them into the earlier groups, most into VI, but others into II, III, IV, and V.

His final draft, which is not in the manuscript and was apparently lost, was the copy for the printer. Thoreau must have sent off some of his copy in late February or early March, for he noted in his journal on March 28, 1854, "Got first proof of 'Walden.'" This referred to the first batch of page proof and not to a first set of proofs of the whole work. In the manuscript of VII, in the midst of a sentence in "Economy," 38, Thoreau noted, "end of 2nd proof"; and on page 64 of the page proof (HM 925) he wrote to the printer, "Will try to make the last part of the Ms. more legible." He sent the copy off in parts and received the page proof in the same way.[5] He probably finished

4. "Where I Lived," 1, 2, 3, and 5; and "Sounds," 5–13; Thoreau revised both passages before the final text of *Walden*.

5. The page proof was the only proof he received; he could not have received anything before it. It was set up with three pages on a sheet. In the first batch of proof Thoreau received five sheets; the first sheet contained the title page and the copyright; each of the other four sheets contained three pages of proof. On the verso of the fifth sheet is written "duplicate proof for the editor." The second batch of proof consisted of four sheets—twelve pages—of proof. The end of the twenty-fourth page of text (the end of the ninth sheet of proof) coincides with the point in the manuscript at which Thoreau wrote "end of 2nd proof." On the verso of the ninth sheet is the direction "Henry D. Thoreau, Concord, Mass." There is no evidence as to the extent of later batches of proof.

the copy for the printer in late April or May. He wrote of the breaking-up of the ice in 1854, "about the 7th of April," in "Spring," 3; and his observation on how long it took for Walden Pond to rise and fall in "The Ponds," 10, is from the journal entry for April 27, 1854; he first put it in *Walden* on a scrap of paper which he attached to a leaf of version VI.

Even when the copy for the printer was done, Thoreau could not rest. On March 31, 1854, he had written in the journal: "In criticising your writing, trust your fine instinct. There are many things which we come very near questioning, but do not question. When I have sent off my manuscripts to the printer, certain objectionable sentences or expressions are sure to obtrude themselves on my attention with force, though I had not consciously suspected them before. My critical instinct then at once breaks the ice and comes to the surface." The page proof allowed him one more opportunity to make a number of small changes for the published text.

And when it was too late for the benefit of others, he made a few corrections in his own copy of *Walden*.[6]

WRIGHT MORRIS

To the Woods †

I went to the woods because I wished to live deliberately, to front only the essential facts of life, and see if I could not learn what it had to teach, and not, when I came to die, discover that I had not lived.

This statement, by one of the world's free men, has captivated and enslaved millions. It is a classic utterance, made with such art that what is not said seems nonexistent, civilization and its ways a mere web of *in*essentials, distracting man from the essential facts of life. The texture of this language and the grain of this thought are one and the same. To fall under its spell is to be in possession of *one* essential self. A sympathetic mind may find the call irresistible. The essential facts of life will seem to be these facts, all others

6. It is in the Abernethy Library, Middlebury College, Middlebury, Vermont. The corrections in it are given by Reginald L. Cook, "Thoreau's Annotations and Corrections in the First Edition of *Walden*," *Thoreau Society Bulletin*, XLII (1953), I.

† From Wright Morris, *The Territory Ahead*, New York, 1957 Pp. 39–50. Copyright 1957, 1958 by Wright Morris. Reprinted by permission of Atheneum Publishers and Wright Morris.

but stratagems, snares, and delusions, although the facts to support such a conclusion are not self-evident. They are implied, but implied with such persuasion they seem facts. That is Thoreau's intention. But his art is greater than his argument. Although he sought to persuade through *facts*, through the testimony of the raw material, it is his craft as a writer that gives his facts conviction, and his example such power. It is his art, not his facts, that sent his readers to the woods.

As André Malraux points out in *The Creative Act*, the artist is launched on his career not by the supremely beautiful face, but by the supremely beautiful painting. It is not just the Woods, but *Thoreau's Woods*, that captivate us. What he chooses to give us is so patently essential—to the picture he is painting—and what he withholds is so plainly inessential, we feel, to life. It is all a matter of selection. Of art, that is.

The American mind, the Yankee imagination, had sap and substance before this man spoke, but I believe we can say it had no grain until Thoreau. It is the natural grain of this mind that still shapes our own. The self-induced captivity of the American mind to some concept of Nature—NATURE writ large—can be traced, it would seem, to the shores of Walden Pond. Here is the first contour map of what we might call our *natural* state of mind.

With his customary intuition concerning things American, D. H. Lawrence, in his *Studies in Classical American Literature*, points this out.

NATURE.
I wish I could write it larger than that.
N A T U R E.
Benjamin [Franklin] overlooked NATURE. But the French Crèvecœur spotted it long before Thoreau and Emerson worked it up. Absolutely the safest thing to get your emotional reactions over is NATURE.

The unmistakable accuracy of this barb makes us wince. Nature —even Nature tooth and claw—is child's play when confronted with *human* nature. The problem, reduced to its essentials, is NATURE v. Human Nature. It was this problem that led Thoreau to take to the woods. But he would not have been led there—he more or less tells us—if he had not believed that taking to the woods was the prevailing tendency of his countrymen.

In *Walden* that prevailing tendency received its classical form. Back to Nature was not new with Thoreau—it had, in fact, lost the gloss Crèvecoeur gave it—but Thoreau endowed it with a civilized respectability. The romantic wash of color is replaced with the essential facts. But the result—since he was an artist—was to heighten the romantic effect. Through the sharp eyes of this capital realist, NATURE, writ large, looked even more inviting, and the realistic myth took precedence over the romantic one. It remains, to this day, a characteristic quality of the American wilderness.

Flight from something, we can say without quibbling, was foreign to Thoreau's mind, and we know that when he turned his back on the city it was *toward* the facts—not away from them. In his own mind he was facing the very facts that his friends and neighbors turned away from, and it is this sentiment, not a romanticized Nature, that gives W*alden* its power. But in a culture of cities, as the country was then becoming, this sentiment went against the very grain of culture, and became, in time, a deliberate rejection of the essential facts of this culture.

In 1845, when Thoreau went to Walden, he had a continental wilderness lying *before* him, and he was hardly in a position to see that he had actually turned his back on the future. Or that the prevailing tendency of Americans was *flight*. Flight, not from what they had found, but from what they had created—the very culture of cities they had labored to establish.

Each of these cultural centers, each of these established towns, became a fragment of Europe and a past to get away from—the prevailing tendency of Americans being what it was. Thoreau did not expose this tendency to examination—he accepted it. It satisfied, after all, the drift and grain of his own mind. He *began* at that point—in a language and a tone similar to that which informed the Declaration of Independence. He established, as that document sought to, certain inalienable human rights. One of them being to take to the woods, if and when you felt the need.

The principle of turning one's back on unpleasant facts—unpleasant because they were so deeply inessential, so foreign, in a way, to our essential Nature—is one *naturally* congenial to the American mind. Thoreau gave this principle its classic utterance. In his spirit, if not in his name, we still take to such woods as we can find. If his genius had been of another kind he might have scrutinized this principle, rather than Nature, but it was his destiny to be the archetypal American. To put, that is, the prevailing tendency to a rigorous test. That he did; that he did and found it wanting, since he both went to the woods and then left them, is an instructive example of how a necessary myth will survive the conflicting facts. The wilderness is now gone, a culture of cities now surrounds us, but the prevailing tendency of Thoreau's countrymen—his more gifted countrymen—is still to withdraw into a private wilderness. William Faulkner is the latest, but he will not be the last, to pitch his wigwam in the pine-scented woods.

If other American classics have been more widely read—and as a rule they would be children's classics—none has left such an impression where it counts the most: on impressionable men. In Thoreau they see the archetypal *man* as well as the American. He is our first provincial with this universal mind. Under the spell of his style his raw material, that little piece of it around Walden Pond, was processed into a universal fact. There it stands, like an act of Nature, having little to do with the man who made it, and, as so often happens, we henceforth have little to do with him. He walks off—he seems to pass like the seasons—leaving us with his pond. With all those facts, essential and inessential, gleaming like a scimitar in the sun, not to mention the problems that his stay in the woods did not resolve.

We have his word for it that Walden was not enough. Is another life of quiet, *very* quiet, desperation all that lies in store? The rest is silence. There is nothing for us to do but go to Walden and see for ourselves.

Somewhere between Walden Pond and Boston—at some point of tension, where these dreams cross—the schizoid soul of the American is polarized. On the one hand we are builders of bridges and cities, we are makers of things and believers in the future. On the other we have a powerful, *private* urge to take to the woods, as we so often do. Sometimes a note left on the bureau, or one tucked into the vest, asks those who still love us to please forgive us, and it usually goes without saying that those who truly love us will understand. After all, it is still the prevailing tendency. To the woods, if we can find them; if we *can't*, then, to the dogs.

It is in the woods at Walden that the shape of things to come is formulated. Here the American mind is divided down its center, fact against fact. At the threshold of our literature the prevailing tendency is given its classic statement and justification. Turn your back on the city, the civilized inessential, and withdraw into the wilderness. Turn your back on those things built with hands, and withdraw into a world not made with hands. The territory ahead lies behind you. *Allons donc!* Take to the woods.

What we have is Nature, NATURE writ large. But it was Thoreau who was the first to remind us that men lead lives of quiet desperation, and another year at Walden, we have reason to believe, he would have been leading one of them. But after two years he had had it. He left the woods, he tells us, for as good a reason as he went there. We have to take that on credit, however, since he does not tell us how it worked out. There is no equally reassuring volume on the world he went back to. Walden was an experiment, he says, and what he learned from it was this: that if a man advances confidently in the direction of his dreams, and endeavors to actually live the life he has imagined, he will meet with a success unexpected in the common hours.

To that we can say *Good!* So he says, and so we believe. But in what direction, pray, now led his dreams? We know only that they led him into the wilderness, not out of it. He does not trouble to tell us in what way his prevailing tendency reversed itself, or, if it did not, how and why it lost its efficacy. No other tendency, of equal inspiration, took its place. Having entered upon and completed his experiment, Thoreau then took eight years to formulate his report, and it stands as the central experiment of his life. And yet we know he went on living. We even know he went on writing. But neither his living nor his writing found another center, another *tendency*, that engaged him like the one that took him to the woods. We might say that having finished with that experiment, he had finished with his life. There is more day to dawn, he reassures us, but he is silent on what day it might be, and in our hearts we feel that the man we know is still in the woods.

What *kind* of man was he? Any number of men, most of them distinguished, have added their touches to his self-portrait. They reaffirm, rather than rearrange, the classical lines. Emerson likened the taking of his arm to the taking of a piece of wood. It would be sound, grainy wood. The elbow honed and polished like the handle of a cane.

But in the main the self-portrait is more than enough. He would ask us to face him as he himself sought to face the facts.

> If you stand right fronting and face to face to a fact, you will see the sun glimmer on both its surfaces, as if it were a cimiter, and feel its sweet edge dividing you through the heart and marrow, and so you will happily conclude your mortal career. Be it life or death, we crave only reality. If we are really dying, let us hear the rattle in our throat and feel the cold in the extremities; if we are alive, let us go about our business.

What business? Ah, there's the rub. Not any ordinary business, certainly, since he has just told you, in no uncertain terms, that in nine chances out of ten your *business* is killing you off. It is why you are dying. It is why, as you read him, he has the ring of truth. It is why the essential facts seem to be that we must go to the woods ourselves if we are to live deep and suck the marrow out of life. It is our busy-ness—if we want to face the facts—that is killing us.

The unexamined paradox is one of many that Thoreau leaves with the reader—forever leaves with him, that is, since a volume on that subject never appeared. *Walden*, like *Huckleberry Finn*, is a *beginning*—the opening chapter of a life, a story, one that en-thralls us, but with all the remaining chapters missing.

A capital realist, the archetypal honest man, when Thoreau had had enough of the woods he left them—but the facts of his life among men are neither essential nor reassuring. What *could* follow on such a beginning? Deep in our hearts we know that the best has been lived, that we have now had it, which is why we don't ask, why we will settle for a pond, a raft, and Huck Finn.

Behind all this talk about facts, and fine talk it is, one fact escapes comment. There is no other business; no other essential business. One leaves the pond to disappear, like an echo, into the wings. The curtain comes down. The lights come on. Can that be the end? It can't—but those are all the facts we are going to get. In the beginning, and a very unforgettable beginning it was, a man went deliberately into the woods. We know that for a fact. But there is very little evidence, of the same order, that he ever came out.

> I should not talk about myself so much [he tells us] if there were anybody else whom I knew as well. Unfortunately I am confined to this by the narrowness of my experience.

The revelation of this statement may lead us to overlook its accuracy. The narrowness of his experience is one of the essential facts in his book. I am not concerned with the absence of those things that we now exploit. On such matters as women and sex we can respect his silence. What he chooses to tell us is much more to the point. The insights of Freud—imaginative in nature—have made it difficult, if not impossible, to face the facts of an age different from our own. I would like to suggest that the myth of Nature—writ large, as Thoreau wrote it—can be as overwhelm-ing, traumatic in fact, as the myth of Sex. It is the myth of Nature that concerns us in Thoreau. He turned to Nature as D. H. Law-rence *turned* to Sex, and both transformed what they saw, what they found, to suit the needs of their genius and their tempera-ment. It is difficult to say which offers the greater handicap. Each man sees, in the mirror of his choice, what he is compelled to see. For all of the material details, the counting of nails and beans, Walden Pond is a mythic, personal vision, and in its depths lurk such facts as it is the genius of the beholder to see. It is on the same map, and no other, as Huck Finn's mighty river, and its memorable facts are the product of the same chemistry, the poet's imagination processing the raw-material facts.

If we now ask Thoreau about his own *business*, he will give us a curious answer. His true profession was, he would have us know, a "saunterer." If this word has a strong romantic coloration—we *see* Thoreau in the woods, but we do not see him saunter—it is still consistent with his role in the myth. The busy man has no time to saunter. In fact, he has no place. One saunters in Nature, plucking a leaf, chewing a twig. It is the saunterer who stops and asks in amazement, "What is the grass?" It is the saunterer who has the time to tell you that it is the flag of his disposition, or better yet, the beautiful uncut hair of the graves. It is the saunterer who leans and loafs at his ease. And with that picture, that telling self-portrait, we know, in our bones, that Thoreau was no saunterer. We know only, thanks to his statement, that he wanted to be. But I believe it no accident, however, that the archetypal saunterer of our dreams, like the archetypal Nature man, Thoreau, began precisely at the point where Thoreau left off. The prevailing tendency, having finished with Thoreau, reappears as a sauntering Song in Walt Whitman, as he makes his way, idly, down the endlessly open road. Walt Whitman, a Kosmos, of Manhattan the son, is that other half of the Nature picture, but this time it is Human Nature—and Walt Whitman's own. Turbulent, fleshy, sensual, eating, drinking, and breeding, Walt Whitman wants space, he wants air, he wants OUT!

Unscrew the locks from the doors!
Unscrew the doors themselves from the jambs!

In theory, if not in practice, in private, if not in public, this was, and still is, the prevailing tendency of his countrymen.

PERRY MILLER

Thoreau in the Context of International Romanticism †

In 1842 Emerson made a special trip to the State House in order to secure a set of reports recently published by the Commonwealth itemizing the flora and fauna of the state. Then, he says, he "set Henry Thoreau on the good track of giving an account of them in the Dial, explaining to him the felicity of the subject for him as it admits of the narrative of all his boatcraft & fishcraft." The young Thoreau meekly followed his master's directive—as a few years later the recalcitrant Thoreau emphatically would not. Margaret Fuller, who did not share Emerson's admiration for the

† From *The New England Quarterly,* by permission of the editors of *NEQ.*
XXIV, 147–59 (June, 1961). Reprinted

rustic genius, had given up the editorship of *The Dial* at the beginning of 1842, and so Emerson was able to print Henry's first original piece in the July issue, under the title "The Natural History of Massachusetts."

Emerson, like many later Thoreauvians, thought of Thoreau as being primarily a naturalist, a rural poet of the meadows and woods, a preternaturally accurate observer (as Emerson was not) of phenomena. Emerson was never to disabuse himself of this misconception, though he had momentary glimmerings of bewilderment and at times almost recognized that Thoreau had a mind. But in the funeral oration for Thoreau, published in the *Atlantic* in 1862, Emerson made an enduring incubus out of his own prejudice by such sentences as "He knew the country like a fox or a bird, and passed through it as freely by paths of his own." If even the sensitive Emerson, with all his chances of first-hand knowledge, held this to be the essential Thoreau, it is no wonder that later admirers, who oddly enough have often taken on some characteristics of a sentimental cult, construe any effort to submit him to a more critical or intellectual analysis as a denigration of their hero.

Yet "The Natural History of Massachusetts" should have warned Emerson, as it still should warn us. Thoreau did indeed demonstrate his vast familiarity with the concrete, the specific, but he pronounced the official reports to be limited and imperfect volumes because they were merely factual. As far as they went, they were admirable, and he was the last to condemn them; yet he was obliged to add "Let us not underrate the value of a fact; it will one day flower in a truth." If Emerson paused over this sentence, he probably smiled with the pleasure of seeing an ingenious variant on one of his favorite themes. Those who like Margaret Fuller or James Russell Lowell dismissed Henry as a bungling imitator of Emerson—even, according to some of them, modeling his nose on Emerson's—would have concluded that here he was commencing his career of stealing neighbor Emerson's apples. Few if any at that time could comprehend, and today the awareness even for the most devoted student is hard to acquire, that this sentence was prophetic of Thoreau's whole artistic endeavor. Yet understanding dawns when we read further into the paragraph and find him saying, ominously, "He has something demoniacal in him, who can discern a law, or couple two facts." What? we should ask at this point—if we are sufficiently jolted— do facts sweetly flower into truths by and of themselves? If so then what need is there of demoniacal assistance? And if it is demoniacal to couple two facts, where does the demon dwell? Could it possibly be that he inhabits what Wordsworth called, and all Yankee Transcendentalists repeated after him, "our meddling intellect" which, according to the high priest of Romantic Naturalism botanizes on grandmother's grave and murders to dissect?

The story of America's initial hostility to Wordsworth—manifested in virtually all departments of the indigenous intelligence—and then of his gradual acceptance as the foremost poet of the age, is a familiar tale. Emerson himself had, in the 1820's, been repelled by him, but in a lecture of 1838 he declared to Boston, and he was later to make the point even more emphatically in *The Dial*, his conversion. Whether Thoreau heard this particular lecture or not, the passage is worth repeating, because it indicates what Thoreau would start with, he never having to learn by a long process of overcoming an inherited opposition, what Emerson with great difficulty had finally grasped but on which Emerson's hold was never to be as tight as Henry's:

> The fame of Wordsworth is one of the most instructive facts in modern literature when it is considered how utterly hostile his genius at first seemed to the reigning taste, & I may add with what feeble poetic talents his great & steadily growing dominion has been established. More than any poet his success has been not his own but that of the Idea or principle which possessed him & which he has rarely succeeded in adequately expressing.

The last sentence is the heart of the drama. In our perspective we may indeed say that Wordsworth succeeded in adequately expressing his great "Idea" only in *The Prelude*, which was not to become public property until after his death in 1850. Yet magnificent as that statement is, and fundamental though it be for *our* understanding of Wordsworth, it is astonishing how in 1850, when it was at long last revealed, the meaning of it had already been absorbed. Thoreau does not often mention Wordsworth, but the very opening segments of the *Journal* show that he hardly needed to. He was already a Wordsworthian, and in that sense a child of the Romantic era.

The original draft of the sentence about the fact flowering into truth was entered in December 1837, when Thoreau was twenty and just out of Harvard College. Even more revealing is a praise of Goethe in the same month which approves of his being satisfied "with giving an exact description of objects as they appear to him." This, Thoreau pontificates, is the trait to be prized, and its skill consists in the device whereby "even the reflections of the author do not interfere with his descriptions." For Thoreau had thus already completely comprehended one of the major problems of the Romantic movement—for that portion of Romanticism preoccupied with the new interpretation of Nature it was the major problem—of striking and maintaining the delicate balance between object and reflection, of fact and truth, of minute observation and generalized concept. There can be no doubt that Thoreau was made aware of the problem at least in part by Emerson's *Nature*, which with its Platonic ascent from the lowly level of "Commodity" into the intellectual vistas of "Prospects" sought to offer an original method for combining the two poles of the Romantic dilemma. But it does seem to me that from the beginning Henry possessed an insight which, though it too must be located within the larger framework of Romantic Naturalism, is very different from Emerson's. The contrast becomes vivid if you put Emerson's famous sentences about becoming a transparent eyeball and about the currents of universal being circulating through him alongside this entry of Thoreau's, on March 3, 1839, on "The Poet":

> He must be something more than natural—even supernatural. Nature will not speak through but along with him. His voice will not proceed from her midst, but, breathing on her, will make her the expression of his thought. He then poetizes when he takes a fact out of nature into spirit. He speaks without reference to time or place. His thought is one world, hers another. He is another Nature,—Nature's brother. Kindly offices do they perform for one another. Each publishes the other's truth.

It was from this duality of vision—what in *Walden* he would call "doubleness" and which, he would say, often made its possessor a bad neighbor—that he was able to extract from the *Journal* and put into "The Natural History" such contradictory assertations as, on the one hand, "Nature will bear the closest inspection; she invites us to lay our eye level with the smallest leaf, and take an insect view of its plain," and then, on the other, invoking in full awareness of its intellectualized nature one of the grand conceptual techniques of Biblical scholarship, this remark, "When I walk in the woods, I am reminded that a wise purveyor has been there before me; my most delicate experience is typified there." If at one and the same time Nature is closely inspected in microscopic detail and yet through the ancient system of typology makes experience intelligible, then Thoreau will have solved the Romantic riddle, have mastered the destructive Romantic Irony. Seen in such a context, his life was an unrelenting exertion to hold this precarious stance. In the end, the impossibility of sustaining it killed him. But not until, at least in *Walden*, he had for a breathless moment, held the two in solution, fused and yet still kept separate, he and Nature publishing each other's truth.

Surely, it was a demoniacal enterprise from start to finish. This is why, it seems to me, that Thoreau can at long last be seen as a major writer of his century, not because he also happened to know boatcraft and fishcraft.

When *The Prelude* was published, the by then great host of Wordsworth's followers found in Book XII a passage which they might well wish he had published in the first decade of the century (when it actually was written), for it would have saved them a great deal of trouble in groping their way to what Emerson called his "Idea." In a magnificent apostrophe to the "Soul of Nature" Wordsworth condemns anew what he held to be the vice of the eighteenth century, its lust for comparing scene with scene, pampering the taste with novelties of color and proportion, and so rendering taste insensible to the spirit of a particular place. He himself had once let his eye tyrannize over him, so that for awhile even he went about seeking for the picturesque,

> Still craving combinations of new forms,
> New pleasure, wider empire for the sight,
> Proud of her own endowments, and rejoiced
> To lay the inner faculties asleep.

Yet all this while he had beside him his sister Dorothy, who finally showed him how to be an enthusiast without permitting the eye to become mistress of the heart.

> She welcomed what was given, and craved no more;
> Whate'er the scene presented to her view
> That was the best, to that she was attuned
> By her benign simplicity of life.

Yet probably this passage would not have been really too helpful to such a creature as Henry because Wordsworth says that Dorothy's freedom from false notions of the picturesque in Nature was a feminine trait, that she was content to remain passively receptive because she was "wise as women are." However, we have become of late increasingly aware that in many of the most characteristic figures of the Romantic movement there flourished a special type of exquisite emotional sensibility, a warmth of temperament and a disposition to let experience come to them rather than that they should go forth, sword in hand, to conquer it. Goethe's *Werther* is the prototype of them all, which the supreme man of action in the era, Napoleon, read and re-read. We may think also of Constant's *Adolphe*, of Keats's *Endymion*, of the cult of Chatterton, of the personality of Robert Schumann. It would be too much to say that these creations or the creators were "feminine" in nature, but they are not robustly masculine as had been Dr. Johnson or Fielding. Each of them, whether an imagined creation or an imaginative creator, is what Thomas Mann (whose comprehension of the Romantic spirit was profound) called a "delicate child of life." In all American literature Henry Thoreau is the one to whom this characterization perfectly applies. Let us remind ourselves, one of the earliest and most appealing of Thoreau's poems is, of course, "Lately, alas, I knew a gentle boy."

So it was not necessary that the example of Dorothy Wordsworth be put before the young Transcendentalists in order that they should learn the inner secret of Romantic receptivity. They had such tuition as Wordsworth's lines on "Tintern Abbey," and on the superiority of an impulse from the vernal wood over all intellectual instruction if only they would learn to come forth from science and art "with a heart/That watches and receives." Above all, they had the "Preface" to the 1800 edition of *Lyrical Ballads*. I do not propose to argue that Thoreau found the origin of his own "Idea" in this document, or even to insist that he read it (though the chances are all on the side that he did). Even if he never looked at it, we can find in it the most precise exposition of his ambition as a writer and his aspiration as an artist.

To read the "Preface" with Thoreau in mind is to realize anew how different was the situation of the Romantic revolutionary in England (as indeed in all Europe) from that of the American. The chief thrust of Wordsworth is against the poetic diction of the Neo-Classical age, the formalized and stereotyped abstract adjectives of Pope and Johnson. His great plea is that poetry use "the real language of men." We comprehend from his fervent argument how terribly dominating Neo-Classical verse had been in literary England. Provincial America endeavored to imitate the mode—witness Freneau and the Connecticut Wits—but we never had a poet who so tyrannized over our native taste as did Pope in England. Hence when youths like Emerson felt the impulse from the vernal wood stirring in their hearts, they had to exert themselves not so much in dethroning a vested interest in technique as merely in liberating themselves from a culture that they now perceived was prosaic and uncreative. They simply had to disassociate themselves from what Emerson pungently called "the corpse-cold Unitarianism of Brattle Street and Harvard College." Or, like Henry, they could resign from all the societies they had never joined—including the Thoreau Society!

Hence what meant the most to them in Wordsworth's "Preface" were the hints he threw out about a new kind of utterance—he was talking about poetry but his prescriptions would apply as well to prose—in which the writer would strive by might and main to look steadily at his subject. The most thrilling paragraph to the generation of Thoreau would be that wherein Wordsworth rejected as idle and unmanly the faintness of heart which, despairing of ever producing a language as fitting for expression of the passion as the real passion itself, abjectly concluded that the artist should become a translator and substitute excellencies of another kind for those which are unattainable in speech. By this specious attempt to surpass his subject, said Wordsworth, the writer condemns his material to an inferior status, and thus slyly exalts himself over it. No, no: fidelity to the thing, strict application to the object, no underestimation of the value of the fact—these convictions and only these will create a literature "not standing upon external testimony, but carried alive into the heart by passion; truth which is its own testimony, which gives competence and confidence to the tribunal to which it appeals, and receives them from the same tribunal."

As we know, Wordsworth had a long struggle explaining to his contemporaries that by his phrases "the language really spoken by men" and his "looking steadily at the subject" he did not mean what we would term photographic reproduction of the scene or of the human face. Romantic Nature was not—for better or worse —what the next generation would salute as "Realism." Wordsworth never taught the neophyte that a daguerreotype of Walden Pond should be esteemed more highly than a truly poetic rendition of it. He insisted that poetry have form, that it cast into metrical arrangements the materials carried alive into the heart, that passion come into literature not as animal cries or exclamations of pain, but as emotion recollected in tranquility. This meant that while no *apriori* concept of the picturesque, or of dignity or of excellence, should be imposed from without, that there would be an organic growth of the concept out of a fervent devotion to objective truth. The fact, in other words, would flower into a truth—*if*, that is, the poet could bring an adequate passion to his portraiture. Thoreau, therefore, would not be betraying or patronizing or insulting his material when he openly admitted that he was "for convenience putting the experience of two years into one." That was not illegitmate manipulation of reality, it was a way of being "something more than natural," of becoming "Nature's brother."

By the time Thoreau graduated from Harvard, this Romantic aesthetic had been widely domesticated in America. The principal agent in reconciling a suspicious public to what had at first seemed a nonsensical or even subversive paradox was landscape painting. In terms comprehensible to the average intelligence the Hudson River School, as historians now label them, were dramatizing Wordsworth's great "Idea." Indeed, I am convinced that one immensely helpful way to deepen our appreciation of what Thoreau was seeking is to look closely at certain pictures of Thomas Cole (not his grandiose tableaus but his smaller scenes), Asher Durand or Thomas Doughty. Especially I would say Durand, for in him appears that union of graphic detail and organizing design which the disciple of Wordsworth ever strove to attain. An influential periodical of the time, the *Knickerbocker*, said of him in 1853—just as *Walden* was receiving its last revision—that "His compositions, while faithful to the truth of detail, combine a beautiful *sentiment*, which is felt by the observer, and it is in this in which his true greatness consists." All the implications of this sentence, advertised by its use of "while" along with "combine," show how, even in the complacent circles which subscribed to the *Knickerbocker*, the Romantic "Idea" had become an orthodoxy. Hence the more opulent in these circles paid high prices for the landscapes of Durand and his fellows. We might surmise that by the same token they should have recognized in *Walden* a prose counterpart to their beloved painters. But, as is a matter of record, they bought the paintings but never the book.

There are a hundred reasons why comfortable citizens of the Republic in 1854 would hang over their fireplace a landscape by Durand or Doughty, at the wildness of which they might gaze without perturbation, and still be horrified at the wildness of *Walden*—if indeed they so much as heard of it. Among these reasons, however, must be enumerated—or at least I shall venture to list it—the fact that Thoreau managed so radical a penetration into "the truth of detail," and then so blatant an assertion of what the *Knickerbocker* called "sentiment," that the "combination"—to use again the catchword of the era—seemed either grotesque or truly demoniacal. Or another way to put it is to say that Henry Thoreau took the basic premise of the Romantic Age more seriously than most romantics were able to accept.

I would not unduly belabor this point, yet I would like to suggest that it indicates the perennial and never quite definable fascination of *Walden*. Thoreau spoke it as bluntly as possible in the chapter he called "Sounds," and most succinctly in the first sentence. Books, he there said, are things in dialect and are provincial, and if we are confined solely to them, "we are in danger of forgetting the language which all things and events speak without metaphor, which alone is copious and standard." Consequently *Walden* is one of the supreme achievements of the Romantic Movement—or to speak accurately, of Romantic Naturalism. Mr. Shanley has proved beyond the shadow of any doubt that it was a conscious, a deliberate creation; it was not and is not some spontaneous impulse from the vernal wood, although unfortunately many of its modern champions pretend that it was. No, it is truly emotion, but emotion ostensibly recollected in tranquility. Yet it is assuredly emotion, passion. There is no substitution for the original experience, there are no excellencies of diction contrived so as to suggest an inferiority of the original to the narration. Still, it is not a mere recital, item by item, atomic moment after moment, of two years beside the pond. It is a magnificent autobiography, faithful in every detail to the setting, arising to the level of a treatise on imagination and taste, and all this without ever becoming didactic. When seen in such a perspective, it can be placed beside *The Prelude*. It is the "growth of a poet's mind," and despite all its wealth of concrete imagery it is centered not upon Nature, but upon Nature's brother, the intelligence of the artist.

I need hardly observe that in this century the entire philosophy of what I call Romantic Naturalism has been attacked from innumerable sides and is generally thought to be completely discredited. In painting, the Hudson River School of representation gave way to a succession of infinitely more sophisticated methods until eventually the object disappeared altogether and an artist simply painted his idea. In poetry the creative impulse for several decades has been calling for a repudiation of the identification of mind with thing, for the formulation of a poetry which shall be entirely intellectual, metaphorical, artificial. That disposition which in recent English writing has been expressed in Yeats, in Ezra Pound, in T. S. Eliot, sees in the artist a manipulator, an inventor of symbols and images, who severs himself from Nature, who deliberately violates her, pillages her for schemes of his own devising. And even Robert Frost, who like Wordsworth insists that poetry must keep close to the language of ordinary human talk, reminds us again and again that we must avoid the pathetic fallacy of assuming any correspondence between human emotions and natural fact. If one is versed in country things, he memorably says, one does not suppose phoebes weep over the desolation of an abandoned farmhouse. Indeed, in one of his most powerful proclamations, "The Most of It," Frost seems to be deriding all the Henry Thoreaus of his past by describing a "he" who kept the universe alone, who wanted from Nature "someone else additional to him" and who received in answer only the sudden eruption from the woods of a great buck, an utterly inhuman beast.

If the twentieth-century judgment of the Romantic aesthetic is correct, then Henry Thoreau is one of its monumental failures and martyrs, along with Shelley and Novalis. Neither he nor they were able to answer the terrible question of whether, once they committed themselves to the proposition that their most delicate experience was typified in Nature, they were thereafter actually writing about Nature—about Walden Pond, for instance—or about nothing more than their delicious experiences. If in reality they were only projecting their emotions onto the Natural setting, if the phoebes do not weep for human miseries, then their effort to find someone additional to themselves was doomed to ghastly defeat. In this view, the career of Henry Thoreau is as tragic as that of King Lear. He too sacrificed himself needlessly to a delusion.

In his first organized statement, Thoreau could say, with all the confidence that a Lear had in the love of his daughters, that when he detects a beauty in any recess of Nature he is reminded of the inexpressible privacy of a life, that he may rest content with nothing more than the sight and the sound. On the premise of that doctrine, he may properly say no more than "I am affected by the sight of the cabins of muskrats," or than "I am the wiser in respect to all knowledges, and better qualified for all fortunes, for knowing that there is a minnow in the brook." In the glowing confidence of these aphorisms lurks the assumption that moral law and natural law contain analogies, and that for this reason the writer may safely record facts without metaphors, since truths are bound to sprout from them. The later portions of Thoreau's *Journal*, those after 1854, with their tedious recordings of mere observations, of measurements, of statistics, seem to attest not only the dwindling of his vitality but the exhaustion of the theory upon which he commenced to be an author in the first place. He immolated himself on the pyre of an untenable concept of literary creation.

And yet, he refuses to be consumed. Expound *Walden*, if you will, as a temporary and so an empty triumph of the Romantic dream, as a work doomed to diminish with the recession of that dream, yet the book refuses to go into the archeological oblivion of, shall I say? Shelley's *The Revolt of Islam*. Robert Frost, while objecting with all his Yankee soul to Thoreau's epistemology, still proclaims that with him Thoreau is a "passion." The obvious answer, or rather the easy one, is that Thoreau was a great writer, and so his pages survive in spite of changes in metaphysical fashions. But that is truly an easy, a luxurious way of salvaging our poet. The more difficult, but I believe the more honest and, in the final accounting, the more laudatory way is to say that the Romantic balance, or its "Idea" of combination, of fusing the fact and the idea, the specific and the general, is still a challenge to the mind and to the artist. Thoreau was *both* a Transcendentalist and a Natural Historian. He never surrendered on either front, though the last years of the *Journal* show how desperate was the effort to keep both standards aloft. He said, in the central conceptual passage of W*alden*, that he wanted to drive life into a corner, to publish its meanness if it proved to be mean, but that if it should turn out to be sublime, then to give a true account of its sublimity. "The universe constantly and obediently answers to our conceptions" was his resolute determination. For what more sublime a cause, even though it be a questionable thesis, can a man expend himself?

THEODORE BAIRD

Corn Grows in the Night †

Anyone who sits down to read straight through the *Bulletins* of the Thoreau Society—whose members collect and print every scrap of news about their author—is bound to notice how variously a literary man can be put to what are after all non-literary uses. Those expectations associated with Swift or Pope or Jane Austen, subtlety of thought and feeling and expression, the creation of a coherent imagined world to which we respond with pleasurable emotion, are subordinated to something large and vague called an influence, a political and social force, a public image, even a property worth dollars and cents. Like the Lincoln of the Lincoln Memorial or Dr. Schweitzer on the cover of *Time*, Thoreau now looms as an international figure. He seems to stand for private rebellion. He is the solitary man against society, appealing to the individual's profound dissatisfaction with the part he must play in earning a living, in just being a member of the human race. Furthermore Thoreau preaches a better life within walking distance: after a left turn you come to a woods and a pond. So it is that Thoreau has even been mentioned in the same breath with Jesus and with Gandhi.

No wonder, then, that a watchful eye finds Thoreau's name in so many odd connections that the *Bulletin* is able to publish in every issue a column of the latest news of their author, how he is put to use in Seattle, what new translation has been made in Spanish. Single sentences of his appear, we are told, on bus cards in such and such a city, and the curious fact is added that these cards are often stolen. He also provides quotations to be used, along with Elbert Hubbard, in the calendars of savings banks, and,

† From in *The Massachusetts Review* (Autumn, 1962) pp. 93–103. Copyright © 1963, The Massachusetts Review, Inc.

along with John Locke, in the prestige advertising of great corporations. His name is invoked on behalf of good causes, as if there
were something about him that would naturally make him a pro-
ponent of homeopathy and vegetarianism, of theosophy and pho-
netic spelling and organic gardening. He has been acknowledged as
their model by a number of people who have taken to the woods
and tried living on woodchuck and purslane or soybeans, and
Paul Elmer More in Shelburne, N H. complacently wrote *A
Hermit's Notes on Thoreau* and actually professed to have read
Walden out of doors. Thoreau has also been loosely associated
with nature as a picture, especially when charmingly recorded by
the camera, and it seemed as proper in 1906 to adorn the edition
of the *Journal* with a series of fine illustrations—snow on pitch
pines, a wildflower—as it did more recently for *Life* to run what is
called a photographic essay on Thoreau. Appropriately, as a
piece of property Thoreau's money value does not seem great.
Of course the Morgan and Huntington Libraries do possess manuscripts. And why not? But a pencil made by Thoreau, an empty
pencil box, a couple of bricks from his birthplace, are modestly
priced, and an ordinary first edition of *Walden*, while more expensive than a Chauncey Depew item, may cost less than a good
Currier and Ives.

Such relations as these are scarcely literary. Of course Thoreau
does have his earnest readers, and some of them make the most
extraordinary claims for their author, as an "influence," as an
instrument useful in locating the good life. Some such assertions
have been made, for example, by Upton Sinclair, Robert W. Service, John Buchan, Bette Davis, Bernard Baruch, Gypsy Rose Lee,
Henry Miller. Thoreau has also had his solitary reader, the one-
book man, puzzling and brooding over the text as if it were a religious document, finding in it a new confidence for trusting in
his own incommunicable inner life. Then 'here are those for whom
the essay on "Civil Disobedience" serves as the classic document
for signing a separate peace treaty and resigning from society. It
is seriously reported that every now and then someone deciding
he will no longer pay his income tax sends a copy of this essay
to the nearest Collector of Internal Revenue as an explanation, as
an intelligible explanation. In other acts of defiance of constituted
authority Thoreau is appealed to. The marchers against a missile
base in Kansas are said to have named Thoreau as a writer who
justified their conduct. So when Dr. Uphaus took a copy of "Civil
Disobedience" with him to his New Hampshire jail he defined for
anyone who knew anything his own position. Curiously it was as
long ago as the 1890's that Thoreau served such purposes in
Britain, and the textbooks tell us that he has had his effect on

Gandhi and the Labour movement. As for the immediate disturbed present, when some token resistance is made at the launching of every submarine, when civil defense regulations are deliberately violated, when riders are on their way to New Orleans and walkers on their way to Moscow, when sitters occupy Whitehall, who can say where in the many aggressive acts of individual conscience Thoreau's name is not a living force? When we read as an item of biographical interest that Kenneth Kaunda has served a prison term in Northern Rhodesia for possessing books advocating non-violence, do we not think back with astonishment to that scene in Concord, Massachusetts, that ordinary scene in which no voices were raised, when Thoreau on his way to the cobbler's was arrested by Sam Staples, the night spent in jail, and the next day the huckleberrying as usual? "The air is filled with sounding boards and the echoes are flying," said John Jay Chapman, speaking in the purest Concord idiom. And so it would seem. Apparently Thoreau's voice does carry from continent to continent. He is heard by all sorts of people, as if he were shouting his most intimate thoughts across Walden Pond, and they know what he means. The separate words may be blurred, but distinct speech, we know, is only for the convenience of those who are hard of hearing.

In addition to the revolutionary, the rebellious, and the crackpot, the English teacher has often made Thoreau into a special property, and again for reasons that can hardly be called literary. Thoreau has been blown up way out of proportion compared with, say, Emerson. He is presented, along with Dostoievski, as a treat for the bright high school student, and, along with Jacques Barzun, as a stimulating writer in the book of readings aimed at shaking loose the thick wits of college freshmen. In the classroom he is used to make quick and easy relations between literature and life. The teacher can begin by quoting this bit of English prose: " 'Pay . . . or be locked up.' I declined to pay." He can describe the night in jail—in all the history of human suffering, how it is remembered —and then allude to the many cells now or lately occupied by the many people, some of them almost children, who have sought arrest because their conscience demanded it. Then there can be quoted the words of the Federal judge—it is unlikely that they will ever be included in a volume of stimulating essays for freshmen— when sentencing for more than a single night, for as much as four years, some pacifists who tried to hinder the launching of a nuclear submarine: "While all of you may be sincerely desirous of moving the world in the direction of peace and goodwill, the court cannot accept your decision to accomplish this highminded end by means of breaking the Federal law." Other examples of organized protest are everywhere so common it is inconceivable that a class would not soon be arguing the rights and wrongs of everything. It may seem then that literature is at last, finally and unmistakably, connected with life, with things that matter.

When a writer is put to such diverse uses, as a thinker of great thoughts, as an example of desirable anti-social behavior, as an authority sanctioning the individual's reliance on his own judgment, as an encourager of organized protest, and, at the lowest level, as a bludgeon to rouse sluggish wits, you have evidence of something extravagant. The attention to Thoreau, and admiration for him, is out of all reasonable bounds. He is, in fact, the center of a cult. At its beginning Lowell protested, and to this day he has never been forgiven. Quite recently when Perry Miller in *Consciousness in Concord* demonstrated in a tone of excusable acrimony that Thoreau has his limitations both as a man and as a writer, the reply was a scream of outrage. Perry Miller noticed that the more readers Thoreau has had "the more they try not to recognize his lineaments." The big nose, the weak chin, the high Yankee style with its frequent tones of querulousness, the extremely self-conscious stylist fitting sentences together, in the comparison made by a contemporary, as if he were working in mosaic, all this is blurred, and as if they were listening to the humming of telegraph wires his readers fill in the words from their own highest yearnings and deepest dissatisfactions.

Nevertheless Thoreau's position as a writer can be located, and let the worst be said first of all. He is an impossible egotist. Why, wrote one of his oldest friends, was he so disappointed with everybody else &c., not even putting it in the form of a question and making the object all inclusive. Thoreau speaks as the exception to every rule, the judge of all the rest of the universe, droning on and on, monotonously didactic, deliberately obscure, about friendship and chastity and the soul and things like that, all the while playing with words, seeing similarities in differences, differences in similarities, punning and turning out paradoxes. No wonder Hawthorne called him an intolerable bore. But Thoreau's own awareness of where he stood in relation to his friends gives us some idea of the high visibility of the Concord air, so clear, dry, and cold it was. He actually says of himself, "My only distinction must be that I am the greatest bore they ever had."

And the portentous tone still comes through to us. Thus he says, for example, "Silence alone is worthy to be heard." The fact is that once you give your mind to this way of talking you can set yourself up as a sage, and with the same effect. Insensibility, one can say, alone is worthy of being felt . . . The invisible alone is worthy of being seen . . . The intangible alone we want to touch . . . The incommunicable . . . The ineffable . . . "Give me that sen-

tence," says Thoreau, "which no intelligence can understand."
Well? The question is answered by Thoreau again from his own
terrible awareness of what he was doing. On the publication of
Walden he wrote down in his *Journal* a list of his faults as a
writer, and he begins with "Paradoxes . . . a style which may be
imitated." Profundity turns out to be a surface obscurity, and that
which no intelligence can understand a trick of style.

To continue the catalogue of faults, Thoreau also enjoys the
easy position of the moralist. You can watch him walk into and
establish the obvious connections. When he sees a sloop off
Chatham dragging for anchors, he goes on in the entirely expected
way: "If the roadsteads of the spiritual ocean could be thus
dragged, what rusty flukes . . ." and so on and on, where the shift
from the material to the spiritual meaning is explicit and traditional. The ocean of life. Throw out the lifeline. A great deal of
Thoreau is like this, obvious, soothing, expected, on the level of
hymn writing and the common cant of sermons.

Having said all this in obvious disparagement, I add that there
is a lot of fun in Thoreau. It is too bad he did not preserve more
bits of conversation with his Uncle Charles, more examples of
human oddity, like that of the man who began to dig through to
China. We have Emerson's word for it that his Concord audience
—how experienced they were in listening to lecturers—laughed
till they cried over his description of his rambles on Cape Cod, and
there is a great deal of laughter still available on the printed page.
Thoreau's humor is like that of another Yankee who sailing alone
around the world repelled the attacks of hostile natives by strewing
his deck with carpet tacks and so reduced their bloodthirstiness
and his own real danger to something more than a little ludicrous.
In his highest flights where Thoreau is at his best there is this same
awareness of the fun of the thing, an awareness that he is playing
the part of a sage, homespun, crackerbarrel, local, living right
there along with the many other sages in Concord. He shows us
how every American can be his own philosopher, and what a
funny idea that is.

As a writer, however, Thoreau must be taken with the utmost
seriousness. "Hardly in the history of literature, wherever we
enter the workshop, is there such devotion to duty," says Perry
Miller, and we can follow the author from one stage to another in
the manufacture of the finished product. First there is the author
out of doors, often—and this comes as a surprise—carrying an
umbrella, sometimes accompanied by his unnamed friend (Channing) and his nameless dog (Peter). We can see him stopping to
write in his notebook, recording frequently in the present tense a
scene or object before his eyes. Later there was the writing up of

these notes and then their revision in the *Journal*. Finally there was the ransacking of the *Journal*, the dovetailing and patching in book and essay, making that rich texture where every sentence and metaphor connect with a constantly enlarging complex of imagery and thought. Indeed it might even be said that part of Thoreau's present importance is a result of the rich material he offers the analytical reader.

Even more remarkable than the intricacy of his arrangements on the page is his extraordinary use of language to communicate the incommunicable, to express those wordless moments when Thoreau stood alone in the presence of his subject. And what, precisely, was that subject? Nature, we say, and everyone knows that nature for Thoreau was but a figure of speech. "—I use a part of the world as a symbol to express my thought," and nature, he says, provides the "raw material of tropes and symbols with which to describe . . . life." Well, yes, of course, nature (whatever that may be) has always served this purpose for the writer, and the other side of the equation—god or love or life—has always been beyond expression. "To walk abroad is, not with eyes, / But thoughts, the fields to see and prize. . . ." Thoreau's fields appear in the plainest, most ordinary terms, pretty good walking and clean in the New England way. In his turn the reader moves across the gap (nature is like—) with confidence, from shrikes and chickadees, toads and snakes, wildflowers in spring and frozen apples in winter, to his most ardent aspirations. Aspirations for what? For something, not evident at first sight in the relation of shrike and chickadee. Call it perfection—"methinks a roseate sunset is preparing."

Almost more than anything else Thoreau is an inspiriting writer, and *Walden* is about the only book I know of written by a genuine author that seems to promise us happiness. "The sun is but a morning star." I say this despite the ambiguities that close analysis does turn up and the incoherence in what can only be called Thoreau's systems of thought. The devoted reader knows what Thoreau is saying, for he speaks directly to the heart, confirming what the heart already knows. Life is good. To speak otherwise is to admit personal failure. "That man who does not believe that each day contains an earlier, more sacred, and auroral hour than he has yet profaned, has despaired of life. . . ." To live well you must master the art of affecting the quality of the day. To learn this art you must know what is happening in the woods at night and at the bottom of streams and on the surface of the quaking bog. You must inspect snowstorms. You must savor the difference between the low growing and the highbush blueberry. He is telling us that life is wild, to use his favorite word, something best understood by, of all people, the red Indians, something still to be felt in the rise and fall of rivers, the flight of geese, the growth of trees, the movement and force that contains winter and death. Such knowledge brings hope and reassurance. From any other point of view this can be seen as a very strange conclusion indeed.

It really isn't very clear, and you either know what Thoreau is talking about or you don't. The art, however, is unmistakable. In the several pages at the end of *Walden* on the railroad cut in spring, a regular set piece, can be demonstrated most beautifully how complex is Thoreau's vision, how, in fact the world of thawing sand and clay becomes a symbol of life itself, for rivers, trees, butterflies, and, most wonderfully, blood vessels. The movement from the plain ordinariness of walking down the B & M tracks to seeing the earth as "living poetry" is grand enough to excite a cheer. There are also simpler examples where he does not rely on the piling up of sentence on sentence to construct a context where a larger meaning seems all but put into words. Sometimes he is simply cryptic. Three times he notices in his *Journal* without preparation or comment that corn grows in the night, and the attentive reader knows that the natural phenomenon so dear to middle western writers is really not what is being talked about. Or consider a fragment of a sentence where, it seems to me, Thoreau is at his very best: "—explore your own higher latitudes—with shiploads of preserved meats to support you, if they be necessary, and pile the empty cans sky-high for a sign." Here Thoreau uses what we take on Sunday mornings to the town dump as symbols for all we discard in our social institutions (Harvard College, the state, the family) in pursuit of our own private aspiration. But that is a stupid beginning of a translation and misses all the fun of the thing. Better leave it in the original Concord, where it is perfectly plain. Only by an effort of the historical imagination is it possible to imagine someone—like Dr. Johnson—so dull, so unwilling to understand, as to profess not to know what Thoreau is talking about. What are these higher latitudes? Why tin cans? A sign for what? Of course you could always try to explain Thoreau's meaning by talking about the search for Franklin, the search for the North-West Passage, the search for—. But no lectures on American Civilization, no close reading of the text, will ever fill in what is meant by that dash. The fact is Thoreau is conveying more than words can ever say. How, you ask, do I know this? I answer, I know that I know.

Small wonder, then, that while everyone is conscious of the limitations of language Thoreau should seem to be a very great man and a very great writer. He is telling us that life must be good, our human capacities are infinite, our inexpressible desires capable of being satisfied. He tells us all this by speaking of the ordinary things of pasture and woodlot and stream. To use his own words, he heard beyond the range of sound and saw beyond the range of sight. He lived in two worlds, and so his life was, as he said, an ecstasy.

The sad truth is that within the short lifetime of forty-five years this vision of the world and this use of language proved not to be durable. Of course Emerson in his funeral sermon tried to insure a happy ending by calling Thoreau "a spirit . . . which effaced its defeats with new triumphs." Would that this were possible, and that this language stood for some recognizable experience. As for the record of Thoreau's failure, it is all written out in the journal.

Once upon a time Thoreau gathered the wild vine of the Assabet. Finally he gathered a measurable quantity of cranberries. Once Thoreau knew that in naming and measuring—the process so satisfying to the ordinary person who gets interested in his surroundings—there is something deadly. Repeatedly he spoke of how the description of a bird or a flower killed for him the direct wordless experience of the object. Yet this vision of wild nature— "What is a man but a mass of thawing clay?"—early began to grow dim, as if it depended simply on being young, as if the failure were in the nervous system itself. Already in 1851—three years before *Walden*—he was asking himself if he were not "narrowed down to the field of the microscope." Later he asks, "Shall I become insensible as a fungus?" And he says, "We begin to die, not in our senses or extremities, but in our divine faculties." In a long passage, he places the blame partly outside himself: "We soon get through with Nature. She excites an expectation she cannot satisfy. . . . There was a time when the beauty and the music were all within, and I sat and listened to my thoughts, and there was a song in them." Along with these and similar passages there are many examples of what can only be called a hardening of the heart. His descriptions of the explosion at the powder mill, of a tree struck by lightning, of an ice storm, are beautifully exact and entirely without regard for violence as a fact, a terrifying fact. Thoreau was not, to use his own contemptuous word, a "feeling" man.

Nature had once been "all but a figure of speech," but with time, alas, the other side of the similitude grew dim and immediate experience finally became more and more fascinating for, as we say, its own sake. Ordinary names are enough for ordinary objects. So when late in life Thoreau found, of all things, three or four pieces of coral in a field near Concord, he does not immediately begin to play with the paradox of the far as near nor does he hear in the rumble of the farmer's wagon crossing a plank bridge the thunder of waves on undream'd shores. Just like anyone else he wonders how these bits of coral came there, and then he moves on to something else. Coral turns out to be coral. And what is wrong with that?

Thoreau's world finally appears as the rich multiplicity of the naturalist. This was a change of direction rather than a choice between opposites. Or to put it another way, it was a change in language, from metaphor expressing the world as a trope or symbol to a more or less technical terminology by which the parts of this world are related one to another. Channing tells us that Thoreau's dream was to compile a calendar of Concord, to "paint a sufficient panorama of the year, which multiplied the image of a day." Another noble ambition. The last volumes of the *Journal*—those printed do not contain all his observations—show him as one obsessed, moving from one thing to another in an endless succession of marvels. He recorded temperatures, the height of rivers, the depth of snow. He took muskrat houses and birds' nests apart to see how they were built and with what materials. He observed the formation of ice. And then one day while counting tree rings he caught cold.

As a story of a man's life or of a writer's career, this does not come out right, and a reader who tries to express his mixed responses to Thoreau may well feel that his dominant emotion is sadness. Here is a man who promises us everything. Consciousness alone, unaided by armies or money or dynamos or political power or tradition, can shape the world to our own expectation. The force of a single mind—if only you write an essay or hire a hall and give a lecture—can do anything. Or in simplest terms and in one of his best sentences, "To affect the quality of the day, that is the highest of arts." Why, then, should life end in counting and measuring and labeling according to Gray's *Botany*? It is hard not to feel there is some kind of defeat here.

Another way to talk about this sadness is for the reader to admit that he is thinking partly of himself and how his own literary expectations have changed. If he responds, as every good reader should do, to Thoreau's most hopeful tones, he must also recognize this susceptibility as weakness. For Thoreau's position as an author when he is talking about the new dawn is remarkable, perhaps the most remarkable thing about him. It is inexcusable. Thoreau speaks as a god.

For Thoreau is not like other men. He does not share the usual human limitations, such as an inability to understand other people, a misplaced confidence in what and how much is known to anyone, wilfulness, a pathetically invincible selfishness, a general stupidity, etc. He knows and understands and judges everything and everybody. And he speaks directly to the reader as one who shares this same godlike capability. For example, when Thoreau says, "The impression made on a wise man is that of universal innocence. Poison is not poisonous after all, nor are any wounds fatal," the reader instantly agrees, for he knows no poisons and bears no wounds, and easily shuts his eyes to what is around him. A single glance in any direction would provide plenty of contradictory evidence. Everywhere people volunteer the information that even in the nearest hills, the first rise in the ground toward the terrible mountains on the horizon, there are rattlesnakes. And history— "Julian attempted to draw the deadly weapon from his side," says Gibbon—supports the proposition that men have died of wounds. And for the fate of unfortunate humanity, living through no choice of their own in this dangerous valley, Thoreau, not a "feeling" man, wastes no compassion. Indeed for the homely and ingenious ways that other people have used to pass the time, to kill time, Thoreau feels nothing but contempt. The daily routine of dusting a collection of bric-a-brac on the mantelpiece, the laborious attempt to do good to other people, the organized pursuit of runaway slaves, the building of a railroad as far west as Fitchburg, the lifelong attempt to pay off the mortgage on the place, the shooting of muskrats and songbirds, the cutting down of every tree in sight, these and an infinite number of similar absurdities do not touch with pity a heart eagerly waiting for the new dawn. And the reader also feels disdain.

Thoreau appears as one who changed the object of his search. In one role he has just made an important discovery, a patch of woods really belonging to the land, going straight back to the red Indian, genuine woods, not yet cut over for firewood nor yet burned up by a couple of Harvard boys cooking a mess of fish. There, in these woods, are plenty of signs, if you will only look. There are bits of coral as well as cairns composed of empty tin cans to indicate that someone has already passed that way in pursuit of a hound, a bay horse, and a turtle dove. We have all had our losses, Thoreau was to explain, and the reader knows about that. The track leads straight away from all human habitation. But is this the way we really want to go? It would seem not. So we turn to the other Thoreau. One world at a time, he said, when he was dying.

RICHARD DRINNON

Thoreau's Politics of the Upright Man †

"In imagination I hie me to Greece as to an enchanted ground," Thoreau declared in his *Journal* and then proved himself as good as his word in his lecture on "The Rights & Duties of the Individual in relation to Government." There was not a major figure in the classical background of anarchism whom Thoreau did not draw upon in some way. Though he may have been unaware of Zeno's strictures against Plato's omnicompetent state, he assuredly honored the Stoic for his individualism, his use of paradox, perhaps his belief in transcendent universal laws, certainly his serenity— "play high, play low," Thoreau observed with delight, "rain, sleet, or snow—it's all the same with the Stoic." He read Ovid with pleasure, used a quotation from the *Metamorphoses* as an epigraph for his *Week on the Concord and Merrimack Rivers,* and must have been well aware of Ovid's nostalgia for a time when there was no state and "everyone of his own will kept faith and did the right." But he found the most dramatic presentation of libertarian views in the *Antigone* of Sophocles. In this great drama of rebellion the central conflict was between the spirited Antigone and her uncle Creon, a not unkind man who had just ascended the throne of Thebes. Corrupted a little already by his power, blinded more than a little by bureaucratic definitions of right and wrong and advancing specious reasons of state as justification for his actions, Creon forbade the burial of the dead traitor Polynices. Driven by love for her slain brother and more by her awareness of the unambiguous commands of the gods to bury the dead, Antigone defied Creon's order. When she was brought before the king, she proudly avowed her defiance:

> For it was not Zeus who proclaimed these to me, nor Justice who dwells with the gods below; it was not they who established these laws among men. Nor did I think that your proclamations were so strong, as, being a mortal, to be able to transcend the unwritten and immovable laws of the gods. For not something now and yesterday, but forever these live, and no one knows from what time they appeared. I was not about to pay the

† From *The Massachusetts Review* (Autumn, 1962) pp. 126–38. Copyright © 1963, The Massachusetts Review, Inc.

Reprinted with permission from *The Massachusetts Review*.

penalty of violating these to the gods, fearing the presumption of any man.[1]

In his lecture on the individual and the state, which became the essay printed first as "Resistance to Civil Government" and later under the famous title "Civil Disobedience," Thoreau echoed Antigone's magnificent lines in his admission that "it costs me less in every sense to incur the penalty of disobedience to the State than it would to obey" and in his declaration that "they only can force me who obey a higher law than I." Like Sophocles' heroine, Thoreau made quite clear his rejection of the Periclean argument of Creon that the highest responsibility of the individual must be to the state and his rejection of the later Platonic assumption of a pleasing harmony between the laws of man and the laws of the gods. The kernel of Thoreau's politics was his belief in a natural or higher law; for the formulation of his essay on this subject, his indebtedness to the Greek tragedian was considerable.

Yet no single work provided Thoreau with his key concept.[2] In his day the doctrine of a fundamental law still covered Massachusetts like a ground fog. It had survived the classical period, had become the eternal law of Aquinas, the anti-papal fundamental law of Wycliffe, and, through Calvin, Milton, and Locke, had flowed across the Atlantic to furnish the colonists with their indispensable "Word of God." The more secular emphasis of the eighteenth century on the "unalienable Rights" possessed by every in-

1. Thoreau's sturdy prose translations in the *Week, Writings (1906)* I, 139–40, may be compared with Gilbert Murray's rhyming verse translation of *Antigone* (London: Allen & Unwin, 1941), 37–38. As Murray remarked in the introduction, Sophocles seemed to have created the ideal virgin martyr of Greek tragedy almost in spite of his intention; it is highly improbable that he set out to create an anarchist heroine. Yet she demonstrated unforgettably a specific instance of the possible gap between justice and state law and the final responsibility the individual owes to those laws which are above and beyond the Creons of this world. In this ultimate sense Antigone was an anarchist heroine—with reason Henry Nevinson pointed this out years ago in an essay on "An Anarchist Play," *Essays in Freedom* (London: Duckworth, 1911), 209–14.
2. Thanks to the careful researches of Ethel Seybold, *Thoreau: The Quest and the Classics* (New Haven: Yale University Press, 1951), 16, 17, 24, 66, 75, we know that Thoreau read the *Antigone* at Harvard and probably twice thereafter, once at the time he

was working up his lecture on the dangers of civil disobedience and once in the 1850's. Unfortunately Miss Seybold overstates her case by making the *Antigone* "probably responsible for one whole section of Thoreau's thought and public expression. From it must have come his concept of the divine law as superior to the civil law, of human right as greater than legal right." I say "unfortunately," because her overstatement has allowed some students to dismiss her valid points with rather fatuous pronouncements that Thoreau was merely an "involuntary classicist," that he was a "romanticist" by nature —whatever all this means. That Thoreau could find plenty of "romance" in the revels of the great god Pan, the mysticism of Orpheus, and the naturalness of Homer seems clear to me. In any event, one major inspiration for "Civil Disobedience" was Sophocles' work, first presented about 441 B.C., well in advance of Étienne de Boétie's *Discourse sur la Servitude Voluntaire,* published in 1577 and suggested as the earliest important source by Edward L. Tinker, *New York Times Book Review,* 29 March 1942.

dividual in a state of nature made little difference in end result—
little difference at least in doctrine, for all along men had thought
it natural for a higher law to be the basis for legislation. In nineteenth-century Massachusetts the existence of a fundamental,
higher law was accepted by radicals such as Alcott and Garrison,
by liberals such as William Ellery Channing, and by conservatives
such as Justice Joseph Story. These older countrymen of Thoreau
were joined by Emerson, whose essay on "Politics," published
five years before "Civil Disobedience," had a more direct influence on the young rebel. To be sure, Emerson approached the
crass Toryism of Chancellor Kent in discussing "higher law" by
attaching it to the power of property. But Emerson was usually
much better—at his worst he could sound like an early incarnation
of Bruce Barton—than his lines on wealth and property would
suggest; most of "Politics" was on the higher ground of a radical
Jeffersonianism:

> Hence the less government we have the better—the fewer laws
> and the less confided power. The antidote to this abuse of
> formal government is the influence of private character, the
> growth of the Individual . . . the appearance of the wise man;
> of whom the existing government is, it must be owned, but a
> shabby imitation. . . . To educate the wise man the State exists,
> and with the appearance of the wise man the State expires. The
> appearance of character makes the State unnecessary. The wise
> man is the State.[3]

Emerson even averred that "good men must not obey the laws too
well."

The similarity of Emerson's point of view and even his language
to Thoreau's must be clear to anyone who has carefully read
"Civil Disobedience." Living where he did when he did, Thoreau
could hardly have escaped the doctrine of a higher law. It was
hardly fortuitous that *all* the most notable American individualist
anarchists—Josiah Warren, Ezra Heywood, William B. Greene,
Joshua K. Ingalls, Stephen Pearl Andrews, Lysander Spooner,
and Benjamin Tucker—came from Thoreau's home state of Massachusetts and were his contemporaries. Tying the development of
American anarchism to native traditions and conditions, Tucker
uttered only a little white exaggeration when he claimed that he
and his fellow anarchists were "simply unterrified Jeffersonian
democrats." [4]

3. *The Complete Essays* (New York: Modern Library, 1940), 431.
4. Quoted in Rudolf Rocker, *Pioneers of American Freedom* (Los Angeles: Rocker Publications Committee, 1949), 150. A more recent and helpful study of early American anarchism is James J. Martin, *Men against the State* (DeKalb, Illinois: Adrian Allen Associates, 1953). The native American anarchists shared with Thoreau yet another Yankee characteristic: they were

Thus the doctrine of higher law, as Benjamin Wright once remarked, logically leads to philosophical anarchism. True, but this truth can be misleading without the warning note that the logic has to be followed out to the end. Half-way covenants can lead to something very different. John Cotton, for instance, believed in a higher law, yet came down on the side of authority and the Massachusetts establishment; Roger Williams believed no less in a higher law, yet came down on the side of freedom and the individual. Like all ideas, that of a higher law could become a weapon in the hands of groups and institutions. For Thomas Aquinas *lex aeterna* meant the supremacy of the church, for Thomas Hobbes the "Law of Nature" meant the supremacy of the state. For Jefferson and Paine, natural law meant revolution and the establishment of a counter state. But for Thoreau it meant no supremacy of church over state or vice versa, or of one state over another, or of one group over another. It meant rather the logical last step of *individual action*. Belief in higher law *plus* practice of individual direct action *equal* anarchism. "I must conclude that Conscience, if that be the name of it," wrote Thoreau in the *Week*, "was not given us for no purpose, or for a hindrance." From Antigone to Bronson Alcott, Thoreau, and Benjamin Tucker, the individuals who acted on the imperatives of their consciences, "cost what it may," were anarchists.[5]

2

So much for the main sources and the master pillars of Thoreau's political position. I have argued that in those crucial matters in which expediency was not applicable, it added up to anarchism. But the question of whether this made him a workaday anarchist lands us in the middle of a tangle. Was Thoreau really an individualist, an anarchist, or both, or neither? Emma Goldman defined

all members of an entrepreneurial professional middle-class which was integral to a relatively simple economy based on farming and trade. Not unnaturally they tended to assume that the interests of all would be best promoted if the individual were left absolutely free to pursue his self-interest. That is to say, just as they developed higher law doctrine to its logical conclusion, so did they take laissez faire theory beyond the liberals to advocate a marketplace literally without political controls. Fortunately Thoreau did not join these anarchists in their preoccupation with currency manipulation, free banking, economic competition. Aside from being more interesting, the trail Thoreau cut for himself promised to lead somewhere.

5. In 1875 Tucker followed Thoreau's example and refused to pay the poll tax of the town of Princeton, Massachusetts; he was imprisoned in Worcester a short while for his refusal—see Martin, *Men against the State*, pp. 203–04. It had almost become a habit in the area. Three years before Thoreau spent his night in jail, Alcott was arrested for not paying his poll tax. Thoreau was probably influenced by his example and by the civil disobedience agitation of William Lloyd Garrison and his followers—see Wendell Glick, " 'Civil Disobedience': Thoreau's Attack upon Relativism," *Western Humanities Review*, VII (Winter 1952–53), 35–42.

anarchism as "the philosophy of a new social order based on liberty unrestricted by man-made law" and once spent an evening in Concord vainly trying to persuade Franklin Sanborn that under this definition Thoreau was an anarchist. Joseph Wood Krutch doubts that Thoreau felt a direct responsibility for any social order, old or new, and stresses his "defiant individualism." [6] Sherman Paul, on the other hand laments that "one of the most persistent errors concerning Thoreau that has never been sufficiently dispelled is that Thoreau was an anarchical individualist." [7] Still, "Thoreau was not an anarchist but an individualist," argues John Haynes Holmes.[8] The tangle becomes impassable with Paul's additional observation that Thoreau "was not objecting to government but to what we now call the State."

There are two main reasons for this muddle. Thoreau was himself partially responsible. His sly satire, his liking for wide margins for his writing, and his fondness for paradox provided ammunition for widely divergent interpretations of "Civil Disobedience." Thus, governments being but expedients, he looks forward to a day when men will be prepared for the motto: "That government is best which governs not at all." The reader proceeds through some lines highly critical of the American government, only to be brought up sharp, in the third paragraph, by the sweet reasonableness of the author: "But, to speak practically and as a citizen, unlike those who call themselves no-government men, I ask for, not at once no government, but *at once* a better government." Those who discount Thoreau's radicalism snap up this sentence which seems clear on the face of it: Do not think me an extremist like the Garrisonians and anarchists, he seems to be saying, but think of me as one who moderately desires a better government now. But is this all he wants? Might he not favor, a *little later*, no government? Shattered by this doubt, the reader is thrown forward into another bitter attack on the American government and on the generic state. It becomes increasingly clear that critics who have tried to put together a governmentalist from Thoreau's writings on politics have humorlessly missed the point. He does indeed say that he will take what he can get from the state, but he also twits himself a little for inconsistency: "In fact, I quietly declare war with the State, after my fashion, though I will still make what use and get what advantage of her I can, as is usual in such cases." Compare Thoreau's wry position here with that of Alex Comfort,

6. Krutch, *Henry David Thoreau* (New York: William Sloane, 1948), 133–35.
7. Paul, *The Shores of America: Thoreau's Inward Exploration* (Urbana: University of Illinois Press, 1958), 75–80, 377. Paul emphasizes Thoreau's willingness to have "governmental interference for the general welfare."
8. Holmes, "Thoreau's 'Civil Disobedience,'" *Christian Century*, LXVI (January-June 1949), 787–89.

the English anarchist, written a hundred years later: "We do not refuse to drive on the left hand side of the road or to subscribe to national health insurance. The sphere of our disobedience is limited to the sphere in which society exceeds its powers and its usefulness. . . ." [9] But let us back up a bit. What was the nature of the "better government" he wanted at once? Obviously it was one that would stay strictly in its place and ungrow—progressively cease to exist. What was the "best government" he could imagine? He has already told us and the essay as a whole supports his declaration: a government "which governs not at all."

But the main obstacle to any clear cut identification of Thoreau's politics has been the uncertain shifting borders of anarchism, liberalism, and socialism in the nineteenth century and after. No series of definitions has succeeded in decisively marking out their frontiers. Stephen Pearl Andrews, for instance, the erudite contemporary of Thoreau, conceived of himself as at one and the same time a believer in the socialism of Charles Fourier and the anarchism of Josiah Warren. The intermingling of socialism and anarchism is further illustrated by Mikhail Bakunin, the founder of communist anarchism, who thought of himself as a socialist and fought Marx for the control of the First International. Even Marx has been called an ultimate anarchist, in the sense that he presumably favored anarchism after the state withered away. But perhaps the closest analogue to Thoreau was William Morris. Working closely with Peter Kropotkin for a number of years, Morris rejected the parliamentarians and joined forces with the libertarians in the Socialist League of the 1880's—the League was eventually taken over completely by anarchists!—and wrote *News from Nowhere* which was anarchist in tone and sentiment. Yet his explanation of why he refused to call himself an anarchist was obviously confused and showed that he was rejecting individualist anarchism and not Kropotkin's communist anarchism.[1]

A somewhat comparable confusion mars a recent attempt to analyze Thoreau's position. He was not "an anarchical individualist," argues Paul, because he went to Walden not "for himself alone but to serve mankind." It would be easy to quote passages from *Walden* which seem to call this contention into question. One example: "What good I do, in the common sense of that word,

9. Quoted by Nicolas Walter, "Disobedience and the New Pacifism," *Anarchy*, No. 14 (April 1962), 113. It is worth noting that Walter thinks "Thoreau wasn't an anarchist," though he believes that "the implications of his action and his essay are purely anarchist. . . ." I am sure that Thoreau would have chuckled or perhaps laughed in his full free way had he known this question would still be debated a hundred years after his death.

1. George Woodcock and Ivan Avakumovic, *The Anarchist Prince* (London: T. V. Boardman, 1950), 216–19. Thoreau's great influence on the English left dates back to this period when many were filled with idealism and with admiration for the "sublime doctrine" of anarchism.

must be aside from my main path, and for the most part wholly unintended." Another: "While my townsmen and women are devoted in so many ways to the good of their fellows, I trust that one at least may be spared to other and less humane pursuits." [2] Yet this would be to read Thoreau literally. Unquestionably, as he informed us in "Civil Disobedience," he was "as desirous of being a good neighbor as I am of being a bad subject." The distinction was crucial. Though he served the state by declaring war on it, in his own way, he served society for a lifetime by trying to understand and explain Concord to itself. The manageable unit of society—unlike the vast abstraction in Washington or even Boston—was drawn to the human scale of Concord and other villages. If men lived simply and as neighbors, informal patterns of voluntary agreement would be established, there would be no need for police and military protection, since "thieving and robbery would be unknown," [3] and there would be freedom and leisure to turn to the things that matter. Thoreau's community consciousness was the essential, dialectical *other* of his individuality. Consider the following from *Walden:*

> It is time that villages were universities, and their elder inhabitants the fellows of universities, with leisure . . . to pursue liberal studies the rest of their lives. Shall the world be confined to one Paris or one Oxford forever? Cannot students be boarded here and get a liberal education under the skies of Concord? . . . Why should our life be in any respect provincial? If we will read newspapers, why not skip the gossip of Boston and take the best newspaper in the world at once. . . . As the nobleman of cultivated taste surrounds himself with whatever conduces to his culture—genius—learning—wit—books—paintings—statuary—music—philosophical instruments and the like; so let the village do. . . . To act collectively is according to the spirit of our institutions. . . . Instead of noblemen, let us have noble villages of men.[4]

One nobleman who also agitated for noble villages was the anarchist Kropotkin. He could have agreed completely with Thoreau's preoccupation with his locality and his readiness to act collectively "in the spirit of our institutions." In *Mutual Aid* (1902),

2. *Walden,* p. 49. All references to *Walden* are to this Norton Critical Edition [Editor].
3. *Walden,* p. 115.
4. *Walden,* p. 73 ff. By all means see Lewis Mumford's fine discussion of Thoreau in his chapter on "Renewal of the Landscape," in *The Brown Decades* (New York: Dover Publications, 1955). 64–72. Mumford credits Thoreau with the achievement of helping "to acclimate the mind of highly sensitive and civilized men to the natural possibilities of the environment" and gives him a major place in the history of regional planning in America. The influence of Thoreau on Paul Goodman, who describes himself as a "community anarchist," is apparent to anyone who has read his and his brother Percival's *Communitas* (Chicago: University of Chicago Press, 1947).

Kropotkin celebrated the vital growth of society in the ancient Greek and medieval cities; he sadly outlined the consequences of the rise of centralization when the state "took possession, in the interest of minorities, of all the judicial, economical, and administrative functions which the village community already had exercised in the interest of all." Like Thoreau, Kropotkin advocated that the community's power be restored and that local individuality and creativity be left free to develop. The closeness of their views —though Kropotkin must have thought Thoreau too much an individualist like Ibsen!—points up the mistake of Sherman Paul and others in equating the "anti-social" with the "anarchical" Society and the state, as Thoreau and Kropotkin were very much aware, should not be confused or identified.

The definition of Emma Goldman quoted above will have to do for our purposes, then, though we must keep in mind its approximate nature and the greased-pole slipperiness of the political theory from which Thoreau's views are so often confidently said to have differed. Under this definition Thoreau was always an anarchist in matters of conscience, an ultimate anarchist for a time "when men are prepared for it," and in the meanwhile an anarchical decentralist. But enough of this attempt to stuff the poet and mystic in one political slot. Actually Thoreau's writings may yet help to explode all our conventional political categories.

3

"We scarcely know whether to call him the last of an older race of men, or the first of one that is to come," admitted an English critic in *The Times Literary Supplement* for 12 July, 1917. "He had the toughness, the stoicism, the unspoilt senses of an Indian, combined with the self-consciousness, the exacting discontent, the susceptibility of the most modern. At times he seems to reach beyond our human powers in what he perceives upon the horizon of humanity." With remarkable insight, the writer had perceived Thoreau's perplexing doubleness and had even touched the edge of his higher, profoundly exciting unity.

Of Thoreau's "unspoilt senses of an Indian" and his passion for the primitive there can be no question. "There is in my nature, methinks," he declared in the *Week*, "a singular yearning toward all wildness." To the end he was convinced that "life consists with wildness." But this conviction did not rest on a sentimental-romantic view of our "rude forefathers." The crude relics of the North American tribes, their improvident carelessness even in the woods, and their "coarse and imperfect use" of nature repelled him. His unpleasant experience of a moose-hunt in Maine led to the reflection: "No wonder that their race is so soon exterminated. I already, and for weeks afterwards, felt my nature the coarser for this part of my woodland experience, and was reminded that our life should be lived as tenderly and daintily as one would pluck a flower." [5] Yet Thoreau never gave up his conviction that, standing so close, Indians had a particularly intimate and vital relationship with nature. "We talk of civilizing the Indian," he wrote in the *Week*, "but that is not the name for his improvement. By the wary independence and aloofness of his dim forest life he preserves his intercourse with his native gods, and is admitted from time to time to a rare and peculiar society with nature. He has glances of starry recognition to which our saloons are strangers."

By way of contrast, "the white man comes, pale as the dawn, with a load of thought, with a slumbering intelligence as a fire raked up, knowing well what he knows, not guessing but calculating; strong in community, yielding obedience to authority; of experienced race; of wonderful, wonderful common sense; dull but capable, slow but persevering, severe but just, of little humor but genuine; a laboring man, despising game and sport; building a house that endures, a framed house. He buys the Indian's moccasins and baskets, then buys his hunting-grounds, and at length forgets where he is buried and plows up his bones." [6] In this list of the bourgeois virtues, the keen, far-reaching social criticism of "Life Without Principle"—first entitled "Higher Law"—and indeed of *Walden* itself is anticipated. Calculating for the main chance, this obedient white man had cut his way through thousands of Indians in order to rush to the gold diggings in California, "reflect the greatest disgrace on mankind," and "live by luck, and so get the means of commanding the labor of others less lucky, without contributing any value to society! And that is called enterprise! I know of no more startling development of the immortality of trade. . . . The hog that gets his living by rooting, stirring up the soil so, would be ashamed of such company." [7] In this powerful essay on "Life Without Principle," he concluded that "there is nothing, not even crime, more opposed to poetry, to philosophy, ay, to life itself, than this incessant business." An economist of importance, as the first chapter of *Walden* may yet prove to a skeptical world, Thoreau saw clearly that the accumulation of wealth really leads to the cheapening of life, to the substitution for man of the less-than-hog-like creature who calculates and lays up money and even fails to root up the soil in the process. "What is

5. Quoted in Albert Keiser, *The Indian in American Literature* (New York: Oxford University Press, 1933), 227.

6. *Works*, I, 52–53; see also 55.

7. "Life without Principle."

called politics," he wrote in "Life Without Principle," "is comparatively something so superficial and unhuman, that practically I have never fairly recognized that it concerns me at all." The war against Mexico, the scramble for territory and power, and other debauches in nationalism were, he trusted, a different manifest destiny from his own. In his letter to Parker Pillsbury on the eve of the fighting at Fort Sumter, he reported that he did "not so much regret the present condition of things in this country (provided I regret it at all) as I do that I ever heard of it. I know one or 2 who have this year, for the first time, read a president's message; but they do not see that this implies a fall in themselves, rather than a rise in the president. Blessed were the days before you read a president's message. Blessed are the young for they do not read the president's message." [8] Yet, despite all these devastating shafts aimed at the institutions reared up by the "pale as dawn" white man, Thoreau honored learning as much or more than any man in America. Far from advocating a return to some preliterate bliss, he advocated, in his chapter on "Reading" in *Walden*, a study of "the oldest and the best" books, whose "authors are a natural and irresistible aristocracy in every society, and, more than kings or emperors, exert an influence on mankind."

Thus Thoreau's doubleness, of which he was well aware: "I find an instinct in me conducting to a mystic spiritual life, and also another to a primitive savage life." It was one of his great achievements to go beyond the polarities of "Civilization and Barbarism" —alternatively attractive poles which drew most of Thoreau's contemporaries helplessly back and forth like metal particles—to come close to a creative fusion: "We go eastward to realize history and study the works of art and literature, retracing the steps of the race," he wrote in the serene summary of his walks. "We go westward as into the future, with a spirit of enterprise and adventure." Thoreau wanted the best for his countrymen from both nature and civilization, past and present. He perceived clearly the meaning of America. It was an opportunity for new beginnings: "The Atlantic is a Lethean stream, in our passage over which we have had an opportunity to forget the Old World and its institutions. If we do not succeed this time, there is perhaps one more chance for the race left before it arrives on the banks of the Styx; and that is in the Lethe of the Pacific, which is three times as wide." Had he lived with unflagging powers for another decade or so, he might have used his laboriously accumulated notebooks of "Extracts re-

8. His reference to "manifest destiny" appeared in his letter to H. G. O. Blake, 27 February, 1853; his letter to Pillsbury was dated 10 April, 1861 —*The Correspondence of Henry David Thoreau*, eds. Walter Harding and Carl Bode (New York: New York University Press, 1958), 296, 611.

lating to the Indians" to show why the aborigines enjoyed "a rare and peculiar society with nature." [9] It is indisputable that his interest in classical mythology, ancient societies, and contemporary tribes was an anthropological concern for the enduring features of life in groups. His interest in savages was much like that of Claude Lévi-Strauss and might have been expressed in the latter's words: "The study of these savages does not reveal a Utopian state in Nature; nor does it make us aware of a perfect society hidden deep in the forests. It helps us to construct a theoretical model of society which corresponds to none that can be observed in reality, but will help us to disentangle 'what in the present nature of Man is original, and what is artificial.' " [1] Thoreau's theoretical model, which came from all his efforts to drive life into a corner and get its measurements, made it clear that the efforts of his neighbors to live for the superfluous made their lives superfluous. Through careful inspection of his model, he was able to see, years before Lenin, that at bottom the state is a club. To cooperate with it, especially in matters of importance, is to deny life, for the state, like a standing army, is organized power and at the disposal of hate. "You must get your living by loving," confidently declared this supposedly narrow village eccentric. Clearly, he aspired to create for his countrymen a "new heaven and a new earth," just as each of Greece's sons had done for her. The look of this new heaven is suggested by a passage in the *Week*. On Saturday, after he and John had made the long pull from Ball's Hill to Carlisle Bridge, they saw "men haying far off in the meadow, their heads waving like the grass which they cut. In the distance the wind seemed to bend all alike. As the night stole over, such a freshness was wafted across the meadow that every blade of cut grass seemed to teem with life."

To this feeling of the correspondence of man to nature, "so that he is at home in her," Thoreau added poetic intuitions of an individualism to come. With his common sense, he realized that the notorious common sense of his countrymen was insane. The important questions were buried under daily rounds of trivia. Living

9. Keiser, *The Indian in American Literature*, 217–18, "cannot but believe that cruel fate robbed the world of a great work dealing in a sanely realistic yet sympathetic . . . manner with the child of nature on the American continent. . . ." Perhaps, though it is possible that the Civil War might have undone Thoreau along with so many others. It should be noted that Thoreau shows, in many passages, an intuitive sense of the distinction, made by such modern students as Mircea Eliade, between cyclical archaic time and progressive, cumulative modern time. His works were organized around the former. Indeed the *Week* might be interpreted as an extended defense of Parmenides's thesis of the permanence of the universe against the Heraclitean progressivism of a nation of boosters (see esp. 54–56, 60, 128, 239, 347, 416). His constant return to the problem of time and its obvious importance for his understanding of man in nature invite a careful, systematic inquiry.
1. Lévi-Strauss, "Tristes Tropiques," *Encounter*, XC (April 1961), 40.

was constantly deferred. No joyful exuberance was allowed to slip by prudence. Thoreau could have joined William Blake in his belief that "Prudence is a rich, ugly old maid, courted by Incapacity." The incapacity was partly the result of a split between the head and the heart, thought and feeling, and the absurd belief that the intellect alone enables man to meet life. In his final summing up, in the essay "Walking," he warned that the most we can hope to achieve is "Sympathy with Intelligence . . . a discovery that there are more things in heaven and earth than are dreamed of in our philosophy." But his neighbors not only had an overfaith in abstract reasoning and in the general efficacy of the intellect; they also distrusted the body. William Blake could thrust through the prudishness of his time to rediscover the body; hemmed in by the moral sentimentalism of his family, by Emersonian etherealness, and his own confirmed virginity, Thoreau had more difficulty. His embarrassing admission—"what the essential difference between man and woman is, that they should be thus attracted to one another, no one has satisfactorily answered"—is indeed, as Krutch points out, "a real howler." [2] Nevertheless, he took a sensuous delight in his body, claiming in the *Week* that "we need pray for no higher heaven than the pure senses can furnish, a purely sensuous life. Our present senses are but rudiments of what they are destined to become." Here is a body mysticism which placed Thoreau in the tradition of Jacob Boehme and William Blake. It presupposed, Norman Brown observes, that "the consciousness strong enough to endure full life would be no longer Apollonian but Dionysian—consciousness which does not observe the limit, but overflows; consciousness which *does not negate any more*.[3] Shocked by phallic forms in nature, the stiff-backed Thoreau yet remarked that he worshipped most constantly at the shrine of Pan —Pan, the upright man of the Arcadian fertility cult, famous for his Dionysiac revels with the mountain nymphs! [4] The vision of individuals with spiritual development and the simple animal strength to affirm their bodies was one of the important contributions of this paradoxical celibate. It was a vision sensed and acted upon, in their own ways, by Isadora Duncan and Emma Goldman and Randolph Bourne and Frank Lloyd Wright. It exerts its appeal to the poetic libertarian strain in radicalism, to men as diverse as e. e. cummings, Karl Shapiro, Henry Miller, Paul Goodman, Kenneth Patchen, Herbert Read, the late Albert Camus and Nicolas Berdyaev. A recent, rather extravagant form is perhaps

2. Krutch, *Thoreau*, 207.
3. Brown, *Life against Death* (Middletown, Conn.: Wesleyan University Press, 1959), 308-11.
4. *Works*, I, 65. I should not place any great reliance on this passage, which apparently was valued in part for its shock value, if it stood alone. It does not.

Allen Ginsberg's notion of "Socialist-Co-op Anarchism." In any form it is revolutionary.

"One thing about Thoreau keeps him very near to me," Walt Whitman remarked. "I refer to his lawlessness—his dissent—his going his absolute own road let hell blaze all it chooses." [5] Thousands of young people know exactly what Whitman meant. A few perhaps can see that Thoreau's death was his greatest achievement, for it showed that his philosophy had taught him how to die—and therefore how to live. Some can appreciate and understand his two years at Walden Pond. But many are ready, like the young Indian lawyer in South Africa in 1907, to be impressed that Thoreau "taught nothing he was not prepared to practice in himself." [6] Like Gandhi, they are ready to draw on Thoreau's "Civil Disobedience" for "a new way" of handling political conflict. Thoreau thereby made another major contribution to radical politics, for anarchism and socialism have traditionally been strong on ends and weak or worse on means. It is true that Thoreau was himself unclear about violence, as his splendid tribute to John Brown and his occasional callow observations on war show—"it is a pity," he wrote a correspondent in 1855, "that we seem to require a war from time to time to assure us that there is any manhood still left in man." [7] Yet he went farther than most in thinking his way through this problem. More importantly, like Antigone he left us the powerful, burning, irresistible appeal of his example. It is as timely as the banner "Unjust Law Exists" which marched beside Camus' "Neither Victims Nor Executioners" in the recent Washington youth demonstrations. It is as timely as Bertrand Russell's sit-down in Trafalgar Square. It may even help us survive the disease called modern history.

5. Quoted by Walter Harding, *A Thoreau Handbook* (New York: New York University Press, 1959), 201.
6. Quoted by George Hendrick, "The Influence of Thoreau's 'Civil Disobedience' on Gandhi's *Satyagraha*," *New England Quarterly*, XXIX (1956), 464.
7. Letter to Thomas Cholmondeley, 7 February 1855—see *Correspondence of Thoreau*, 371.

Bibliography

The best source of bibliographical information on Thoreau is the essay, "Thoreau," by Lewis Leary, in the volume, *Eight American Authors: a Review of Research and Criticism*, edited by Floyd Stovall, originally published by the Modern Language Association in 1956, and subsequently reprinted with a "Bibliographical Supplement: a Selective Check List, 1955-1962," by W. W. Norton and Company, Inc. (1963). For material published since 1962, the best source is the annual "MLA International Bibliography" published in May of each year as a supplement of *PMLA* by the Modern Language Association. The following selective bibliography includes only those works that are generally available in most libraries.

THOREAU: BIBLIOGRAPHIES AND EDITIONS

F. H. Allen, *Bibliography of Henry David Thoreau* (1908).
William White, "A Henry David Thoreau Bibliography, 1908-1937," *Bulletin of Bibliography,* 1938-39.
Carvel Collins, "Contribution to a Bibliography of Thoreau, 1938-1945," *Bulletin of Bibliography,* 1946-47.
The Writings of Henry David Thoreau, 20 vols. (1906).
Collected Poems of Henry Thoreau, ed. Carl Bode (1943); rev. ed. (1964).
Journals, eds. Bradford Torrey and Francis H. Allen with a foreword by Henry Seidel Canby, 14 vols. (1949).
The Correspondence of Henry David Thoreau, eds. Carl Bode and Walter Harding (1958).

THOREAU: BIOGRAPHIES

H. S. Salt, *The Life of Henry David Thoreau* (1890).
Ellery Channing, *Thoreau: The Poet-Naturalist,* ed. F. B. Sanborn (1902).
F. B. Sanborn, *The Life of Henry David Thoreau* (1917).
Leon Bazalgette, *Henry Thoreau, Bachelor of Nature,* trans. Van Wyck Brooks (1924).
Brooks Atkinson, *Henry Thoreau, the Cosmic Yankee* (1927).
H. S. Canby, *Thoreau* (1939).
Milton Meltzer and Walter Harding, *A Thoreau Profile* (1962).

THOREAU: CRITICISM

Raymond Adams, "Thoreau and Science," *Scientific Monthly* (1945).
———, "Thoreau's Sources for Resistance to Civil Government," *Studies in Philology* (1945).
J. P. Brawner, "Thoreau as Wit and Humorist," *South Atlantic Quarterly* (1945).
H. S. Canby, "Thoreau and the Machine Age," *Yale Review* (1931).
Arthur Christy, *The Orient in American Transcendentalism* (1931).
R. L. Cook, *Passage to Walden* (1949).
J. B. Dabb, "Thoreau—the Adventurer as Economist," *Yale Review* (1947).
Frank Davidson, "Thoreau's Hound, Bay Horse, and Turtle-Dove," *New England Quarterly* (1954).
Norman Foerster, "The Intellectual Heritage of Thoreau," *Texas Review* (1917).
———, "Thoreau as Artist," *Saturday Review* (1921).
Wendell Glick, "Thoreau's Attack on Relativism," *Western Humanities Review* (1952-53).
J. J. Kwait, "Thoreau's Philosophical Apprenticeship," *New England Quarterly* (1945).
Joseph Leach, "Thoreau's Borrowings in *Walden*," *Notes and Queries* (1943).
F. W. Lorch, "Thoreau and the Organic Principle of Poetry," *PMLA* (1938).
Sherman Paul, "The Wise Silence: Sound as the Agency of Correspondence in Thoreau," *New England Quarterly* (1949).

Paul Schwaber, "Thoreau's Development in *Walden*," *Criticism* (1963).
Ethel Seybolt, *Thoreau: The Quest and the Classics* (1951).
Randall Stewart, "The Growth of Thoreau's Reputation," *College English* (1947).
H. W. Wells, "An Evaluation of Thoreau's Poetry," *American Literature* (1944).
George Whicher, *Walden Revisted* (1945).
Paul O. Williams, "The Concept of Inspiration in Thoreau's Poetry," *PMLA* (1964).